The Only **DOS** book you'll ever need

SECOND EDITION

About the author

Since 1981, Doug Lowe has authored 15 computer books on both PC and mainframe computer subjects. He is widely respected for his ability to translate complex computer subjects into layman's terms so that both new and experienced users can understand the underlying concepts and apply this knowledge in practical ways.

Doug co-authored the first edition of *The Only DOS Book You'll Ever Need* in 1991. Now, he's completely revised the book in this second edition to reflect the practical use of DOS today.

About the cover

Kate Solari Baker is the creator of the drawing, *Still Waters #4*, that is featured on the cover of this book. Kate has studied with Wayne Thiebaud at the Santa Fe Institute of Fine Arts and exhibits her work in Marin County and San Francisco. She considers her work to be primarily drawings, but because of her layering technique with chalk pastels, she achieves a "painterly" look.

In addition to our support and concern for the environment, Mike Murach & Associates, Inc., has chosen to show our support for the fine arts by featuring works from California artists on the covers of our technical books. How appropriate, then, that Kate Baker says about her work, "My subject most recently has been Northern Californian scenes with an emphasis on the rivers, lakes, and wetlands so necessary for our survival."

The Only DOS book you'll ever need

SECOND EDITION

Doug Lowe

Mike Murach & Associates

2560 West Shaw Lane, Suite 101, Fresno, California 93711-2765

(209) 440-9071

Production team

Editor
Anne Prince

Graphics designer
Steve Ehlers

Other books for PC users

The Least You Need to Know about DOS

Crash Course: Windows 95 & NT 4.0
Crash Course: Word 97
Crash Course: Excel 97
Crash Course: Word 95
Crash Course: Excel 95
Work like a PRO with Word for Windows 95
Work like a PRO with Excel for Windows 95

The Least You Need to Know about Windows 3.1
Work like a PRO with Word 6 for Windows
Word 6 for Windows: The Mail Merge feature
Work like a PRO with Excel 5 for Windows
Excel 5 for Windows: Lists, pivot tables, and external databases

20 19 18 17 16 15 14 13 12 11 10 9 8 7 6 5 4 3

ISBN: 0-911625-71-2

Library of Congress Cataloging-in-Publication Data

Lowe, Doug.
The only DOS book you'll ever need / Doug Lowe.—2nd ed.
p. cm.
Includes index.
ISBN 0-911625-71-2
1. Operating systems (Computers) 2. MS-DOS (Computer file) 3. PC -DOS (Computer file) I. Title.
QA76.76.063L68 1993
005.4'469—dc20 93-859
CIP

Contents

Preface

DOS has been the operating system of choice for personal computers ever since IBM introduced the first PC in 1981. Since then, there have been at least ten versions of DOS. The current version, 6.0, was introduced in the Spring of 1993. Each version has improved upon the previous version in many ways. DOS 6.0 improves upon its predecessor (DOS 5.0) by providing better memory management, on-the-fly disk compression, a high-speed backup utility, virus protection, and many more new features.

Yet for all of its improvements, DOS remains a source of confusion for most of its users. Most users take quickly to application programs like *Lotus 1-2-3* or *WordPerfect*, but are intimidated by the thought of learning how to use DOS with its arcane commands, cryptic error messages, and incomprehensible manual. And yet, sooner or later, every computer user realizes that you can't ignore DOS forever. You must use DOS to start your application programs. You must use DOS to keep track of the files and directories on your hard disk. And you must use DOS to perform the many routine tasks that need to be done periodically to keep your computer in efficient operating condition. In short, you can't use your PC effectively without a working knowledge of DOS.

That's where this book comes in. It will give you the working knowledge of DOS you need to use your PC effectively. Plus, it will serve as a valuable reference once you've learned the basics of DOS. As a reference, this book is quick and easy to use, whether you need to quickly jog your memory on some detail you've forgotten or you've decided it's time to learn an advanced feature of DOS that you haven't tackled yet.

How this book is different from the rest

With literally hundreds of books available on DOS, what makes this book different from all the others? Several things.

First, this book is organized so that you can get the information you need quickly. Most of the chapters stand on their own, so you can read them in any order you wish once you've read the first six chapters. For example, if you want to learn how to partition and format a hard disk, you can go straight to chapter 22 and learn how. If you want to learn how to create DOS shell menus, go straight to chapter 13. To learn how to protect your computer from viruses, go straight to chapter 17. The information isn't buried in some obscure corner of the book or spread throughout three or four different chapters the way it is in so many other books.

Second, this book depends heavily on well-designed illustrations and figures that show you quickly how to use a particular command or help you understand a difficult concept. Just page through this book and look at the illustrations and figures, and compare them with the illustrations and figures in other DOS books. In particular, look at the figures that show you how to use DOS commands. They clearly explain how you use the important parameters and switches, and they back up that explanation with realistic examples that show you how to apply the command to everyday tasks. These figures not only make it easier to learn how to use the command in the first place, but also serve as excellent references if you need a refresher later on.

Third, this book emphasizes the practical. It doesn't cover every DOS command and option just because it's there. Nor does it encourage you to make a career of learning every nook and cranny of DOS. Instead, it presents DOS as a series of skills you should master so you can get the most from your application software and from your PC. This doesn't mean that this book ignores commands and features just because they're "advanced." On the contrary, a large portion of this book is devoted to showing you how to use advanced DOS skills. But these advanced skills are always presented within a framework of practical application.

Who this book is for

This book is for anyone who uses a PC and wants to learn more about DOS. It makes few assumptions about your experience, knowledge, or skill level. And it makes few assumptions about the type of PC you're using or the version of DOS you're using. So this book is appropriate for you whether you've just purchased your first computer or you've been using a computer for years. And it's appropriate whether you're using an old AT-style computer with a 30MB hard disk or a new 486DX2 system with a 250MB hard disk. However, this book does assume you're using a hard disk.

This book is slanted towards the two most recent versions of DOS: 5.0 and 6.0. But if you're using an earlier version, you don't need to worry. Whenever I present a feature that isn't available under all versions of DOS, I'll be sure to point out which version of DOS introduced the feature. So you'll find this book useful even if you're using an older version of DOS. (If you're not sure what version of DOS you're using, you'll learn how to find out in chapter 4.)

Also, I assume that your computer is put together and that you have at least some experience using it. This book won't teach you how to assemble your computer, how to turn your computer on, how to put paper in the printer, and so on. Some experience working with an application program such as a word processor or spreadsheet program is a plus, but not an absolute requirement. Beyond these few assumptions, this book teaches you everything you need to know about DOS to get the most from your application programs and from your PC.

What this book does

If you'll look at the table of contents, you'll see that this book is divided into seven sections. The first two sections comprise a basic tutorial for new users. In the two chapters in section 1, you'll learn the concepts and terms that apply to your computer's hardware and software. Once you're familiar with these concepts and terms, you'll be ready to learn the basics of using DOS. If you're already familiar with hardware and software basics, you can probably skip these chapters. Skim through them quickly to be sure.

In section 2, you'll learn how to use the basic DOS functions that every PC user should know about. You'll learn how DOS organizes data on your hard disk into files and directories so you can access any file on the disk, how to use some basic DOS commands, how to set up your AUTOEXEC.BAT file so DOS gets started properly, and how to start your application programs. You should read these chapters in sequence.

In section 3, you'll learn the DOS skills that are essential to using your PC productively, no matter what application programs you use or what version of DOS you use. You'll learn how to set up and manage the directories on your hard disk; how to work with data on diskettes; how to back up the data on your hard disk; how to prevent, detect, and recover from disk errors; and how to make your PC run faster without buying new hardware. I wrote these chapters so they are independent of one another, so you can read them in any sequence you wish.

In section 4, you'll learn how to use the DOS shell, which comes with DOS 5.0 and 6.0 (the shells in the two versions are nearly identical). Here, you'll learn how to set up menus, how to manage your directories and files, and how to use the DOS shell's task switching capabilities so you can quickly switch from one application to another. The chapters in this section are also independent of one another, although you should read chapter 12 first because it presents an overall introduction to the shell.

Section 5 contains one chapter for each of the new utility programs that comes with DOS 6.0. These utilities include: *Microsoft Backup*, a high-speed backup program that can back up your hard disk data up to four times faster than the older DOS Backup command; *Microsoft Anti-Virus*, which detects and removes harmful computer viruses from your system; *DoubleSpace*, which compresses data so that the capacity of your hard disk is effectively doubled; *Microsoft Defrag*, which improves the stability and performance of your hard disk by reorganizing the data stored on it; *Interlnk* and *Power*, which make portable computers easier to use; and *Microsoft Diagnostics*, which displays a variety of useful information about your system. If you have DOS 6.0, the chapters in this section will teach you how to use these programs. If you don't yet have DOS 6.0, you can read through these chapters to see if you should upgrade to DOS 6.0. Because these chapters are independent of one another, you can read them in any order you wish.

The four chapters in section 6 all relate to setting up your system's configuration. Here, you'll learn how to partition and format a hard disk (chapter 22), how to upgrade to DOS 6.0 (chapter 23), how to set up your CONFIG.SYS and AUTOEXEC.BAT files (chapter 24), and how to configure your computer's memory for optimum use (chapter 25). Two of these chapters also include features that are new with DOS 6.0. Chapter 24 presents DOS 6.0 enhancements to CONFIG.SYS that let you set up multiple configurations, and chapter 25 presents a DOS 6.0 utility called *MemMaker*, which automates the chore of optimizing your memory configuration. Although these chapters are mostly independent of one another, chapter 25 builds on the configuration information presented in chapter 24. As a result, you should read those two chapters in sequence.

Finally, in section 7, you'll learn some additional advanced DOS skills. In chapter 26, you'll learn how to use advanced DOS commands and techniques. Then, in chapter 27, you'll learn how to create advanced batch files. These chapters are independent of one another, so you can read them in any order you wish.

Is this really the only DOS book you'll ever need?

I think so. If you look at the other DOS books on the market today, you'll find that they fall into several categories. There are introductory books for novice users. There are advanced books for experienced users who want to know everything there is to know. There are books for users of earlier versions of DOS who want to know just about the new features of DOS 6.0. There are books on specific aspects of using DOS, such as managing your hard disk or writing batch files. And there are reference books that describe every DOS command in reference format.

This book covers all these bases. If you're a novice user, the first two sections of this book will get you going as well as any other book will. If you want to become a power user, the last two sections will teach you everything you need to know about configuring your system, using advanced commands, and writing batch files. If you want to learn how to use the new features of DOS 6.0, section 5 is just what you need. And if you want a good reference, I don't think you'll find a better one anywhere.

Other books may go into greater depth on a particular aspect of using DOS. For example, an entire book on writing batch files will probably cover that subject in more detail than you'll find in this book. But, for the vast majority of computer users, the information you'll find in this book on writing batch files is more than you'll ever need. The same holds true for memory management, hard disk management, virus protection, and so on. You might find books that cover each of these subjects in greater depth. But unless you have an unusual situation, you'll find all you need to know about those subjects within these pages.

Conclusion

I wrote this book because there are too many DOS books on the shelves of bookstores already, yet few of them teach you what you really need to know. Enough said.

My hope is that through the skills you'll learn from this book, you'll become a more efficient, effective, and productive computer user. I hope this book helps you become more confident and saves you some frustration along the way. If you have any comments or suggestions for the next edition of this book, please let me know by using the postage-paid comment form at the back of the book. I look forward to hearing from you.

Doug Lowe
February, 1993

Section 1

An introduction to Personal Computers

Before you can use DOS effectively, you need to understand the concepts and terms that apply to the PC you're using. So the two chapters in this section provide you with the background you need. In chapter 1, you'll learn the hardware concepts and terms that every PC user should know. In chapter 2, you'll learn the software concepts and terms that every DOS user should know.

If you're already familiar with PC hardware, you can probably skip chapter 1. But you ought to at least skim the chapter to make sure you know the concepts and terms it presents. On the other hand, you should probably read chapter 2 even if you are familiar with PC software. This chapter presents some concepts that will make it easier for you to learn how to use DOS. It also presents some terms that will direct you to other chapters in this book.

Chapter 1

Hardware concepts and terms for every PC user

Do you know what kind of processor your PC has? Do you know the difference between internal memory and disk storage? Do you know the difference between double-density and high-density diskettes? Do you know why you usually lose your work when a power failure takes place while you're using an application program? Are you familiar with the terms listed in the first group at the end of this chapter?

If you've answered "yes" to all those questions, you can probably skip this chapter and go on to chapter 2. But if you've answered "no" to any of them, you should read this chapter. To use a PC effectively, you need to have a basic understanding of the equipment, or *hardware*, you're using. That's why this chapter presents the hardware concepts and terms that every PC user should know.

An introduction to PCs

In 1981, IBM introduced a microcomputer called the IBM *Personal Computer*, or *PC*. Today, the term *PC* can be used to refer to the original IBM PC, the IBM PC/XT (or just *XT*), the IBM PC/AT (or just *AT*), and the IBM *PS/2*. The term can also be used to refer to PCs that aren't made by IBM, like those made by Compaq, Tandy, and Dell. The PCs that aren't made by IBM are often called *clones* or *compatibles* because they work just like IBM PCs.

As I explained in the preface, this book is for people who use PCs. But it doesn't matter whether you have an XT, an AT, a PS/2, or an IBM compatible. Although one PC may be faster than another, DOS works the same on all of them.

The physical components of a PC

Figure 1-1 shows a typical PC. As you can see, it consists of five physical components: a printer, a monitor, a keyboard, a mouse, and a systems unit. In a portable PC, the monitor, keyboard, and systems unit are combined into a single carrying case. But on most other systems, these units are separate and can be purchased separately. Because you're probably familiar with these five components already, I'll just describe them briefly.

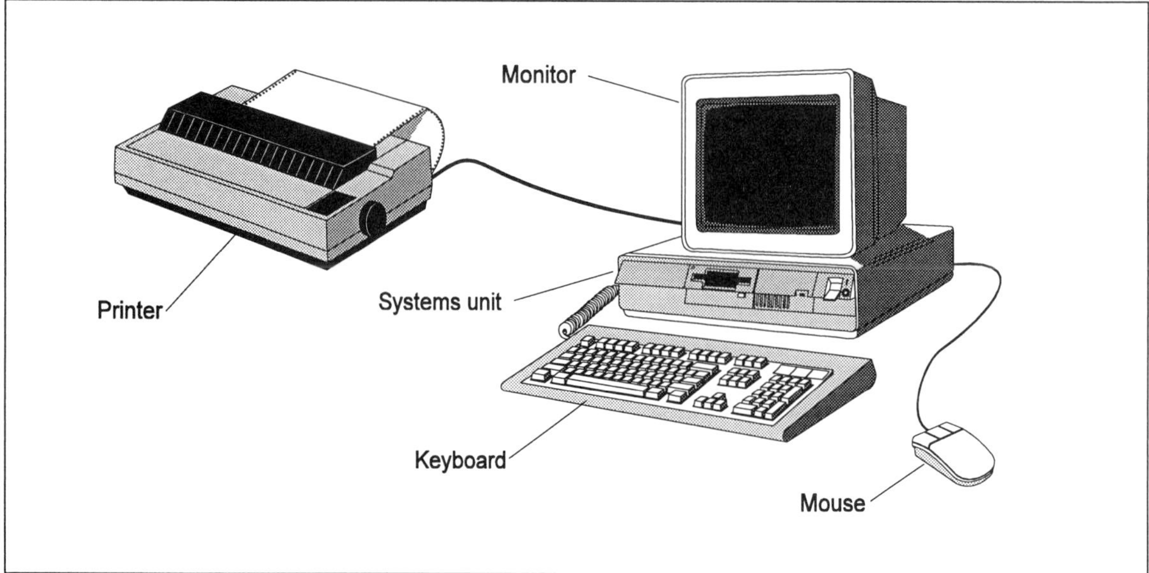

Figure 1-1 The physical components of a PC

The systems unit The *systems unit* is the unit that the other physical components are connected to. This unit can also be referred to as the *electronics unit* or the *systems chassis*. As you will soon learn, this unit contains the processor that controls the operations of the PC. In contrast, the four other physical components are input and output devices.

The monitor The *monitor* is an output device that can also be referred to as a *display*, a *screen*, or a *CRT* (which stands for *Cathode Ray Tube*). *Monochrome monitors* can display only one color, which is usually green or amber on a dark background, but *color monitors* can display a variety of colors. Today, most PCs are sold with a color monitor.

Like a television set, a monitor uses dot patterns to display characters and images. The individual dots are called *pixels*, which is short for *picture elements*. The more pixels a monitor can display, the higher its *resolution* and the sharper its image. Not surprisingly, high-resolution monitors cost more than low-resolution monitors, just as color monitors cost more than monochrome monitors.

When a monitor displays images, it can do so in two modes. In *text mode*, data is displayed on the screen in the form of characters. In this mode, most monitors display data in 25 rows of 80 characters each for a total of 2,000 characters on the screen. In *graphics mode*, however, all of the pixels on the screen can be independently controlled. Then, the monitor can display complex diagrams and shapes. Since

Adapter	Standard resolution
Monochrome Display Adapter (MDA)	720x348
Color Graphics Adapter (CGA)	640x200
Enhanced Graphics Adapter (EGA)	640x350
Video Graphics Array (VGA)	640x480
Super VGA (SVGA)	800x600
High-resolution VGA (HRVGA)	1024x768

Figure 1-2 A summary of monitor characteristics

graphics mode is considerably slower than text mode, most programs work in text mode unless they need the extra capabilities offered by graphics mode.

When a monitor is in operation, its images are controlled by an electronic *display adapter* within the systems unit. This display adapter can come as a separate circuit card that's installed in the systems unit, or it can be an integral part of the system unit's main circuit board.

Today, monitors for PCs are available in six standard forms that are related to their display adapters as summarized in figure 1-2. The *Monochrome Display Adapter*, or *MDA*, is for the basic monochrome monitor. Because the original IBM version of the MDA could display only text, an MDA monitor couldn't display graphic images like a *Lotus 1-2-3* graph. However, a monochrome graphics display adapter called *Hercules* soon became so popular that almost all monochrome monitors and display adapters now support it. The other five display adapters in figure 1-2 are for progressively better color graphics monitors: *CGA* stands for *Color Graphics Adapter*; *EGA* for *Enhanced Graphics Adapter*; *VGA* for *Video Graphics Array; SVGA* for *Super VGA*; and *HRVGA* for *High-Resolution VGA*. Most PCs sold today come with SVGA or better monitors and adapters.

You should realize that there are other display adapters in widespread use besides the standard ones listed in figure 1-2. For example, large-screen monochrome monitors are common for desktop publishing applications. These display adapters have resolutions that range from 1024x1024 to as high as 2048x1536, and they are usually used with 19- or 20-inch monitors. Because they display black characters on a white background, they're often called *paper-white monitors*.

The keyboard The *keyboard* is the main input device of a PC. Although it resembles the keyboard of a typewriter, a PC keyboard has more keys, as you can see in figure 1-3. This figure shows the two most common types of PC keyboards: the 84-key and the 101-key keyboards. Although the 84-key keyboard was the original keyboard for the AT, the 101-key keyboard is now a standard component of all PS/2s and most other PCs.

If you study the keyboards in figure 1-3, you can see that they have several types of keys. First, the keyboards include a full set of typewriter keys. Second, they have a numeric pad on the right side of the keyboard in the same arrangement as the ten keys on a calculator. They also have either ten or twelve function keys, depending on the type of keyboard, numbered F1, F2, F3, and so on. And they have some special control keys, such as the Escape key (Esc), the Control key (Ctrl), the Alternate key (Alt), the Page-up and Page-down keys, and so on.

The Arrow keys move the *cursor* on the screen of a monitor. The cursor is the underline or highlight that identifies a specific character or area of a screen. As a result, the Arrow keys are often called *cursor control keys.*

If you have an 84-key keyboard on your PC, you have to know how the Num-lock key works on it. Within the ten-key numeric pad of that keyboard, every key but the 5-key has a control function. For instance, the 7-key is also the Home key; the 8-key is also the Up arrow key; and the 9-key is also the Page-up (Pg-up) key. If the Num-lock light is on, each of the keys represents its decimal value or the decimal point. If the Num-lock light is off, each of the keys represents its control function. To turn the Num-lock light on or off, you press the Num-lock key.

Because this doubling up of keyboard meanings can cause some entry errors, most people prefer the 101-key keyboard shown in figure 1-3. Here, the control functions of the ten-key pad are duplicated on control keys that are located between the typewriter keys and the numeric pad. Then, if you keep the Num-lock light lit, you can use the control pad for control functions and the numeric pad for numeric entries.

The mouse A *mouse* is a small hand-held input device that has two or three buttons on it. If you've ever used a mouse or seen one used, you know that it's just a pointing device. When you move the mouse across a table top (or across a *mouse pad* on the table top), a pointer on the monitor moves in the same direction. This pointer on the monitor is called the *mouse cursor*.

With a little practice, you can easily and quickly move the mouse cursor anywhere on the screen. Then, you can *click* or *double-click* the buttons on top of the mouse to perform various actions. If you *click-and-drag* a mouse, you can highlight portions of the screen.

Exactly how you use a mouse, or whether you can use a mouse at all, depends on the programs you're using. For instance, the early releases of DOS didn't provide for the use of a mouse. More recent releases do let you use a mouse for certain functions, though. So in this book, I'll show you how to perform those functions using either a mouse or the keyboard.

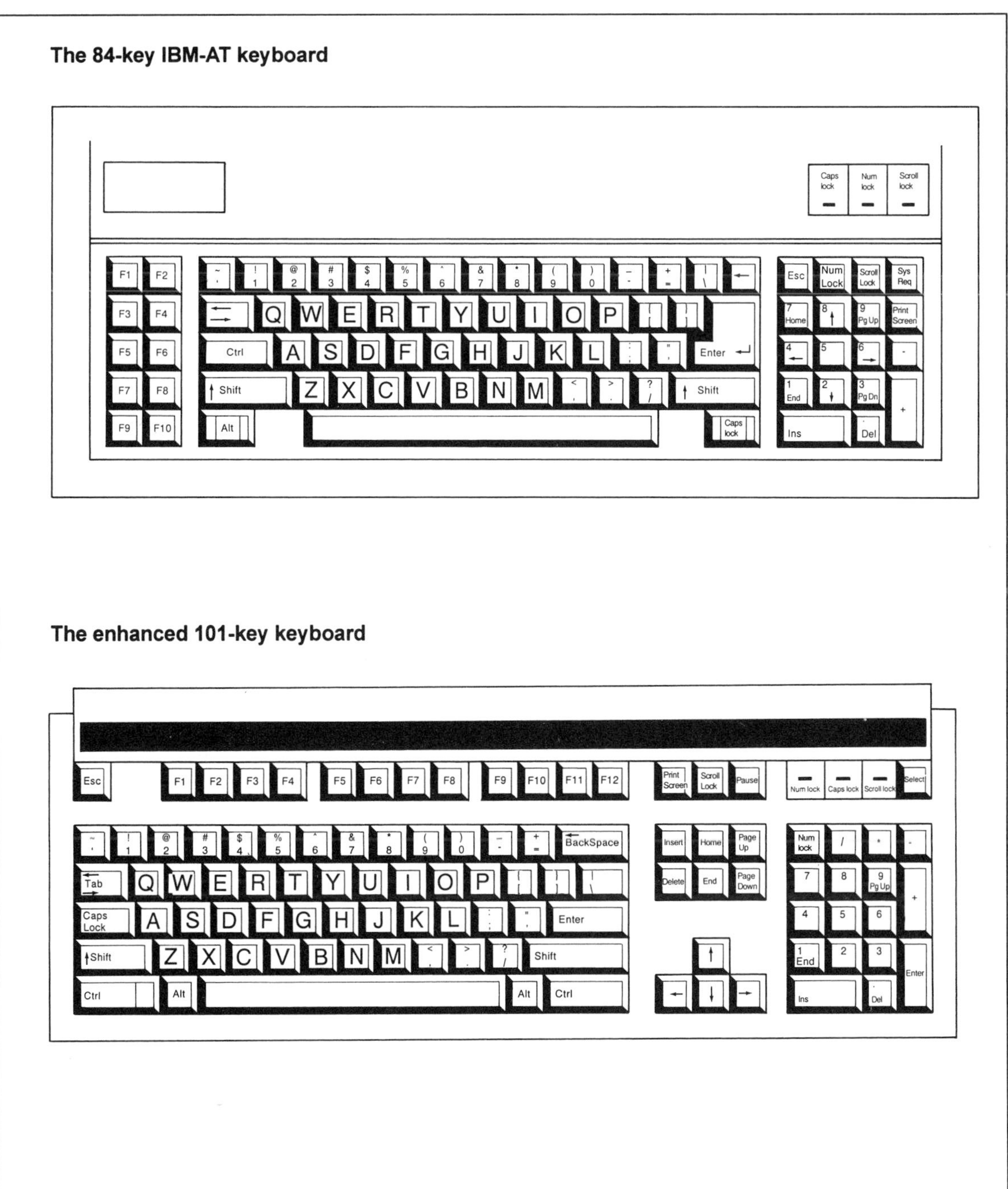

Figure 1-3 The two most common types of PC keyboards

The printer The *printer* is an output device. Although many different kinds of printers have been developed, the most widely used printers today are dot-matrix printers and laser printers.

A *dot-matrix printer* works by striking small pins against an inked ribbon. The resulting dots form characters or graphic images on the paper. Today, most dot-matrix printers are either 9-pin or 24-pin printers. As you might expect, 24-pin printers print with better quality than 9-pin printers. But both can print text in two different modes: *draft mode* and *letter quality mode*. Not surprisingly, the draft mode is faster, but the letter quality mode is easier to read. For instance, my 24-pin printer prints at 216 cps (characters per second) in draft mode and 72 cps in letter quality mode. As a result, I sometimes print a document in draft mode first, then use letter quality mode for the final copy that other people will see.

Today, dot-matrix printers can print text characters in more than one size and more than one typeface, or *font*. They can print type styles such as italics and boldface. They can print graphics such as charts and diagrams. And they can handle cut forms as well as continuous forms. In general, the more you pay for a dot-matrix printer, the faster it prints and the more features it comes with.

In contrast to dot-matrix printers, *laser printers* work on the same principle as photocopiers. These printers are not only faster than dot-matrix printers, but they're also quieter (since no pins are striking the paper) and they print with better quality. Today, most laser printers print at 300 dpi (dots per inch), but 600 dpi printers are also available. Naturally, the print quality (or resolution) of a laser printer depends on the number of dots per inch, and high-resolution printers are more expensive than low-resolution printers.

At one time, dot-matrix printers were far less expensive than laser printers, and far more common. But as laser printer prices have dropped, the quality and speed they provide have made them more and more popular. In fact, nowadays most people at least consider purchasing a laser printer instead of a dot-matrix printer when they buy a PC. And many businesses are making laser printers available to employees in every department.

Whether you use a dot-matrix or a laser printer, the printer cable goes from the printer to a *printer port* on the back of your systems unit. The printer port can be either a *parallel port* or a *serial port*, and various dot-matrix and laser printers use either one type of port or the other. You don't have to worry about attaching your printer cable to the wrong type of port because it won't fit. But you do have to make sure that your systems unit has the right type of port for your printer.

Fortunately, most PCs today come with both a parallel and a serial port. In fact, your systems unit may have two serial ports and two parallel ports. If it does, you must make sure that you plug your printer cable into the correct parallel or serial port. If your PC doesn't have the type of port you need for a printer, you can add the right port to your systems unit without much trouble.

The primary components of the systems unit

If you've ever opened up the systems unit of a PC, you know that it is full of electronic components. These components are attached to electronic cards that are inserted into the unit. Although you don't have to understand how any of these components work, you should have a conceptual idea of what the primary components are and what they do.

Figure 1-4 is a conceptual drawing of the components of a typical PC. Within the systems unit, you can see four primary components: the diskette drive or drives, the hard disk, internal memory, and the processor.

The diskette drive or drives A *diskette* is the actual recording medium on which data is stored, and the *diskette drive* is the device that writes data on the diskette and reads data from the diskette. Diskettes are also called *floppy disks*, but I'll refer to them as diskettes throughout this book. To read data from a diskette or write data on a diskette, you insert the diskette into the slot on a diskette drive and close the drive's latch (if it has a latch).

Figure 1-5 illustrates the sizes of the diskettes that can be used with PCs. Originally, all PCs, XTs, and ATs used 5-1/4 inch diskettes, and all PS/2s used the newer 3-1/2 inch diskettes. Today, however, most PCs come with 3-1/2 inch diskette drives, and many come with both a 5-1/4 and a 3-1/2 inch drive.

The amount of data you can store on a diskette depends on its size and on whether it's a *double-density* diskette, a *high-density* diskette, or, in the case of 3-1/2 inch diskettes, an *extended-density* diskette. Each type has a different storage capacity that is measured in *bytes* of data. For practical purposes, you can think of one byte of data as one character of data, and you can think of a character as a letter, a digit (0-9), or a special character such as #, %, or &. Thus, ten bytes of diskette storage are required to store the word *impossible*; four bytes are required to store the number *4188*; and two bytes are required to store *$9*.

For 5-1/4 inch double-density diskettes, the storage capacity is 360,000 bytes, or 360KB (where *K* stands for 1,000, *B* stands for bytes, and *KB* stands for *kilobyte*, which is approximately 1,000 bytes). In contrast, high-density diskettes allow for 1,200KB, or 1.2MB (where *M* stands for 1,000,000, *B* stands for byte, and *MB* stands for *megabyte*, which is approximately one million bytes). For 3-1/2 inch diskettes, double-density capacity is 720KB, high-density capacity is 1.44MB, and extended-density capacity is 2.88MB.

If you're curious about why I said one KB is approximately 1,000 bytes and one MB is approximately 1,000,000 bytes, it has to do with the way computers perform arithmetic. Strictly speaking, one KB is 1,024 bytes and one MB is 1,048,576 bytes. This is because computers often work with powers of two rather than with powers of ten, and 1,024 and 1,048,576 are powers of two (2^{10} and 2^{20}). Only computer specialists need to be aware of this distinction, however. For most purposes, its safe to think of one KB as 1,000 bytes and one MB as 1,000,000 bytes.

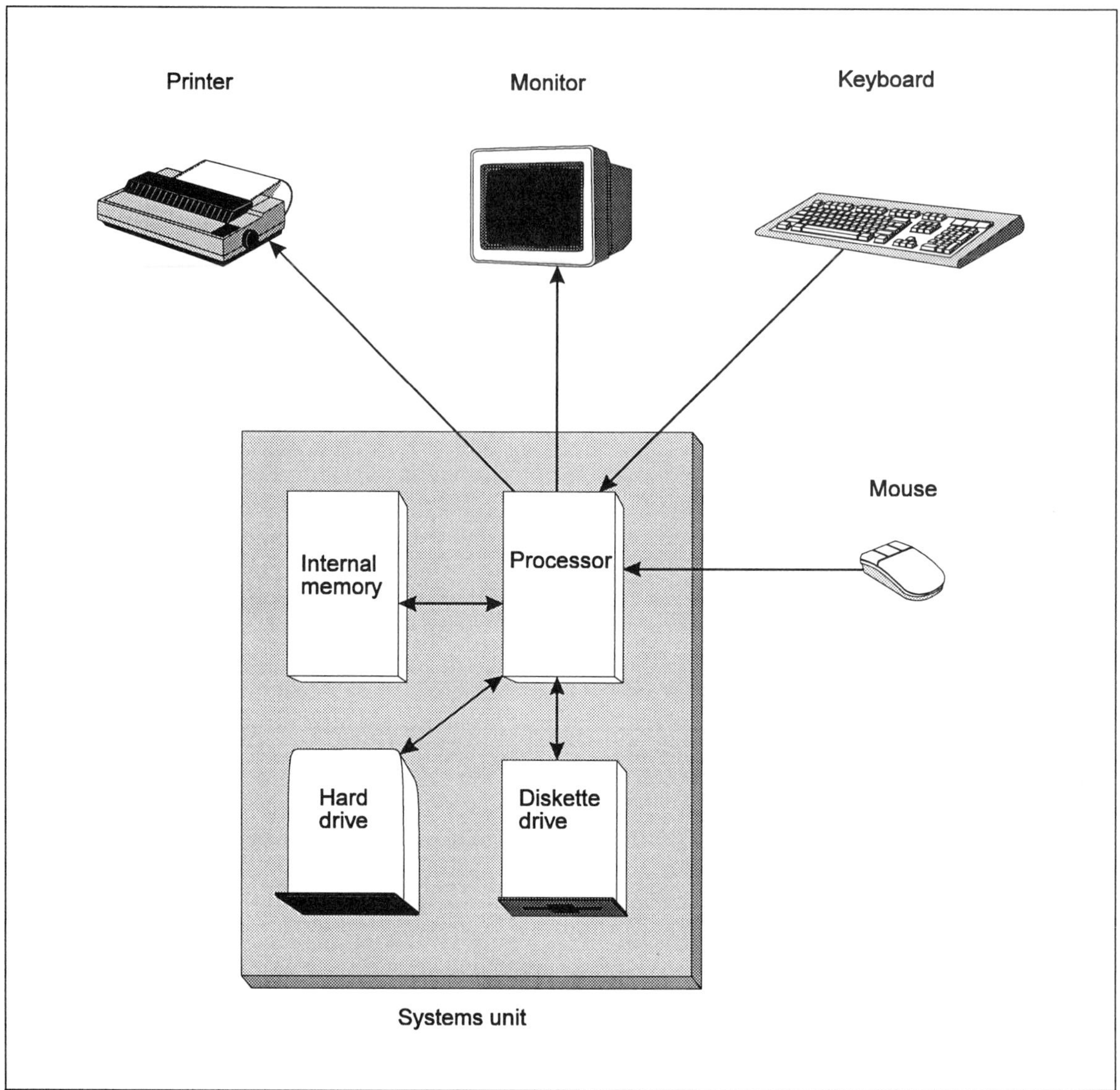

Figure 1-4 The internal components of the systems unit

Figure 1-6 summarizes the diskette sizes and capacities. Because the labelling for diskettes is often confusing, this figure also lists the common labelling designations for each type of diskette.

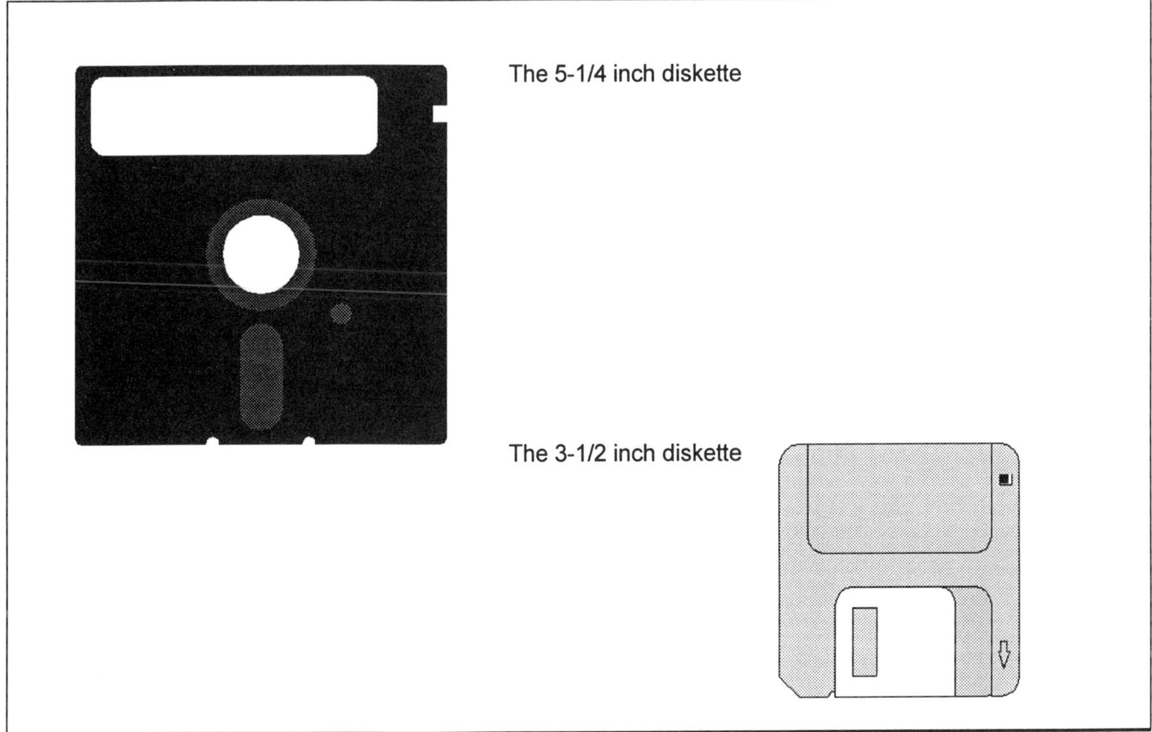

Figure 1-5 The two diskette sizes

When you use a diskette to transfer data from one PC to another, you must make sure that you're using a diskette that is the right size and capacity for the system you're transferring the data to. For example, on older PCs like the XT, a 5-1/4 inch diskette drive can usually only read and write double-density diskettes. However, a 5-1/4 inch drive on an AT can read and write either double- or high-density diskettes. As a result, you must use double-density diskettes to transfer data between an XT and an AT.

Likewise, if you have a PC with both a 3-1/2 inch and a 5-1/4 inch drive and you want to copy data from one to the other, you must make sure that the diskette you're copying to has enough room on it. For example, if you copy from a high-density 3-1/2 inch diskette to a double-density 5-1/4 inch diskette, you'll probably run into trouble. That's because the 3-1/2 inch diskette may have up to 1.44 MB of data on it, while the 5-1/4 inch diskette can hold only 360KB.

The hard disk In contrast to diskettes, a *hard disk* is installed inside the systems unit, and the recording medium and the drive are sealed together in a single unit. As a result, a hard disk can't be removed from the PC the way a diskette can. That's why

Size	Capacity	Common labelling notation
5-1/4"	360KB	5-1/4" Double-Sided Double-Density 5-1/4" DSDD
5-1/4"	1.2MB	5-1/4" Double-Sided High-Density 5-1/4" DSHD
3-1/2"	720KB	3-1/2" Double-Sided Double-Density 3-1/2" 2DD 3-1/2" 1.0M formatted capacity
3-1/2"	1.44MB	3-1/2" Double-Sided High-Density 3-1/2" 2HD 3-1/2" 2.0M formatted capacity
3-1/2"	2.88MB	3-1/2" Double-Sided Extended-Density 3-1/2" 2ED 3-1/2" 4.0M formatted capacity

Figure 1-6 A summary of diskette characteristics

hard disks are sometimes called *fixed disks*. In this book, though, I'll use the term *hard disk*.

Today, most hard disks have capacities of 40MB or more, and you can buy hard disks with capacities of 1,000MB or more. To put that into perspective, consider that one megabyte of disk storage can hold about 500 pages of word processing text. So an 80MB hard disk can hold 40,000 pages of text, while a 1.2MB diskette can hold only about 600 pages. To look at it another way, an 80MB disk can store the equivalent of about 66 diskettes that have a capacity of 1.2MB.

To give you some idea of how a hard disk works, figure 1-7 is a drawing of a typical hard disk after the protective cover has been removed. In this device, data is recorded on both sides of three disk platters that are stacked on a spindle. When the disk drive is in operation, the spindle assembly rotates at a speed of 3,600 revolutions per minute, or 60 times per second.

The top and bottom surface of each disk platter is coated with a material that contains magnetic particles. This surface can be used to store information in the form of magnetic codes. To write data on this surface or to read data from it, there is one *read/write head* for each surface. As a result, a disk drive with three platters and six disk surfaces has six read/write heads. When the disk is operating, the read/write heads don't actually touch the surfaces of the disks. Instead, they float on cushions of air that are about 1/100,000 of an inch thick.

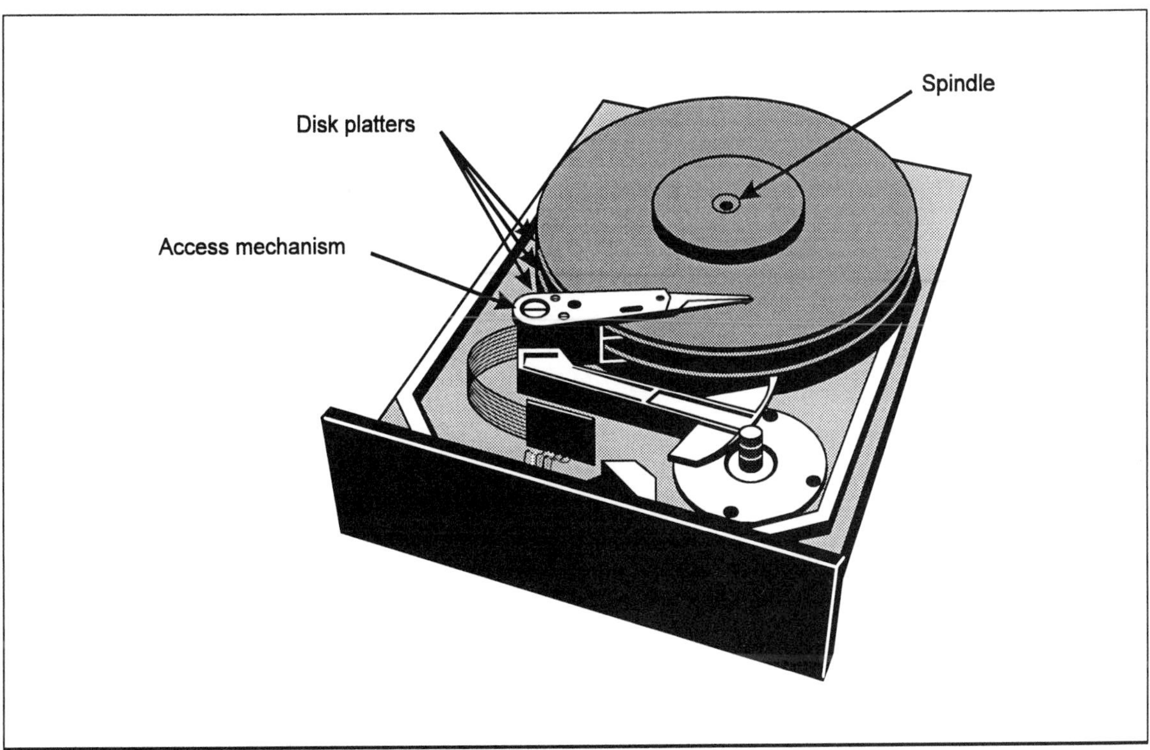

Figure 1-7 The primary components of a hard disk

The read/write heads record data on the disk surfaces in a series of concentric circles called *tracks*, as illustrated in figure 1-8. The number of tracks on each recording surface depends on the make and model of the disk drive. For instance, the Seagate ST-1144 hard disk has 1,024 tracks on each surface.

When the access mechanism is moved to a track, all of the read/write heads are moved at once. If, for example, a hard disk has six recording surfaces, all six read/write heads are moved to the same track when the access mechanism is moved. These six tracks can be referred to as one *cylinder* of data. If, for example, the access mechanism is moved to the 75th cylinder, all six tracks in the cylinder can be read or written without moving the access mechanism again.

As shown in figure 1-9, each track on each disk surface is divided into a fixed number of *sectors*. In general, each sector of a hard disk can store 512 bytes of data, and most hard disks have 17 sectors per track. At 1,024 tracks per surface, that's 17,408 sectors per surface. Then, if the hard disk has seven platters and fourteen recording surfaces, the entire disk has 243,712 sectors. At 512 bytes per sector, that's more than 120MB of data. Because each sector on a disk has a unique sector number, the disk drive can directly access any sector on the disk.

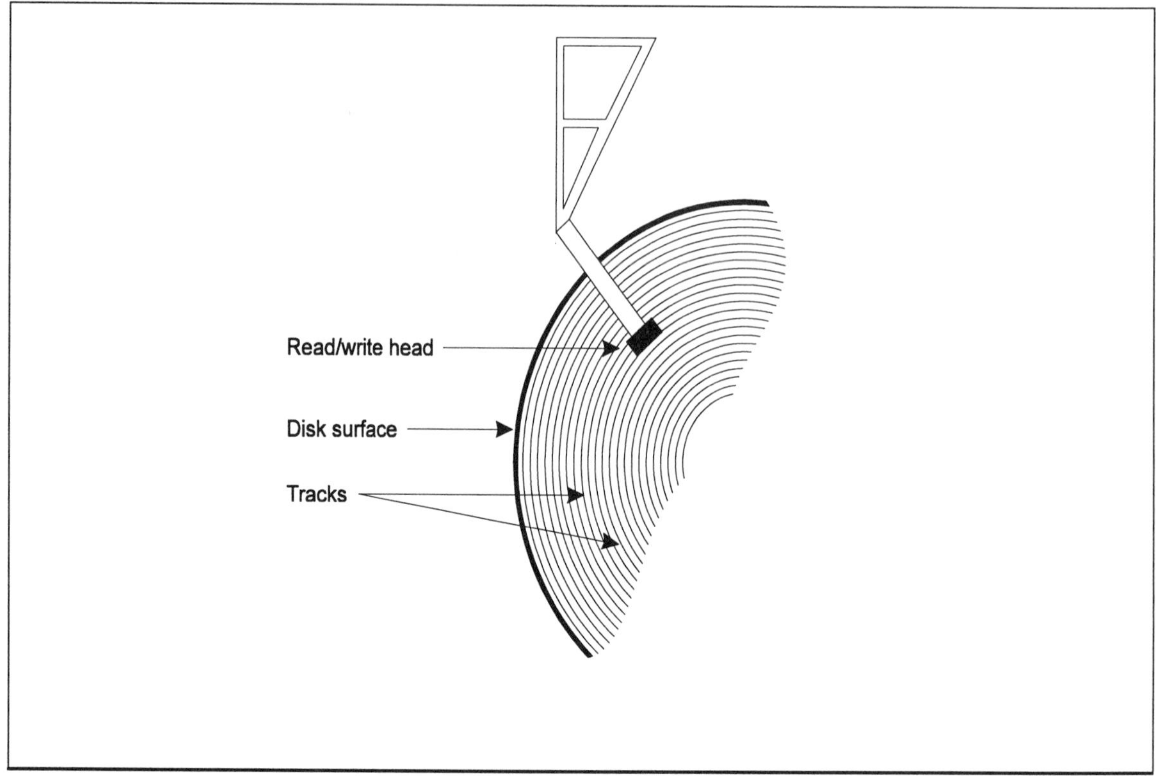

Figure 1-8 The tracks on the surface of a disk platter

To read or write a sector, the disk drive goes through four phases. First, the access mechanism is moved to the track that contains the desired sector. If, for example, the sector is on the 212th track, the access mechanism moves to the 212th cylinder. Second, the read/write head that is on the correct surface is turned on. Third, the disk drive waits until the desired sector rotates around to the read/write head. Fourth, the disk drive reads or writes the sector.

Today, the *access speeds* for hard disks are typically from 19 to 65 *milliseconds* (thousandths of a second). That means it takes less than one-tenth of a second to access any sector on a hard disk, even though a typical hard disk contains more than 40,000 sectors. Once a sector has been accessed, it can be read or written by the hard disk.

Because you can store so much data on a hard disk, you have to manage a hard disk more carefully than you manage diskettes. In particular, you have to use directories to organize the data on a hard disk. And you have to back up the data on a hard disk so you won't lose it in the event of a hardware or software problem. As you read this book, you'll realize that one of its major purposes is to teach you skills that help you get the most from your hard disk.

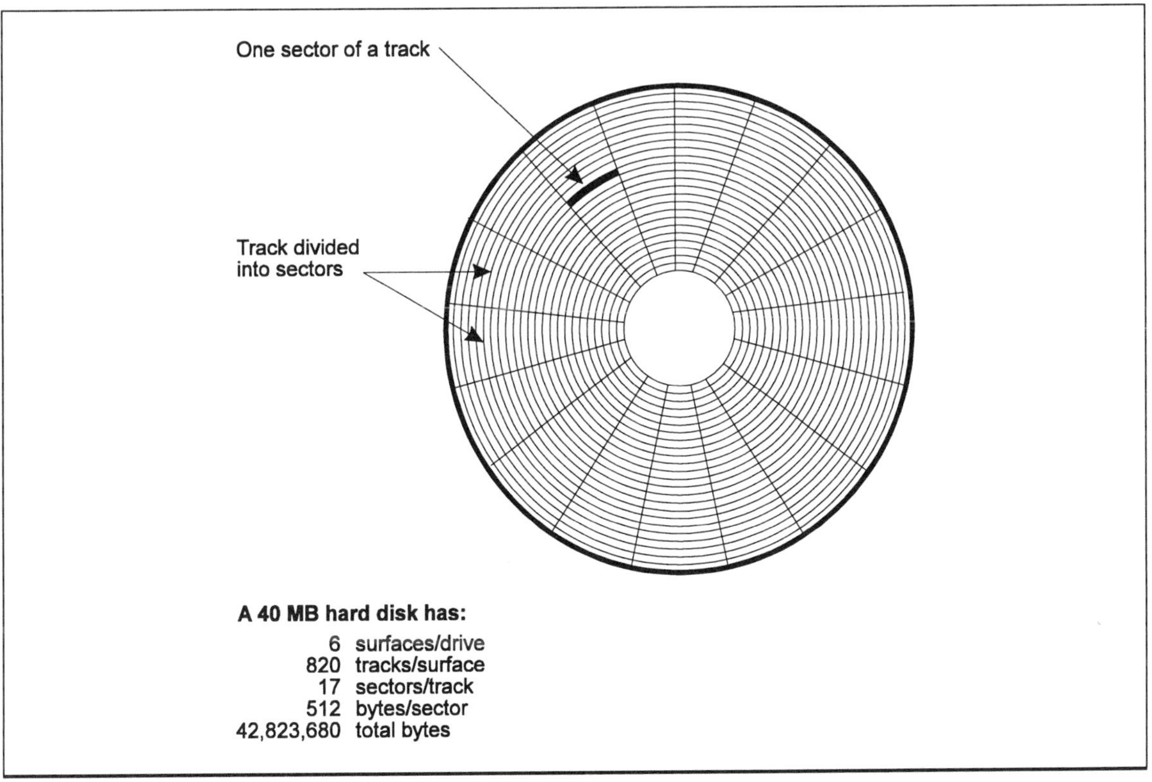

Figure 1-9 Tracks and sectors on one surface of a hard disk

Now that you're familiar with the operation of a hard disk, you should realize the same concepts and terms apply to diskettes and diskette drives. Both the 5-1/4 inch and 3-1/2 inch diskettes have a single disk platter, and data can be recorded on both sides of the diskette. However, the standard-capacity, 5-1/4 inch diskette has only 40 tracks per surface and nine sectors per track, and the high-capacity diskette has only 80 tracks per surface and 15 sectors per track. Similarly, the standard-capacity 3-1/2 inch diskette has 80 tracks per surface with nine sectors per track, and the high-capacity diskette has 80 tracks with 18 sectors per track. As a result, the capacity of a diskette is only a fraction of the capacity of a hard disk.

Because a hard disk rotates at 3,600 revolutions per minute and a diskette is stopped between operations, a hard disk can read and write sectors much faster than a diskette drive. Similarly, the access time of a hard disk is usually a small fraction of the access time for a diskette drive. From a practical point of view, this means you are rarely delayed for more than a second or two by the operations of a hard disk. In contrast, diskette operations are often so slow that they're frustrating.

Since your PC has a hard disk, you probably won't use diskettes much because all of your programs will be stored on the hard disk. However, you still need at least one diskette drive on your PC. You'll use it to back up the data on your hard disk to diskettes, to install new programs from diskettes to your hard disk, and to transfer data from one PC to another.

Internal memory Before your PC can operate on the data that is stored on a diskette or a hard disk, the data must be read into the *internal memory* of the systems unit. This memory can also be called *internal storage* or *RAM* (for *Random Access Memory*), but I'll refer to it as internal memory throughout this book.

Like diskette or hard disk storage, the capacity of internal memory is measured in kilobytes or megabytes. Although the original PCs were typically sold with less than 1MB of internal memory, PCs today are usually sold with 2MB or 4MB of internal memory. The most powerful PCs are sold with 8MB, 16MB, or even 32MB of internal memory.

Because you'll hear the term used sooner or later, you should probably know that each byte of data stored on disk or in memory is actually made up of eight electronic components called *bits*. As data is stored in a byte, each bit is turned off or on to form a code. The standard code for the off-on combinations is called *ASCII* (pronounced as′-key), and this code can be used to store one letter, number, or special character in each byte of data. However, the bits can also be used to store data in other coded forms.

In contrast to the access speeds for hard disks, which are measured in milliseconds (thousandths of a second), the access speeds for internal memory are measured in *nanoseconds* (billionths of a second). This means data can be accessed thousands of times faster in internal memory than it can be in hard disk storage. From a practical point of view, this means operations that take place in internal memory happen so fast that you're not aware of them. In contrast, you often notice a delay when your PC accesses its hard disk.

Because a program must be stored in internal memory before it can be used, each program requires a specific amount of internal memory. For instance, *WordPerfect* 5.1 requires a PC with at least 384KB of internal memory, and *Lotus 1-2-3* release 3.4 requires 1MB of internal memory. However, because the PC was originally designed for a maximum of 640KB, only a few programs require more than 640KB of memory.

This first 640KB of internal memory can be referred to as *conventional memory*. If your PC doesn't have a full 640KB of conventional memory (the first PCs had only 128KB) and you want to use a program that requires more memory than your PC has, you can add more conventional memory to it. On some PCs, you can do that by buying memory chips that you plug into the *motherboard*, the main electronic circuit board of your systems unit. On other PCs, you must buy a *memory expansion card* that you plug into an *expansion slot* within the systems unit. In either case, you have to open the systems unit's case before you can add the memory.

There are four other types of memory you might hear mentioned: *extended memory*, *expanded memory*, *high memory*, and *upper memory*. These all refer to memory above and beyond the conventional 640K that's available under DOS. To explain the differences between these types of memory and describe how each is used is beyond the scope of this introductory chapter. You'll learn more about memory in chapter 25 when I show you how to make the most of your computer's memory using the memory management features of DOS versions 5.0 and 6.0.

You should realize, though, that there is a difference between extended and expanded memory. So before you add memory, you must make sure it's the right kind for the program that will use it, and it's the right kind for your system. I'll have more to say about extended and expanded memory in chapter 25.

When you're using a PC, your current work is stored in internal memory. However, the data in internal memory is erased when the power for the PC is turned off, either deliberately or due to a power failure. That's why you must store your work to diskette or hard disk storage before you turn your PC off. Otherwise, your work is lost. In contrast to internal memory, diskettes and hard disks retain the data that has been stored on them whether the power is on or not.

The processor If you look back to figure 1-4, you can see that all of the components I've described so far are connected to the *processor*. When a program is in operation, the processor controls all of the other components of the PC by executing the instructions of the program. Other terms for a processor are *microprocessor*, *central processing unit*, and *CPU*, but I'll use the term *processor* throughout this book.

The basic function of the processor is to execute any of the 100 or so instructions a PC is designed to perform. Some of these instructions perform arithmetic calculations like adding or multiplying. Other instructions make decisions by comparing two values and acting on the result of the comparison. Still other instructions communicate with devices like the keyboard, monitor, or hard disk.

In a PC, the entire processor is contained in a single *microprocessor chip*. Most of these chips are manufactured by Intel and have names like the 8088, the 80286, the 80386, and the 80486, as summarized in figure 1-10. As you can see, the shortened versions of the chip names are the 286, the 386SX, the 386, the 486, and so on. (A few other manufacturers have recently begun manufacturing processor chips that are compatible with the Intel chips. But DOS and your application programs work the same, whether your PC uses a genuine Intel chip or a compatible.)

Because the processor controls all of the operations of a PC, the speed of the processor can have an important effect on how fast a program runs on your PC. One measure of processor speed is *clock speed*. In general, the faster the clock speed, the faster the computer operates. The clock speed of the original IBM PC was 4.77 million cycles per second, or 4.77Mhz (*Mhz* stands for *Megahertz*). Today, as you can see in figure 1-10, some processors have clock speeds in the 25 to 66Mhz range.

You should realize, though, that clock speed isn't the only factor that influences your processor's speed. Which processor chip your system is based on often makes an

Processor names	Abbreviated names	Clock speeds
8088	None	4.77 - 10Mhz
80286	286	6 - 20Mhz
80386SX	386SX	16 - 20Mhz
80386DX	386	16 - 33Mhz
80486SX	486SX	25 - 33Mhz
80486DX	486	25 - 50Mhz
80486DX2	486DX2	50 - 66Mhz

Figure 1-10 A summary of PC processors

even bigger difference than the clock speed of the processor. For example, the 286 is inherently faster than the 8088. Thus, a 286 running at a clock speed of 8Mhz is about five times as fast as an 8088 running at 8Mhz. Similarly, a 386 running at 20Mhz is about three times as fast as a 286 running at 20Mhz. And a 486 is about half again as fast as a 386 running at the same speed.

One reason the 80286 is inherently faster than the 8088 is that it works on 16 bits (two bytes) at a time instead of 8 bits (one byte). As a result, you can refer to a 286 as a 16-bit processor and to an 8088 as an 8-bit processor. That explains why a 10Mhz 286 works at least twice as fast as a 10Mhz 8088. Similarly, the 386 is a 32-bit processor, and that explains why a 20Mhz 386 is at least twice as fast as a 20Mhz 286.

This is a simplified explanation of processor speed because there's more to it than just the chip the processor is based on and how many bits the processor works on at a time. Also, whenever you consider processor speed, you should realize that it is only one measure of the speed of your PC. When it comes to getting work done, the speed of your hard disk is often more important than the speed of your processor.

Besides performance, you should know that different processors provide different technical features. Some programs are designed to take advantage of some of the features of a specific processor, and some even require a specific processor. Release 3.1 of *Lotus 1-2-3*, for example, requires that you have at least a 286 processor so it can use some of the special features that are provided by the more advanced processors. In contrast, release 2.3 of *Lotus 1-2-3* works with all processors from the 8088 on.

Some perspective on hardware

Throughout this chapter, I've tried to simplify the concepts and keep the number of new terms to a minimum. In general, I've tried to present only those PC concepts you need to know to use your software effectively. And I've tried to present only those terms that you're most likely to encounter in manuals and in magazine articles.

Nevertheless, this chapter presents more than you need to know about hardware if all you want to do is use your PC effectively. As a result, you shouldn't feel that you need to know all of the terms in this chapter before you continue. That's why I've divided them into two groups. If you're familiar with the terms in the first group that follows, you're ready to go on to the next chapter.

Terms you should be familiar with before you continue

hardware
personal computer
PC
XT
monitor
monochrome monitor
color monitor
keyboard
cursor
cursor control keys
mouse
mouse cursor
printer
dot-matrix printer
laser printer
diskette
AT
PS/2
compatible
systems unit
diskette drive
double-density
high-density
extended-density
byte
kilobyte (KB)
megabyte (MB)
hard disk
internal memory
conventional memory
processor
microprocessor chip

Objectives

1. List the primary physical components of a PC.
2. List the primary components of a systems unit.
3. Explain why you should save your work before you turn the PC off.

Other terms presented in this chapter

clone
electronics unit
systems chassis
display
screen
CRT
Cathode Ray Tube
resolution
pixel
picture element
text mode
graphics mode
display adapter
Monochrome Display Adapter
MDA
CGA
Color Graphics Adapter
EGA
Enhanced Graphics Adapter
VGA
Video Graphics Array
SVGA
Super VGA
HRVGA

High-resolution VGA
paper-white monitors
mouse pad
click
double-click
click-and-drag
draft mode
letter quality mode
font
printer port
parallel port
serial port
floppy disk
fixed disk
read/write head
track
cylinder
sector
access speed
milliseconds
internal storage
RAM
Random Access Memory
bit
ASCII
nanosecond
motherboard
memory expansion card
expansion slot
extended memory
expanded memory
high memory
upper memory
microprocessor
central processing unit
CPU
clock speed
Megahertz (Mhz)

Chapter 2

Software concepts and terms for every DOS user

Do you know the difference between an application program and an operating system program? Do you know what the primary functions of DOS are? Do you know what happens when you use the DOS command processor to start an application program? Do you know you can buy utility programs that will help you perform some functions more quickly and easily than you can with DOS?

Unless you can answer an unqualified "yes" to those questions, you should read this chapter before you go on to the next one. To use a PC effectively, you must have a basic understanding of PC *software*. The term *software* refers to the *programs* that direct the operations of the PC hardware. When you complete this chapter, you'll have the software background you need for learning how to use DOS.

The two types of programs every PC requires

In broad terms, PC software can be divided into two types: application programs and operating system programs. To do work on your PC, you need both types of programs. In case you're not already familiar with both types, here's some information about each.

Application programs An *application program* is a program you use to do your work. It lets you *apply* your PC to the jobs that you want to do on a PC. For instance, *WordPerfect* is a word processing program that lets you apply your PC to jobs like writing letters, memos, and reports. And *Lotus 1-2-3* is an application program that lets you apply your PC to the job of creating spreadsheets.

Figure 2-1 lists three of the most popular types of application programs: word processing, spreadsheet, and database programs. This figure also lists some of the most popular programs of each type. If you've used a PC at all, you've probably used one or more of these programs.

When you use a *word processing program*, you prepare *documents* like letters, memos, or reports. When you use a *spreadsheet program*, you prepare *spreadsheets* like budgets or profit projections. And when you use a *database program*, you create and maintain a *database* like an employee, customer, or vendor database. Once you

Program type	Examples	Operates upon
Word processing	*WordPerfect* *Microsoft Word*	Documents
Spreadsheet	*Lotus 1-2-3* *Quattro Pro*	Spreadsheets
Database	*dBase IV* *Paradox* *Q&A*	Records within a database

Figure 2-1 Three of the most popular types of application programs

establish a database, you can extract information from it in the form of reports and other documents.

Word processing, spreadsheet, and database programs are considered to be *general-purpose programs* because you can use them for so many different jobs. But many other kinds of general-purpose programs are also available. For instance, *presentation graphics programs* let you create charts, diagrams, and other graphic presentations. *Desktop publishing programs* let you create documents with published quality. And *integrated programs* combine the features of several different types of general-purpose programs. *Microsoft Works*, for example, provides word processing, spreadsheet, database, graphics, and communications features, all in one program.

In contrast to general-purpose programs, some programs are designed for special, narrowly-defined purposes. For example, you can buy a program that will help you manage rental properties, a program that will help you manage accounts receivables for a retail business, and a program that will analyze the quality of your writing. In fact, so many application programs are available today, it's difficult to categorize them.

Operating system programs An *operating system* is a program that lets your application programs run on your PC. For instance, an operating system lets you load an application program into internal memory so you can use it. An operating system also provides functions that let your application programs read a file from a disk drive, print on a printer, and so on.

The concept of an operating system is elusive because much of what the operating system does goes on without your knowing about it. When you save your work on a hard disk, for example, it is the operating system, not the application program, that actually writes the data on the disk. In other words, your application program communicates with the operating system without your knowing about it. Without the operating system, your application program wouldn't work.

Operating system	Current version	Characteristics	Special requirements
DOS	6.0	640K memory limit	None
Windows	3.1	4,096MB memory limit Multi-tasking capabilities Graphical user interface Runs DOS or *Windows* programs	80286 processor (80386 recommended) 1MB internal memory (4MB recommended) 8MB disk space
OS/2	2.0	4,096MB memory limit Multi-tasking capabilities Graphical user interface Runs DOS, *Windows*, or OS/2 programs	80386 processor 4MB internal memory (8MB recommended) 15MB disk space

Figure 2-2 The three operating systems for PCs

Figure 2-2 presents the three main operating systems you can use on a single-user PC today: *DOS*, *Microsoft Windows*, and *OS/2*. DOS (pronounced *doss*) is short for *Disk Operating System*. It's the most widely-used operating system, and it's the subject of this book.

Windows gets its name from the fact that it provides a *graphical user interface* (or *GUI*, pronounced *gooey*) built around the idea of dividing your screen into one or more rectangular areas called "windows." Each window can contain a different application program, and you can use the mouse to move or resize a window to arrange the information on your screen just the way you want it. One of the most compelling reasons for using *Windows* is that it lets you run more than one application program at a time. Another benefit of *Windows* is that it doesn't suffer from the 640K memory limit of DOS. Under *Windows*, your application programs can access as much internal memory as is available on your PC. Most PCs sold today come with both DOS and *Windows* already installed.

OS/2, which is short for *Operating System/2*, was designed to eventually replace DOS as a more powerful and more reliable operating system. Like *Microsoft Windows*, OS/2 uses a graphical user interface with resizable windows in which you can run your application programs; it lets you run more than one program at once; and it doesn't limit your application programs to 640K of internal memory. Although most experts agree that OS/2 is a technically superior operating system, DOS and *Windows* continue to dominate because of the huge number of PCs already using DOS and the perception that OS/2 is more difficult to install and maintain than DOS or *Windows*.

When you purchase an application program for your PC, make sure you get a version that's compatible with the operating system you're using. All of the operating systems listed in figure 2-2 can run DOS application programs. But if you're using *Windows*, you're better off purchasing *Windows* versions of your application programs. That way, your applications can take full advantage of *Windows*' advanced features. If you're running OS/2 version 2.0, you can run DOS or *Windows* applications, or you can purchase OS/2 versions of your applications (if you can find them; few software vendors have produced OS/2 versions of their programs).

As I mentioned, DOS is by far the most widely-used operating system on PCs today, and that won't change for awhile. It doesn't look as if OS/2 will overcome DOS, but *Windows* is becoming more popular all the time. If you're using *Windows*, this book will be useful, but you'll want to read an introductory *Windows* book as well. (I recommend *The Least You Need to Know about Windows*, by Steve Eckols.) If you're an OS/2 user, however, this book won't help much.

When DOS is sold by Microsoft Corporation, the company that created it, it's called *MS-DOS*; when it's sold by IBM Corporation, it's called *PC-DOS*; and some PC manufacturers provide their own modified versions of DOS. Fortunately, all of the manufacturers' versions work essentially the same way, so I'll use the term *DOS* in this book to apply to all of them.

What DOS provides

When you turn on a hard disk PC, it starts by loading a portion of DOS into internal memory. This portion of DOS occupies a portion of internal memory, usually from 40 to 70KB in size, as shown in the schematic drawing in figure 2-3. Because this portion of DOS remains in internal memory until you turn off your PC, DOS functions are available to you and your application programs whenever your PC is running.

In general terms, DOS provides three types of functions: command processing, DOS services, and DOS commands. You need to have a basic understanding of all three of these functions to use your PC effectively.

Command processing The DOS *command processor* is loaded into internal memory when you start your PC. When the command processor is in control of the system, it displays a *command prompt* like the one shown in figure 2-4. Generally, this command prompt is displayed when your PC finishes its start-up procedure.

When the command prompt is displayed, the command processor is waiting for you to enter a command. For instance, you normally enter the letters *wp* to start *WordPerfect* and the numbers *123* to start *Lotus 1-2-3*. You can also start DOS commands from the command prompt, as you will learn in a moment.

Figure 2-5 illustrates how DOS uses the command processor to switch from one application program to another. When you start your PC, the DOS command processor is loaded into the internal memory of your system along with some other parts of DOS. As I mentioned earlier, this portion of DOS resides in internal memory

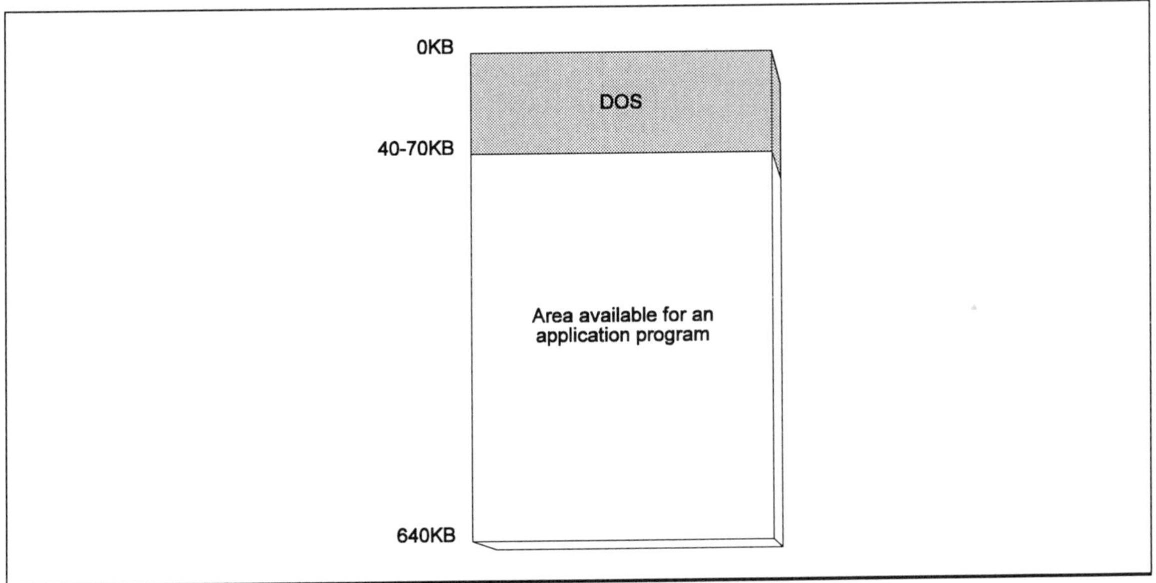

Figure 2-3 The contents of internal memory after DOS has been loaded into it

whenever the PC is in operation. This is indicated by the contents of internal memory in step 1 of the figure.

When you enter *wp* at the command prompt, the command processor loads *WordPerfect* from the hard disk into internal memory, as shown in step 2. This is called *loading a program*. Then, the command processor passes control of the PC to the first instruction of the *WordPerfect* program. When you instruct *WordPerfect* to retrieve a document, it copies the document file from the disk into internal memory. This is called *loading a file*. When you finish your word processing activities and exit the *WordPerfect* program, control is passed back to the command processor, as shown in step 3. Then, the memory used by *WordPerfect* and the document is released, and the command processor waits for another command from the PC user.

When you enter *123* at the command prompt as shown in step 4 of figure 2-5, the command processor loads *Lotus 1-2-3* into internal memory as shown in step 5. Then, the command processor passes control to the first instruction of the application program. When you finish your spreadsheet work and exit the *Lotus 1-2-3* program, control is passed back to the command processor as shown in step 6. Then, the command processor waits for your next command. In this way, the command processor lets you switch from one program to the next.

This figure also shows why it's crucial to save the file you've been working on before you exit from an application program. If you look back at step 4, you'll see that, once you've exited from a program, DOS treats the internal memory used by the program as though it were unused. So if you don't save the file you've been working on before you exit, your work will be lost.

Figure 2-4 A typical DOS command prompt

DOS services When an application program is running, DOS provides *DOS services* to the program. Some of the most important of these services are called *input/output services*, or *I/O services*. These services make it possible for the application program to receive input from the input devices of the PC and to give output through the output devices of the PC.

To illustrate, figure 2-6 shows how DOS provides I/O services when an application program wants to retrieve data from a hard disk. Here, you can see that an application program doesn't access disk data directly. Instead, it requests DOS to do the work for it. In step 1, the application program asks DOS to retrieve data from the disk. In step 2, DOS directs the disk device to read the requested data. In step 3, the disk device reads the data and sends it back to DOS. Finally, in step 4, DOS returns the requested data to the application program.

Actually, this process is much more complicated than figure 2-6 indicates. For example, DOS must be able to retrieve data from any type of disk drive, whether it's a 5-1/4 inch or 3-1/2 inch diskette drive, a 30MB hard disk, or a 300MB hard disk. In addition, DOS must be able to handle a variety of error conditions that might be encountered. For example, what if the data can't be found? Or what if a hardware failure occurs? By taking care of these kinds of details, DOS insures that all application programs handle disk access in a consistent manner.

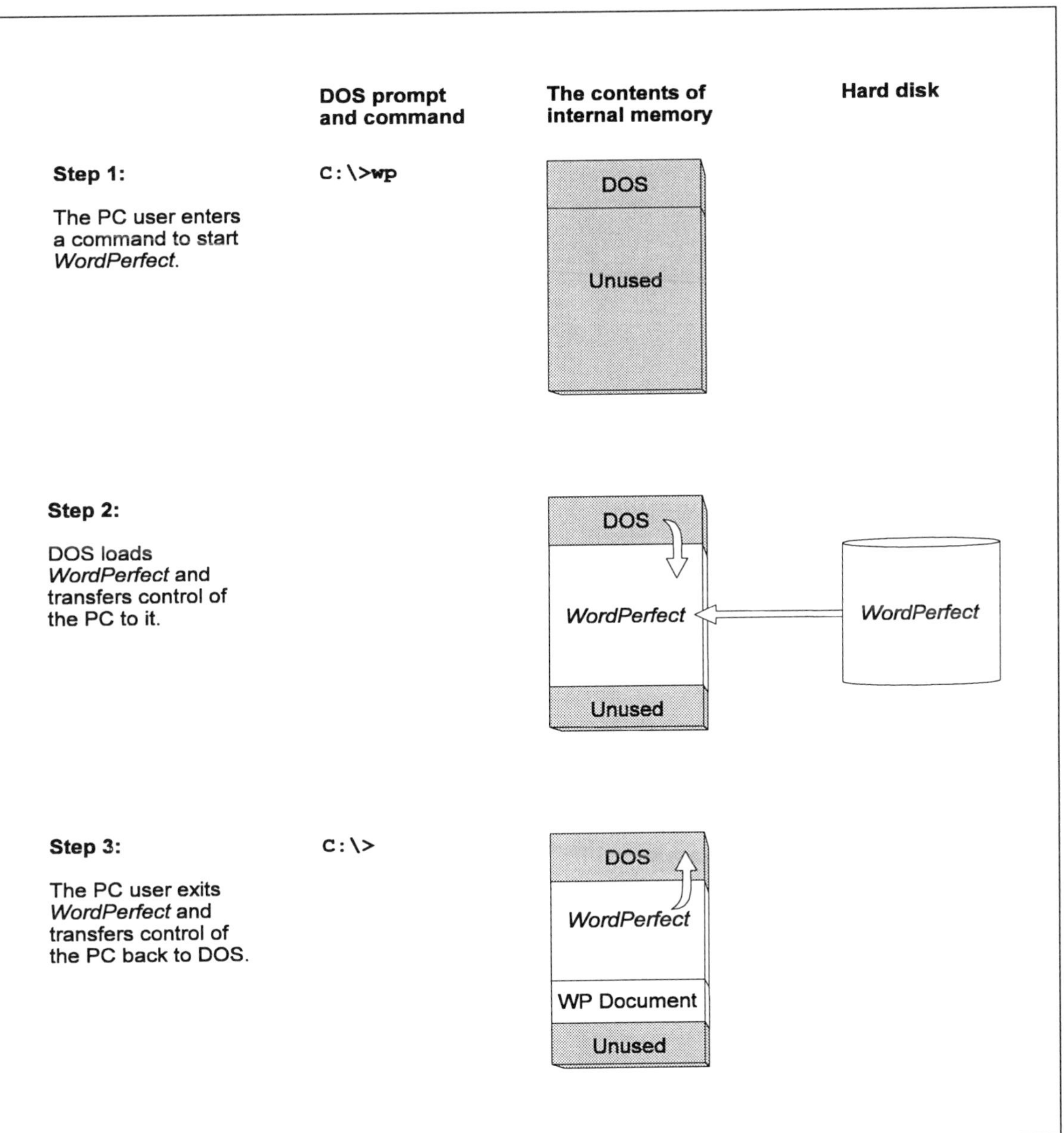
DOS prompt and command
The contents of internal memory
Hard disk
Step 1:
The PC user enters a command to start WordPerfect.
C:\>wp
DOS
Unused
Step 2:
DOS loads WordPerfect and transfers control of the PC to it.
DOS
WordPerfect
Unused
WordPerfect
Step 3:
The PC user exits WordPerfect and transfers control of the PC back to DOS.
C:\>
DOS
WordPerfect
WP Document
Unused

Figure 2-5 How DOS goes from one application program to the next (part 1 of 2)

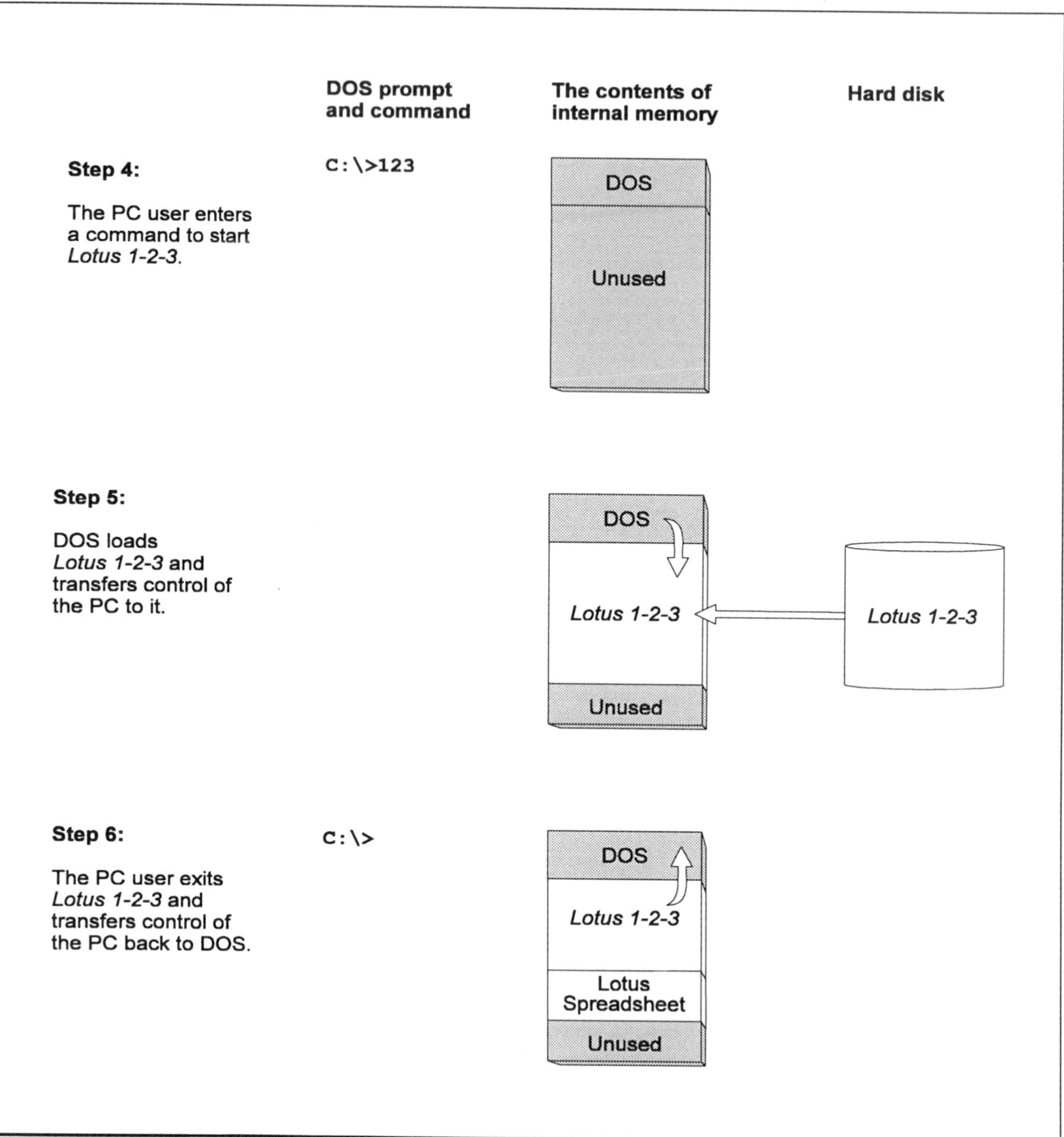

Figure 2-5 How DOS goes from one application program to the next (part 2 of 2)

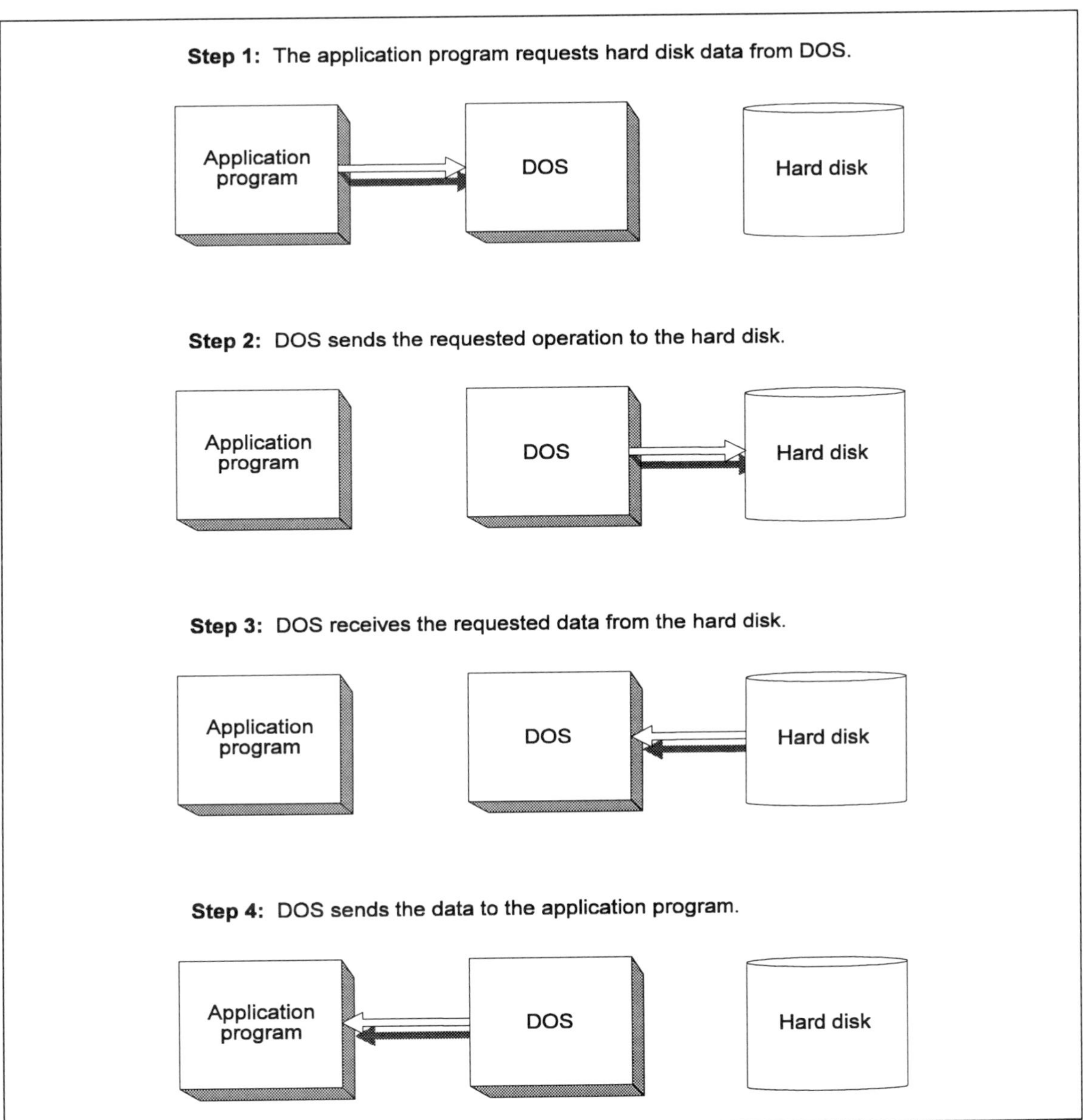
Step 1: The application program requests hard disk data from DOS.
Application program
DOS
Hard disk
Step 2: DOS sends the requested operation to the hard disk.
Application program
DOS
Hard disk
Step 3: DOS receives the requested data from the hard disk.
Application program
DOS
Hard disk
Step 4: DOS sends the data to the application program.
Application program
DOS
Hard disk

Figure 2-6 How DOS provides an input service to an application program

As part of its services, DOS also manages all of the files that are stored on a hard disk or diskette. In DOS terms, each document, spreadsheet, database, or program on a hard disk or diskette is called a *file*. So although you might think of a file as a document file, a spreadsheet file, a database file, or a program file, DOS makes no distinction between them. It manages all of the files in the same way.

To keep track of the files, DOS requires that they be organized into *directories*. Then, in the directory entry for each file, DOS records the file name, the disk location, the file size in bytes, the date the file was last changed, and the time the file was last changed. As a result, an application program doesn't have to know these details when it requests an input or output operation for a disk file. Instead, the application program has to supply just the name of the file and the name of the directory that contains the file. In the next chapter, you'll learn how to refer to the files and directories you use on a DOS system.

Because you only use DOS services through your application programs, you don't have to be concerned about them. Most of the time, in fact, you won't even be aware that the services have been provided for you. When something goes wrong with a service request, though, you sometimes get a message directly from DOS. Then, it's obvious that the DOS services are in use.

DOS commands In addition to the DOS services that you use indirectly through an application program, DOS provides commands that you can use directly from the command prompt. Most of these commands let you manage the files and directories on a disk. But some provide other types of functions.

Figure 2-7 presents twelve typical *DOS commands*, organized by type. The first group, for example, provides functions you can use to manage the files on a disk. These commands let you delete, rename, or copy one or more files. The other commands provide functions for managing directories, backing up the files on a hard disk, and so on.

In sections 2 and 3 of this book, you'll learn how to use these and other DOS commands. You'll also learn when and how to use them for maximum efficiency.

How DOS has evolved

Over the years, DOS has changed substantially, as summarized in figure 2-8. Here, you can see that each new version of DOS is given a *version number* like 2.0 or 3.3. In general, a change in the first digit of a version number means a major revision of the program; a change in the digits to the right of the decimal point means a minor revision. This is true for application programs as well as for DOS. If you want to find out what version of DOS you have on your system, just type *ver* at the command prompt and press the Enter key.

As you can see in figure 2-8, the original version of DOS was a modest operating system that was designed for diskette systems. Later versions provided for hardware developments like hard disks, 1.2MB diskette drives, 3-1/2 inch diskette drives, and hard disks larger than 32MB. Later versions also provided new commands, capabilities, and features.

Command type	Command	Function
File management	**DEL**	Deletes one or more files from disk storage.
	REN	Renames one or more files in disk storage.
	COPY	Copies one or more files from one disk location to another.
Directory management	**MD**	Makes a new directory.
	RD	Removes an empty directory.
Backup	**BACKUP**	Copies the files and directories on a hard disk to a series of diskettes.
	RESTORE	Copies the backup files and directories on a series of diskettes to a hard disk.
Date and time	**DATE**	Requests the current date and sets the internal clock using this information.
	TIME	Requests the current time and sets the internal clock using this information.
Error checking and recovery	**CHKDSK**	Checks a disk for errors and attempts to correct the errors.
Information display	**VER**	Displays the version of DOS in use.
	DIR	Displays the files and directories on a disk drive.

Figure 2-7 Twelve typical DOS commands

Although you can use this book with any version of DOS that's 2.0 or later, you probably are using a version of DOS that's 3.0 or later. If you're using a version of DOS that's earlier than 3.0, you probably should upgrade to DOS 6.0 as soon as you can. Nevertheless, I'll let you know whenever I present a DOS feature that requires a version more recent than 2.0.

DOS 1.0 When DOS 1.0 was introduced by Microsoft Corporation in 1981, it was one of three operating systems you could buy for the original IBM PC. Within just a year or two, though, DOS became the dominant operating system for the IBM PC.

Version	Conventional memory required	Major improvements
1.0	8KB	
2.0	24KB	Support for hard disks Directories
3.0	37KB	Support for 1.2MB diskette drives
3.1	39KB	Support for networks
3.2	46KB	Support for 3-1/2 inch diskette drives
3.3	55KB	Multiple logical drives on a hard disk New commands
4.0	70KB	Support for hard disk drives of more than 32MB Extended memory support DOS shell
5.0	60KB 18KB (if upper memory is used)	Less conventional memory required Improved use of extended memory Task switching Full-screen editor New DOS shell and other utility programs
6.0	63KB 106KB (with DBLSPACE in conventional memory) 20KB (if upper memory is used)	New utility programs, including high-speed backup, anti-virus, and disk defragmentor Improved configuration options Disk compression to double disk space Support for portable computers

Figure 2-8 The evolution of DOS

Although DOS 1.0 was a limited operating system, it was adequate for most users of the original PCs.

DOS 2.0 through 3.3 As new hardware became available, Microsoft updated DOS to support the new devices. When IBM introduced the PC/XT computer with its hard disk, for example, Microsoft introduced DOS 2.0. This new version of DOS provided I/O services for hard disks along with support for user-defined directories that help you organize the many files you can store on a hard disk. Similarly, DOS 3.0 added support for the 1.2MB diskette drives that came with the IBM AT. DOS 3.1 added network support; DOS 3.2 added support for the 3-1/2 inch diskette drives; and DOS 3.3 let you create two or more logical drives on a hard disk to get around the 32MB limitation for a hard disk.

DOS 4.0 through 5.0 With DOS 4.0, several new features were added. When you use DOS 4.0, you can set up a hard disk of more than 32MB as one logical drive, which you couldn't do with DOS 3.3. You can also take advantage of the extended memory that's already installed in most 80286 and 80386 PCs.

With DOS 5.0, you get all the benefits of DOS 4.0, but DOS works more efficiently. In particular, DOS 5.0 uses less conventional memory than DOS 4.0. It uses extended memory more efficiently than DOS 4.0. It allows you to switch more quickly between application programs. And it provides several new programs that make DOS easier to use.

With both DOS 4.0 and DOS 5.0, you also get a program called the *DOS shell*. One of the purposes of this program is to make it easier for you to use DOS. When you use the shell, you can set up your system so a screen like one of the ones in figure 2-9 is displayed whenever you start your PC. Then, you can use the modules of the DOS shell to manage files and directories, to execute DOS commands, and to start your application programs without ever entering DOS commands at the command prompt.

Although I haven't discussed DOS 6.0 yet, you should know that its shell is nearly identical to the DOS 5.0 shell. So when you start the DOS 6.0 shell, you'll see a screen like the one in the bottom of figure 2-9.

Although the shell makes it easier for you, you still have to know how DOS commands work. So you should read sections 2 and 3 of this book before you learn how to use the shell for your version of DOS. Then, you can learn how to use the 5.0/6.0 shell in section 4 of this book. (I don't cover the DOS 4.0 shell in this book because it's not widely used.)

DOS 6.0 With DOS 6.0, Microsoft again added several new features that make DOS more versatile and easier to use. In particular, the new DOS 6.0 Backup utility makes doing backups faster and easier. In addition, DOS 6.0 includes a feature called *DoubleSpace* that increases the capacity of your disk drive by compressing data that's stored on it. DOS 6.0 also includes an anti-virus program, a disk defragmenter, new configuration options, and support for portable computers. I'll discuss all of these features later in this book.

Utility programs that improve upon DOS

From its beginning in 1981, DOS has never been all that people have wanted it to be. As a result, many *utility programs* (or just *utilities*) have been developed to improve upon DOS. Some of these utilities provide functions that DOS doesn't provide. And some perform functions better than DOS performs them.

The first screen of the DOS 4.0 shell

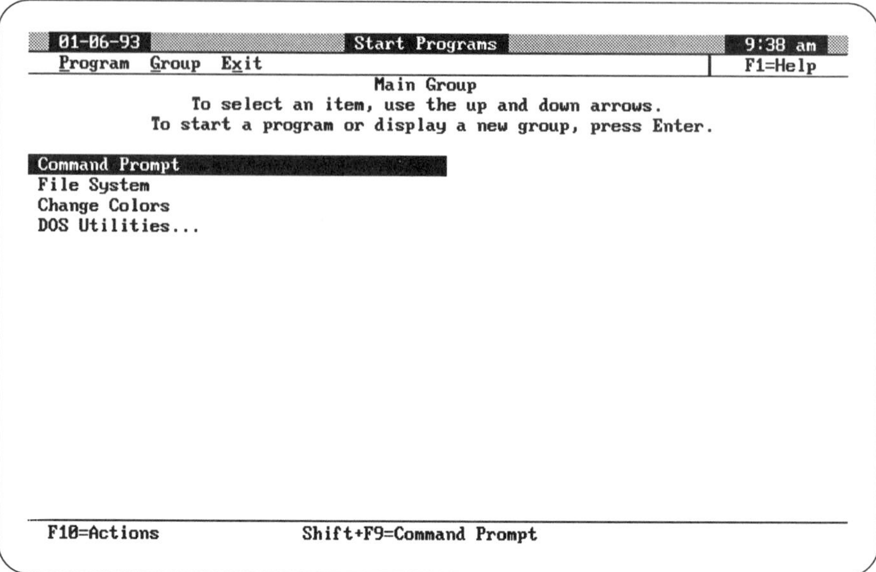

The first screen of the DOS 5.0/6.0 shell

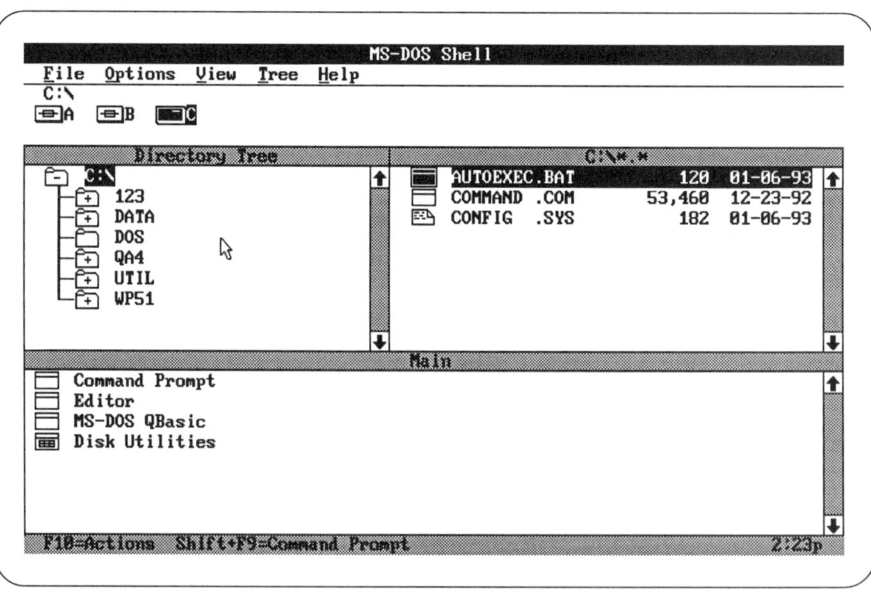

Figure 2-9 The opening screens of the DOS 4.0 and DOS 5.0/6.0 shells

If you're like most PC users, one or more of these utilities can help you use your PC more effectively. Some of these programs are available commercially from the same distributors that sell application programs. Some are available at no charge or at just a nominal charge. And some that weren't available with earlier versions of DOS now come with DOS 5.0 or DOS 6.0.

Some perspective on software

The evolution of PC software since 1981 has been impressive. During that time, we've gone from small application programs that performed a limited number of functions to large programs that perform more functions than the average user knows what to do with. We've gone from programs that worked only in text mode on monochrome monitors to programs that use both text and graphic modes on color monitors. And we've gone from programs that printed text only in one font to programs that can print complex graphics as well as text in many fonts.

Although application programs have gotten easier to use, DOS hasn't. As a result, most PC users still have a difficult time using DOS effectively, just as they did back in the early 1980s. In fact, most PC users seem to avoid DOS whenever they can. They have to learn how to use DOS to start their application programs, of course, but that's all many of them want to know.

Unfortunately, you need to know more than that if you want to get the maximum benefit from your PC. If you don't know how to use DOS, you won't be able to manage your files and directories as effectively as you should, so they'll eventually get out of control. You won't back up your files as efficiently or as frequently as you should, so you won't be protected from a hard disk disaster. If someone changes the way your PC is set up, you may not even be able to start your application programs. And whenever something goes wrong, you'll be at the mercy of someone who does know DOS.

That's why the next two sections in this book will teach you the DOS skills all PC users should have. In section 2, you'll learn the DOS skills you need for working with your application programs. In section 3, you'll learn additional skills that will save you time and trouble each day. Once you've mastered these skills, you'll be able to use your PC effectively.

Terms

software
program
application program
word processing program
document
spreadsheet program
spreadsheet
database program
database
general-purpose program
presentation graphics program
desktop publishing program
integrated program
operating system
DOS
Windows
OS/2
Disk Operating System

graphical user interface (GUI)
Operating System/2
MS-DOS
PC-DOS
command processor
command prompt
loading a program
loading a file
DOS service
input/output service
I/O service
file
directory
DOS command
version number
DOS shell
utility program
utility

Objectives

1. Describe the primary difference between an application program and an operating system program.
2. In general terms, explain how command processing works on a DOS system.
3. In general terms, explain how a DOS I/O service for a disk device works when an application program is in operation.
4. Explain the significance of the digits before and after the decimal point in the version number for a software product.
5. Describe the purpose of the DOS shell.
6. Describe the purpose of a utility program.

Section 2

A short course in DOS for every PC user

When you use an application program on a PC, you need to know something about DOS. At the least, you need to know how to identify DOS drives, directories, and files so you can save and retrieve your work files. But you should also know how to start your application programs from the command prompt. And if you have to enter the same set of commands each day after you turn your PC on, you should know how to start up your PC so it executes those commands automatically. These are the skills you'll learn in this section.

When you finish this section, your PC and its software will be less mysterious to you. You'll understand how to use directories and files as you save and retrieve your work files. You'll know how to use 11 DOS commands. You'll always be able to start your application programs, no matter who used the PC last or for what purpose. And if you normally start your programs from a shell, you'll find you'll be using the shell more effectively.

Chapter 3

How to identify DOS drives, directories, files, and paths

Although most application programs today try to shield you from the intricacies of DOS, all of them use DOS specifications for files. As a result, you should know how to refer to DOS disk drives, directories, and files, whether or not you ever use DOS itself. In this chapter, you'll learn how to refer to any file on a DOS system by specifying its drive, directory, and file name.

To start, you'll learn how to give a complete file specification for any file on a DOS system. Then, you'll learn what the default drive and current directory are and how they affect your file specifications. Last, you'll learn how to use DOS file specifications within your application programs.

How to specify the drive, path, and file name for any DOS file

Whenever you use an application program or DOS to access a file, you have to specify what file you want to access and where the file is located. You supply this information using a *file specification.* A complete file specification consists of three parts: a drive, a path, and a file name. Figure 3-1 shows complete specifications for a file on a diskette and for a file on a hard disk. Now, I'll explain what each part of a file specification is.

The drive DOS identifies a PC's hard disk drive and diskette drives by letters. For instance, the first diskette drive on every system is always drive A, and the second diskette drive, if there is one, is always drive B.

The hard disk, or at least the first portion of it, is always identified as drive C, even on a single-diskette system where there isn't a drive B. However, one hard disk can be divided into more than one drive, as shown in figure 3-2. Then, the first drive is drive C; the second is drive D; and so on.

This division of a hard disk into more than one drive originally started because DOS was unable to manage hard disks that had capacities larger than 32MB. As a

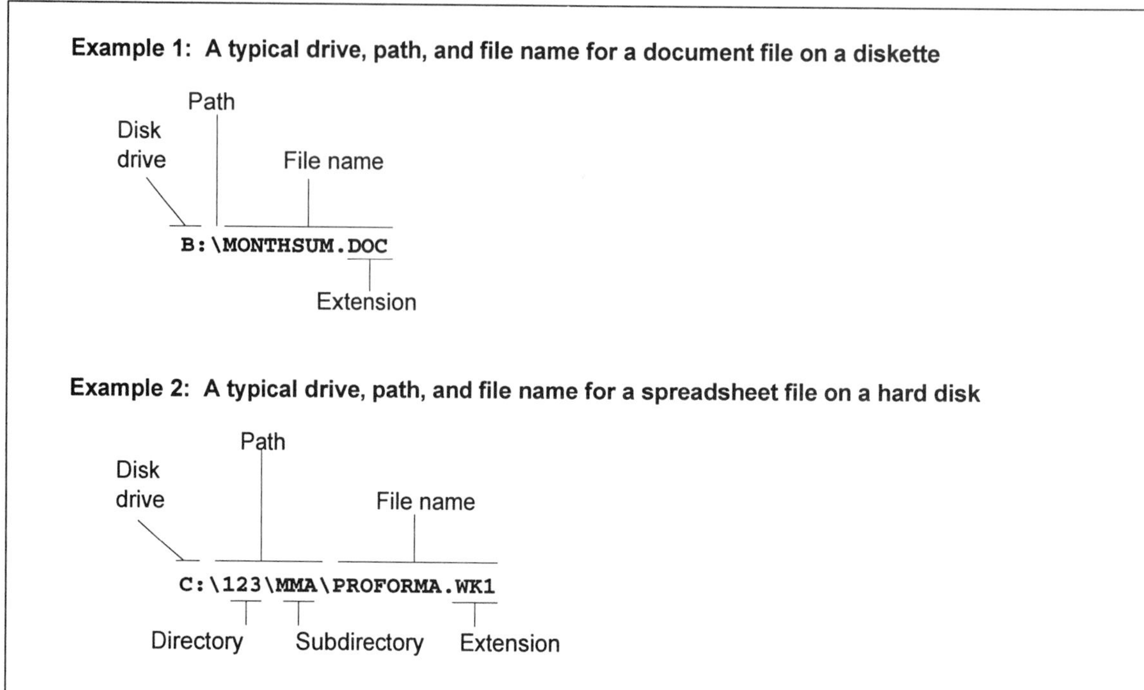

Figure 3-1 Typical drives, paths, and file names for word processing and spreadsheet files

result, a 120MB hard disk had to be divided into four 30MB drives. DOS 3.3 was the first version of DOS to provide for this division directly. Before DOS 3.3, you had to use non-standard software to divide a drive larger than 32MB into smaller, usable drives. Today, DOS 4.0 through 6.0 can treat an entire 120MB disk as the C drive, and it's uncommon to find a large hard disk broken down into more than two drives.

In PC and DOS literature, these drives are often referred to as *logical drives* to distinguish them from the hard disk, or physical disk drive. Thus, one physical drive can be divided into two or more logical drives. From a practical point of view, however, you can think of each logical drive as a physical drive. As a result, I won't distinguish between the two in the remainder of this book. I'll simply refer to disk drives by letter, as in "the C drive" or "the D drive."

In this book, I assume that your hard disk has already been set up for you. At the least, then, you know that your PC has a C drive. In the next chapter, I'll show you how to find out whether your PC has other drives and how to find out the capacity of each drive.

To specify the disk drive in a file specification, you always give the drive letter followed by a colon. In figure 3-1, you can see that example 1 specifies the B drive, which is the second diskette drive of a PC. Example 2 specifies the C drive.

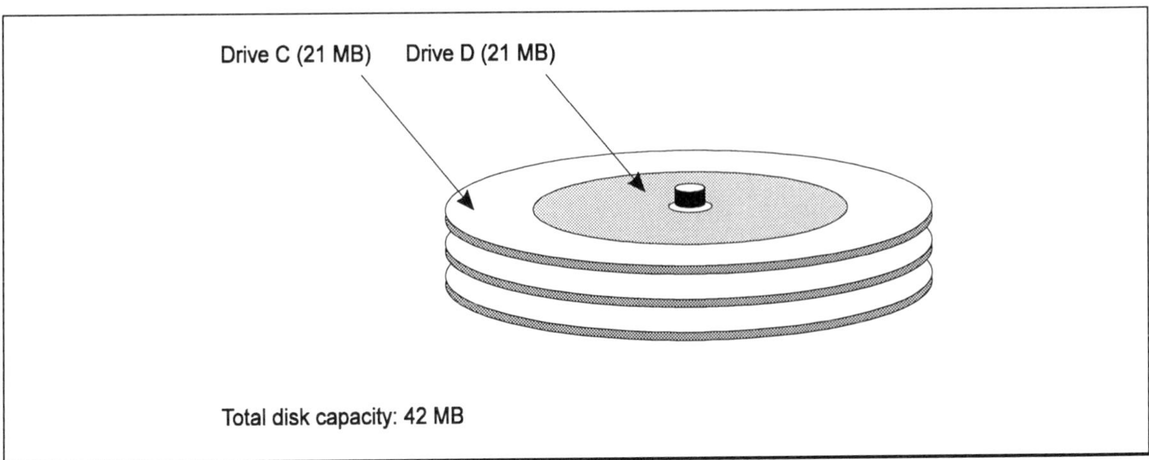

Figure 3-2 Two drives on one hard disk

The path In chapter 2, I mentioned that DOS has you organize or group files into *directories*. The 1,368 files on my system, for example, are organized into 39 different directories. These directories are just a special type of file that DOS uses to keep track of the names and locations of the files that are stored on a disk. On a DOS system, every file must be stored in a directory.

Figure 3-3 illustrates a typical directory structure for a hard disk. For each hard disk or diskette, the top-level directory is always called the *root directory*. In this figure, the root directory contains references to five other directories named DOS, UTIL, WP51, 123, and QA. These directories contain the files for DOS, for some utility programs, for *WordPerfect*, for *Lotus 1-2-3*, and for *Q&A*.

Because one directory can contain entries for other directories, the subordinate directories can be referred to as *subdirectories*. In figure 3-3, for instance, the WP51 directory has two subdirectories named MMA and PROJ1, and the 123 directory has two subdirectories named MMA and DOUG. These subdirectories are just like any other directory; they're just subordinate to a higher-level directory. As a result, subdirectories can also be referred to as directories.

The *path* of a file specification identifies the directory for the file. More specifically, the path tells DOS how to get from the root directory to the directory that contains the entry for the file you want. In the directory structure in figure 3-3, the shaded path goes from the root directory to the WP51 directory to the PROJ1 directory.

Below the directory structure in figure 3-3, you can see the specifications for the paths of the eleven directories shown in the structure. The first backslash (\ ) represents the root directory. The level-1 directories are identified by the backslash followed by the directory name, as in \DOS, \UTIL, \WP51, \123, and \QA. And the level-2 directories, or subdirectories, are identified by the backslash, the level-1 directory name, another backslash, and the level-2 directory name, as in \WP51\MMA and \WP51\PROJ1.

Note in figure 3-3 that \PROJ1 isn't a valid path. To be valid, it must be preceded by its directory as in this path: \WP51\PROJ1. Note also that the same subdirectory name can be used within more than one directory. Thus, an MMA directory is subordinate to the WP51 directory, the 123 directory, and the QA directory. For DOS to tell these three directories apart, they must be referred to as \WP51\MMA, \123\MMA, and \QA\MMA.

If you refer back to figure 3-1, you can see that the path in the first example is just the root directory. The path in the second example, however, is the MMA subdirectory within the 123 directory within the root directory.

The file name Whenever you save a new file on a hard disk or a diskette, whether you use DOS or an application program, you need to be able to create a valid *file name* for it. If you refer back to figure 3-1, you can see that a file name can be separated into two parts by a period. The part that comes before the period is required. I'll refer to this as the *name* portion of the file name. The part after the period is optional and is called the *extension*.

Figure 3-4 gives the rules for forming valid file names. If you use just letters and numbers in your names, you don't have to worry about the special characters listed in rule 3. Then, you just have to make sure that the name before the period is from one to eight characters and that the extension is from one to three characters. However, you may find that you can benefit from using characters like the hyphen (-) in file names. So don't completely rule out these other characters. Note also in rule 4 that DOS doesn't care whether you use uppercase or lowercase letters when you specify a file name. Both are treated the same. As you can see in the last two examples of valid file names, you can omit the period if you don't specify an extension.

Although extensions are optional, many programs use them. For instance, *Lotus 1-2-3* uses WK1 or WK3 as the extension for the spreadsheet files you create, and *Microsoft Word* uses DOC as the extension for the document files you create. When you use these programs, though, you don't have to include the extension when you create a file name because the application program adds it automatically.

How the default drive and current directory affect a file specification

Whenever your PC is running, one and only one drive is the DOS *default drive*. In fact, DOS displays the default drive as part of its command prompt. Similarly, one directory is identified as the *current directory* for each drive. When you use DOS, you don't have to specify the drive and path in a file specification if the file is in the current directory on the default drive.

Some application programs work that way too. They assume that the DOS default drive and current directory are intended whenever the drive and path are

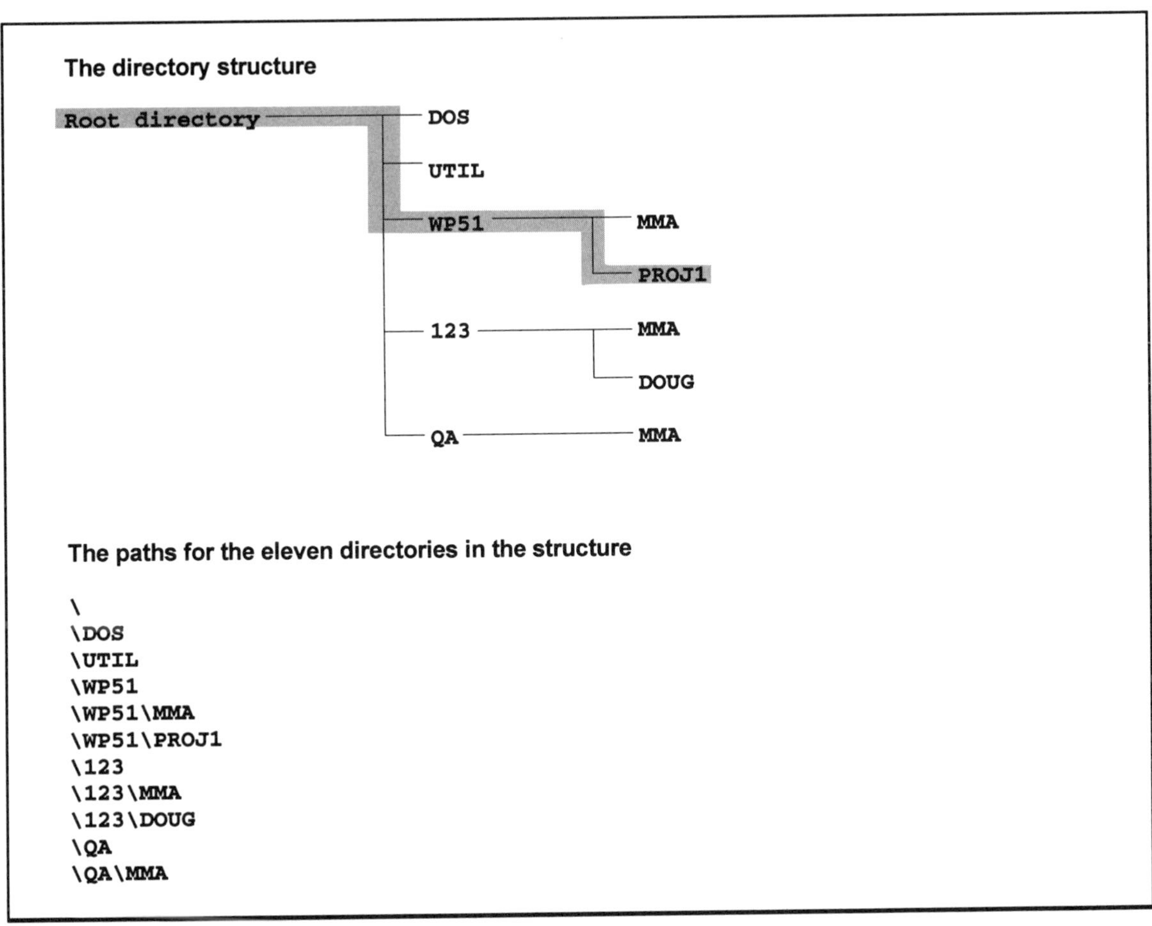

Figure 3-3 The paths for the directories of a hard disk

omitted from a file specification. That can simplify your file specifications considerably because it often means that you have to specify only the file name. *WordPerfect*, for example, looks for a file in the current directory on the default drive whenever the drive and path are omitted from a file specification.

In contrast, some application programs have their own default drives and directories. When you use one of these programs to save or access files, the DOS default drive and current directory don't matter. Instead, the program looks for a file in its own default directory on its own default drive. For example, *Lotus 1-2-3* and *Q&A* are programs that keep track of their own default directories and drives. Then, when the file you want is in the program's default directory on the default drive, you can omit the drive and path from the file specification.

You should also realize that the current directory can affect how DOS interprets the path you use in a file specification. If you begin the path with a backslash, the directory path begins with the root directory. In this case, the current directory has no effect on the path. However, if you do not begin the path with a backslash, the path begins at the current directory rather than the root directory. In that case, you can omit the current directory from the path.

To illustrate, suppose you want to access a file named JAN93.WK1 in the 123\MMA directory. If you use a complete path, like this:

```
\123\MMA\JAN93.WK1
```

the path will access the file no matter which directory is current. However, if the 123 directory is current, you can start the path like this:

```
MMA\JAN93.WK1
```

Because the first backslash is omitted, DOS looks for the MMA subdirectory in the current directory (123) rather than in the root directory.

Although omitting the current directory information from the path can sometimes save you a few keystrokes, it can also create problems. For example, suppose you believe the 123 directory is current, but in reality the current directory is WKDOCS. Then, when you save a file using the path MMA\JAN93.WK1, the JAN93.WK1 file will be saved in the WKDOCS\MMA directory, not in 123\MMA. As a result, you should give the complete directory path whenever you aren't certain what the current directory is.

How to use file specifications in application programs

Once you understand DOS file specifications, you shouldn't have any trouble using them in your application programs. With some programs, the complete file specifications appear on the screen so you can see the drive and path for each file you save or retrieve. Figure 3-5, for example, shows the screen *Lotus 1-2-3* displays when you save or retrieve a file. As you can see in the second line of the screen, *Lotus* displays the complete drive and path it uses for the file. Then, if the drive and directory are set to the ones you want to use, all you have to do is enter a file name to retrieve or save a file. If the drive and directory aren't the ones you want, you can set them the way you want them before you retrieve or save a file.

Other programs, however, don't always display complete specifications. When you use the Save or Retrieve commands in *WordPerfect*, for example, you get the prompts shown in figure 3-6. But these prompts don't tell you what the drive and path are. Then, if you enter just the file name for a Save command, that file will be saved in the current directory on the default drive. But if the default drive and directory are not the ones you think they are, you won't know where your file is getting stored.

To avoid problems, you should make sure you know what the defaults are whenever you give an incomplete file specification. If you don't know, you should give the complete specification, which includes the drive and path. Then, the file will

The rules for forming file names

1. The name must consist of from one to eight characters.
2. The extension is optional. If you have one, it must be from one to three characters, and it must be separated from the name by a period as in this example:

   `MONTHSUM.JAN`
3. You can use any character in the name or the extension except for the space and any of these characters:

   `. , < > ? / : ; " ' [ ] | \ + = *`
4. You can use either lowercase or uppercase letters in the name or the extension of a file name, but they are treated the same. As a result, the two names that follow are the same:

   `MONTHSUM.JAN` and `monthsum.jan`

Valid file names

```
JAN93.WK1
letter.doc
5-16-92.doc
FEB93RPT
ltr10-21
```

Invalid file names

`JANUARY93.WK1`	(The name is more than 8 characters.)
`JAN:93.WK1`	(The colon is an invalid character.)
`JAN93.TEXT`	(The extension is more than 3 characters.)

Figure 3-4 The rules for forming file names

always be stored on the drive and directory given by the complete file specification, no matter what the default drive and directory are.

How to use the * wildcard in the file specification for an application program

If you look closely at the file specification in the second line of figure 3-5, you'll see that it contains an asterisk:

```
C:\123\MMA\*.WK1
```

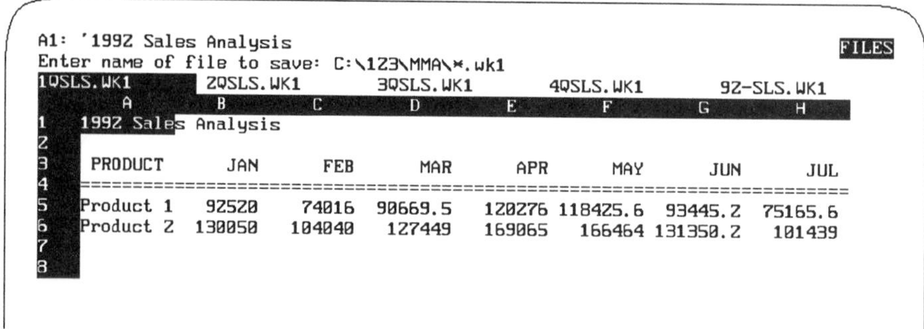

Figure 3-5 The drive and directory information that *Lotus 1-2-3* displays when you save or retrieve a file

This * is one of the two types of *wildcards* that DOS provides. It is called the * *wildcard*, and it represents one or more characters of any kind. As a result, this *Lotus* command displays all the files that have an extension of WK1. Since only spreadsheets have this extension, this command displays all the spreadsheets in the directory, but not any other kinds of files.

Some common forms of file names that contain wildcards are illustrated in figure 3-7. As you can see, *.* refers to files with any name before the period and any extension; *.WK1 refers to files with an extension of WK1; *.DOC refers to files with an extension of DOC; and *. refers to files that don't have an extension. Many application programs use simple wildcard specifications like these.

In chapter 4, you'll learn how to use simple forms of the * wildcard in DOS commands. Then, in chapter 7, you'll learn how to use the * wildcard in more complex forms, and you'll learn how to use the ? wildcard. In the meantime, you don't have to use * wildcards at all. You just have to understand what they mean in the specifications displayed by your programs.

If you do change a wildcard specification that is displayed by an application program, you should realize that the function that is going to be performed will be changed accordingly. For example, if you use *WordPerfect's* List command to display the files in a directory, *WordPerfect* gives you a prompt like this that shows the default directory:

```
Dir C:\WP51\PROJ1\*.*
```

If you change the *.* specification to *.DOC and then press the Enter key, *WordPerfect* will list only the files that have an extension of DOC, not all the files in the directory. Sometimes, it makes sense to change a specification in this way so the application program does its function on just those files you specify.

The prompt for the Save command

```
Document to be saved:
```

The prompt for the Retrieve command

```
Document to be retrieved:
```

Figure 3-6 The *WordPerfect* prompts for the Save and Retrieve commands

Wildcard example	Meaning
`*.*`	All files (any name, any extension)
`*.WK1`	All files with an extension of WK1
`*.DOC`	All files with an extension of DOC
`*.`	All files without any extension

Figure 3-7 Some common forms of file specifications that contain * wildcards

Some perspective on DOS drives, paths, and file names

In the next chapter, you'll see how drives, paths, and file names are used in DOS commands. You'll also realize that a typical DOS system has to keep track of hundreds of files stored in a dozen or more directories. Because directories and files can easily get out of control when you use several application programs, chapter 7 will show you how to manage the directories and files on your system.

Terms

file specification
logical drive
directory
root directory
subdirectory
path
file name
extension
default drive
current directory
wildcard
* wildcard

Objectives

1. Given the drive, directory, subdirectory, and name for a file, type a complete specification for the file.
2. Given the default drive and current directory of a file and given a complete file specification for the file, type the shortest file specification that will identify the file.

Exercises

1. Give the complete file specification for a file named MMASLS with the extension WK1 that's stored in the WK1 directory on drive D.
2. Give the complete file specification for a file named MMASLS with the extension WK1 that's stored in the MMA directory, which is subordinate to the 123 directory on drive C.
3. Give the complete file specification for a file named REPORT1 (no extension) that's stored in the \DOC\MIKE directory on drive D.
4. Give the complete file specification for a file named REPORT1.DOC that's stored in the directory named MIKE, which is subordinate to the WP51 directory on drive C.
5. The current directory is \WP51 and the current drive is C. What's the shortest file specification you can use for accessing a file with this specification: C:\WP51\MMA\MONRPT.DOC?
6. The current directory is \WP51 and the current drive is C. What's the shortest file specification you can use for accessing a file with this specification: C:\123\MMA\MONSLS.WK1?
7. The current directory is \WP51\MMA and the current drive is C. What's the shortest file specification you can use for accessing a file with this specification: C\123\MMA\MONSLS.WK1?
8. The current directory is \123\MMA and the current drive is D. What's the shortest file specification you can use for accessing a file with this specification: C:\123\MMA\MONSLS.WK1?

Chapter 4

How to use DOS commands to start your application programs

In this chapter, you'll learn how to enter a DOS command, you'll learn about the two types of DOS commands, and you'll learn how to use 11 of the DOS commands. You'll also learn three skills that will help you enter DOS commands more efficiently, you'll learn how to start an application program from the DOS prompt, and you'll learn how to use the DOS 5.0 and DOS 6.0 Help features. When you complete this chapter, you'll understand why you'll want to use DOS commands in the first place. And you'll start to take control of your PC.

As you read this chapter, you can try the DOS commands on your own PC right after you read about them. Or you can read the entire chapter first and then try the DOS commands using the figures as guidelines. If you would like more direction as you experiment with the commands, you can do the guided exercises at the end of the chapter. As you experiment on your own PC, you'll see how your system varies from the system used for the examples in this book.

What DOS does when you start your PC

If your PC has a hard disk, DOS is stored on it. So to start your system, all you have to do is turn on the monitor and the systems unit. If all of the components of your PC are connected to a surge protector or some other single power source, all you have to do is throw the switch on that unit.

Before you turn the systems unit on, though, you must make sure that you don't have a diskette in drive A and that the door of drive A is open. If drive A contains a diskette, your PC looks for DOS on the diskette instead of the hard disk. Then, if the diskette doesn't have DOS on it, your PC will display an error message. At that time, you can take the diskette out of drive A and restart your systems unit.

When you start your PC, it automatically performs two functions. First, it checks itself to make sure it's working properly. This is called the *self-test*, or *POST (Power-On-Self-Test)* routine. If anything goes wrong during this test, the PC displays an error message. On most PCs, the self-test takes just a few seconds. On others, it takes much longer. During this time, your monitor may look as though nothing is happening. But since you can't do any work on your PC until the self-test is over, you just have to wait.

Second, the PC loads DOS from the C drive of the hard disk. This is called *booting the system*, which comes from the expression "pulling yourself up by your own bootstraps." During this process, DOS loads itself into internal memory and prepares itself to execute your application programs.

The DOS command prompt As DOS initializes itself, it may display several messages on the monitor. It may also ask you to enter the date and time. Eventually, though, DOS should display either the *command prompt* or a DOS shell. If the DOS shell appears, you can press the F3 key to exit from the shell and get to the prompt. If some other program appears instead of the DOS shell, exit from it and get to the prompt. You have to be at the DOS prompt before you can try the commands presented in this chapter.

In its standard form, the prompt looks like this:

```
C>
```

This prompt displays just the default drive. However, some PCs are set up so the prompt displays the current directory along with the default drive in this form:

```
C:\123\MMA>
```

No matter what the prompt looks like, though, it means that the DOS command processor is waiting for your command.

How to enter and correct a DOS command

To enter a DOS command, you type in the command at the command prompt and press the Enter key. That's all there is to it. On some keyboards, the Enter key is called the Return key. And on other keyboards, the Enter key is marked only with this symbol: (↵). Throughout this book, though, I'll refer to this key as the Enter key, no matter how it's marked on your keyboard.

Although you always have to press the Enter key to enter a command, I won't indicate that in the examples in this book. Instead, I'll just assume you know that you have to press the Enter key after each command. I'll also assume you know that the command always comes right after the (>) symbol in the command prompt. As a result, this example:

```
C>dir a:
```

means to type *dir a:* and press the Enter key.

With few exceptions, DOS doesn't care whether you use uppercase or lowercase letters in commands. So whenever possible, I'll use lowercase letters for them. This will help you tell the commands from the DOS prompts and messages, which are displayed in uppercase letters.

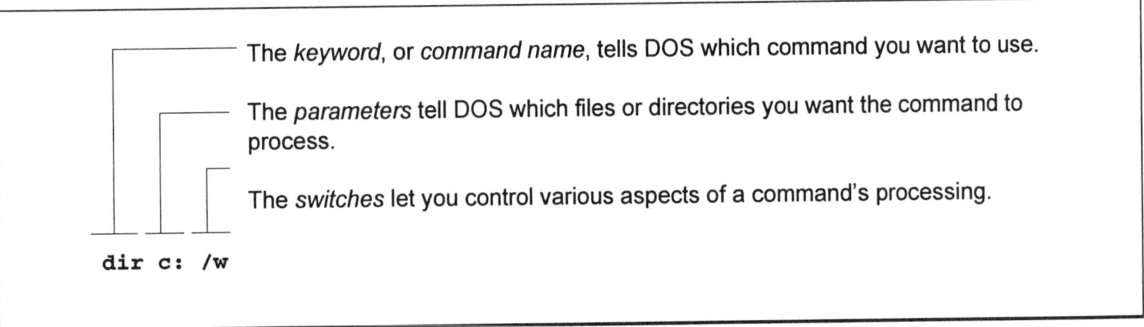

The *keyword*, or *command name*, tells DOS which command you want to use.
The *parameters* tell DOS which files or directories you want the command to process.
The *switches* let you control various aspects of a command's processing.
dir c: /w

Figure 4-1 The basic format of a DOS command

The basic format of a DOS command Figure 4-1 gives the basic format for any DOS command. As you can see, a command can consist of three parts. The first part is the *keyword*. Since it identifies the command, it can also be called the *command name*. The second part consists of one or more *parameters*; they tell DOS what drives, directories, or files the command should work on. The third part consists of one or more *switches*; they tell DOS which variations of the command you want.

As you will see in a moment, some command formats consist of a keyword only; some consist of a keyword and parameters; and some consist of a keyword, parameters, and switches. You'll also see that the parameters and switches are often optional. In figure 4-1, for example, the Directory command contains a keyword (dir), one parameter (c:), and one switch (/w). But Directory commands can also be used without parameters and without switches.

When you enter a command at the command prompt, you must separate the parts of a command so DOS can tell what they are. Normally, you do this by typing in one or more spaces between the parts. So if a command consists of the keyword, a parameter, and a switch, you normally enter it like this:

```
C>dir \dos /w
```

Here, the keyword is *dir*; the parameter is *\dos*; and the switch is */w*.

For the examples in this book, the parts of a command are always separated by one or more spaces. You should realize, though, that DOS also recognizes the backslash and the slash as separators. As a result, DOS interprets this command:

```
dir\dos/w
```

as though it were written as:

```
dir \dos /w
```

Key	Function
F1	Retypes one character from the last command you've entered each time you press this key.
F3	Retypes all of the characters from the last command you entered.

Figure 4-2 Keystrokes that help you correct or repeat a command

Nevertheless, it's usually best to separate the parts of a command with spaces. That way, the commands are easier to read, and you can be sure that DOS is going to interpret them the way you mean them.

If you're a little confused at this point by the use of both slashes and backslashes in a command, you're not alone. The use of both leads to typing errors even for experienced DOS users. You use the backslash in parameters and the regular slash in switches. You don't always need a backslash in a parameter, though. And not all switches start with a slash, although most of them do.

How to correct or repeat a command If you make a mistake entering a command, but you notice it before you press the Enter key, you can just backspace and correct it. If you press the Enter key before you realize you made a mistake, DOS will display an error message that indicates something is wrong with your command. One way to correct it is to enter the entire command again in its corrected form.

However, you can also use the two Function keys shown in figure 4-2 to help you correct a command. If a command is lengthy, using one of these keys is usually more efficient than entering the entire command again. If, for example, you press the F3 key after you get an error message from DOS, all of the characters from the last command that you entered appear at the new prompt. Then, you can backspace and make the required corrections. You can also use this key if you want to repeat the execution of a command.

If you press the F1 key after you get an error message from DOS, the first character of the last command appears at the new prompt. If you press the F1 key again, the second character appears, and so on. Then, you can continue to press the F1 key until you reach the part of the last command that needs to be corrected. When you reach that point, you can make the necessary correction and type the rest of the command.

If you're using DOS 5.0 or DOS 6.0, you can also recall and correct commands using the Doskey feature. To activate this feature, you enter the command name, *doskey*, at the command prompt. After that, you can use the keystrokes summarized in figure 4-3 to recall or edit commands. If you experiment with these keystrokes for a few minutes, you'll see how easy it is to use this feature.

Keys for recalling commands	Function
↑	Recalls the command you issued before the one displayed.
↓	Recalls the command you issued after the one displayed.
F7	Displays all commands stored in memory along with a number that identifies each command.
Alt+F7	Erases all commands stored in memory.
F8	Searches memory for a command that matches the first portion of a command that you have typed at the command prompt.
F9	Recalls a command by the number assigned to it.

Keys for editing commands	Function
←	Moves the cursor back one character.
→	Moves the cursor forward one character.
Ctrl+←	Moves the cursor back one word.
Ctrl+→	Moves the cursor forward one word.
Home	Moves the cursor to the beginning of the command.
End	Moves the cursor to the end of the command.
Esc	Clears the command from the command prompt.
Del	Deletes the character at the cursor position.
Ins	Toggles between the Insert and Typeover modes. When the Typeover mode is activated, the cursor is an underline. When the Insert mode is activated, the cursor is a block.

Figure 4-3 The most useful keys of the Doskey feature

If someone else has set up your PC, the Doskey feature may be activated when you turn your PC on. Then, you don't have to activate it before you use it. In the next chapter, you'll learn how to set up your PC so it starts the way you want it to.

The two types of DOS commands

When you use DOS, you should realize that there are two types of commands: internal commands and external commands. Although DOS is always able to find and execute its internal commands, you sometimes need to tell DOS where to find its external commands.

Internal commands As I explained in chapter 2, part of DOS stays in the internal memory of your systems unit whenever your PC is turned on. This portion of DOS includes the command processor, and it also includes many of the DOS commands.

The commands that DOS keeps in internal memory are known as *internal commands*. Because they are always in internal memory, DOS always knows where to find them. Also, it doesn't have to load them from disk storage into internal memory before it can execute them. To use one of these commands, all you ever have to do is enter the command name at the command prompt.

External commands If a command isn't kept in internal memory, it's called an *external command*. Each of these commands is stored in a disk file called a *command file*. On a DOS system, the names of command files always have an extension of COM or EXE. Usually, these command files for DOS functions are stored in the DOS directory on one of the drives of your PC. On some older systems, however, you'll find the DOS command files in the root directory of the C drive. (If you're using a system that's set up like this, you should consider updating to a new version of DOS.)

Before DOS can execute an external command, it must find the command file for the command and load the command into internal memory. But not all systems are set up so DOS is able to find the external commands for its own functions. If yours isn't, you should set the current directory to the one that contains the DOS external command files before you try to execute one of them. You'll learn how to do that in a moment. Then, because DOS always looks in the current directory for the requested command file, it will be able to find and execute its external commands.

On the other hand, some systems are set up so DOS can always find its external command files. Then, you can execute an external command the same way you execute an internal command. You just enter it at the command prompt. In the next chapter, you'll learn how to set up your system so DOS always knows where to find its external command files.

How to use 11 DOS commands

Figure 4-4 gives the formats and functions for 11 DOS commands. In these formats, I've used uppercase letters for the keyword and switches for each command, and I've used lowercase letters for the parameters. If the parameters or switches are optional, I've enclosed them in brackets [ ]. I've also used the abbreviation *spec* for the word

Name	Format	Function
Clear screen	`CLS`	Clears the monitor screen.
Prompt	`PROMPT $p$g`	Changes the format of the command prompt so it shows the default drive and current directory.
Change drive	`Drive-spec`	Changes the default drive to the drive specified.
Directory	`DIR [file-spec][/P] [/W]`	Displays a directory listing for the specified files. The switches let you control how the command displays the listing.
Change directory	`CD [directory-spec]`	Changes the current directory. If the parameter is omitted, this command displays the path of the current directory.
Version	`VER`	Displays a message that tells what version of DOS is installed.
Date	`DATE`	Lets you inspect and change the current date.
Time	`TIME`	Lets you inspect and change the current time.
Check disk	`CHKDSK [drive-spec]`	Displays messages about the disk drive that's specified and about the PC's internal memory.
Type	`TYPE file-spec`	Displays the contents of a text file.
Print	`PRINT file-spec`	Prints the contents of a text file.

Figure 4-4 Eleven DOS commands

specification. This is the notation that's used in most DOS manuals, and it's the one that's used throughout this book.

When I selected the commands for this chapter, I used three guidelines. First, I wanted to present a range of commands that represent the types of functions that DOS commands can perform. Second, I wanted to present commands that help you understand DOS. Third, I wanted to present commands that you are likely to use right away. As a result, all of the commands in figure 4-4 serve one or more of these purposes.

Of the 11 commands in figure 4-4, only two are external commands. These are the Check-disk and Print commands. By the time you get to these commands, you'll know how to change the current directory to the one that contains the command files for these commands, so you shouldn't have any trouble using them.

To use the commands in figure 4-4, you start by entering the keyword. Next, if the command requires parameters or switches, you enter them, making sure that you use one or more spaces to separate the parts of the command. Then, when you've got the command the way you want it, you press the Enter key so DOS will execute it.

When you enter a command, I recommend that you use lowercase letters for all its parts. Because DOS treats uppercase and lowercase letters the same, this won't affect your commands in any way. But it will make it easier for you to enter them.

The Clear-screen command The Clear-screen command clears the screen of any messages and puts the command prompt at the top of the screen. It has no parameters or switches. You can use this command to clear the screen before you issue a command that displays information.

The Prompt command When the command prompt is in its standard form (C>), it tells you what the default drive is, but it doesn't tell you what the current directory is. To change the form of the prompt so it does tell you what the current directory is, you use the Prompt command with the parameter shown in figure 4-4: pg.

The use of this command is illustrated in the first line of figure 4-5. (I've shaded the commands in this figure so you can see the command prompts more easily.) After the Prompt command is executed, the prompt is changed to show that the current directory for the C drive is the root directory (C:\>). Then, if the current directory is changed to the DOS directory, the prompt will look like this:

```
C:\DOS>
```

This enhanced form of the prompt stays in effect until you turn your PC off.

Most likely, your PC is already set up to display the current drive and directory in the command prompt. If so, you shouldn't ever have to use the Prompt command. But if your PC isn't set up this way, you should always use Prompt pg. Then, in chapter 5, you can learn how to set up your PC so it starts the way you want it to. After that, you won't have to use the Prompt command any more.

The Change-drive command To use the Change-drive command, you just type the letter of the drive that you want as the default drive followed by a colon. When you press the Enter key, DOS changes the default drive and displays the new default drive in the command prompt. To illustrate, the first three Change-drive commands in figure 4-5 change the drive from C to A, from A to B, and from B to D.

To find out how many drives your hard disk is divided into, you can issue the Change-drive command to change from the C drive to the D drive. If DOS doesn't display a message that tells you there is no D drive, you can continue with the E, F, and G drives until you get a message that says there's no such drive. In figure 4-5, the

```
C>prompt $p$g

C:\>a:

A:\>b:

B:\>d:

D:\>e:
Invalid drive specification

D:\>
```

Figure 4-5 The Prompt command and four examples of how to use the Change-drive command

last Change-drive command tries to change the default drive to the E drive, but DOS displays an error message that says that the drive doesn't exist. As a result, you know that the C and D drives are the only valid drives for the hard disk.

The Directory command The Directory command displays a directory listing of the directory or file you specify in the file specification parameter. If you enter the command without a file specification, DOS displays a listing of the current directory on the default drive. As a result, the Directory command in figure 4-6 displays the root directory for the C drive. This directory listing consists of five entries for each file. From left to right, they are the name of the file, the file extension, the size of the file in bytes, the date the file was last changed, and the time the file was last changed.

Note that this directory listing doesn't include the period that separates the name portion of the file name from the extension. Instead, it lists the name portions in the first column of the listing and the extension in the second column. So the root directory that's listed in figure 4-6 contains three files named

```
COMMAND.COM
CONFIG.SYS
AUTOEXEC.BAT
```

To read a directory listing properly, you must mentally convert the file names in the listing to this form.

In figure 4-6, the directory listing contains six directories as indicated by <DIR> in the column that gives the file size. Although a directory name can have an extension, most don't. Remember, though, a directory is just a special type of file that contains entries for other files.

Incidentally, the three files that are listed in figure 4-6 must always be stored in the root directory of the C drive, so you shouldn't delete them. The first one, COMMAND.COM , contains the DOS command processor and other DOS

```
C:\>dir

 Volume in drive C is HD42

 Volume Serial Number is 1983-5D30
 Directory of C:\


DOS          <DIR>          8-05-92   2:55p
COMMAND  COM         53022  10-26-92   6:00a
CONFIG   SYS           135  12-03-92  11:41a
QA4          <DIR>         12-03-92   1:06p
AUTOEXEC BAT            91  12-04-92   1:19p
WP51         <DIR>         12-03-92  12:34p
123          <DIR>         12-03-92   1:22p
UTIL         <DIR>         12-03-92   2:04p
DATA         <DIR>         12-03-92   2:08p
        9 File(s)    53277 bytes
                  24786944 bytes free

C:\>
```

Figure 4-6 The operation of the Directory command

commands that are stored in internal memory, so it's critical to the operation of your system. Similarly, the CONFIG.SYS file contains information about your system that is required for it to function properly. And the AUTOEXEC.BAT file tells your system what commands to execute as part of its start-up procedure. (Actually, it's possible to move the COMMAND.COM file to another directory. You'll learn how to do that in chapter 24. Until then, leave COMMAND.COM in the root directory.)

If you look at the format for the Directory command in figure 4-7, you can see two of the switches that are available for it. The independent operation of these switches is illustrated in figure 4-7, but you can use both of these switches in a single Directory command. In figure 4-7, I've shaded the commands to distinguish them from the command output. As you can see, the /W switch causes DOS to display a directory in a wide format with only the name and extension for each file. And the /P switch causes DOS to pause when the screen is filled. Then, when you press any key on the keyboard, the directory command displays the next screen full of entries and pauses again. If you don't use this switch for a directory that fills more than one screen, the directory entries scroll by so fast you can't read them, and the scrolling continues until the last screen of entries is displayed.

If you look again at the directory displays in figure 4-7, you can see that they start with entries for a directory designated by a single period (.) and for another directory designated by two periods (..). You'll always see these entries for a directory that isn't the root directory because DOS uses them to keep track of where it

The format of the Directory command

```
DIR [file-spec] [/P] [/W]
```

The /W switch displays the directory listing in a wide format

```
C:\>dir \wp51 /w

 Volume in drive C is HD42
 Volume Serial Number is 1983-5D30
 Directory of  C:\WP51

[.]             [..]            INSTALL.EXE     STANDARD.CRS    WP.LRS
CONVERT.EXE     GRAPHCNV.EXE    GRAB.COM        MACROCNV.EXE    WPINFO.EXE
CURSOR.COM      FIXBIOS.COM     SPELL.EXE       CHARACTR.DOC    WP51-386.PIF
WP51-286.PIF    WP-PIF.DVP      NWPSETUP.EXE    WPHELP.FIL      ALTRNAT.WPK
MACROS.WPK      ENHANCED.WPK    SHORTCUT.WPK    EQUATION.WPK    LABELS.WPM
CODES.WPM       REVEALBX.WPM    REVEALCO.WPM    REVEALTX.WPM    FOOTEND.WPM
ENDFOOT.WPM     INLINE.WPM      LIBRARY.STY     WP.EXE          PRINTER.TST
WP.FIL          KEYS.MRS        WP.MRS          WPSMALL.DRS     STANDARD.IRS
STANDARD.PRS    STANDARD.VRS    WP.QRS          WP{WP}US.LEX    WP{WP}.SPW
WP{WP}US.HYC    WP{WP}US.THS    EGA512.FRS      EGAITAL.FRS     EGASMC.FRS
EGAUND.FRS      HRF12.FRS       HRF6.FRS        VGAUND.FRS      VGASMC.FRS
VGAITAL.FRS     VGA512.FRS      8514A.VRS       ATI.VRS         GENIUS.VRS
INCOLOR.VRS     PARADISE.VRS    VIDEO7.VRS      WP.DRS          WPDM1.ALL
WPHP1.ALL       WP51.INS        WP{WP}US.LCN    EPFX1050.PRS    WP{WP}.SET
EPLQ850.PRS     HPLASEII.PRS
       72 file(s)     3463870 bytes
                     24778752 bytes free
```

The /P switch pauses the directory listing after it fills the screen

```
C:\>dir \wp51 /p

 Volume in drive C is HD42
 Volume Serial Number is 1983-5D30
 Directory of C:\WP51

.                      12-03-92   12:34p
..                     12-03-92   12:34p
INSTALL  EXE     55808 02-07-90   12:00p
STANDARD CRS      2555 02-07-90   12:00p
WP       LRS     18971 02-07-90   12:00p
CONVERT  EXE    109049 02-07-90   12:00p
GRAPHCNV EXE    111104 02-07-90   12:00p
GRAB     COM     16450 02-07-90   12:00p
MACROCNV EXE     26063 02-07-90   12:00p
WPINFO   EXE      8704 02-07-90   12:00p
CURSOR   COM      1452 02-07-90   12:00p
FIXBIOS  COM        50 02-07-90   12:00p
SPELL    EXE     55808 02-07-90   12:00p
CHARACTR DOC     43029 02-07-90   12:00p
WP51-386 PIF       369 02-07-90   12:00p
WP51-286 PIF       369 02-07-90   12:00p
WP-PIF   DVP       416 02-07-90   12:00p
NWPSETUP EXE     28672 02-07-90   12:00p
WPHELP   FIL    188832 02-07-90   12:00p
Press any key to continue . . .
```

Figure 4-7 How the /W and /P switches of the Directory command affect the screen display

The format of the Change-directory command

```
CD [directory-spec]
```

Examples

```
C:\>cd \dos

C:\DOS>cd \

C:\>cd \dos

C:\DOS>cd \wp51

C:\WP51>cd mma

C:\WP51\MMA>cd \123\mma

C:\123\MMA>
```

Figure 4-8 Six examples of how to change directories with the Change-directory command

is in the directory structure. The single period represents an entry for the current directory, and the double period represents an entry for the parent directory.

The *parent directory* is just the directory that the current directory is immediately subordinate to. In figure 4-7, the parent directory is the root directory on drive C. I mention this because you'll sometimes see the dots and the term *parent directory* when you're using an application program.

The Change-directory command The Change-directory command lets you change the current directory, as illustrated in figure 4-8. Here, you can see the results of each command by noticing how the DOS command prompt changes. The first command changes the current directory from the root directory to the DOS directory, so the command prompt changes from C:\> to C:\DOS>. The second command changes the current directory back to the root directory. And so on.

When you start the parameter of a Change-directory command with a backslash, DOS assumes that your specification starts with the root directory. When you start the parameter without a backslash, DOS assumes that the parameter is a subdirectory contained within the current directory, as illustrated by the fifth command in figure 4-8. Here, this command:

```
cd mma
```

changes the current directory from C:\WP51 to C:\WP51\MMA.

```
C:\>ver

MS-DOS Version 6.00
```

Figure 4-9 The operation of the Version command

The Version command Figure 4-9 shows how to use the Version command. As you can see, this command displays a message that tells what version of DOS you're using. Since some application programs require specific versions of DOS, this command can tell you whether you have the right version of DOS for the program you're trying to use.

The Date and Time commands Figure 4-10 shows you how to use the Date and Time commands. Here, I've shaded the commands as well as the date and time entries made by the PC user. If you don't want to make any changes to the date or time that's displayed, just press the Enter key when DOS asks you for a new value, and you'll return to the command prompt.

If your PC displays these commands as part of your startup procedure, you probably know how to use them already. But you should realize that you can issue them from the DOS prompt whenever you need to check or correct the date or time.

If your system doesn't have a battery-powered internal clock, you should enter the correct date and time each time you start the PC. Otherwise, the date and time that are stored in the directory information for a new or updated file won't be correct. Also, the date and time won't be correct when one of your application programs gets this information from the system.

On the other hand, if your system has an internal clock, both the date and time should be kept current for you. Then, when one of your application programs gets the current date or time from the system, it should be correct. Internal clocks aren't always accurate, though, so you should check the time periodically and adjust it if necessary. And twice a year, you'll need to set the clock when the time changes to standard time and back again to daylight savings time.

The versions of DOS before 4.0 use a 24-hour clock. As a result, 4:09 p.m. must be entered into the system as 16:09. Beginning with DOS 4.0, however, this changed. Although you can still enter the time in 24-hour form, you can also enter 4:09 p.m. as 4:09pm or 4:09p, as shown in figure 4-10.

The Check-disk command Figure 4-11 shows you how to use the Check-disk command to display information about a specific disk. Here again, I've shaded the commands to separate them from the data that's displayed by DOS. Note that the first Check-disk command doesn't specify a disk drive, so it operates on the default drive, which is drive C. In contrast, the second command specifies drive B, a diskette drive.

```
C:\>date
Current date is Tue 02-10-1993
Enter new date (mm-dd-yy): 02-1-93

C:\>time
Current time is 4:06:56.37p
Enter new time: 4:09p
```

Figure 4-10 The operation of the Date and Time commands

As you can see, the Check-disk command shows the total number of bytes of storage available on each disk, how that storage is used, and how much storage is available for new files. When you need to know whether a hard disk or diskette has enough space for a program or data file, you can use this command to find out.

Each command breaks the disk storage down to show how many bytes of storage are used for *hidden files* (files that DOS doesn't want you to access), how many for directories, and how many for user files. This command also shows how many bytes are in *bad sectors*. These are units of disk space that are damaged, so they can't store data reliably. Since DOS knows about these bad sectors and doesn't use them, they're nothing to worry about. In fact, most disks have some bad sectors.

In DOS 4.0 and later versions, this command also displays information about the *allocation units* on the disk. An allocation unit is the smallest unit of storage that's used for a file. Even if a file contains only one byte of data, it uses a whole allocation unit. So there have to be enough allocation units available for a file, as well as enough disk space, or the file won't fit on the disk. As you can see in figure 4-11, the size of an allocation unit differs depending on the disk.

The last two lines of information for each drive tell how many bytes of conventional internal memory your system has and how many bytes aren't being used. In figure 4-11, these lines tell you that the PC has 655,360 bytes (640KB) of memory, and that 584,512 are free. If you subtract the second number from the first, you can see that 70,848 bytes of memory are used.

Besides displaying the information shown in figure 4-11, the Check-disk command looks for various types of disk errors. If it finds any, it displays messages about these errors along with the other information. If you get one of these error messages, you often need to get technical help. In chapter 10, you'll learn what these messages are and what you should do about them.

Unlike the commands I've presented so far in this chapter, the Check-disk command is an external command. As a result, DOS may not be able to find its command file when you issue the command. If it can't, DOS will display this message:

```
Bad command or file name
```

If that happens, you can use the Change-directory command to change the current directory to the one that contains the DOS files.

The format of the Check-disk command

```
CHKDSK [drive-spec]
```

Example 1

```
C:\>chkdsk

Volume HD42        created 08-05-1992 2:49p
Volume Serial Number is 1983-5D30

  44363776 bytes total disk space
     79872 bytes in 2 hidden files
     40960 bytes in 15 directories
  19443712 bytes in 569 user files
     20480 bytes in bad sectors
  24778752 bytes available on disk

      2048 bytes in each allocation unit
     21662 total allocation units on disk
     12099 available allocation units on disk

    655360 total bytes memory
    584512 bytes free
```

Example 2

```
C:\>chkdsk b:

    362496 bytes total disk space
    155648 bytes in 10 user files
    206848 bytes available on disk

      1024 bytes in each allocation unit
       354 total allocation units on disk
       202 available allocation units on disk

    655360 total bytes memory
    584512 bytes free

C:\>
```

Figure 4-11 The operation of the Check-disk command

The Type and Print commands The Type command lets you display the contents of a file; the Print command lets you print the contents of a file. However, these commands work only on *text files*. These files contain only characters that are in a standard code called ASCII. As a result, you can't use these commands to display or print the contents of the data files used by your application programs, such as word processing, spreadsheet, or database files.

Figure 4-12 shows how I used these commands to display and print the contents of a DOS text file named CONFIG.SYS. Since the commands don't specify a drive or directory for the CONFIG.SYS file, DOS looked for it in the current directory (the root directory) on the default drive (the C drive). As you can see, this file contains seven lines of text.

Since the Print command is another external command, you may have to change the current directory to the one that contains the DOS files before you issue the Print command. Also, the Print command displays a message like the one in figure 4-12 that asks you to name the list device. If your system has been set up properly, all you have to do is press the Enter key when this message appears.

You can use the Type and Print commands to display or print the contents of the README files that come with software products. These are text files that usually contain corrections and changes to the manuals that come with the products. Because the files are often lengthy, it's usually better to print them than to display them. But if you want to read a file while it's displayed, you can control the scrolling of the text by using the Pause key, as I'll explain in a moment.

Three skills that will help you use DOS commands more effectively

To use DOS commands effectively, you should know how to use the keyboard to help control the operation of a command. You should know how to handle the most common DOS error messages. And you should know how to use simple forms of the * wildcard.

How to use the keyboard to control the operation of a command

Figure 4-13 presents keystrokes and keystroke combinations that you can use to control the operation of a command. First, you can use the Esc key to cancel a command before you press the Enter key. Then, you can enter the command again.

Second, you can stop the scrolling of the display screen by pressing the Pause key. This can be useful when you use the Type command to display a lengthy text file, or when you use the Directory command to display a lengthy directory. If your keyboard doesn't provide a Pause key, you can stop the scrolling by holding down the Ctrl key and then pressing the key for the letter S. Then to continue the scrolling, you can press any key.

Third, you can interrupt the execution of a command and cancel it by holding down the Ctrl key then pressing the Pause or Break key. If, for example, the Type command is displaying the contents of a lengthy text file, you can cancel the

The formats of the Type and Print commands

```
TYPE file-spec

PRINT file-spec
```

The display of the Type and Print commands

```
C:\>type config.sys
DEVICE=C:\DOS\SETVER.EXE
FILES=30
BUFFERS=30
DEVICE=C:\DOS\HIMEM.SYS
STACKS=9,256
SHELL=C:\DOS\COMMAND.COM C:\DOS\  /p
DOS=HIGH

C:\>print config.sys
Name of list device [PRN]:
Resident part of PRINT installed


  C:\CONFIG.SYS is currently being printed

C:\>
```

The printed output of the Print command

```
DEVICE=C:\DOS\SETVER.EXE
FILES=30
BUFFERS=30
DEVICE=C:\DOS\HIMEM.SYS
STACKS=9,256
SHELL=C:\DOS\COMMAND.COM C:\DOS\  /p
DOS=HIGH
```

Figure 4-12 The operation of the Type and Print commands

command by pressing those keys. If your keyboard doesn't have a Pause key, you can cancel a command by holding down the Ctrl key and then pressing the letter C.

Fourth, if you want to print the output of a command that's displayed on the screen, you can hold down the Shift key and then press the Print-screen key. This is often useful if you want to print the output from a Directory command. However, this

Keystrokes	Alternates	Function
Esc		Cancels the command you've entered without trying to execute it.
Pause	Ctrl+S	Stops the scrolling of the display screen; any key restarts it.
Crtl+Pause	Ctrl+C	Interrupts the execution of the command and cancels it.
Print-screen		Prints whatever is displayed on the screen.
Ctrl+Print-screen		Starts or stops the printing of whatever is displayed on the screen as DOS commands are executed.

Figure 4-13 Keystrokes and keystroke combinations that can help you control the DOS commands

keystroke combination only prints what's displayed on the screen, not any part of the display that has already scrolled off the screen.

Fifth, if you want to print whatever is displayed on the screen as DOS commands are executed, you can hold down the Ctrl key and then press the Print-screen key. From that time on, whatever is displayed on the screen is also printed on the printer. To stop the printing, you press this keystroke combination again.

How to handle the most common DOS error messages If you've been trying the commands on your own system as you've read this chapter, you've probably encountered one or more *DOS error messages*. Some of the ones you'll see most often are shown in figure 4-14.

As you can see in the first example, if you spell the keyword of a command wrong, DOS will tell you that you've used a "bad command or file name." However, DOS also displays this message when it can't find the command file you tried to execute. If, for example, you haven't changed the current directory to the program directory before you issue the command for starting an application program, you'll usually get this error message.

The second example shows you the message you get if DOS can't find the file you've specified within a command: "File not found." Here, DOS looks for a file named WP.EXE in the current directory, but none exists. That may be because the file's been deleted somehow. But sometimes you get this message because you've entered the file name wrong. And sometimes you get it because you didn't give a complete file specification, and the file isn't in the current directory of the default drive. Then, to correct the problem, all you have to do is give a complete specification.

If you include a parameter or switch that isn't valid for a command, DOS gives you the message "Invalid parameter" or "Invalid switch" as shown in the third

Example 1:
```
C:\>promp $p$g
Bad command or file name
```

Example 2:
```
C:\>dir wp.exe
Volume in drive C is HD42
Volume Serial Number is 1983-5D30
Directory of C:\

File not found
```

Example 3:
```
C:\>dir /d
Invalid switch -  d
```

Example 4:
```
C:\>a:
Not ready reading drive A
Abort, Retry, Fail? f
Current drive is no longer valid>c:

C:\>
```

Figure 4-14 The most common DOS error messages as they appear on your screen

example. If you're using DOS 4.0 or later, the message tells you which parameter or switch is invalid; for earlier versions of DOS, you have to check the format of the command to find out what's wrong. Then, to correct the problem, you just reissue the command in its proper form. Often, you get this message when you accidentally use a slash (/) instead of a backslash (\) within a path specification.

The last message in figure 4-14 is this:

```
Not ready reading drive A
Abort, Retry, Fail?
```

You get this message when you specify diskette drive A, but that drive doesn't contain a diskette or the door for that drive isn't closed. Often, you get this message because you forgot to put the diskette in drive A before you issued a command that requires the drive. Then, to correct the problem, you put the diskette in the drive, close the door, and enter the letter R for Retry.

If you get that error message because you specified drive A by accident, you just enter the letter F for Fail. Then, DOS may display this error message as shown in figure 4-14:

```
Current drive is no longer valid>
```

Wildcard example	Meaning
`*.*`	All files (any name, any extension)
`*.com`	All files with COM as the extension
`*.`	All files that don't have extensions
`C1.*`	All files named C1 no matter what the extensions are
`C*.*`	All files with names that start with the letter C no matter what the extensions are

Figure 4-15 Common uses of the * wildcard

This means that DOS no longer knows what its default drive should be. To correct this problem, you just enter a drive specification like C: to reset the default drive.

Although DOS has many other error messages, these are the most common ones. If DOS displays a message you're not familiar with, you can usually figure out what's wrong by carefully inspecting the command you entered. Otherwise, you can look in the back of your DOS manual to see if it has a summary of the DOS error messages. If it does, this summary should tell you how to respond to each message.

How to use simple forms of the * wildcard in your commands DOS provides two *wildcards* that you can use within the file specifications of DOS commands. In chapter 7, you'll learn how to use both of them to help you manage the files on a hard disk. However, I'm going to introduce you to some simple forms of the * *wildcard* (asterisk wildcard) now so you can start using them right away.

The * wildcard represents one or more characters of any kind. It is used within the file name portion of a file specification so a command can operate on more than one file. Some simple forms of file names that use this wildcard are illustrated in figure 4-15. As you can see, *.* refers to files with any name before the period and any extension. As a result, it refers to all the files in a directory. In the other examples in figure 4-15, you can see how this wildcard is used to represent all files with the extension of COM, all files with no extension, and so on.

Perhaps the best way to get comfortable with the use of this wildcard is to practice using it in Directory commands, as shown in figure 4-16. Here, the first command displays only the files with COM as the extension. The second command displays only the files with EXE as the extension. The third command displays all of the files named CHKDSK, no matter what the extensions are (only one file is displayed). And the last command displays all the files with names that start with C and have COM as the extension.

Example 1

A Directory command that displays all the files in the current directory that have an extension of COM.

```
C:\DOS>dir *.com /w

 Volume in drive C is DRIVE_C
 Volume Serial Number is 1982-730B
 Directory of  C:\DOS

FORMAT.COM       KEYB.COM         SYS.COM          DISKCOMP.COM     DISKCOPY.COM
MIRROR.COM       DOSSHELL.COM     MODE.COM         MSHERC.COM       ASSIGN.COM
HELP.COM         EDIT.COM         GRAFTABL.COM     DISK.COM         DISKCOPY.COM
MORE.COM         GRAPHICS.COM     TREE.COM         DOSKEY.COM       LOADFIX.COM
VSAFE.COM        COMMAND.COM
       22 file(s)      327796 bytes
                     71249920 bytes free
```

Example 2

A Directory command that displays all the files in the current directory that have an extension of EXE.

```
C:\DOS>dir *.exe /w

 Volume in drive C is DRIVE_C
 Volume Serial Number is 1982-730B
 Directory of  C:\DOS

NLSFUNC.EXE      DEBUG.EXE        EXPAND.EXE       FDISK.EXE        EDLIN.EXE
ATTRIB.EXE       DEFRAG.EXE       INTERLNK.EXE     INTERSVR.EXE     MSD.EXE
POWER.EXE        DOSSWAP.EXE      SETVER.EXE       SMARTMON.EXE     FASTOPEN.EXE
RECOVER.EXE      SHARE.EXE        PRINT.EXE        MEM.EXE          XCOPY.EXE
DOSHELP.EXE      BACKUP.EXE       COMP.EXE         QBASIC.EXE       APPEND.EXE
CHKDSK.EXE       FC.EXE           FIND.EXE         EXE2BIN.EXE      LABEL.EXE
JOIN.EXE         RESTORE.EXE      SORT.EXE         DOSSHELL.EXE     REPLACE.EXE
SUBST.EXE        UNDELETE.EXE     MSAV.EXE         MEMMAKER.EXE     SIZER.EXE
MSBACKUP.EXE     DBLSPACE.EXE     DELOLDOS.EXE     EMM386.EXE       SMARTDRV.EXE
       45 file(s)     2101817 bytes
                     71248820 bytes free
```

Example 3

A directory command that displays all the files in the current directory named CHKDSK no matter what the extensions are.

```
C:\DOS>dir chkdsk.*

 Volume in drive C is DRIVE_C
 Volume Serial Number is 1982-730B
 Directory of  C:\DOS

CHKDSK   EXE       16216 10-26-92   6:00A
        1 file(s)         16216 bytes
                      71249920 byte free
```

Figure 4-16 The use of the * wildcard in four Directory commands (part 1 of 2)

Example 4

A Directory command that displays all the files in the current directory with names that start with C and have COM as the extension.

```
C:\DOS>dir c*.com

 Volume in drive C is DRIVE_C
 Volume Serial Number is 1982-730B
 Directory of  C:\DOS

CHOICE   COM       1754 10-26-92   6:00a
COMMAND  COM      53022 10-26-92   6:00 a
        2 file(s)        54776 bytes
                      71249920 bytes free

C:\DOS>
```

Figure 4-16 The use of the * wildcard in four Directory commands (part 2 of 2)

How to start an application program from the DOS command prompt

Now that you know how to start internal and external commands from the command prompt, you should also be able to start any application program from there. You should be able to do this easily when you know what directory the program is in and what the name of the program is. You should also be able to do this if you know the name of the program but you can't remember the name of the directory it's in.

How to start a program when you know its directory When you talk about a word processing or spreadsheet program, it sounds like you're talking about a single program file. However, if you use the Directory command to display the files in the directory for an application program, you'll see that a typical application program consists of many files. For instance, if you look back at figure 4-7, you'll see that my directory for *WordPerfect 5.1* contains 72 files. Many of these files contain supporting data that *WordPerfect* uses, like tables, dictionaries, and thesauruses. But eleven of the files are command files. Command files always have file names with an extension of COM or EXE, and DOS can execute them as commands.

To start an application program, you need to know the name of the command file that's designed to start the program. Then, you enter this name *without* the COM or EXE extension to start the program. For instance, the name of the starting command file for *WordPerfect* is WP.EXE, so WP is the command name that starts the program. The name of the starting command file for *Lotus 1-2-3* is 123.EXE, so 123 is the command name that starts the program. Although a program may consist of more than one command file, only one of the files is designed to start the program.

Example 1: Starting *WordPerfect* 5.1 from the WP51 directory with the name WP

```
C:\>cd \wp51
C:\WP51>wp
```

Example 2: Starting *Lotus 1-2-3* from the 123 directory with the name 123

```
C:\WP51>cd \123
C:\123>123
```

Example 3: Starting *Q&A* from the QA4 directory with the name QA

```
C:\123>cd \qa4
C:\QA4>qa
```

Figure 4-17 How to start an application program when you know its directory and name

If you don't know the name of the command file that starts the program, you can look in its program manual to get the correct name. Otherwise, you can use the Directory command to list the files in the directory. If you look for files with COM and EXE extensions, you can usually figure out which file is the one that is designed to start the program. To help you in your search, you can use wildcard file specifications in the Directory command, like this:

```
dir *.exe

dir *.com
```

Then, the Directory command will list only the files with the extension you specify.

Before you execute the starting command file, though, you often need to change the current directory to the one that contains the program's files. This is illustrated in figure 4-17, which shows you how to start three different programs: *WordPerfect*, *Lotus 1-2-3*, and *Q&A*. In all three examples, the first command is a Change-directory command that sets the current directory to the one that contains the program. The second command is the command name that starts the program. You can start programs in other ways, but this procedure is the only one that works on all systems for all programs.

Of course, these examples assume that all program directories are on the C drive. If they aren't, you have to use a three-step procedure for starting a program from the command prompt. First, use the Change-drive command to change the default drive to the one that contains the program directory you want. Second, use the Change-directory command to change the current directory to the program directory. Third, enter the name of the command file that starts the program.

Although you can use the procedure shown in figure 4-17 to start any command or program, sometimes you don't have to change to the program's directory before you issue the command. In the next chapter, for example, I'll show you how to set up your system so DOS will know where to look for the application programs that you use most frequently.

If you're using a version of DOS that's 3.0 or later, you can also start a program without changing to the directory it's in by coding its path along with its command name. If, for example, *WordPerfect* is in the WP51 directory on the C drive, you can start it with this command:

```
c:\wp51\wp
```

This command tells DOS to look in the WP51 directory on the C drive for a command file named WP.COM or WP.EXE.

Before you try to start a program this way, you should realize that it won't work with many application programs. For instance, many releases of *Lotus 1-2-3* require that the current directory be set to the program directory before the program is run. That way, the program can find the files it requires for operation. As a result, you have to use the method in figure 4-17 for starting programs like these.

How to start a program when you don't know its directory If you're working on someone else's PC or you're trying to start a program that you use infrequently, you may not remember the name of the directory it's in. Usually, though, you'll be able to start the program by using the commands you've learned in this chapter.

To find the directory for a program, you can start by using the Directory command to display the root directory on the C drive. Often, this directory will contain the program directories for the system, and you'll be able to figure out which directory contains the program you're trying to start. If the root directory on the C drive doesn't contain the directory you're looking for, you can display the root directories of the other drives. One of these directories ought to contain the directory you're looking for.

Once you know the drive and path of the program directory, you can start the program in three steps or less. First, use the Change-drive command to set the default drive to the one that contains the program directory. Second, use the Change-directory command to set the current directory to the program directory. Third, enter the name of the command file that is designed to start the program.

How to use the DOS 5.0 and 6.0 Help features

Unlike earlier versions of DOS, versions 5.0 and 6.0 both provide *Help features* that you can use to get information about the format and switches of a command. Figure 4-18 summarizes the three ways that you can get Help information for a command in either DOS 5.0 or DOS 6.0. As you can tell from this figure, the two versions of the Help feature are very different. So I'll present them one at a time. You only have to read about the feature that's available on your PC.

Format	Example	DOS 5.0 function	DOS 6.0 function
`HELP`	`C:\>help`	Displays a brief summary of the function of each DOS command.	Goes into the full-screen Help feature; displays a list of DOS 6.0 commands so you can choose the one you want to know about.
`HELP command-name`	`C:\>help dir`	Displays the syntax for the named command with a brief explanation of each syntax element.	Goes into the full-screen Help feature and displays Help information for the named command.
`Command-name /?`	`C:\>dir /?`	Displays the syntax for the named command with a brief explanation of each syntax element.	Displays brief Help information for the command at the command prompt (like the Help information given by the DOS 5.0 Help feature).

Figure 4-18 Three ways to use the DOS 5.0 and 6.0 Help features

The DOS 5.0 Help feature The Help information provided by DOS 5.0 is limited. If you enter just the command name, *help*, DOS 5.0 displays a brief summary of the function of each DOS command. If you enter the word *help* followed by another command name, DOS 5.0 displays the Help information for that command. This includes the command format and a one- or two-line explanation of each element in the format. And if you enter the name of the command that you want information for followed by /?, you get the same Help information that you get when you enter *help* followed by the command name.

The DOS 5.0 Help feature may save you from looking up commands in the DOS reference manual when you're already familiar with the command and you just need to be reminded of its syntax. But if you need more detailed information about what the command does, you'll probably have to use the reference manual.

The DOS 6.0 Help feature In contrast to the DOS 5.0 Help feature, the DOS 6.0 Help feature provides a complete, easy-to-use command reference. So complete, in fact, that DOS 6.0 doesn't come with a separate reference manual. So unless you

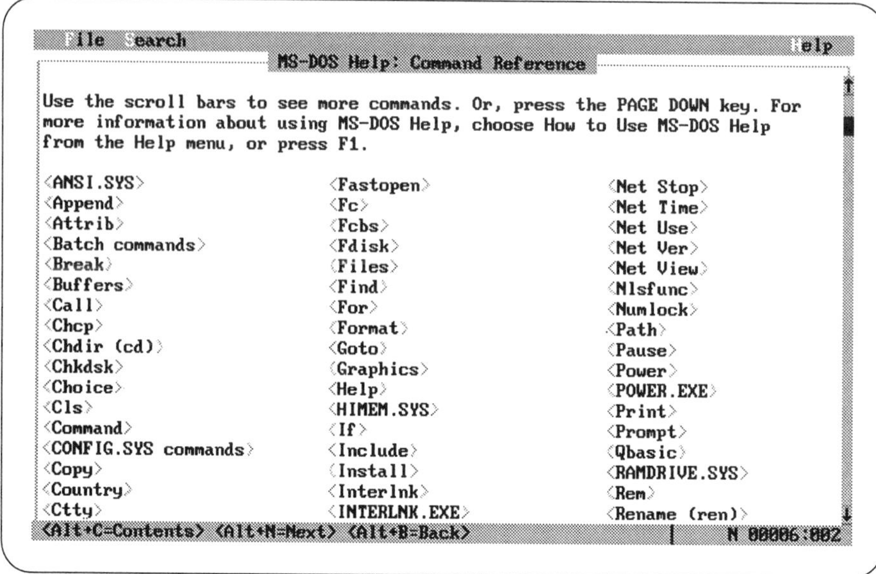

Figure 4-19 The opening screen of DOS 6.0's full-screen Help feature, MS-DOS Help

use only a few simple DOS commands that you have memorized, I think you'll use this Help feature often.

To access Help information in DOS 6.0, you can use the same three formats that you use in DOS 5.0, as shown in figure 4-18. But only the third format, a command name followed by /?, works the same as in DOS 5.0. It displays the command syntax and a brief explanation of each syntax element. In contrast, the other two formats take you into DOS 6.0's full-screen Help feature, called MS-DOS Help.

If you enter the command name, *help*, by itself, DOS 6.0 displays a screen like the one in figure 4-19. As you can see, this is a table of contents for all the DOS 6.0 commands. To move the cursor around within this table of contents, you use the cursor control keys, the Page-up and Page-down keys, and the Tab key. For example, if you want to see what additional commands there are, you can use the Down arrow key or the Page-down key to display another screenful of entries. To move from one entry to another, you can use the Tab key to move the cursor forward one entry, and the Shift+Tab key combination to move back to the previous entry.

If you're using a mouse, you can also scroll through the table of contents using the *scroll bar* at the right side of the Help screen. You can scroll one line at a time by clicking on the arrow at the top or bottom of the scroll bar. If you hold the mouse button down on the arrow instead of clicking on it, the lines scroll continuously until you release the button. You can also scroll through varying numbers of lines using the highlighted portion of the scroll bar, called the *scroll box*. To do that, move the mouse cursor to the scroll box, then hold down the left mouse button while you move the

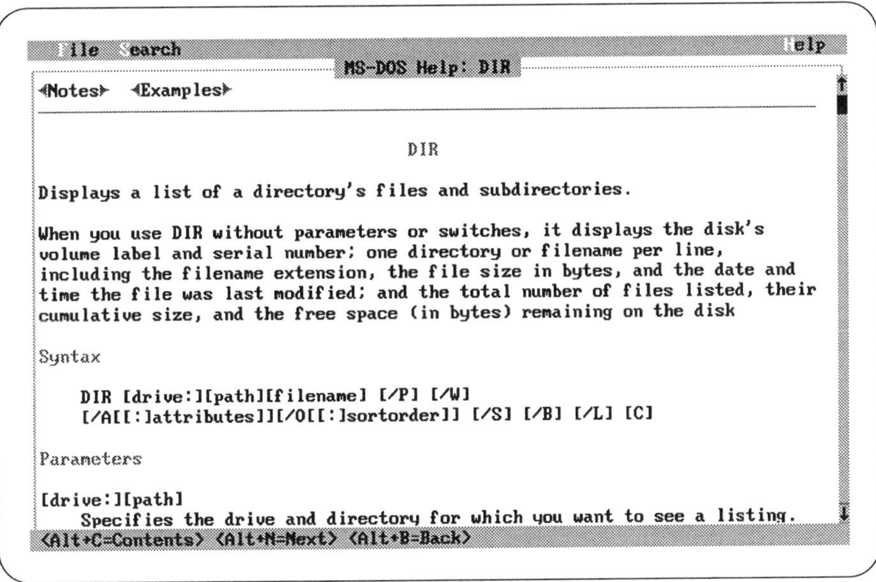

Figure 4-20 The first screen of syntax information for the Directory command

scroll box to a new position. When you release the mouse button, the Help text scrolls to its new position.

To get Help information on a specific command, you move the cursor to the command name and press the Enter key. Or, click on the command name using the mouse. Then, DOS 6.0 displays extensive information on the syntax of the command. For example, figure 4-20 shows the first syntax screen for the Directory command. Again, you can use the Arrow keys and the Page-up and Page-down keys or the scroll bar to scroll through this information and find out what you need to know.

You can also press the Tab key to move the cursor to the "Notes" or "Examples" options that appear near the top of the screen. Then, when you press the Enter key, the Help feature displays additional information on how to use the command. If you're using a mouse, simply click on one of these options to display this information.

You can also use the Tab key to move to other topics that are highlighted throughout the text. For example, the last screen of the Directory command syntax, shown in figure 4-21, refers to the TREE and DBLSPACE commands. Notice that these commands are enclosed in angle brackets (< >) so they're easily identified. To get information on a highlighted topic, place the cursor on it and press the Enter key or click on it with the mouse.

At any point, if you want to go back to the table of contents, you can press the Alt+C key combination. If you want to move back through the screens you've already looked at, one at a time, you can press the Alt+B key combination. If you want to move forward to the next Help topic, you can press the Alt+N key combination. If you're using a mouse, you can activate these functions by clicking on the appropriate

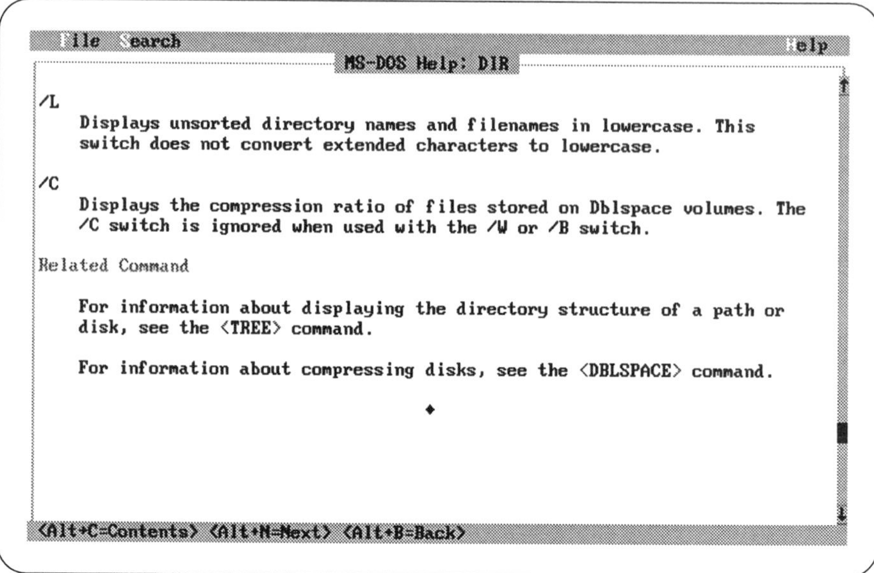

Figure 4-21 The last screen of syntax information for the Directory command

option at the bottom of the screen. You can also press the F1 key at any time to find out more about how MS-DOS Help works.

At the top of the screens in figures 4-19, 4-20, and 4-21, you can see that MS-DOS Help provides you with three *menus*: File, Search, and Help. These menus allow you to do certain tasks within MS-DOS Help. Figure 4-22, for example, shows the options on the File menu. Here, the Print option allows you to get a printed copy of Help information, and the Exit option lets you exit MS-DOS Help and return to the command prompt.

To select a menu option, you press the Alt key to activate the menu system. Then, you can continue in one of two ways. You can move the cursor to the menu you want, press Enter to open the menu, move the cursor to the menu command you want, and press Enter to start the command. Or, you can press the letter that's highlighted in the menu name to open the menu, and then press the letter that's highlighted in the menu command to start the command. If you're using a mouse, you can select these options and commands by clicking on them.

The second Help command format in figure 4-18 also activates MS-DOS Help. But instead of taking you to the table of contents, it takes you directly to the first syntax screen for the command you specify. For example, if you enter the command

```
help dir
```

at the command prompt, DOS 6.0 will take you to the screen shown in figure 4-20. At this point, you can move through MS-DOS Help just as if you had entered at the table of contents screen.

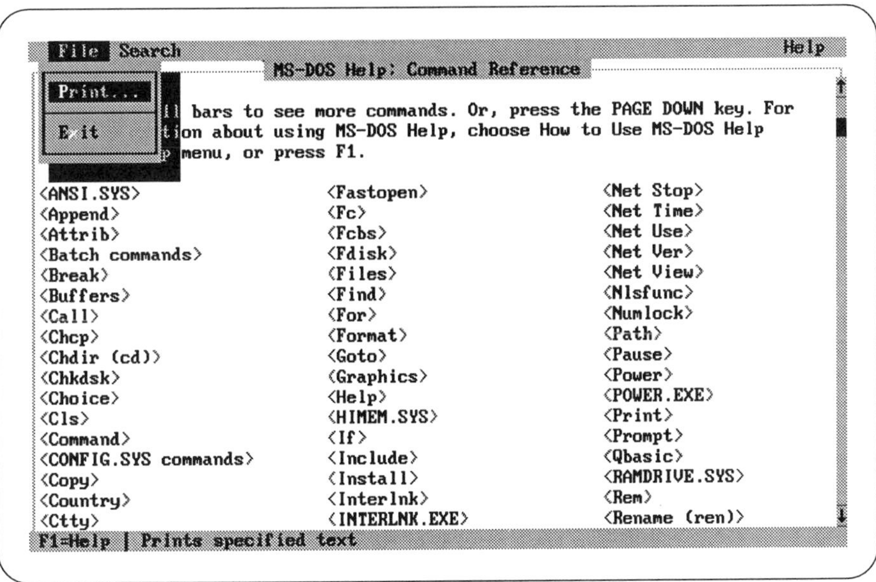

Figure 4-22 The File menu of MS-DOS Help

How to shut down your PC

In general, you shouldn't turn your PC off when you're using an application program. If you do, you'll lose the work that is stored in internal memory. Instead, you should save your work and exit properly from the application program. Then, when DOS displays the command prompt, you can turn off your PC. It's also a good idea to remove diskettes from the diskette drives before you turn your system off, but that isn't essential.

How to restart your PC without turning it off and on

Occasionally, you may need to restart your PC because you've gotten hung up by a software or hardware problem. To do that, you can shut down your PC as described above and then turn it on again. Or you can press this key combination: Ctrl+Alt+Delete. This means to press the Delete key while holding down both the Ctrl and Alt keys. This boots DOS, but doesn't force the PC to go through its self-test again.

To guard against losing any of your work, you should use this key combination only when you're at the command prompt. In other words, if you're in the middle of an application program, exit properly from the program before you restart your PC. In the next chapter, I'll show you a specific instance when this key combination comes in handy.

Some perspective on DOS

The hardest part about learning to use DOS is getting started. Before you can do much of anything, you need to know how to enter a command, what the command formats are, how to use various keystroke combinations to control the execution of the commands, and how to handle DOS error messages. It also helps if you know something about wildcards.

Now that you've seen how 11 of the DOS commands work, you should have a better idea of why you need to learn DOS. First, you often have to use DOS commands to start your application programs. Second, you can do some jobs with DOS commands that you can't do any other way. For instance, you can set the date and time of your system, and you can check the available capacity of your hard disk.

Perhaps the most important reason for learning DOS, though, is that it helps you understand your system. In general, the more you learn about DOS, the more you take control of your system. As much as the software developers would like you to believe that you can use an application program without any knowledge of DOS, that just isn't true.

On the other hand, I'm not suggesting that you learn how to use every DOS command. Because it's obvious that you're not getting application work done when you're using DOS, you should use DOS commands only when they can help you work more productively. That's why the remaining chapters in this section show you how to use DOS commands for specific jobs that you have to do to use your PC effectively.

Terms

self-test
POST (Power-On-Self-Test)
booting the system
command prompt
keyword
command name
parameter
switch
internal command
external command
command file
parent directory
hidden file
bad sector
allocation unit
text file
DOS error message
wildcard
* wildcard
Help feature
scroll bar
scroll box
menu

Objectives

1. Given the directory name and the command name for a program, start the program from the command prompt.
2. Given a drive and directory, use a DOS command to display a list of the files in the directory.

3. Use a DOS command to find out what version of DOS your PC is using.
4. Use DOS commands to check the system date and time and to correct them if they're inaccurate.
5. Use a DOS command to find out what directories are in the current path.
6. Use a DOS command to find out how much storage is available on any of the disk drives on your system.
7. Use a DOS command to display or print any text file on your PC.
8. Use the proper combination of commands to start any external command, even if the DOS directory isn't in the list established by the Path command.

Exercises

1. Use the Version command to find out what version of DOS you're using on your PC. Then, use the Clear-screen command to clear the screen.
2. Use the Prompt command as shown in figure 4-5 to change the prompt so the current directory is displayed.
3. Use the Change-drive command to find out what drive letters are valid on your system. Then, use the Clear-screen command to clear the screen.
4. Use the Date and Time commands to find out whether the date and time are set correctly for your system. If they aren't, correct them.
5. Use the Directory command to display the directory listing for the root directory of the C drive. If the listing for this directory is more than one screen long, use the /P switch to display the directory again. Next, use the /W switch to display the directory again. While the listing is displayed, note the names of the directories that are listed. Then, find the entries for the COMMAND.COM, CONFIG.SYS, and AUTOEXEC.BAT files. If you can't find one for the AUTOEXEC.BAT file, you're going to want to create one after you read the next chapter.
6. If there are no directories in the root directory of the C drive, use the Directory command to display the directories that are stored in the root directory of the D drive. While the directory is displayed, note the names of the directories that are listed.
7. Use the Change-directory command to change from one of the directories to another. Note how the command prompt changes as the current directory changes. If your system has both C and D drives, experiment with the Change-drive and Change-directory commands so you see that each drive has its own current directory.
8. Find out which directory contains the DOS files for your system. Normally, that directory will be on the C drive, and it will be named DOS. On some systems, however, all of the DOS files will be stored in the root directory of the C drive.

To find out whether a directory contains the DOS files, use the Directory command with the *.COM file specification to list only the COM files. If the directory contains the DOS files, you should be able to find entries for the CHKDSK.COM and PRINT.COM files in the directory listing if you're using DOS 4.0 or earlier. If you're using DOS 5.0 or 6.0, you should be able to find entries for the DOSSHELL.COM and DOSKEY.COM files.

9. Use the Change-directory command to change the directory to the one that contains the DOS files. Next, use the Directory command with the /P and /W switches to display the current directory. Then, experiment with the keystrokes and keystroke combinations in figure 4-13 to see how they work when you use Directory commands to display the current directory. Last, experiment with * wildcards as shown in figure 4-16 to see how they work when you use Directory commands to display the current directory.

10. With the current directory set to the one that contains the DOS files, use the Check-disk command to find out the capacities of the disk drives on your system. You can do this for the diskette drives as well as for the hard disk drives, but remember that the A drive on some PCs can handle both standard and high capacity diskettes. Then, the capacity depends on the diskette, not the drive.

11. To see if your system is set up so that DOS knows where its files are, change the directory to the root directory and try the Check-disk command again. If DOS issues a message saying that the command is invalid, DOS doesn't know where to find its files. In the next chapter, I'll show you how to fix this.

12. Use the Type and Print commands to display and print the CONFIG.SYS file in the root directory of the C drive. Next, use the Type command to display the COMMAND.COM file in the root directory of the C drive. Since this isn't a text file, the command won't work properly.

13. To see how the F3 key works, press it to run your last command again. Then, press the Enter key, so you're ready to see how the F1 key works. Next, press the F1 key several times to see the results. The functions for these keys are summarized in figure 4-2.

14. Put a diskette in the A drive. Next, use the Directory command to display its contents. Then, remove the diskette and run the last command again. When DOS displays its error message, put the diskette back in the drive and enter the letter R to retry the command.

15. If you're using DOS 5.0 or 6.0, enter the word *doskey* at the command prompt and press the Enter key to activate the Doskey feature. Then, enter a few commands such as a Type command to display the CONFIG.SYS file and a Change-directory command to make \DOS the current directory. Next, press the Up arrow key to recall the previous command. Next, press the F7 key to display all the commands in memory. Then, experiment with the other keystrokes in figure 4-3 to see how the Doskey feature works.

16. If you're using DOS 5.0, enter the word *help* at the command prompt to display the Help summary. Next, use the summary to get the Help information for the Directory command. Then, use the two other ways shown in figure 4-18 to get the Help information for the Directory command.

17. If you're using DOS 6.0, enter the word *help* at the command prompt to display the first screen of the full-screen Help feature. Next, use the keyboard or the mouse to display Help information for the Directory command. Then, use the other ways shown in figure 4-18 to get the Help information for the Directory command.

Chapter 5

How to set up the AUTOEXEC.BAT file so DOS gets started right

When you start your PC, DOS looks for two files in the root directory of the C drive. The first, CONFIG.SYS, contains special configuration commands that tell DOS how to initialize itself. The second, AUTOEXEC.BAT, contains one or more DOS commands that are always executed when you start your PC. If DOS can't find an AUTOEXEC.BAT file in the root directory of drive C, it executes the Date and Time commands.

The AUTOEXEC.BAT file is simply a list of DOS commands, as shown in the sample in figure 5-1. Because it can contain any commands, it can have a significant effect on the way your system starts up and works. At the least, it will save you from having to enter the same set of commands at the DOS prompt each time you start your PC.

In this chapter, you'll learn which commands you should consider including in your AUTOEXEC.BAT file and why. Then, you'll learn four methods for creating or changing the file. Last, you'll learn how to test your file without turning the PC off and on.

Before you start, however, you should realize that an AUTOEXEC.BAT file is a *batch file*. A batch file is a file that contains one or more DOS commands. The file names for all batch files have BAT as the extension so DOS can distinguish them from other types of files. The only difference between the AUTOEXEC batch file and other batch files is that the AUTOEXEC file is automatically executed when the system is started. Consequently, much of what you learn in this chapter applies to any batch file.

```
echo off
prompt $p$g
path=c:\dos;c:\util
cls
```

Figure 5-1 A typical AUTOEXEC.BAT file

Commands to use in your AUTOEXEC.BAT file

Although the AUTOEXEC.BAT file in figure 5-1 is a simple one, the commands it contains are typical of those you'll want to include in your own AUTOEXEC.BAT. The Echo command isn't crucial for getting your PC started up smoothly, but it is useful, so I'll show you how it works in this section. In contrast, the Prompt and Path commands are critical in getting your PC set up right, so you should always include them in your AUTOEXEC.BAT. And you'll also want to include other commands, like the Clear-screen command, that you normally enter each time you turn on your PC.

How to use the Echo command in a batch file Figure 5-2 presents the Echo command, a command designed specifically for batch files. You can use it to specify whether or not you want batch file commands displayed as they are executed. You can also use it to display messages.

In the batch file in figure 5-1, OFF is specified, so the commands in the file aren't displayed (or "echoed") as they are executed. However, if the commands in the batch file generate any messages, these messages are displayed. Since ON is the default condition, you need to use an ECHO ON command only if an ECHO OFF command has been issued previously.

If the parameter is anything other than ON or OFF, the Echo command treats it as a message you want displayed on the monitor. The message is displayed whether or not the current Echo status is "on" or "off." This is illustrated by the third and fourth examples in figure 5-2, and I'll show you how this works in an AUTOEXEC.BAT file later in this chapter.

Why you should include the Prompt and Path commands in your AUTOEXEC.BAT file In general, the AUTOEXEC.BAT file should include at least two commands. One should be a Prompt command like the second command in figure 5-1. As you learned in chapter 4, this command tells DOS to display the default drive and current directory in the command prompt.

The other command that should be included in the AUTOEXEC.BAT file is a Path command that establishes the list of directories that DOS searches whenever it receives a command. When DOS receives an external command or a program name, it always starts by looking for the command or program file in the current directory. Then, if a Path command is in effect, DOS continues the search by looking through

Format

```
ECHO [ON][OFF][message]
```

Function

If the parameter is ON, this command tells DOS to display all batch file commands as they are executed. If the parameter is OFF, this command tells DOS not to display the batch file commands as they are executed. The OFF parameter stays in effect until the next Echo command is executed. If there's a Message parameter, the message is displayed. If no parameters are used, DOS displays a message that tells whether the Echo status is on or off.

Examples

```
echo on

echo off

echo Please record your PC time at the computer center
echo after each session.
```

Figure 5-2 The Echo command for use in batch files

the directories given in the list. This list stays in effect until another Path command is issued. In figure 5-1, the Path command tells DOS to search two directories on the C drive in this order: first DOS, then UTIL.

At the least, the Path command in the AUTOEXEC.BAT file should include the DOS directory. Then, DOS will always know where to find its external commands. In addition, the Path command should include the directory that contains the other batch files for your system. On many systems, these files are in the UTIL directory or the BAT directory.

Beyond this, you may want to include one or more of the directories that contain application programs, but that depends on the requirements of your programs. Often, you don't gain anything by putting the directory of an application program in the directory list because the current directory has to be set to the program directory anyway before you can start the program. Then, since DOS always starts its search for a command in the current directory, it never gets to the directory list.

Since DOS doesn't use the Path command when it's looking for data files, you shouldn't include data directories in your Path command. Similarly, you shouldn't include the root directory of the C drive in your Path command unless it contains command or batch files that aren't executed automatically as part of the start-up procedure.

In general, you shouldn't include diskette drives in your Path command either. If you do, DOS will search them when it can't find a command in the directories that precede the diskette directories in the search path. Then, if you don't have a diskette in the drive that's specified, DOS will display an error message indicating that the drive isn't ready. That just slows you down.

Other commands to consider for your AUTOEXEC.BAT file Beyond the Path and Prompt commands, your AUTOEXEC.BAT file should contain whatever commands are appropriate for your system. For example, if you enter the same series of commands each time you start your PC, you should put those commands in this file. And some hardware components require that special commands be put in this file.

To illustrate expanded versions of AUTOEXEC.BAT files, figure 5-3 presents three more. The first file ends with several Echo commands that display a message for the PC user who starts the system. The second file ends with two commands that start an application program (*Lotus 1-2-3*). This is useful if you regularly use just one program. Then, you don't have to start the program from the command prompt each time you use the PC. The third file ends with a Dosshell command that starts the DOS 5.0/6.0 shell. If you don't end the AUTOEXEC.BAT file with this command, DOS 5.0 or 6.0 will start with the command prompt just like earlier versions of DOS. The third file also includes a Doskey command. It activates the Doskey feature that I explained in chapter 4. If you use DOS 5.0 or 6.0, your AUTOEXEC.BAT file should probably include this command so this feature is always available to you.

Four ways to create or change an AUTOEXEC.BAT file

Now that you've seen how the AUTOEXEC.BAT file works, you can decide whether or not your own AUTOEXEC.BAT file is adequate for your system. To begin, use the Directory command to check the root directory of the C drive to find out whether your PC has an AUTOEXEC.BAT file. If it doesn't, you definitely should create one. If it does, you can use the Type or Print command to look at the contents of the file. Then, if the file doesn't contain the proper Prompt and Path commands, you should take the time to change it. (Before you make any changes, be sure to use a Print command to get a printout of the existing file so you have a backup copy in case the changes don't work.) If you decide that you are going to create or change your AUTOEXEC.BAT file, please read on. Otherwise, you can skip this section.

Because the AUTOEXEC.BAT file is just a text file, you can use several different methods to create or change it. No matter what version of DOS you're using, you can use the Copy command to create a simple text file. If you have a text editor on your PC like the one that comes with DOS 5.0 or 6.0, the easiest way to work with a text file is to use that editor. If you have a word processing program like *WordPerfect* that makes it easy to work with text files, you can use that for creating and changing the AUTOEXEC.BAT file. And if none of these three methods works for you, you can use the Edlin program that comes with all versions of DOS except

An AUTOEXEC.BAT file that displays a message

```
echo off
prompt $p$g
path=c:\dos;c:\util
cls
echo Please record your PC time at the computer center when
echo you're done. We're trying to keep track of the usage of
echo each system this month.
echo Thanks for your cooperation.
```

An AUTOEXEC.BAT file that starts *Lotus 1-2-3*

```
echo off
prompt $p$g
path=c:\dos;c:\util
cd \123
123
```

An AUTOEXEC.BAT file that starts the DOS 5.0/6.0 shell

```
echo off
prompt $p$g
path=c:\dos;c:\util
doskey
dosshell
```

Figure 5-3 Expanded versions of AUTOEXEC.BAT files

6.0. (If you upgraded to DOS 6.0 from an earlier version of DOS, Edlin will still be in your \DOS directory. But if you purchased your computer with DOS 6.0 already installed, Edlin won't be available.) These methods are now presented in the sequence I've just given, but remember that you need to know how to use only one of them.

How to use the Copy command to create or change a batch file One of the easiest ways to create a new batch file is to use a special form of the DOS Copy command, as illustrated in figure 5-4. Here, the first parameter in the Copy command is the word CON, which means that the source file will come from the keyboard, or console, of the PC. The second parameter specifies the name that you want to use for the batch file that the command will create. When you issue the Copy command using these parameters, DOS automatically moves the cursor to the next line so you're ready to type in the commands for the batch file.

The format of the Copy command to create a batch file

```
COPY CON file-spec
```

The operation of the Copy command

```
C:\>copy con c:autoexec.bat
echo off
prompt $p$g
path=c:\dos;c:\util
cls
^Z
         1 File(s) copied

C:\>
```

Figure 5-4 How to use a special form of the Copy command to create the AUTOEXEC.BAT file

After you've entered the commands that you want in the batch file, you enter an end-of-file character, which appears as ^Z. To make this entry, you hold down the Ctrl key while you press the letter Z. Or you can press the F6 key. Although this entry appears as two characters on the monitor, it's read as a single character that tells DOS that the source file contains no more commands. To complete the Copy command, you press the Enter key. Then, DOS copies the commands you entered into the file you specified.

If you want to change an existing batch file, you can still use the Copy command. You just create a new file with the same name as the file you want to change. Then, when you end the command, the original file will be replaced with the file you created. Obviously, though, this isn't efficient because you have to enter a whole file even if you want to change only one character.

How to use a full-screen text editor to create or change a batch file

A full-screen *text editor* is a program that is designed for creating and changing text files. Unlike the Copy command, a text editor lets you change existing batch files. Also, a full-screen text editor is easier to use and is more flexible than the other programs presented here. So you'll probably want to use a full-screen text editor if you have one.

Most shell utilities, like *PC Tools*, come with a text editor. And both DOS 5.0 and 6.0 provide a full-screen text editor called *Edit*. To start the DOS 5.0/6.0 text editor, you type *edit* followed by the name of the file you want to edit, as in this example:

```
C:\>edit autoexec.bat
```

This starts the Edit program and displays the file you specified, as shown in figure 5-5.

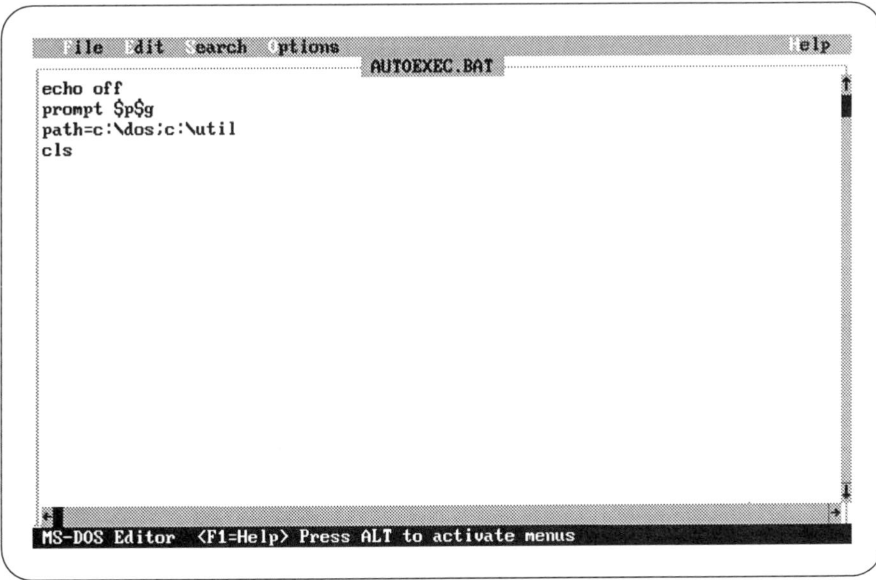

Figure 5-5 A batch file displayed by the DOS 5.0/6.0 Edit program

If you're creating a new file, you just start adding commands to the file. If you're modifying an existing file, you make the necessary modifications. When you're done with the file, you save it to the hard disk.

Like a word processing program, the Edit program lets you use the Arrow keys to move the cursor where you want it, and any text you type will be added at the cursor location. In addition, you can use the Delete or Backspace keys to delete characters. And you can use the Insert key to change from Insert to Typeover mode or vice versa.

You can also highlight the text you want to copy, move, or delete. To do that, you move the cursor to the beginning of the text. Then, you hold down the Shift key as you use the Arrow keys to highlight the text you want to edit. You can also highlight text using the mouse. To do that, you move the mouse pointer to the beginning of the text. Then, you press and hold down the left mouse button as you move the pointer to highlight the text.

The Edit program also provides menus that make it easier to select the commands that you need to edit a file. Figure 5-6, for example, shows the commands on the Edit menu. Here, the Cut command temporarily deletes the highlighted text; the Copy command copies the highlighted text; the Paste command inserts text that you deleted using the Cut command; and the Clear command permanently deletes the highlighted text.

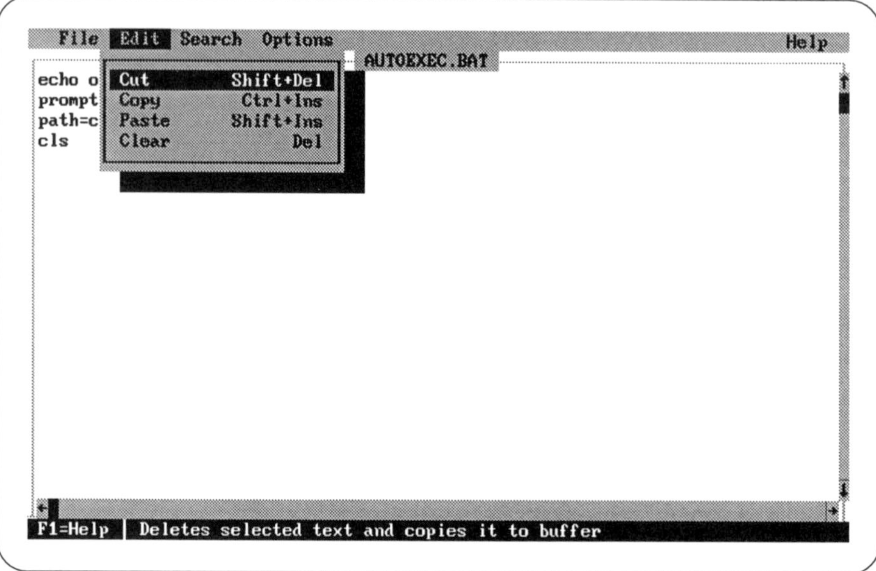

Figure 5-6 The Edit menu of the DOS 5.0/6.0 Edit program

To select one of the commands the Edit program provides, you press the Alt key to activate the menu system. Then, you can use two techniques. You can use the Left and Right arrow keys to move to the menu you want, press the Enter key to open the menu, then use the Down arrow key to move to the command you want, and press the Enter key again to start the command. Or you can press the key for the letter that's highlighted in the menu name to open the menu, and then press the key for the letter that's highlighted in the command to start the command. If you have a mouse, you can also select a menu or command by clicking on it.

After you have created or edited a file, you save it using one of the commands on the File menu shown in figure 5-7. Here, the New command clears the screen so you can create a new file. The Open command loads an existing file from disk storage so you can edit it. The Save command saves the file using the current file name. The Save-as command lets you specify the file name you want to use to save the file. The Print command prints the file. And the Exit command stops the program and returns you to the command prompt.

Although this is just a brief introduction to the Edit program, that's all you need to know for editing small files. If you work with this program for a few minutes, you'll see that it's quite easy to use. So if you have DOS 5.0 or 6.0, you'll probably want to use this program for creating and changing your AUTOEXEC.BAT file.

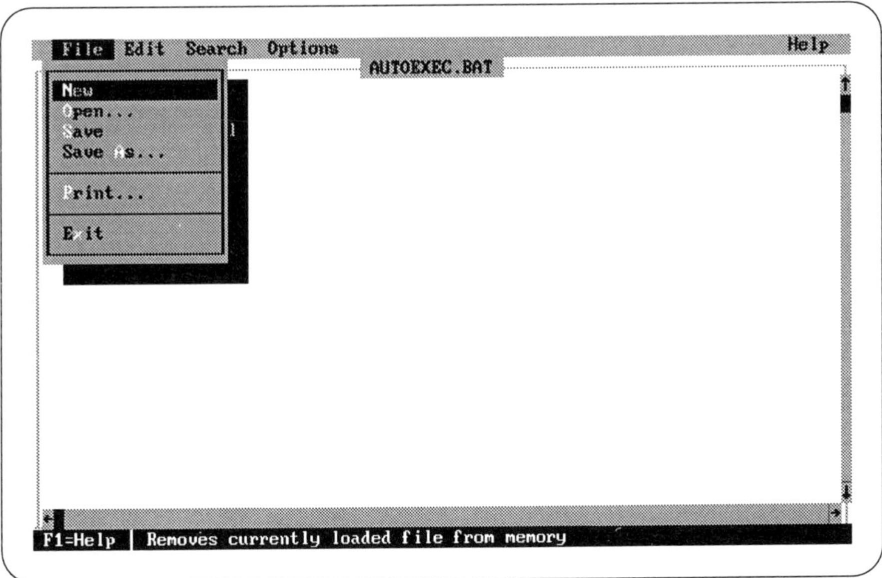

Figure 5-7 The File menu of the DOS 5.0/6.0 Edit program

How to use a word processing program to create or change a batch file If you don't want to use the Copy command and if you don't have a text editor, you can use the text feature of your word processing program to create and change batch files. In this case, you must make sure that you retrieve an existing batch file as a text file, not as a word processing file. Also, after you create a new batch file or change an existing one, you must make sure you save the file as a text file, not as a word processing file.

When you use *WordPerfect*, for example, you use the Text-in feature to retrieve a batch file. Then, you use the regular word processing commands to change the file. When you're done, you use the Text-out feature to save the file as a DOS text file. Not all word processing programs make it that easy to work with text files, though, so this isn't always practical with other programs.

How to use Edlin to create or change a batch file Edlin is a program that you can use to create or change a batch file or any other text file. But unlike a text editor, Edlin lets you edit only one line at a time. This makes Edlin awkward to use when compared to a text editor. In addition, the Edlin commands are likely to be confusing at first. So if you have another method you can use for editing batch files, you'll probably want to skip this information on Edlin.

Figure 5-8 presents some of Edlin's most useful commands. As you can see, the formats of these commands use line numbers and single letters to invoke functions.

Edlin commands

Name	Format	Function
Insert	`(line-number)I`	Inserts one or more lines before the line number indicated.
Edit	`line-number`	Edits the line indicated by the line number.
Delete	`(line-number or numbers)D`	Deletes the line or lines indicated by the line numbers.
List	`L`	Lists the current version of the file.
End	`E`	Ends the editing session and saves the file.
Quit	`Q`	Quits the editing session without saving the file.

Keystrokes for the Edit command

Key	Editing function
F1	Copies one character from the old line.
F3	Copies the remaining characters in the old line.
Delete	Skips one character in the old line, thus deleting it.
Insert	Starts or stops the insertion of the characters you type in the new line.

Keystrokes for the Insert command

Keys	Editing function
Ctrl+Pause or Ctrl+C	Ends the Insert command.

Figure 5-8 A summary of the most useful commands and keystrokes for Edlin

```
C:\DOS>edlin c:\autoexec.bat
End of input file

*L          1:*echo off
            2: prompt $p$g
            3: path=c:\dos;c:\util
            4: cls
*1
            1:*echo off
            1:*echo on
*4D
*L
            1: echo on
            2: prompt $p$g
            3: path=c:\dos;c:\util
*4I
            4:*cd \wp51
            5:*wp
            6:*^C
*L
            1: echo on
            2: prompt $p$g
            3: path=c:\dos;c:\util
            4: cd \wp51
            5: wp
*E

C:\DOS>
```

Figure 5-9 How to use Edlin to modify a batch file

This figure also shows the most useful keystrokes that you can use to edit a line or insert lines into a batch file.

In figure 5-9, you can see how Edlin is used to change an AUTOEXEC.BAT file. Here, all of the entries made by the PC user are shaded. The file specification that's entered with the Edlin command indicates the file you want to edit or create. If this file doesn't exist, Edlin assumes you're creating a new file. If the file does exist, Edlin displays the following message:

```
End of input file
```

Then, on the next line, it displays an asterisk (*) that indicates it's waiting for a command.

In figure 5-9, the first command is the letter L. (I entered the commands in uppercase letters in this example so you can distinguish between the letter L and the number 1.) This List command tells Edlin to list the current version of the file. As you can see, the file consists of four commands.

The second command in figure 5-9 is the line number 1. Because no command code is given with the line number, this tells Edlin that you want to edit line 1. In this case, the ECHO OFF command is changed to an ECHO ON command so the commands in the batch file will be displayed as they are executed. When you edit a line, you can use the F1 or F3 key to copy one or more characters from the old version of the line. You can also use the Delete and Insert keys to delete or insert characters within a line.

The third command in figure 5-9 (4d) tells Edlin to delete the fourth line in the file. Then, the fourth command (l) tells Edlin to list the current version of the file. Now, the file has only three lines because one has been deleted.

The fifth command in figure 5-9 (4i) tells Edlin that lines are going to be inserted into the file before the fourth line. Since the file has only three lines, the lines are inserted after the last line in the file. Because you can insert one or more lines with this command, you need to tell Edlin when you're through. To do this, you hold down the Ctrl key and press the letter C. Note that this is the same keystroke combination you use to cancel a command that's being executed by DOS. When this combination is used within Edlin, it appears as ^C, and it ends the Insert command.

The sixth command in figure 5-9 is the List command again; it lists the changed version of the file. Since the file is now in the form that the user wants, the next command is the End command. The keystroke for this command is the letter E. This command ends Edlin and saves the edited file. As a result, the command prompt appears on the monitor. If you want to end Edlin without saving the edited file, you enter the letter Q for the Quit command.

Although Edlin is a bit confusing when you first start to use it, you can get used to it after a short time. That's particularly true if you limit yourself to the commands and keystrokes shown in figure 5-8. Although Edlin provides several other commands and several other keystrokes and keystroke combinations, they just make Edlin that much harder to use.

When you use Edlin to edit an existing file, it automatically creates a backup file for you. If, for example, you're editing the AUTOEXEC.BAT file, Edlin saves the original version of the file under the name AUTOEXEC.BAK. Then, if the new version of the file doesn't work right, you still have the original version to work with. To reinstate the original as the AUTOEXEC.BAT file, you can use this Copy command:

```
copy c:\autoexec.bak c:\autoexec.bat
```

The use of this command is explained in chapter 7.

If you're using Edlin to create a new batch file, you get this message after you enter the command and file name at the command prompt:

```
New file
```

Then, you use the Insert command to insert the commands you want in the batch file. After you enter the last command, you turn off the Insert command using the Ctrl+C key combination. Next, you save the file and return to the prompt by pressing the letter E.

How to test an AUTOEXEC.BAT file

When you finish creating or changing an AUTOEXEC.BAT file, you should test it to make sure it works right. One way to do that is to turn the PC off and turn it back on again. Then, the PC performs its self-test and boots DOS. As part of the booting process, the commands in the AUTOEXEC.BAT file are executed.

A more efficient way to restart DOS is to use the key combination I introduced in chapter 4: Ctrl+Alt+Delete. This boots DOS, but doesn't force the PC to go through its self-test again.

Some perspective on the AUTOEXEC.BAT file

Once you have your AUTOEXEC.BAT set up properly, you shouldn't have to change it unless you change some of the hardware components of your system or add a program to your system that requires a special command. If, for example, you add a mouse to your PC, you may have to add a command to the AUTOEXEC.BAT file. Similarly, if you add a shell program to your system and you want to start it from AUTOEXEC.BAT, you may have to add a command to the file. That's not always necessary, though. Even if you add new hardware or software to your system, many installation programs make the required AUTOEXEC.BAT changes for you.

So you shouldn't have to spend much time working with your AUTOEXEC.BAT file. However, from time to time, you may want to add or change commands that will coordinate with the commands in other batch files that you write. So the next chapter will show you how to do that.

Terms

batch file
text editor

Objectives

1. In general terms, list the directories that should be included in the Path command in the AUTOEXEC.BAT file.
2. List four types of commands or programs you can use to create or change any batch file, including the AUTOEXEC.BAT file.
3. Check whether you have an AUTOEXEC.BAT file on your PC. If not, create an appropriate one using one of the commands or programs that's available to you.
4. If you already have an AUTOEXEC.BAT file on your PC, make changes to it as needed using one of the commands or programs that's available to you.

Exercises

Before you modify an existing AUTOEXEC.BAT file, it's always a good idea to have a backup copy. Then, you can reinstate the original file if the changes you make don't work right. So before you do exercises 3 or 4, make a backup copy of your existing AUTOEXEC.BAT file.

1. Enter a Path command without any parameters at the command prompt to see if a path has been established on your PC.
2. Use a Directory command to see whether the root directory of the C drive contains an AUTOEXEC.BAT file. If it does, use the Type or Print command to display or print the file.
3. Create a new AUTOEXEC.BAT file or modify the existing one so it includes a Path command with a different path than the one that was displayed when you did exercise 1. If you don't understand what some of the commands in an existing file do, don't delete or modify them because they may have an important effect on your system. To test your AUTOEXEC.BAT file, press the Ctrl+Alt+Delete key combination to restart the PC. Then, enter a Path command without any parameters to make sure the new path has been established properly.
4. Create a new AUTOEXEC.BAT file or modify the existing one so it works the way you want it to. At the least, this file should include both a Prompt and a Path command. If you don't understand what some of the commands in an existing file do, don't delete or modify them because they may have an important effect on your system. To test your AUTOEXEC.BAT file, press the Ctrl+Alt+Delete key combination to restart the PC. Then, use the system to make sure the AUTOEXEC.BAT file has set it up correctly.

Chapter 6

How to use batch files to start your programs

As you learned in chapter 5, a batch file is a file that contains one or more DOS commands and has a file name with BAT as the extension. When you use a batch file, DOS gets its commands from the file instead of from the command prompt. As a result, the commands in the batch file are executed in the order in which they appear in the file. To execute a batch file other than the AUTOEXEC.BAT file, you just enter the name of the batch file at the command prompt without its BAT extension.

In this chapter, you'll learn to create simple batch files that make it easier to start your programs. First, you'll learn three techniques for starting an application program from a batch file. Next, you'll learn how to create batch files that accept parameters. Finally, you'll learn four guidelines that will help you manage your batch files. Throughout this chapter, I assume that you already know how to create and change a batch file using the methods that I presented in chapter 5.

Three ways to start an application program from a batch file

Whether you're issuing commands at the command prompt or from a batch file, there are three methods you can use to start an application program, as shown in figure 6-1. I presented the first two methods in chapter 4, so I'll just review them briefly here. As you will see, two of these methods can't be used for certain programs. But you should understand all three methods so you can select the one that's best for each of your programs.

Method 1: Set the default drive and current directory to the program directory before issuing the command name In the first example in figure 6-1, the first two commands set the default drive and the current directory to those that contain the program. Then, the third command starts the program. This method will work no matter what version of DOS you're using or what application program you're trying to start.

Method 2: Enter the program's path along with the command name (DOS 3.0 or later) If you're using a version of DOS that's 3.0 or later, you can

Method 1: Set the default drive and current directory to the program directory

```
c:
cd \wp51
wp
```

Method 2: Enter the program's path along with the program name (DOS 3.0 or later)

```
c:\wp51\wp
```

Method 3: Include the program's directory in the Path command in the AUTOEXEC.BAT file and enter just the program name in the batch file

```
wp
```

Figure 6-1 Three ways to start an application program from a batch file

code a program's path along with its program name. This is illustrated by the second example in figure 6-1. This command tells DOS to look on the C drive in the WP51 directory for a program named WP.

As I said in chapter 4, though, this method won't work with many application programs. For instance, most releases of *Lotus 1-2-3* require that the current directory be set to the program directory before the program is run. As a result, you have to use the first method in figure 6-1 for starting programs like these.

Method 3: Include the program's directory in the Path command in the AUTOEXEC.BAT file and enter just the program name With some programs, you can add the program directory to the Path command in your AUTOEXEC.BAT file. Then, DOS searches through the directories in the Path command list until it finds the program to be executed. To start the program, you enter just its command name. This is illustrated by the third example in figure 6-1.

In general, I recommend you use methods 1 and 2 rather than this method. That's because each directory you include in the Path command can cause DOS to spend more time searching directories whenever you run an external command or application program. Also, this method won't work for programs that require the current directory to be set to the program directory.

How to use parameters with a batch file

As you already know, many DOS commands accept parameters. The Directory command, for instance, accepts parameters that specify which drive and directory you want to display. And the Type command accepts a parameter that specifies the file you want to display.

A batch file named WP.BAT that provides for one parameter

```
c:
cd \wp51
wp %1
```

A command that starts the batch file and specifies which file to retrieve

```
C:\>wp mma\slsrpt
```

Figure 6-2 How to use a replaceable parameter in a batch file

Similarly, many application programs accept one or more parameters. When you start *WordPerfect*, for example, you can use a parameter to specify the name of the file that you want the program to retrieve, as in this example:

```
C:\WP51>wp \wp51\mma\c1figs
```

Here, the file name specification includes the directory and subdirectory the file is in. Then, after DOS loads the program, *WordPerfect* retrieves the file you specified. Many application programs provide for a retrieval parameter like this, and some programs provide for other parameters as well.

You can also use parameters like this in batch files. To do that, you code a *replaceable parameter* in the appropriate command in the batch file. This parameter consists of the character %, followed by a number (1 for the first replaceable parameter, 2 for the second one, and so on). Then, you enter the value for the replaceable parameter in the command that you use to execute the batch file.

For example, suppose you want to create a batch file named WP.BAT that starts *WordPerfect* and provides for a file name parameter. Figure 6-2 shows how you can do this. Notice the third line of the batch file:

```
wp %1
```

Here, the %1 is the replaceable parameter. When DOS executes this line of the batch file, it replaces the %1 with the value of the first parameter you entered when you started the batch file. So if you start the batch file using the command shown in the figure, DOS substitutes MMA\SLSRPT for %1 when it executes the third line. As a result, *WordPerfect* will retrieve the SLSRPT file in the MMA subdirectory as its initial document.

As I said before, you can use more than one replaceable parameter in a batch file. You just use %2 for the second parameter, %3 for the third parameter, and so on. Then, you enter the actual values as additional parameters on the command that starts the batch file. Although DOS lets you use as many parameters as you want, you'll rarely need more than one or two.

The 123.BAT file

```
c:
cd \123
123
cd \
cls
```

The command that starts the 123.BAT file

```
C:\>123
```

The WP.BAT file for use with DOS 3.0 or later

```
c:
cd \wp51\mma
\wp51\wp %1
cd \
cls
```

The command that starts the WP.BAT file

```
C:\>wp file-specification
```

Figure 6-3 Typical batch files for starting a spreadsheet and a word processing program

Two examples of batch files that start application programs

With this as background, you should understand the examples of batch files in figure 6-3. They start a spreadsheet and a word processing program.

A batch file for starting *Lotus 1-2-3* The first batch file in figure 6-3 starts *Lotus 1-2-3*. Because most releases of this program require that the current directory be set to the program directory, this batch file uses the first method in figure 6-1. It doesn't provide for any replaceable parameters because *Lotus 1-2-3* won't accept a parameter that lets you specify the spreadsheet file that you want to retrieve first.

Notice that this file contains two commands after the command that starts *Lotus 1-2-3*. These two commands aren't executed until the PC user exits from *Lotus*. Then, the first command changes the current directory to the root directory, and the second one clears the monitor screen. At that point, the batch file is finished executing, so DOS displays the command prompt and waits for the next command.

Also notice that the batch file name and the name for the command file that starts the program are the same. If this seems too confusing to you, you can give the batch file a different name, like 123GO.BAT. Then, to start the batch file, you would enter 123GO at the command prompt.

```
Enter:

     WP  - to run WordPerfect
     123 - to run Lotus 1-2-3
     QA  - to run Q&A

C:\>
```

Figure 6-4 A simple menu for three batch files that start application programs

A batch file for starting *WordPerfect* The second batch file in figure 6-3 starts *WordPerfect* 5.1. Its file name is WP.BAT, so once again, the command you use to start the batch file is the same as the command you use to start the program itself.

The second command in this batch file sets the current directory to the data directory before starting the program. This saves time, because you don't have to use *WordPerfect* to change the current directory to your data directory once the program is started. Also, because this batch file provides for one replaceable parameter, you can specify the first file that you want to work on when you execute the batch file.

For example, if the first file you want to work on is named MONTHEND, you start the program by issuing this command at the prompt:

```
C:\>wp monthend
```

Because this batch file sets the current directory to the data directory before it starts the word processing program, this command causes *WordPerfect* to retrieve the file named MONTHEND from the MMA directory within the WP51 directory.

Unfortunately, you can't use this batch file with a version of DOS that precedes 3.0. That's because the third command specifies the path for the word processing program, and earlier versions of DOS don't let you do that.

How to use batch files to create program menus

For most people, batch files like those in figure 6-3 are adequate. Once you set a batch file up, it saves you a dozen or more keystrokes each time you use it. More important, you don't have to remember the specific directory names and program names for each program you use. You have to remember only the names of the batch files.

If appropriate, though, you can take batch files one step further so they create a simple menu system. If, for example, a PC is used infrequently by several different users, a menu like the one in figure 6-4 will help the users remember what programs are available and how to start them.

Figure 6-5 shows how you can use a series of batch files to create a menu system like the one in figure 6-4. Here, the menu is kept in a text file named MENU.TXT and is displayed by a batch file named MENU.BAT. To display this menu, each batch file including the AUTOEXEC.BAT file ends by starting the MENU.BAT file. As a result, whenever you start the PC or exit from an application program, the menu file is displayed on the screen. Then, when you enter one of the choices from the menu, DOS executes the corresponding batch file to start the program.

In general, I recommend that you avoid using batch files to set up a menu system because you can easily spend more time maintaining it than it's worth. Each time you add a program to the PC, you have to change the menu text file and create a new batch file. Each time you delete a program, you have to change the menu text file and delete a batch file. If you reorganize your directories, you may have to change several of the batch files. And if you don't make these changes, the menu stytem gets out of date so it loses its value.

That's why I recommend you think twice before you take the time to set up a menu system with batch files. If you still think a menu system will improve operations, you should consider getting a utility program for creating menus or using the DOS 5.0/6.0 shell. But if you must create a menu system with batch files, DOS 6.0 includes a new command, Choice, that will help you do that. I'll cover the Choice command in chapter 27.

Four guidelines for using batch files

If you use batch files correctly, they don't take much time to set up or maintain. And they improve your efficiency. To use your batch files to best advantage, though, you should follow the guidelines in figure 6-6.

Keep your batch files simple Besides the commands you've learned so far in this book, DOS provides many others that are specifically designed for use in batch files. These commands make it possible for you to create batch files that do elaborate functions. But even without these commands, it's tempting to try to do too much with a batch file.

So the first guideline is to keep your batch files simple. Most of the time that means your batch files should have just four or five commands, like the batch files in figure 6-3. If your batch files are more complicated than those, you're likely to find that you're spending more time using DOS and less time using your application programs to do productive work.

Store your batch files in a utility or batch file directory To keep your batch files under control, you should store them all in the same directory. Then, you can use one Directory command to list all of them when you need to review what you have on your system. On my system, I keep all of the batch files in a directory named UTIL that includes some utility programs. However, you can also keep your batch files in their own directory. A good name for this directory is BAT.

The AUTOEXEC.BAT file

```
echo off
prompt $p$g
path=c:\dos;c:\util
menu.bat
```

The MENU.BAT file

```
cls
type c:\util\menu.txt
```

The text file named MENU.TXT in the UTIL directory

```
Enter:

     WP  - to run WordPerfect
     123 - to run Lotus 1-2-3
     QA  - to run Q&A
```

The WP.BAT file in the UTIL directory

```
echo off
cd \wp51\mma
\wp51\wp %1
cd \
menu.bat
```

The 123.BAT file in the UTIL directory

```
echo off
cd \123
123
cd \
menu.bat
```

The QA.BAT file in the UTIL directory

```
echo off
cd \qa
qa %1
cd \
menu.bat
```

Figure 6-5 A text file and four batch files that create a menu system

1. Keep your batch files simple.
2. Store your batch files in a utility or batch file directory.
3. Make sure the directory that contains your batch files is in the path that's established by the AUTOEXEC.BAT file.
4. Make sure you understand how DOS searches for commands so your batch files work correctly.

Figure 6-6 Four guidelines for using batch files

Make sure the directory that contains your batch files is in the path that's established by the AUTOEXEC.BAT file To execute the commands in a batch file, DOS needs to be able to find the file. As a result, you should put the directory that contains your batch files in the list established by the Path command in the AUTOEXEC.BAT file. If, for example, your batch files are stored in the UTIL directory, your AUTOEXEC.BAT file should include a Path command like this:

```
path=c:\dos;c:\util
```

This will get your PC started right.

Make sure you understand how DOS searches for commands so your batch files work correctly When DOS receives a command, it always starts looking for it in the current directory. If it doesn't find the command there, it searches through the directories in the current directory list, one directory at a time. In each directory, DOS looks first for a COM file, then for an EXE file, and last for a BAT file.

If you use the same name for a batch file that is used for a COM or EXE file, this search order can cause a problem as illustrated by the batch file in figure 6-7. Here, the WP.BAT file is in the UTIL directory. Then, when the WP command is entered at the command prompt, DOS starts the batch file because it finds the WP.BAT file in the UTIL directory before it finds a WP.COM or WP.EXE file in another directory. After the second command in this batch file changes the current directory to WP51\MMA, the third command issues the WP command to start *WordPerfect*. That's when the problem starts.

First, DOS looks for a WP file in the current directory, C:\WP51\MMA. When it doesn't find one in this data directory, it starts searching the directories listed in the Path command. If you look at the Path command in the AUTOEXEC.BAT file, you can see that the UTIL directory is before the WP51 directory in the search list. That means that DOS finds the WP.BAT file before it finds the WP.EXE file. As a result, the WP command in this batch file starts the batch file again, not *WordPerfect*. This starts a loop that will continue until you restart the system.

The AUTOEXEC.BAT file

```
echo off
prompt $p$g
path=c:\dos;c:\util;c:\wp51
cls
```

The WP.BAT file in the UTIL directory

```
echo on
cd \wp51\mma
wp %1
cd \
cls
```

The command that starts the batch file

```
C:\>wp
```

Figure 6-7 A batch file that won't work correctly

If you're using DOS 3.0 or later, the best way to solve this problem is to include the program's path along with its name in the batch file. For example, the third line of the WP.BAT file in figure 6-7 should be:

```
\wp51\wp %1
```

That's the way it is in the WP.BAT file in figure 6-3. Then, DOS looks for the program in the correct directory, and you get the result you want.

Another solution is to use a name for the batch file that is different from the name for the program's command file. If, for example, you name the batch file WPGO.BAT, the file will work the way you want it to.

A third solution is to change the current directory to the one that contains the program instead of the one that contains the data before you issue the program command. This, of course, is the solution you'll have to use if you have an early version of DOS.

Incidentally, it might seem logical to try and solve this problem by changing the Path command in the AUTOEXEC.BAT file as follows:

```
PATH=C:\DOS;C:\WP51;C:\UTIL
```

Then, the batch file would be able to find the WP.EXE file in the WP51 directory. The problem here is that if you entered WP at the command prompt to start your batch file, DOS would find the WP.EXE file in the WP51 directory instead of the WP.BAT file in the UTIL directory. So you would be starting *WordPerfect* instead of executing the batch file.

Some perspective on batch files

Once you know how to create and maintain a batch file, you should be able to set one up in just a few minutes. Although each batch file saves you just a few keystrokes each time you use it, this set-up time pays off because it simplifies your operational procedures. As a result, you don't have to remember as many DOS details to use your application programs.

Once you've set up a batch file for starting an application program, you can execute the batch file in several ways. If, for example, you want to start the same application program each time you turn on your PC, you can include the command for the batch file that starts the application in the AUTOEXEC.BAT file. In other words, a batch file can execute other batch files. You can also execute a batch file from the DOS shell or from another shell utility. And you can execute a batch file from the command prompt.

Although this chapter shows you how to use batch files just for starting application programs, you can also use them for simplifying DOS commands. In chapter 9, for example, you'll learn how to use a batch file to simplify the use of the Backup command. By using the batch file instead of entering the command, you don't have to remember the details of using the command.

With this in mind, you should consider using a batch file to simplify your operational procedures whenever you're bothered by the continual need to remember DOS details. Once you've got your batch files set up, you'll spend more time using your application programs and less time using DOS.

Term

replaceable parameter

Objectives

1. Given the drive, directory, and command name for a program, list the commands for a batch file that will start the program. If the program provides for a replaceable parameter, the batch file should provide for one too. If the program lets you set the data directory to the one you want to use before you start the program, the batch file should provide for that too.
2. Create a simple menu system using batch files that lets you execute the application programs you use frequently.
3. Describe the search sequence that DOS uses when it looks for an EXE, COM or BAT file.

Exercises

1. Start one of your application programs from the command prompt by using the second technique in figure 6-1. But remember, if the program requires that the current directory be set to the program's directory, this technique won't work properly.

2. Use Directory commands to see which of the directories (if any) contain batch files. You can do that by using this wildcard specification: *.BAT . If only one of the directories is used for batch files, make sure that this directory is listed in the Path command in the AUTOEXEC.BAT file.

3. Create a batch file for starting one of your application programs. If the program allows one or more parameters, set up the batch file so it accommodates them. Store the batch file in a directory that's appropriate for batch files. If none is, you can temporarily store it in the root directory of the C drive. Then, in the next chapter, you'll learn how to create and organize your directories. To test your batch file, enter its name at the command prompt. If its directory isn't listed in the current path, you must change the current directory to the one that contains the batch file before you enter the name of the batch file.

Section 3

Essential DOS skills

The five chapters in this section present a variety of DOS skills that every PC user should have. Since these chapters are independent of each other, you can read them in whatever order you wish.

In chapter 7, you'll learn how to manage the directories and files on your hard disk. In chapter 8, you'll learn how to work with diskettes. In chapter 9, you'll learn how to back up the files on your hard disk to diskettes using the DOS Backup command. In chapter 10, you'll learn how to prevent, detect, and recover from disk problems. And in chapter 11, you'll learn how to make your PC run faster without buying new hardware. These are essential skills for all PC users no matter what application programs they use. Although you can perform some of the functions presented in these chapters by using a shell utility or an application program like *WordPerfect*, you can do them more efficiently if you understand how to do them from the command prompt in DOS.

Chapter 7

How to manage the directories and files on a hard disk

When you use a hard disk, its directories and files can quickly get out of control. If you use three or four different application programs for a year or two, it's not unusual to have more than one thousand files spread over a couple dozen directories. By that time, you're likely to have dozens of files that you no longer need and at least a few files that you need but can't find. That's why it's important that you learn how to do an effective job of managing your directories and files.

In this chapter, you'll learn how to use seven DOS commands to manage your directories and five commands to manage your files. Next, you'll learn how to use the two DOS wildcards within the commands for managing files. Then, you'll learn how to use the directory commands and file commands together for some common maintenance tasks. Last, you'll learn 12 guidelines that will help you manage your directories and files more effectively.

If you have a shell program on your PC that makes it easy to manage directories and files, you should use it for most of those tasks. But you should also know how to manage directories and files from the command prompt for at least two reasons. First, you can perform some file management jobs more efficiently from the command prompt. Second, you'll be able to use your shell program more effectively if you understand how the shell functions are done with DOS commands. All a shell program does is convert the functions that you request into DOS commands so you don't have to be concerned about the details of the commands.

Seven commands for working with directories

Figure 7-1 summarizes seven commands you can use for working with directories. As you can see, their formats are simple. So you shouldn't have any trouble learning to use these commands. And since you're already familiar with the first two commands, I'll just expand on their use here.

Name	Format	Function
Directory	`DIR [file-spec] [/P] [/W] [/S][/O[:order]] [/A[:attrib]]`	Displays a directory listing for the specified files. The switches control the display as summarized in figure 7-2.
Change directory	`CD [directory-spec]`	Changes the current directory. If the directory parameter is omitted, this command displays the path of the current directory.
Make directory	`MD directory-spec`	Creates a new directory.
Remove directory	`RD directory-spec`	Removes a directory. The directory must be empty before it can be removed. Also, you can't remove a directory when it's the current directory.
Tree	`TREE [drive-spec] [/F]`	Displays the directory structure for a drive. The /F switch also causes a display of the files within each directory.
Move	`MOVE dir-spec-1 dir-spec-2`	New in DOS 6.0. Renames a directory. The drive and path in the second directory specification must be the same as in the first directory specification.
Delete tree	`DELTREE dir-spec`	New in DOS 6.0. Deletes a directory and all its subdirectories and files. Use this command with caution.

Figure 7-1 Seven commands for working with directories

The Directory command As you already know, the Directory command displays the contents of a directory. This command has a variety of switches you can use to control the format of its display and the types of files it includes. Figure 7-2 summarizes the function of five of these switches. I showed you how to use the /P and /W switches in chapter 4. Now, I'll show you how to use the /S, /O, and /A switches. These switches were introduced with DOS 5.0, so you can't use them if you're using an earlier version of DOS.

When you use the /S switch, DOS not only displays the contents of the directory you've specified, but it also displays the contents of any subdirectories that are subordinate to that directory. You'll probably use this switch most often for finding a file when you can't remember what subdirectory it's in. In that case, you enter the file name as part of the file specification in the command, and DOS looks for the file name in the specified directory and all its subdirectories. Then, DOS displays a listing for each of the files it finds with that name.

The format of the Directory command for DOS 5.0 and 6.0

```
DIR [file-spec] [/P] [/W] [/S] [/O[:order]] [/A[:attrib]]
```

Switch meanings

`/P`	Pauses the listing after it fills the screen.
`/W`	Displays the listing in a wide display format.
`/S`	DOS 5.0 and 6.0 switch that searches for files in subordinate subdirectories.
`/O[:order]`	DOS 5.0 and 6.0 switch that displays the files in the specified order. For *order*, you can specify:

N	Alphabetical order by file name
-N	Reverse alphabetical order by file name
E	Alphabetical order by extension
-E	Reverse alphabetical order by extension
D	Date order, oldest files first
-D	Date order, newest files first
S	Size order, smallest files first
-S	Size order, largest files first
G	List directories before files
-G	List directories after files

If you specify /O but omit *order*, directories are displayed first in alphabetic order followed by files in alphabetic order. The colon that precedes *order* is optional.

`/A[:attrib]` DOS 5.0 and 6.0 switch that lists files only if they have the specified attribute. For *attrib*, you can specify:

A	List files whose archive bit is set
-A	Do not list files whose archive bit is set
D	List directories
-D	Do not list directories
H	List hidden files
-H	Do not list hidden files
R	List read-only files
-R	Do not list read-only files
S	List system files
-S	Do not list system files

If you specify /A but omit *attrib*, all files are displayed. The colon that precedes *attrib* is optional.

Figure 7-2 The Directory command for DOS 5.0 and 6.0

In figure 7-3, for example, I used the /S switch to find out the path for a file named ADV92. DOS looked through all of the directories on the C drive starting with the current directory (the root directory) and found two files with that name. The complete paths and file names for each one are:

```
123\FILES\ADV92.WK1
WP51\MKTG\ADV92
```

The /O switch was introduced with DOS 5.0 to let you control the order of the Directory command results. If you omit this switch, the command lists the contents of the directory in whatever order the entries appear in the directory. In most cases, the result is a mix of files and subdirectories in no apparent order. The examples in figure 7-4 show how you can use this switch to display the contents of a directory in a more meaningful order. Example 1 lists the subdirectories first in alphabetical order, followed by the files in alphabetical order. Example 2 lists the files first in decreasing size order, followed by the subdirectories in decreasing size order.

Example 3 in figure 7-4 shows you how to use the /A switch. This switch lets you choose the files that are displayed depending on their *attributes*. Because I specified the D attribute in the example, this command will list only directories. I also included the /O switch so the directories are listed in alphabetical order. If you enter the Directory command without the /A switch, it displays all files except hidden and system files. If you enter the /A switch without specifying any attributes, all files are listed. You'll learn more about file attributes in chapters 14 and 26. Then, the different attributes you can use with this switch will make more sense to you.

The Change-directory command As you already know, you use this command to change the current directory. But there's another form of this command that is often useful:

```
cd ..
```

The two dots in the directory specification represent the parent directory. The parent directory is always the directory in the path that immediately precedes the current directory. So with this specification, you can change the current directory to the parent directory.

The Make-directory command You use the Make-directory command to make a new directory. As you can see in figure 7-1, you enter a directory specification in this command to indicate the directory you want to create. This specification gives the name of the new directory, and it also locates the new directory within the directory structure of the drive. You'll learn how to use this command for directory maintenance tasks later in this chapter.

When you name a directory, you use the same naming rules that you use for files. Thus, a directory name can be up to eight characters long with an extension of up to three characters. In practice, though, it makes sense to create short, meaningful directory names with no extensions.

```
C:\>dir adv92 /s

 Volume in drive C is DRIVE_C
 Volume Serial Number is 1911-0C02

Directory of C:\123\FILES

ADV92    WK1     11818 12-16-92   1:25p
        1 file(s)      11818 bytes

Directory of C:\WP51\MKTG

ADV92             2819 10-22-92   3:19p
        1 file(s)       2819 bytes

Total files listed:
        2 file(s)      14637 bytes
                   134680576 bytes free

C:\>
```

Figure 7-3 The use of the /S switch in the Directory command for DOS 5.0 and 6.0

Example 1: A Directory command that lists subdirectories in alphabetical order, followed by files in alphabetical order.

```
C:\>dir /o
```

Example 2: A Directory command that lists files in decreasing size order, followed by subdirectories in decreasing size order.

```
C:\>dir /o:-s /o:-g
```

Example 3: A Directory command that lists only subdirectories (no files) in alphabetical order.

```
C:\>dir /a:d /o:n
```

Figure 7-4 The use of the /O and /A switches in the Directory command for DOS 5.0 and 6.0

The Remove-directory command You use this command to remove a directory. However, you can't remove a directory with this command if it contains any subdirectories or files. (If you have DOS 6.0, you can use the Delete-tree command to do this. I'll cover that command in a moment.) And you can't remove a directory if it's the current directory. You'll learn how to use this command for directory maintenance tasks later in this chapter.

The Tree command If you have more than a few directories on your PC, it's hard to visualize the directory structure. The Tree command is designed to help you review that structure. It displays the directories on a disk drive. If you use the /F switch, it also displays the files in each directory.

To illustrate, figure 7-5 shows the output that's displayed by the Tree command for versions of DOS before 4.0. As you can see, this command displays a list of the directories and the subdirectories that they contain. Unfortunately, it's difficult to work with this information in this form, so this command isn't used much.

In contrast, figure 7-6 shows how the output of the Tree command is displayed for DOS 4.0 and later versions. With these versions, this command displays a graphic tree that gives you a quick view of the directory structure. In general, the more directories you have on your drives, the more valuable the graphic tree structure becomes and the less valuable the old-style tree listing becomes.

The Move command (DOS 6.0) The Move command introduced in DOS 6.0 is designed to move files from one directory to another, as you'll see later in this chapter. However, it also lets you change the name of a directory, as in this example:

```
C:\>move \wp51\mma \wp51\rpts
```

Here, the subdirectory named MMA is renamed RPTS. Note that the directory you're renaming can't be the current directory.

As you'll see later in this chapter, you have to enter a whole series of commands to rename a directory without the Move command. So although you won't have to rename directories very often, you'll want to use this command whenever you do.

The Delete-tree command (DOS 6.0) As I mentioned a moment ago, you can't use the Remove-directory command to delete a directory that contains any subdirectories or files. But in DOS 6.0, the Delete-tree command has been introduced for that purpose. For example, if you enter the command

```
C:\>deltree c:\wp51\mma
```

DOS displays a message like this:

```
Delete directory "c:\wp51\mma" and all its subdirectories? [yn]
```

Then, if you enter Y, DOS deletes the directory and all of its subordinates.

```
C:\>tree

DIRECTORY PATH LISTING

Path: \DOS

Sub directories:  None


Path: \UTIL

Sub directories:  None


Path: \WP51

Sub directories:  MMA
                  PROJ1


Path:  \123

Sub directories:  MMA
                  DOUG


Path:  \QA4

Sub directories:  MMA
```

Figure 7-5 The output displayed by the Tree command in DOS versions before 4.0

As you might imagine, you can do a lot of damage with this command, destroying months of work with just a few keystrokes. So don't use it unless you're sure you want to delete the entire directory, no matter what files and subdirectories it contains.

Five commands for working with files

Figure 7-7 summarizes five commands you can use for working with files. You can use all of these commands to operate on a single file or on multiple files. However, to operate on multiple files with the Copy, Delete, and Rename commands, you have to use wildcards. I'll show you how to use wildcards with these commands later. For now, just concentrate on learning how to use these commands on single files.

```
C:\>tree
Directory PATH listing
C:.
  ├──DOS
  ├──UTIL
  ├──WP51
  │   ├──MMA
  │   └──PROJ1
  ├──123
  │   ├──MMA
  │   └──DOUG
  └──QA4
      └──MMA
```

Figure 7-6 The output displayed by the Tree command for DOS 4.0 and later versions

The Copy command You use the Copy command to copy files. You can use this command to copy files within a single directory, from one directory to another, from the hard disk to a diskette, or from a diskette to a hard disk. As a result, you're likely to use the Copy command frequently.

If you look at the format of the Copy command shown in figure 7-7, you can see that it has two parameters. The first parameter is the file specification for the *source file*: the file that's going to be copied. The second parameter is the file specification for the *target file*: the file that's going to be created by the Copy command.

Figure 7-8 shows five examples of Copy commands along with explanations of what happens when they are executed. In all of these examples, the command prompt tells you what the default drive and current directory are. If you specify the drive, directory, and file name for both the source and target files, it doesn't matter what the default drive and the current directory are. But if you omit the drive specification for a file, the default drive is assumed. And if you omit the directory specification, the current directory is assumed.

If you omit the file name for the target file, DOS uses the file name of the source file for the target file. Since that's frequently what you want, you'll often omit the target file name, whether or not you give a drive and directory specification. For instance, example 2 gives a drive and directory specification but no file name, and example 4 gives a drive specification but no file name.

When you use the Copy command, you must realize that it will replace an existing file if the file specification for the target file is the same as one for an existing file. Worse, DOS will replace the existing file without warning you that it's going to be replaced. If, for example, you copy a file named C1.DOC to a diskette that already has a file named C1.DOC on it, DOS will replace the existing file with the new file. Although that might be what you want, you must use the Copy command with care so you don't replace files accidentally.

Name	Format	Function
Copy	`COPY source-spec [target-spec]`	Copies the file identified by the source specification to the path and file name given by the target specification. If the target specification is omitted, this command copies the source file to the current directory on the current drive using the source file name for the target file.
Xcopy	`XCOPY source-spec [target-spec] [/S] [/E] [/P]`	Copies the files identified by the source specification to the files identified by the target specification. The switch meanings are summarized in figure 7-9. This command is available in DOS 3.2 and later versions.
Delete	`DEL file-spec [/P]`	Deletes the file identified by the file specification. The /P switch provided by DOS 4.0 and later versions of DOS asks you for confirmation before the file is deleted.
Rename	`REN source-spec target-spec`	Renames the file identified by the source specification with the name given in the target specification. You cannot specify a drive and directory in the target specification; you can only rename the file within the same directory.
Move	`MOVE source-spec-1 [source-spec-2] target-spec`	New in DOS 6.0. Moves the file or files identified by the source specifications to the target specification. If more than one file is specified, the target specification must be a directory name. If only one file is specified, you can also rename it by including a file name in the target specification.

Figure 7-7 Five commands for working with files

The Xcopy command The Xcopy command is similar to the Copy command, but it lets you copy all the files in a directory and its subdirectories at once. To do that, you enter the command with the /S switch, as shown in figure 7-9, and enter a directory name instead of a file name as the source specification. In example 1, DOS

The format of the Copy command

```
COPY source-spec [target-spec]
```

Example 1: A Copy command that copies the file named ADMGOALS.TXT in the current directory to a new file named ADMGOALS.BAK in the same directory.

```
C:\WP51\MMA>copy admgoals.txt admgoals.bak
```

Example 2: A Copy command that copies the file named ADMGOALS.TXT in the current directory to a file with the same name in the WP51\MMA93 directory on the D drive.

```
C:\WP51\MMA>copy admgoals.txt d:\wp51\mma93
```

Example 3: A Copy command that copies the file named ADMGOALS.TXT in the WP51\MMA directory on the C drive to a new file with the same name in the current directory on the default drive.

```
D:\DATA\MMA93>copy c:\wp51\mma\admgoals.txt
```

Example 4: A Copy command that copies the file named ADMGOALS.TXT in the current directory to a file with the same name on a diskette in the A drive.

```
C:\WP51\MMA>copy admgoals.txt a:
```

Example 5: An invalid Copy command that tries to copy a file within the current directory but doesn't give a name for the new file.

```
C:\WP51\MMA>copy admgoals.txt
```

Figure 7-8 The Copy command

will copy all the files in the MMA directory and its subordinates to the root directory of the D drive, using the same file and subdirectory names as they have on the C drive.

In example 2, I included a directory name in the target specification. Here, DOS will create a directory named MMA on the D drive, then copy all the files in the MMA directory and its subordinates from the C drive to the MMA directory on the D drive. Notice that I followed the directory name in the target specification with a backslash. If you omit the backslash, DOS won't know if the specification is a file name or a directory name and will prompt you to indicate which it is. So it's best to avoid this confusion by including the backslash.

Example 3 shows how you can use the Xcopy command to copy the entire contents of one diskette to another. Here, I used the /E switch so that even empty subdirectories are reproduced on the target drive. In chapter 8, you'll learn how to use the Diskcopy command to perform a similar function. Unless the diskette is nearly full, however, it's faster to copy it using the Xcopy command as shown.

The format of the Xcopy command

```
XCOPY source-spec [target-spec] [/S] [/E] [/P]
```

Switch meanings

`/S`	Copies files from subordinate subdirectories.
`/E`	Recreates the entire subdirectory structure in the target directory, including empty subdirectories. Use only with the /S switch.
`/P`	Prompts the user before copying each file.

Example 1: An Xcopy command that copies all files from the MMA directory and its subdirectories on the C drive to the root directory on the D drive.

```
C:\>xcopy mma d: /s
```

Example 2: An Xcopy command that creates an MMA directory on the D drive, then copies all files from the MMA directory and its subdirectories on the C drive to the MMA directory on the D drive.

```
C:\>xcopy mma d:\mma\ /s
```

Example 3: An Xcopy command that copies all files and subdirectories (including empty subdirectories) from the diskette in the A drive to the diskette in the B drive.

```
C:\>xcopy a: b: /s /e
```

Figure 7-9 The Xcopy command

You can also use the /P switch on the Xcopy command. When you use this switch, Xcopy displays the name of each file before copying it and asks you if you want to copy it. It's useful when the target directory contains files you don't want to overwrite with files from the source directory.

Although you can copy multiple files with a single Copy command as I'll show you later in this chapter, you can't copy an entire directory structure with Copy as you can with Xcopy. What's more, Xcopy works by reading in as much data as it can, then writing files to the target. In contrast, Copy works on one file at a time. In some cases, this makes Xcopy faster, especially when you're reading or writing files from diskette. So you'll probably use Xcopy often when you're copying files.

The Delete command You use the Delete command to remove a file from a directory. In this command, the file specification identifies the file that you want to delete. If you use the /P switch, the Delete command asks you for confirmation before it deletes the file. This usually isn't necessary when you're deleting a single file, but it's a good precaution when you're deleting multiple files. You'll see an example of

The format of the Delete command

```
DEL file-spec [/P]
```

Example 1: A Delete command that deletes the file named ADMGOALS.TXT from the current directory.

```
C:\WP51\MMA>del admgoals.txt
```

Example 2: A Delete command that deletes the file named ADMGOALS.WK1 from the WK1 directory on the D drive.

```
C:\WP51\MMA>del d:\wk1\admgoals.wk1
```

Example 3: A Delete command that asks you for confirmation before deleting the file named ADMGOALS.WK1 from the WK1 directory on the D drive.

```
C:\WP51\MMA>del d:\wk1\admgoals.wk1 /p

D:\WK1\ADMGOALS.WK1,  Delete (Y/N)?
```

Figure 7-10 The Delete command

that later in this chapter. (The /P switch was introduced in DOS 4.0, so it's not available to you if you have an earlier version of DOS.)

Figure 7-10 shows three examples of the Delete command. In example 1, the command deletes a file named ADMGOALS.TXT from the current directory. In example 2, the command gives a complete file specification to delete a file named ADMGOALS.WK1 from the WK1 directory on the D drive. In example 3, the /P switch causes DOS to ask you for confirmation before it deletes the file.

The Rename command You use the Rename command to change the name of a file. In this command, the source specification identifies the file you want to rename, and the target specification gives the new name for the file. Note, however, that you can't specify a drive and directory in the target specification because this command can only rename a file; it can't move the file to another directory.

Figure 7-11 shows three examples of Rename commands. In example 1, the command renames a file named REVSUM.TXT in the current directory to REVSUM92.TXT. In example 2, the command renames a file named REVSUM.WK1 in the WK1 directory on the D drive to REVSUM92.WK1. In example 3, the command is invalid because its target specification includes drive and directory information.

The format of the Rename command

```
REN source-spec target-spec
```

Example 1: A Rename command that renames REVSUM.TXT in the current directory to REVSUM92.TXT.

```
C:\WP51\MMA>ren revsum.txt revsum92.txt
```

Example 2: A Rename command that renames REVSUM.WK1 in the WK1 directory on the D drive to REVSUM92.WK1.

```
C:\WP51\MMA>ren d:\wk1\revsum.wk1 revsum92.wk1
```

Example 3: An invalid Rename command that tries to rename a file in the current directory with a target file specification that's in another drive and directory.

```
C:\WP51\MMA>ren revsum92.txt d:\wk1\revsum92.txt
```

Figure 7-11 The Rename command

The Move command (DOS 6.0) You've already seen how to rename a directory with the DOS 6.0 Move command. You can also use this command to move one or more files on your system. And you can use it to rename a single file as you move the file.

Figure 7-12 shows six examples of Move commands. In example 1, the command moves a file named WP.BAT from the UTIL directory to the BAT directory. In example 2, the command moves a file named MONTHEND.WK1 from the C drive to the A drive. In example 3, the command moves a file named EOMJAN.WK1 down one step in the directory structure by moving it from the 123 directory on the C drive to the 123\92RECS directory. In example 4, the command moves a file from one drive and directory to another and changes its name at the same time. So the file that was named REVSUM92.DOC is now called REVENUE.92. Example 5 shows how to move two files at the same time. It moves the files named C1.DOC and C1FIGS.DOC from the MMA directory on the C drive to the directory named DOSBK. In this case, the target specification must be a directory name.

With what you know about the operation of the Copy command, you might expect that you could omit the target directory from the Move command in example 5 since the intended target directory is the current directory. You can't do that, however, because the Move command requires a target specification. If you omitted the target directory from the command in example 5, Move would assume that the second file specification was the target, and the command wouldn't work as you intended.

The format of the Move command

```
MOVE source-spec-1 [source-spec-2...] target-spec
```

Example 1: A Move command that moves the file named WP.BAT from the current directory to the BAT directory on the default drive.

```
C:\UTIL>move wp.bat \bat
```

Example 2: A Move command that moves the file named MONTHEND.WK1 from the current directory on the C drive to the A drive.

```
C:\123>move monthend.wk1 a:
```

Example 3: A Move command that moves the file named EOMJAN.WK1 from the 123 directory on the C drive to the 123\92RECS directory.

```
C:\>move 123\eomjan.wk1 123\92recs
```

Example 4: A Move command that moves the file named REVSUM92.DOC from the current directory on the C drive to the DATA directory on the D drive and renames the file REVENUE.92.

```
C:\WP51\MMA>move revsum92.doc d:\data\revenue.92
```

Example 5: A Move command that moves two files, C1.DOC and C1FIGS.DOC, from the MMA directory on the C drive to the \DOSBK directory.

```
C:\DOSBK>move \mma\c1.doc \mma\c1figs.doc \dosbk
```

Example 6: A Move command that uses a period in the target specification to move two files to the current directory.

```
C:\DOSBK>move \mma\c1.doc \mma\c1figs.doc .
```

Figure 7-12 The Move command

Instead of entering the name of the current directory for the target specification as in example 5, you can use the shortcut illustrated in example 6. Here, I entered a period for the target specification. When you do that, DOS substitutes the current directory for the period.

Like the Copy command, the Move command will overwrite existing files in the target directory without warning. So be careful whenever you use it to move files into a directory that already has files in it.

Wildcard	Meaning
`*`	One or more characters of any kind
`?`	One character of any kind

Example	Meaning
`*.*`	All files (any name, any extension)
`*.com`	All files with COM as the extension
`*.`	All files that don't have an extension
`c1.*`	All files named C1 no matter what the extension is
`c*.*`	All files with names that start with C
`c?.*`	All files with one- or two-character file names that start with C
`c?.com`	All files with one- or two-character file names that start with C and have an extension of COM
`c???????.`	All files with file names that start with C and that don't have an extension (same as c*.)
`????.exe`	All files with one-, two-, three-, or four-character file names that have an extension of EXE

Figure 7-13 The * and ? wildcards

How to use wildcards within a DOS command

DOS provides two *wildcards* that you can use within the file specifications of DOS commands. These wildcards are summarized in figure 7-13. When you use wildcards within a command, a single DOS command can operate on more than one file.

You already know a little bit about the ** wildcard* (asterisk wildcard). It represents one or more characters of any kind, and it is the wildcard that you'll use the most. Sometimes, this wildcard is called the *star wildcard*, and a specification like *.* is referred to as "star-dot-star." This wildcard makes it easy for a single command to operate on all the files within a directory or all the files in a directory that have a specific extension.

The *? wildcard* (question mark wildcard) represents one character of any kind. Although you may never need it, it can be useful once in a while. It's used to select files that have any character in each ? wildcard position. For instance, the specification

```
C?FIGS
```

includes files with names like C1FIGS, C2FIGS, and C9FIGS, but it excludes files with names like C19FIGS and C20FIGS.

Perhaps the best way to get comfortable with the use of wildcards is to practice using them in Directory commands, as illustrated in figure 7-14. Here, the first command displays only the files with COM as the extension. The second command displays the files that have an extension of COM and that start with the letter M. The third command displays the files that have no extension and that start with the letter M. The fourth command uses ? wildcards to display file names of four characters or less that start with the letter M and that have COM as the extension. The fifth command uses ? wildcards to display file names of three characters or less no matter what the extensions are.

Once you're sure that you know how wildcards work, you can use them in Copy, Xcopy, and Rename commands as illustrated in figure 7-15. Here, the examples only show the use of * wildcards, but you can use ? wildcards whenever they are appropriate.

If you have any doubt about the way wildcards are going to work in Delete commands, I recommend that you use a two-step procedure like the one in figure 7-16. In step 1, you use the Directory command with the file specification for the files you want to delete. Then, if the correct files are displayed, use exactly the same file specification in a Delete command, as shown in step 2.

Remember that if you have DOS 4.0 or later, you can use the /P switch to avoid deleting the wrong files. When you use this switch, the Delete command asks you for confirmation before it deletes a file. If you respond with Y when DOS asks you if you want to delete a file, the file is deleted. If you respond with N, the command proceeds to the next file specified by the command or ends the command if no other files are specified.

In DOS 6.0, you can also use wildcards with the Move command, but you can't use them as widely as you can in some of the other commands. Figure 7-17 gives you two examples. The first example works just as you've seen the wildcards work in other commands. The second example, however, is an invalid command because it includes a wildcard in the target specification. Although you can code a Copy command like this, when you're moving multiple files the target specification must be a directory name, and the wildcard indicates a file name.

Typical command sequences for managing directories and files

Although the versions of DOS before DOS 6.0 provide commands for making a new directory and removing an empty directory, they don't provide commands for renaming a directory, for removing a directory that contains files, or for moving a directory and its files from one point in the directory structure to another. To do these tasks, you have to use a combination of DOS commands. With DOS 6.0, you can use the Move command to rename a directory, and you can use the Delete-tree command to delete a directory that contains files, but you still have to use a combination of commands to move a directory and its files.

Example 1

A Directory command that displays all the files in the current directory that have an extension of COM.

```
C:\DOS>dir *.com /w

 Volume in drive C has no label
 Volume Serial Number is 1983-5D30
 Directory of C:\DOS

FORMAT.COM      KEYB.COM        SYS.COM         UNFORMAT.COM    CHOICE.COM
MIRROR.COM      DOSSHELL.COM    MODE.COM        GRAFTABL.COM    HELP.COM
EDIT.COM        MSHERC.COM      ASSIGN.COM      DISKCOMP.COM    DISKCOPY.COM
MORE.COM        GRAPHICS.COM    TREE.COM        DOSKEY.COM      LOADFIX.COM
VSAFE.COM       COMMAND.COM
       22 file(s)     327796 bytes
                    25636864 bytes free

C:\DOS>
```

Example 2

A Directory command that displays all the files in the current directory with names that start with the letter M and have an extension of COM.

```
C:\DOS>dir m*.com

 Volume in drive C has no label
 Volume Serial Number is 1983-5D30
 Directory of C:\DOS

MIRROR   COM     18169 04-09-91   5:00a
MODE     COM     23537 10-26-92   6:00a
MSHERC   COM      6934 04-09-91   5:00a
MORE     COM      2618 10-26-92   6:00a
        4 file(s)      51258 bytes
                    25636864 bytes free

C:\DOS>
```

Example 3

A Directory command that displays all the files in the current directory with names that start with the letter M and have no extension.

```
C:\DOS>dir m*.

 Volume in drive C has no label
 Volume Serial Number is 1983-5D30
 Directory of C:\DOS

File not found

C:\DOS>
```

Figure 7-14 The use of wildcards in Directory commands (part 1 of 2)

Example 4

A Directory command that displays all the files in the current directory with names that start with the letter M and are four characters or less and have an extension of COM.

```
C:\DOS>dir m???.com

 Volume in drive C has no label
 Volume Serial Number is 1983-5D30
 Directory of C:\DOS

MODE     COM      23537 10-26-92   6:00a
MORE     COM       2618 10-26-92   6:00a
        2 file(s)      26155 bytes
                    25636864 bytes free

C:\DOS>
```

Example 5

A Directory command that displays all the files in the current directory that have file names of three characters or less.

```
C:\DOS>dir ???

 Volume in drive C has no label
 Volume Serial Number is 1983-5D30
 Directory of C:\DOS

.
    12-15-92   8:50a
..
    12-15-92   8:50a
EGA      SYS       4885 10-26-92   6:00a
EGA      CPI      58873 10-26-92   6:00a
SYS      COM      13440 10-26-92   6:00a
MSD      EXE     158428 10-26-92   6:00a
MEM      EXE      30470 10-26-92   6:00a
LCD      CPI      10753 04-09-91   5:00a
FC       EXE      18650 10-26-92   6:00a
XMA      TXT       5408 12-19-88  12:00a
       10 file(s)     300907 bytes
                    25636864 bytes free

C:\DOS>
```

Figure 7-14 The use of wildcards in Directory commands (part 2 of 2)

When you use a shell program for managing directories and files, you can do most directory functions more easily than you can from the command prompt. For instance, the DOS 5.0/6.0 shell provides specific functions for creating, renaming, and deleting directories. As a result, you don't have to know how to do these functions from the command prompt. However, the DOS 5.0/6.0 shell doesn't provide a function for moving a directory and its files from one point in the directory structure

Example 1: A Copy command that copies all of the files in the WP51\MMA directory on the C drive to a diskette in the A drive.

```
C:\>copy \wp51\mma\*.* a:
```

Example 2: A Copy command that copies all of the files on the diskette in the A drive to the current directory.

```
C:\DATA\123>copy a:*.*
```

Example 3: A Copy command and an Xcopy command that copy all of the files with an extension of WK1 in the current directory to a diskette in the A drive.

```
C:\DATA\123>copy *.wk1 a:
C:\DATA\123>xcopy *.wk1 a:
```

Example 4: A Rename command that renames all files named PRSUM in the current directory, no matter what the extensions are, to PRSUM93.

```
C:WP51\MMA>ren prsum.* prsum93.*
```

Example 5: A Rename command that changes the extensions of all files in the current directory with the extension of WK1 to the extension of BAK.

```
C:\123\MMA>ren *.wk1 *.bak
```

Figure 7-15 The use of wildcards in Copy, Xcopy, and Rename commands

Step 1: Use the Directory command with the wildcard specification that you intend to use in the Delete command.

```
C:\>dir d:\wp51\mma\*.bak
```

Step 2: If the files that are displayed are the ones that you want to delete, use the Delete command with exactly the same wildcard specification that you used in step 1.

```
C:\>del d:\wp51\mma\*.bak
```

Figure 7-16 How to use wildcards in Delete commands

to another, and it doesn't provide a function for deleting a directory that contains files. To do either of these tasks, you must use the series of DOS commands that I'll describe in a moment. You can start these commands from the command prompt or from the shell, but you must understand what has to be done before you can do it.

Example 1: A Move command that moves all of the files with an extension of 92 from the current directory to a diskette in the A drive.

```
C:\DATA\WP51>move *.92 a:
```

Example 2: A Move command that's invalid because it includes a wildcard in the target specification. (The wildcard indicates a file name, and the target specification must be a directory name when you're moving multiple files.)

```
C:\DATA\WP51>move *.92 a:\*.old
```

Figure 7-17 The use of wildcards in Move commands

How to create a new directory Figure 7-18 shows you two ways to use the Make-directory command when you want to create a new directory. In example 1, the Change-directory command changes the current directory to the one that the new directory should be subordinate to. Then, the Make-directory command specifies only the new directory name as a parameter. In example 2, the Make-directory command includes a complete path for the new directory.

How to remove a directory Figure 7-19 shows you one way to remove a directory from a drive if you're using a version of DOS that's earlier than DOS 6.0. In step 1, you change the current directory to the one that you want to remove. In step 2, you delete all the files in the directory because a directory has to be empty before you can remove it. When you use wildcard specifications to delete all of the files in a directory, DOS displays the message

```
Are you sure (Y/N)?
```

to give you a chance to change your mind. If you are sure, you respond with Y. In step 3, you use the Change-directory command to change the current directory to the root directory because you can't use the Remove-directory command to remove the current directory. And in step 4, you use the Remove-directory command to remove the empty directory.

This example assumes that the QA4\COLLEGE directory doesn't contain any subdirectories. But if a directory does contain subdirectories, you must first use this procedure to delete the files from each subdirectory and remove the subdirectory. Then, when the directory is completely empty, you can remove it.

Example 1

```
C:\>cd \123

C:\123>md becky
```

Example 2

```
C:\>md \123\becky
```

Figure 7-18 Two ways to make a new directory named 123\BECKY

For versions of DOS before DOS 6.0

Step 1: Change the current directory to the one that you want to remove.

```
C:\>cd \qa4\college
```

Step 2: Delete all the files in the directory.

```
C:\QA4\COLLEGE>del *.*
All files in directory will be deleted!
Are you sure (Y/N)?y
```

Step 3: Change the current directory to the root directory.

```
C:\QA4\COLLEGE>cd \
```

Step 4: Remove the empty directory.

```
C:\>rd \qa4\college

C:\>
```

For DOS 6.0

```
C:\>deltree \qa4\college
Delete directory "\qa4\college" and all its subdirectories?[yn]y
Deleting \qa4\college...

C:\>
```

Figure 7-19 How to remove a directory named QA4\COLLEGE

If you like, you can simplify the procedure in figure 7-19 by specifying the directory path in the Delete command. Then, you can delete the files and remove the directory with just two commands:

```
C:\>del \qa4\college\*.*
All files in directory will be deleted!
Are you sure (Y/N)?y

C:\>rd \qa4\college
```

Figure 7-19 also shows how to remove a directory in DOS 6.0. As you can see, all you have to do is issue a Delete-tree command for the directory and press Y when DOS asks you for confirmation. Then, DOS will delete the directory and all its subdirectories and files.

How to rename a directory Because there's no single DOS command for renaming a directory in the versions of DOS before DOS 6.0, you have to use the combination of commands shown in figure 7-20. In step 1, you use the Make-directory command to create a directory with the new name you want to use for the existing directory. In step 2, you copy all of the files in the existing directory to the new directory. In step 3, you delete all the files in the existing directory. In step 4, you remove the existing directory from the disk. The result is a renamed directory.

Unfortunately, to use this technique, you must have enough space on your hard disk to hold two copies of the files in the directory. If you don't have enough free disk space, you have to delete some files before you begin. In addition, the process is more complicated if the directory you want to rename has subdirectories. In that case, you must copy and delete each of those subdirectories as well. (If you're using DOS 3.2 or a later version, you can use the Xcopy command with the /S switch instead of the Copy command to copy all the subdirectories with a single command.)

DOS 6.0 makes it much easier to rename a directory. As you can see in figure 7-20, all you have to do is enter a Move command that specifies the current directory name and the new directory name. DOS makes all the adjustments needed to identify the files in the directory according to their new path names.

How to move a directory There's no single DOS command for moving a directory from one point in a directory structure to another. Also, as I mentioned earlier, the DOS 5.0/6.0 shell doesn't provide for this function. As a result, you have to use a combination of commands to move a directory, as shown in figure 7-21.

As you can see, moving a directory using a version of DOS before DOS 6.0 requires basically the same steps as renaming a directory, so I won't go through the commands again. Remember, though, the process is more complicated if the directory you want to move has subdirectories, unless you're using DOS 3.2 or later. Beginning with DOS 3.2, you can use the Xcopy command with the /S switch to copy the directory and all its subdirectories in a single command.

For versions of DOS before DOS 6.0

Step 1: Create a directory that has the new name you want to use for the existing directory.

```
C:\>md \123\mma92
```

Step 2: Copy the files from the old directory to the new directory using the Copy or Xcopy command.

```
C:\>copy \123\mma\*.* \123\mma92
BALSHEET.WK1
PROFORMA.WK1
SALARIES.WK1
MKTGEXP.WK1
ADMEXP.WK1
       5 File(s) copied
```

Step 3: Delete the files in the old directory.

```
C:\>del \123\mma\*.*
All files in directory will be deleted!
Are you sure (Y/N)?y
```

Step 4: Remove the old directory.

```
C:\>rd \123\mma

C:\>
```

For DOS 6.0

```
C:\>move \123\mma 123\mma92
C:\123\MMA ⇒ C:\123\MMA92 [ok]
```

Figure 7-20 How to rename a directory from 123\MMA to 123\MMA92

If you're using DOS 6.0, the procedure for moving a directory is simpler because you can use a single Move command in place of the Copy and Delete commands. And you don't need to change the current directory to the new directory before issuing the Move command. You have to specify the directory in the target specification anyway, since you're moving multiple files. If the directory you want to move contains subdirectories, use the Xcopy command with the /S switch to copy the directories to their new position in the directory tree. Then use the Delete-tree command to delete the old directory and its subdirectories.

For versions of DOS before DOS 6.0

Step 1: Make a new directory in the location that you want to move the old directory to.

```
C:\>md \mma
```

Step 2: Change the current directory to the new directory.

```
C:\>cd \mma
```

Step 3: Copy the files from the old directory to the new directory using the Copy or Xcopy command.

```
C:\MMA>copy \123\mma\*.*
BALSHEET.WK1
PROFORMA.WK1
SALARIES.WK1
MKTGEXP.WK1
ADMEXP.WK1
       5 File(s) copied
```

Step 4: Delete the files in the old directory.

```
C:\MMA>del \123\mma\*.*
All files in directory will be deleted!
Are you sure (Y/N)?y
```

Step 5: Remove the old directory.

```
C:\>rd \123\mma
```

For DOS 6.0

Step 1: Make a new directory in the location that you want to move the old directory to.

```
C:\>md \mma
```

Step 2: Move the files from the old directory to the new directory.

```
C:\>move \123\mma\*.* c:\mma
C:\123\MMA\BALSHEET.WK1 = C:\MMA\BALSHEET.WK1 [ok]
C:\123\MMA\PROFORMA.WK1 = C:\MMA\PROFORMA.WK1 [ok]
C:\123\MMA\SALARIES.WK1 = C:\MMA\SALARIES.WK1 [ok]
C:\123\MMA\MKTGEXP.WK1 = C:\MMA\MKTGEXP.WK1 [ok]
C:\123\MMA\ADMEXP.WK1 = C:\MMA\ADMEXP.WK1 [ok]
```

Step 3: Remove the old directory.

```
C:\>rd \123\mma
```

Figure 7-21 How to move the 123\MMA directory to a new directory named MMA

1. Keep the number of files in the root directory to a minimum.
2. Don't use more than two directory levels below the root directory.
3. Use simple directory names.
4. Store DOS files in a DOS directory.
5. Store utility programs in a utility directory.
6. Store all batch files in one directory.
7. Store application programs in their own directories.
8. Store data files in logically organized data directories.
9. Keep your data directories small.
10. Don't keep files you don't need.
11. Use consistent file names.
12. Include the file name in the heading of each document that's prepared from a file.

Figure 7-22 Twelve guidelines for managing directories and files

Twelve guidelines for managing your directories and files

Now that you've learned the commands for managing your directories and files, here are 12 guidelines that will help you do a better job of managing them whether you use the DOS commands or a shell. Because these guidelines are all straightforward, I'll go through them quickly. They are summarized in figure 7-22.

Keep the number of files in the root directory to a minimum If you keep only a few files in the root directory, it's easier to manage the directories and files on your system. In general, the root directory of each drive should contain only entries for subordinate directories. In addition, the root directory of the C drive must contain the COMMAND.COM, CONFIG.SYS, and AUTOEXEC.BAT files.

You can't always keep other files out of the root directory, though, because some application programs and utility programs put files of their own in the root directory of the default drive. For example, *PC Tools* routinely puts files in my root directory. Nevertheless, you shouldn't put any more files in your root directory than are required. Instead, you should store your files in directories that help you keep them organized.

Don't use more than two directory levels below the root directory
Sometimes, it's tempting to use more than two levels of directories below the root directory. For instance, you start by adding a directory (WP) for your word processing program that's subordinate to the root directory. Next, you add a data directory

(WP\PROJECTA) for the files you'll create as part of an extensive writing project. Then, because several of you are working on the project, you are tempted to add more directories that are subordinate to the PROJECTA subdirectory. That way, there's a directory for each person's work: WP\PROJECTA\DOUG, WP\PROJECTA\ANNE, and so on.

As tempting as this may be from an organizational point of view, you should resist doing this because it leads to paths that are too long for efficiency. After you enter the complete path specifications a few times, you'll be convinced of that. Also, you can get the same effect without going to a third structural level. Just make the directories for each person as well as the PROJECTA directory subordinate to the word processing directory. Or make the PROJECTA directory subordinate to the root directory instead of the word processing directory. Either way, by limiting yourself to two directory levels below the root directory, you'll simplify your directory and file management.

Use simple directory names You'll type directory and subdirectory names often as you use your PC, so keep them short and simple like the ones illustrated in this book. Don't use special characters in your directory names because they're more difficult to type than letters and numbers, and don't use extensions in your directory names either. For program directories, try to use the name suggested by the program's installation instructions. For data directories, try to use a short but meaningful name.

Store DOS files in a DOS directory Many users keep all of their DOS files in the root directory of the C drive. But rather than clutter up the root directory, I suggest that you store the DOS files (except for COMMAND.COM, CONFIG.SYS, and AUTOEXEC.BAT) in a directory named DOS. Then, add the DOS directory to the Path command in your AUTOEXEC.BAT file.

If your DOS files are already stored in the root directory, you can move them to a DOS directory. But you may have to work around other files that are in the root directory. As a result, you'll need to perform six steps to move your DOS files to a DOS directory. First, create a DOS directory that's subordinate to the root directory. Second, copy all of the files from the root directory to the DOS directory. Third, delete all of the files in the root directory. Fourth, copy the COMMAND.COM, CONFIG.SYS, and AUTOEXEC.BAT files, and any files that aren't DOS files from the DOS directory to the root directory. Fifth, delete the COMMAND.COM, CONFIG.SYS, and AUTOEXEC.BAT files, and any files that aren't a part of DOS from the DOS directory. Sixth, add the DOS directory to the Path command in the AUTOEXEC.BAT file.

Store utility programs in a utility directory If you own any utility programs, I suggest you store them in a directory named UTIL. Then, add the UTIL directory to the Path command in your AUTOEXEC.BAT file. If you purchase a large utility that comes with many files, you can create a separate directory for that program.

Store all batch files in one directory I mentioned this in chapter 6, but it's worth repeating. To control the batch files on your system, you should store them in one directory. This can be the UTIL directory, or you can create a separate directory for them named BAT or BATCH. If you create a separate directory, you should add it to the Path command in your AUTOEXEC.BAT file.

Store application programs in their own directories Because most application programs require dozens of files, you should store each program in its own directory and make that directory subordinate to the root directory. If you look back to the tree in figure 7-6, you can see three directories for application programs: WP51 for *WordPerfect*; 123 for *Lotus 1-2-3*; and QA4 for *Q&A*.

Store data files in logically organized data directories Although some programs require it, you shouldn't store data files in program directories if you can avoid it. Otherwise, your program directories will quickly become unmanageable. Instead, you should store your data files in logically organized data directories.

Figure 7-23 illustrates five ways to organize data directories. In the first structure, word processing documents are stored in a directory called DOC, and spreadsheets are stored in a directory called WK1 (the normal extension for *Lotus 1-2-3* spreadsheets). This one-level structure is sensible if you don't have too much software or data on your system.

In the second structure in figure 7-23, the two data directories (DOC and WK1) are subordinate to a directory named DATA. And all of the program directories are subordinate to the root directory. As chapter 9 explains, this two-level structure can simplify your backup procedures.

The third structure in figure 7-23 is a two-level structure that's organized by application program. Here, the data directories are subordinate to the program directories. As a result, you know that the MEMOS, LETTERS, and REPORTS directories contain word processing documents. And you know that the CORP and DEPT directories contain spreadsheets.

The fourth structure in figure 7-23 is a two-level structure that's organized by project. Here, the DOC directories contain word processing documents related to each of the two projects, and the WK1 directories contain spreadsheets related to the projects.

The last structure in figure 7-23 is a two-level structure that's organized by PC user. This is sensible when several people use the same PC. Then, the users decide how they want to organize their subdirectories.

The point I'm trying to make is that there should be some logic to the structure of your directories. If there is, it will be easier for you to manage your files. You'll also be able to find whatever files you're looking for.

Keep your data directories small At some point, a data directory holds so many files that it becomes unmanageable. Then, it's time to delete files you no longer need. It may also be time to regroup the files into two or more subdirectories based on

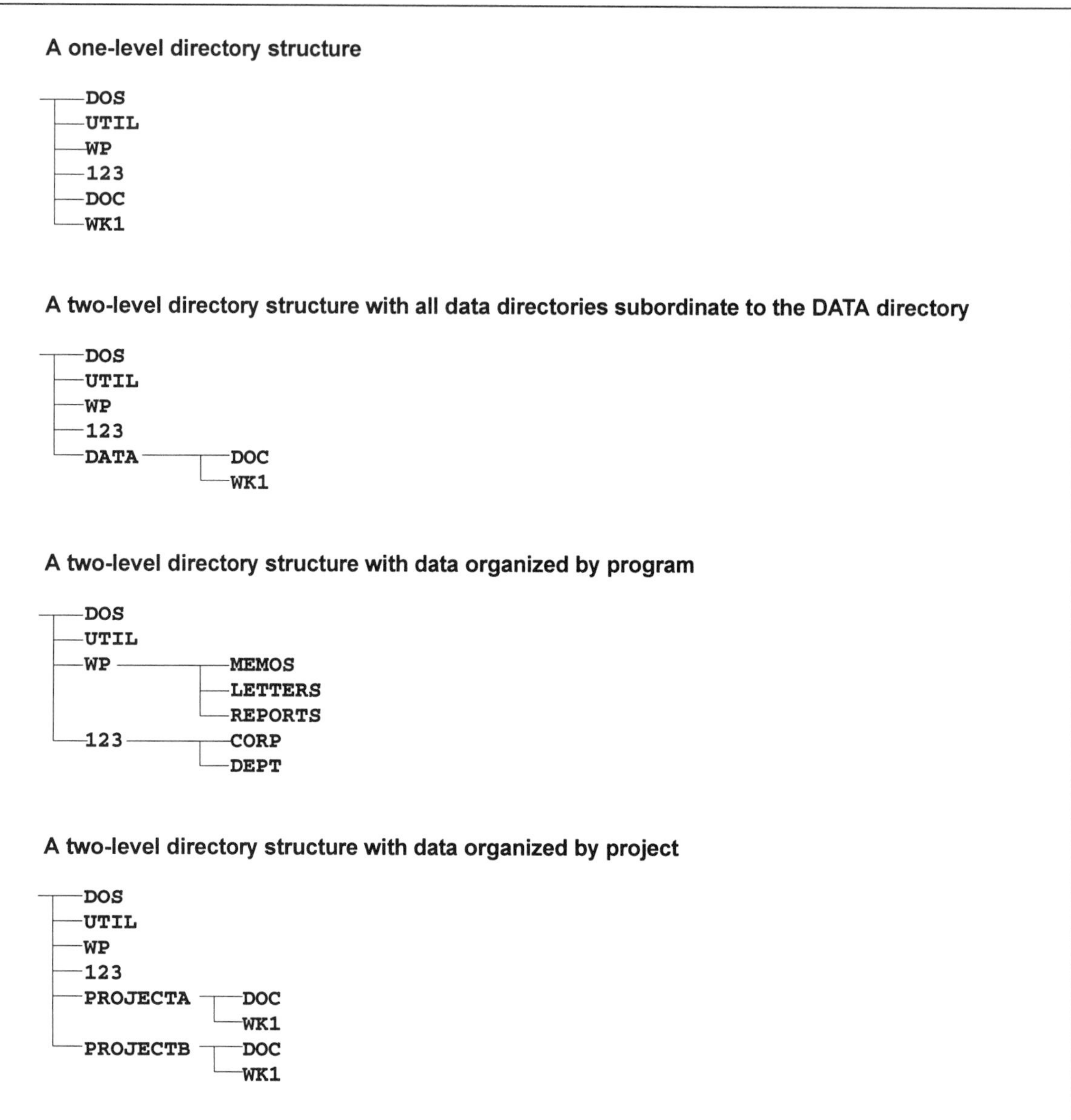

Figure 7-23 Five ways to organize data directories (part 1 of 2)

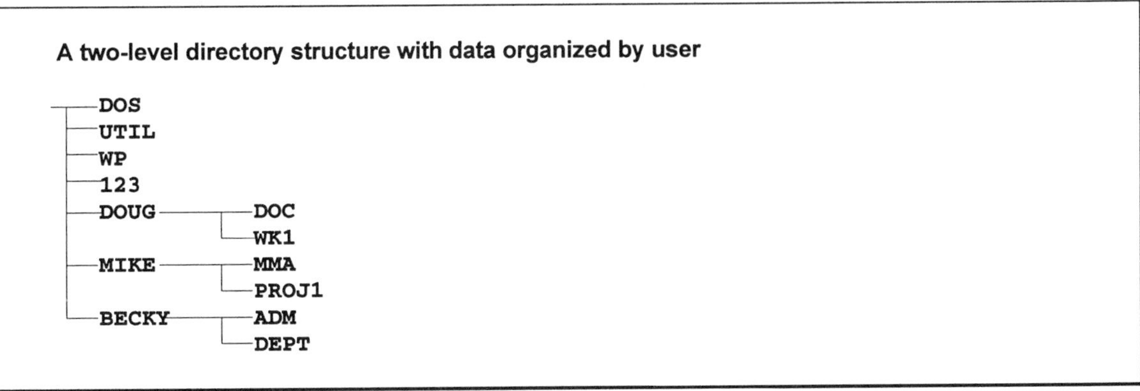

Figure 7-23 Five ways to organize data directories (part 2 of 2)

some logical structure. If you keep your data directories small, you'll be able to manage your files more effectively.

Don't keep files you don't need This guideline is pretty obvious, and it's closely related to the previous one. However, I've included it as a separate guideline because most PC users don't follow it. Since they've usually got millions of bytes of free space on their disk drives, they just don't worry about a few unnecessary files. But the few files add up, and eventually the clutter makes it more difficult to manage the directories and files.

For instance, many PC users keep a copy of each letter they write on their systems. But they rarely refer to any of them. Similarly, they keep several versions of reports and proposals on their systems, but they use only the final versions. If you're guilty of either of these practices, delete the files you never use and you'll simplify file management.

To complicate matters, some programs automatically create files you don't need. For instance, many programs create backup files for each file you work on so you won't lose your work in case of a power failure. Normally, these files have a distinctive extension such as BAK or BK. Also, some programs create temporary files while you're using them. If you end the program normally, these files are deleted. But if you don't, these files with extensions like TMP, $$$, or 001 stay on your system. Occasionally, then, you should take a few minutes to delete the backup and temporary files that have accumulated. You can delete them by using a wildcard with an appropriate extension as in this command:

```
C:\WORD>del *.tmp
```

Use consistent file names A good file name is one that is descriptive enough to tell you what's in the file, and distinct enough to distinguish it from other files with similar names. Unfortunately, you can't always create good file names with a limit of eight characters for the name and three for the extension. That's why it's so important that you organize your data files in logical directories and that you keep those directories small.

Within each data directory, you should try to create file names that are consistent. In a word processing directory, for example, you may want to use the extension RPT for reports, LTR for letters, and MEM for memos. If the program doesn't let you use your own extensions, you can start the file names with three-character identifiers. Similarly, you may want to start spreadsheet names with PF for proforma analyses, SLS for sales summaries, and FIN for financial summaries. Although this consistency may not help you find the exact file you're looking for, it will at least help you narrow down the possibilities.

Include the file name in the heading of each document that's prepared from a file Because you can't always create distinctive file names, you should include the file name in the heading of any document or spreadsheet that's printed from a file. Then, if you want to modify the document, you look for a file with that name in the directory that's logically related to it. Usually, you don't need to include the path along with a file name in the heading, but if there's any chance for confusion, include the path too.

How a shell program can help you manage directories and files

If you follow the 12 guidelines I've just presented, you can do an effective job of managing your directories and files whether or not you use a shell program. If you're not using a shell program, though, you should probably consider getting one.

To start, you can learn how to use the DOS 5.0/6.0 shell for managing directories and files in chapter 14 of this book. If you like that shell, you can upgrade from your current version of DOS to DOS 6.0. Otherwise, you can install a commercial shell program on your system without changing your current version of DOS.

From a practical point of view, it's usually best to use some combination of DOS commands and shell functions to manage your directories and files. If you want to carefully select files for deletion by reviewing their names and creation dates, a shell is usually more efficient. But if you want to copy or delete entire directories or portions of directories that can be selected by wildcards, the DOS commands are usually more efficient.

Terms

attribute
source file
target file
wildcard
* wildcard
star wildcard
? wildcard

Objectives

1. Given a drive specification, use the Tree command to display the directory structure of the drive.
2. Given a directory specification, use the appropriate commands to move it, to rename it, to remove it, or to add a new directory of that name to your system.
3. Given file specifications, use the appropriate commands with or without wildcards to copy, delete, rename, or move one or more files.

Exercises

1. Use the Directory command to experiment with the * and ? wildcards until you understand how they work.
2. Copy all the files that start with A, C, or D from your DOS directory to an empty diskette in drive A. That will require three Copy commands with wildcards. Next, change the default drive to drive A. Then, use the Directory command to get a directory listing of the files in the current directory of the default drive.
3. Use the Make-directory command to create a COM directory on the diskette in the A drive. Next, copy all the files in the root directory of the C drive with an extension of COM to the COM directory. Then, use Directory commands to list the files in the root directory and the COM directory to make sure your commands worked correctly.
4. Use a single Rename command to rename all the files in the COM directory on the diskette in the A drive so the extensions are CBK. Then, use a Directory command to list the files in the COM directory to make sure the Rename command worked correctly.
5. Change the name of the COM directory to CBK. If you're using DOS 6.0, do this using the Move command.
6. Remove the CBK directory from the diskette in the A drive. If you're using DOS 6.0, do this using the Delete-tree command.
7. Use the Directory command to get directory listings of the root directories on the drives of your hard disk. Do these directories contain acceptable minimums of files? Are the DOS files in the root directory of the C drive? Are any other programs in the root directory of the C drive? What directory and file reorganization do these listings suggest?
8. Run the Tree command for the C drive of your system to see what output you get. If you have other drives on your hard disk, run the Tree command for those drives too. How are the program directories on your system organized? How are the data directories organized? What directory and file reorganization is suggested by the current directory structure?

Chapter 8

How to work with diskettes

When a PC has a hard disk, you won't have much need for diskettes. Most of the time, you'll retrieve the files you need from the hard disk, and you'll save the files you create on the hard disk.

Nevertheless, one diskette drive is an essential component of a hard disk system because the hard disk isn't removable. As a result, software for a hard disk system is usually delivered on diskettes. You often use diskettes when you want to transfer data from one PC to another. And the most common way to back up a hard disk is to transfer its data to diskettes.

In this chapter, you'll learn how to work with diskettes. First, I'll review the diskette characteristics I presented in the first chapter. Then, I'll present two DOS commands you can use when you work with diskettes. Last, I'll present three specific skills that are related to diskette use.

When you finish this chapter, you will know how to use diskettes for transferring data from one system to another. You will also know how to work with diskettes when you use them for backing up data as presented in the next chapter. You need to have these skills whether or not you use a shell program on your PC.

A review of diskette characteristics

In chapter 1, I described the two types of diskettes that are in widespread use today: the 5-1/4 inch diskette and the 3-1/2 inch diskette. Now, I'll review some of the characteristics of these diskettes. These characteristics are summarized in figure 8-1.

5-1/4 inch diskettes These diskettes are most commonly used with PCs, XTs, and ATs. The double-density capacity is 360KB; the high-density capacity is 1.2MB. Although a 1.2MB diskette drive can read and write both types of diskettes, a 360KB drive can read and write only double-density diskettes.

Although 5-1/4 inch diskettes are tough, they're not indestructible. In fact, reading and writing errors often occur when you use this type of diskette. So to get the best results from them, you should handle them with care. That means you shouldn't write on them with a pencil or a ballpoint pen; you shouldn't touch the surface that's exposed through the diskette opening; you shouldn't get them close to anything magnetic (including paper clips that have been in a magnetic paper clip

Size	Capacity	Common labelling notation	Tracks	Sectors per track
5-1/4"	360KB	5-1/4" Double-Sided Double-Density 5-1/4" DSDD	40	9
5-1/4"	1.2MB	5-1/4" Double-Sided High-Density 5-1/4" DSHD	80	15
3-1/2"	720KB	3-1/2" Double-Sided Double-Density 3-1/2" 2DD 3-1/2" 1.0M formatted capacity	80	9
3-1/2"	1.44MB	3-1/2" Double-Sided High-Density 3-1/2" 2HD 3-1/2" 2.0M formatted capacity	80	18
3-1/2"	2.88MB	3-1/2" Double-Sided Extended-Density 3-1/2" 2ED 3-1/2" 4.0M formatted capacity	80	36

Figure 8-1 A summary of diskette characteristics

holder); and you shouldn't leave them anywhere that will expose them to extremes of heat or cold. You should also keep them in their protective sleeves when they're not in use.

3-1/2 inch diskettes Although these diskettes were popularized by laptop computers and the PS/2s, you can now get a 3-1/2 inch drive for other types of PCs. The double-density capacity is 720KB; the high-density capacity is 1.44MB; and the extended-density capacity is 2.88MB. Here again, a 2.88MB diskette drive can read and write all three types of diskettes, a 1.44MB drive can read and write both double-density and high-density diskettes, and a 720KB drive can read and write only double-density diskettes.

These diskettes are more reliable than the 5-1/4 inch diskettes, so reading and writing errors rarely occur when you use them. Also, these diskettes don't require as much care. With sensible handling, you shouldn't have any problems with them.

Two commands for working with diskettes

Figure 8-2 summarizes the two commands you need for formatting and copying entire diskettes. Otherwise, you use the same file handling commands for diskettes that you use for hard disks, including the Copy, Xcopy, Delete, Rename, and Move commands

The format of the Format command

```
FORMAT drive-spec [/4] [/N:sectors] [/T:tracks] [/F:capacity]
                  [/Q] [/S] [/U]
```

Function

This command formats a diskette for use by DOS. To format a diskette in the default format of the diskette drive, you don't need any switches. Otherwise, you must use one or more of the switches as illustrated in figure 8-3.

Switch meanings

/4	Formats a 360KB diskette in a 1.2MB drive.
/N:sectors **/T:tracks**	DOS 3.2 and 3.3 switches used to format a double-density diskette on a higher-capacity drive.
/F:capacity	DOS 4.0 replacement for the /N and /T switches.
/Q	DOS 5.0 switch for reformatting a diskette quickly (only for use on previously formatted diskettes).
/S	Formats a system diskette that's used to boot DOS.
/U	DOS 5.0 and 6.0 switch that destroys all the data on a disk. Since it prevents you from recovering the data on the disk after it's formatted, it's typically used only with unformatted diskettes.

The format of the Diskcopy command

```
DISKCOPY source-drive target-drive
```

Function

This command copies an entire diskette including any directories and all of its files. It works most efficiently if you copy the diskette in one drive to a diskette in another drive. But you can also use this command when your PC has only one diskette drive.

Figure 8-2 Two commands for working with diskettes

that are covered in chapter 7. You can also use the directory commands covered in chapter 7, although the root directory is usually the only directory you need on a diskette.

The Format command Before a diskette can be used, it has to be formatted. Although you can buy diskettes that are already formatted, you can also buy unformatted diskettes. If you do, you have to use the Format command to format them.

The Format command prepares the surface of the diskette so it can record information. It does this by defining the tracks on a diskette, setting up the root directory for the diskette, and checking the reliability of the diskette. The Format command also creates the *File Allocation Table*, or *FAT*, which DOS uses to keep track of the location of files on the diskette.

If you're using a version of DOS before 5.0 and you format a diskette that already has data on it, all of its data is destroyed. Similarly, if you unintentionally format your hard disk, all of its data is destroyed. To avoid this disaster, you should make sure that the drive specification in this command is always drive A or drive B. If you specify drive C, DOS will give you a warning message. But if you ignore it, the disaster is in progress.

If you're using DOS 5.0 or 6.0, DOS still gives you a warning message if you specify drive C. But even if you ignore the message, the data on the disk isn't destroyed. That's because beginning with DOS 5.0, the Format command does a *safe format*. With a safe format, DOS clears the File Allocation Table and the root directory, but leaves the data in place. That way, you can easily unformat a disk if you format it in error. Unformatting a hard disk is not a totally reliable procedure, however. So you still want to be careful when you use the Format command. I'll have more to say about unformatting disks in chapter 10.

Figure 8-3 gives you several examples of the Format command. The first example shows you how to enter the command when the capacity of the diskette and the drive match up, as, for example, when you format a 3-1/2 inch high-density diskette in a 1.44MB drive. As you can see, no switches are required; the only parameter is the drive specification. Then, the command formats the diskette with the default format of the drive. This is the way you'll enter the command most of the time.

The next four examples in figure 8-3 show you how to enter this command when you want to use a drive with a higher capacity to format a diskette with a lower capacity. Here, the switches tell DOS what the formatting requirements are. In the second example, the /4 switch tells DOS the diskette capacity is only 360KB even though the drive capacity is 1.2MB. In the third example, the switches specify the number of tracks and sectors for a 720KB diskette. In the fourth and fifth examples, the /F switch that was introduced in DOS 4.0 simplifies the command syntax; you just specify the capacity of the diskette you're formatting, not the number of tracks and sectors it can contain. If you frequently use commands in any one of these forms, you may want to set up batch files for them so you don't have to remember how to enter the switches.

The sixth example in figure 8-3 shows how you can use the /Q switch introduced in DOS 5.0 to reformat a diskette quickly. When you use this switch, DOS doesn't format every track on the diskette. Instead, DOS just erases the directory and file entries on the diskette. This reduces the time required to reformat a previously formatted diskette. However, you can't use the /Q switch to format an unformatted

Example 1: How to format a diskette in the default format of the drive

```
C:\>format a:
```

Example 2: How to format a 360KB diskette in a 1.2MB drive

```
C:\>format a: /4
```

Example 3: How to format a 720KB diskette in a 1.44MB drive (DOS 3.2 and 3.3)

```
C:\>format a: /n:9 /t:80
```

Example 4: How to format a 720KB diskette in a 1.44MB drive or a 2.88MB drive (DOS 4.0 and later versions)

```
C:\>format a: /f:720
```

Example 5: How to format a 1.44MB diskette in a 2.88MB drive

```
C:\>format a: /f:1440
```

Example 6: How to reformat a diskette quickly (DOS 5.0 and 6.0)

```
C:\>format a: /q
```

Example 7: How to format a system diskette

```
C:\>format a: /s
```

Example 8: How to format a diskette and destroy any data it contains (DOS 5.0 and 6.0)

```
C:\>format a: /u
```

Figure 8-3 How to use the Format command

diskette. Because it doesn't do any actual formatting, it only works on previously formatted diskettes.

The seventh example in figure 8-3 shows you how to use the /S switch. When you use this switch with the Format command, it copies three DOS files from the hard disk to the diskette after it finishes formatting the diskette. One of the files is the COMMAND.COM file. The other two files are hidden files so they won't show up in a directory listing. When you use the /S switch, the default drive has to be the C drive, so DOS can find the three files it needs. After you format a diskette in this way, you can use it to boot DOS from the A drive. I'll explain more about this in a moment when I tell you about preparing a system diskette.

The last example in figure 8-3 shows you how to use the /U switch that was introduced with DOS 5.0. This switch causes all the data on the disk to be destroyed. With versions of DOS before 5.0, this was the default. With DOS 5.0 and 6.0, the default is to do a safe format, which leaves the data in place as I described earlier.

```
C:\>format a:
Insert new diskette for drive A:
and press ENTER when ready...

Checking existing disk format.
Saving UNFORMAT information.
Verifying 1.44M
Format complete.

Volume label (11 characters, ENTER for none)?

   1457664 bytes total disk space
   1457664 bytes available on disk

       512 bytes in each allocation unit.
      2847 allocation units available on disk.

Volume Serial Number is 3D39-12EE

Format another (Y/N)?n

C:\>
```

Figure 8-4 The operation of the Format command

Since a safe format protects you from destroying data unintentionally, I recommend you use the /U switch only for unformatted diskettes. In fact, you should always use this switch for unformatted diskettes because it reduces their formatting time dramatically.

Figure 8-4 shows the Format command in operation. When you issue the command, DOS prompts you to insert the diskette to be formatted into the disk drive. After you insert the diskette and close the drive door (if it has a door), you press the Enter key to start the formatting. As DOS formats the disk, it displays its progress. If you're using DOS 3.3 or earlier, it displays the track and side that's currently being formatted. If you're using DOS 4.0 or later, it displays the percent of the disk that has been formatted.

When DOS has completed the formatting operation, it displays storage information like that shown in figure 8-4. This information includes the total number of bytes on the diskette, the number of bytes in bad sectors (if any), and the number of bytes of available disk storage. If there are bad sectors on the diskette, you don't have to worry about them; DOS locks them out and doesn't use them to store data. In DOS 4.0 and later versions, DOS also displays information about the allocation units on the diskette.

After DOS has formatted one diskette, it asks if you want to format another. If you respond with a Y for Yes, DOS repeats the process I just described. If you have just opened a box of diskettes, it's often worth taking the time to format all of them.

With some versions of DOS, the Format command displays a message that asks you to supply a *volume label* for the diskette that's going to be formatted. You can see this message displayed in the middle of figure 8-4. Because you don't need to assign a volume label to a diskette, you can just press the Enter key to ignore the message.

If you're using DOS 5.0 or 6.0, you'll also see the group of messages at the beginning of the Format operation in figure 8-4. The message I want you to notice in particular is the second one, "Saving UNFORMAT information." This means that DOS is performing a safe format, as I described earlier.

The Diskcopy command Occasionally, you'll want to make a copy of an entire diskette. Then, you can use the Diskcopy command. Because this command copies the entire *source diskette*, whether it's filled with data or not, all data on the *target diskette* is destroyed. So choose your target diskette carefully. You should also know that you can't use this command to copy a diskette of one capacity onto a diskette of another capacity.

If you have two drives on your system, you enter this command as shown in the first example in figure 8-5. (I've shaded the Diskcopy commands in this figure so you can see them more easily.) Then, DOS tells you to put the source diskette (the diskette you want to copy) in the A drive and the target diskette (the diskette you want to create) in the B drive. When the copy operation is finished, DOS asks if you want to copy another diskette.

If you have only one drive on your system, you enter the command as shown in the second example in figure 8-5. After DOS tells you to put the source diskette in drive A, this command reads as much data as it can from the source diskette into internal memory. If, for example, your PC has 640KB of memory and you're copying a 360KB diskette, this command reads the entire diskette into internal memory. Next, the command asks you to remove the source diskette from the drive and insert the target diskette. When you do that, the data in memory is copied onto the target diskette. If the entire diskette can't be read into internal memory all at once, the command repeats this procedure until all the data has been copied to the target diskette.

With some versions of DOS, you can use an unformatted diskette for the target diskette of a Diskcopy command. For instance, all versions of PC-DOS will automatically format the target diskette if it's not already formatted. However, the versions of MS-DOS before 4.0 require that you format the target diskette before you use this command.

As I mentioned in the last chapter, you can also use the Xcopy command to copy all of the files from one diskette to another. Xcopy can be faster than Diskcopy if the diskette doesn't have many files. And Xcopy lets you copy files between diskettes with different capacities as long as there's enough space on the target diskette to accommodate all of the files on the source diskette.

The format of the Diskcopy command

```
DISKCOPY source-drive target-drive
```

Example 1

How to copy a diskette from one drive to another

```
C:\>diskcopy a: b:

Insert SOURCE diskette in drive A:

Insert TARGET diskette in drive B:

Press any key to continue . . .

Copying 80 tracks
18 sectors per track, 2 side(s)


Copy another diskette (Y/N)?n

C:\>
```

Example 2

How to copy a diskette using only one diskette drive

```
C:\>diskcopy a: a:

Insert SOURCE diskette in drive A:

Press any key to continue . . .

Copying 80 tracks
18 sectors per track, 2 side(s)

Insert TARGET diskette in drive A:

Press any key to continue . . .


Copy another diskette (Y/N)?n

C:\>
```

Figure 8-5 The operation of the Diskcopy command

Example 1: A Copy command that copies a file named PROJSUM.WK1 from the PROJECTB directory of the C drive to the diskette in the A drive.

```
C:\>copy \projectb\projsum.wk1 a:
```

Example 2: A Copy command that copies all the files in the BECKY directory on the C drive to the diskette in the A drive.

```
C:\>copy \becky\*.* a:
```

Example 3: A Copy command that copies all the files with the DOC extension from the current directory on the hard disk to the diskette in the A drive.

```
C:\DATA\MMA>copy *.doc a:
```

Figure 8-6 How to use the Copy command for copying selected files to a diskette

Three related skills

The Format and Diskcopy commands are the only new commands you need to know to work specifically with diskettes. Along with those commands, though, you should also know how to do the skills that follow.

How to use diskettes to transfer data from one PC to another Figure 8-6 shows you how to copy data from a hard disk to a diskette. The first example shows you how to copy just one file; the second example shows you how to use wildcards to copy all the files in a directory; and the third example shows you how to copy just the files in a directory that have a specific extension. Once you have the data copied to a diskette, you can use the Copy command to copy the data to the hard disk of another PC.

You should realize, though, that you can't use the Copy command to copy a file that is larger than the capacity of a single diskette. Similarly, you can't use this command to copy all the files in a directory if the files require more bytes than are available on a single diskette. In either case, the Copy command is cancelled when it tries to copy a file that requires more bytes than are in the remaining capacity of the diskette. To get around this limitation, you can use the Backup command that is presented in chapter 9.

You should also be aware of the compatibility problems you can encounter when you transfer files from one PC to another. The most obvious problem is trying to read a high- or extended-density diskette in a drive with a lower capacity. Although that won't work, you should remember that a higher-capacity drive is able to read a lower-capacity diskette. As a result, you shouldn't have any trouble transferring data from a PC with a 360KB drive to a PC with a higher-capacity drive.

When you want to transfer data from a higher-capacity drive to a lower-capacity drive, you should use the lower-capacity drive to do the formatting whenever possible. If the diskettes are formatted by the higher-capacity drive, they may be incompatible with the lower-capacity drive due to some technical differences in how the two types of drives do the formatting.

How to write-protect a diskette Occasionally, you may want to protect the files on a diskette so no one can delete them or destroy them by reformatting the diskette. You can provide this protection by *write-protecting* the diskette. Then, DOS can read data from the diskette, but it can't change the data on the diskette in any way.

Figure 8-7 shows how to write protect a diskette. For a 5-1/4 inch diskette, you cover the notch on the diskette with one of the write-protect tabs that comes with a box of diskettes. For a 3-1/2 inch diskette, you slide the plastic tab on the diskette up to open the write-protect window.

When you use a program or command that tries to write on a write-protected diskette, DOS displays a message like this:

```
Write protect error writing drive A
Abort, Retry, Fail?
```

If that happens, you can remove the write protection, put the diskette back in the drive, and reply with an *R* for retry. Or, you can reply with an *A* for abort. But you should never replace the write-protected diskette with another diskette and reply with an *R* for retry. If you do, the data won't be written in the right location on the replacement diskette. Although DOS won't alert you to the problem, it won't be able to retrieve the file correctly later on.

How to prepare a system diskette Normally, when you start your PC, it boots the DOS files it needs from the hard disk. Sometimes, though, you will want to boot your PC from a diskette. If, for example, something goes wrong with the hard disk, you may have to boot from a diskette to get your PC started again. For this purpose, you need a special type of diskette called a *system disk*, or *system diskette*. This diskette contains the files that DOS needs for getting itself started.

If you have DOS 3.3 or an earlier version, the easiest way to prepare a system diskette is to use the Diskcopy command to make a copy of the system diskette that DOS came with. For most versions of DOS, you'll use the diskette labelled "DOS diskette" or "DOS Operating Diskette." If you have a later version of DOS, you can't use the Diskcopy command to copy the system diskette that comes with DOS. Instead, you must use the installation program to create a system diskette.

Sometimes, you will want to customize your system diskette instead of making an exact duplicate of the DOS system diskette. For example, you may want to put just a few of the DOS commands on the diskette. Then, you'll have room on the diskette for a utility program or a small application program.

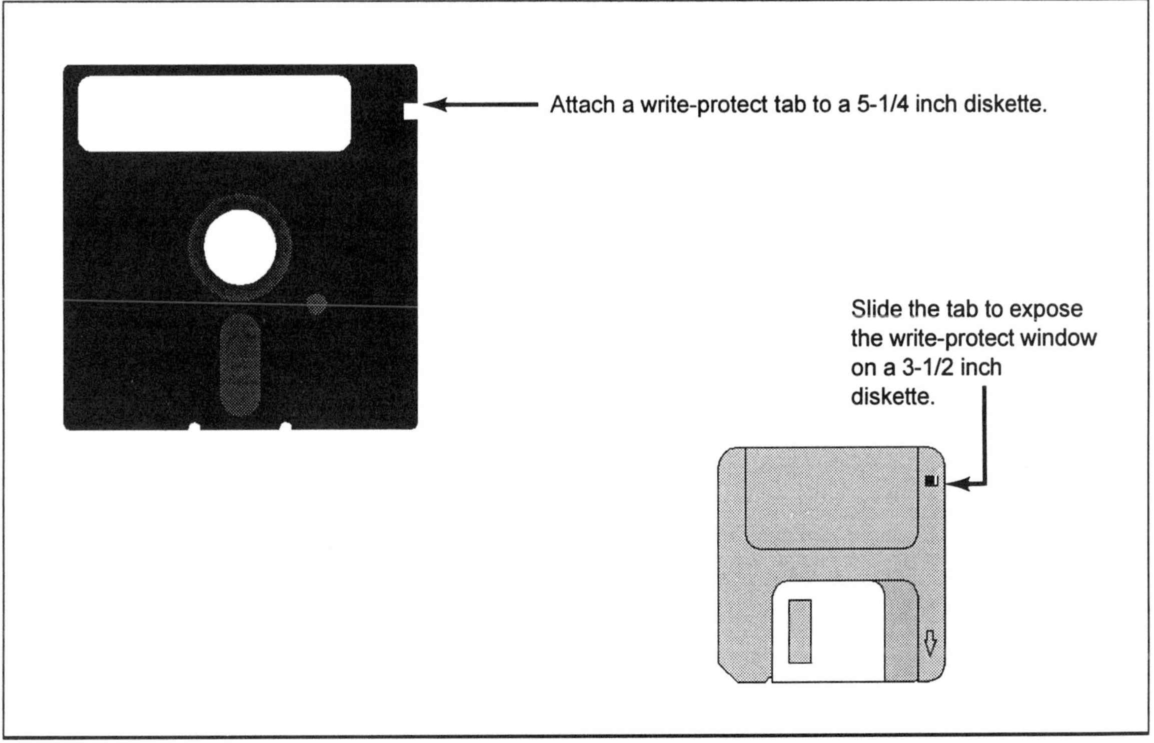
Attach a write-protect tab to a 5-1/4 inch diskette.
Slide the tab to expose the write-protect window on a 3-1/2 inch diskette.

Figure 8-7 How to write-protect a diskette

To customize a system diskette, you use the Format command with the /S switch (and any of the other switches you have to use), as in the seventh example in figure 8-3. Then, DOS copies three files onto the diskette: the COMMAND.COM file and two hidden files. After that, you can copy whatever DOS command files you want to use from the hard disk. You can also copy the program files for the utility or application programs that you want to put on the diskette. This procedure works with all versions of DOS.

Some perspective on diskettes for hard disk users

As I said at the start of this chapter, you shouldn't have much need for diskettes if you have a hard disk system. However, they're still the best medium for transferring data from one PC to another (unless your PC is connected to a network). And, as you'll learn in chapter 9, they're still the least expensive medium for backing up the data on a hard disk.

Terms

File Allocation Table
FAT
safe format
volume label
source diskette
target diskette
write-protection
system disk
system diskette

Objectives

1. Describe the differences between diskettes in terms of diskette size and capacity.
2. Given a double-density, a high-density, or an extended-density diskette, format it in a drive of the same or a higher capacity.
3. Given a diskette of any capacity, copy it in its entirety using one or two drives.
4. Given the specifications for one or more files that can be stored on a single diskette, transfer them from one PC to another. You should be able to do this even if one of the PCs has a higher capacity drive than the other one.
5. Given any type of diskette, write-protect the data on it.
6. Use the Format command to create a system diskette.

Exercises

1. Use the Directory command to display the directory of a diskette in the A drive. Next, if the diskette is unformatted or if you don't need any of the files on the diskette, use the Format command to format the diskette in the default format of your A drive. Then, use the Directory command to display the directory of the newly formatted diskette.
2. Use the Copy command to copy all of the files in a directory on the hard disk to a diskette in the A or B drive. If possible, choose a directory that exceeds the capacity of a single diskette. When the command is finished, use the Directory command to display the directory of the diskette.
3. Use the Diskcopy command to copy the files on the diskette you've just created to another diskette.
4. Use the Format command to create a system disk from your hard disk. Then, restart the PC with the system disk in the A drive to make sure that it works.

Chapter 9

How to back up a hard disk using the Backup command

Eventually, the hard disk on your PC will fail, and all of the data on it will be lost. This could happen the first month you have the disk drive, or it could happen after five years of heavy use. But even before it fails, you can lose all the data on the disk by an operational error like someone accidentally reformatting drive C. You can also lose all the data due to theft, fire, or vandalism.

Sooner or later, you'll also lose one or more of the files on your hard disk due to a programming or an operating error. If, for example, you're working on two proposals at the same time and you replace the first one on the disk with the second one, the first one is lost. Or, if while using the Delete command you accidentally delete all the files in the current directory when you meant to delete all of the files on the diskette in the A drive, dozens of files may be lost. Mistakes like that happen to even the most proficient PC users.

So think about it right now. Can you afford to lose all of the data on your hard disk? Can you afford to lose one of your largest and most important files? If you can't, you should protect yourself by *backing up* your hard disk to diskettes. Then, if a disaster happens, you can recover from it by *restoring* the diskette files to the hard disk.

In this chapter, you'll learn how to back up and restore the files on your hard disk using the DOS Backup and Restore commands that come with all versions of DOS before DOS 6.0. Since many PC users don't back up their disks regularly because backup takes too long, the emphasis will be on efficient backup procedures. After you learn how to use the Backup and Restore commands, you'll learn three ways to design your backups and six guidelines that will help you do your backups as quickly and as effectively as possible. Then, you'll learn about two hardware improvements and one software improvement that can make your backups even more efficient.

In DOS 6.0, the Backup command has been replaced by a backup utility called *Microsoft Backup*. If you upgrade to DOS 6.0 from an earlier version of DOS, the installation procedure will retain the Backup command on your system. But if you get DOS 6.0 on a new PC, you won't get the Backup command at all. That's no problem, because *Microsoft Backup* is far easier to use than the DOS commands. And, if you still need the Backup command, you can get it by purchasing the DOS 6.0 supplemental program diskette from Microsoft. (DOS 6.0 does include the Restore command. So if you've been backing up your data with the Backup command, you can still use the Restore command under DOS 6.0 to restore it.)

I'll present the *Microsoft Backup* utility in chapter 16. But even if you use this utility to do your backups, I recommend you read this chapter. That's because you need to know about the backup concepts and guidelines presented here, regardless of how you back up your system. However, you can skim over the details of using the DOS commands if you like.

Two types of backup

The key to efficient backups is realizing that there are two kinds of backups. These are illustrated in figure 9-1. Here, the system is backed up on Monday using a *full backup*. On the other days of the week, the system is backed up using an *incremental backup*.

Full backup Most computer users think of a full backup as a backup of every file on a drive. And, in fact, the term *full backup* is used quite often to mean just that. But a full backup doesn't have to include all the files on a drive. For example, it may consist of only the files in a single directory, or it may even consist of a single file. What distinguishes a full backup from other types of backups is that all the files you specify are backed up whether or not they've changed since the last backup. This will make more sense in a minute when I describe incremental backups. For now, keep in mind that when a hard disk fails, the full backup is the starting point for recovery.

In general, full backups are time consuming, particularly if they include all the files on a drive as in figure 9-1. If, for example, you have 20MB of files on a hard disk and you're using 1.2MB or 1.44MB diskettes, a full backup can take 30 minutes. And it will take even longer if you're using 360KB or 720KB diskettes. That's why you'll want to use some combination of full and incremental backups.

Incremental backup In contrast to a full backup, an incremental backup is a backup of just the files that have been created or changed since the last backup. This is illustrated in figure 9-1 by the procedures for Tuesday through Friday. Even if you have hundreds of files on your system, you probably use only a few files each day. As a result, incremental backups are much faster than full backups. On my PC, for example, I do an incremental backup of my hard drive each day before I leave the office, and that procedure usually takes less than 30 seconds.

Incremental backups are possible because the directory entry for each file on a DOS system has an *archive bit*. This bit indicates whether or not the file needs to be backed up. Whenever you create or change a file, this bit is set so the Backup command knows that the file should be backed up during an incremental backup. Then, when the Backup command is executed, all of the archive bits are reset so they

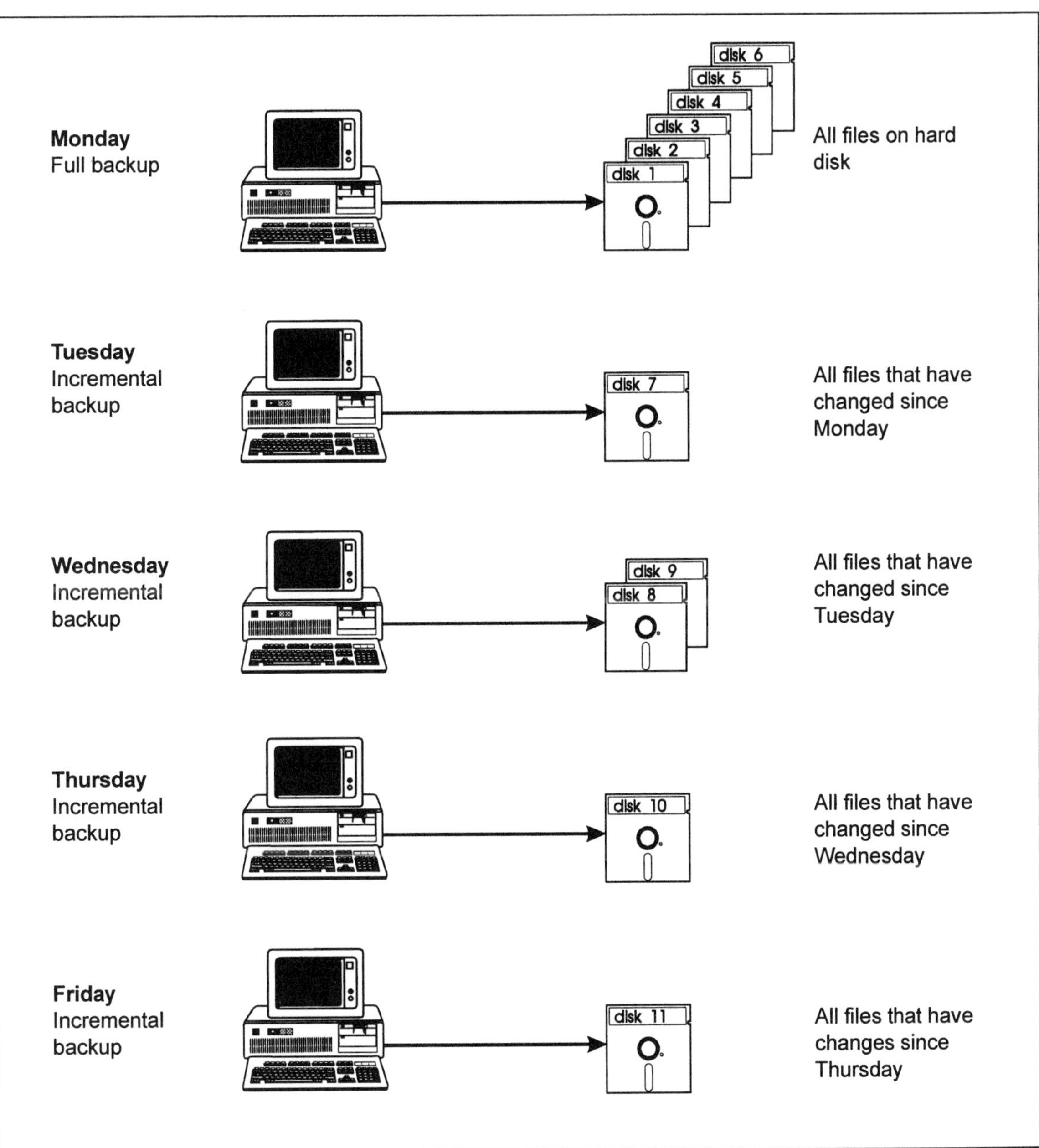

Figure 9-1 A weekly schedule of full and incremental backups

The format of the Backup command

```
BACKUP source-spec target-spec [/S] [/M] [/A] [/L] [/F]
```

Switch meanings

/S	Includes files that are in the subdirectories of the specified directory.
/M	Backs up only those files that have been modified since the last backup.
/A	Adds the new files to the files that are already on the backup diskette (DOS 3.3 or later).
/L	Creates a log file named BACKUP.LOG in the root directory of the source disk.
/F	Formats a backup diskette before using it if the diskette isn't already formatted. (DOS 3.3, but not 4.0 or later because this is done automatically by those versions of DOS.)

The format of the Restore command

```
RESTORE source-spec target-spec [/S]
```

Switch meaning

/S	Restores all files in all subdirectories.

Figure 9-2 The Backup and Restore commands

won't be backed up the next time. Usually, when you use an application program, only the data files that you work on are changed, so your program files aren't included in an incremental backup.

Two commands for backing up data and restoring it

Figure 9-2 summarizes the two DOS commands for backing up and restoring a hard disk. Although you should use the Backup command frequently, you only use the Restore command when you need to restore data to your hard disk.

The Backup command If you study the Backup command in figure 9-2, you can see that this command backs up the files in the source specification to the target specification. When you use this command, the source specification is for one or more files on the hard disk, while the target specification is a diskette drive. When the command is run, the files in the source specification are backed up to the diskette drive. Any data on the diskette in the drive is lost; it's overwritten by the backup data.

The format of the Backup command

```
BACKUP source-spec target-spec [/S] [/M] [/A] [/L] [/F]
```

Example 1: A Backup command that backs up all the files on a drive whether or not they've been changed since the last backup (full backup).

```
C:\>backup c:\*.* a: /s
```

Example 2: A Backup command that backs up only those files on a drive that have been changed since the last backup (separate incremental backup).

```
C:\>backup c:\*.* a: /s /m
```

Example 3: A Backup command that does an appended incremental backup of all the files on a drive (DOS 3.3 or later).

```
C:\>backup c:\*.* a: /s /m /a
```

Example 4: A Backup command that backs up all the files on a drive using unformatted diskettes (DOS 3.3 or later).

```
C:\>backup c:\*.* a: /s /f
```

Example 5: A Backup command that backs up all the files on a drive and creates a log file.

```
C:\>backup c:\*.* a: /s /l
```

Example 6: A Backup command that backs up all the files in one data directory.

```
C:\>backup c:\123\mma\*.* a:
```

Figure 9-3 How to use the Backup command

Figure 9-3 shows how to use the Backup command. Here, the first command does a full backup of the C drive. In this case, the /S switch is required because it tells DOS to include the files in all the subdirectories of the source specification. If the /S switch wasn't included, only the root directory would be backed up.

When a backup is in progress, DOS displays messages that tell you which diskette to insert into the drive next. For instance, a message like this is displayed when the command needs diskette number 3:

```
Insert backup diskette 03 in drive A:
WARNING! Files in the target drive
A:\ root directory will be erased
Press any key to continue . . .
```

As you can see, you need to label and number your backup diskettes so you can keep them organized.

The second example in figure 9-3 shows how to use the Backup command to do an incremental backup of all the files on the C drive. Here, the /S switch tells DOS to include subdirectories, and the /M switch tells it to do an incremental backup. Since I didn't include the /A switch in this example, the backed up files will be directed to a new diskette. This type of backup is called a *separate incremental backup*. If you look back to figure 9-1, you'll see that it illustrates separate incremental backups because each backup starts with a new diskette.

The third example in figure 9-3 shows the use of the /A switch. When it is used, DOS prompts you to insert the last backup diskette into the drive. Then, the backed up files are added to this diskette. Since this saves diskettes, you usually want to use this switch for incremental backups. Then, you can refer to the backup as an *appended incremental backup* because the new files are appended to the last diskette in the set. Remember, though, that you can only do an appended backup with a version of DOS that's 3.3 or later.

The fourth command in figure 9-3 shows you how to back up files to unformatted diskettes using DOS 3.3 and the /F switch. This switch causes DOS to format the diskettes as it backs up data to them. And it will work for either a full or an incremental backup. You don't need to use this switch if you're using DOS 4.0 or a later version of DOS because these versions automatically format unformatted diskettes before using them for a backup.

The fifth command in figure 9-3 shows the use of the /L switch for creating a log file. This file is a text file that contains the name of every file that is backed up along with the number of the diskette that the file is on. It's useful if you need to restore only a few selected files from a backup that consists of several diskettes. Then, you can find out what diskette the files are on by using the Type command to display the log file or the Print command to print it. Once you know what diskette a file is on, you can start the restore using that diskette instead of having to search through all the backup diskettes for the file.

The log file is named BACKUP.LOG, and it's stored in the root directory of the source drive. If the file already exists when the Backup command is issued, the new log is added to the end of the old log. Since you usually don't want that, you should delete the BACKUP.LOG file before using the Backup command with the /L switch.

The last command in figure 9-3 shows you how to back up just one directory on a hard disk. This is useful when you work on the files in only one directory. And it's usually better than the DOS Copy command because the Backup command will use as many diskettes as are needed for the backup operation. It will also back up a single file that is so large it can't be stored on a single diskette. In contrast, the Copy command stops as soon as the first diskette is full.

If you use the Directory command to display the root directory of a backup diskette, you'll realize that the Backup command doesn't work at all like a Copy command. Instead of one entry for each file that has been backed up, you'll find just two directory entries for an entire backup diskette. One entry is for a file named BACKUP; the other is for a file named CONTROL. The first file contains all the files

The format of the Restore command

```
RESTORE source-spec target-spec [/S]
```

Example 1: A Restore command that restores all the files from a full backup of a drive.

```
C:\>restore a: c:\*.* /s
```

Example 2: A Restore command that restores all the files from a backup of the QA4\DATA directory.

```
C:\>restore a: c:\qa4\data\*.*
```

Example 3: A Restore command that restores a single file from a full backup of all the files on a drive.

```
C:\>restore a: c:\account\dist5.dbf
```

Figure 9-4 How to use the Restore command

that have been backed up to the diskette; the second one contains control information that is required for the proper operation of the Backup and Restore commands. Both file names have a 3-digit extension that identifies the sequence of the backup diskette. For example, on the first backup diskette, the file extensions are .001; on the second diskette, .002; and so on. Note that if you do appended incremental backups, these sequence numbers are continued when you use a new diskette. But each separate incremental backup begins again with sequence 001. One way DOS uses these file extensions is to make sure that you insert the backup diskettes in the correct sequence when you're restoring files.

The Restore command Because the Backup command stores data in a special format, you must use the Restore command to restore files that have been backed up. You can't use the Copy command.

The first example in figure 9-4 shows you how to use the Restore command if you want to restore all of the files from a full backup of the C drive. Because the /S switch is used, this command will restore the files in all of the subdirectories. If you insert all of the backup diskettes in the sequence they were created, this command restores all the files from a full backup as well as all the files from the appended incremental backups that were done after the full backup. If the incremental backups are on separate diskettes, however, the restore operation stops at the end of the full backup. Then, you have to issue the same Restore command again for each incremental diskette to restore the most recent versions of all your files.

The second example in figure 9-4 shows you how to use this command if you want to restore the files from just one directory of a backup. Because this command is entered in an unusual way, you should take a moment to study it. As you can see, the A drive is given as the source drive, just as you would expect. However, the directory that you want restored from the A drive is given in the target specification. In this example, all the files in the QA4\DATA directory are restored. Note that the *.* designation is included in the target specification so that DOS knows it's a directory name, not a file name. Also note that you must specify the directory you want to restore whether the backup consists of all the files on the drive or only the files from one directory, as in the example. When the Restore command is executed, the restored files are always stored in the directory that they were backed up from.

If you've done appended incremental backups, a Restore command for a directory will restore all the files in the directory from the full backup as well as any applicable files from the incremental backups. However, if the incremental backups are on separate diskettes, you'll have to issue additional Restore commands for those diskettes. That way, you'll be sure you've restored the most recent versions of all the files in the directory.

The third example in figure 9-4 shows you how to use the Restore command if you want to restore just one file from a full backup. As you can see, the A drive is given as the source drive, and the path and name of the file that you want restored from the A drive are given in the target specification. Again, the restored file is always stored in the directory that it was backed up from.

Whether you restore one file or many, the Restore command has you insert each diskette from your set of backup diskettes. As a result, if you're restoring only one file, you may spend several minutes inserting diskettes before you get to the one that has the file you want restored.

An alternative is to use a log file to find out what backup diskette contains the file you want to restore. Then, you can speed up the restoration process by inserting just the diskette that contains that file. If that diskette is other than the first one, DOS will display a message telling you that the diskette is out of sequence. However, this is only a warning message; DOS lets you continue with the diskette simply by pressing the Enter key. Of course, to use a log file, you must have created one when you did the backup you're using for the restore operation. Although a log file may be useful in this situation, if you don't need to restore single files often, it may not be worth the trouble to create and use one.

When you're restoring a single file, the Restore command works a little differently than it does when you're restoring a full directory or drive. Even if you use appended incremental backups, DOS doesn't look on all the backup diskettes for the file you're restoring. Instead, it stops the restore operation when it comes to the end of the first diskette that contains the file. Even though that diskette may contain more than one version of the file, it may not contain the most recent version. To make sure you get the most recent version, you have to issue a Restore command for each diskette that contains incremental backup data in the order they were backed up. If you used appended incremental backups, that means you'll start each restore operation with a diskette other than the first one. So when DOS tells you the diskette is out of sequence, just press the Enter key.

Even if it takes several minutes to restore a file, you'll be delighted to discover that the file has been restored, and you haven't lost all the hard work that went into it. If you ever have to restore hundreds of files, you'll be thankful indeed that you took the time to do an effective job of backing up your hard disk.

Three ways to back up your hard disk

To make your backups as tolerable as possible, you should design them so they're as efficient and easy as possible. That almost certainly means you should use incremental backups in combination with full backups. But that can also mean you should do two different sets of backups: one for program files and one for data files.

Here, then, are three practical ways to run your backups. If you're like most PC users, one of these methods will be appropriate for your system. If you don't use your system often enough to justify daily backups, you can use the same methods on a less frequent backup schedule.

Daily backup of all files If you want to keep your backups as simple as possible, don't distinguish between program and data files. Then, you can back up your hard disk by doing a full backup of all the files on the first day of each month or each week and an incremental backup of all the files on the other days of the month or week. That way, all the files on your hard disk are backed up daily.

However, because program files usually don't change, you spend more time doing backups than you need to when you use this method. If, for example, your hard disk has 6MB of files on it but only 2MB of data files, you're backing up 4MB of files unnecessarily. To improve the efficiency of your backups, you can use one of the two methods that follow.

Daily backup of data drive and periodic backup of program drive On my PC, all the program files are stored on drive C, and all the data files are stored on drive D. Then, I do a full backup of drive C once a month, and I don't do daily incremental backups for this drive. In contrast, I do a full backup for drive D on every Monday, and I do daily incremental backups for this drive the rest of the week. By using separate backup procedures for the program drive and the data drive, my total backup time for the month is less than 30 minutes.

If you buy a new PC or a hard disk, you can easily set up the drives so you can use this method of backup. I'll explain how to do that in chapter 22. But it's time consuming to set up the drives in this way after you've used a PC for a while. Often, it takes several hours to back up the hard disk, repartition it into two or more drives, and restore the old files to the new drives. As a result, you may be better off using a different backup method.

Daily backup of data directories and periodic backup of program directories If you commonly work within several data directories, you can sometimes simplify your backup procedures by reorganizing your directories. If, for

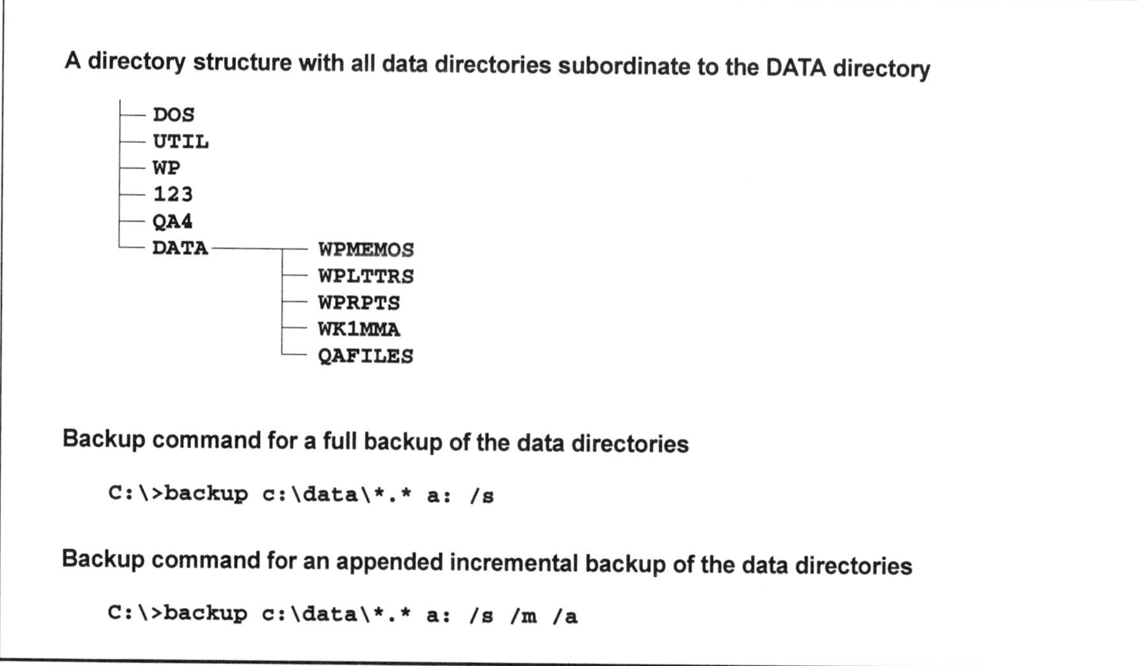
A directory structure with all data directories subordinate to the DATA directory

```
├── DOS
├── UTIL
├── WP
├── 123
├── QA4
└── DATA ──┬── WPMEMOS
           ├── WPLTTRS
           ├── WPRPTS
           ├── WK1MMA
           └── QAFILES
```

Backup command for a full backup of the data directories

```
C:\>backup c:\data\*.* a: /s
```

Backup command for an appended incremental backup of the data directories

```
C:\>backup c:\data\*.* a: /s /m /a
```

Figure 9-5 A directory structure that can simplify backups

example, all of your data directories are subordinate to one data directory as shown in figure 9-5, you can back them up using one command for a full backup and another one for an incremental backup. By combining a backup procedure for the entire hard disk with a backup procedure for the DATA directory and its subordinates, you can reduce the time you spend doing your daily backups.

Six guidelines for simple and reliable backups

Now that you know how to back up your hard disk, here are six guidelines for simple and reliable backups. They are summarized in figure 9-6.

Set a schedule for your backups Because backing up a hard disk takes time away from your other activities, it's always tempting to skip your backup procedure for a day, a week, or a month. Even if you're doing incremental backups that take less than a minute each, it's tempting to skip them. Before long, you won't even remember the last time you did a backup.

That's why it's important to set a schedule for your backups. How often should you do them? That depends on how much you use your system. If, for example, you use your system more than four hours a day, you should probably do daily backups. If you use your system just an hour or two a day, you can perhaps get by with weekly

1. Set a schedule for your backups.
2. Use batch files to automate your backups.
3. Delete unnecessary files before you do a full backup.
4. Keep your diskettes organized.
5. Keep a log of your backups.
6. Consider keeping two sets of backups.

Figure 9-6 Six guidelines for simple and reliable backups

backups, but you're going to be better off with daily backups. As a rule of thumb, you should schedule your backups so you'll never lose more work than you can afford to lose when a disk failure occurs. Then, you should stick to your schedule.

If you do one backup for program files and one for data files, you should set a separate schedule for each type of backup. For instance, you can schedule program backups once a month and data backups daily.

If you want to schedule both full and incremental backups, you can set full backups for a day like the first day of each month, the first day of each week, the last day of each month, or the last day of each week. Just schedule your full backups on days that usually provide the free time you need for this task. Then, schedule incremental backups on the other days. But if you don't want to schedule days for full backups, you can just do them whenever the number of diskettes you've used for incremental backups gets unwieldy.

Use batch files to automate your backups Once you've designed and scheduled your backups, you should put the commands in batch files to make them easier to use. In figure 9-7, for example, you can see one batch file for a full backup of the C drive and one for an incremental backup. Once you create these files, you don't have to remember the details for entering the Backup command each time you do a backup. Instead, you can execute these batch files from the command prompt or from a shell program.

Delete unnecessary files before you do a full backup Often, it's quicker and easier to delete unnecessary files than it is to back them up. So before you start a full backup, it's worth taking a few minutes to see if your hard disk has any directories or files that you no longer need. If you find some and delete them, your backups will run more quickly, and your directories and files will be more manageable.

Example 1: A batch file that does a full backup of drive C.

```
BACKFULL.BAT

backup c:\*.* a: /s
```

Example 2: A batch file that does an incremental backup of drive C.

```
BACKINC.BAT

backup c:\*.* a: /s /m /a
```

Figure 9-7 Two batch files for backups

Keep your diskettes organized This is obvious, but I think it's worth mentioning. By all means keep your diskettes organized by labelling and numbering your backup diskettes and your diskette boxes. That way, you'll be able to run your backups as efficiently as possible. Also, if you ever have to use the Restore command, you'll be able to present the diskettes in the proper sequence so the command will work the way you want it to.

In general, the label for a backup diskette should indicate the drive or directory that the backup is for. It should also give the sequence number of the diskette within the backup procedure. However, a diskette label shouldn't indicate whether it is for a full or incremental backup. If, for example, the full backup ended with diskette 6 and the first incremental backup started with diskette 7, you shouldn't indicate this on the diskette labels. And you shouldn't write the date of the backup on the labels. Instead, because this information is likely to change with each backup you do, you should record it in a backup log.

Keep a log of your backups When you use more than one type of backup, you can easily lose track of what type of backup you should be doing and which diskette you should start with. That's why you should keep a log of the backups you run. You don't need anything elaborate for this, so a simple form like the one in figure 9-8 will do.

In this log, you can see that the PC user does a full backup of the C drive on the last work day of the month. That backup includes both program and data directories, so it protects against a complete failure of the hard disk. For the rest of the month, the user does a full backup of just the data directories on each Monday and incremental backups of just the data directories on the other days of the week. By using a separate procedure for backing up data files, the user can keep backup time to a minimum and never be in danger of losing more than a day's work. But without a backup log, a system like this can get out of control.

Backup Log			
Date	**Drive/Path**	**Backup Type**	**Last disk**
3/30	C:	Full	12
4/2	C:\data	Full	2
4/3		Incremental	3
4/4			3
4/5			3
4/6			4
4/9	C:\data	Full	2
4/10		Incremental	3
4/11			3
4/12			4
4/13			4
4/16	C:\data	Full	2
4/17		Incremental	3
4/18			3
4/19			3
4/20			3
4/23	C:\data	Full	2
4/24		Incremental	3
4/25			3
4/26			3
4/27			3
4/30	C:	Full	12
5/1	C:\data	Full	2
5/2		Incremental	3
5/3			4
5/4			4

Figure 9-8 A simple backup log

Consider keeping two sets of backups As you use diskettes, occasionally you'll find that one you've used in the past without any trouble has become unreadable. If that happens to one of the diskettes in your backup set, it means you can't restore the data from that diskette. So you may want to keep two backup sets for your hard drive. When you have two sets of backups, you alternate the sets each time you do a backup. If, for example, you do full backups weekly and incremental backups daily, you use a different backup set each week.

If you decide to keep a second set of backups, the label for each diskette should indicate which backup set it's a part of. And you should record which set you're using for each backup on your backup log. It's also a good idea to keep each backup set in a different place. For example, you can keep one set in your desk, and the second set in the office safe. Then, if one whole set is destroyed, you still have the second set.

Two hardware improvements that can simplify backups

If your backups take so long that you often skip them, you should do whatever you can to make them quicker and easier. One way to make an improvement in your backup procedures is to add a new hardware component to your system. Two components that can help are a high-capacity diskette drive and a backup tape drive.

A high-capacity diskette drive If you don't already have a high-capacity diskette drive on your system, buying one can quickly improve backups. Since the 1.2MB diskettes have about four times the capacity of the 360KB diskettes, you only have to use one-fourth as many diskettes. Similarly, you only have to use one-half as many diskettes if you add a 1.44MB diskette drive to a PC with only a 720KB drive, and a 2.88MB drive will cut that number by half again. At a price of about $100 for a 1.44MB drive or $225 for a 2.44MB drive, this purchase can simplify your backups so you're more likely to do them as scheduled.

A backup tape drive Backup tape drives are becoming more and more popular all the time. That's because they're faster and have far larger capacities than diskettes. In fact, if you get a tape drive with a large enough capacity, you can run a full backup unattended because you don't have to insert diskettes as the backup program runs. You can also set up the backup program so it runs automatically after you've gone home.

A backup tape drive records data on a special high-capacity tape that's enclosed in a removable cartridge. Most tape drives fit in the space allocated for a diskette drive in the systems unit of a PC. The two most common tape drives for individual PCs are 120MB drives, available for about $200, and 250MB drives, for about $300. At these prices, a tape drive can easily justify its cost by reducing the time and trouble of doing regular backups.

The only drawback to tape is that *Microsoft Backup*, the backup utility in DOS 6.0, doesn't support it. However, most tape drives come with their own backup utility. And most commercial backup utilities support tape drives.

How a commercial backup utility can improve backups

If your backup requirements are simple, the DOS Backup and Restore commands may be all that you need. For most PC users who don't have DOS 6.0, however, a commercial *backup utility* like *Central Point Backup*, *Fastback Plus*, or *Norton Backup* will pay for itself in less than a year. In general, backup utility programs are much faster than the DOS commands, and they're also easier to use. But, as with hardware improvements, the most important benefit of a backup utility is not the time you save by using one. It's the fact that you're far more likely to do scheduled backups because they take less time.

As you'll see in chapter 16, the DOS 6.0 backup utility, *Microsoft Backup*, is far more flexible and easier to use than the DOS Backup and Restore commands. But it still isn't as fast as most commercial backup utilities, and it doesn't support tape backup. So even if you have DOS 6.0, you may still be interested in getting a commercial backup utility. You'll be better able to decide that after you've learned to use *Microsoft Backup*.

If you don't have DOS 6.0 but you're thinking about getting a commercial backup utility, I suggest you read chapter 16 on *Microsoft Backup. I*t will give you some idea of what a backup utility has to offer. And, if you're considering upgrading to DOS 6.0 for some of its other features, you may decide that *Microsoft Backup* will be an adequate backup utility for you.

Terms

backing up a hard disk
restoring a hard disk
full backup
incremental backup
archive bit
separate incremental backup
appended incremental backup
log file
backup utility

Objectives

1. Explain the difference between a full backup and an incremental backup.
2. Explain the difference between a separate incremental backup and an appended incremental backup.
3. Use the Backup command to do a full backup of a specified drive or directory, with or without subdirectories.
4. Use the Backup command to do a separate incremental backup or an appended incremental backup of a specified drive or directory, with or without subdirectories.
5. Use the Restore command to restore an entire set of backup diskettes, a directory, or a file.
6. Describe an efficient method of backup for your PC and your work habits.
7. Explain how a commercial backup utility can improve backup procedures.

Exercises

1. Use the Backup command to do a full backup of all the files in one of the data directories of your hard disk to diskettes in the A drive. Next, use the Directory command to display the directories of the backup diskettes.
2. Modify one of the files that you backed up in exercise 1, but not a file that you can't afford to lose. Then, do an incremental backup of all the files in the data directory that you used for exercise 1.
3. Delete the file that you modified in exercise 2. Then, use the Restore command to restore the modified version of it.
4. Run a full backup of all the files on the hard disk and record the time that it takes. Also, record the details of the backup using a simple backup log like the one in figure 9-8.
5. Using the methods and guidelines given in this chapter, evaluate your backup needs and establish backup procedures for your system. If you've read chapter 6, create batch files for the Backup commands required by your procedure.

Chapter 10

How to prevent, detect, and recover from disk problems and user errors

As I mentioned in the last chapter, all disk drives will eventually fail. When that happens, the result is often the loss of all data on the drive. However, many disk drive problems are not so catastrophic. Sometimes, a small portion of the disk recording surface becomes unusable. This doesn't make the entire drive fail, but data can't be stored reliably in the unusable portion of the disk.

Besides physical failures, programming errors and user errors can cause you to lose data. A programming error or a power failure can also corrupt the DOS directory structure, which can also cause you to lose data. When any of these situations occur, you may be able to recover the data using the DOS recovery commands you'll learn in this chapter. After you read this chapter, though, I hope you'll realize that the best way to protect your hard disk files is to back them up on a regular basis.

How to use the Label command to prevent an accidental reformatting of your hard disk

In chapter 8, I mentioned that you can accidentally reformat your hard disk if you specify the wrong drive when you use the Format command. That shouldn't happen if you pay attention to the messages, but it's possible. And, if you're using a version of DOS before 5.0, all of the files on the drive are lost.

With DOS versions 3.2 to 4.0, you can prevent an accidental reformatting by putting a *volume label* on each drive of a hard disk. Normally, you do this when you format the hard disk. To find out if the drives on your hard disk have volume labels, you can use the Volume command. If they don't have labels, you can use the Label command to put them on the drives after they've been formatted.

Figure 10-1 shows you how to use the Volume and Label commands. The information that's displayed when you enter the Volume command depends on the version of DOS you're using. If you're using DOS 4.0, the Volume command displays the volume label, if there is one, and the volume serial number. But before DOS 4.0, disk drives weren't assigned volume serial numbers, so only the volume label is displayed.

When you enter the Label command, DOS asks you for the volume label. A volume label can have up to 11 characters, and I recommend you use as many of those characters as you can so it won't be easy for someone else to duplicate the label by accident. In figure 10-1, I used DISK1-VOL1 as the label for the C drive. If you have more than one drive on your hard disk, be sure to put a different volume label on each of the drives. Once you've put a volume label on a drive, you can't reformat it without entering the label, as illustrated in the bottom of figure 10-1. Although DOS 5.0 and 6.0 don't provide this safeguard, these versions have other features that will help prevent the loss of data. I'll discuss those features later in this chapter.

How to use the Check-disk command to detect and fix disk problems

In chapter 4, I showed you how to use the Check-disk command to find out the capacities of a PC's hard disk and internal memory. I also pointed out that this command summarizes the number of bad sectors on each drive. What I didn't mention in chapter 4 is that the Check-disk command also summarizes other types of disk errors. And it can help you fix some types of errors.

When DOS stores a file on a hard disk, it divides each file into small pieces called *allocation units*. (In versions of DOS before 4.0, allocation units are referred to as *clusters*.) Each allocation unit consists of a group of sectors. The number of sectors in each allocation unit depends on the size of the disk. To keep track of these allocation units, DOS uses a special area of the hard disk called the *File Allocation Table*, or *FAT*. If this table becomes inaccurate due to a hardware or a software problem, DOS isn't able to correctly access all of the files on the hard disk.

When you run the Check-disk command, it checks the FAT for errors. If it finds any, it displays error messages. Two types of problems that you should be aware of are *lost allocation units* and *cross-linked files*.

What to do if CHKDSK reports lost allocation units *Lost allocation units* are allocation units that the FAT says contain data, but that aren't part of any file. Usually, they're created when you turn off your PC before exiting from a program or when you press the Ctrl+Alt+Delete keys to restart your PC while a program is running. Since both of these actions are fairly common, lost allocation units are fairly common. In fact, lost allocation units account for most of the errors detected by the Check-disk command.

Figure 10-2 illustrates the messages displayed by the Check-disk command when it detects one or more lost allocation units. Here, the command found 412 lost allocation units in eight chains. Since a *chain* is a sequence of related allocation units, all of the allocation units in a chain are usually related to the same file. That's why the last of the error messages in figure 10-2 asks if DOS should convert the lost chains to

How to find out if a hard drive has a label

```
C:\>vol

Volume in drive C has no label
Volume Serial Number is 1A24-7880

C:\>
```

How to label an unlabelled hard drive (DOS 3.2 and later)

```
C:\>label

Volume in drive C has no label

Volume label (11 characters, ENTER for none)?disk1-vol1

C:\>
```

How a volume label can prevent an accidental reformatting of a hard drive (DOS 3.2 to 4.0)

```
C:\>format c:
Enter current volume label for drive C:
Invalid Volume ID
Format terminated

C:\>
```

Figure 10-1 How to use the Volume and Label commands

files. However, DOS won't do the conversion even if you answer with the letter Y. Before DOS can convert the chains, you have to rerun the Check-disk command using the /F switch.

When you rerun the command using the /F switch, DOS converts the eight chains to the eight files listed in part 2 of figure 10-2 starting with FILE0001.CHK. These files are stored in the root directory of the drive that the chains were on. Then, you can display each of the eight files to see whether it contains data that is still useful. If it does, rename the file and move it to an appropriate data directory. If it doesn't, delete the file. Usually, the chains don't contain data that you need anymore, but sometimes they do. That's more likely to happen if you discover the allocation units right after they become lost.

What to do if CHKDSK reports cross-linked files *Cross-linked files* occur when the FAT indicates that one or more allocation units belong to two or more

A Check-disk command that reports lost allocation units

```
C:\>chkdsk

Volume DISK1-VOL1  created 01-15-1993 2:34p
Volume Serial Number is 1A24-7880

Errors found, F parameter not specified.
Corrections will not be written to disk.

412 lost allocation units found in 8 chains
Convert lost chains to files (Y/N)?n

 170266624 bytes total disk space
     86016 bytes in 3 hidden files
    348160 bytes in 76 directories
 105775104 bytes in 2513 user files
  64057344 bytes available on disk

      4096 bytes in each allocation unit
     41569 total allocation units on disk
     15639 available allocation units on disk

    655360 total bytes memory
    497136 bytes free

C:\>
```

A Check-disk command that converts the lost chains to files using the /F switch

```
C:\>chkdsk /f

Volume DISK1-VOL1  created 01-15-1993 2:34p
Volume Serial Number is 1A24-7880

412 lost allocation units found in 8 chains
Convert lost chains to files (Y/N)?y
```

Figure 10-2 What to do when the Check-disk command reports lost allocation units (part 1 of 2)

files at the same time. Then, when the Check-disk command checks the FAT, it discovers this type of error and displays error messages like those in figure 10-3. Here, a file named 1CHOICE.SCR is cross linked with a file named WORKS.EPS.

The files created from the eight lost chains

```
FILE0001.CHK
FILE0002.CHK
FILE0003.CHK
FILE0004.CHK
FILE0005.CHK
FILE0006.CHK
FILE0007.CHK
FILE0008.CHK
```

What to do with the files created from the lost chains

1. Display the files to see if they contain anything useful, and rename them if they do.
2. Delete all the files that you haven't renamed.

Figure 10-2 What to do when the Check-disk command reports lost allocation units (part 2 of 2)

Although the Check-disk command can detect cross-linked files, it can't correct them. So you have to correct them yourself by using the steps summarized in figure 10-3. If you have backup copies of the cross-linked files, restore them and the problem may disappear. But if you didn't detect this problem early enough, the backup copies may be corrupted too. Then, you can try to restore the files from earlier copies. Or, if any of the cross-linked files are program files, you can copy them back onto the system from the original program diskettes.

If you can't restore the files from backup copies, you can correct the cross linking by copying the cross-linked files. Since the copied files won't be cross linked, you can then delete the cross-linked versions. However, at least one of the copied files will be damaged. As a result, you'll have to use the appropriate application program to carefully examine the copied files, and then do what you can to repair them.

What to do if CHKDSK reports other errors Lost allocation units and cross-linked files are the most common types of errors that the Check-disk command reports, so they're the only ones I'll present in this chapter. If the Check-disk command reports other types of errors, you can turn to the section on error messages in your DOS manual for an explanation of the message. Even if the explanation doesn't make much sense to you, you should be able to figure out whether the /F switch can help correct the problem. If it can, run the command again with the /F switch on.

If the problem can't be fixed, you have to reformat the hard disk. This corrects all problems by creating a new File Allocation Table. Then, you have to restore the files that were on the disk from your backup diskettes.

Why you shouldn't use the DOS Recover command for fixing bad sectors

When you format a hard disk or a diskette, DOS locks out the *bad sectors* that are already on the disk. When you run the Check-disk command, it summarizes the bad sectors that were locked out when the disk was formatted. This is nothing to be concerned about because hard disks come from the manufacturer with bad sectors.

Instead, it's the bad sectors that aren't locked out that you have to worry about. These are the sectors that go bad as you use the disk. When part of a file is stored in one of these sectors, DOS either won't be able to access some of the data in the file, or it won't be able to access the file at all.

Although versions of DOS before 6.0 provide a Recover command that looks like it could be used to recover data from bad sectors, you shouldn't use it for two reasons. First, you can use this command only after you discover a file is damaged, so some or all of the data is lost already. Second, if you give a drive specification instead of a file specification as the parameter, this command tries to recover the entire drive. To start, it removes all the directories on the drive and moves all the files into the root directory. Then, it renames all of the files on the drive in sequence starting with FILE001.REC. The only way to recover from this disaster is to restore the entire drive from your backup diskettes.

Since this second reason is so compelling, I suggest that you remove the Recover command from your system. To do that, just delete the file named RECOVER.COM from your DOS directory. If you have more than an occasional disk problem that you need to recover from, you should buy an advanced disk utility.

How to use DOS 5.0 and 6.0 commands for recovering from user errors

DOS 5.0 has three helpful commands you can use to recover files that you've lost because of user errors. The Undelete command lets you recover files that you deleted accidentally. The Unformat command lets you recover data from a hard disk that you formatted accidentally. And the Mirror command improves the success of the Undelete and Unformat commands.

DOS 6.0 also includes the Undelete and Unformat commands, but the Mirror command has been dropped. If you upgraded to DOS 6.0 from an earlier version of DOS, the Mirror command will still be available. If you purchased your computer with DOS 6.0 already installed, you must order the DOS 6.0 supplemental program diskette to obtain the Mirror command. DOS 6.0 includes most of the functions of the Mirror command with the Delete and Format commands. I'll cover the new function of the DOS 6.0 Undelete command separately after I show you how to use the DOS 5.0 and 6.0 Undelete command to recover files. And I'll tell you about the new function of the Format command when I present the Unformat command.

How to use the Undelete command to recover files The Undelete command can often recover a file because DOS doesn't actually erase a file's contents when it deletes it. Instead, DOS changes the first character of the directory entry for

A Check-disk command that reports cross-linked files

```
C:\>chkdsk

Volume DISK1-VOL1  created 01-15-1993 2:34p
Volume Serial Number is 1A24-7880

Errors found, F parameter not specified.
Corrections will not be written to disk.

C:\HSG\1CHOICE.SCR
   is cross linked on allocation unit 5812
C:\HSG\WORKS.EPS
   is cross linked on allocation unit 5812

170266624 bytes total disk space
     86016 bytes in 3 hidden files
    348160 bytes in 76 directories
 105775104 bytes in 2513 user files
  64057344 bytes available on disk

      4096 bytes in each allocation unit
     41569 total allocation units on disk
     15639 available allocation units on disk

    655360 total bytes memory
    497136 bytes free

C:\>
```

How to fix the cross-linked files

1. If you have backup copies of the files, restore them. Then, check to see whether the backup copies were cross linked too.
2. If the files are still cross linked, restore them from earlier backup copies.
3. If the files are still cross linked, copy the files and delete the original versions. The copied files won't be cross linked, but at least one of them will be damaged.

Figure 10-3 What to do when the Check-disk command reports cross-linked files

the file to indicate that the file has been deleted. DOS also changes the File Allocation Table to indicate that the disk space occupied by the file is available for use. But the file's contents stay in that space until DOS writes over the space with another file. When you use the Undelete command, it restores the directory entry and the File Allocation Table to the way they were before the file was deleted.

The format of the Undelete command for recovering files

```
UNDELETE [file-spec]
```

How to undelete all batch files in the current directory

```
C:\>undelete *.bat

UNDELETE - A delete protection facility
Copyright (C) 1987-1993 Central Point Software, Inc.
All rights reserved.

Directory: C:\
File Specifications: AUTOEXEC.BAT

    Delete Sentry control file not found.

    Deletion-tracking file not found.

    MS-DOS directory contains    1 deleted files.
    Of those,    1 files may be recovered.

Using the MS-DOS directory method.

      ?UTOEXEC BAT      344  1-08-93  3:43p  ...A  Undelete (Y/N)?y
      Please type the first character for ?UTOEXEC.BAT: a

File successfully undeleted.


C:\>
```

Figure 10-4 How to use the Undelete command to recover files

Beginning with DOS 3.3, DOS uses an improved method for allocating disk space to files. With this new method, DOS is less likely to write another file over the disk space occupied by a deleted file. So your chances of recovering a deleted file are improved.

Figure 10-4 shows how you use the Undelete command to recover files. Here, I used a wildcard file specification to undelete all batch files in the current directory. Because DOS replaces the first character of a file name with a delete character when the file is deleted, DOS lists each deleted file using a question mark for the first character as shown here. This means that DOS doesn't know what the first character of the file name should be.

So when you answer with the letter Y to indicate that you want to undelete the file, the command asks you to enter the first character of the file name. After you do that, DOS tries to undelete the file. In this example, the command was successful.

If an undelete function isn't successful, the command attempts to recover as much of the file as possible. Then, you can load the file using the program you used to create it so you can fix the file. Since this is a tedious process, you probably won't want to use this procedure unless the file is critical and you don't have a backup copy of it.

The more you use your PC after you delete a file, the less chance there is that you'll be able to undelete that file successfully. So as soon as you realize that you accidentally deleted a file, you should try to undelete it.

How to use the DOS 6.0 Undelete command to improve file recovery

If you're using DOS 6.0, you can also use the Undelete command to help improve the odds of recovering a deleted file. The Undelete command provides two levels of protection above the standard protection provided by DOS: delete tracking level and delete sentry level. When you use the *delete tracking* function of Undelete, it loads a *memory resident program* that keeps track of the file name and File Allocation Table information for files you delete. That way, you can almost always recover a file as long as DOS hasn't put another file in the deleted file's disk space.

When you use the *delete sentry* function of Undelete, it loads a memory resident program that provides even greater protection than the delete tracking function. If you delete a file with delete sentry in effect, the memory resident program moves the file to another location in a hidden directory named SENTRY. Then, if you need to recover the file, the Undelete command moves it back.

To start either of these levels of protection, you use the format of the Undelete command presented in figure 10-5. To start delete sentry protection, use the /S switch. To start delete tracking protection, use the /T switch. Usually you'll code this command in your AUTOEXEC.BAT file so it's executed automatically when you start your system.

The first time you use the Undelete command to start delete sentry or delete tracking protection, it creates a file name UNDELETE.INI in the DOS directory. This file contains information that determines what happens when a file is deleted. For example, it tells Undelete whether delete sentry or delete tracking protection is active. Although you provide Undelete with some of this information when you start the memory resident program, you can change some of the information only by editing the DELETE.INI file. UNDELETE.INI is a simple text file, so you can edit it using the Edit command.

The bottom part of figure 10-5 shows the DELETE.INI file that was created by the Undelete command in the figure. Although I won't describe this file in detail, there are two values in particular you might want to change. I've shaded them in the figure.

The Days value indicates how long a deleted file is to be kept in the SENTRY directory. The default is seven days. The Percentage value indicates the maximum percent of your hard disk the SENTRY directory can occupy. If you delete a file that will put the percentage over this amount, Undelete deletes the oldest files in the directory to make room for the newly deleted file.

Both delete tracking and delete sentry require additional memory and disk storage to operate. For delete tracking, these requirements are minimal. So if you have DOS 6.0, there's no reason for you not to use at least the delete tracking level of protection. And, although delete sentry can use a large amount of disk space, you can restrict that amount by changing the Days and Percentage values in the UNDELETE.INI file as I described a moment ago. So, if you need the added protection delete sentry provides, there should be no reason for you not to use it.

Incidentally, DOS 6.0 also provides a *Windows* version of the Undelete command. It provides the same features as the DOS version, but it takes advantage of the more friendly *Windows* interface.

How to use the Unformat command If you accidentally reformat your hard disk, you can often recover its data using the Unformat command. This command reconstructs the File Allocation Table, the directories, and the directory entries on the disk. However, this command can't always recover all the data on the disk so you should use it with caution.

If you use the DOS 5.0 Mirror command, which I'll describe in a minute, you can improve the chances of being able to unformat a disk. You can also improve the chances of unformatting a disk simply by using DOS 5.0 or 6.0. That's because when you use the DOS 5.0 or 6.0 Format command to format a disk, it does a safe format as I described in chapter 8. With a safe format, the data on the disk isn't destroyed. Instead, the Format command simply clears the File Allocation Table and the root directory. But even before it does that, it makes a copy of the File Allocation Table and the root directory. That makes it more likely that DOS will be able to unformat the drive if you should need to do that.

Figure 10-6 shows how you use the Unformat command. Here, I booted the system from a system diskette that contains the Unformat command. As the Unformat command reconstructs the data on the disk, it displays the warnings and messages shown here. After you use this command, you should check to see how many of the files and directories it was able to recover. If the command didn't recover all the data that was on the hard disk, you have to finish the task by recreating directories, copying files, and restoring backups.

How to use the DOS 5.0 Mirror command to improve file recovery

The Mirror command makes an extra copy of the root directory and the File Allocation Table for a drive. Then, when you delete a file, the Undelete command can use the old File Allocation Table to help recover that file. Also, if you format a disk, the Unformat program can use the old root directory and File Allocation Table to help recover all the directories and files on the disk.

When you use the delete tracking function of the Mirror command, it loads a memory resident program that keeps track of the file name and File Allocation Table

The format of the DOS 6.0 Undelete command for improving file recovery

```
UNDELETE /S[drive-spec] /Tdrive-spec
```

Switch meanings

/S	Loads a memory resident program that provides delete sentry level protection for deleted files.
/T	Loads a memory resident program that provides delete tracking level protection for deleted files.

A command that starts delete sentry level protection for drive C

```
UNDELETE /sc
```

The DELETE.INI file

```
[configuration]
archive=FALSE
days=7
percentage=20
[sentry.drives]
C=
[mirror.drives]
[sentry.files]
s_files=*.* -*.tmp -*.vm? -*.woa -*.swp -*.spl -*.rmg -*.img -*.thm -*.dov
[defaults]
d.sentry=TRUE
d.tracker=FALSE
```

Figure 10-5 How to use the DOS 6.0 Undelete command to improve file recovery

information for every file you delete. Thus, the Undelete function can almost always recover a deleted file as long as DOS hasn't put another file in the deleted file's disk space.

Figure 10-7 shows you how to use the Mirror command. As you can see, the /T switch starts the delete tracking function for each hard drive. Because this function provides an extra level of protection for your files, you should start the Mirror command with delete tracking from your AUTOEXEC.BAT file.

The Mirror command also has the ability to save a copy of your partition table on a diskette. (The partition table is the portion of your disk that keeps track of any partitions or logical drives you've created using the DOS Fdisk program, which you'll

The format of the DOS 5.0/6.0 Unformat command

```
UNFORMAT drive-spec
```

How to unformat drive C

```
A:\>a: unformat c:

Restores the system area of your disk by using the image file created
by the MIRROR command.

   WARNING !!        WARNING !!

This command should be used only to recover from the inadvertent use of
the FORMAT command or the RECOVER command.  Any other use of the UNFORMAT
command may cause you to lose data!  Files modified since the MIRROR image
file was created may be lost.

Searching disk for MIRROR image.

The LAST time the MIRROR or FORMAT command was used was 10:17 on 01-19-93.

The MIRROR image file has been validated.

Are you SURE you want to update the SYSTEM area of your drive C (Y/N)?y

The system area of drive C has been rebuilt.

You may need to restart the system.

A:\>
```

Figure 10-6 How to use the DOS 5.0/6.0 Unformat command

learn about in chapter 22.) To make a copy of your partition table, use a Mirror command like this:

```
C:\mirror /partn
```

When you do, mirror will prompt you to insert the diskette you want it to copy the partition table to. When Mirror is finished, be sure to label this diskette clearly and store it in a safe place.

If for some reason your hard disk becomes unusable because of an error in its partition table, you can reconstruct the partition table with the Unformat command, like this:

```
A:\unformat /partn
```

Then, Unformat will instruct you to insert the diskette that contains the partition table and attempt to recreate your partitions.

The format of the Mirror command

```
MIRROR drive-spec /Tdrive-letter
```

Example 1: A Mirror command that saves the directory and FAT for the current drive.

```
mirror
```

Example 2: A Mirror command that saves the directory and FAT for drives C and D.

```
mirror c: d:
```

Example 3: A Mirror command that saves the directory and FAT for drives C and D, and starts delete tracking for drive D.

```
mirror c: d: /td
```

An AUTOEXEC.BAT file that saves the directory and FAT for drives C and D, and starts delete tracking for drives C and D.

```
path=c:\;d:\;d:\dos;d:\util;d:\pctools
prompt $p$g
fastopen c:=10 d:=50
mirror c: d: /tc /td
mouse
dosshell
```

Figure 10-7 How to use the DOS 5.0 Mirror command

Although the DOS 6.0 Undelete command eliminates the need to use Mirror for delete tracking, it doesn't replace the Mirror command's ability to protect your partition table. This function alone may justify obtaining the DOS 6.0 supplemental diskette, which contains the Mirror command.

Why you should consider buying an advanced disk utility

As you can see, DOS just doesn't provide that much help when it comes to preventing, detecting, and recovering from disk problems. And only DOS 5.0 and 6.0 provide commands for recovering files you've deleted accidentally. That's why you should consider buying an advanced disk utility. These programs usually provide several functions that can improve the reliability of your disk operations.

First, an advanced disk utility can detect and lock out bad sectors that occur after a disk has been formatted. It can also help recover files that are stored in bad sectors. And some utilities can actually fix bad sectors so they can be used again. If you have an advanced disk utility, you can run it once every two or three months to detect bad sectors, lock them out, and recover the files that are affected by them.

Second, an advanced disk utility can *unfragment* the *fragmented files* on a hard disk. This means combining the allocation units of a file that are in several different areas of a hard disk (the fragments) and putting them into one continuous series of allocation units. This *fragmentation* occurs because DOS stores a new file in the first available disk space that it finds. If this space isn't large enough for the entire file, DOS stores as much of the file as it can and looks for the next available space. It continues in this way until the entire file is stored on the disk. Although file fragmentation isn't a problem in itself, it can contribute to disk problems like lost allocation units and cross-linked files. If you have an advanced disk utility, you can run it once every two or three months to unfragment the files on a system and thus reduce the likelihood of disk problems. If you're using DOS 6.0, you can use the *Microsoft Defrag* utility to unfragment files. I'll cover *Microsoft Defrag* in chapter 19.

Third, an advanced disk utility can undelete a file that you've accidentally deleted. Generally, the undelete functions provided by a disk utility are more thorough than the Undelete command DOS 5.0 and 6.0 provide. For example, advanced disk utilities can undelete deleted subdirectories as well as files. And if you don't have DOS 5.0 or 6.0, the disk utility gives you recovery features you don't already have.

Terms

volume label
allocation unit
cluster
File Allocation Table
FAT
lost allocation unit
cross-linked file
chain
bad sector
delete tracking
delete sentry
memory resident program
unfragment
fragmented file
fragmentation

Objectives

1. For each hard drive on your PC, determine if the drive has a volume label assigned to it. If it doesn't, assign one to it.
2. Determine if your hard disk has any lost allocation units or cross-linked files. If it does, correct those conditions.
3. If you have DOS 5.0 or 6.0, use the commands available with these versions to assist you in recovering data that has been accidentally deleted or destroyed by the Delete or Format command.

Exercises

1. Use the Volume command on each drive of your hard disk to see if the drive has a label. If the drive doesn't have a label, use the Label command and the guidelines presented in this chapter to assign one to the drive.

2. Run the Check-disk command for each of the drives on your hard disk. If the command reports that there are lost allocation units or cross-liked files, use the procedures you learned in this chapter to correct these problems.

3. Explain why you shouldn't use the DOS Recover command for fixing bad sectors of your hard disk. Then, delete the file named RECOVER.COM from your DOS directory.

4. If you have DOS 5.0, use the Mirror command to start delete tracking. Then, delete a file and use the Undelete command to restore it.

5. If you have DOS 6.0, use the Undelete command to start delete tracking or delete sentry protection. Then, delete a file and use the Undelete command to restore it.

6. Describe the three ways an advanced disk utility can help you prevent, detect, and recover from disk problems better than DOS can.

Chapter 11

How to improve your PC's performance without buying new hardware

Do you ever wish that your PC would run faster? For instance, do you ever wish that it didn't take so long to load an application program from the hard disk to internal memory? That it didn't take so long for the cursor to move across the screen? Or that you could continue working while your printer prints?

If your answer to any of these questions is "yes," you may be interested to know that you can often improve the performance of a PC without buying new hardware. To do that, you can use a couple of the commands and functions available with some versions of DOS. You can also use special-purpose utility programs. In this chapter, I'll present both of these options.

How to use two DOS commands that can speed up disk operations

DOS provides two commands that can speed up disk operations. The Buffers command has been a part of DOS since version 2.0, so you most likely have it on your system. The Fastopen command, however, didn't become available until version 3.3.

The Buffers command To improve the performance of hard disk operations, DOS sets up small areas in internal memory called *buffers*. These buffers are used to hold data that has been read from the hard disk. Then, when a program asks DOS to get more data from the hard disk, DOS first checks the buffers to see whether the data is already in internal memory. If it is, DOS gets the data from the buffer, which is faster than getting it from the hard disk. If the data isn't already in a buffer, DOS reads the data from the hard disk into the buffer that held the least recent data.

By default, DOS sets up a small number of buffers. For instance, DOS versions 2.0 through 3.2 set up either two or three buffers based on the type of PC you're using. Later versions of DOS set up the buffers based on the amount of internal memory your PC has.

Usually, you can improve the performance of your PC by setting up more buffers than the DOS default. To do that, you put a Buffers command in the CONFIG.SYS file for your PC. To modify this batch file, you can use any of the methods described in chapter 5. And you can put the Buffers command anywhere in the file because the location doesn't matter. Then, after you've modified the CONFIG.SYS file, you should restart your system to put the command into effect.

Figure 11-1 summarizes the format of the Buffers command. As you can see, the first parameter on this command for all versions of DOS is the number of buffers. No matter what version of DOS you use, I recommend that you set up between 16 and 30 buffers. If you set up fewer than 16, you won't get the full benefit from this command. And if you set up more than 30, your PC may actually slow down because DOS will have trouble managing the buffers efficiently.

With DOS 4.0 or a later version, you can use a second parameter on the Buffers command. Under DOS 4.0, this parameter sets up what DOS calls *read ahead sectors*. Under DOS 5.0 and 6.0, this parameter sets up what DOS calls a *secondary buffer cache*. Either way, this parameter can often improve the overall performance of your PC by reducing the number of times DOS must access the hard disk. That's why I recommend that you specify a number from four to eight as the second parameter in your Buffers command.

The Fastopen command The more directories and files you have on your hard disk, the longer it takes DOS to find a file because DOS has to look through more directory entries. However, if you have DOS 3.3 or a later version, you can speed up these searching operations by using the Fastopen command. This command sets up special areas in internal memory for the most recent directory information. Then, if DOS can find the directory information it needs in the Fastopen memory, it doesn't have to search for it on the hard disk, so the search time is reduced.

Figure 11-2 summarizes the Fastopen command for DOS 3.3. Its only parameter is the number of directory entries for the drive. If you have more than one drive on your hard disk, you enter one parameter for each of the drives. For each drive, I recommend that you set up space for 50 directory entries. In figure 11-2, the commands in both examples set up Fastopen space for the last 50 files accessed on the C drive. The command in the second example also sets up space for the last 50 files accessed on the D drive. When you use the Fastopen command, you put it in your AUTOEXEC.BAT file anywhere after the Path command that identifies its directory.

Figure 11-3 summarizes this command for DOS 4.0. In this format, you can specify *continuous space buffers* as well as directory entries. The continuous space buffers improve performance when a fragmented file is accessed by a program. This is a file that is split over more than one disk area. For each drive on your hard disk, I recommend 50 directory entries and 200 continuous space buffers.

The format of the Buffers command for DOS 2.0 through 3.3

```
BUFFERS=number-of-buffers
```

The format of the Buffers command for DOS 4.0

```
BUFFERS=number-of-buffers[,read-ahead-sectors]
```

The format of the Buffers command for DOS 5.0 and 6.0

```
BUFFERS=number-of-buffers[,secondary-buffer-cache]
```

Example 1: A Buffers command that sets up 20 buffers.

```
buffers=20
```

Example 2: A Buffers command that sets up 20 buffers and 8 read ahead sectors (DOS 4.0) or 8 secondary buffers (DOS 5.0 and 6.0).

```
buffers=20,8
```

Figure 11-1 How to use the Buffers command in the CONFIG.SYS file

The format of the Fastopen command for DOS 3.3

```
FASTOPEN drive-spec=number-of-directory-entries
```

Example 1: A Fastopen command that specifies 50 directory entries for drive C.

```
fastopen c:=50
```

Example 2: A Fastopen command that specifies 50 directory entries for both drives C and D.

```
fastopen c:=50 d:=50
```

Figure 11-2 How to use the DOS 3.3 Fastopen command in the AUTOEXEC.BAT file

Although you can put a Fastopen command in the AUTOEXEC.BAT file of DOS 4.0, you can also use an Install command to load Fastopen from the CONFIG.SYS file, as shown in the third example in figure 11-3. In fact, when you install DOS 4.0 on your system, an Install command to load Fastopen is automatically put in your CONFIG.SYS file. If you want to change the parameters in the Fastopen

The format of the Fastopen command for DOS 4.0

```
FASTOPEN  drive-spec=(number-of-directory-entries,
                      continuous-space-buffers)
```

Example 1: A Fastopen command that specifies 50 directory entries and 200 continuous space buffers for drive C.

```
fastopen c:=(50,200)
```

Example 2: A Fastopen command that specifies 50 directory entries and 200 continuous space buffers for both drives C and D.

```
fastopen c:=(50,200) d:=(50,200)
```

Example 3: An Install command that loads Fastopen from your CONFIG.SYS file.

```
install=c:\dos\fastopen.exe c:=(50,200) d:=(50,200)
```

Figure 11-3 How to use the DOS 4.0 Fastopen command

command, you can either modify the existing command or replace it. Notice that when the Fastopen command is in the CONFIG.SYS file, you must specify its drive and path because DOS processes the CONFIG.SYS file before it executes the Path command in the AUTOEXEC.BAT file.

Figure 11-4 summarizes the Fastopen command for DOS 5.0 and 6.0. This command uses basically the same command format as DOS 3.3. However, you can use the Install command to load Fastopen from the CONFIG.SYS file. In addition, you can use the /X switch to use EMS memory for Fastopen as long as the expanded memory conforms to the EEMS standard. When you do that, more conventional memory is left for your application programs.

How to use Smartdrive to improve disk performance

The Buffers and Fastopen commands will speed up disk operations on your PC, but the speed improvement will probably be barely noticeable. In contrast, more recent versions of DOS come with a program called Smartdrive that may give you a dramatic improvement in disk performance. Smartdrive creates a *disk cache* (pronounced *cash*), which is nothing more than a large buffer that holds thousands of disk sectors. Smartdrive intelligently manages the disk data stored in the cache, keeping recently used data in the cache, anticipating which data your programs will need so it can read the data from the disk ahead of time, and deciding which cached data should be discarded to free up additional disk space.

The format of the Fastopen command for DOS 5.0 and 6.0

```
FASTOPEN drive-spec=number-of-directory-entries [/X]
```

Example 1: A Fastopen command that specifies 50 directory entries for drive C.

```
fastopen c:=50
```

Example 2: A Fastopen command that specifies 50 directory entries for both drives C and D.

```
fastopen c:=50 d:=50
```

Example 3: An Install command in the CONFIG.SYS file that uses conventional memory for Fastopen.

```
install=c:\dos\fastopen.exe c:=50 d:=50
```

Example 4: An Install command in the CONFIG.SYS file that uses EMS memory for Fastopen.

```
install=c:\dos\fastopen.exe c:=50 d:=50 /x
```

Figure 11-4 How to use the DOS 5.0 and 6.0 Fastopen command

To create a large enough cache to make disk caching worthwhile, your PC needs to have additional memory available. If your PC is relatively new, it probably has 4MB or more of total memory, with 3MB of available extended memory. If that's the case, you should dedicate as much of this memory as possible to Smartdrive. If you have an older 286-based PC with 1MB of internal memory, you probably have a 384KB block of extended memory you can use for disk caching. And if you have an older 286 or perhaps an 8086-based PC, you might have expanded memory available.

Smartdrive was originally introduced with DOS 4.0 and *Windows* 3.0. The Smartdrive program included with DOS 5.0 was the same as the DOS 4.0 version of Smartdrive. You activate this version of Smartdrive by including a statement that starts it in your CONFIG.SYS file. DOS 6.0 and *Windows* 3.1 come with a newer version of Smartdrive that speeds up disk access even more than the older Smartdrive version. You activate the DOS 6.0/*Windows* 3.1 version of Smartdrive by including a command in your AUTOEXEC.BAT file rather than in your CONFIG.SYS file. If your PC has DOS 5.0 and *Windows* 3.1, you should use the newer version of Smartdrive found in the WINDOWS directory rather than the older version found in the DOS directory.

Both versions of Smartdrive are designed to work cooperatively with *Microsoft Windows*. As a result, you can allocate nearly all of your available extended memory to Smartdrive without worrying about running out of memory for *Windows*. If

Windows requires additional memory, it can tell Smartdrive to reduce the size of its cache to free up memory. When *Windows* is finished with the memory, it returns it to Smartdrive.

Whichever version of Smartdrive you use, you should reduce the number of buffers specified by the Buffers command in the CONFIG.SYS file to a minimum when you use Smartdrive. Otherwise, your PC will be slowed down because it will have to look through both the buffers and the cache whenever a disk operation is requested by an application program. You can minimize the buffers by including a Buffers command like this:

```
buffers=2
```

Or, you can omit the Buffers command and let DOS use its default number of buffers which, as I've already pointed out, is small.

How to use the DOS 4.0 and 5.0 version of Smartdrive With DOS 4.0 and 5.0, you activate Smartdrive by including a Device command for it in your CONFIG.SYS file, as shown in figure 11-5. On the Smartdrive Device command, you specify the amount of memory you want Smartdrive to initially allocate to its cache. You specify the cache size in term of kilobytes. Thus, example 1 creates a 384KB disk cache and example 2 creates a 2MB cache (each MB is 1,024KB, so 2MB is 2,048KB). In addition, example 2 specifies that *Windows* should not be allowed to shrink the Smartdrive cache below 512KB.

If your PC doesn't have extended memory but does have expanded memory available, you can tell Smartdrive to create the cache in expanded memory by using the /A switch. If you have both extended and expanded memory, you should use the extended memory for the Smartdrive cache because it's faster.

How to use the DOS 6.0 version of Smartdrive DOS 6.0 includes a new version of Smartdrive that improves the overall performance of your disk by caching not only read operations, but write operations as well. In other words, when an application program saves a file to disk, it doesn't have to wait for the data to actually be written to the disk. Instead, once the data has been moved to the cache, the program continues. Later, the Smartdrive program takes care of actually writing the data to the disk. Because moving the data to the cache is much faster than writing it to the disk, the performance increase for some applications can be dramatic.

Unfortunately, write caching does involve a certain amount of risk. Once your data has been moved into the cache, your program assumes that it's been safely written to the disk. If a power failure should occur after the data has been moved to the cache but before it's been written to the disk, the data is lost. However, the odds of that happening are slim enough that the risk is outweighed by the performance improvement you get from write caching. And, to make write caching as safe as possible, Smartdrive makes sure that no write-cached data stays in the cache longer than five seconds before being written to disk. Most data gets written to the disk long before those five seconds have elapsed.

The format of the Device command for Smartdrive (DOS 4.0 and 5.0)

```
DEVICE=C:\DOS\SMARTDRV.SYS [initial-size] [minimum-size] [/A]
```

Explanation

initial-size The number of kilobytes Smartdrive is to use initially for its cache. The value must be between 128 and 8192. If you omit *initial-size*, 256KB is assumed.

minimum-size The minimum number of kilobytes in the Smartdrive cache when *Windows* is running. If *minimum-size* is omitted, 0KB is assumed.

/A Tells Smartdrive to use expanded memory for the cache. If you omit this switch, Smartdrive uses extended memory.

Example 1: A Device command that creates a 384KB Smartdrive cache using extended memory.

```
device=c:\dos\smartdrv.sys 384
```

Example 2: A Device command that creates a 2MB Smartdrive cache using extended memory and allows *Windows* to shrink the cache to no less than 512KB.

```
device=c:\dos\smartdrv.sys 2048 512
```

Figure 11-5 How to add a Device command for Smartdrive to your CONFIG.SYS file with DOS 4.0 and 5.0

When you use the new version of Smartdrive, however, you do need to be careful about turning off your PC. If you reboot your PC by pressing Ctrl+Alt+Del, Smartdrive detects the reboot and writes any pending data to disk. But if you simply shut down your PC, pending data may be left in the Smartdrive cache. To make sure that doesn't happen, always reboot your PC by pressing Ctrl+Alt+Del before turning it off. Or just make sure your PC has been idle for at least five seconds before turning it off.

Unlike the older version of Smartdrive, you activate the DOS 6.0 version of Smartdrive by including a Smartdrv command in your AUTOEXEC.BAT file rather than in your CONFIG.SYS file. Figure 11-6 shows the format for the Smartdrv command. In most cases, you'll want to specify the initial cache size and the minimum cache size; these parameters work the same as they do for the older version of Smartdrive. Example 1 shows how you might set up a 286 PC with 1MB of total memory with a 384KB cache. Example 2 shows a Smartdrv command for a computer with 4MB of extended memory. This command allocates the entire 4MB to Smartdrive, but specifies that *Windows* should not be allowed to shrink the cache below 512KB. And example 3 shows how you can set up a similar Smartdrive cache, but disable write caching for the C drive. Then, Smartdrive will cache only read operations.

The format of the Smartdrv command for DOS 6.0

```
SMARTDRV [drive[+|-]...] [initial-size] [minimum-size]
```

Explanation

`drive[+|-]`	Specifies the drives to cache. If you specify a drive letter without + or -, read caching is enabled for the drive. If you specify a drive letter followed by +, both read and write caching are enabled for the drive. If you specify a drive letter followed by -, the drive is not cached. If you don't specify any drive letters, diskettes drives are read cached, and hard drives are read and write cached.
`initial-size`	The number of kilobytes Smartdrive is to initially use for its cache. If you omit *initial-size*, the default depends on the amount of extended memory available: Smartdrive will use 1MB if you have up to 4MB of extended memory; if you have more than that, Smardrive will use 2MB.
`minimum-size`	The minimum number of kilobytes in the Smartdrive cache when *Windows* is running. If omitted, the default depends on the amount of extended memory available: 256KB for 1 to 2MB available memory, 512KB for 2 to 4MB available memory, 1MB for for 4 to 6MB available memory, and 2MB for more than 6MB available memory.

Example 1: A Smartdrv command that creates a 384KB Smartdrive cache.

```
smartdrv 384
```

Example 2: A Smartdrv command that creates a 4MB Smartdrive cache and allows *Windows* to shrink the cache to no less than 512KB.

```
smartdrv 4096 512
```

Example 3: A Smartdrv command that creates a 4MB Smartdrive cache that's used only for read caching on drive C and that allows *Windows* to shrink the cache to no less than 512KB.

```
smartdrv c 4096 512
```

Figure 11-6 How to add a Smartdrv command to your AUTOEXEC.BAT file for DOS 6.0

Although Smartdrive supports a few other switches, you don't need to worry about them unless you're interested in squeezing as much performance out of Smartdrive as possible. In that case, you can consult DOS 6.0 on-line Help to see the format of these switches. Then, you can experiment with various switch settings. Because the optimum settings for these switches varies from one system to the next, there's no way to make a blanket recommendation. For most systems, though, the increase in performance you can expect from this experimentation is so slight that it's not worth the effort.

Incidentally, when you install DOS 6.0 or *Windows* 3.1, the Setup program automatically adds a Smartdrv command to your AUTOEXEC.BAT file. But you should double-check your AUTOEXEC.BAT file to make sure that Setup configured the Smartdrv command the way you want it.

Setup may also add a Device command like this to your CONFIG.SYS file:

```
device=c:\dos\smartdrv.exe /double_buffer
```

This statement enables a Smartdrive feature called *double-buffering*, which is required to support certain disk controllers when you use the EMM386.EXE memory manager or when you use *Windows*. The Setup program examines your system to determine if double-buffering is necessary and adds this CONFIG.SYS statement if it is. Unfortunately, Setup is overcautious and may install double-buffering when it's not really necessary. If Setup added this Device command to your CONFIG.SYS file and you think it might be unnecessary, follow the procedure described in DOS 6.0 on-line Help to determine if you can remove it.

The Smartdrv command does have two additional switches you can use after Smartdrive has been started from your AUTOEXEC.BAT file. Figure 11-7 shows how you can use these switches. Example 1 shows how you can use the /S switch to display status information about Smartdrive. Here, you can see which drives are being cached, how large the cache is, and how many disk requests were for data that was already in the cache ("cache hits") and how many required access to the disk because the requested data wasn't already in the cache ("cache misses"). Also notice that this display is for version 4.1 of Smartdrive, which is the version that comes with DOS 6.0.

Example 2 in figure 11-7 shows how you can use the Smartdrv command to force Smartdrive to write all pending data to the disk. You probably won't use this command often, but if you have a batch file that runs a utility program that reboots your computer and you use Smartdrive's write-caching feature, you should add this command immediately before the reboot command. This is required because many of these reboot utilities do not cooperate with Smartdrive to make sure that data isn't lost.

How to speed up the cursor with DOS 4.0 or a later version

As you become more proficient with PC programs, your speed improves. Eventually, you may work so fast that the speed of the cursor slows you down. Then, it's helpful to be able to speed the cursor up. Today, some application programs have their own facilities for controlling the speed of the cursor, but many still don't.

If you have DOS 4.0 or a later version and if you have a PC with a 286, 386, or 486 processor, you can use the Mode command to speed up the cursor. This command is summarized in figure 11-8. The Rate parameter is a value from 1 to 32 that controls how many times a key is repeated in a second. The Delay parameter is a value from 1

Example 1

A Smartdrv command that displays additional status information about Smartdrive.

```
C:\>smartdrv /s
Microsoft SMARTDrive Disk Cache version 4.1
Copyright 1991,1993 Microsoft Corp.

Room for 64 elements of 8,192 bytes each
There have been 2,629 cache hits
    and 2,590 cache misses

Cache size: 524,288 bytes
Cache size while running Windows: 524,288 bytes

            Disk Caching Status
drive   read cache   write cache   buffering
--------------------------------------------
  A:       yes          no            no
  B:       yes          no            no
  C:       yes          yes           no

For help, type "Smartdrv /?".

C:\>
```

Example 2

A Smartdrv command that forces Smartdrive to write any data in its cache to the hard disk.

```
C:\>smartdrv /c
```

Figure 11-7 Two DOS 6.0 Smartdrv commands you might use after Smartdrive is started

to 8 under DOS 4.0, or 1 to 4 under DOS 5.0 and DOS 6.0. This parameter controls the delay before a keystroke is repeated when the key is held down. Both of these values apply to all keystrokes, but they are most evident when you use the cursor control keys.

To find out what settings of the Rate and Delay parameters are best for you, you must experiment with them. To do that, enter a Mode command at the command prompt. Then, start an application program and see how the settings work. If the cursor is too fast or too slow, exit from the program and try another Mode command with adjusted settings. When you find the settings that work the best, you can put the Mode command anywhere in your AUTOEXEC.BAT file.

The format of the Mode command for DOS 4.0

```
MODE CON RATE=value-from-1-to-32 DELAY=value-from-1-to-8
```

The format of the Mode command for DOS 5.0 and 6.0

```
MODE CON RATE=value-from-1-to-32 DELAY=value-from-1-to-4
```

A Mode command that sets the number of times a key is repeated in a second to 32 and the delay before a keystroke is repeated to 2

```
mode con rate=32 delay=2
```

Figure 11-8 How to use the Mode command to increase the speed of the cursor under DOS 4.0, 5.0, and 6.0 if you have a 286, 386, or 486 processor

How to use the DOS Print command so you can keep working while your printer is printing

Some application programs let you continue working while the printer is printing. If, for example, you're using *WordPerfect* to print a 20-page document, you can continue working on that document or on other documents while the printer is in use. Although this doesn't actually speed up your PC, it lets you work faster so the effect is the same.

Unfortunately, many application programs don't let you work while the printer is in use. So if you are printing a 20-page report from a word processing program or 2,000 labels from a database program, you just have to wait for the printing to be completed before you can resume your PC work.

Although DOS provides a Print command that lets you continue to use your application programs while your printer prints, it isn't an efficient solution for this problem. I'll present this command anyway because it's an acceptable solution in some situations.

When you use the Print command, your application programs print to disk files instead of directly to the printer. Since most application programs provide this capability, you shouldn't have any trouble creating these *print files*. Although you can give these files whatever names you want, it makes sense to use PRT as the extension for them so you can identify them as print files later on.

After you create the print files, you exit from the application program you've been using. Then, you use the Print command summarized in figure 11-9 to print the print files in the *DOS background*. When you specify one or more print files in a Print command without any switches, the files are put in a *print queue*. Then, DOS prints the files in this queue in the order of entry. By default, this queue can hold up to ten files at one time. After you've placed all the print files in the queue, you restart your application program and continue work while the printer prints.

The first time you issue a Print command after you start your PC, DOS asks you for the name of the printer device. If you want to avoid this, you can put a Print command with the /D switch in the AUTOEXEC.BAT file. As part of this switch, you can identify the printer device as illustrated in the first example in figure 11-9.

As you continue your work, you can add more files to the print queue by issuing other Print commands as in the second example in figure 11-9. You can also cancel the printing of one or more files by issuing the print command with the /C switch, as illustrated in the third example. Notice that the switch comes before the file specifications for the file or files to be removed from the queue. If you want to terminate the printing for all files in the queue, you use the /T switch as in the fourth example. And if you want to display a list of all the files that are still in the queue, you issue a Print command without any parameters or switches as in the fifth example.

Actually, the print queue contains the names of the print files, not the files themselves. As a result, the print files remain after the files in the queue have been printed, cancelled, or terminated. That means you should delete the print files after you're done with them. If you used PRT as the extension for your print files, you can easily find them and delete them.

Does this sound like it's more trouble than it's worth? It is unless your printing jobs are lengthy. If, for example, a printing job takes two hours, using this command is worth the effort. But if you print many short jobs, it isn't.

If you do find yourself using the Print command frequently, you should consider buying a commercial *print spooling utility*. These programs give you all the benefits of printing in background mode, and they work automatically. The spooling program creates the print file, queues it, and deletes it after the file prints so that you don't have to.

Task switching and multi-tasking utilities

If you frequently switch from one program to another, task switching and multi-tasking utilities can help you work more efficiently. A *task switching utility* lets you load two or more programs into internal memory at the same time and lets you switch between them. If, for example, you frequently use *Lotus 1-2-3* and *WordPerfect*, you can load them both, then switch between them without having to exit from one before you switch to the other. You switch between the programs by pressing a pre-defined key combination.

Like a task switching utility, a *multi-tasking utility* lets you load two or more programs and switch between them. However, a task switching utility actually runs only one program at a time. In contrast, a multi-tasking utility runs two or more programs concurrently. That means you can see more than one program at a time on your monitor. And it means that you can more easily transfer data between programs.

The format of the Print command

```
PRINT [/D:device] [/C] [/T] file-specification
```

Switch meanings

`/D` Sets the device name for the printer. You can use a Print command with this switch in the AUTOEXEC.BAT file. Then, the command won't ask for the device name the first time you enter it from the command line. PRN is the name for the first parallel port; LPT2 is the name for the second parallel port; and COM1 is the name for the first serial port.

`/C` Cancels the printing for all of the files named in the command. This removes the named files from the print queue. If a named file is being printed, the printing is stopped, a message is printed, the paper is advanced to the top of the next page, and the printer's alarm is sounded (if there is one).

`/T` Terminates the printing. This removes all of the files from the print queue. If a file is being printed, the printing is stopped, a message is printed, the paper is advanced to the top of the next page, and the printer's alarm is sounded (if there is one).

Exampe 1: A Print command in the AUTOEXEC.BAT file that gives the device name for the printer.

```
print /d:prn
```

Example 2: Three Print commands that add one or more files to the print queue.

```
print report5.prt
print labels.prt report1.prt report2.prt
print \q\mma\*.prt
```

Example 3: A Print command that removes three files from the print queue.

```
print /c labels.prt report1.prt report5.prt
```

Example 4: A Print command that terminates all the files in the print queue.

```
print /t
```

Example 5: A Print command that displays a list of all the files in the print queue.

```
print
```

Figure 11-9 How to use the Print command to overlap printing with other tasks

As you'll learn in chapter 15, DOS 5.0 and 6.0 include a simple task switching feature as part of their shell programs. And if you use *Microsoft Windows*, you can do true multi-tasking. Several popular commercial utility programs also provide task switching or multi-tasking capabilities.

Some perspective on PC performance

The techniques you've learned in this chapter can often have a dramatic effect on your PC's speed, especially for certain applications. You should realize, however, that none of these techniques can improve your PC's performace beyond the limits of its hardware. In other words, if you're using an older 286 PC that's running at a clock speed of 12Mhz, no amount of fiddling with buffers, Fastopen, or disk caches will make it run as fast at a 486 PC that's runiing at 33Mhz. As a result, you should run software that's appropriate for your PC. For example, don't try to run *Windows* on a 286 running at 12Mhz. Instead, use DOS-based applications.

Terms

buffer
read ahead sectors
secondary buffer cache
continuous space buffers
disk caching
disk cache
double-buffering
cursor control utility
print file
DOS background
print queue
print spooling utility
task switching utility
multi-tasking utility

Objectives

1. Use the DOS commands and the disk caching program presented in this chapter to speed up disk operations on your system.
2. Use a DOS command to set the cursor speed so it works best for you.
3. Use a DOS command to overlap printing with other tasks.

Exercises

1. Use the Type or Print command to display or print the CONFIG.SYS file that's in the root directory of the C drive. Does the Buffers command provide for at least 16 buffers? If you're using DOS 4.0 or a later version, is a Fastopen command installed?
2. Use the Type or Print command to display or print the AUTOEXEC.BAT file that's in the root directory of the C drive. If you're using DOS 3.3, does the file include a Fastopen command? If you're using DOS 4.0 or a later version, does the file include a Mode command that sets the cursor speed?

3. If the CONFIG.SYS or AUTOEXEC.BAT files aren't set up the way they should be, modify them. If you don't understand what some of the commands in the old files do, don't delete or modify them because they may have an important effect on your system. When in doubt, be sure to make a backup copy of the old file before you modify it so you can reinstate the old file if the new one doesn't work right. To test your new files, press the Ctrl+Alt+Delete key combination to restart the PC. Then, see how the changes affect the performance of your system.

4. If you're using DOS 4.0 or 5.0 and you don't have *Microsoft Windows* 3.1, inspect the CONFIG.SYS file to see if there's a device command for Smartdrive. If there isn't, add one. If you're using DOS 6.0 or if you have *Windows* 3.1, inspect your AUTOEXEC.BAT file to see if it includes a Smartdrv command. If it doesn't, add one.

5. If you added Smartdrive in exercise 4, or if you already have it on your PC, check the Buffers command in your CONFIG.SYS file (if there is one). If you have a Buffers command, do you need to minimize it? If you do, edit the command and reset the number of buffers to 2. Or, omit the Buffers command and let DOS use its default number of buffers.

Section 4

How to use the DOS 5.0 or 6.0 shell

Since the introduction of the IBM PC and DOS in 1981, users have complained that DOS is hard to use. To a large extent, that's why *shell programs* have become popular. These programs let you perform many of the functions provided by DOS commands without forcing you to know the details of the commands themselves.

Beginning with DOS 4.0, Microsoft included a shell program with DOS called the *DOS shell*. With DOS 5.0, Microsoft significantly improved the shell program. The DOS 6.0 shell is nearly identical to the DOS 5.0 shell. Although some commercial shell programs still provide advanced features that aren't found in the DOS 5.0 and 6.0 shells, the 5.0/6.0 shell provides most of the shell features you're likely to want. It also includes a few features that aren't found in any commercial shell programs. And it's easy to use. So if you have DOS 5.0 or 6.0 on your PC and you aren't already using another shell, I definitely recommend that you use the DOS shell.

If you have DOS 5.0 or 6.0, the four chapters in this section will show you how to use the DOS shell. In chapter 12, you'll be introduced to the basic functions of the shell. In chapter 13, you'll learn how to use the shell to create and use menus to start your application programs. In chapter 14, you'll learn how to use the shell to manage the directories and files on your hard disk. And in chapter 15, you'll learn how to use the task switching capabilities of the shell to quickly switch between application programs. When you finish this section, you'll be able to use the DOS shell for most DOS functions.

If you don't have DOS 5.0 or 6.0 on your PC, you can read this section to see what the shell can do and how it works. Then, you can decide for yourself whether upgrading to DOS 6.0 is worth the effort. If you like the idea of using a shell but you don't want to upgrade to DOS 6.0, you can consider the purchase of a commercial shell program.

Chapter 12

An introduction to the DOS shell

In this chapter, I'll introduce you to the shell by presenting a brief overview of its menu and file management functions. Then, in chapters 13 and 14, I'll show you how to use these shell functions in detail. In chapter 15, I'll present the task-switching functions that the DOS shell provides.

As you will soon see, the quickest way to learn how to use a shell is to experiment with it. That's why the chapters in this section don't present detailed instructions for using the shell. Instead, they present general operational procedures for using the shell, and they introduce you to the capabilities of the shell. Once you have this background, you shouldn't have much trouble using the shell because most of its operations are self-explanatory.

If your PC has a mouse, you'll want to use it with the DOS shell because it simplifies some of the operations. However, you can also use the shell with the keyboard. Throughout this section of the book, I'll show you how to perform a function using both a mouse and the keyboard.

An overview of the DOS shell

Before you learn how to use the DOS shell, you should know that it provides functions you can use for three distinct purposes. First, it provides a program-list function that lets you start your application programs by selecting choices from a menu rather than by typing commands. Second, it provides file management functions that let you manage your directories and files without remembering the details of DOS command formats. Third, it provides task-switching functions that let you load several programs into memory at once and switch from one to another with just a few keystrokes.

How to start the DOS shell If you want to start the DOS shell every time you start your computer, you should include the Dosshell command in your AUTOEXEC.BAT file. Dosshell is the name of the program file that starts the shell.

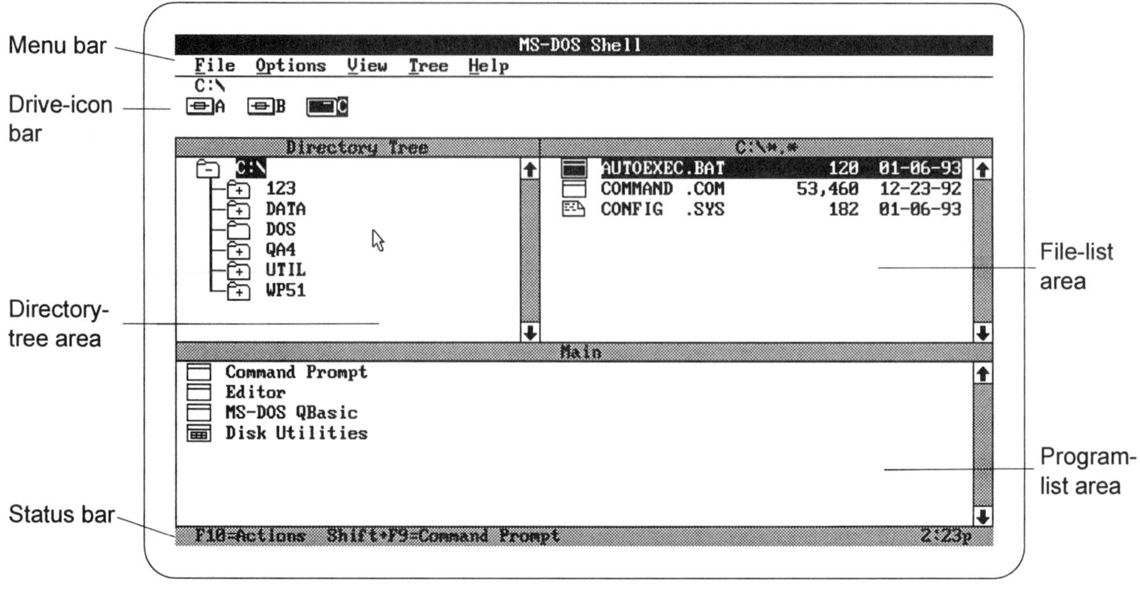

Figure 12-1 The first screen of the DOS 5.0/6.0 shell

If your shell isn't started by the AUTOEXEC.BAT file, you can start it any time by entering the Dosshell command at the prompt.

The DOS shell display When you start the shell, it displays the screen shown in figure 12-1. This is the standard display, but you should know that you can select other display options. If you or someone else has used the shell previously and selected another display option, your screen won't look like this one. In just a moment, I'll show you how to reset your display to the one shown here.

In figure 12-1, you can see that the DOS shell displays a *menu bar* at the top of the screen. You use this menu bar to select DOS shell functions. Below the menu bar are the *drive icons* in the *drive-icon bar*. These icons represent each disk drive on your system, and you use them to select the drive you want to use. Below the drive icons, the display is divided into two areas: the *directory-tree area* and the *file-list area*. You use these two areas to manage your files and directories. The next area is the *program-list area*. You use it to start DOS utilities and application programs. At the bottom of the screen, the *status bar* displays the current time and indicates any function keys or keystroke combinations you can use to perform functions.

If the DOS shell display on your PC uses the same basic layout, but it looks slightly different from the one in figure 12-1, you're probably using a different monitor than the one I used for the figures. Also, I used the shell in graphics mode because it uses some graphics symbols. So if you're running the shell in text mode, your screen won't look exactly like the one in figure 12-1.

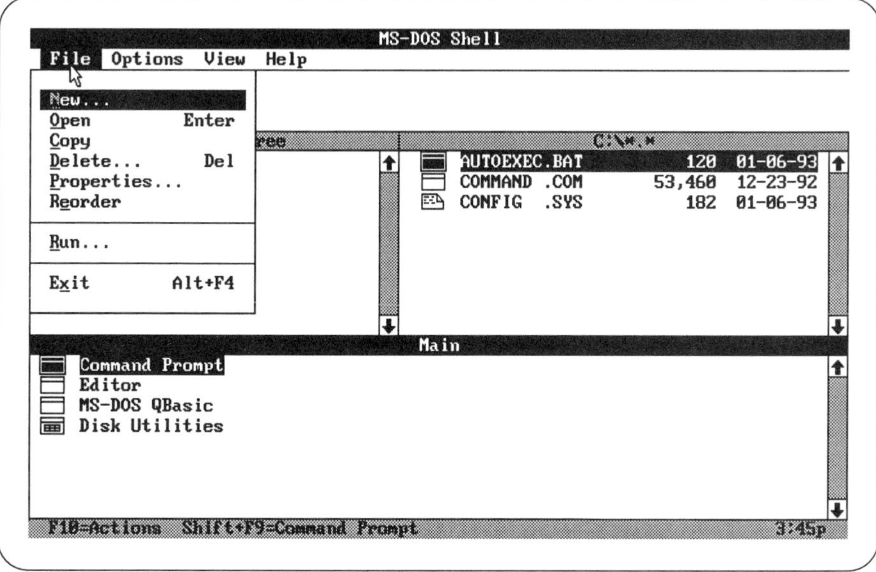

Figure 12-2 The File menu when the program-list area is active

When you use the DOS shell, only one of the areas on the display is active at a time. If you're using a color monitor, the DOS shell identifies the active area by using a different color in the area's title bar. If you're using a monochrome monitor, the DOS shell identifies the active area by placing a small arrow next to the current item within the area.

To use one of the areas of the DOS shell, you must first make that area active. If you have a mouse, you just move the mouse cursor to the area you want to activate and press the left mouse button. This is referred to as *clicking the mouse*. If you don't have a mouse, you use the Tab key to move from one area to the next. Each time you press the Tab key, the next screen area is activated. As a result, you sometimes have to press the Tab key several times to activate the area you want.

How to use the pull-down menus The menu bar in figure 12-1 contains five menu items: File, Options, View, Tree, and Help. To select one of these menu items, just click on it with the mouse. When you do that, a *pull-down menu* is displayed. For example, figure 12-2 shows the pull-down menu that's displayed when you click on the File menu item when the program-list area is activated. As you can see, this menu has eight functions: New, Open, Copy, Delete, Properties, Reorder, Run, and Exit. To select one of these functions, you just point to it with the mouse cursor and click again.

If you don't have a mouse, you can use three techniques to use the pull-down menus. One, you can activate the menu bar by pressing the F10 key. Then, you can pull down a menu by pressing the underlined letter of the menu you want (F for File, O for Options, and so on). Two, you can press the F10 key to activate the menu bar and then use the cursor keys to move the highlight to the menu you want and press the Enter key. Three, you can hold down the Alt key while pressing the underlined letter of the menu you want.

Once you've pulled a menu down, you can use the keyboard to select a function by pressing the underlined letter of the function you want (for example, O for Open). Or you can use the cursor keys to move the highlight to the function and then press the Enter key.

You can also execute some of the functions on the pull-down menus by using the *shortcut keys*. If a function has a shortcut key, it's listed to the right of the function name on the pull-down menu. In figure 12-2, the pull-down menu shows shortcut keys for the Open, Delete, and Exit functions. So, for example, instead of selecting the File menu then selecting the Exit function to exit from the DOS shell, you can simply press Alt+F4.

Although the shortcut keys can be useful, particularly if you use a function frequently, I won't present them for most of the DOS shell functions. Instead, I'll show you how to execute functions using the pull-down menus. Once you become familiar with the functions available from the pull-down menus, you can use the shortcut keys if you choose to.

If you're running the DOS shell on your PC as you read this chapter and if the DOS shell display is different than the one in figure 12-1, take a moment now to change the display. First, select the View menu from the menu bar. Then, select the Program/File-list view from the menu. Now, your display should match the figures in this chapter.

When you use the DOS shell, you'll probably notice that the items in the menu bar change as you move from one area to another. When the program-list area is active, for example, the Tree menu is removed from the menu bar. In addition, the functions that appear in the pull-down menus vary depending on which area of the shell is active. In some cases, menu functions are displayed in grey to show that they're unavailable because they don't apply to the area that's active. (On a monochrome monitor, these functions aren't displayed at all.) When you're using the directory-tree area, for example, the Copy function of the File menu isn't available because you can't copy a directory.

How to get Help information from the DOS shell Whenever you're using the DOS shell, you can get information from the Help facility by pressing the F1 key. This information is displayed in a *window* as shown in figure 12-3, and it always relates to whatever you're trying to do at the time. If, for example, you press the F1 key while you're using the file-list area, you get the information shown in this figure. As you can see, the Help information explains what the file list does.

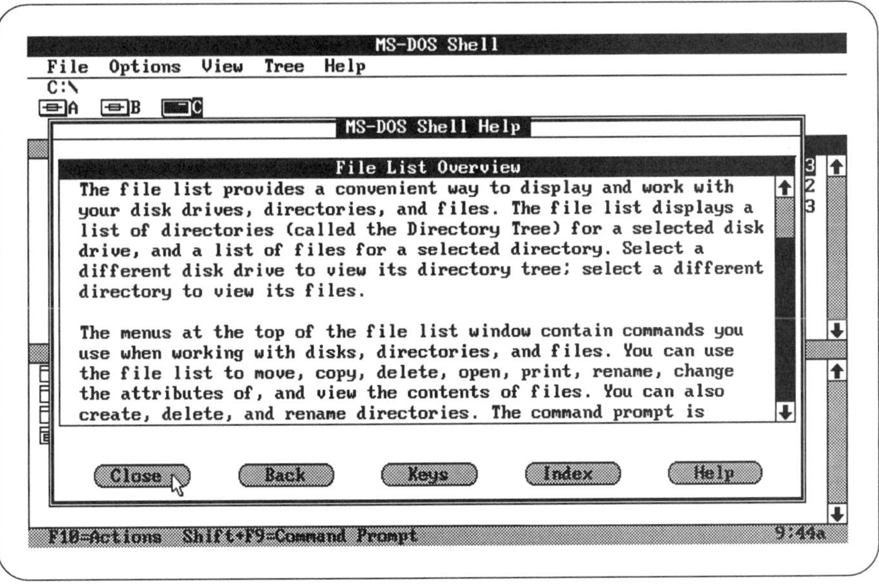

Figure 12-3 One of the Help facility windows that's displayed when you press the F1 key

The five ovals at the bottom of the Help window are called *buttons*. To use any one of the button functions, you click on it with the mouse. You can also start one of these functions by using the Tab key to move the cursor to the desired button and then pressing the Enter key. For instance, you can cancel the Help function by clicking the mouse on the Close button, or you can move the cursor to it and then press the Enter key.

The Help button in figure 12-3 provides information about how to use the Help facility. The Index button displays an index of topics within the Help facility. By using it, you can skip directly to any Help subject that's available. The Keys button displays a list of all the functions that can be performed by keyboard and function keys when you're using the DOS shell. And the Back button moves you to the previous Help screen.

How to exit from the DOS shell You can exit from the DOS shell in two different ways. To exit from the shell completely and return to the DOS prompt, you select the Exit option from the File menu. If you want to start the DOS shell again after you use this command, you must enter DOSSHELL at the command prompt.

If you just want to exit from the shell temporarily, you can press the Shift+F9 key combination as indicated by the status bar, or you can select the Command-prompt option from the Main program list. Either way, the DOS command prompt is displayed. To return to the DOS shell, you just type the word "exit" at the prompt and press the Enter key.

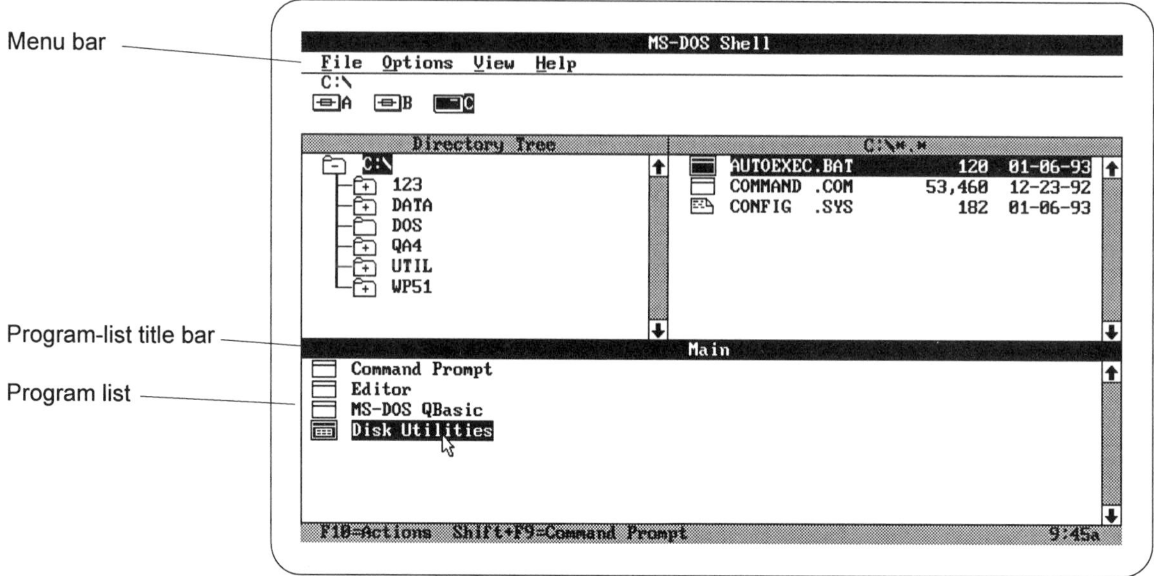

Figure 12-4 The components of the shell that provide the program-list functions

An introduction to the program-list functions of the shell

A *program list* is a menu that you can use for starting your application programs or DOS utilities. When you first install the DOS shell, the program-list area contains a program list with just a few options that let you execute some of the more useful DOS commands. In this chapter, I'll show you how to use the default program list provided with the DOS shell. In the next chapter, you'll learn how to customize that program list by adding options to it that start your application programs.

The components of the DOS shell that provide the program-list functions Figure 12-4 identifies the components of the DOS shell you use to perform program-list functions. The *menu bar* displays the menu choices that are available when you're working with the program list: File, Options, View, and Help. The *program-list title bar* shows the name of the program list that's currently displayed. Here, the *Main program list* is active and it has four options displayed in the program-list area: Command Prompt, Editor, MS-DOS QBasic, and Disk Utilities.

In figure 12-4, you can see that the first three options of the Main program list have plain boxes to the left of them. That means these options start programs or functions. The last option, however, has a box with a pattern of smaller boxes in it. That means it leads to another program list. You can think of the Main program list and its subordinate program lists as a multi-level menu system. And you can think of

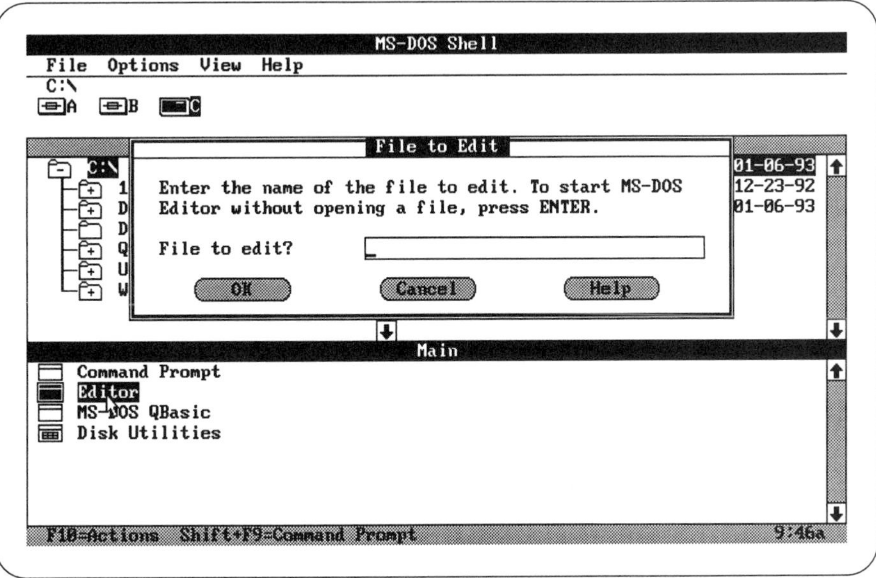

Figure 12-5 The dialog box for the Editor option of the main program list

the options in these program lists as menu choices. You'll understand how these two types of program lists work before you complete this chapter.

How to select an option from the Main program list To select one of the options on the Main program list, you move the mouse cursor to it and press the left mouse button twice in rapid succession. This is referred to as *double-clicking the mouse*. If you don't have a mouse, you must first press the Tab key one or more times to activate this area of the shell. Then you use the cursor control keys to highlight your selection, and you press the Enter key to execute it.

How to start the Edit program The Editor option starts the Edit program that I showed you how to use in chapter 5. This full-screen text editor makes it easy to edit batch files. When you select the Editor, the DOS shell starts by displaying the *dialog box* shown in figure 12-5. After you type in the file specification and press the Enter key, DOS starts the Edit program and loads the file you specified.

How to use the Disk-utilities program list When you select the Disk-utilities option from the Main program list, the DOS shell displays a list of utilities that varies depending on whether you're using DOS 5.0 or 6.0. Figure 12-6 shows the DOS 5.0 Disk-utilities program list. Here, the Diskcopy option runs the DOS Diskcopy command, the Backup-fixed-disk option runs the DOS Backup

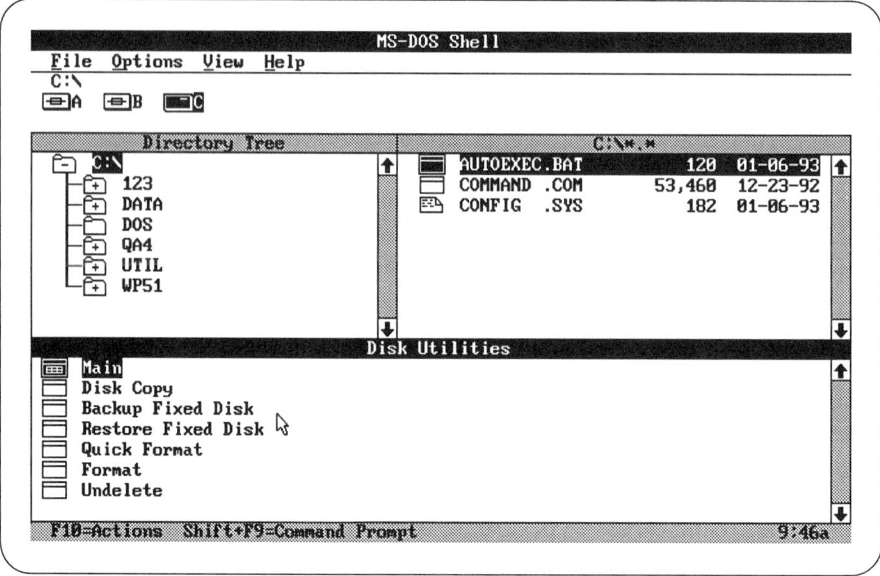

Figure 12-6 The Disk-utilities program list for the DOS 5.0 shell

command, and so on. Figure 12-7 shows the DOS 6.0 version of the Disk-utilities program list. It's the same as the DOS 5.0 version, except that the outdated Backup and Restore options have been replaced by options that run the newer DOS 6.0 Backup and Anti-Virus utilities. You'll learn about these utilities in chapters 16 and 17. (Incidentally, if you upgraded from DOS 5.0 to 6.0, the DOS shell will probably continue to display the DOS 5.0 version of the Disk-utilities program list. You can skip ahead to chapter 23 if you want to learn how to upgrade the DOS shell so it displays the DOS 6.0 version of this list.)

When you select one of these options, a dialog box asks for parameters. To illustrate, figure 12-8 shows the dialog box you get when you select the Format option. Here, the default drive is drive A. So if you want to format a 720KB diskette in drive B, which is a 1.44MB drive, you have to type in the following information:

```
b: /f:720
```

These are the parameters I presented in chapter 8 when I showed you how to format a diskette using the Format command at the DOS prompt. So even though you're using the DOS shell, you have to know the details of the command.

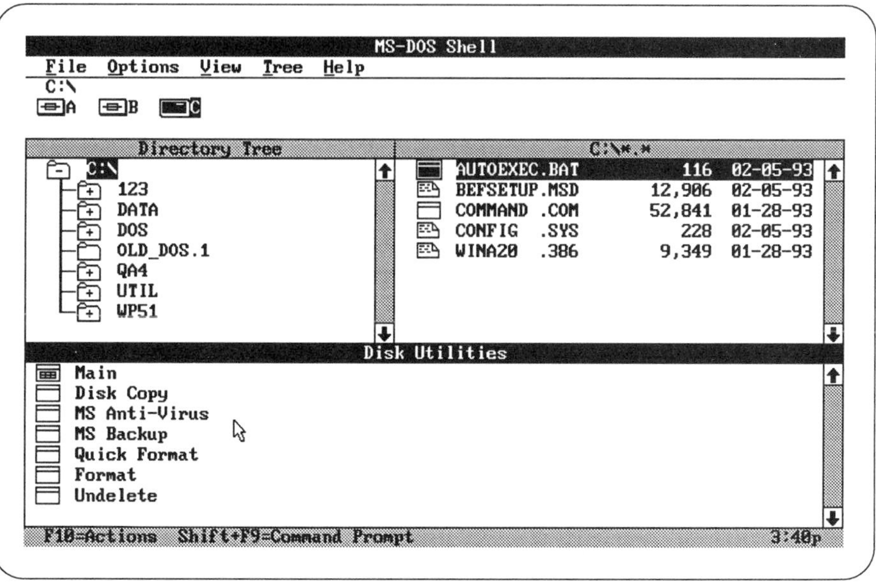

Figure 12-7 The Disk-utilities program list for the DOS 6.0 shell

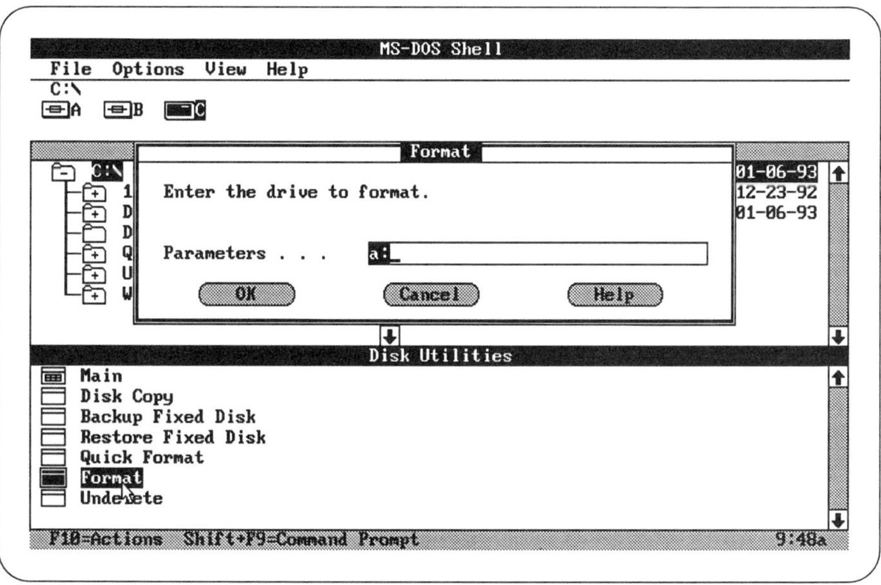

Figure 12-8 The dialog box for the Format option in the Disk-utilities program list

An introduction to the file-management functions of the shell

When you use the DOS shell to manage files, you use the directory-tree and file-list areas of the screen. After I introduce you to these and other components, I'll show you how to change the default drive, change the current directory, scroll through a file list, scroll through a directory tree, and select files. I'll also show you the functions available from the File menu for managing files.

The components of the DOS shell that provide file-management functions Figure 12-9 identifies the components you use to manage files. You're already familiar with the menu bar. If the directory-tree or file-list area is active, the menu bar displays five choices for pull-down menus: File, Options, View, Tree, and Help.

The drive-icon bar displays the drives and highlights the default drive. If your monitor is in graphics mode, the shell uses a symbol to indicate whether a drive is a diskette drive or a hard drive. In addition, the *path bar* displays the default drive and path. In figure 12-9, this bar specifies the root directory on the C drive.

The directory-tree area presents a *directory tree*, which is a graphic representation of the default drive's directory structure. If your monitor is in graphics mode, folders represent directories, and plus signs on those folders identify directories that have subdirectories that aren't displayed. One directory is highlighted to identify it as the current directory.

The file-list area displays a *file list*, which is a list of the files of the current directory in a format that is similar to one displayed by the Directory command. In graphics mode, a symbol next to each file indicates whether the file is a program file or a data file. This symbol is called a *file icon*. The *selection cursor* is a bar in this area that's used to select files by highlighting them.

How to change the default drive To change the default drive, you can use the mouse to click on the drive you want in the drive-icon bar. If you don't have a mouse, you can hold down the Ctrl key while you press the letter of the drive you want. Or you can press the Tab key until the drive-icon bar becomes active. Then, you can use the cursor control keys to highlight the drive that you want and press the Enter key.

How to change the current directory To change the current directory, you can use the mouse to click on the directory you want. If you don't have a mouse, you must first use the Tab key to activate the directory-tree area. Then, you use the cursor control keys to highlight the directory you want and press the Enter key.

How to scroll through a file list If a directory has more files than can be displayed in the file-list area at one time, you can scroll through the list to view all of the files. The easiest way to do that is by using the cursor control keys to move through the list one line at a time, or by using the Page-up and Page-down keys to move through the list one screen at a time.

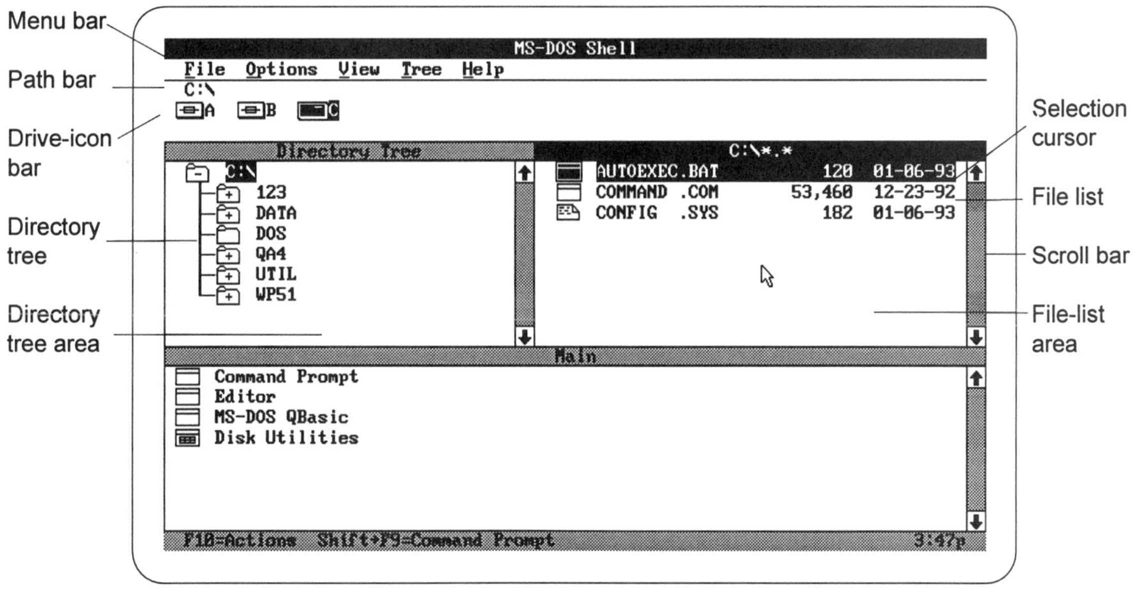

Figure 12-9 The components of the shell that provide the file-management functions

You can also scroll through the list with a mouse by using the *scroll bar* to the right of the file list. You can scroll down one line at a time by clicking on the arrow at the bottom of the scroll bar. Similarly, you can scroll up one line at a time by clicking on the arrow at the top of the scroll bar.

To scroll through varying numbers of lines with the mouse, you move the mouse cursor to the portion of the scroll bar called the *scroll box* as illustrated in part 1 of figure 12-10. Then, you hold down the left mouse button while you move the scroll box to the new position. As you move the mouse, the file list scrolls to its new position, as you can see in part two of figure 12-10. Notice that the file named ATTRIB.EXE, which was at the bottom of the file list in part 1, has been scrolled off of the list in part 2.

To help you gauge your position when you use the scroll bar, the height of the scroll box indicates the relative size of the file list. For instance, the scroll box in figure 12-9 occupies the entire scroll bar, which means that all of the files in the directory are displayed. In contrast, the scroll box in figure 12-10 indicates that about one-fifth of the files in the directory are displayed. In part 1, the scroll box indicates that the files in the first part of the directory are displayed. In part 2, the box indicates that the files in the middle part of the directory are displayed.

How to scroll through a directory tree If a drive has more directories than can be displayed in the directory-tree area at one time, you can scroll through the directory tree just as you can the file list. Again, the easiest way to do that is by using the cursor control keys to move the tree display one line at a time or by using the Page-up and Page-down keys to move the tree one screen at a time.

You can also scroll through the directory tree with a mouse by using the scroll bar to the right of the directory tree. You can scroll up or down one line at a time by clicking on one of the arrows at the top or bottom of the scroll bar. And you can scroll varying amounts by moving the scroll box.

Figure 12-11 shows how the shell displays a typical directory structure. Here, plus signs (+) on folders indicate that these directories have at least one subdirectory. To expand a directory so you can see these subdirectories, you move the mouse to the directory folder as shown in part 1. When you click the mouse, the directory is *expanded* to display any subdirectories as shown in part 2. To use the keyboard to expand a directory, you press the Tab key to activate the directory-tree area. Then, you use the cursor control keys to move to the desired directory. When you press the Plus sign key, the DOS shell expands the directory.

When a directory has been expanded, a minus sign (-) is displayed in the directory folder to indicate that you can *collapse* the directory. To collapse an expanded directory using a mouse, you just click on the folder. To collapse a directory using the keyboard, you move the highlight to the folder and press the Minus sign key.

The DOS shell also provides commands you can use to expand and collapse directories. You access these commands from the Tree menu. With them, you can expand one directory or all of the directories on the tree, and you can collapse a directory.

How to select files When you use DOS commands, you enter the names of the files you want to process as parameters. In contrast, when you use the DOS shell, you don't enter file names. Instead, you select the files you want to process before you start a command. Then, when you select the command that you want from a menu, all the files you selected are processed. To delete files, for example, you first select all the files you want to delete. Next, you select the Delete command from the File menu. All the selected files are then deleted.

You can use three techniques to select files using a mouse. First, you can select a single file by moving the mouse cursor to the file in the file list and clicking on it. After you select a file, it's highlighted.

Second, you can select several files by holding down the Ctrl key as you click on each file. If you click on a file that's already selected while holding down the Ctrl key, the file is deselected. With this technique, you can select any number of files from anywhere in the file display as shown in figure 12-12.

Third, you can select a group of files that are listed together. First, you move the mouse cursor to the first file in the group and click on it, as shown in part 1 of figure 12-13. Next, you move the mouse cursor to the last file in the group you want to select. Then, you hold down the Shift key as you click on the file. All the files in the

Part 1:

Put the mouse cursor on the scroll box.

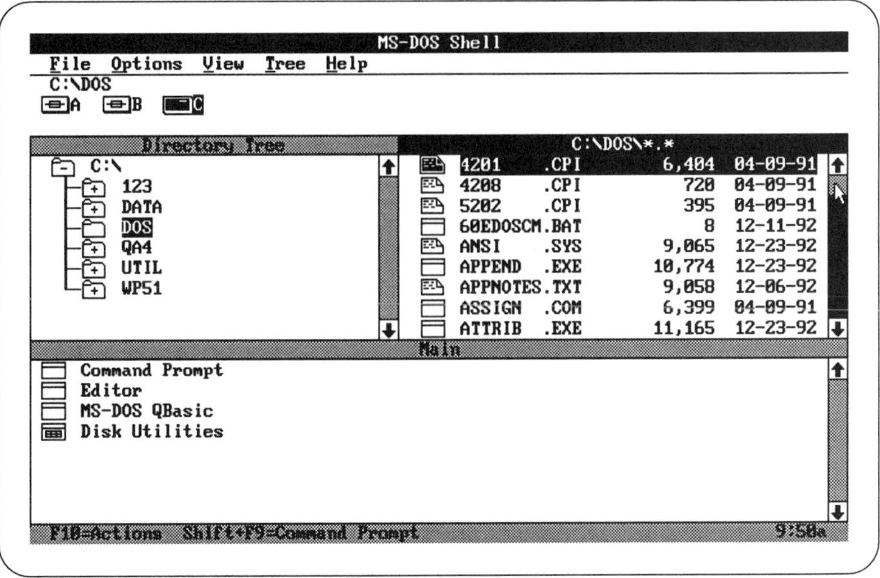

Part 2:

While holding down the left mouse button, drag the scroll box to the new file position.

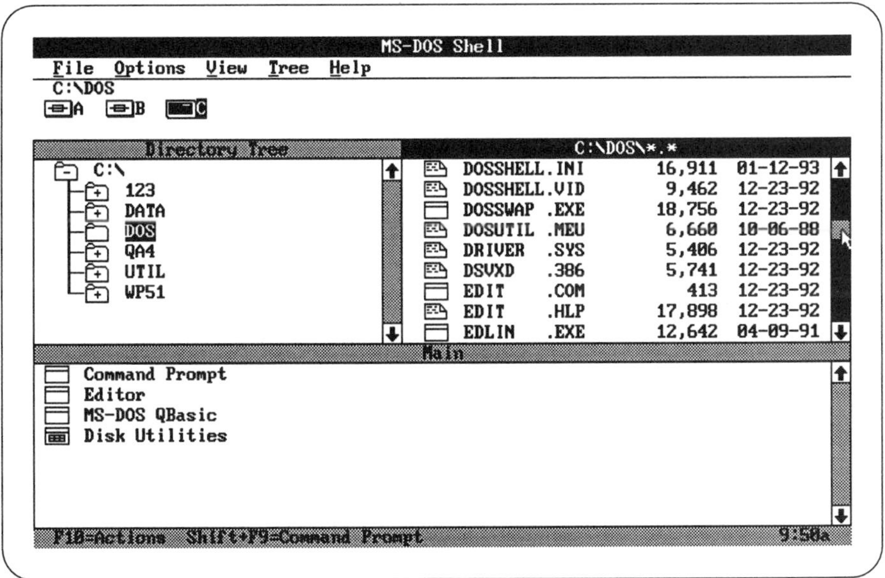

Figure 12-10 How to use the scroll bar to scroll through the file list

Part 1:

Move the mouse cursor to the folder of the directory you want to expand and click the mouse.

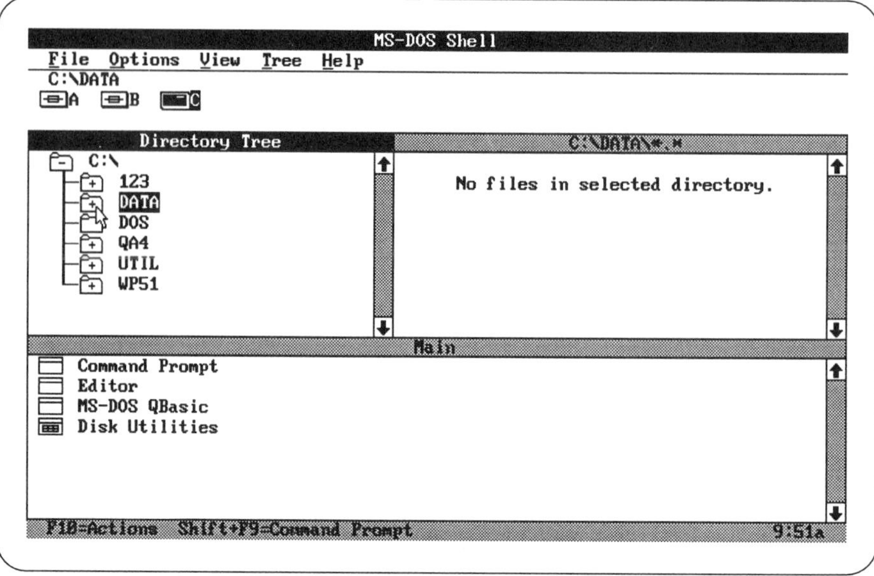

Part 2:

The expanded directory is then displayed.

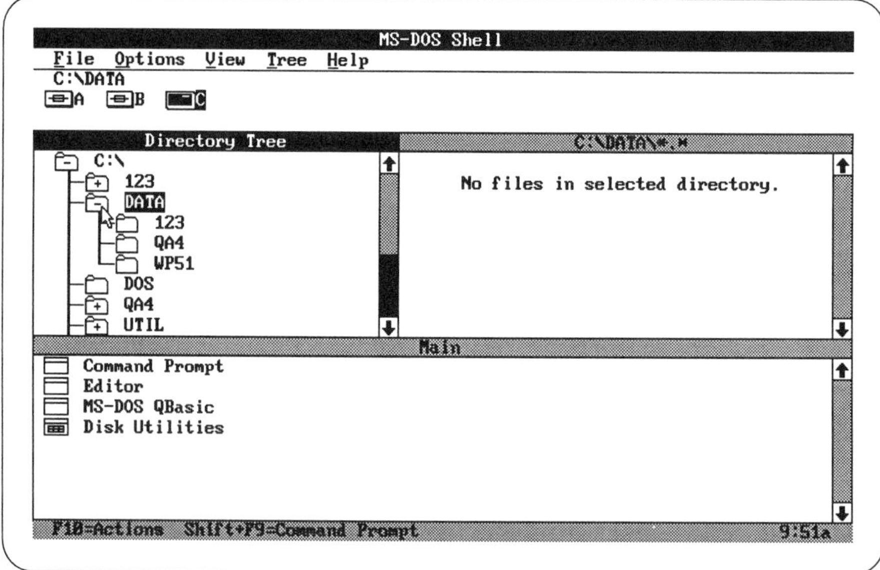

Figure 12-11 How to expand a directory

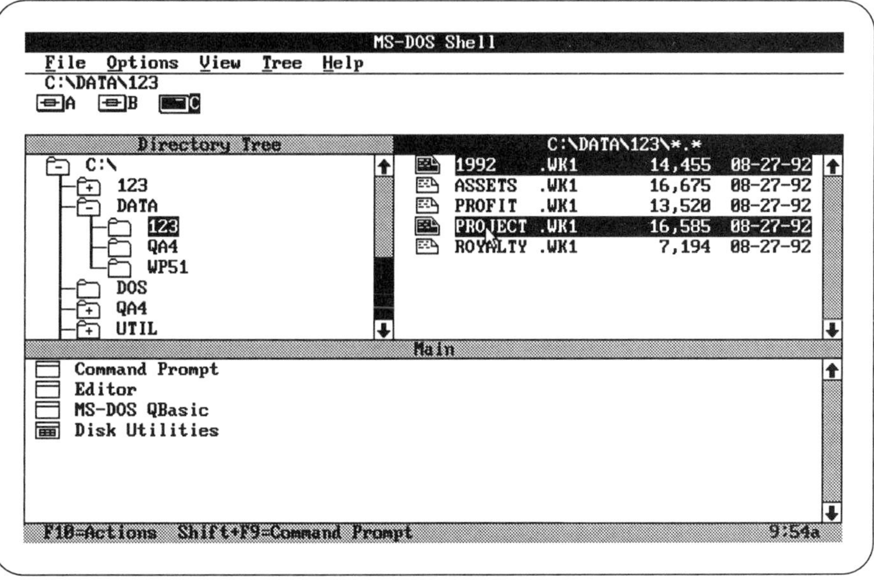

Figure 12-12 Two files selected by holding down the Ctrl key as you click the mouse on each file

group are then selected, as shown in part 2 of figure 12-13. If you need to cancel all the files you've selected, just click the mouse on any file.

To select a single file with the keyboard, you use the cursor control keys to move the selection cursor to the file. To select several files, you press the Shift-F8 key combination to turn on Add mode. Then, you use the cursor control keys to move to each file you want to select and press the Space bar. If you press the Space bar on a file that's already selected while Add mode is on, the file is deselected. To turn Add mode off, you press the Shift+F8 keys again. To select a group of files, you hold down the Shift key and use the cursor control keys to select the group. If you need to cancel all the files you've selected, just press the Space bar.

Functions available from the pull-down menus If you look again at figure 12-9, you can see that when the file-list area is active, the menu bar contains these five selections: File, Options, View, Tree, and Help. The pull-down menu you'll use the most as you work with files and directories is the File menu, shown in figure 12-14. As you can see, it provides several groups of functions. Many of these functions correspond to familiar DOS commands, such as Copy, Delete, and Rename. Other functions, such as Associate, are unique to the shell. You'll learn how to use all of these functions in chapter 14.

Part 1:

Select the first file in the group, then move the mouse cursor to the last file in the group.

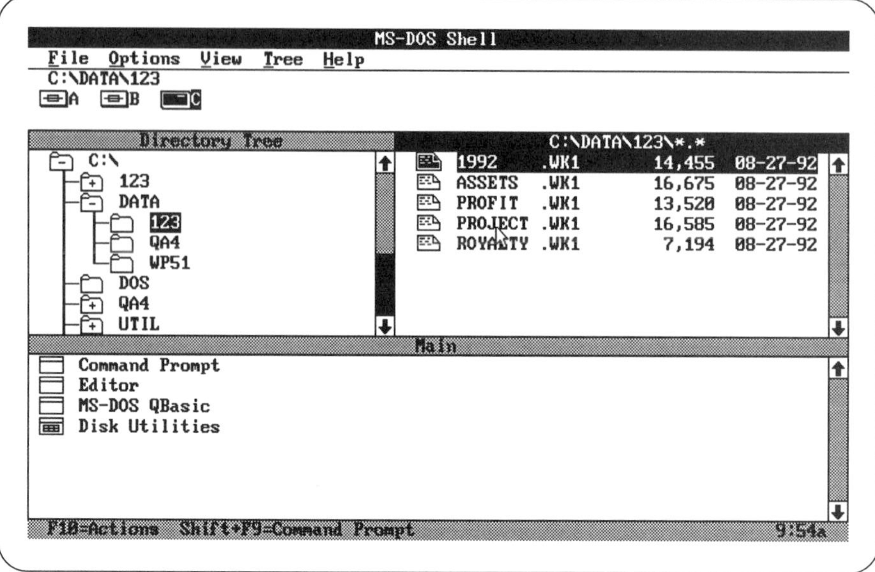

Part 2:

Select the group by holding down the Shift key while you click the mouse on the last file.

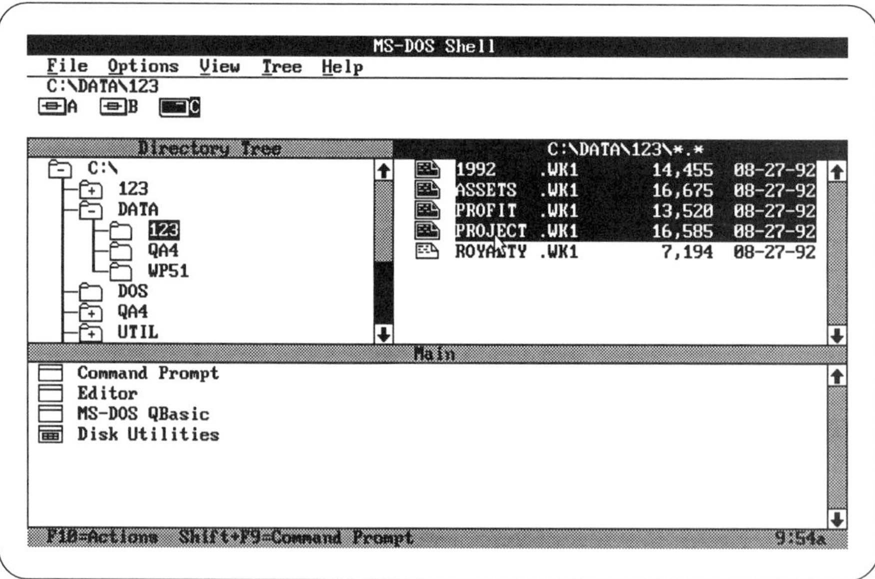

Figure 12-13 How to select a group of files

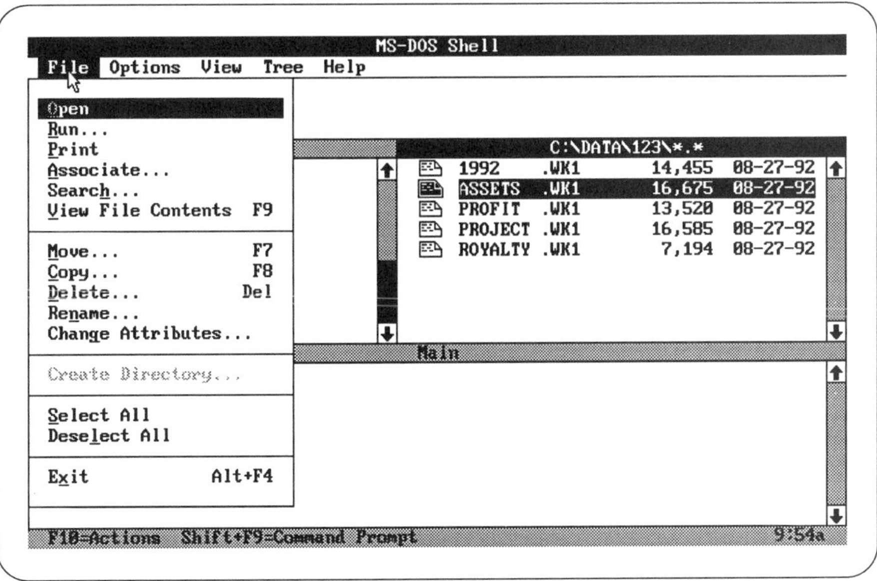

Figure 12-14 The File menu when the file-list area is active

How to start a command or program from the file-list area

When you use the DOS shell, you can start any command or program from the file-list area. To do this with a mouse, you double-click on the command or program file in the file list. To do this with the keyboard, you use the cursor control keys to highlight the command or program file and then press the Enter key.

Since you can use this method to start any file with a COM or EXE extension, you can start any of the external DOS commands in this way. You can also start batch files this way. If, for example, you have already stored one batch file for each of your application programs in the UTIL directory, you just change the current directory to UTIL, select the batch file you want to execute, and start the batch file using one of the techniques I just mentioned.

Some perspective on the DOS shell

If you use the DOS shell only for starting commands and programs, you won't get much benefit from it. In fact, if you already use batch files to start your application programs, you can probably start them faster from the command prompt than you can from the shell. Similarly, if you already know how to use the DOS commands, you can probably run them faster from the command prompt than you can from the Disk-utilities program list in the shell.

In the next chapter, though, you'll learn how to use the DOS shell to create and use menus to start your application programs. Then, in chapter 14, you'll learn how to use the shell to manage directories and files. After you finish these chapters, you'll have a better idea of how the DOS shell can help you work more efficiently.

Terms

shell program
DOS shell
menu bar
drive icon
drive-icon bar
directory-tree area
file-list area
program-list area
status bar
clicking the mouse
pull-down menu
shortcut key
window
button
program list
menu bar
program-list title bar
main program list
double-clicking the mouse
dialog box
path bar
directory tree
file list
file icon
selection cursor
scroll bar
scroll box
expand a directory
collapse a directory

Objectives

1. Start a program or function from the program-list area.
2. Given file specifications for one or more files, select the files from the file-list area.
3. Start a command or program from the file-list area.

Chapter 13

How to use the DOS shell to create and use menus

The program-list functions of the DOS shell make it easy for you to create menus for starting your application programs. Once you create the menus, you can start your application programs more easily from a program list than you can from the file list. All you have to do to start a program is double click the mouse on the selection you want. Or if you don't have a mouse, you just highlight the selection you want and press the Enter key.

In this chapter, you'll learn how to use the program-list functions to create your own menus. You'll also learn how to customize the items on a menu so they start your programs the way you want them to. If you've read the last chapter, you already know the general techniques for using the DOS shell, so this chapter should be easy to follow. When you finish this chapter, you should be able to set up menus for your own programs in just a few minutes.

The menu structure of the program-list area

The program-list area in figure 13-1 shows the Main program list. When you install DOS 5.0 or 6.0, this screen automatically has the four options shown here: Command Prompt, Editor, MS-DOS QBasic, and Disk Utilities. As you can see, the first three options have plain boxes to the left of them to indicate that they start programs. The last option, however, has a box with a pattern of smaller boxes in it. This symbol indicates that this option leads to another program list.

When you use the DOS shell, you can create a multi-level menu system. The Main program list can lead to other program lists, and those program lists can lead to still others. For most users, though, a two-level menu structure is adequate. So the menu structure consists of just the Main program list and the program lists that it leads to.

If you use just two or three application programs, it's probably best to add them to the Main program list shown in figure 13-1. If, on the other hand, you use several programs, it's probably best to create a program list for them that's subordinate to the Main program list. You can call this something like "Applications."

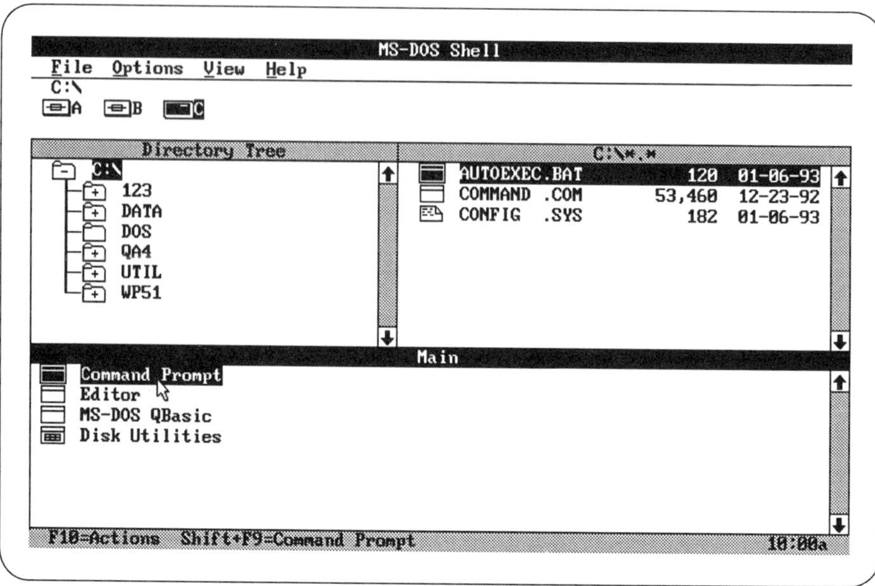

Figure 13-1 The Main program list

How to add a program list to the Main program list

To add a program list to the Main program list, you activate the program-list area and pull down the File menu as shown in figure 13-2. As you can see, it provides eight functions: New, Open, Copy. Delete, Properties, Reorder, Run, and Exit. In this chapter, I'll show you how to use only the New and Properties functions because all the others are easy to use once you know how to use these two.

Figure 13-3 shows the dialog boxes that appear when you select the New function from the File menu. The dialog box in part 1 lets you specify whether you want to add a new *program group* or a new *program item* to the current list. In this case, I've selected the Program-group option to add a subordinate program list to the Main program list. Here, *program group* is just another name for a program list.

The dialog box in part 2 lets you enter information to identify the new program list. The Title entry is the name of the list that will be added to the Main program list. This entry can be up to 23 characters long, and it's the only required entry for this dialog box.

The Help-text entry can be used if you want Help information to be available for the program group. If you make an entry, the text is displayed when the PC user presses the F1 key while the group is highlighted. Usually, though, the purpose of a program group is obvious so there's no reason to include a Help-text entry.

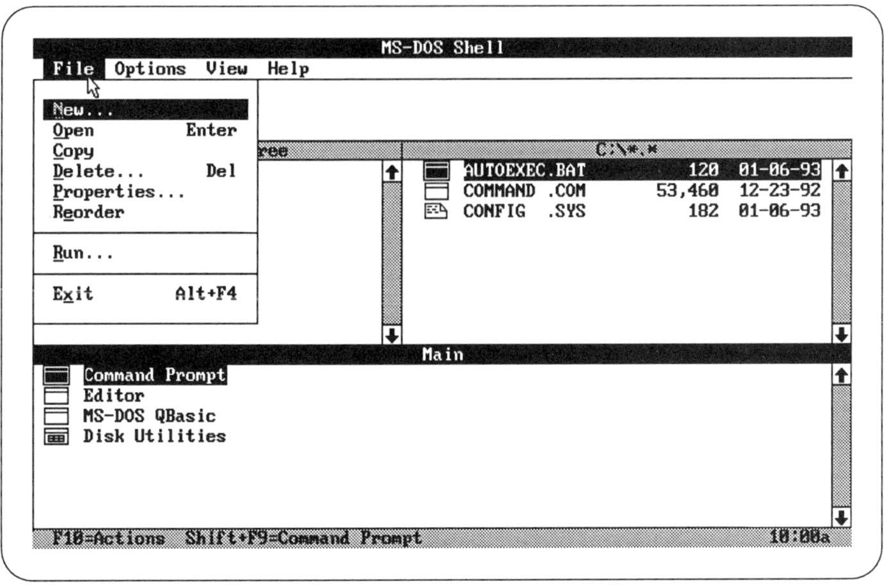

Figure 13-2 The File menu when the program-list area is active

The Password entry can be used if you want to restrict access to the new program list. Then, only a PC user who knows the password can use the programs in the program list. Since passwords have a limited use, you usually leave this entry blank.

After you've completed the entries in this dialog box, use the OK button to add the program list to the Main program list. In figure 13-4, you can see how the Title entry in figure 13-3 is displayed after this list has been added to the Main program list. Also notice that the Applications option has a box with a grid of smaller boxes in it to indicate that it leads to another program list.

How to add a program to a program list

To add a program to a program list, you select the program list in the Main program list that you want to add a program to. If, for example, you want to add a program to the Applications program list, you first select the Applications program list from the Main program list. Then, the shell displays the screen shown in figure 13-5. Notice that the title bar now tells you that you're in the Applications program list. As you can see, the Applications program list is empty except for the option that takes you back to the Main program list.

Part 1:

First, you select the New option from the File menu. Then, you choose the Program-group option in the first dialog box.

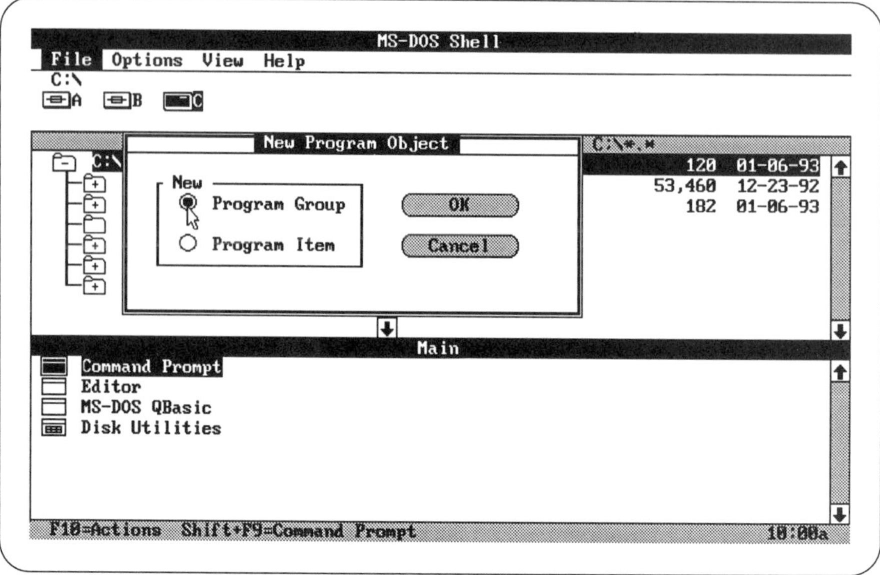

Part 2:

Next, you fill in the entries in the second dialog box that create and identify the new program list.

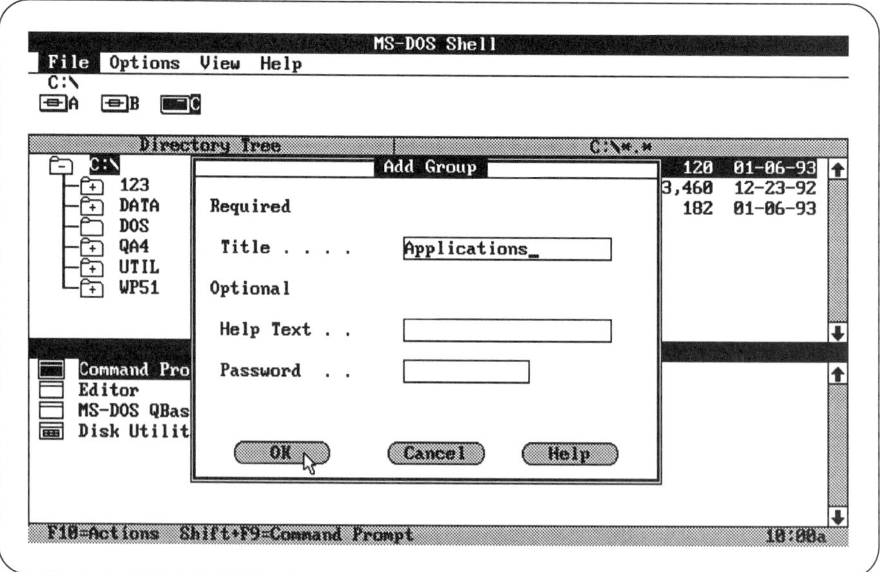

Figure 13-3 How to add a program list to the main program list

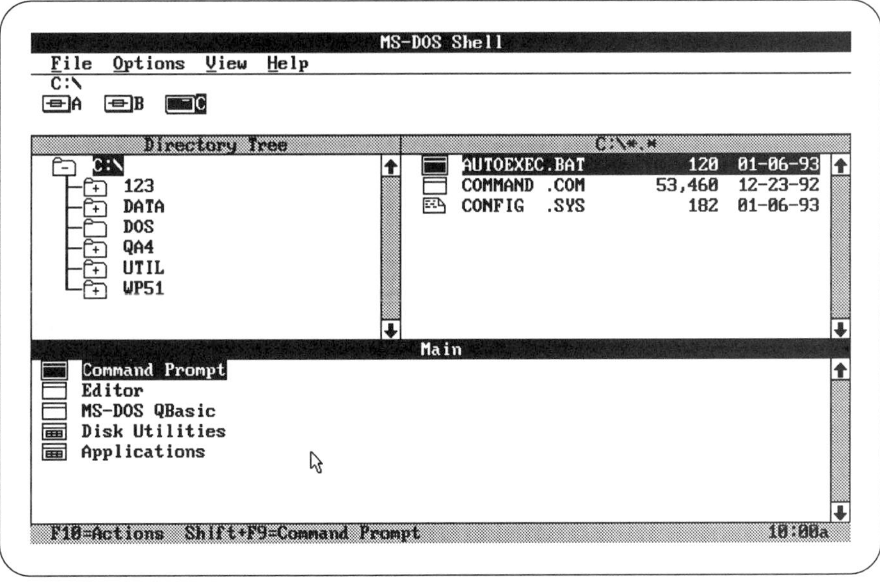

Figure 13-4 The main program list with the Applications option created by the dialog boxes in figure 13-3

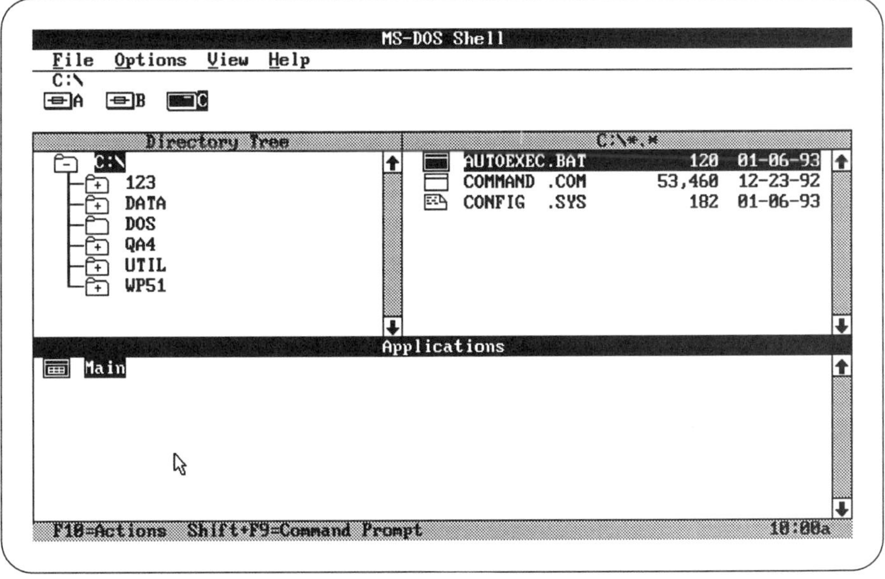

Figure 13-5 The empty program list of the Applications option

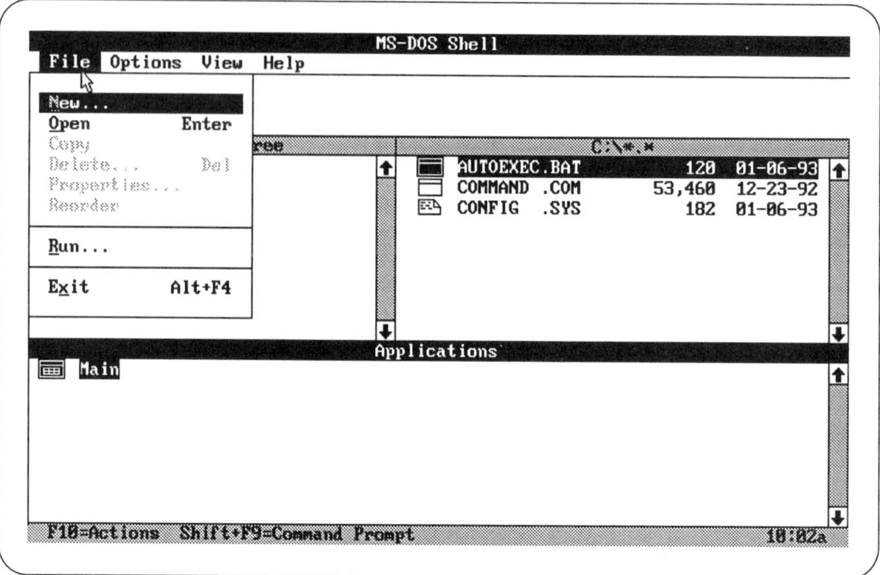

Figure 13-6 The File menu that's displayed for an empty program list

Next, pull down the File menu as shown in figure 13-6. Because the Applications program list is empty, only four options are available on the menu. Select the New option. When you do, the dialog boxes in figure 13-7 appear.

The dialog box in part 1 of figure 13-7 lets you specify whether you want to add a new program group or program item to the current list. In this case, I've selected the Program-item option to add a program to a program list. Here, the term *program item* just refers to the menu item that will start the program that's being added to the program list.

The dialog box in part 2 lets you enter information that's needed to start the program. The first required entry is the Title entry. This establishes the title that will be used in the subordinate program list. In this example, the title that will appear on the program list is *Lotus 1-2-3*.

The second required entry is the Commands entry. For this entry, you can enter one or more commands, provided you don't exceed 256 characters. When you enter more than one command, you separate each command with a space, a semicolon (;), and another space. In part 2 of figure 13-7, you can see that the Command entry contains these three DOS commands:

```
c: ; cd \123 ; 123
```

The first command changes the default drive to the C drive; the second command changes the current directory to the 123 directory; and the third command starts *Lotus*

Part 1:

After you select the program list that you want to add a program to, you select the New option from the File menu. Then, you choose the Program-item option in the first dialog box.

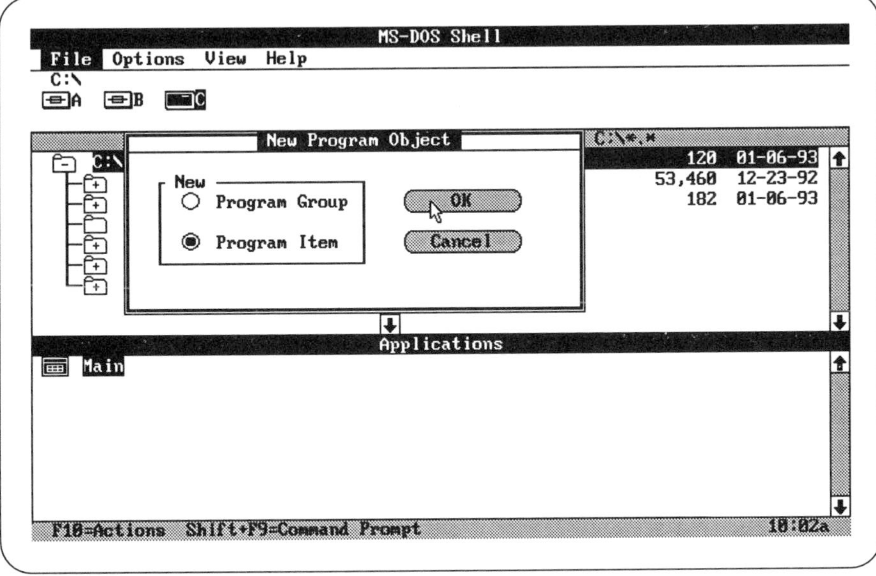

Part 2:

Next, you fill in the entries in the second dialog box that will identify and start the application program.

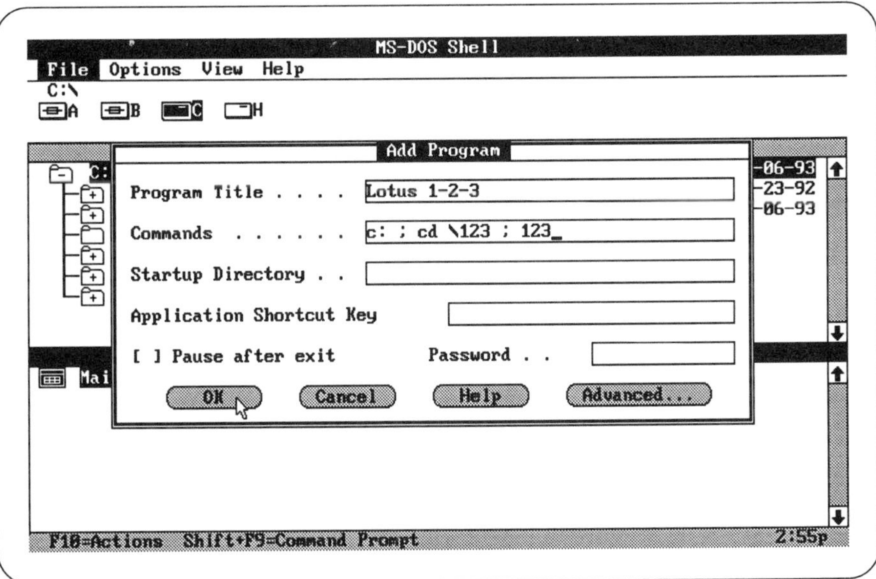

Figure 13-7 How to add a program to a program list

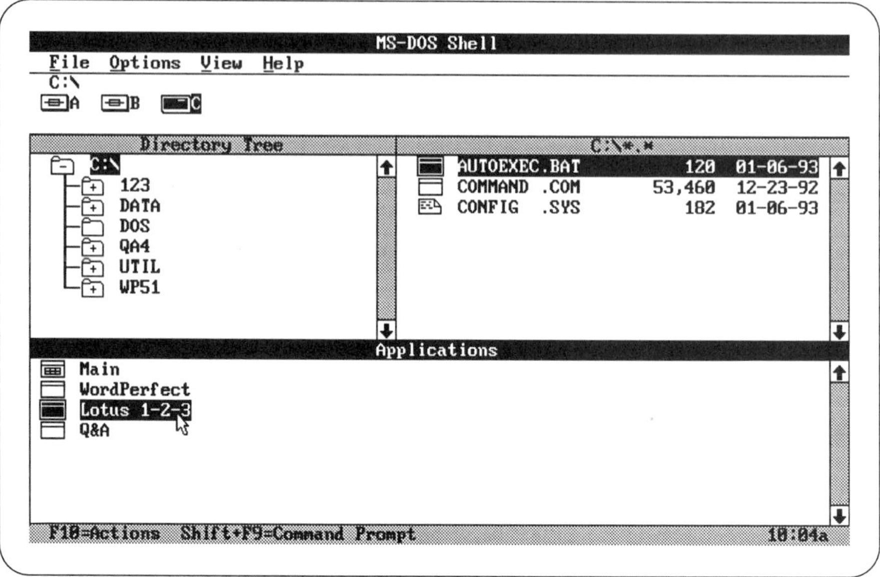

Figure 13-8 The options of the Applications program list

1-2-3. If you already have a batch file set up for starting *Lotus 1-2-3* that contains these three commands, you can simplify your Commands entry by entering only the command for the batch file.

As you can see, the last three entries are optional. The Startup-directory entry lets you specify the data directory that you want to use with the program. However, this doesn't work with many programs. The Applications-shortcut-key entry lets you assign a special keystroke combination to an application program. I'll show you how to use this entry in chapter 15 when I explain the task switching capabilities of DOS 5.0 and 6.0. The Pause-after-exit entry lets you return to the shell immediately after you exit an application program, or it lets you pause and press a key before you return to the shell. And the Password entry lets you assign a password that restricts access to the program. Most of the time, you'll leave these entries blank.

After you've added one application program to a program list, you'll see how easy it is. Then, you can add the other application programs you use to the list. If you want to reorder the program items in a list, you put the highlight on the program item you want to move, and you execute the Reorder function from the File menu. When I finished adding programs to my Applications group, it looked like the one in figure 13-8.

How to set up a customized dialog box for a program item

If the command that starts an application program accepts parameters, you can set up a customized dialog box so you can enter the parameter when you start the program. For instance, you can set up a dialog box for *WordPerfect* that accepts the file name for the first document to be processed by the program.

Figure 13-9 shows you how to create a customized dialog box. First, you highlight the application program in the program list. Then, you select the Properties function from the File menu to get the dialog box shown in part 1 of figure 13-9. Next, you enter a replaceable parameter in the command that starts the program. Here, the replaceable parameter (%1) after the WP command lets you enter a file name when you start *WordPerfect*. In this example, I've used the Startup-directory entry to specify a starting data directory because this works with *WordPerfect*.

Part 2 of figure 13-9 shows the dialog box that the DOS shell displays next. You use the Window-title entry to identify the customized dialog box. You use the Program-information entry to explain how you use the box. You use the Prompt-message entry to prompt for the parameter. And you use the Default-parameters entry to specify a default parameter (if you want one).

After you set up a dialog box like this one, the DOS shell displays it every time you use the program list to start the program. Figure 13-10, for example, shows the dialog box that's displayed as a result of the entries in figure 13-9. Here, the box prompts you for the file you want to use with *WordPerfect* and offers the file named LETTER as a default. At this box, you can either accept the default file specification or type in the one for the file you want to use. After you use the OK button, the DOS shell starts *WordPerfect* and loads the file you specified.

How to modify a program item in a program list

The DOS shell makes it easy for you to modify program items after you've created them. First, you highlight the item you want to change. Then, you select the Properties function from the File menu. The same dialog boxes you used to create the item are then displayed so you can change any of the entries. The new settings are put into effect as soon as you complete the process.

Some perspective on the DOS shell

Without much trouble, you should now be able to set up the menus you need for starting all of your application programs. This can simplify the operation of your PC. And it can be particularly valuable if your PC is used by several people who have trouble starting programs from the DOS prompt.

If you compare the use of the program lists of the DOS shell to the use of batch files, you'll realize that you can start programs just as fast from batch files at the command prompt as you can from the shell. However, you can usually add a program to a program list faster than you can create a batch file for starting a program. Also,

Part 1:

After you select the program from the program list, pull down the File menu and choose the Properties option so you can type a replaceable parameter in the command line of the dialog box.

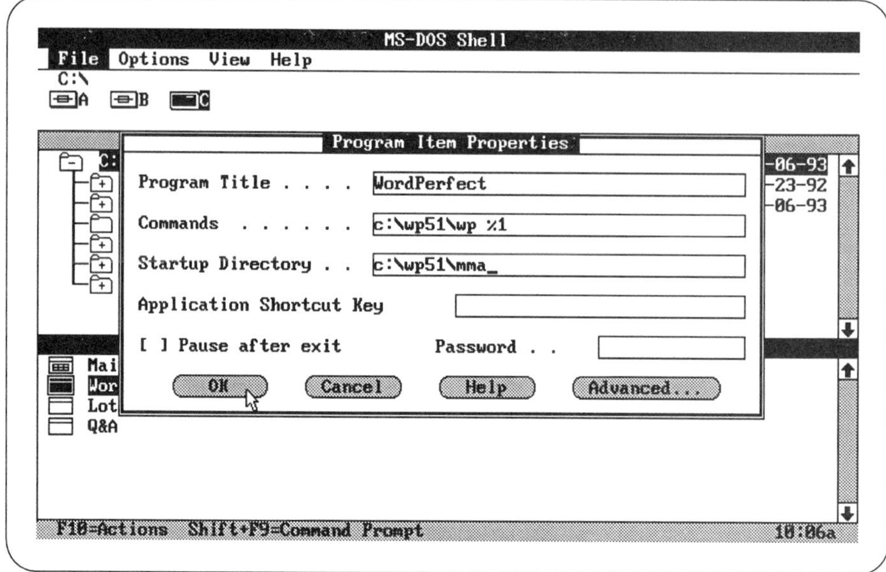

Part 2:

In the second dialog box, you create the text of the customized box and the default value for the replaceable parameter.

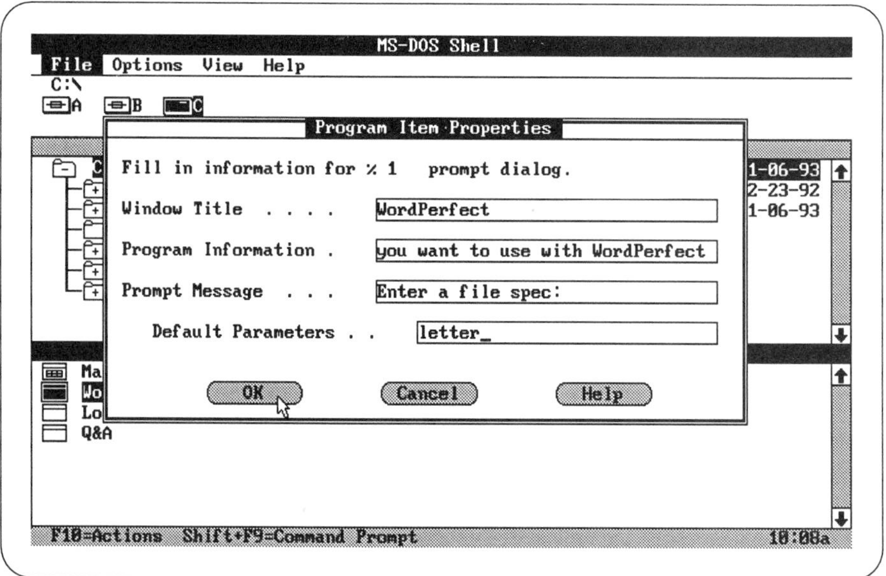

Figure 13-9 How to create a customized dialog box for a program item

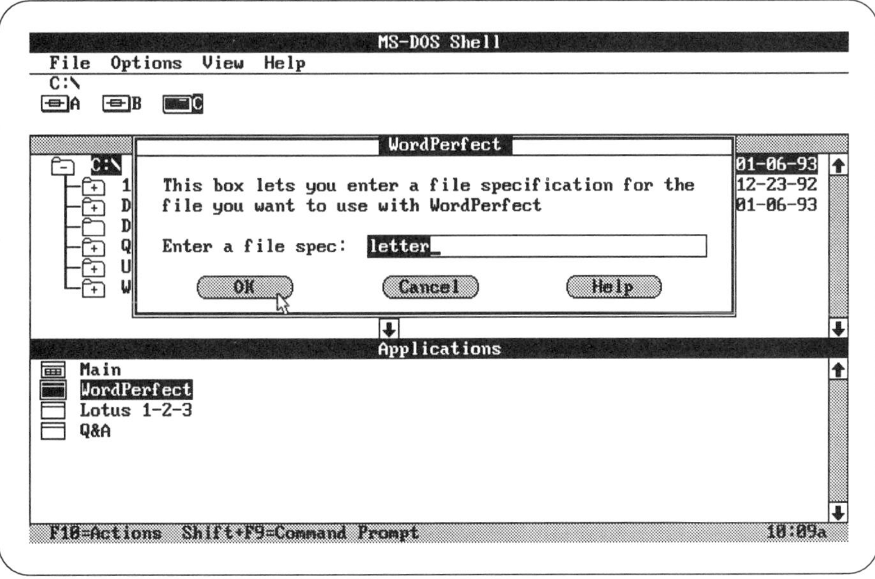

Figure 13-10 The customized dialog box created by the entries in figure 13-9

program lists make the PC easier to use because you don't have to remember the names of batch files. As a result, the menu capability of the DOS shell is clearly an improvement upon the capabilities of earlier versions of DOS.

Terms

program group
program item

Objectives

1. Set up your program-list area so that it includes all the application programs you run regularly.
2. If any programs in your program-list area let you enter parameters when you start them, set up customized dialog boxes for them.

Chapter 14

How to use the DOS shell to manage directories and files

In this chapter, you'll learn how to use the DOS shell to manage directories and files. First, I'll review how you use the directory-tree and the file-list areas to select files for a function. Then, I'll show you how to use the functions of the pull-down menus for these areas. Because you learned the basic techniques for using the DOS shell in chapter 12, you should be able to move quickly through this chapter.

How to use the directory-tree and file-list areas to select files

Before you perform a function on a file or group of files from the DOS shell, you have to select the files. To review how you do that, figure 14-1 shows the DOS shell screen. To select a file using a mouse, you first click on the directory that contains the file or files you want to select. If required, you click on the appropriate directory folder to expand the directory listing. Then, to select a single file, you just click on that file in the file list. To select several files, you hold down the Ctrl key as you click the mouse. If you click on a file that's already selected while holding down the Ctrl key, the file is deselected. And to select a group of files, you select the first file of the group. Then, you move the cursor to the last file in the group and hold down the Shift key as you click the mouse. To cancel your selection, just click the mouse on another file and start the selection process again.

To select a file using the keyboard, you use the cursor control keys to highlight the file. To select several files, you press the Shift+F8 key combination to turn on Add mode. Then, you move to each file you want to select and press the Space bar. If you press the Space bar on a file that's already selected while Add mode is on, the file is deselected. And to select a group of files, you hold down the Shift key as you press the cursor control keys. If you change your mind after you have selected files, you can cancel the selection by pressing the Space bar. After you select a file, it's highlighted in the file list as shown in figure 14-2. Here, two files have been selected.

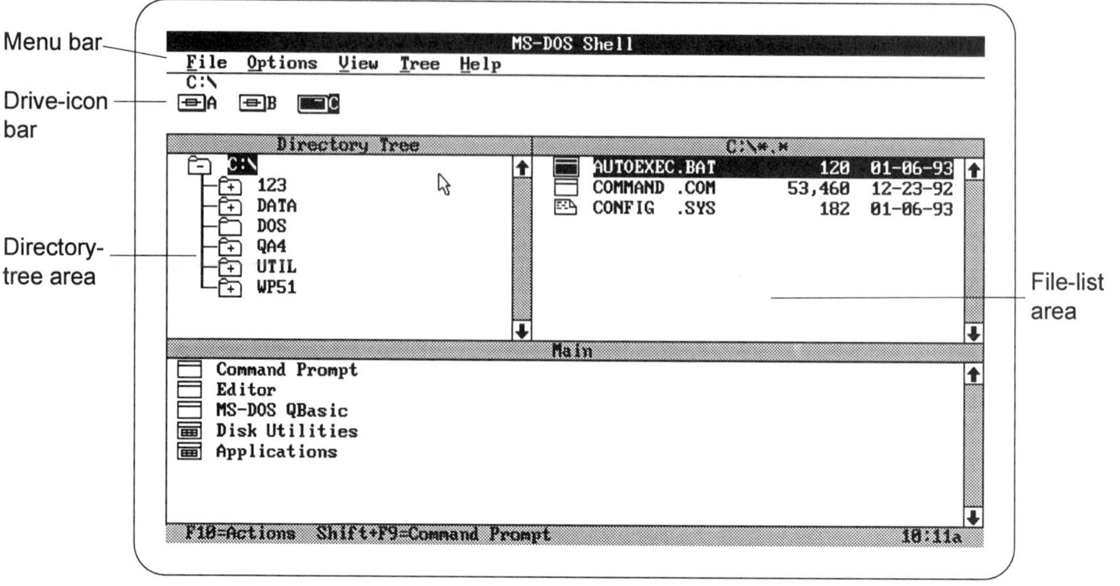

Figure 14-1 The four components of the DOS shell you use to manage directories and files

How to use the File menu for the file-list area

Figure 14-3 shows the File menu for the file-list area. When you pull this menu down while the file-list area is active, the menu offers the 14 functions shown. You use these functions to manage files. Although you may never need some of these functions, I'll go through all of them now so you know how they work.

The Open function You use the Open function to start the command or batch file you've selected. These are files that have extensions of COM, EXE, or BAT. Although you can start a program this way, it's quicker to start one by executing the program's batch file from the file-list area.

The Run function The Run function lets you execute a DOS command from inside the shell. So if you want to use a DOS command to delete all the files in a directory or to copy all the files on a diskette, you don't have to exit from the shell to get to the prompt.

Figure 14-4 shows the dialog box that's displayed when you select the Run function. Here, I've typed in a command to copy all the files from the diskette in drive A to the DATA\WP51 directory on drive C. Occasionally, entering a command in this way is more efficient than using the DOS shell for the task.

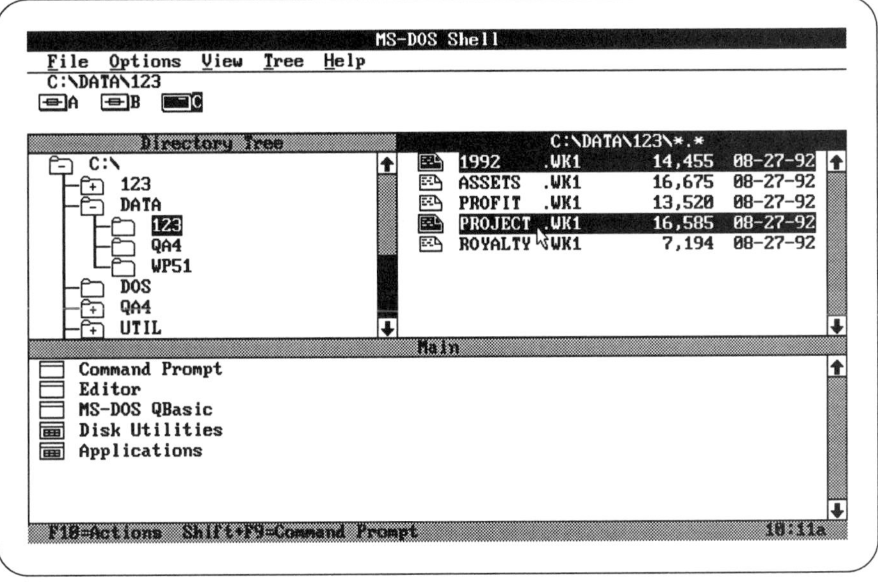

Figure 14-2 Two files selected from the file list

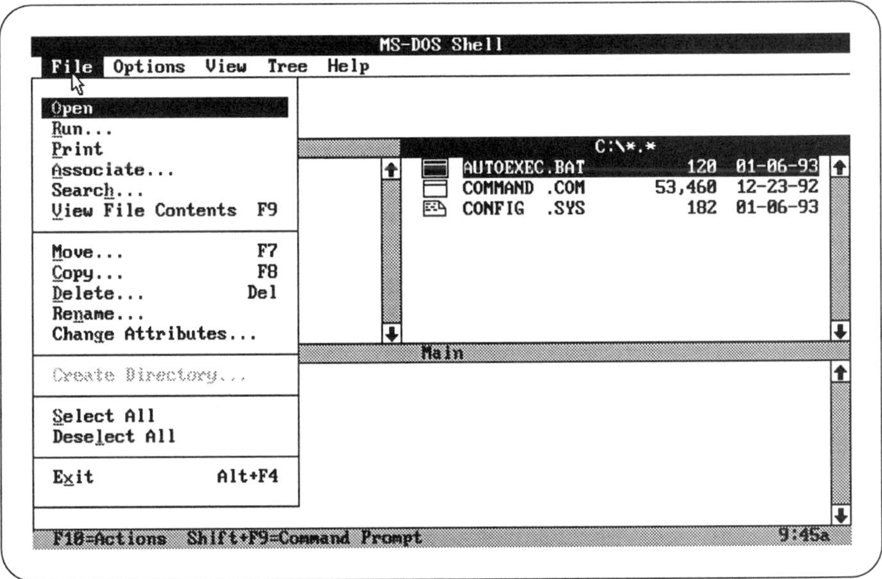

Figure 14-3 The File menu for the file-list area

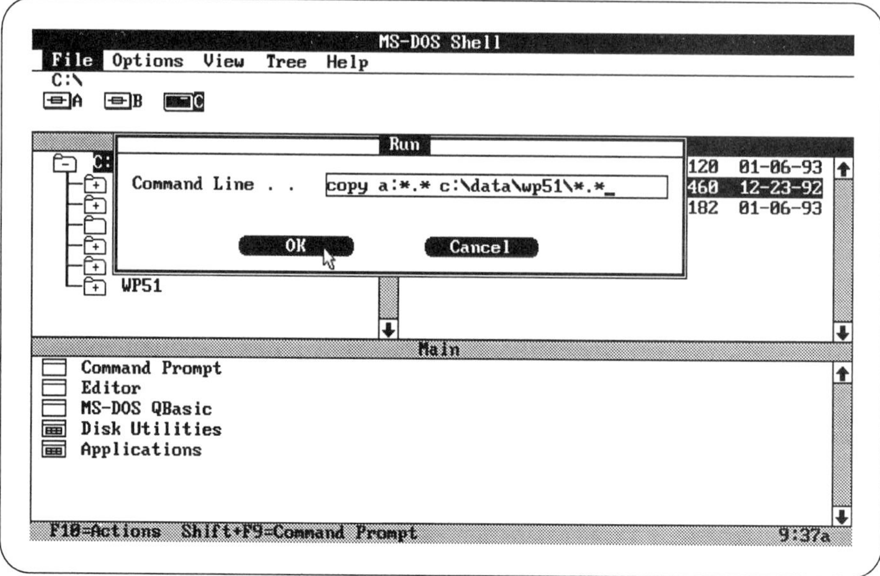

Figure 14-4 The dialog box for the Run function

The Print function The Print function uses the DOS Print command to print up to ten selected files. When you use this function, the files are printed in *background mode*, which means you can use your PC for other jobs while the files are printed.

Before you can use this function, though, the DOS Print command must be executed. When you install DOS 5.0 or 6.0, you can put a Print command in your AUTOEXEC.BAT file so it will be executed each time you start your PC. However, if you don't have the Print command in your AUTOEXEC.BAT file, you must execute it on your own before you use the Print function. To do that, you can enter the Print command without any parameters at the command prompt. Or you can execute the PRINT.EXE file in your DOS directory from the DOS shell.

When you use the Print function, you should realize that you can print files only if they're in standard ASCII format. That means you can't use this function to print word processing, spreadsheet, or database files unless you convert them to print files first. As I explained in chapter 11, though, most application programs allow you to create these print files.

The Associate function The Associate function lets you associate an application program with its data files. Once you've done that, you can start an application program from the file-list area by selecting one of the program's data files instead of selecting the program file itself. The advantage is that the data file you

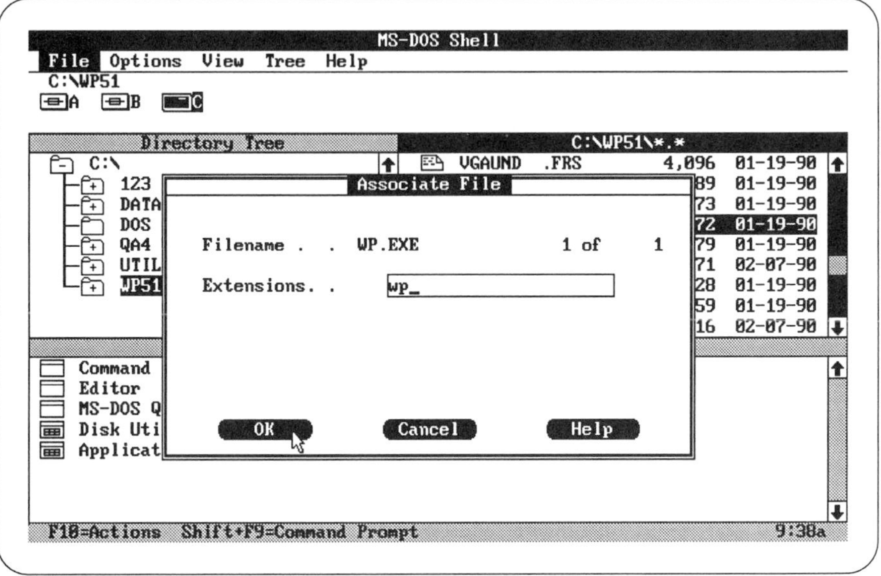

Figure 14-5 The dialog box for the Associate function

select is loaded automatically when the program is started. If, for example, you've associated the application program *WordPerfect* with files that have WP as the extension, you can start *WordPerfect* and load a document by double-clicking on any file with the WP extension. If you don't have a mouse, you can start *WordPerfect* by highlighting any file with the WP extension and pressing the Enter key.

To associate an application program with its data files, you first select the application program file. Then, you select the Associate function from the File menu. When you do that, the DOS shell displays a dialog box like the one in figure 14-5. Here, you type in one or more extensions that are used for the program's data files.

The Associate function will work only with programs that let you specify a data file as the first parameter in the command you use to start the program. As a result, you can't use this function with a program like *Lotus 1-2-3*. Also, this function will work only if a program's data files have consistent extensions. If a program doesn't automatically add extensions, you can establish your own standard extensions for use with the Associate function. For instance, I use WP as the extension for all of my *WordPerfect* data files.

The Search function The Search function makes it easy to find files. It lists all the files on a disk drive that match the file name you specify, and it shows the directory for each file. This command also accepts wildcards.

Figure 14-6 shows the Search function in use. Part 1 shows the dialog box that the DOS shell displays when you select the Search function. At this box, you type in the name of the file you want to find. Here, for example, I entered a file specification to find all the spreadsheet files on the disk. The screen in part 2 shows the list of files that match the file specification in part 1.

The View-file-contents function The View-file-contents function displays the contents of a selected file. You can use it to help you verify that a file in the list is in fact the one you want. If the file is a text file, this function displays its contents as shown in figure 14-7. Here, the contents of the CONFIG.SYS file are displayed. Since batch files are text files, you can use this function to display their contents.

If a file isn't a text file or the DOS shell doesn't recognize it as such, this function displays the file contents in *hex code*. Even if you're familiar with this code, this display format usually doesn't help you identify a file. As a result, this function is useful only for text files.

The Move function The Move function copies files, and then it deletes the originals. To use the Move function, you first select the files you want to move. Then, when you select this function from the File menu, a dialog box like the one in figure 14-8 is displayed. The From field lists the file or files you've selected, and the To field lets you specify the path for the new location. Here, I've entered C:\DATA\123\ as the destination for the file.

If you're working in graphics mode and you have a mouse, you can also use another technique to move files. Figure 14-9 illustrates how you move files using this technique. First, select the files you want to move. Then, put the cursor on the file icon next to one of the selected files, press the left mouse button, and hold it down. While you hold down the button, *drag* a copy of the icon to the directory where you want to move the files, as shown in part 2. When you release the mouse button, the DOS shell displays the dialog box shown in part 3. At this box, you can confirm or cancel the move function.

The Copy function The Copy function works much like the Move function. After you select the files you want to copy and select the Copy function, it displays a dialog box so you can specify where you want to copy the files. Then, it makes copies of the files in the new location.

You can also use the mouse technique to copy files. First, select the files you want to copy. Then, after you click the mouse on one of the file icons, hold down the Ctrl key and drag the icon to the drive or directory you want to use. When you release the mouse button, the DOS shell displays a dialog box like the one it uses for the Move function so you can either confirm the function or cancel it.

Part 1:

Type in the file specification for the search.

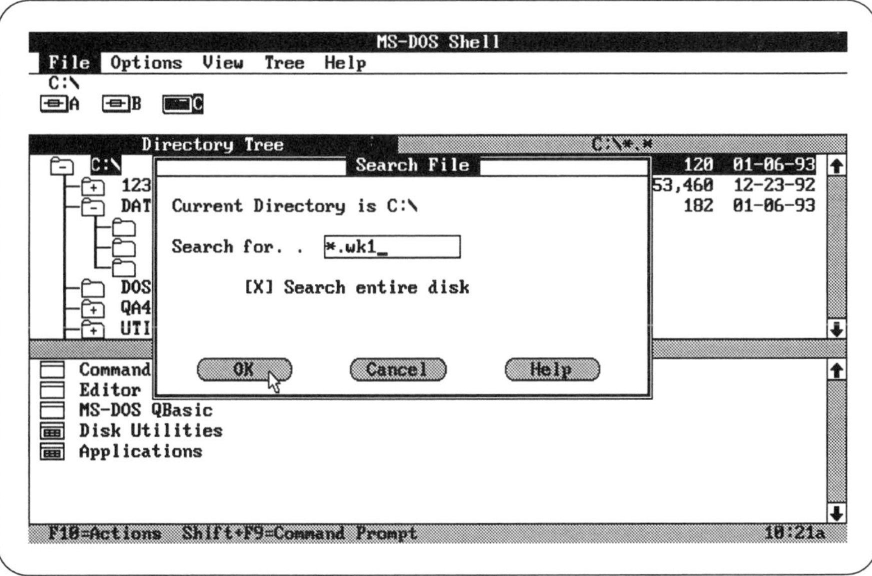

Part 2:

The list of files that matched the search specification is displayed.

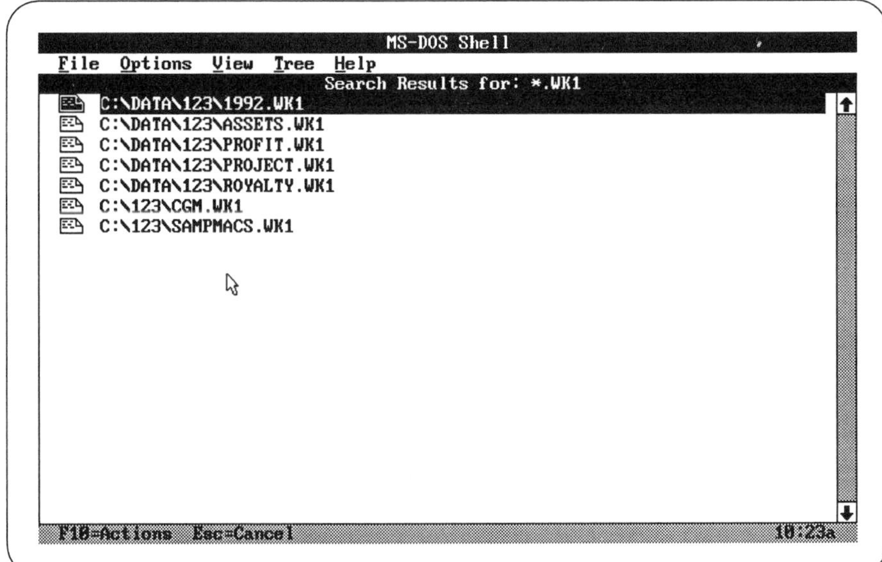

Figure 14-6 How to use the Search function

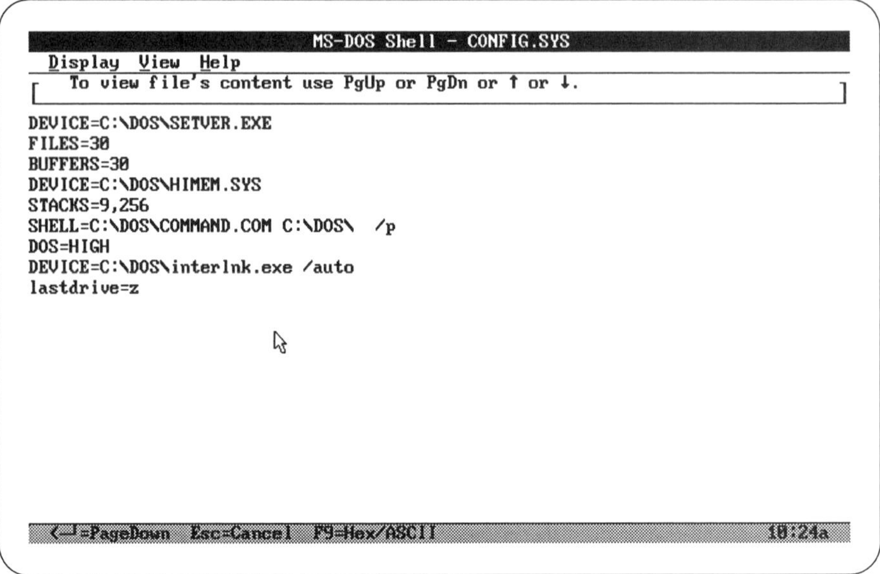

Figure 14-7 How the View-file-contents function displays a text file

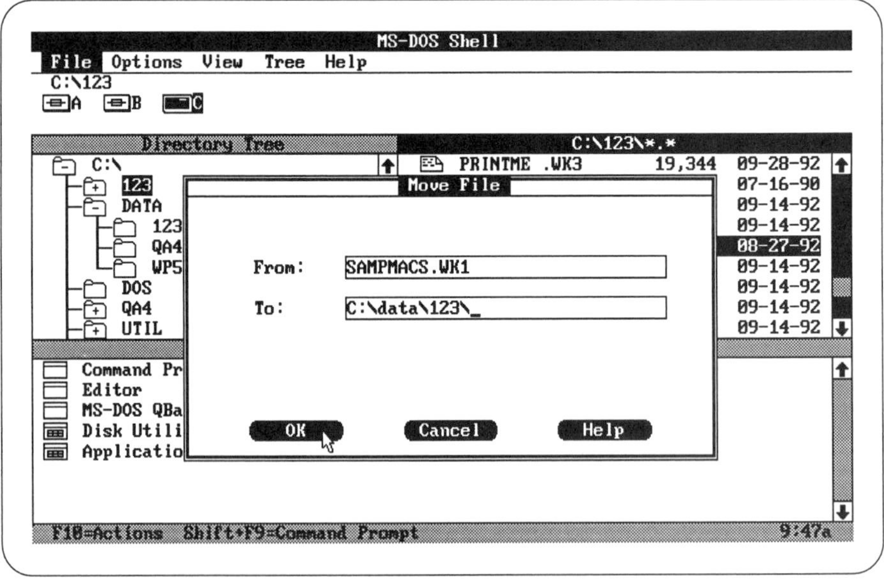

Figure 14-8 The dialog box for the Move function for moving files

Part 1:

Select the file, then click the mouse cursor on the file icon and hold down the left mouse button.

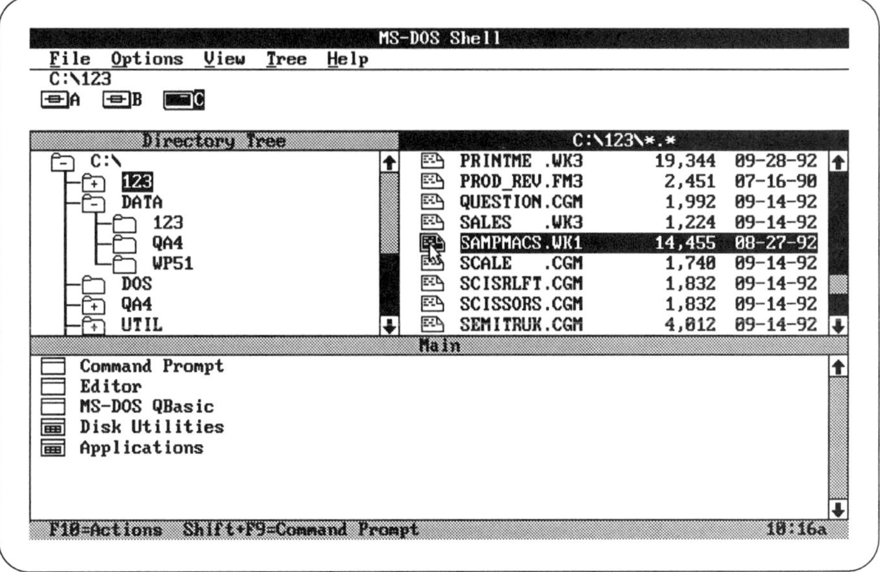

Part 2:

Drag the file icon to the directory you want to move the file to and release the mouse button.

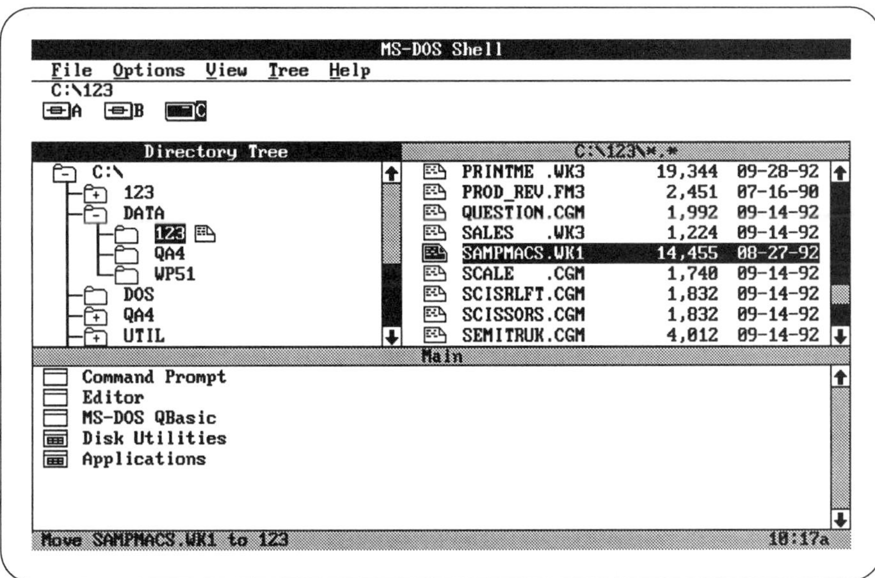

Figure 14-9 How to use the mouse to move a file (parts 1 and 2 of 3)

Part 3:

Use the dialog box to confirm the move or cancel the function.

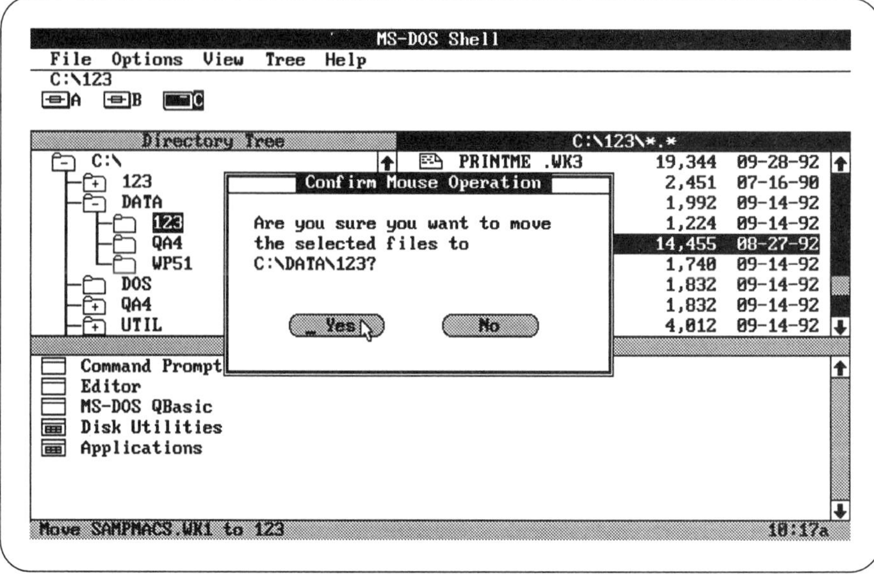

Figure 14-9 How to use the mouse to move a file (part 3 of 3)

The Delete function To use the Delete function, you first select the files you want to delete. Then, after you select the Delete function from the File menu, dialog boxes like the ones in figure 14-10 are displayed. The box shown in part 1 lists the files you selected. Here, you can confirm that you want to delete these files, or you can cancel the Delete function.

If you select OK from the first dialog box, a dialog box like the one in part 2 is displayed for each file. Then, you can delete the file, skip the file, or cancel the Delete function for the remaining files. In a moment, you'll learn how to use the Confirmation function of the Options menu to activate or deactivate this second dialog box.

The Rename function To rename one or more files within a directory, you first select the files you want to rename. Then, after you select the Rename function from the File menu, a dialog box like the one in figure 14-11 is displayed for each file you've selected. Here, you can enter the new name for the file or cancel the function for the remaining files.

Part 1:

After you select the files, you can confirm or cancel the Delete function.

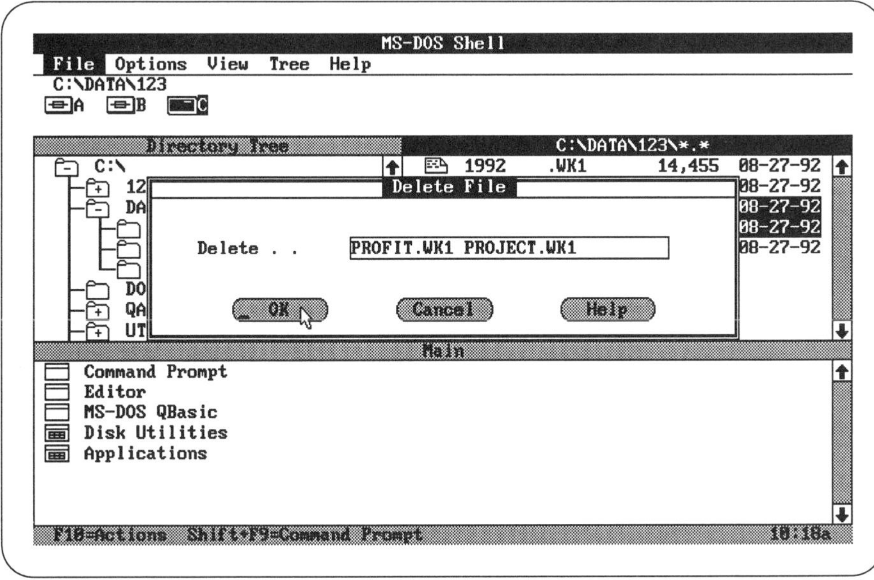

Part 2:

Confirm or cancel the Delete function for each selected file.

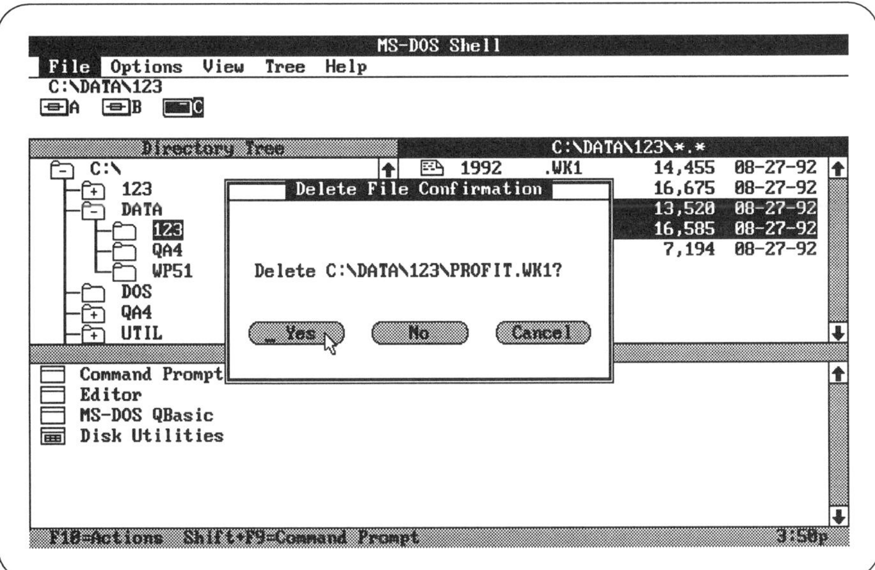

Figure 14-10 How to use the Delete function to delete files

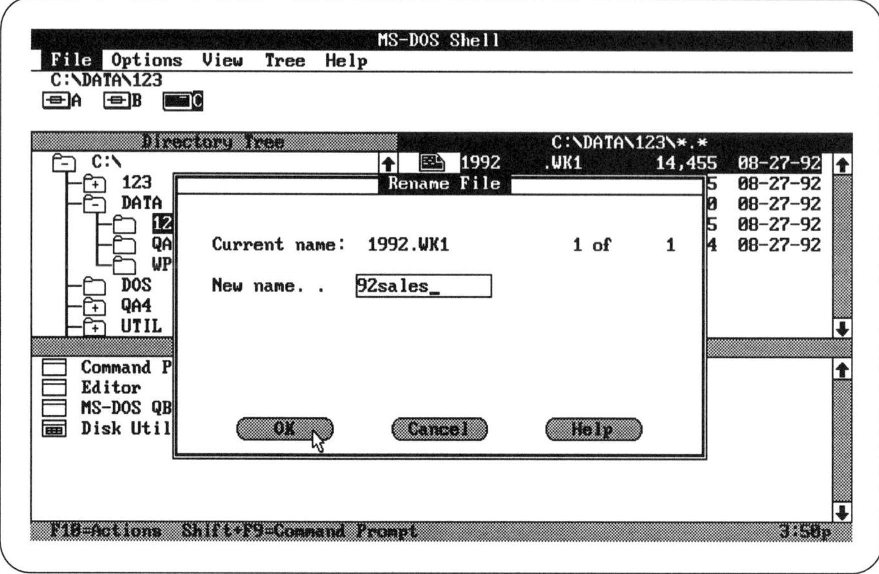

Figure 14-11 The dialog box for the Rename function for renaming files

The Change-attribute function Although you probably won't want to use this function, you can use it to change the four *file attributes* that are associated with a file. These attributes are:

1. The *hidden attribute*, which indicates that a file should not be displayed in a directory listing.
2. The *system attribute*, which indicates that the file is used by the operating system.
3. The *read-only attribute*, which indicates that a file cannot be modified or deleted.
4. The *archive attribute*, which indicates that the file has been modified and should be backed up.

To change one or more of these attributes, you select the files. Then, after you select the Change-attribute function from the File menu, the DOS shell guides you through a series of dialog boxes that specify the attribute changes.

The Select-all and Deselect-all functions When you use the Select-all function, all the files in the file list are selected. That way, you don't have to select the files one at a time. This saves you time when the file list is long and fills several screens. You can use this function when you want to move, copy, or delete all of the files in a directory.

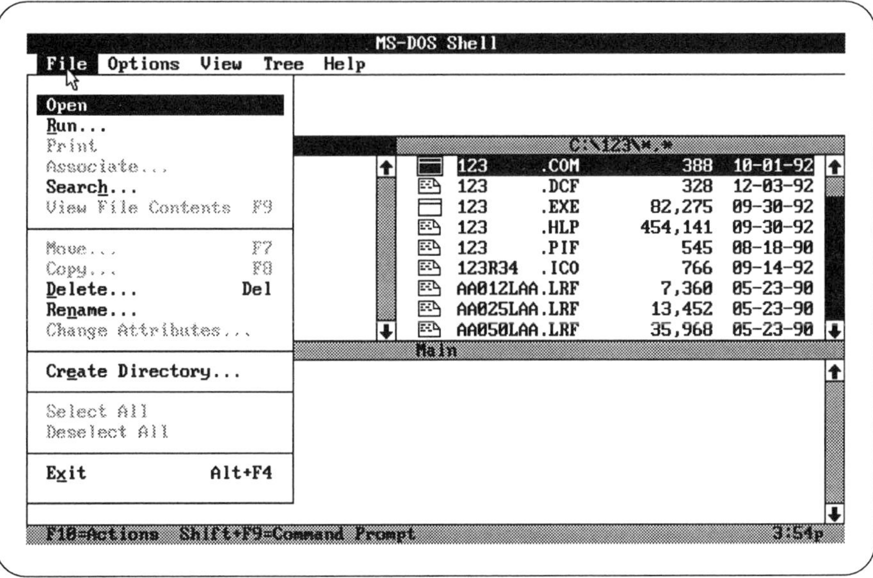

Figure 14-12 The File menu for the directory-tree area

When you use the Deselect-all function, all the selected files are deselected. Since it's usually easier to deselect files using the mouse or the keyboard, you probably won't use this function often. But it can be useful if the Select-across-directories function is on. Then, you can deselect all the selected files, no matter what directory they're in. I'll present the Select-across-directories function later in this chapter.

The Exit function You've already learned that the Exit function stops the DOS shell program and returns you to the DOS command prompt. To start the shell again, you must enter DOSSHELL from the command prompt.

How to use the File menu for the directory-tree area

Figure 14-12 shows the File menu that's available when the directory-tree area is active. Here, I'll show you how to use the three functions you use to manage your directories: the Delete, Rename, and Create-directory functions. Even though the Delete and Rename functions are the same names assigned to functions on the File menu for the file-list area, they perform different functions when the directory-tree area is active.

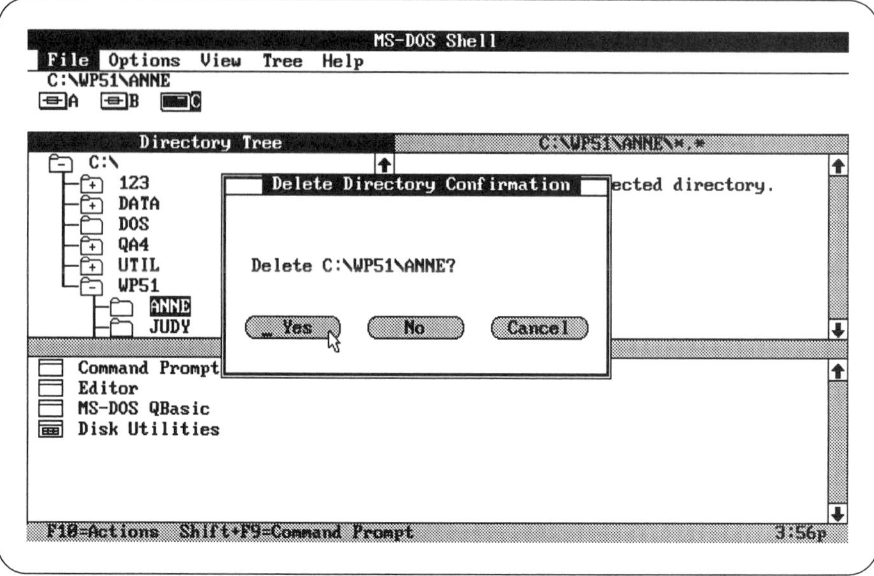

Figure 14-13 The dialog box for the Delete function for deleting directories

The Delete function To delete a directory, you first select the directory you want to delete. Next, you select the Delete function from the File menu. The DOS shell then displays the dialog box shown in figure 14-13. At this box, you can confirm the function or cancel it.

If the directory you're trying to delete isn't empty, the DOS shell displays the dialog box shown in figure 14-14. That's because you can't delete a directory that contains files or subdirectories.

The Rename function To rename a directory, you first select the directory you want to rename. Next, you select the Rename function from the File menu. The DOS shell then displays the dialog box shown in figure 14-15. At this box, you can type in a new name for the directory. If you're using DOS 5.0, this is a valuable function because there isn't a DOS 5.0 command that lets you rename a directory. With DOS 6.0, however, you can rename a directory using the Move command.

The Create-directory function To create a directory, you first select the appropriate drive. Then, you select the directory you want the new directory to be subordinate to. If you're creating a top-level directory, you'll select the root directory. Next, you select the Create-directory function from the File menu. The DOS shell then displays the dialog box shown in figure 14-16. At this box, you enter the name of

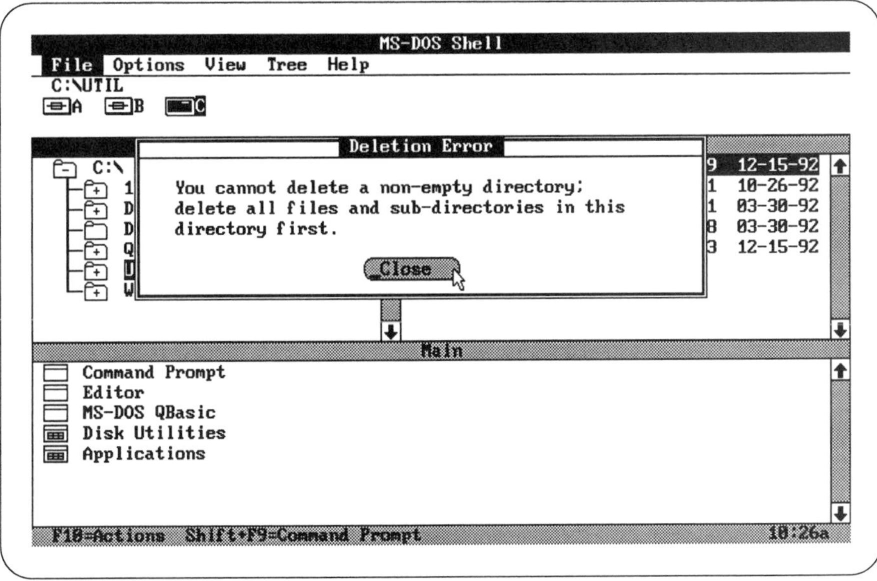

Figure 14-14 The dialog box that's displayed when you try to delete a directory that isn't empty

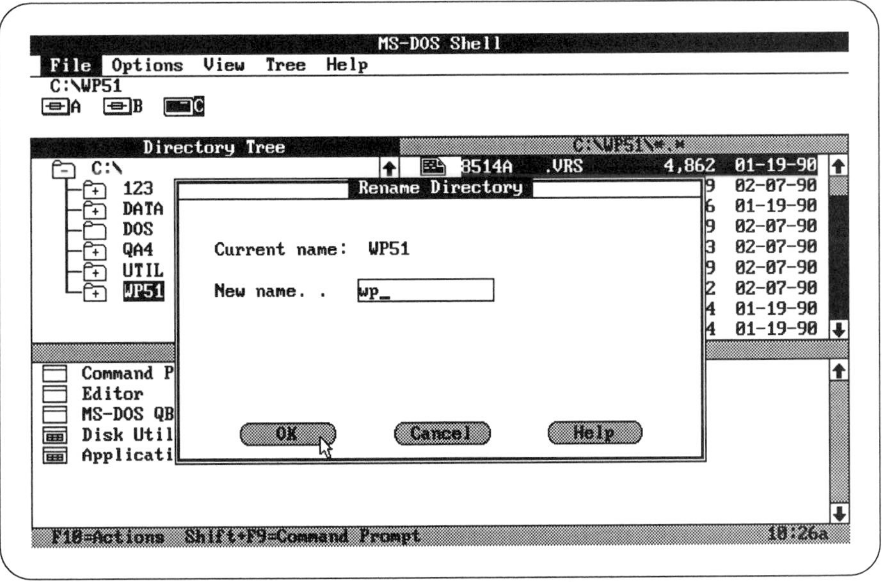

Figure 14-15 The dialog box for the Rename function for renaming directories

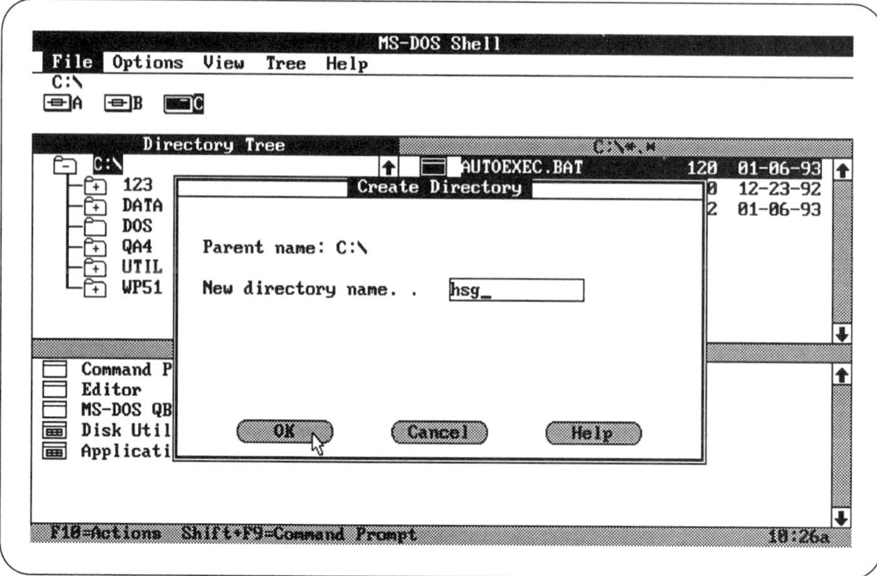

Figure 14-16 The dialog box for the Create-directory function

the new directory. After the function in figure 14-16 is executed, a directory named HSG will be created in the root directory.

How to use the functions of the Options menu

Figure 14-17 shows the Options menu. When you pull down this menu, it offers the seven functions shown here. Generally, you use these functions to set up the DOS shell so it works the way you want it to. Although you probably won't need to do that often, you may occasionally want to change one of these options. So I'll explain when and how to use all these functions now, except for the Enable-task-swapper function. I'll show you how to use the Enable-task-swapper function in the next chapter.

The Confirmation function Figure 14-18 shows the dialog box that's displayed when you select the Confirmation function from the Options menu. Here, an X next to an option indicates it's on. To turn an option on or off, you click on it with the mouse. With the keyboard, you use the cursor control keys to move the highlight from one option to the next, and you use the Space bar to turn an option on or off.

The Confirm-on-delete option specifies whether the DOS shell should ask for confirmation before it deletes a file. If this option is on, a dialog box like the one in

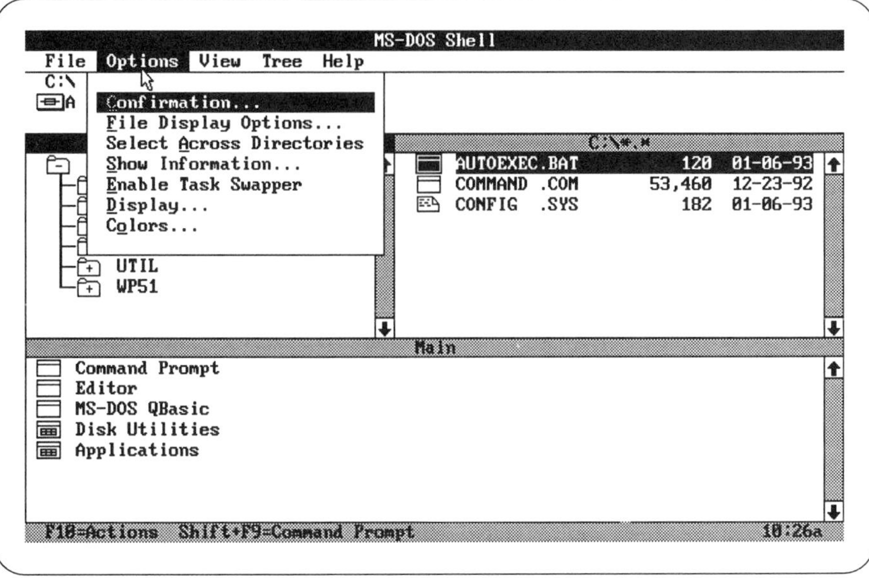

Figure 14-17 The Options menu

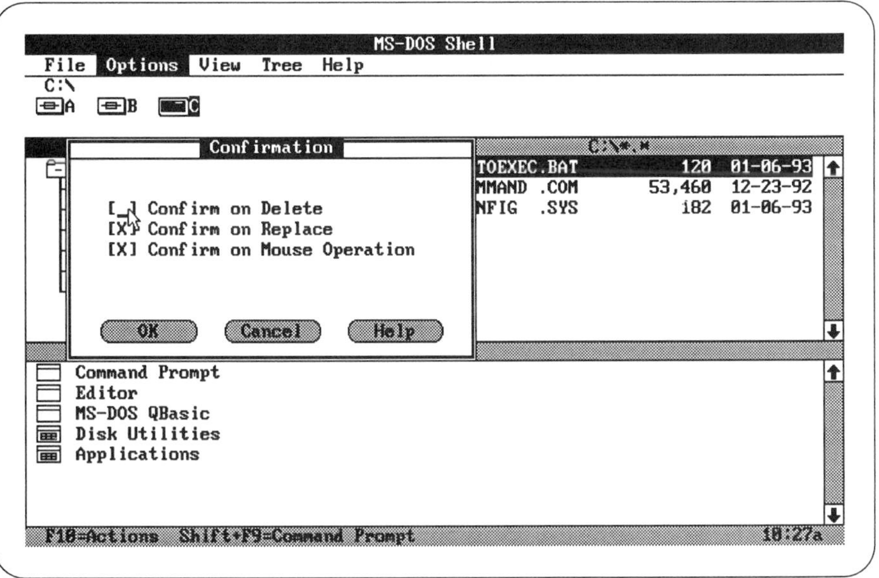

Figure 14-18 The dialog box for the Confirmation function

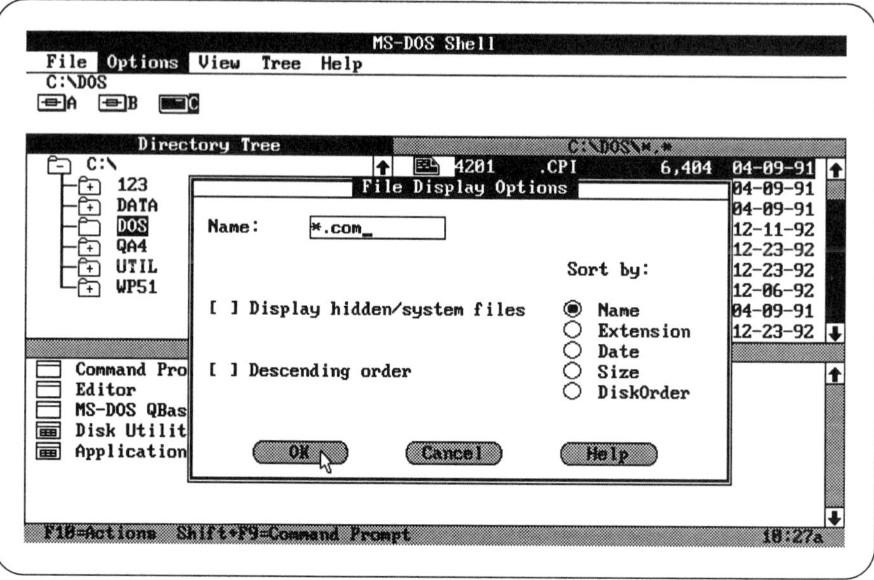

Figure 14-19 The dialog box for the File-display-options function

part 2 of figure 14-10 is displayed each time a file is about to be deleted by the Delete function. As a general rule, you should leave this option on so you won't accidentally delete any files. However, as you become more familiar with the DOS shell, you may want to turn this option off.

The Confirm-on-replace option helps protect files from being accidentally replaced when you use the Copy and Move functions. When this option is on, a Copy or Move function asks for confirmation before replacing an existing file with a new file. In contrast, the DOS Copy command replaces existing files without asking for confirmation. Although this option should be on most of the time, you may want to turn it off when you are deliberately replacing existing files with new ones of the same name.

The Confirm-on-mouse-operation option specifies whether the DOS shell should ask for confirmation before it executes a move or copy operation that you perform using the mouse techniques I showed you earlier. If this option is on, a dialog box is displayed before the function is executed. This box tells you whether you're copying or moving a file, and it gives you a chance to cancel the function. So I recommend that you keep this option on.

The File-display-options function Figure 14-19 shows the dialog box that's displayed when you select the File-display-options function. The default setting for the Name field is *.*. That means all of the files in the current directory are displayed

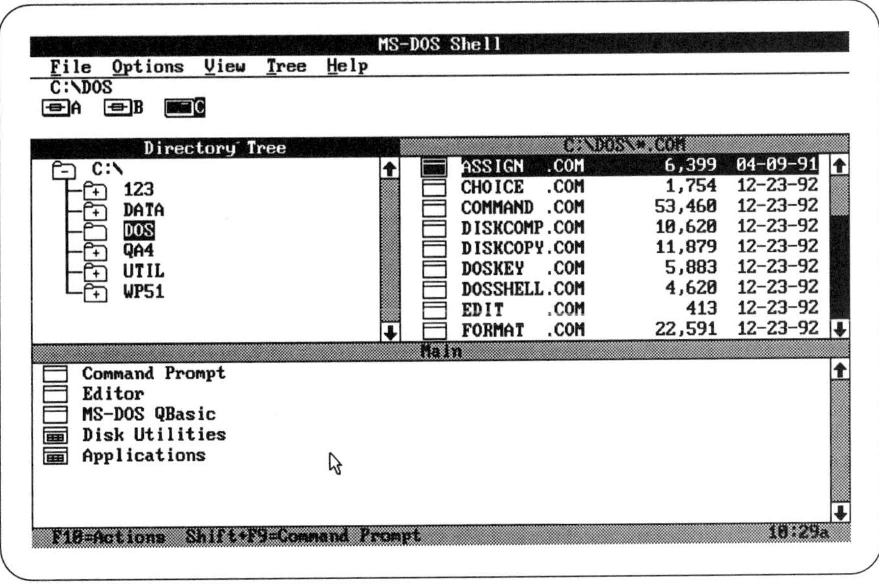

Figure 14-20 The file-list display that results from the selections in figure 14-19

in the file-list area. However, you can change this default setting by entering a file name using wildcards. Here, for example, I entered *.COM to display only the files with an extension of COM. Figure 14-20 shows how the file list looks with this setting in effect.

If you want the files of a directory to be displayed in sequence by name, extension, date, size, or location in the directory, you can use the Sort-by fields in the dialog box. To select one of these fields with a mouse, you just click on the appropriate button. To select a field with the keyboard, you use the Tab key to activate the Sort-by portion of the dialog box. Then, you use the cursor control keys to select the field you want.

If you want to copy, move, rename, or delete files based on a wildcard specification, you can use this function to enter the wildcard specification. Then, you can use the Select-all function of the File menu to select all the files that match the wildcard.

The Select-across-directories function This function controls what happens to selected files when you change directories. If this function is off, all selected files are deselected when you change from one directory to another. That way, files from only one directory at a time can be selected. If this function is on, files are not deselected when you change directories. As a result, you can select files from more than one directory on your hard disk.

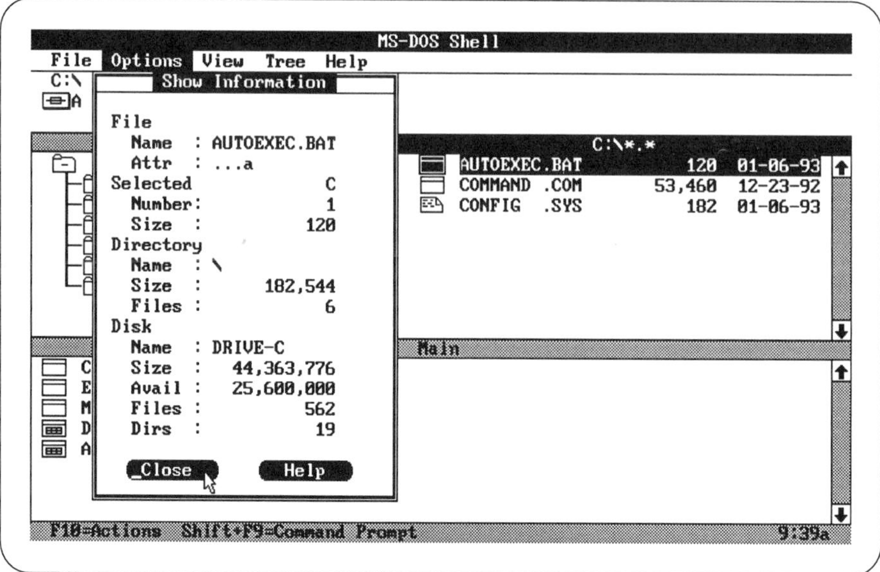

Figure 14-21 The file information that's displayed by the Show-information function

To turn on the Select-across-directories function, you execute it from the Option menu using either the mouse or the keyboard. When you do, a small dot appears next to the function name to show that it is on. To turn this function off, you execute it again. Although the Select-across-directories function should be off most of the time, you may want to use it occasionally for simplifying file maintenance.

The Show-information function When you select this function, the DOS shell presents information about the current file, directory, and disk as shown in figure 14-21. If you examine this figure for a moment, you'll see that it gives the name of the current file; its attributes (*...a* means the archive attribute is on); the size of the file; the name and size of the current directory; and the name and size of the default disk.

The Display function Figure 14-22 shows the dialog box that's displayed when you select the Display function. This box lets you specify whether you want to use *text* or *graphics mode* for the DOS shell screen. If your monitor can display graphics, you'll generally want to select this option because it can make the DOS shell easier to use. You can also specify the number of lines you want to display on your screen.

The options that are available in figure 14-22 depend on the type of monitor you have. The options shown here, for instance, are the ones available with a VGA

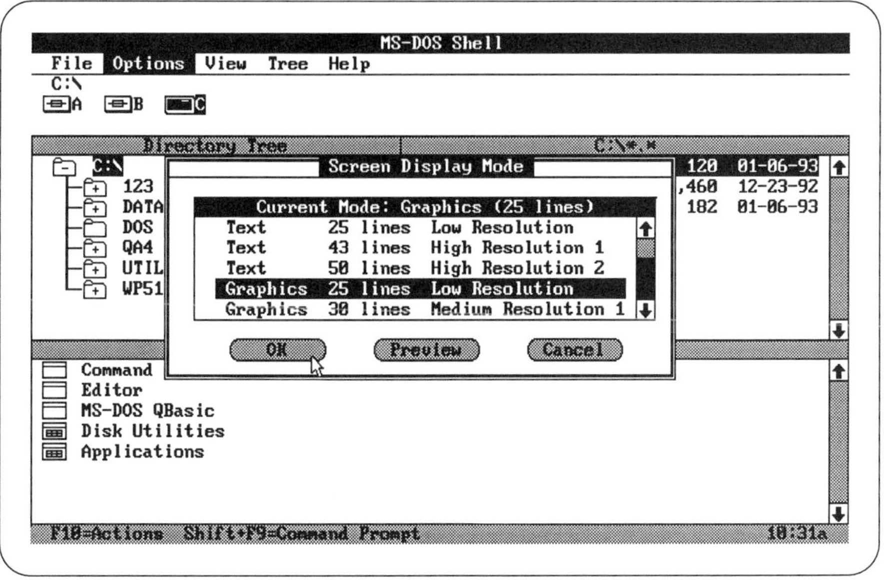

Figure 14-22 The dialog box for the Display function

monitor. So if you have a different type of monitor, the DOS shell will offer you some different options.

The Colors function Figure 14-23 shows the dialog box that's displayed when you select the Colors function from the Options menu. This box lets you select the color scheme you want to use. Of course, if you don't have a color monitor, many of the options shown here aren't available.

How to use the functions of the View menu

Figure 14-24 shows the seven functions available from the View menu. (The Program/File-lists function is dimmed because it's already active.) The first five functions change the format of the DOS shell screen. These different screen formats are called *views*. Although you probably won't use more than one or two of these views, I'll explain them all so you know how they work.

Before I present these views, you should know that if you change views, the new view remains in effect until you select another view. Even when you exit from the DOS shell and start it again, it won't return to the default view. Instead, it will use the view that was active when you last exited from the DOS shell.

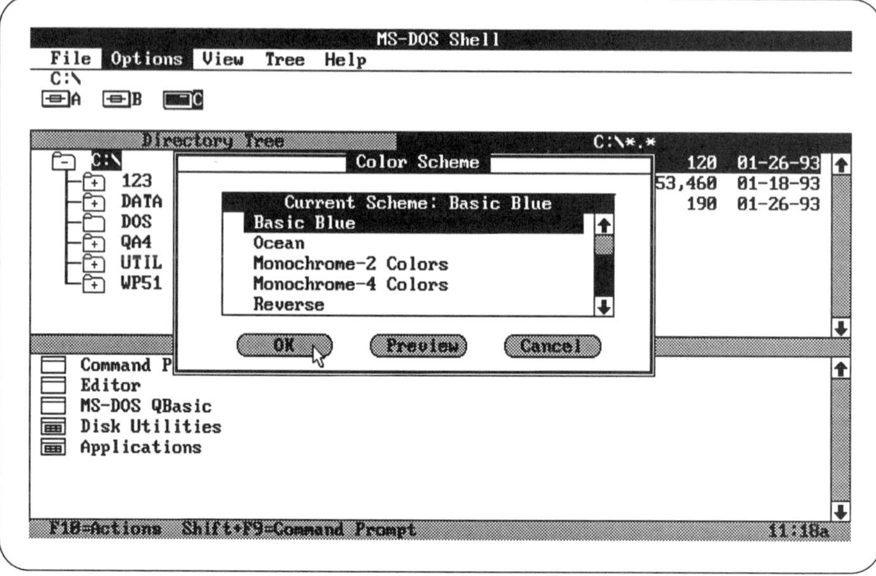

Figure 14-23 The dialog box for the Colors function

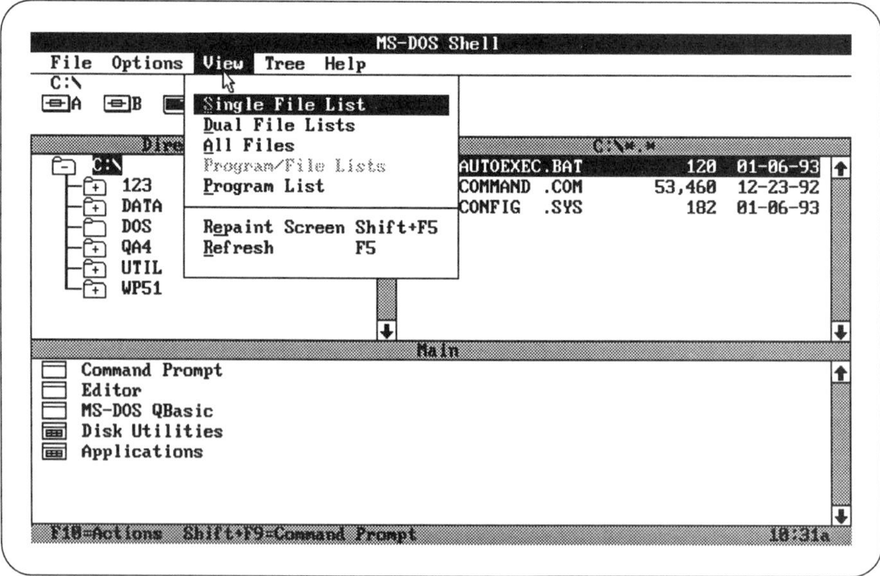

Figure 14-24 The View menu

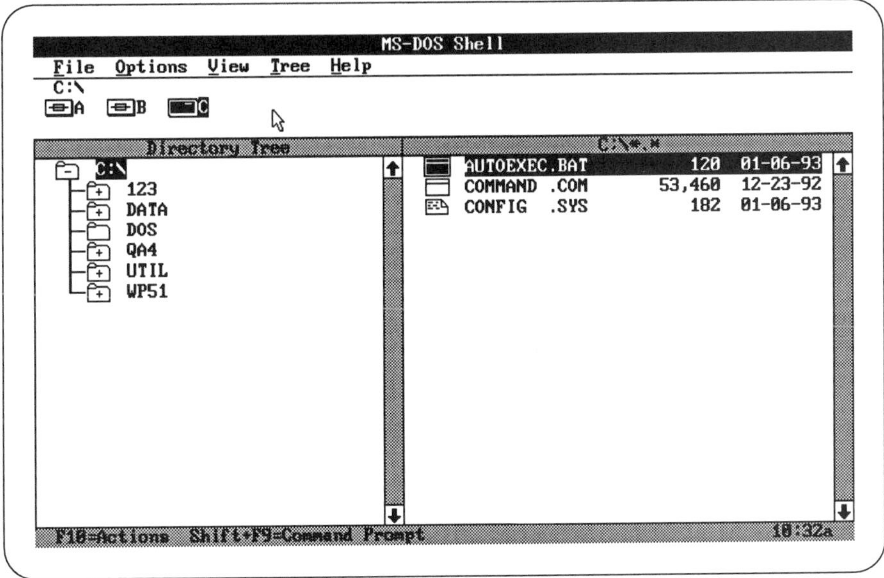

Figure 14-25 How the screen looks in Single-file-list view

The Single-file-list view Figure 14-25 shows the Single-file-list view. This view displays the directory-tree and file-list areas, but not the program-list area. As a result, you can see more files and directories on the screen than you can using the default view. Sometimes, this is helpful when you perform maintenance tasks that involve many files or directories.

The Dual-file-lists view Figure 14-26 shows the Dual-file-lists view. This view lets you display the files from two directories at the same time. As a result, the Dual-file-lists view makes it easier for you to compare the files in two directories and to copy or move files from one directory or drive to another.

The All-files view Figure 14-27 shows the All-files view. When you activate this view, the DOS shell temporarily removes the directory structure from your files and treats all of the files on your hard disk as if they were in one directory. And the directory tree on the left of the screen is replaced by a file information box. This box contains the same information that's displayed when you use the Show- information function from the Options menu. As you scroll through the file list, the file information in the box changes to reflect the file that's highlighted.

The All-files view is rather hard to use. In part, that's because the directory information that's displayed for each file lists only the name of the lowest-level directory, not the complete path for the directory. If, for example, a file is in the

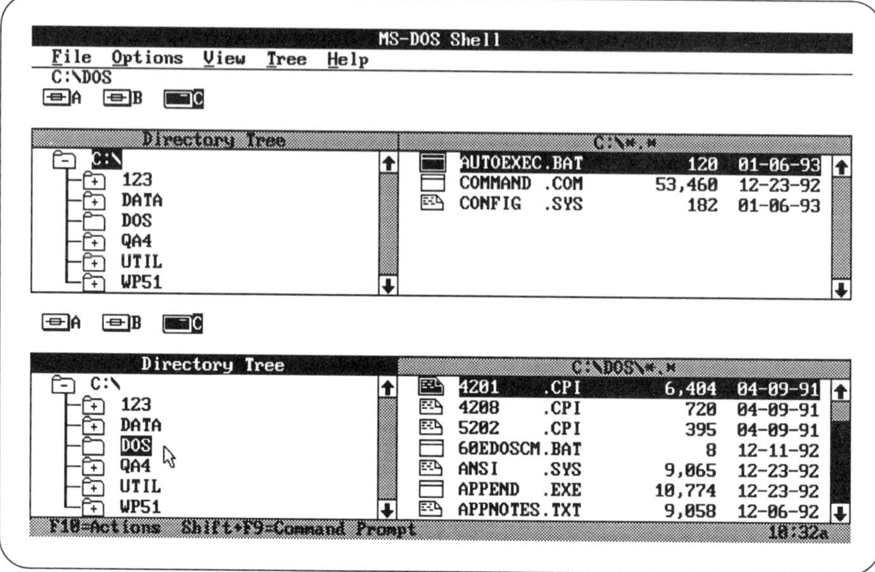

Figure 14-26 How the screen looks in Dual-file-lists view

```
MS-DOS Shell
File Options View Tree Help
C:\123
A B C
                                   *.*
                           123      .BAT        29  12-15-92   2:29p
File                       123      .COM       388  10-01-92   9:30p
  Name  : 123.EXE          123      .DCF       328  12-03-92   1:32p
  Attr  : ...a             123      .EXE    82,275  09-30-92   9:07p
Selected           C       123      .HLP   454,141  09-30-92   4:12p
  Number:          1       123      .PIF       545  08-18-90   2:52p
  Size  :     82,275       123R34   .ICO       766  09-14-92   6:13p
Directory                  1992     .WK1    14,455  08-27-92   1:06p
  Name  : 123              4201     .CPI     6,404  04-09-91   5:00a
  Size  :  2,078,129       4208     .CPI       720  04-09-91   5:00a
  Files :        162       5202     .CPI       395  04-09-91   5:00a
Disk                       60EDOSCM.BAT          8  12-11-92   2:27p
  Name  : DRIVE-C          8514A    .VRS     4,862  01-19-90  12:00p
  Size  :   44,363,776     AA0003   .TDF       504  03-13-90   2:05p
  Avail :   25,600,000     AA012LAA.LRF      7,360  05-23-90  12:00p
  Files :          562     AA025LAA.LRF     13,452  05-23-90  12:00p
  Dirs  :           19     AA050LAA.LRF     35,968  05-23-90  12:00p
                           AC017LAA.LRF      9,240  05-23-90  12:00p
F10=Actions  Shift+F9=Command Prompt                             9:44a
```

Figure 14-27 How the screen looks in All-files view

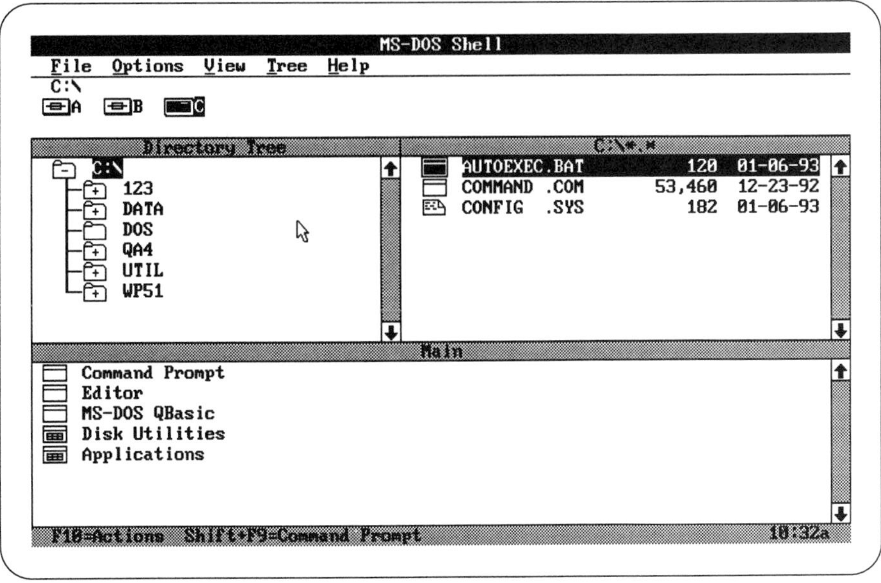

Figure 14-28 How the screen looks in Program/File-lists view

QA4\DATA directory, the directory name will appear as DATA. So if you also have a WP51\DATA directory, you can't tell which DATA directory the file is in.

The Program/File-lists view Figure 14-28 shows the Program/File-lists view. You should already recognize this view because it's the one I've used throughout this section. It's also the default view, so it's the one that's active when you start the DOS shell for the first time.

The Program-list view Figure 14-29 shows the Program-list view. As you can see, it displays only the program-list area. As a result, this view is most useful if you want to set up a PC for other people to use and you don't want them to manage the files and directories on the hard disk.

The Refresh and Repaint functions The Refresh and Repaint functions on the View menu perform operations that help keep the shell working correctly. The Refresh function causes the DOS shell to rescan the disk to find out what directories and files are on the disk. You may need to use this function in three situations: (1) if you exit temporarily from the DOS shell to get to the command prompt and enter a command that changes the directories or files; (2) if you execute a program or command from the file or program list that changes the directories or files; and (3) if the current drive is a diskette drive and you change the diskette. You need to refresh

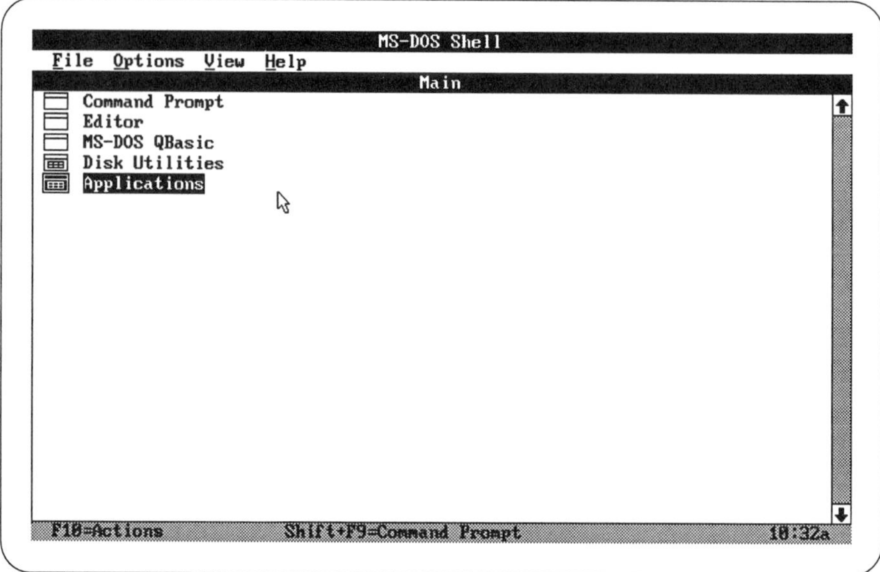

Figure 14-29 How the screen looks in Program-list view

the display in these situations because the shell doesn't know that the information on the disk has changed. That's because even though the shell may be active when these functions are performed, the functions are actually performed outside of the shell.

The Repaint function redraws the DOS shell screen in the event that the screen is corrupted by unwanted characters. Since this should happen rarely, you won't have to use this function as often as you use the Refresh function.

Some perspective on the DOS shell

If you compare the capabilities that are provided by the DOS shell for managing directories and files with the DOS commands that are available at the command prompt, you'll realize that the shell can make it easier for you to manage your directories and files. The directory-tree area makes it easy for you to see, modify, and use the structure of your directories. The selection techniques make it easy for you to select the files for a function. And the pull-down menus make it easy for you to start functions after you've selected the files. As a result, it's easy to create, delete, and rename directories when you use the DOS shell. It's also easy to copy, move, delete, and rename files.

In practice, though, you'll probably use some combination of shell functions and DOS commands for managing directories and files. If, for example, you want to delete all of the files in a directory, you can do so by entering just one Delete command at the DOS prompt. And if you want to copy all of the files in a directory to a diskette, you can do so by entering just one Copy command at the DOS prompt.

Terms

background mode
hex code
dragging a mouse
file attribute
hidden attribute
system attribute
read-only attribute
archive attribute
text mode
graphics mode
view

Objectives

1. Use the functions of the Options and View menus to set up the DOS shell so it works the way you want it to.
2. Given file specifications, use the appropriate functions of the File menu to move, copy, delete, or rename one or more files.
3. Given a directory specification, use the appropriate functions of the File menu to delete it, rename it, or create it.
4. Use the appropriate functions of the File menu to start a command or batch file, execute a DOS command, print files, and associate an application program with its data files.

Chapter 15

How to use the DOS shell to switch between programs quickly

If you frequently switch from one program to another, the DOS shell provides a feature called the Task Swapper that can help you switch between programs more quickly. The capability this feature provides is commonly referred to as *task switching* or *task swapping*. This feature isn't available with earlier versions of DOS, and you can use this feature only through the DOS shell. Also, this feature may not work with older versions of some application programs, so there's a chance that you won't be able to use it with all of your application programs.

In this chapter, you'll learn how to use the Task Swapper. First, I'll explain how the Task Swapper works. Next, you'll learn how to activate the Task Swapper and switch between application programs. Then, you'll learn how to set up and use the Task Swapper to switch between programs more efficiently. Because you've already learned the basic techniques for using the DOS shell, you should be able to move quickly through this chapter.

An introduction to the Task Swapper

When you use the Task Swapper, you can load two or more application programs and switch between them without having to exit from one program before you switch to the next. Each program that's running under the Task Swapper is called an *active task*. You can, for example, start *WordPerfect* and begin work on a report. Then, you can start *Lotus 1-2-3* and load a spreadsheet file to review some data. When you use the Task Swapper to switch back to *WordPerfect*, it returns you to the place where you were last working on the report. As a result, you don't have to start *WordPerfect*, load the report, and find your place again.

Figure 15-1 illustrates how this process works. When the first task is active, *WordPerfect* and a working document are loaded and are running in internal memory, while the second task, *Lotus 1-2-3* and a spreadsheet file, are stored on disk. When

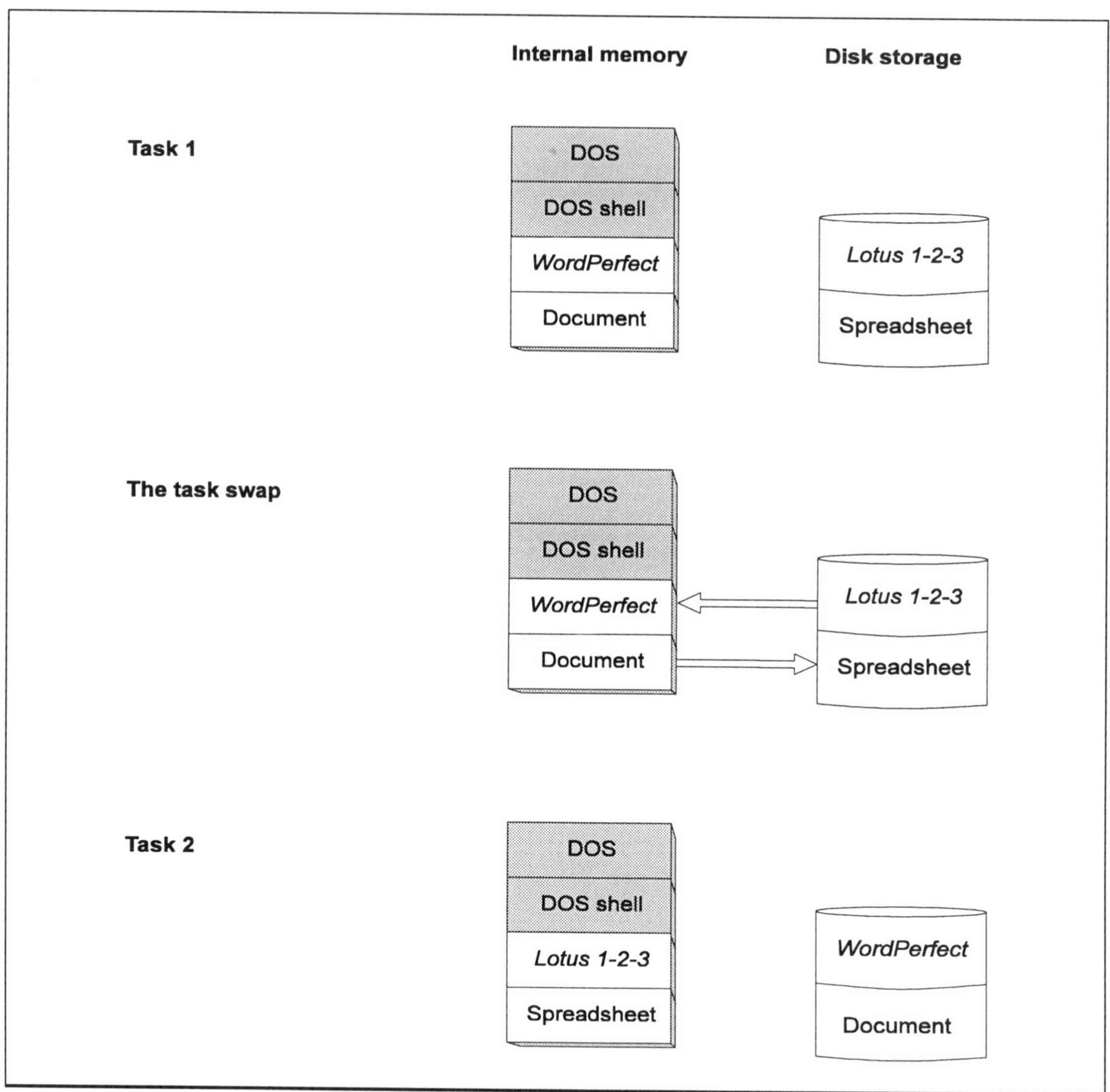

Figure 15-1 How the Task Swapper uses internal memory and disk storage to switch between two programs

you perform the task swap, *WordPerfect* and the working document are transferred to disk storage, and *Lotus 1-2-3* and the current spreadsheet file are transferred to internal memory. When you switch back to *WordPerfect*, the process is repeated.

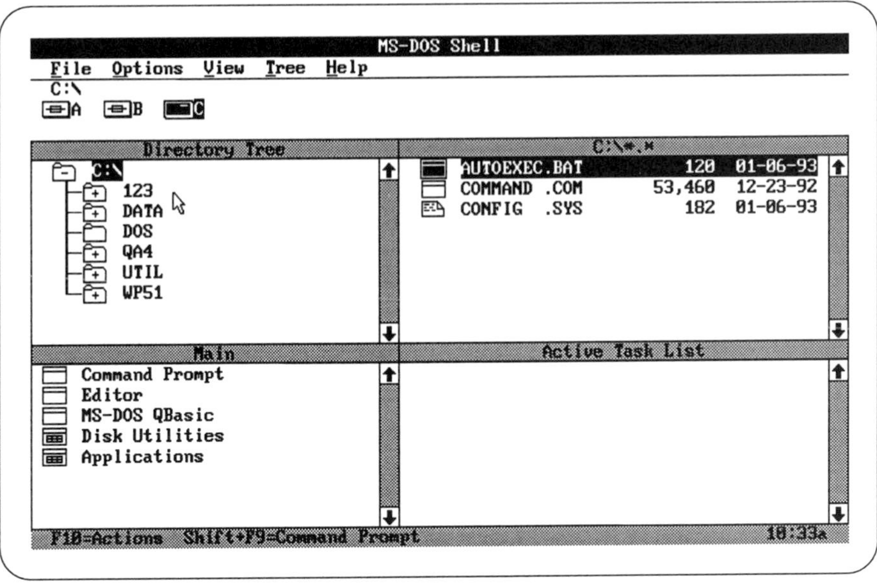

Figure 15-2 The DOS 5.0/6.0 shell with the Task Swapper enabled

How to use the Task Swapper

To use the Task Swapper, you begin by enabling it. Next, you load your application programs so they become active tasks. Then, after you learn a few keystroke combinations to switch between active tasks, you're ready to use the Task Swapper.

How to enable the Task Swapper To enable the Task Swapper, you select the Enable-task-swapper function from the Options menu. The DOS shell then displays an *active task list* in the bottom right portion of the screen, as shown in figure 15-2. After the Task Swapper is enabled, you can load your application programs into it.

How to load programs and switch between them In figure 15-3, you can see that two applications programs have been loaded into the active task list. To load a program, you start it from the program list. If you have a mouse, just double-click on the appropriate program in the program list. Or if you're using the keyboard, highlight the appropriate program and press the Enter key. The DOS shell then starts the program and automatically adds it to the active task list. To load another program, you first use the Ctrl+Esc keystroke combination to switch back to the DOS shell. Then, you start the next program you want from the program list.

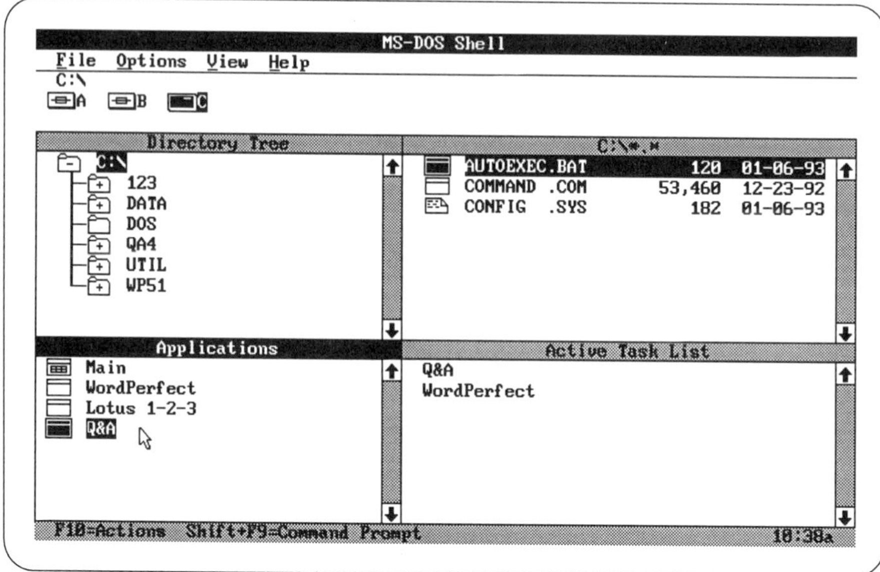

Figure 15-3 Two application programs that have been loaded in the active task list

After you've loaded your programs, you can switch between them using the active task list instead of the program list. To switch to the *WordPerfect* task in figure 15-3, for example, you just double-click on the *WordPerfect* entry in the active task list. Then, when you want to switch to the next task, you use the Ctrl+Esc key combination to return to the DOS shell. Now, you can switch to *Q&A* by double clicking on the *Q&A* task entry.

How to switch between programs more efficiently

The Task Swapper also lets you switch between active tasks without using the DOS shell as an intermediate step. To do that, you use special keystroke combinations that DOS 5.0 and 6.0 provide. Or you can assign your own keystroke combinations to each program.

Special keystroke combinations Figure 15-4 presents the keystroke combinations you can use to switch between programs. You'll probably use the first two most often. The Ctrl+Esc combination always switches you back to the DOS shell. The Alt+Tab key combination switches you back to the most recent task. If you just used the DOS shell, for example, this key combination will return you to the shell. But if you switched from another application program, it will return you to that

Keystrokes	Function
Ctrl+Esc	Switches from the current application program to the DOS shell.
Alt+Tab	As you hold down the Alt key and repeatedly press the Tab key, you cycle through the active task list. As the list cycles, the title of each program is displayed at the top of the screen. When you release the Alt key, the Task Swapper switches you to the program you selected.
Alt+Esc	Switches to the next application program on the active task list.
Shift+Alt+Esc	Switches to the previous application program on the active task list.

Figure 15-4 The special keystrokes you can use to switch between programs

program. With the Alt+Tab key combination, you can also cycle through the programs on the active task list by holding down the Alt key as you repeatedly press the Tab key. Each time you press the Tab key, it shows the title of the next active task at the top of the screen. When you release the Alt key, you're switched to the task that's displayed.

The last two key combinations are Alt+Esc and Shift+Alt+Esc. You can use these to switch to the next program on the active task list or to the previous program on the active task list. Most of the time, though, it's easier to switch tasks using the Alt+Tab key combination.

How to assign a keystroke combination to a program In addition to the keystrokes you've learned so far, you can assign a unique keystroke combination to a program. You can, for example, assign the keystroke combination Alt+W to *WordPerfect.* Then, whenever *WordPerfect* is in the active task list, you can switch directly to it by pressing the Alt+W key combination. Note that if you assign a keystroke combination to a program while the program is in the active task list, you can't use the keystroke combination until you unload the program and load it again.

Figure 15-5 shows the dialog box you use to assign a keystroke combination to a program. To get to this box, you first activate the program-list area and select the appropriate program from the list. Then, after you pull down the File menu, you select the Properties function. In the dialog box, you use the Application-shortcut-key entry to assign a keystroke combination to the program. To do this, you press the actual keystroke combination you want to use. You can use the Alt, Ctrl, or Shift key in combination with another key.

Since you learned how to use the first three entries of this box in chapter 13 to create an option for a program list, most of this procedure should be familiar. In fact, now that you know about assigning key combinations, you'll probably make the assignment when you create the option.

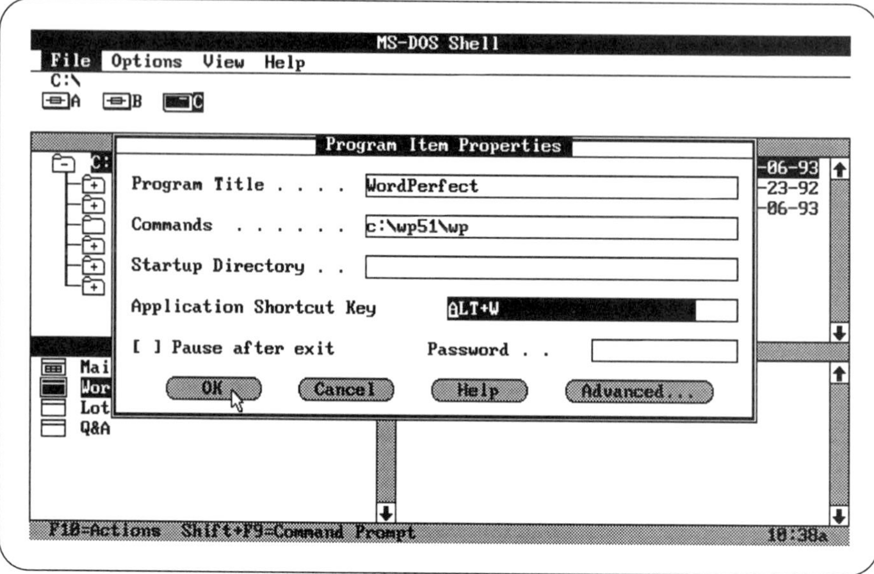

Figure 15-5 The dialog box that you use to assign a keystroke combination to a program

Figure 15-6 shows how programs are displayed on the active task list after you've assigned a keystroke combination to them. This list shows that *WordPerfect* is started by the Alt+W key combination, and *Q&A* is started by the Alt+A key combination.

Some perspective on the Task Swapper

Without much trouble, you should be able to use the task swapping capabilities of the DOS shell. If you occasionally need to switch between two or more programs, the Task Swapper can help you work more efficiently. However, on some PCs the Task Swapper is just too slow to be practical. In addition, the Task Swapper may not work correctly with some older versions of application programs. As a result, you may find that you're better off running only one program at a time.

If you have a 386 or 486 PC with at least 2MB of memory, you may want to consider a utility that provides true *multi-tasking* capabilities. These utilities actually let two or more application programs run concurrently on your PC. Consequently, you can view and run two or more programs in small windows, each of which is displayed on a portion of the screen. This makes it possible to transfer data between two programs, and it makes it easier to switch between programs quickly. Also, these utilities often let your application programs run more efficiently. Today, the most popular multitasking utility is *Windows*.

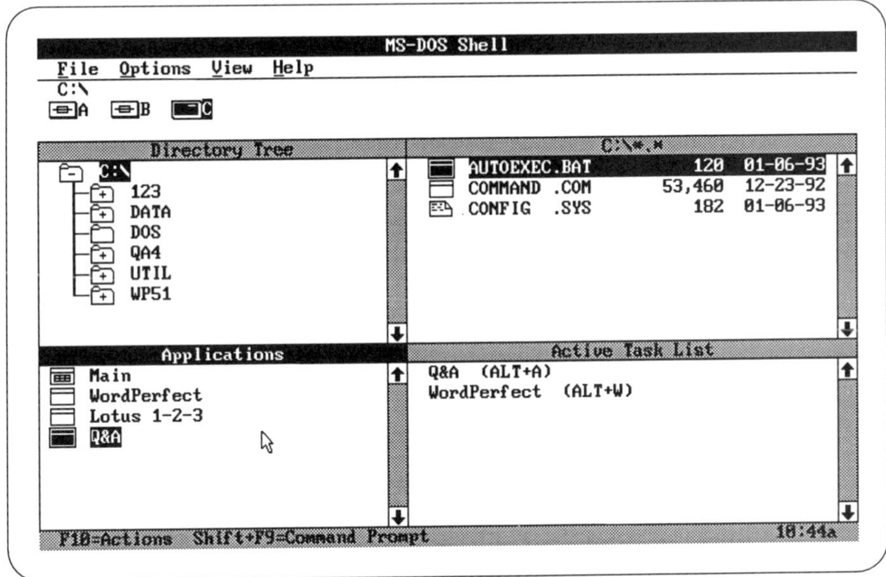

Figure 15-6 Two programs that have had keystroke combinations assigned to them

Terms

task switching
task swapping
active task
active task list
multi-tasking

Objectives

1. Describe how the task swapper uses internal memory and disk storage to switch between tasks.
2. After enabling the task swapper, load two or more programs from the program-list area and switch between them.
3. If you frequently have two or more programs in the active task list at the same time, assign keystroke combinations to these programs.

Section 5

The DOS 6.0 utilities

The most significant new features of DOS 6.0 are its utility programs. These programs provide functions that were previously available only if you purchased third-party utility programs, such as *PC Tools* or *The Norton Utilities*. The six chapters in this section teach you how to use these utility programs:

- In chapter 16, you'll learn how to use *Microsoft Backup*, a high-speed backup program that can back up your hard disk data up to four times faster than the older DOS Backup command.
- In chapter 17, you'll learn how to use *Microsoft Anti-Virus*, which detects and removes harmful computer viruses from your system.
- In chapter 18, you'll learn how to use *DoubleSpace*, which compresses the data on your hard disk so its capacity is effectively doubled.
- In chapter 19, you'll learn how to use *Microsoft Defrag*, which improves the stability and performance of your hard disk by reorganizing the data stored on it.
- In chapter 20, you'll learn how to use *Interlnk* and *Power*, which make portable computers easier to use.
- In chapter 21, you'll learn how to use *Microsoft Diagnostics*, which displays a variety of useful information about your system.

If you have DOS 6.0, the chapters in this section will teach you how to use these programs. If you don't yet have DOS 6.0, you can read through these chapters to see if you should upgrade to DOS 6.0. Because these chapters are independent of one another, you can read them in any order you wish.

Incidentally, DOS 6.0 comes with another utility program called *MemMaker*, which helps you optimize your computer's memory configuration. It's covered in chapter 25, along with other techniques for optimizing your computer's memory.

Chapter 16

Microsoft Backup

The DOS Backup command is both hard to use and slow. That's why backup utilities have become popular. These utilities let you back up your hard disk in a fraction of the time that it takes when you use the DOS Backup command. They're also easier to use than the Backup command, and the backups they do are more reliable than those done by the Backup command.

The most important benefit of a backup utility, though, is the fact that you're more likely to do regular backups when they take only a minute or two a day. Then, whether you lose just one file, all the files in a directory, or all the files on your hard disk, it won't be a disaster. Instead, you'll be able to restore whatever files you've lost.

Prior to DOS 6.0, the only way to get a backup utility was to purchase one. The most popular of these utilities are *Central Point Backup* by Central Point Software and *Norton Backup* by Symantec. With DOS 6.0, Microsoft includes a backup program called *Microsoft Backup*. Microsoft Backup is actually a scaled back version of *Norton Backup*. Although it's not as fast and sophisticated as *Central Point Backup* or *Norton Backup*, it's so much better than the DOS Backup command that you shouldn't even consider using the DOS Backup command if you have DOS 6.0.

In this chapter, I'll introduce you to the major features of Microsoft Backup. First, I'll point out the main differences between Microsoft Backup and the DOS Backup command. Next, I'll show you the operational details of using this full-screen utility. Then, I'll show you how to use the four main functions of Microsoft Backup to get your system set up right, to back up data, to restore data, and to verify the accuracy of your backups.

Why Microsoft Backup is better than the Backup command

Microsoft Backup provides many of the features of other popular backup utilities, as listed in figure 16-1. Its main advantages over the DOS Backup command are improved speed, ease of use, and file compression capabilities.

Speed Figure 16-2 gives you some idea of how Microsoft Backup can improve on the speed of the DOS Backup command. Although this chart just summarizes the data from an informal test on my own system, I think the message is clear. Microsoft

Features of Microsoft Backup

- Full, incremental, and differential backups
- Faster backups
- Saved backup configurations
- File compression

Figure 16-1 Features of the DOS 6.0 Backup utility, Microsoft Backup

Backup can reduce the time you take for backups by 75 percent or more. This means a backup that takes 20 minutes when you use the DOS Backup command will probably take less than 5 minutes when you use Microsoft Backup.

To operate at increased speed, Microsoft Backup uses an advanced hardware feature called *DMA*, or *Direct Memory Access*. Because Microsoft Backup doesn't use DMA as aggressively as commercial backup utilities, such as Central Point Backup and Norton Backup, these programs are even faster than Microsoft Backup.

Ease of use As you learned in chapter 9, the switches of the Backup command make it difficult to use. In contrast, Microsoft Backup provides features that make it easy to use. For instance, it provides menus you use to select options. In addition, it lets you create saved backup configurations. That means that you can save the specifications for a backup procedure after you get it set up the way you want it. Then, you can run the backup procedure the next time just by loading the saved configuration.

File compression Microsoft Backup gives you the option of *compressing* the data in the files that it backs up. This means the files take up less space on the diskettes than they do on the hard disk. In the chart in figure 16-2, you can see the number of diskettes required by Microsoft Backup compared to the Backup command.

Although file compression isn't an essential feature of a backup utility, it can increase backup speed because it reduces the amount of data that has to be written on the backup diskettes. Also, it provides a minor savings in diskette costs. Because data files can be compressed more than program files, this feature means the most when you're backing up data files. In general, the more data you have on your hard disk, the more useful this feature becomes.

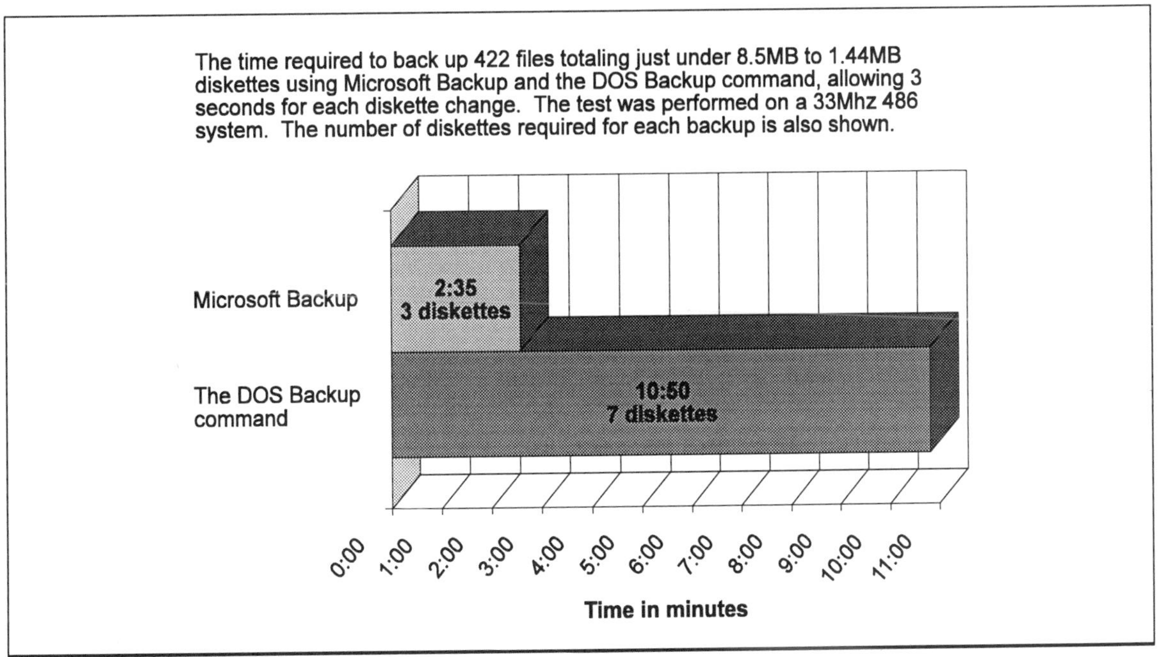
The time required to back up 422 files totaling just under 8.5MB to 1.44MB diskettes using Microsoft Backup and the DOS Backup command, allowing 3 seconds for each diskette change. The test was performed on a 33Mhz 486 system. The number of diskettes required for each backup is also shown.
Microsoft Backup
2:35
3 diskettes
The DOS Backup command
10:50
7 diskettes
0:00
1:00
2:00
3:00
4:00
5:00
6:00
7:00
8:00
9:00
10:00
11:00
Time in minutes

Figure 16-2 A performance comparison of Microsoft Backup (DOS 6.0) and the DOS Backup command

Three types of backups: full, incremental, and differential

In chapter 9, I introduced you to the two major types of backups: full and incremental. Both of these are supported by Microsoft Backup, as well as the DOS Backup command. I also presented the concept of appended incremental backups, supported by DOS 3.3 and later versions of DOS. Unfortunately, Microsoft Backup does *not* support appended incremental backups. So you'll have to use a separate diskette each time you do an incremental backup, as shown in figure 16-3. Now, I want to introduce you to one other type of backup that is supported by Microsoft Backup: differential backups.

Differential backups As I said in chapter 9, when you do an incremental backup, the archive bit on each file is turned off, indicating that the file has been backed up. In contrast, the archive bit isn't turned off during a *differential backup*. As a result, a differential backup is a backup of all the files that have been created or changed since the last full backup, even if they have been backed up in a previous differential backup. You can't do this type of backup with the DOS Backup command.

To illustrate how you can use differential backups, figure 16-4 shows a weekly schedule of one full and four differential backups. As you can see, each differential backup requires only diskette 7. Since the diskettes for a differential backup include

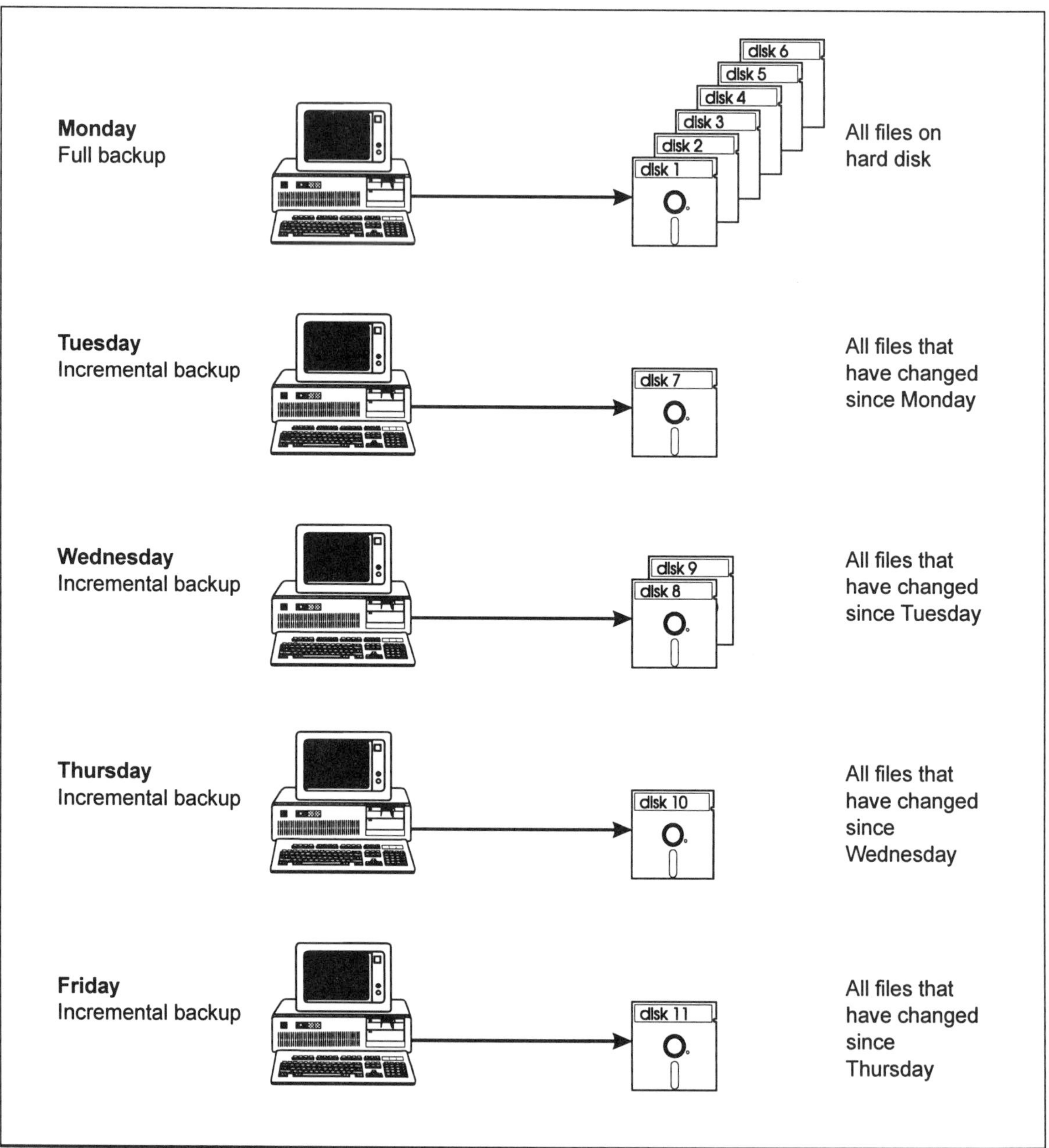

Figure 16-3 A weekly schedule of full and separate incremental backups

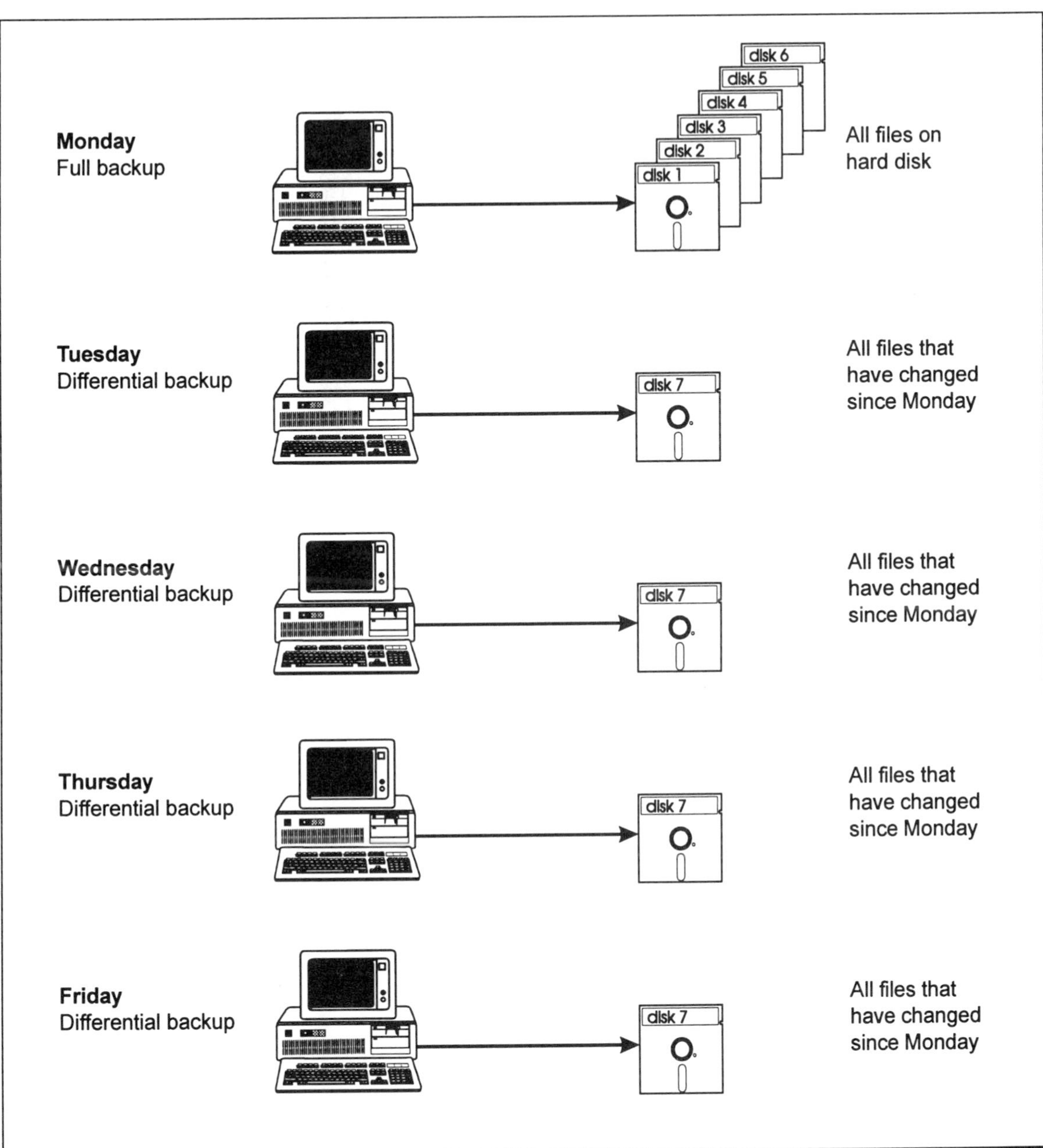

Figure 16-4 A weekly schedule of full and differential backups

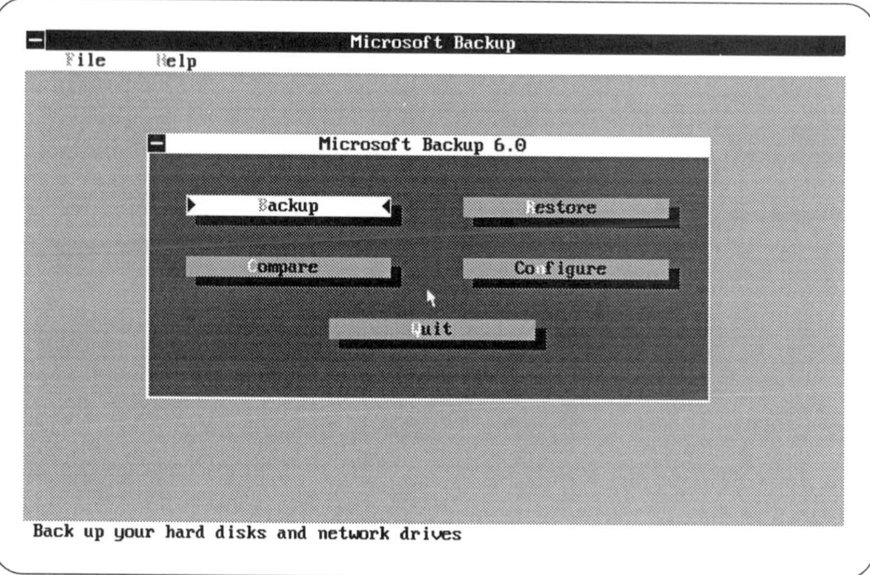

Figure 16-5 The opening screen for Microsoft Backup

only one version of each backed-up file, a schedule of differential backups is likely to require fewer diskettes than a schedule of separate incremental backups. However, the differential backups will take longer on the average than the incremental backups. That's because you have to back up more files each time, unless you're working on the same files every day.

If you do work on the same files each day, you may want to consider differential backups because they will be just as fast as incremental backups, and they won't require as many diskettes. You should be aware, though, that if you use the same diskette for each differential backup as shown in figure 16-4, you can lose a whole week's work if the diskette goes bad. So it's a good idea to alternate between diskettes for each differential backup. Then, if one diskette goes bad, you won't lose more than one day's work.

An overview of Microsoft Backup

To start Microsoft Backup, you enter the program name MSBACKUP at the command prompt. When you do, the screen in figure 16-5 is displayed. As you can see, Microsoft Backup provides four functions: Backup, Restore, Compare, and Configure. I'll show you how to use all of these functions in this chapter. But first, I'll show you how to activate functions from Microsoft Backup, how to use the pull-down menus, and how to get Help information.

How to activate Backup functions The rectangles that contain the Backup functions are called *buttons*. To activate one of these functions, move the mouse cursor to the item and press the left mouse button. This is referred to as *clicking the mouse*. If you don't have a mouse, you can activate a function by pressing its *shortcut key*. The shortcut key is the letter in the function name that's highlighted. If you're using a color monitor, the shortcut key is in a contrasting color. If you're using a black and white monitor, the shortcut key is in reverse video. For example, the shortcut key for the Backup function is B.

You can also activate a function by pressing the Tab key until the function is selected, then pressing the Enter key. A selected function is identified by two arrowheads on the left and right ends of the button. If you're using a color monitor, the selected function is also highlighted. Notice that when a function is selected, a brief description of the function appears on the bottom line of the screen.

Once you've activated a function, you can exit from it by pressing the Escape key. If the function has a Cancel button, you can also exit by selecting that button. And, if you're using graphics mode, you can exit by double-clicking the mouse on the *system box* in the top left corner of the screen. To exit from Microsoft Backup, select the Quit button or double-click on the system box.

How to use the pull-down menus You can also activate functions from the *menu bar* at the top of the screen. The menu bar on all the screens in Microsoft Backup contains only two menu items: File and Help. To activate one of these menu items, you click the mouse on it. When you do that, a *pull-down menu* is displayed. For example, figure 16-6 shows the pull-down menu that's displayed when you activate the File menu item. As you can see, this menu has seven functions. To activate one of these functions, you just point to it with the mouse cursor and click again.

If you don't have a mouse, you can activate a menu item using its shortcut key. In this case, you must hold down the Alt key while pressing the shortcut key. You can also press F10 to activate the File menu. Then, you can activate a function from the menu by pressing its shortcut key, or you can use the cursor keys to highlight the function and then press the Enter key.

How to get Help information Whenever you're using Microsoft Backup, you can get information from the Help facility by pressing the F1 key. This information is displayed in a *window* as shown in figure 16-7, and it always relates to whatever you're trying to do at the time. For example, I pressed F1 when the Backup button was selected to get the Help information in figure 16-7.

To scroll through the Help text, you can use the cursor control keys or the Page-up and Page-down keys. If you're using a mouse, you can also scroll using the *scroll bar* at the right side of the Help window. You can scroll one line at a time by clicking on the arrow at the top or bottom of the scroll bar. Or, you can scroll through varying numbers of lines using the portion of the scroll bar called the *scroll box*.

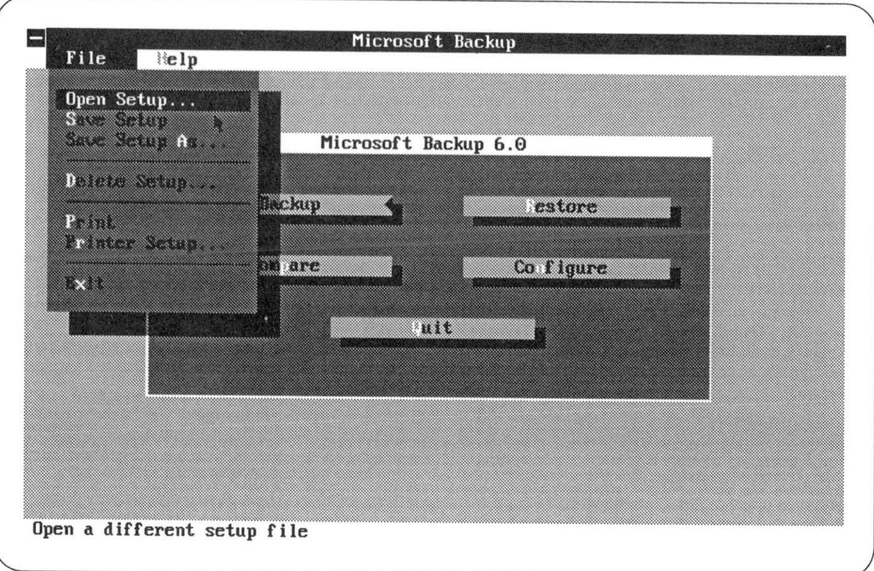

Figure 16-6 The File menu

The scroll box reflects the position of the screen information relative to the full text. For example, when the scroll box is at the top of the scroll bar, as in figure 16-7, the screen displays the beginning of the Help text. When the scroll box is near the middle of the scroll bar, the screen displays the middle part of the Help text. To scroll through the text, move the mouse cursor to the scroll box, then hold down the left mouse button while you move the scroll box to a new position. As you move the mouse, the Help text scrolls to its new position.

To use one of the button functions at the bottom of the Help screen, you click on it with the mouse. You can also start one of these functions by using the Tab key and the cursor control keys to move the cursor to the desired button and then pressing the Enter key. The Topics button displays the Help index. The Previous button displays the previous Help topic. The Next button displays the next Help topic. And the Cancel button exits from Help.

How to use the Configure function before you run your first backup

Figure 16-8 shows the Configure screen that's displayed when you select the Configure function from the opening screen of Microsoft Backup. The first time you use this utility, you should make sure that the video, mouse, and backup devices options are set correctly for your system. They should be set up properly, but if you ever need to change one of these options, simply click the mouse anywhere in the box

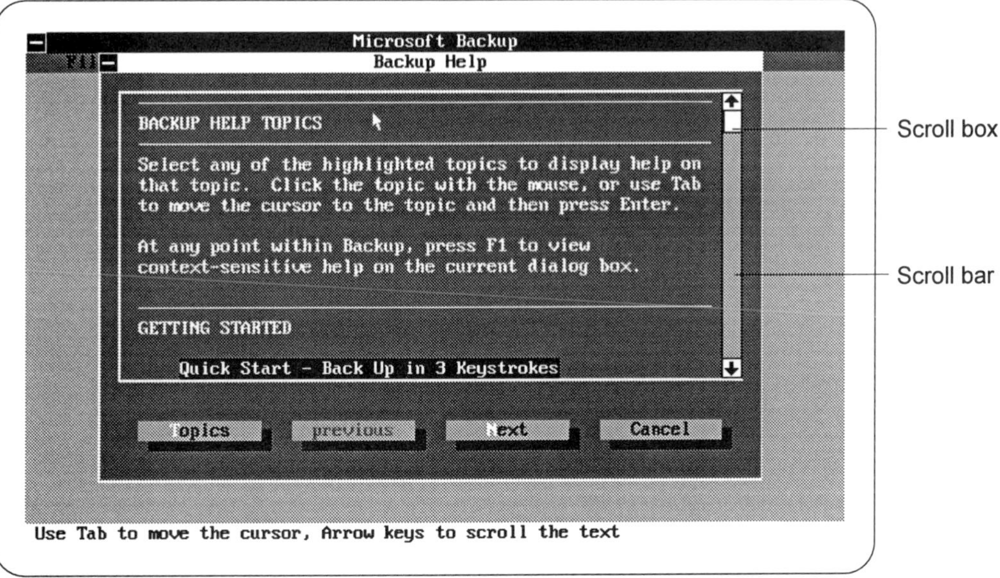

Figure 16-7 A Help facility window

that contains the option. Then, a *dialog box* appears that allows you to select the right value for the option. To display these dialog boxes using the keyboard, highlight the option box using the Tab key, then press the Enter key.

You should also run the compatibility test once for each backup device you use on your system. You start the compatibility test by clicking on its button or by highlighting it and pressing the Enter key. The compatibility test makes sure that Microsoft Backup is compatible with the backup device you're using.

How to use the Backup function to back up data

When you select the Backup function from the opening screen, the Backup screen in figure 16-9 is displayed. From this screen, you can select the type of backup you want to do, the files to be backed up, the drive where the files are to be backed up, and a setup file that contains the specifications for the backup. The settings you see in figure 16-9 are the defaults provided by Microsoft Backup the first time you use it. This screen also tells you the number of files selected for the backup, the number of diskettes that will be required for the backup, and the estimated time to perform the backup. As you can see, there are no files currently selected for the backup. You can also select the Options button from this screen to set backup options. And you can select the Start-backup button to start a backup. To use Microsoft Backup efficiently, you need to know how to use all of these features.

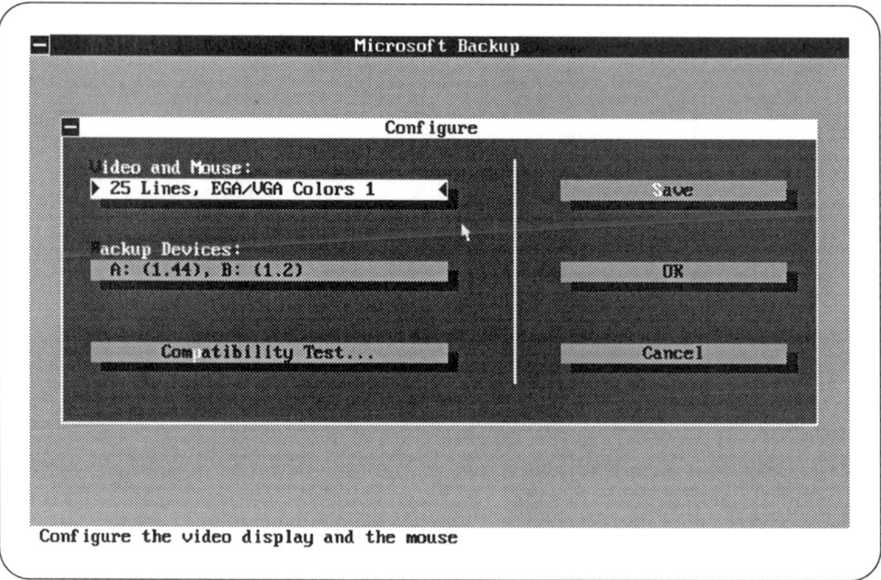

Figure 16-8 The Configure screen

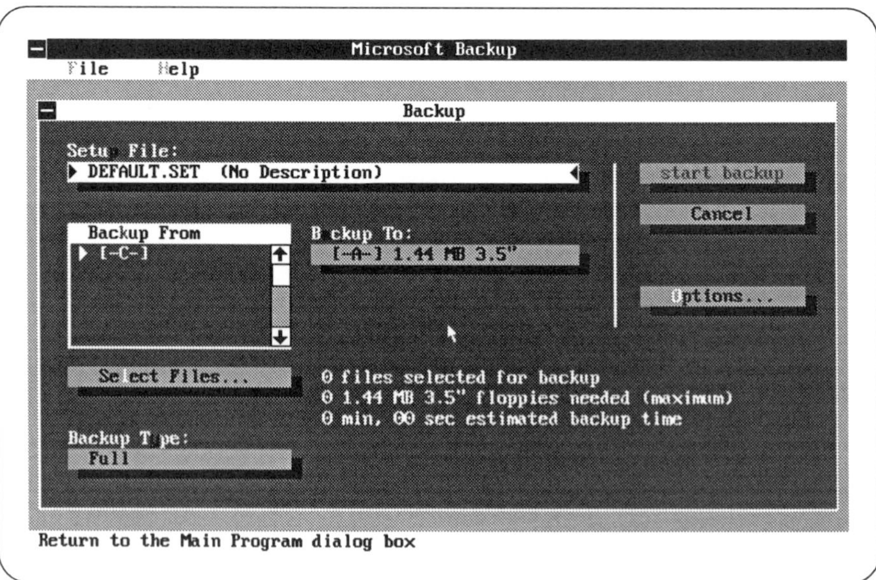

Figure 16-9 The Backup screen

The Disk-backup-options dialog box

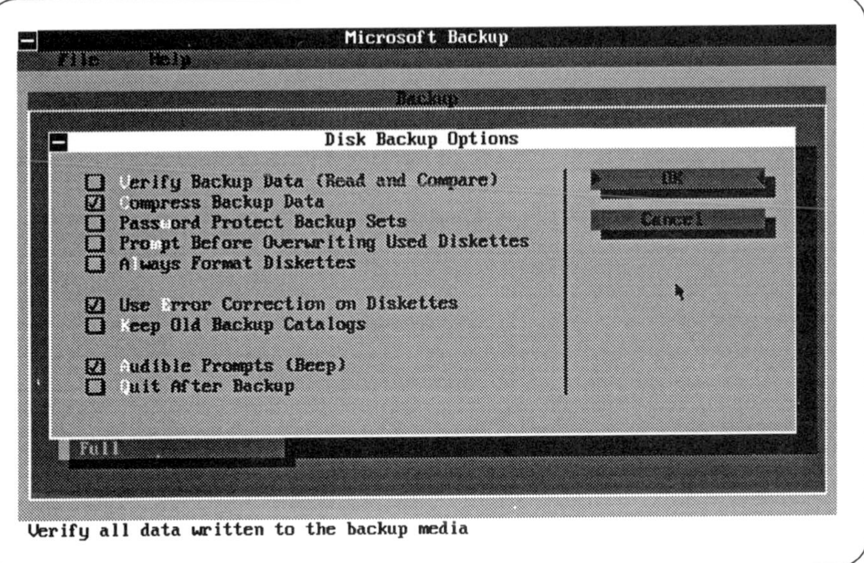

Option	Function
Verify Backup Data	Causes Microsoft Backup to verify the data written to the backup diskettes. Because this nearly doubles the time required for a backup, we recommend you select the Use-error-correction-on-diskettes option instead.
Compress Backup Data	Minimizes the number of diskettes required and the time required for a backup. Use this option for your backups.

Figure 16-10 How to set the backup options (part 1 of 2)

How to set backup options Before you start a backup, you should set the backup options. To do that, you select the Options button from the Backup screen. Then, the dialog box in figure 16-10 is displayed. To select or deselect an option, click the mouse on the box to the left of the option. Or, use the cursor control keys to move to a box and press the Space bar. When an option is selected, a check mark appears in the box.

Option	Function
Password Protect Backup Sets	Allows you to assign a password to your backup diskettes.
Prompt Before Overwriting Used Diskettes	Causes Microsoft Backup to warn you if you insert a backup diskette that contains data. Because this option requires you to confirm every diskette you reuse, it adds to your backup time. So if you always use the same sets of diskettes for backups and know you aren't destroying any data that you need, you won't want to select this option.
Always Format Diskettes	Formats each backup diskette before data is written to it. Since this is time-consuming, you usually won't select this option. Then, only unformatted diskettes are formatted.
Use Error Correction on Diskettes	Writes information to each backup diskette that can help recover the data from the diskette if it's damaged. Use this option instead of the Verify-backup-data option.
Keep Old Backup Catalogs	Keeps a record of previous backups. Since this isn't usually necessary, you probably won't select this option.
Audible Prompts	Causes your workstation to beep whenever Microsoft Backup requires your attention (for example, when you need to insert the next backup diskette).
Quit After Backup	Causes Microsoft Backup to end automatically when the backup is complete.

Figure 16-10 How to set the backup options (part 2 of 2)

In figure 16-10, I've set the options the way I think you'll use them most often. If you look at the option descriptions at the bottom of the figure, you'll see that the first two options I've set provide for file compression and data-recovery safeguards; the third one causes Microsoft Backup to beep whenever you need to provide information to the backup operation. Usually, you will set these options just once so they'll be used in all your backup procedures.

How to do a full backup Figure 16-11 shows you how to do a full backup once you've specified the backup options. In part 1 of the figure, the default settings for the backup are in effect, so no files are selected for the backup. The first thing you need to do, then, is select the files you want to back up.

The Backup-from box displays all the drives on your hard disk. To include or exclude an entire drive from the backup, click the right mouse button on the drive designator in this box (you can also double-click the left mouse button) or highlight the drive designator using the Tab key or the cursor control keys and press the Space bar. For example, if you click on the designator for drive C, an "All files" message appears, indicating that all the files on drive C are selected. Values for the three messages to the right of the Select-files box also appear, as shown in part 2 of figure 16-11. If you click on the C drive designator again, the "All-files" message and the values disappear. You can also select specific files and directories to be backed up. I'll show you how to do that later in this chapter.

If you want to change the drive where the data will be backed up, click the mouse on the Backup-to option box or highlight the box and press the Enter key. Then, a dialog box is displayed that lists all the backup drives so you can select the right one.

Once you're ready to start the backup, you select the Start-backup button. Then, a dialog box like the one in part 3 of figure 16-11 is displayed. This tells you to insert the first diskette into the backup drive. After you insert the diskette, press the Enter key or click on the Continue button.

During the backup, you'll see a screen like the one in part 4 of figure 16-11. This screen shows you the files and directories as they're backed up as well as the progress of the backup.

When a backup diskette becomes full, Microsoft Backup displays a message like the one in part 5 of figure 16-11. (The message is to the right of the drive letter at the top of the Diskette-progress box.) Then, when you insert the next diskette, the backup continues. If you don't respond by inserting the next diskette within a few seconds, a dialog box like the one I showed you in part 3 of the figure is displayed. Then, after you insert the next diskette, you have to press the Enter key or click on the Continue button.

Part 6 of the figure shows the type of summary information you get when the backup procedure is finished. Here, you can see that the backup time for almost 23MB of data was only 6 minutes and 17 seconds. You can also see that the file compression for these files was 2.5 percent, so only 7 diskettes were required for the backup.

How to do an incremental or differential backup The procedure for doing an incremental or differential backup is almost identical to the procedure for a full backup. The only difference is that you have to change the Backup-type option on the Backup screen. To do that, click the mouse on the Backup-type option box or

Part 1:

To back up an entire drive, move the cursor to the drive designator in the Backup-from box and press the Space bar or click the right mouse button.

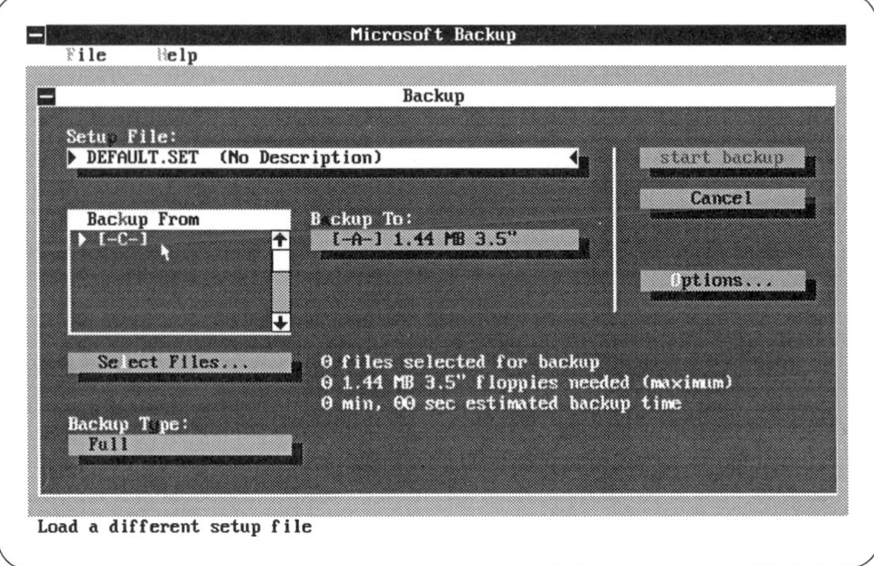

Part 2:

The "All files" message appears in the Backup-from box and the messages to the right of the Select-files box tell you how many files will be backed up, how many diskettes the backup will require, and the estimated backup time. Select the Start-backup button to begin the backup.

Microsoft Backup
File Help
Backup
Setup File:
DEFAULT.SET (No Description)
Start Backup
Cancel
Backup From
[-C-] All files
Backup To:
[-A-] 1.44 MB 3.5"
Options...
Select Files...
686 files (with catalog) selected for backup
18 1.44 MB 3.5" floppies needed (maximum)
11 min, 48 sec estimated backup time
Backup Type:
Full
Press Spacebar or right mouse button to select entire drives

Figure 16-11 How to do a full backup (parts 1 and 2 of 6)

Part 3:

Before the backup starts, Microsoft Backup prompts you for the first diskette. After inserting the diskette, press the Enter key or click on the Continue button.

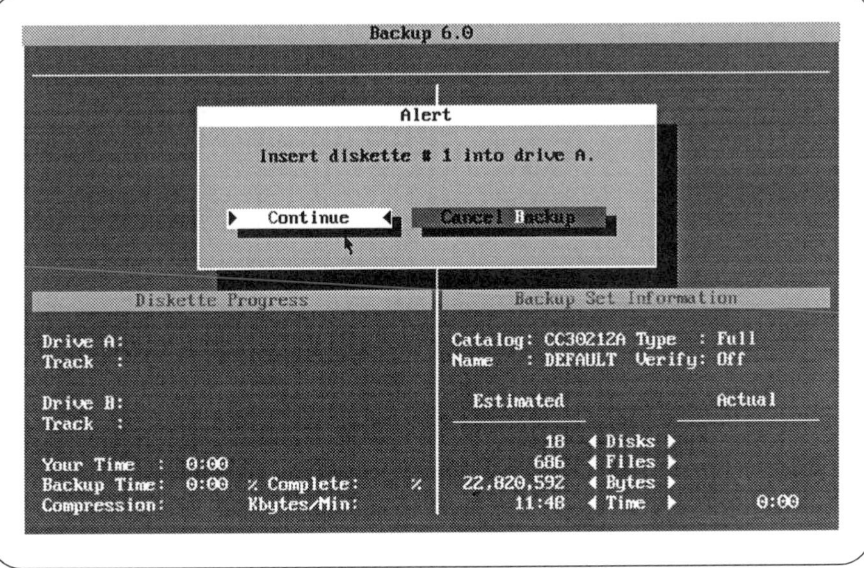

Part 4:

While Microsoft Backup is working, the values in the Diskette-progress and Backup-set-information boxes change to show you how the backup is progressing.

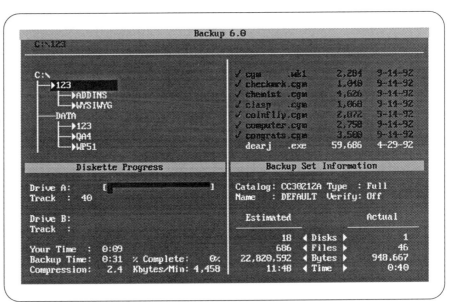

Figure 16-11 How to do a full backup (parts 3 and 4 of 6)

Part 5:

When a diskette becomes full, Microsoft Backup prompts you to insert the next diskette.

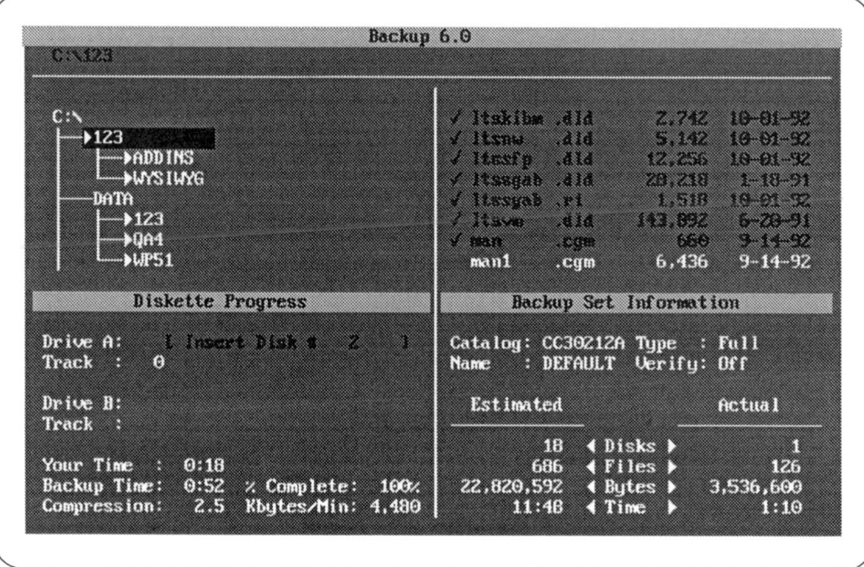

Part 6:

At the end of the backup, Microsoft Backup gives you summary information. Press the Enter key or click on the OK button to return to the opening Backup screen.

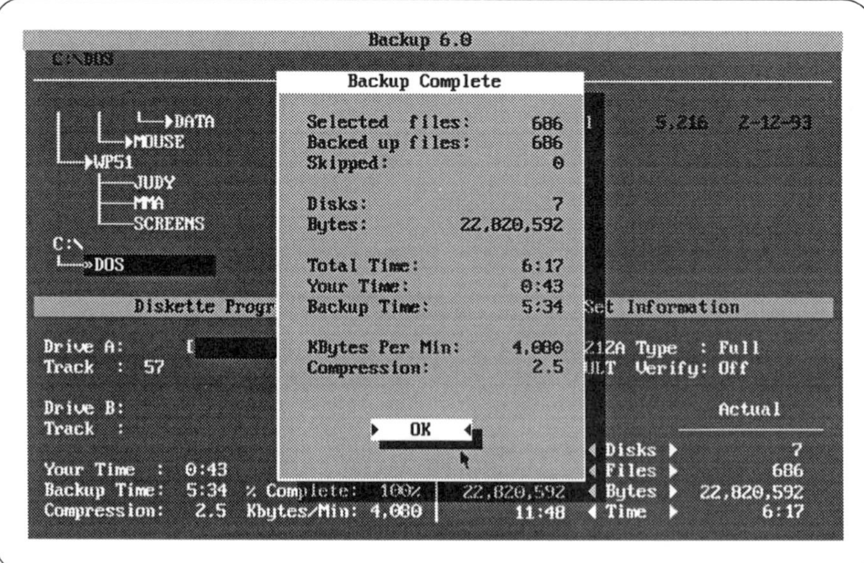

Figure 16-11 How to do a full backup (parts 5 and 6 of 6)

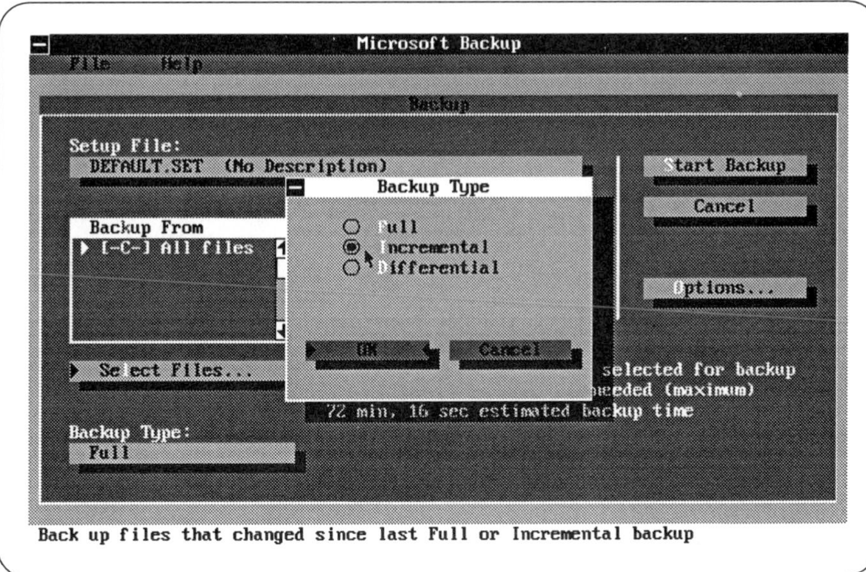

Figure 16-12 How to select the backup type

highlight it and press the Enter key. When you do, a dialog box like the one in figure 16-12 is displayed. Then, select the option you want by clicking on it with the mouse or by pressing the Space bar. Once you've selected the backup type, you're ready to start your backup.

How to select files for a backup In chapter 9, I showed you how you can simplify backups by organizing your directories so that all data directories are subordinate to one directory. Then, you can do a periodic backup of the program directories and a daily backup of the data directories. To do that, you'll need to select the directories you want to back up. Figure 16-13 shows you how to back up a single data directory.

In part 1, you can see that no files are selected for the backup. The current drive is C, indicated by the arrowhead to the left of the drive designator. If you have more than one hard drive on your system, you can change the current drive by clicking on it with the mouse. Or, you can tab to the Backup-from box, then use the cursor control keys to highlight the drive you want.

Next, select the Select-files option. When you do, the screen in part 2 of the figure is displayed. Here, the left side of the screen contains the directory structure of the drive you selected and the right side of the screen contains a list of the files in the current directory. If a directory is selected for the backup, it has an arrowhead pointing to it. If a file is selected, it has a check mark in front of it.

Part 1:

If you don't want to back up an entire drive, select the Select-files function to specify which directories or files should be backed up.

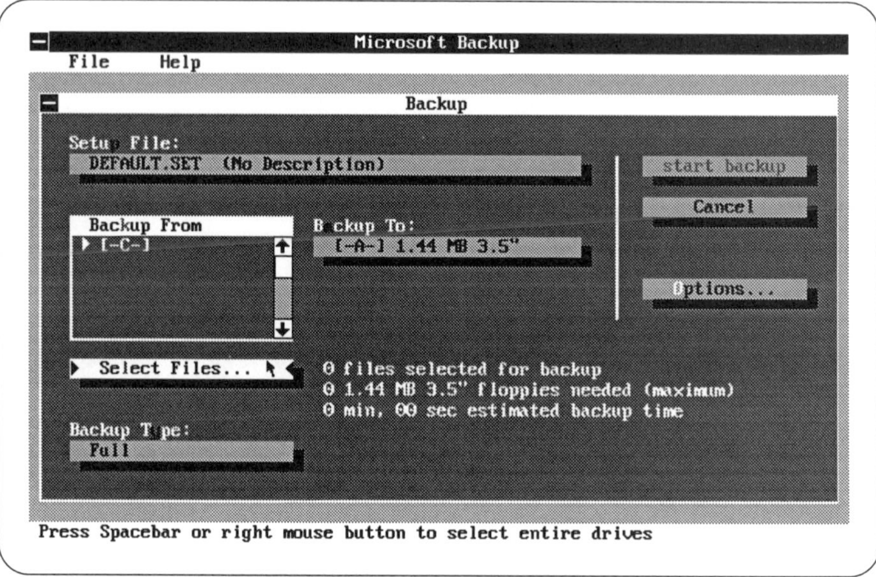

Part 2:

The Select-files screen displays a listing of all the files on the selected drive. The left part of the screen shows the directory structure, while the right part of the screen shows the files in the highlighted directory.

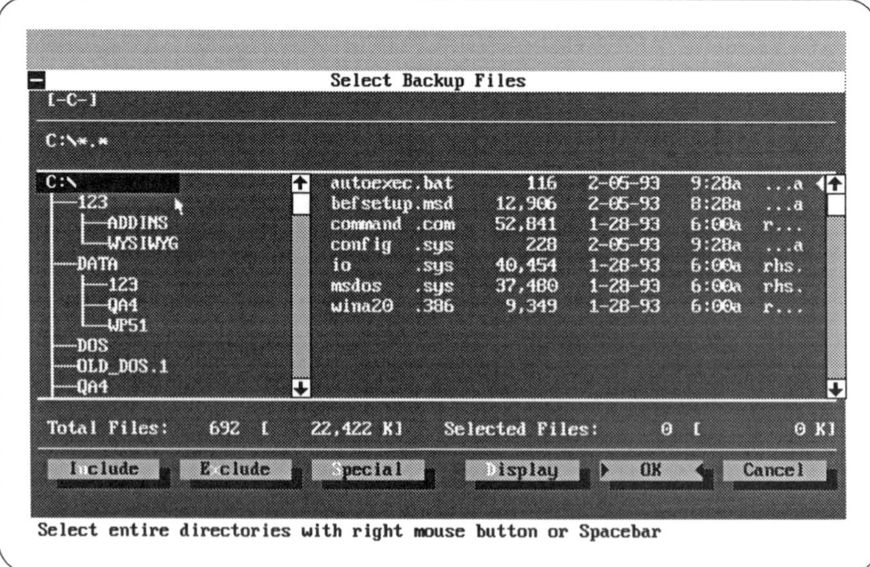

Figure 16-13 How to select files for a backup (parts 1 and 2 of 4)

Part 3:

Move the cursor to the directory you want to back up, and press the Space bar or click the right mouse button to select all the files in it. To select only certain files, move the cursor to the file names and select them individually. When you've selected the files, select the OK button or press the Enter key to return to the Backup screen.

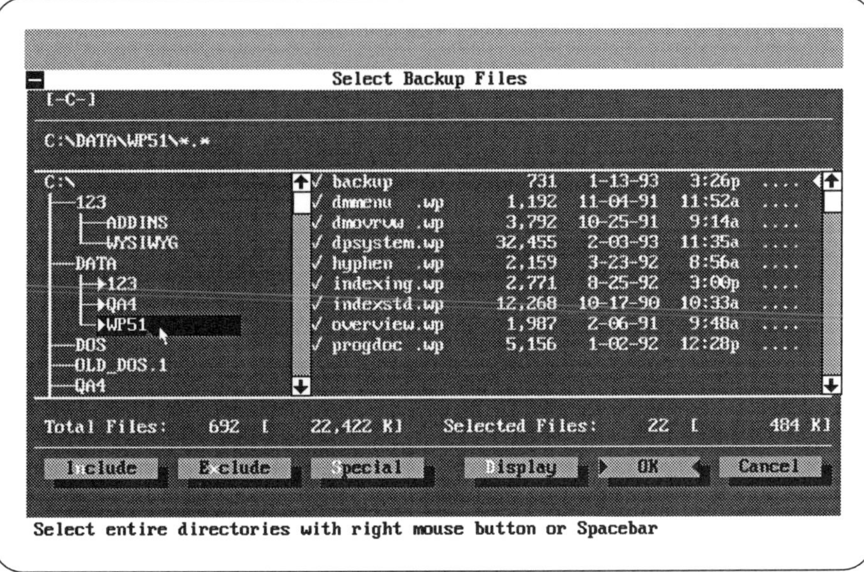

Part 4:

The messages to the right of the Select-files box show how many files have been selected and what the backup requirements are.

Microsoft Backup
File Help
Backup
Setup File:
DEFAULT.SET (No Description)
Start Backup
Cancel
Backup From
[-C-] Some files
Backup To:
[-A-] 1.44 MB 3.5"
Options...
Select Files...
22 files (with catalog) selected for backup
1 1.44 MB 3.5" floppy needed
0 min, 17 sec estimated backup time
Backup Type:
Full
Select specific files for backup

Figure 16-13 How to select files for a backup (parts 3 and 4 of 4)

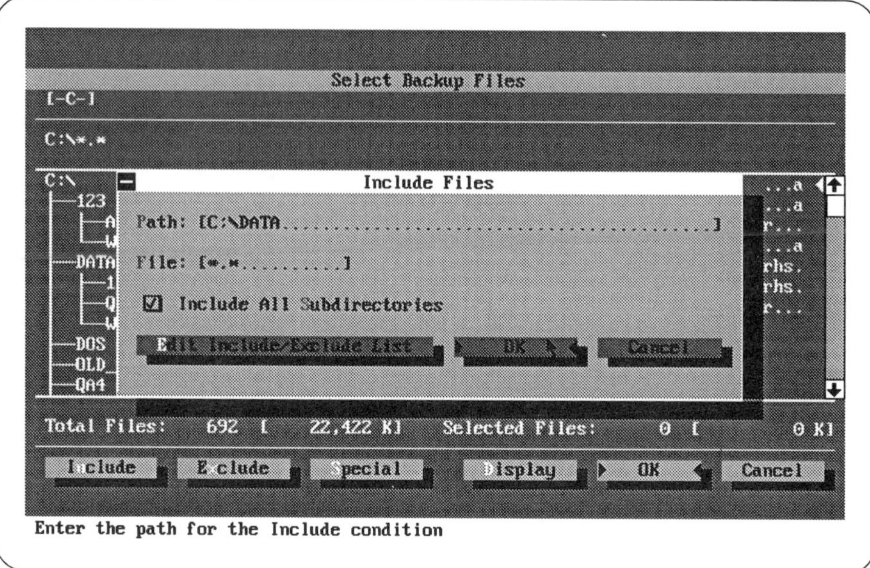

Figure 16-14 The dialog box for the Include option for selecting files

As you can see in part 2, no directories are selected. To select a directory, click the right mouse button on it or highlight the directory and press the Space bar. In part 3, you can see that I've selected all the directories subordinate to the DATA directory. I didn't select the DATA directory itself because it doesn't contain any files, just directories. Note that if you select a directory that contains subdirectories, the subdirectories are *not* automatically selected. You have to select each directory individually. When you return to the Backup screen, you'll see it shows that some of the files on drive C are selected for the backup, as in part 4 of the figure.

If you look back to parts 2 and 3 of figure 16-13, you'll see several buttons at the bottom of the screens. The Include and Exclude buttons let you select specific files or groups of files to be included in or excluded from the backup. For example, if you select the Include button, the dialog box in figure 16-14 is displayed. Here, the Path field defaults to the directory that's currently highlighted. In the File field, you can enter any file specification. The default is for all files to be included (*.*). If you select the Include-all-subdirectories option, any files that match the file specification in all subdirectories are included. In figure 16-14, I specified that all files in the DATA directory and all of its subdirectories are to be included in the backup. So the result is the same as in figure 16-13.

Every time you enter a file specification using the Include or Exclude option, Microsoft Backup adds it to an Include/Exclude list. If you want to, you can edit the

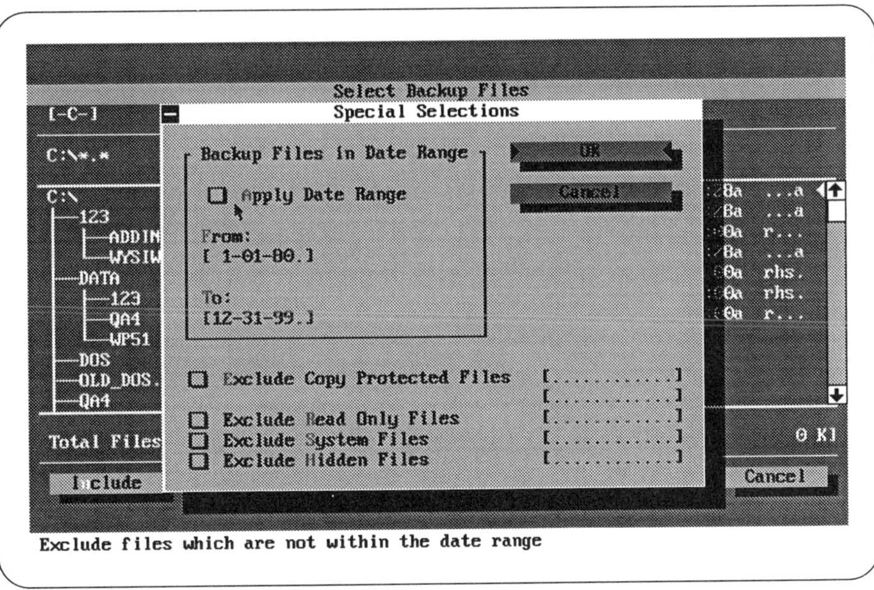

Figure 16-15 The dialog box for the Special option for selecting files

Include/Exclude list directly by selecting the Edit option from the Include or Exclude dialog box.

The Special button at the bottom of the Select-backup-files screen lets you specify a date range for the files to be backed up. Figure 16-15 shows the dialog box that's displayed when you select the Special option. If you enter a date and select the Apply-date-range option, files that weren't created within the date range are excluded from the backup. Note that files that fall within the date range aren't necessarily backed up. You also have to select the files you want to include in the backup.

You can also exclude special types of files from a backup using the Special-selections dialog box. To exclude read-only, system, or hidden files, select the appropriate option. To exclude copy-protected files, select the Exclude-copy-protected-files option and enter the file names in the spaces provided at the right.

Finally, the Display button on the Select-backup-files screen lets you control how the files are displayed on the screen. Figure 16-16 shows the dialog box that's displayed when you select this option. Here, you can sort the files by name, extension, size, date, or attribute, you can group selected files at the beginning of the display, and you can enter a file specification using the * wildcard so only files that match the specification are displayed.

How to use a setup file To simplify your backup procedures, you can save the specifications for a backup in a *setup file*. Then, you don't have to select the

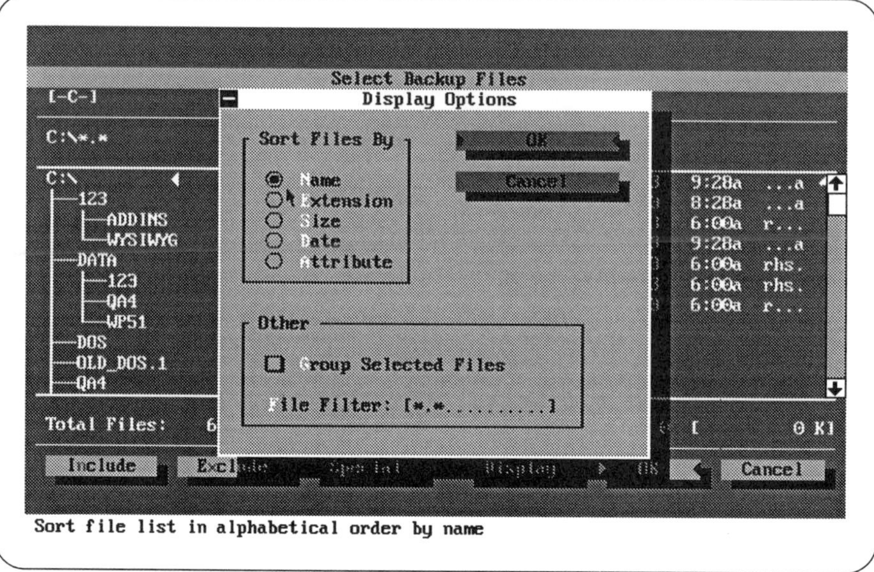

Figure 16-16 The dialog box for the Display option for selecting files

functions and options for a specific backup procedure the next time you want to repeat the backup. Instead, you just load the setup file and start the backup. Microsoft Backup lets you save a backup configuration using the Save-setup and Save-setup-as functions from the File menu, shown in part 1 of figure 16-17. You use the Save-setup function to change a setup file you saved previously. You use the Save-setup-as function to create a new setup file.

After you've configured a backup by setting the drives, directories, and options the way you want them, select the Save-setup-as function. When you do, a dialog box like the one in part 2 of figure 16-17 lets you name the setup file and enter a description for it. Here, I've used the name DATAC for a backup of the data files on drive C. In part 3, you can see that the configuration file has been saved in the file named DATAC.SET.

To load a setup file, you can use the Open-setup function of the File menu, or you can select the Setup-file option box to display a list of setup files, like the one in figure 16-18. After you select the file you want, you're ready to start the backup. Because setup files simplify the use of Microsoft Backup, I recommend that you create one for each backup procedure you run.

You can also load a setup file automatically when you start Microsoft Backup. To do that, specify the name of the setup file following the program name at the command prompt, like this:

```
C:\>msbackup datac
```

Part 1:

To create a new setup file, set the backup specifications on the Backup screen. Then, pull down the File menu and select the Save-setup-as function.

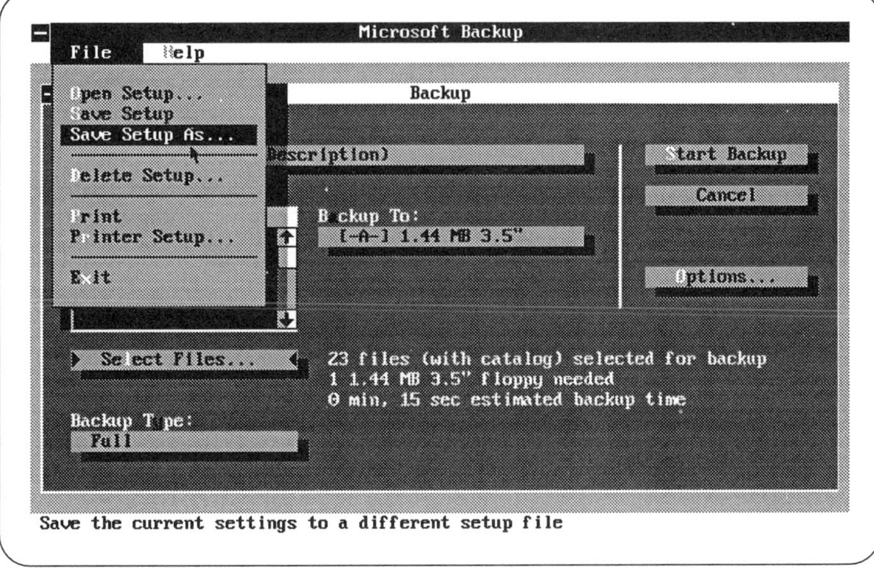

Part 2:

In the dialog box, enter the file name of the new setup file and a file description if desired. Then, select the Save button.

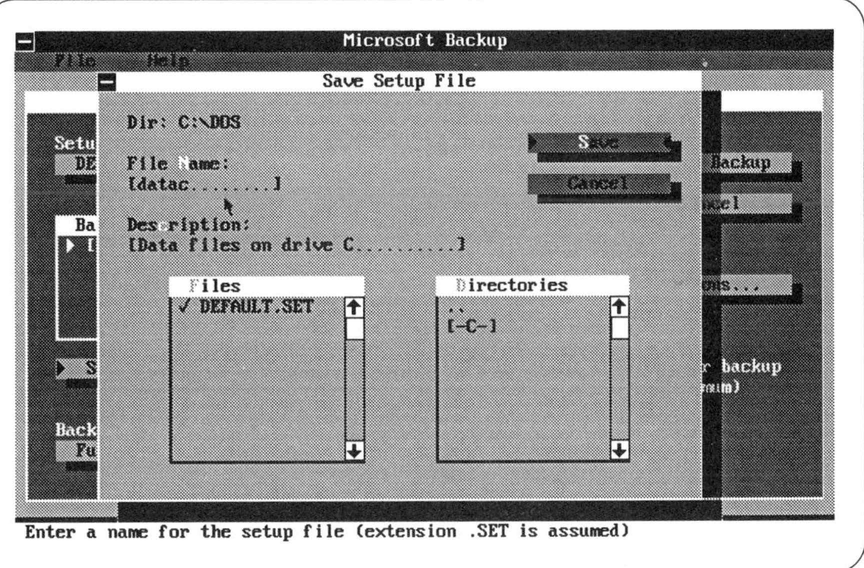

Figure 16-17 How to save the specifications for a backup in a setup file (parts 1 and 2 of 3)

Part 3:

Microsoft Backup saves the backup specifications in the setup file and returns to the Backup screen. The Setup-file box shows the new setup file name.

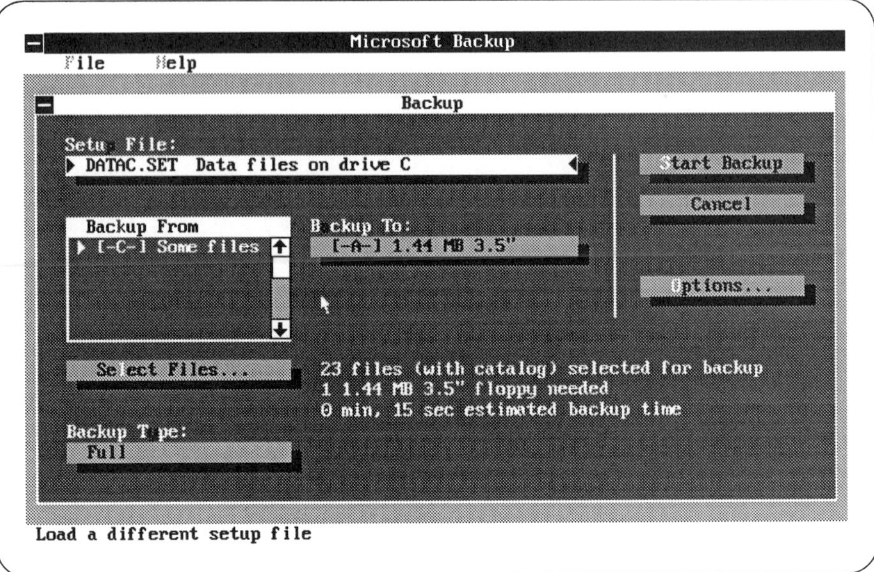

Figure 16-17 How to save the specifications for a backup in a setup file (part 3 of 3)

Since MSBACKUP is the name of Microsoft Backup, this command starts the program using DATAC as the name of the setup file.

If you use setup files, it's best if you use the same file for all types of backups of the same data. For example, I use the DATAC setup file for both full and incremental backups of my data files. Because I have the backup type set to incremental in the setup file, that means I have to change it to full whenever I do a full backup. Although this is a slight inconvenience, it makes restoring the data easier, as you'll see in a moment.

How to use the Restore function to restore files

Before you use the Restore function of Microsoft Backup, you need to understand how it uses catalogs to keep track of the directories and files that are backed up. So, I'll begin this section by describing those catalogs. Then, I'll show you how to load a catalog for a restore operation, how to select files for the restore, and how to set restore options.

Catalogs When you use Microsoft Backup, it automatically keeps track of the directories and files that have been backed up in a *backup catalog*. Microsoft Backup keeps this history information on the hard disk as well as on the last diskette of a

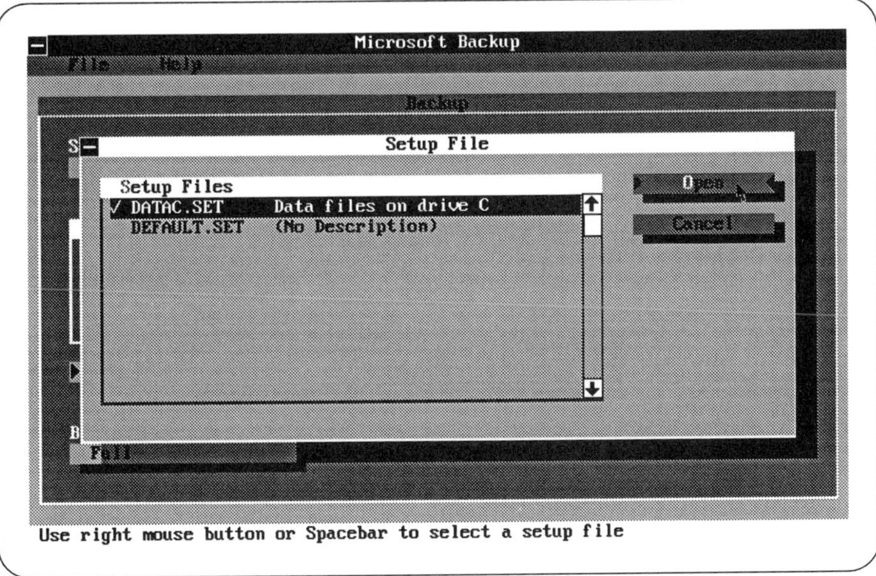

Figure 16-18 The dialog box for the Setup-file option

backup set. That way, if the catalog on the hard disk is damaged, you can retrieve the catalog from the backup set.

The name that's given to a backup catalog consists of the drive indicators, date, sequence of the backup, and type of backup. Specifically, a catalog name has the format illustrated in figure 16-19. So, a catalog named CC21123A.FUL is for the first full backup of data on drive C done on 11/23/92.

When you do a full backup, Microsoft Backup creates a *master catalog* in addition to the backup catalog. The master catalog keeps track of all of the backups in a *backup cycle*. A backup cycle consists of a full backup, plus any intermediate backups done up until the next full backup. For example, if you do a full backup of your data every Monday and incremental or differential backups Tuesday through Friday, the backup cycle consists of the full backup and all four incremental backups. When you do another full backup the following Monday, a new backup cycle begins. Note that all the backups in a cycle must use the same setup file. That's why you should use the same setup file for both full and incremental backups, as I explained earlier. The name of the master catalog is the same as the setup file, with the extension CAT. So the file named DATAC.CAT is the master catalog for all backups done using the setup file named DATAC.

Position	Description
1	The first drive backed up
2	The last drive backed up
3	The last digit of the current year
4-5	The current month
6-7	The current day
8	The sequence of the backup for the day, if more than one backup is done of the same data
Extension	FUL for full backup; INC for incremental backup; DIF for differential backup

Example

CC21123A.FUL	The first full backup of data on drive C done on 11/23/92.

Figure 16-19 The format of a file name for a backup catalog

How to load a catalog Figure 16-20 shows the Restore screen for Microsoft Backup. The default catalog is the one for the most recent backup. In this case, it's the incremental backup of drive C done on 2-14-93. To select a different catalog, select the Catalog button. When you do, the dialog box in figure 16-21 is displayed, showing you all the catalogs on the hard disk. By the way, you can also display a list similar to the one in figure 16-21 by pressing the Enter key or clicking on the Backup-set-catalog option box. However, the dialog box that's displayed doesn't include the Retrieve, Rebuild, and Delete functions. I'll describe these functions in a minute.

The catalog list in figure 16-21 contains four files. The third one, CC30212A.FUL, is for a full backup of the data files on drive C. The first and the second catalogs, CC30213A.INC and CC30214A.INC, are for incremental backups of the data on drive C. And the last one, DATAC.CAT, is the master catalog for the backup of data files on drive C. To select a catalog, click on it with the right mouse button, or use the cursor control keys to highlight the catalog and press the Space bar.

Normally, you'll restore from the master catalog. When you do, Microsoft Backup restores each backup set in the backup cycle in order. For example, if you load the DATAC master catalog in figure 16-21, the full backup, CC30212A.FUL is restored, followed by the two incremental backups. Without the master catalog, you'd have to restore each backup set in a separate operation. So the master catalog simplifies the restore process.

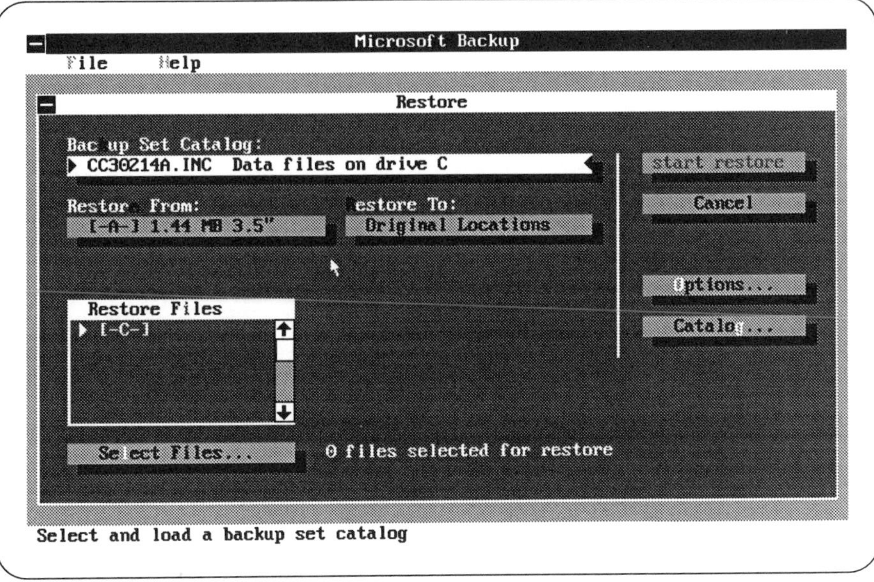

Figure 16-20 The Restore screen

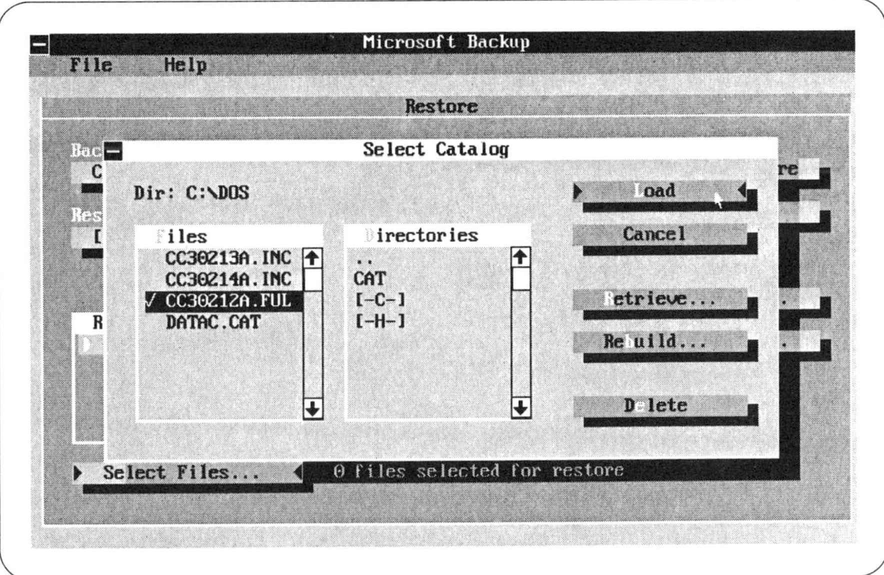

Figure 16-21 The dialog box for the Catalog function

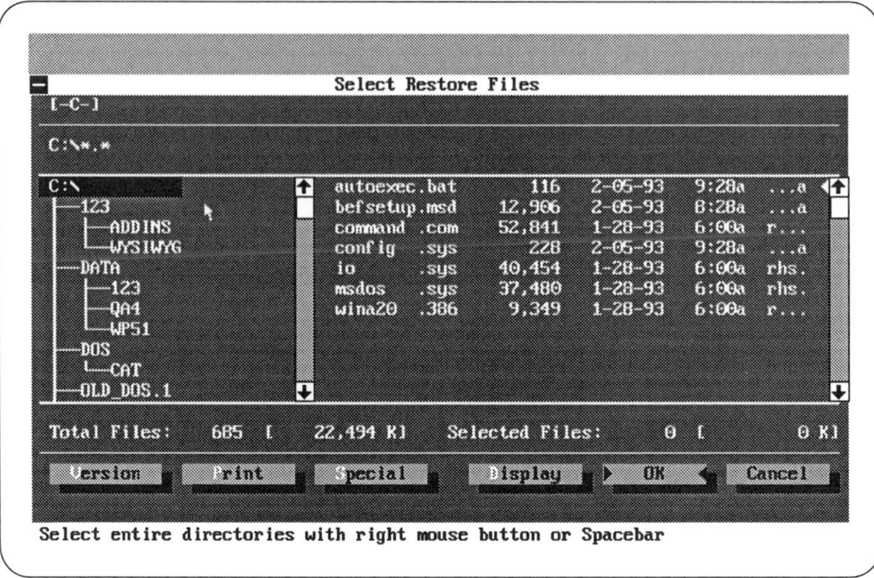

Figure 16-22 The Select-files screen for the Restore function

Before I go on, you should notice three additional functions on the Select-catalog screen: Retrieve, Rebuild, and Delete. You use Rebuild if the catalog you want to use for the restore isn't available on the hard disk. This is the case, for example, if you just formatted your hard disk. Then, you can retrieve the backup catalog from the last diskette of the backup set you want to restore. And if for some reason both copies of the catalog are unavailable or if one or more of the backup diskettes are damaged, you can use the Rebuild function to rebuild a partial catalog from the available backup diskettes. You use the Delete function to delete a catalog file.

How to select the files to restore After you select the catalog for the restore, you select the files you want to restore. You select files the same way you do for a backup. So to restore all the files in the specified catalog, click the right mouse button on the drive designator, or highlight the drive designator and press the Space bar, and the "All files" message will appear. To restore selected files, select the Select-files option, and mark the files you want to restore.

When you select the Select-files option, a screen like the one in figure 16-22 is displayed. This screen is identical to the Select-files screen for the Backup function except for the first two functions at the bottom of the screen. The Print function lets you print the catalog file you've selected, and the Version function lets you select the version of files you want to restore.

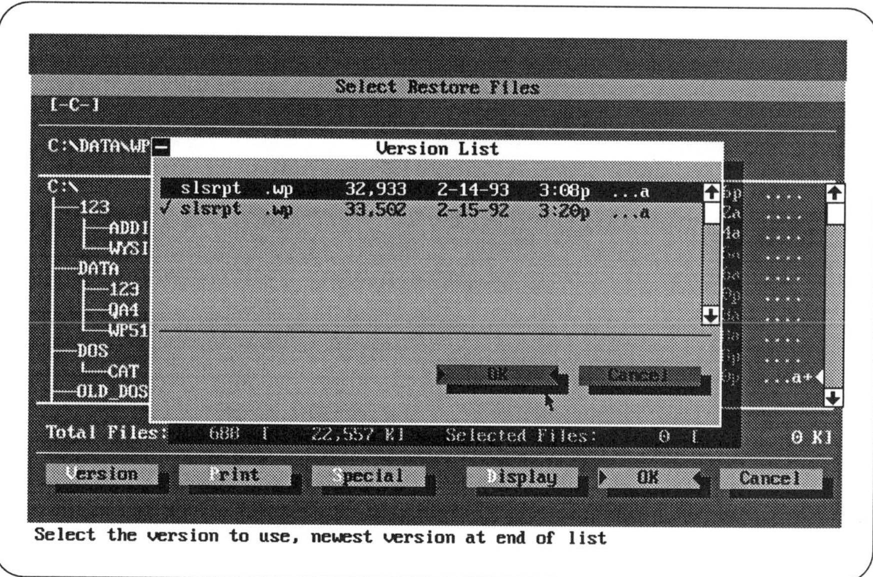

Figure 16-23 How to restore a version of a file other than the most recent one

By default, Microsoft Backup restores the most recent version of a file. But occasionally, you may need to restore an earlier version of a file. For example, if a file becomes damaged and you don't realize it until after you've made one or more backups of the damaged file, you might want to restore an undamaged version of the file from an earlier backup.

To use the Version function, you must select a master catalog for the restore operation so that all the versions of files in the backup cycle are available. Then, you highlight the file on the Select-files screen and select the Version function. When you do, a dialog box like the one in figure 16-23 is displayed. From this dialog box, you can select a version by clicking the right mouse button on it or by highlighting the version and pressing the Space bar. Note that the dates and times in this display are when the file was created or modified last, not when the file was backed up.

How to set restore options Before you do a restore for the first time, you should make sure the options are set the way you want them. Figure 16-24 shows the dialog box you see when you select the Options button on the Restore screen; the figure also includes a brief description of each option. Once you've set these options, they stay in effect until you change them. But you'll probably want to check them whenever you restore files to make sure they're appropriate for the type of restore operation you're doing.

The Disk-restore-options dialog box

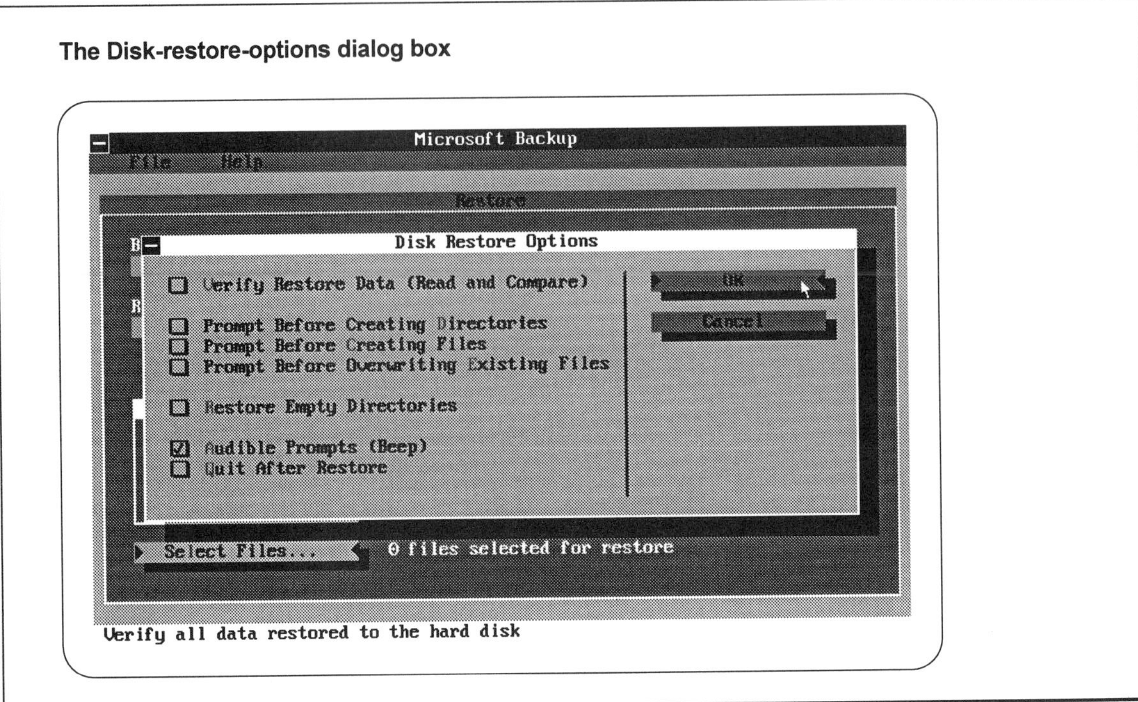

Figure 16-24 How to set the restore options (part 1 of 2)

You should also make sure the Restore-to option on the Restore screen is set properly before you begin a restore. Typically, you'll restore the data to its original location. But you can also restore to another drive or another directory, something you can't do with the DOS Backup command.

How to use the Compare function to verify a backup

The Compare function is similar to the Restore function, as you can see from the Compare screen in figure 16-25. The main difference is that instead of restoring selected files from a backup, it compares the backed up files to the original. You may want to use this function occasionally following a backup to assure yourself that your backups are reliable. Because the Compare function takes extra time, however, you won't want to run it each time you do a backup.

Option	Function
Verify Restore Data	Causes Microsoft Backup to verify the data restored to the hard disk. This adds a lot of time to the restore operation, but you may want to select this option, depending on what files you're restoring.
Prompt Before Creating Directories	Asks you for verification before creating a directory that doesn't already exist on the hard disk.
Prompt Before Creating Files	Asks you for verification before creating a file that doesn't already exist on the hard disk.
Prompt Before Overwriting Existing Files	Warns you if there's already an existing copy of the file you're restoring on the hard disk. You can either skip the file or restore it at that point.
Restore Empty Directories	Restores a complete directory structure, including directories that don't have any files selected for the restore. So if the restore operation comes to a directory that doesn't exist on the hard disk, it restores that directory; it doesn't restore any files in the directory, though, unless they're selected.
Audible Prompts	Causes your workstation to beep whenever Microsoft Backup requires your attention (for example, when you need to insert the next backup diskette).
Quit After Restore	Causes Microsoft Backup to end automatically when the restore operation is complete.

Figure 16-24 How to set the restore options (part 2 of 2)

Microsoft Backup for *Windows*

Besides the DOS version of Microsoft Backup, DOS 6.0 also includes a *Windows* version of the program called *Microsoft Backup for Windows*. Aside from the obvious differences that result from the *Windows* user interface, the *Windows* version of Microsoft Backup is nearly identical to the DOS version. As a result, you should have no trouble applying what you've learned in this chapter to the *Windows* version.

Figure 16-26 shows the main window for Microsoft Backup for *Windows*. Here, the large buttons across the top of the main window correspond to the buttons displayed by the DOS version's opening screen (figure 16-5). The controls displayed in the bottom portion of this window vary depending on which function you've

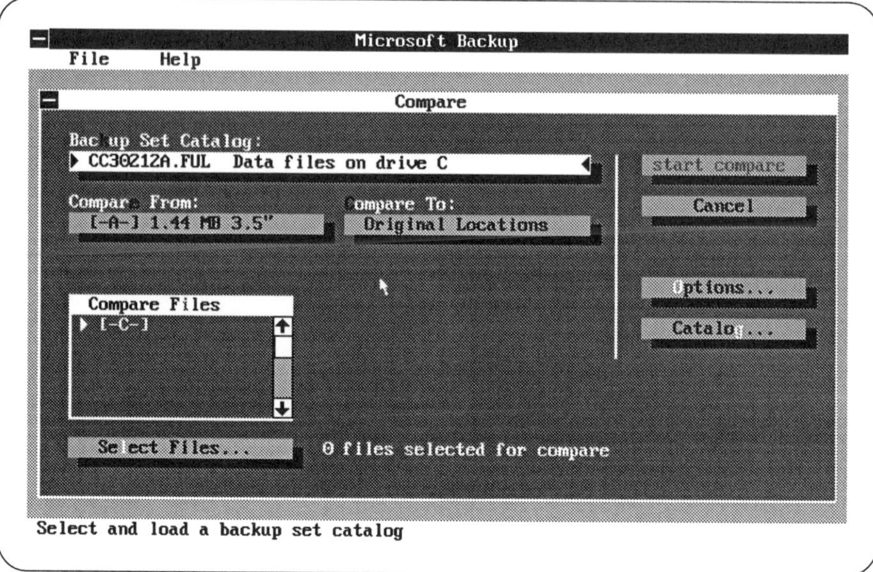

Figure 16-25 The Compare screen

selected. Here, the backup controls are displayed. Using these controls, you can select the drive or drives to back up from, the drive to back up to, and the type of backup. In addition, you can click on the Select-files button to select which files you want to back up or the Options button to specify backup options.

When you click on the Start-backup button, Microsoft Backup for *Windows* displays the Backup-progress window shown in figure 16-27. Here, you can see that this window displays essentially the same information displayed by the DOS version's progress screen (part 4 of figure 16-11).

Incidentally, the backup diskettes created by the DOS and *Windows* versions of Microsoft Backup are compatible with one another. So, you can use the *Windows* version to restore files from a backup created by the DOS version, or vice-versa. If you're a *Windows* user, you'll probably want to use the *Windows* version rather than the DOS version. Not only is it easier to use because of the more friendly *Windows* user interface, but you can use *Windows*' multi-tasking capabilities to do other work while you back up your files.

Some perspective on Microsoft Backup

At this point, you may be wondering if Microsoft Backup is really easier to use than the DOS Backup command. After all, you have to enter only a few keystrokes to use

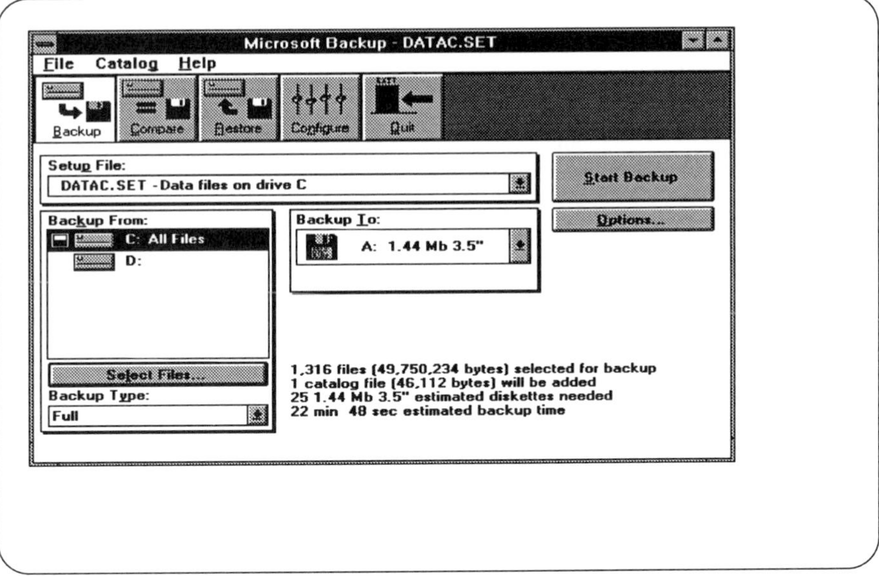

Figure 16-26 The main window for Microsoft Backup for *Windows*

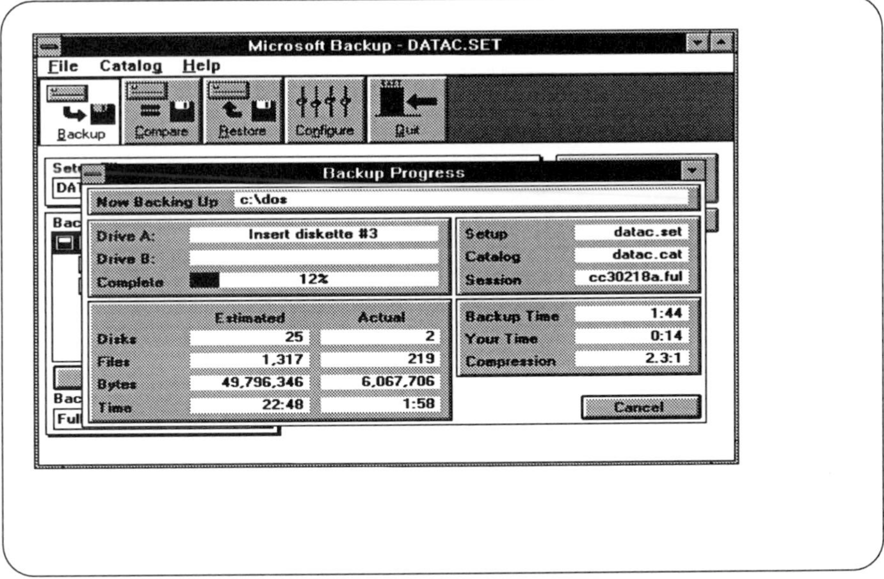

Figure 16-27 The Backup-progress window for Microsoft Backup for *Windows*

the Backup command, whereas Microsoft Backup has dozens of options you need to know about. These options, though, give you more control over your backups than you have with the Backup command. So even if they seem confusing right now, I think you'll appreciate the flexibility they provide once you try them out. And remember, you need to set many of these options only once, so you won't have to worry about them after that.

Because Microsoft Backup provides for so many options, it's adequate for most PC users. But if your backup needs are extensive, you may want to consider purchasing a commercial backup utility. In general, commercial utilities have three advantages over Microsoft Backup: (1) they're even faster than Microsoft Backup (they use DMA more aggressively); (2) they support backups to tape drives; and (3) you can set up a backup to run automatically. If any of these capabilities are essential to your backup strategy, then by all means consider purchasing a commercial utility.

Terms

DMA
Direct Memory Access
file compression
differential backup
button
click the mouse
shortcut key
system box
menu bar
pull-down menu
window
scroll bar
scroll box
dialog box
setup file
backup catalog
backup set
master catalog
backup cycle

Objectives

1. Explain the difference between a differential backup and an incremental backup.
2. Use Microsoft Backup to do a full backup of a specified drive or directory.
3. Use Microsoft Backup to do an incremental or differential backup of a specified drive or directory.
4. Use Microsoft Backup to restore an entire backup set, a directory, or a file.
5. Establish backup procedures for your system using Microsoft Backup.

Chapter 17

Microsoft Anti-Virus

Computer viruses have received a lot of publicity in recent years. Unfortunately, much of the information spread about computer viruses in the press has been confusing or misleading. As a result, many computer users don't have a clear idea of what a computer virus is, how computer viruses spread, and what computer viruses can and cannot do. And they aren't certain whether or not they should be concerned about protecting their systems from computer viruses.

Until now, if you have been concerned about computer viruses, you had to purchase an anti-virus program such as *Central Point Anti-Virus* or *Norton Antivirus*. Now, DOS 6.0 comes with *Microsoft Anti-Virus*, which can detect computer viruses and prevent them from entering your system. Microsoft Anti-Virus is actually a scaled back version of *Central Point Anti-Virus*. Although *Central Point Anti-Virus* has several features Microsoft Anti-Virus doesn't, their basic virus scanning features are the same.

In this chapter, you'll learn what computer viruses are and how to use Microsoft Anti-Virus to protect your PC from viruses. Fortunately, the techniques for detecting a known virus are reliable. So if you follow the advice given in this chapter, the odds of a virus damaging your PC are slim.

If you don't have DOS 6.0 or an anti-virus program, you should read this chapter anyway. At the least, it will give you some ideas for protecting your PC from viruses even if you don't have an anti-virus program. And, it might convince you to upgrade to DOS 6.0 or to purchase an anti-virus program.

What is a virus?

A *computer virus* is a special type of computer program that's designed so that it can reproduce itself. This *self-replicating* capability is what makes computer viruses potentially harmful. Once a virus is present on a computer system, it will attempt to infect other computer systems, often by copying itself to every diskette accessed by the computer. Then, if any of those diskettes are used in another computer system, that computer becomes infected, and the virus spreads. Alternatively, if the infected computer is attached to a local area network, the virus may try to spread to other computers via the network.

Virus type	Characteristics
Boot sector	Infects disk boot sector Activated when system is booted from disk Spreads by infecting other disks
Program infector	Infects executable program files (.EXE, .COM, .SYS) Activated when program is run Spreads by infecting other program files

Figure 17-1 Two types of computer viruses

Most computer viruses do more than just secretly replicate themselves. After a certain time period, on a particular date, or when a certain event occurs, most viruses reveal their presence. Some simply display a message, such as "Gotcha!" Others do obvious damage to your system by reformatting your hard disk or scrambling your hard disk so it is completely inaccessible. Still others do more subtle damage, such as cross-linking files at random. You won't notice this problem until you try to access the corrupted files.

Strictly speaking, a program must be self-replicating for it to be considered a virus. However, the term *virus* is often used to refer to any computer program that can potentially damage your computer system, whether it can reproduce itself or not. For example, you might find a game program on a computer bulletin board that formats your hard disk instead of playing a game with you. This kind of program is called a *trojan horse*. If the trojan horse program doesn't itself do damage but instead plants a virus in your computer, the trojan horse program is sometimes called a *dropper*.

Two types of computer viruses and how they spread

To understand how computer viruses spread, you need to know about the two main types of computer viruses: *boot sector viruses* and *program infector viruses*. Figure 17-1 summarizes their characteristics.

Boot sector viruses To understand what a boot sector virus is and how it works, you need to know that every disk contains a *boot sector*. This sector contains a small program, called the *loader program*, that is executed whenever the computer is booted from the disk. If the disk is a floppy disk, the boot sector is located in the first sector on the disk. If the disk is a hard disk, the first sector on the disk contains the *partition table*, which indicates the number and location of each partition on the drive. Then, the first sector of each partition contains a boot sector.

Boot sector viruses work by replacing the normal loader program with a special loader program that loads the virus program into internal memory as a part of the boot process. If the virus was loaded from a diskette, it then quickly copies itself to your hard disk's boot sector, thus infecting your system. This can happen even if you try to boot from a non-system diskette. That's because even though the system can't be booted from a non-system diskette, the loader program on the diskette is still executed when you attempt to boot from it.

To illustrate, suppose a friend or colleague gives you a diskette that has some data files you need. Not realizing that the diskette's boot sector has been infected by a virus, you insert the diskette into your A drive and copy the files. So far, your PC hasn't been infected, even though you've copied files from an infected diskette. But suppose after working on the files for a while, you turn off your PC and go home for the night, not realizing that you've left the infected diskette in your PC. When you come in the next morning and start your PC, you get a "Non-system disk..." message, so you remove the diskette and press a key to boot from the hard drive. Unfortunately, before the infected diskette's loader program displayed the "Non-system disk..." message, it copied itself into your hard drive's boot sector. Now your system is infected by the virus.

Once your PC is infected, the virus is loaded into memory every time you start your PC. Then, the virus monitors diskette activity and copies itself into the boot sector of any diskette you read or write data to. So even if you just display a diskette's directory with the DIR command, the virus copies itself. This is how boot sector viruses spread from computer to computer.

Program infector viruses Program infector viruses copy themselves into individual program files (programs with EXE or COM extensions) rather than into boot sectors. When the virus infects a program file, it sets itself up so that when you run the infected program, you're actually running the virus without realizing it. The virus quickly does its work, infecting other program files, deleting files, or subtly corrupting your File Allocation Table. Then, it transfers control to the original program. If the virus is well written, you'll hardly notice the delay.

Program infector viruses can be spread from one computer to another when you share a program with another user via diskette. Or, if your computer is attached to a network, the virus can infect a program that resides on a network file server. Then, still more computers on the network can be infected.

The five most common computer viruses

Although over 1500 computer viruses are currently known to exist, the vast majority of them are extremely rare. As I write this, virus experts estimate that as many as 85 percent of all virus infections can be attributed to the five viruses listed in figure 17-2. Experts also estimate a known list of nine other viruses account for nearly all of the

Virus	Type	Symptoms
Stoned	Boot sector	Infects drive C and any diskettes accessed. When the system is booted, a message such as "Your computer is now stoned" is displayed. Has many variants, some of which destroy hard disk data.
Jerusalem	Program infector	After running 30 minutes, PC operations slow by 10 percent and a black box is displayed in lower left corner of screen. Any infected program run on Friday the 13th is deleted.
Michelangelo	Boot sector	Reduces available conventional memory by 2KB. Erases the first 9MB of drive C on March 6 of any year.
Joshi	Boot sector	Displays "Happy Birthday Joshi" on January 5 of any year. The user must type "Happy Birthday Joshi" to continue.
Azusa	Boot sector	Disables communication and serial ports every 32nd time the computer is booted. May corrupt data on diskette drives.

Figure 17-2 The five most common computer viruses

rest. The remaining computer viruses account for less than one percent of all virus infections combined. Of course, this might change as new viruses are discovered.

The most common virus is called the Stoned virus. This virus was first discovered in 1988, and experts estimate that it is responsible for 40 percent or more of all virus infections in the United States. Fortunately, it is relatively benign. In its most basic form, it just displays the message "Your PC is now stoned" randomly, about once every eight times you boot your computer. There are many variations of this virus, each displaying a slightly different message. Some of the variations also damage data on your hard drive.

Unlike the Stoned virus, the Jerusalem and Michelangelo viruses aren't so benign. The Jerusalem virus has a variety of ill effects. It slows down your PC by 10 percent, infects any program file you execute, and deletes any infected program you run on Friday the 13th. The Michelangelo virus erases the first 9MB of your disk drive when you boot your computer on March 6. Since the first 9MB of your drive includes the partition table, boot sector, root directory, and File Allocation Table, this renders the entire drive unreadable. The only way to recover is to repartition and reformat the drive, then restore from a full backup. Like the Stoned virus, there are

1. Regularly back up the data on your hard disk.
2. Use a virus scanning program periodically to scan for viruses on your hard disk.
3. Use a virus scanning program to scan for viruses on all diskettes that aren't your own.
4. Add a memory resident virus scanning program to your AUTOEXEC.BAT file.
5. Create an emergency boot diskette with virus tools and disk reconstruction tools.

Figure 17-3 Five ways to protect your PC from virus infection and damage

many variations of these viruses that go by different names and have different symptoms.

The other two viruses in figure 17-2, Joshi and Azusa, are less common. The Joshi virus displays the message "Happy birthday Joshi" on January 5 of every year. Before you can continue, you must respond by typing "Happy birthday Joshi." Other than this inconvenience, the Joshi virus doesn't do any damage. The Azusa virus intermittently disables your printer and communication ports and may scramble diskette data.

Five ways to protect your PC from viruses

The only surefire way to prevent your PC from encountering a virus is to keep it completely isolated. If you never use someone else's diskette, never use a modem, never connect your PC to a network, never install new software, and never take your computer to a repair shop or allow a technician or consultant to work on it, you'll never be exposed to a computer virus. Obviously, this just isn't realistic. But there are steps you can take to minimize your exposure to viruses.

Figure 17-3 lists five ways to reduce the risk of your PC being infected by a virus or suffering irreparable damage as a result of a virus infection. The first item on the list is an essential part of using your computer: regularly back up the data on your hard disk. If you don't know how to do this, you should read the chapters on backups in this book. A common misconception of viruses is that backups are useless against them because you're backing up data that may have already been corrupted by the virus. While this may be true, if a computer virus trashes your hard disk, the only way to recover may be to restore your backups. Then, once you've restored the disk, you can remove the virus. If you don't have backups, you'll have no way to recover.

Second, use an anti-virus program such as Microsoft Anti-Virus to check your hard disk for signs of virus infection. How often depends on how you use your PC. If you frequently install new software, access bulletin boards, or share diskettes with friends or colleagues, you might want to do this as often as once a week. If you work mostly in isolation, you can determine how often you need to scan your hard disk, if you need to at all. Whether or not you scan your hard disk periodically, I recommend you always use an anti-virus program to check for viruses after your PC has been to a computer repair shop or worked on by a computer technician. Because computer shops, technicians, and repair centers work on so many computers, some experts consider them to be the leading spreader of computer viruses.

Third, use an anti-virus program to scan any diskette you use in your system that isn't your own. For example, if you get a diskette from a friend, scan if first before using it. And before you install a new program, scan the distribution diskettes to make sure they are not infected. Although unlikely, there have been documented cases of viruses found on shrink-wrapped software. New unformatted diskettes are safe, but if you purchase your blank diskettes already formatted, you should scan them too.

Fourth, add a memory resident virus protection program to your AUTOEXEC.BAT file. Microsoft Anti-Virus includes a program called VSAFE that continuously monitors your system for signs of computer viruses. If you add a VSAFE command to your AUTOEXEC.BAT file, VSAFE will always be on the watch for viruses. You'll learn how to use VSAFE later in this chapter.

Finally, create an emergency system diskette so you'll be able to boot your system if you detect a virus or if a virus renders your hard disk unusable. To do that, format the disk using the /S switch. Then, copy the DOS Format and Fdisk commands to the diskette. In addition, copy your backup and anti-virus programs to the diskette, along with any other utility programs you have that might be useful. (Be sure to scan your system for viruses before you create this diskette. You don't want it to be infected by a virus!)

How to use Microsoft Anti-Virus

Microsoft Anti-Virus consists of three programs: MSAV, MWAV, and VSAFE. MSAV is the DOS version of Microsoft Anti-Virus. It scans your entire system looking for signs of known viruses and can remove any virus it finds. MWAV is the *Windows* version of Microsoft Anti-Virus. It performs the same functions as the MSAV program, but from within *Windows*. And VSAFE is a memory resident virus scanner that constantly monitors your system for signs of computer viruses. For the highest level of protection against viruses, you should scan your computer periodically using MSAV or MWAV and include the VSAFE program in your AUTOEXEC.BAT file.

How to scan your system for viruses using MSAV You use the MSAV program to scan your system for viruses and remove any viruses it finds. To start the MSAV program, type the command MSAV without parameters at the DOS prompt:

```
C:\>msav
```

MSAV displays its opening screen, shown in figure 17-4. Here, MSAV presents its basic functions: Detect, Detect-and-clean, Select-new-drive, Options, and Exit. Like

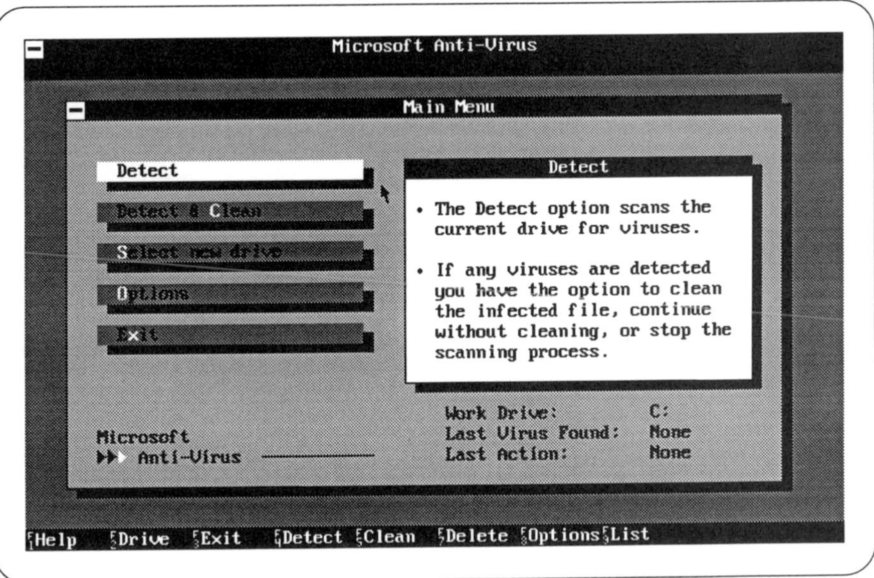

Figure 17-4 The opening screen for MSAV

the other DOS 6.0 utilities, you can select any of these functions by clicking on the appropriate button with the mouse, using the Tab key to highlight the button and pressing the Enter key, or pressing the highlighted letter for each function (D for Detect, C for Detect & Clean, etc.).

You can also select a function using the function keys listed at the bottom of the screen. Here, you have three additional functions to select from: Help, Delete, and List. With the Help function, you can get additional information on using Microsoft Anti-Virus. This feature is similar to the Help features available with other DOS 6.0 utilities, so I won't describe it here. The Delete function lets you delete the checksum files that are created during a virus scan. I'll tell you about these files when I present the MSAV options. The List option lists all known viruses that MSAV scans for.

You can use either the Detect or Detect-and-clean function to detect and remove viruses. If you use the Detect-and-clean function, MSAV automatically removes any viruses it finds. If you use the Detect function, MSAV asks you what to do if it finds a virus. You'll probably use Detect only if you need more control over the action that's taken when a virus is found.

When you select the Detect-and-clean function, MSAV begins by scanning conventional memory for active viruses. Part 1 of figure 17-5 shows the MSAV display during this check. On most systems, this should take only a few seconds.

Part 1:

When you select the Detect-and-clean function from the opening screen, MSAV begins by scanning conventional memory.

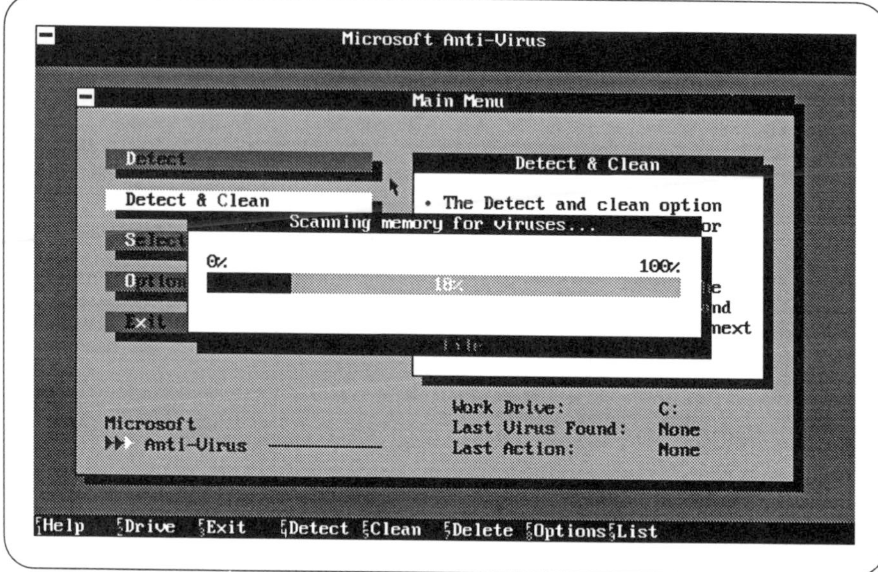

Part 2:

If no virus is found in conventional memory, MSAV scans the current drive.

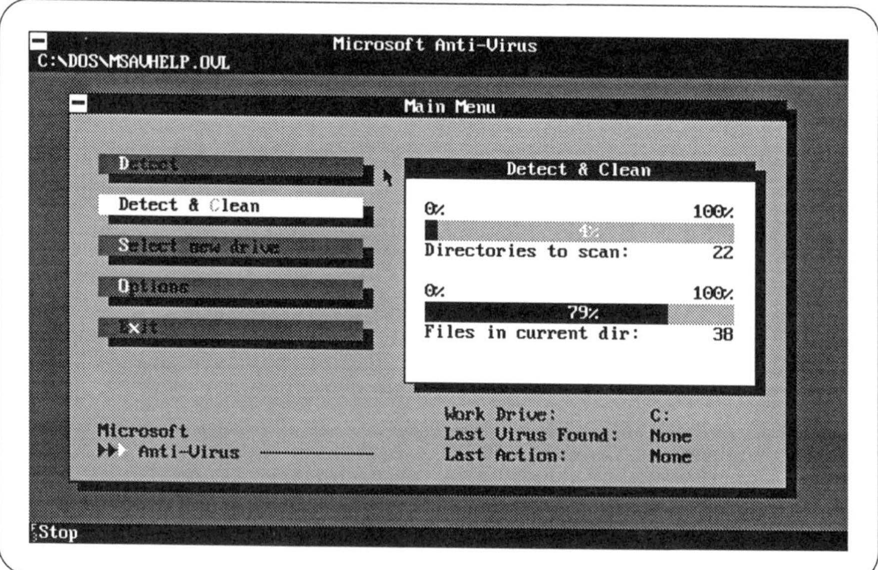

Figure 17-5 How to detect and remove viruses using MSAV (parts 1 and 2 of 3)

Part 3:

When MSAV completes the Detect-and-clean operation, it displays the results.

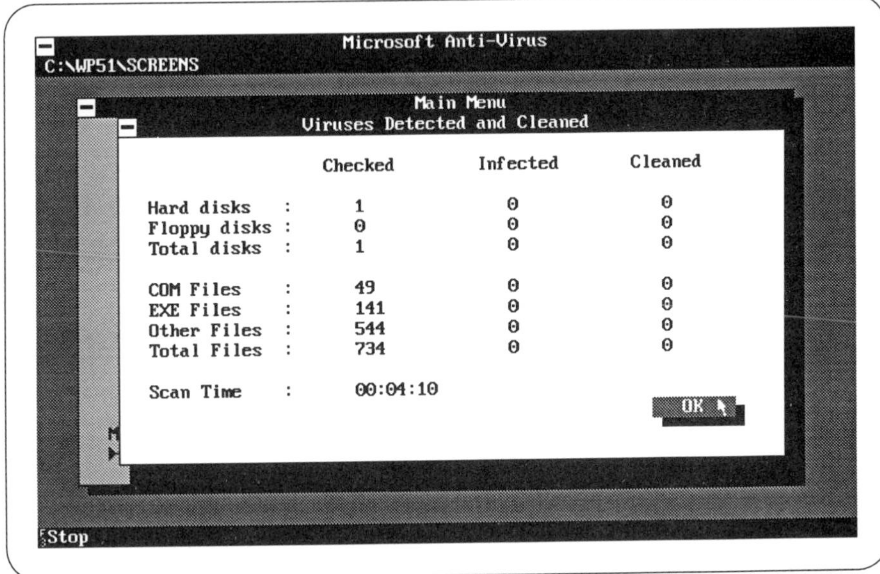

Figure 17-5 How to detect and remove viruses using MSAV (part 3 of 3)

(MSAV doesn't scan high memory, above 640K, because no known viruses load there.)

Assuming that no virus is found, MSAV then begins scanning the current drive. The current drive is indicated by the field labeled Work Drive near the bottom right of the screen. In figure 17-5, the current drive is C.

Part 2 of figure 17-5 shows the MSAV display during the scan of the current drive. The time required to perform this check depends on the type and speed of your processor, the amount of data on the disk, and the MSAV options currently in effect. On my 33Mhz 486 system, this check takes about 2-1/2 minutes to scan a 145MB drive with 100MB of data using MSAV's default options. On a slower system, this scan may take considerably longer. In a moment, I'll show you how you can adjust MSAV's options to reduce the amount of time required to scan the disk.

When the scan is complete, MSAV displays the results of the scan as shown in part 3 of figure 17-5. Here, you can see the number of files scanned, the number of files infected and cleaned, and the total time taken. In this case, no virus infections were found.

If you want to scan the contents of another drive, you can use the Select-new-drive function. When you do, MSAV displays a drive bar across the top of the screen, as figure 17-6 shows. Then, you can pick the drive to scan by clicking on it with the mouse, tabbing to it and pressing the Enter key, or typing the drive letter on the keyboard. This function is useful when you want to scan a diskette for a virus before

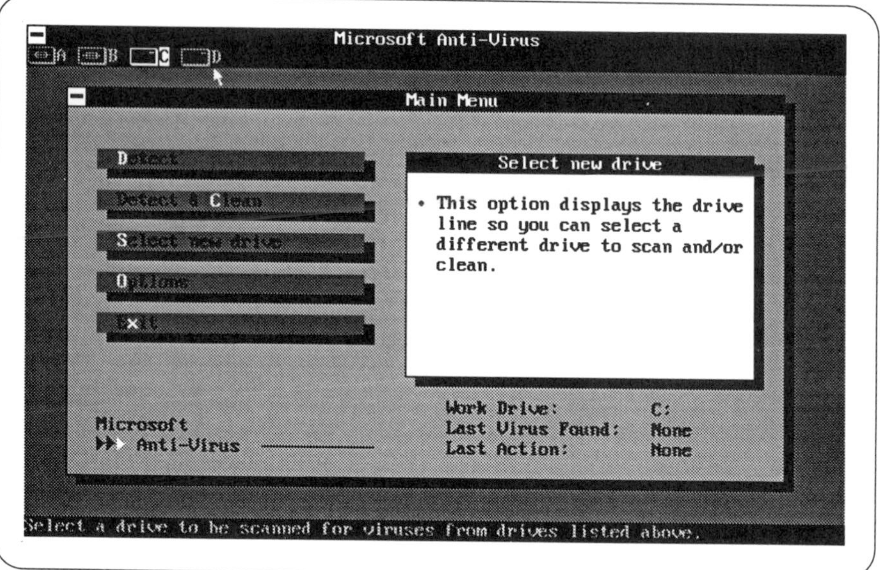

Figure 17-6 How to select a different drive to be scanned

you use it in your PC. You can also select drives to scan by typing command line parameters. I'll show you how to do that in a moment.

How to set MSAV options If you select the Options function, MSAV displays the options dialog box shown in part 1 of figure 17-7. The options that are checked are the ones I recommend you use under normal circumstances. Figure 17-7 also gives a brief description of each of these options. I'll describe the first three options in more detail next. You should have no problem understanding the remaining options.

The first three options, Verify-integrity, Create-new-checksums, and Create-checksums-on-floppy, work together. Create-new-checksums creates a file named CHKLIST.MS in every directory on the disk. This file contains information about each executable file in the directory, including a checksum value that's calculated from the file. Then, when you run MSAV again, the Verify-integrity option causes MSAV to recalculate the checksum value for each file and check it against the value stored in the CHKLIST.MS file. If the checksum has changed, it means that the executable file has been changed, possibly because of a virus. Then, MSAV displays a dialog box like the one in figure 17-8. If you know that something other than a virus caused the file to change, you can select the Update function. Then, MSAV updates the checksum file with the new file information and continues the scan. You can also delete the file, continue the scan, or stop the scan.

Because some executable files change themselves as a normal part of their operation, it's likely that you'll see a dialog box like the one in figure 17-8 at some point. You'll also get this type of error when you update software and the

The MSAVE options dialog box

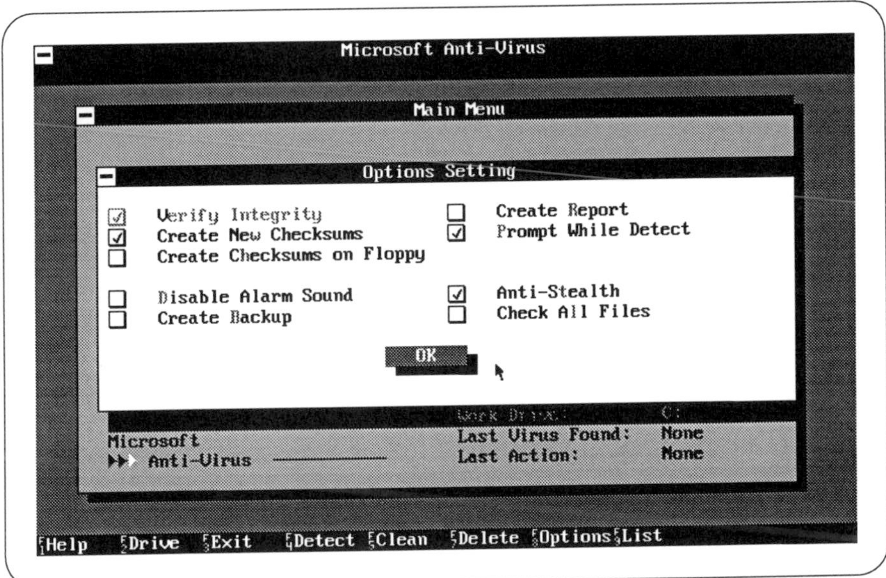

Option	Function
Verify Integrity	Checks for changes in executable files. I recommend that you turn this option on.
Create New Checksums	Creates a file named CHKLIST.MS in every directory on a hard disk as it is scanned. This file contains information about each executable file in the directory, including a checksum value that's calculated from the file. The checksum value is used by the Verify-integrity option to determine if an executable file has changed. I recommend that you turn this option on.
Create Checksums on Floppy	Same as Create-New-Checksums options, except it creates CHKLIST.MS files on a floppy disk as it is scanned.
Disable Alarm Sound	Tells MSAV not to beep when it detects a possible virus problem.
Create Backup	Creates a backup copy of a file before it attempts to remove a virus from it.

Figure 17-7 How to set the options for MSAV (part 1 of 2)

Option	Function
Create Report	Creates a report file named MSAV.RPT in the root directory of the work drive that indicates the date and time of the virus scan and the number of viruses found and removed.
Prompt While Detect	Displays a dialog box whenever MSAV encounters a virus during a Detect operation. If a boot sector virus is found, this dialog box gives you the options of removing the virus, ignoring it and continuing, or stopping the scan. If a program infector virus is found, the dialog box also contains the name of the virus and the file that contains it, and an additional option to delete the file. I recommend that you turn this option on.
Anti-Stealth	Scans for viruses called stealth viruses. This requires more sophisticated detection techniques and slows down the scan. I recommend that you turn this option on.
Check All files	Scans all files on the selected drive. If this option is off, only executable files are scanned.

Figure 17-7 How to set the options for MSAV (part 2 of 2)

Verify-integrity option is on. In that case, it's best to turn the Verify-integrity option off the first time you scan after the update. Then, turn the Verify-integrity option back on and scan again to verify all the executable files on the disk.

Each time you scan a disk with the Create-checksums option selected, MSAV automatically updates the CHKLIST.MS file, adding information for new program files and removing information for program files you've deleted. Because this might cause a problem on a write-protected diskette, the Create-new-checksums option doesn't create CHKLIST.MS files when you scan a diskette. To create these files on a diskette, you must select the Create-checksums-on-floppy option.

Although the Create-new-checksums option clutters your disk with CHKLIST.MS files, I recommend you use it and the Verify-integrity option. The checksum files are relatively small (27 bytes for each program file in a directory), and the extra time it takes to recalculate and compare the checksums is small.

How to use MSAV command-line options If you include the MSAV command in a batch file, you'll probably want to execute the program without user intervention. To do that, you need to know about some of the command options that

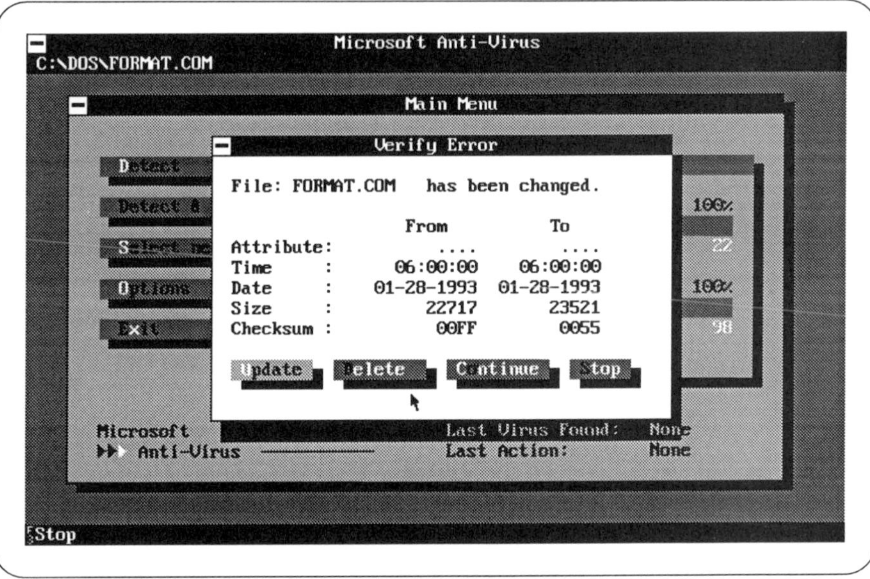

Figure 17-8 The dialog box that's displayed when MSAV detects a change in an executable file

are available. Figure 17-9 shows the format of the MSAV command, along with an explanation of its most useful switches and two examples.

As you can see, you can specify up to three drive letters on the command to direct MSAV to scan specific drives. Or, you can specify a directory for MSAV to scan by including a path. The first example in figure 17-9 shows how you can invoke MSAV to scan the diskette in drive A. If you wanted to scan and clean the diskette, you'd include the /C switch. Although scan is the default, you can specify scan explicitly by including the /S switch.

If you omit both the drive and path specification from the MSAV command, you'll want to code either the /A or /L switch. Both of these switches tell MSAV to scan all hard drives. The difference between the two is that if you're attached to a network, /A will scan network drives as well as local drives, while /L will scan local drives only. So the second example in figure 17-9 will scan and clean all local drives except A and B.

If you invoke MSAV using either of the examples in figure 17-9, MSAV will still display its full-screen interface as it executes. You can suppress that display by including the /P switch on the command line. Then, MSAV simply displays informational messages as it executes. You can also use the /N switch to suppress the full-screen interface, but it also suppresses all informational messages, including those that alert you to possible viruses. So you probably won't want to use this option. If you do, however, you should also include the /R option to create a report. Then, when MSAV finishes executing, you can display or print the report to see if any viruses were detected.

The format of the MSAV command

```
MSAV [drive:] [drive:] [drive:] [switches]
```
or
```
MSAV [path] [switches]
```

Switch meanings

`/S`	Scans the specified drives. This is the default.
`/C`	Scans and cleans the specified drives.
`/R`	Creates a report.
`/A`	Scans all drives except A and B.
`/L`	Scans all local drives except A and B.
`/P`	Uses a command-line interface instead of the full-screen interface.
`/N`	Uses a command-line interface and suppresses informational messages.
`/F`	Suppresses the file name display when /P or /N is used.
`/?`	Displays help information.
`/VIDEO`	Displays help information for video and mouse options.

Example 1: An MSAVE command that automatically scans the A drive.

```
msav a:
```

Example 2: An MSAVE command that automatically scans and cleans all local hard drives.

```
msav /l /c
```

Figure 17-9 The MSAV command

If you include /N or /P on an MSAV command, you can also include the /F switch. This switch suppresses the list of file names MSAV displays as it executes. Since MSAV displays the list of files rapidly, you probably won't pay much attention to it. So you can disable the display if you prefer not to see it.

The last two switches, /? and /VIDEO, display Help information for MSAV. You learned how the /? switch works for all DOS commands in chapter 4. The /VIDEO switch displays information on the video and mouse options you can include on the MSAV command. You probably won't need to use any of these options, so I don't present them here.

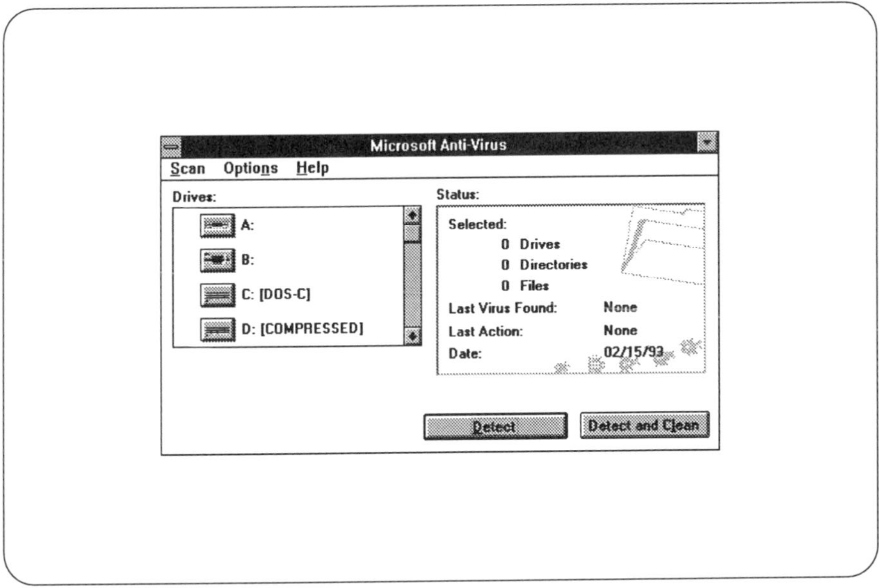

Figure 17-10 Microsoft Anti-Virus for *Windows*

How to scan your system for viruses using Microsoft Anti-Virus for *Windows* DOS 6.0 also comes with a *Windows* version of Microsoft Anti-Virus. To start it, you double click the Microsoft Anti-Virus for *Windows* icon in the Microsoft Tools program group. Microsoft Anti-Virus for *Windows* displays the window shown in figure 17-10. Unlike the MSAV program, Microsoft Anti-Virus for *Windows* requires that you select a drive before starting a scan. To do that, you just click on one of the drive icons. You can select more than one drive to scan by clicking on additional drive icons.

Like most *Windows* applications, you use pull-down menus to access most of the functions for Microsoft Anti-Virus for *Windows*. The Scan menu provides functions for Detect, Detect-and-clean, Delete-checksum-files, and Virus-list. These functions work the same as they do for the DOS version. You can also activate the Detect and Detect-and-clean functions by clicking on the buttons at the bottom right corner of the window. The Options menu lets you access a dialog box where you set options. Here again, the options are the same as for the DOS version.

How to prevent a virus from entering your system using VSAFE The MSAV program can detect the presence of a virus on your system and remove it, but it can't actually prevent a virus from entering your system. To do that, you need to use the VSAFE program. VSAFE is a memory resident program supplied with DOS 6.0 that constantly monitors your system for signs of virus infection and displays a warning message at the first sign of virus activity. It can automatically check the boot sector of diskettes you access for known viruses, scan executable files when you execute them or copy them onto your hard drive, and prevent virus programs from altering your hard disk's boot sector or partition table or performing a low-level format on your hard drive.

To use VSAFE, all you have to do is include a VSAFE command in your AUTOEXEC.BAT file. Figure 17-11 presents the format of the VSAFE command. The first eight switches in figure 17-11 correspond to eight VSAFE options that determine what virus checks VSAFE will perform. To turn an option on, include the corresponding switch on the VSAFE command. The options that correspond to the /1, /4, /5, and /6 switches are on by default, so you don't need to include them on the VSAFE command unless you want to turn them off. To turn one of these options off, follow the switch with a minus sign (-) as in the example at the bottom of figure 17-10. (You can also turn an option on by following it with a plus sign (+), but the sign isn't necessary.)

You can also change the VSAFE options after VSAFE is loaded by using its *hotkey*, Alt+V. When you press the hotkey combination, VSAFE interrupts whatever program you're running and displays the control panel shown in figure 17-12. This control panel shows which of eight types of virus checks VSAFE is currently performing. By pressing the keys 1 through 8, you can turn any of these checks on or off.

The VSAFE command switches let you specify other options as well. For example, you can use the /NE or /NX switches to tell VSAFE what type of memory it should use. You can use the /A*x* or /C*x* switches to specify a different hotkey, just in case you use an application program that uses the Alt+V combination. In the example at the bottom of figure 17-11, I coded the switch /CV to change the hotkey to Ctrl+V. If you use a network and the commands that load the network drivers come after the VSAFE command in your AUTOEXEC.BAT file, you should specify the /N switch on the VSAFE command. The /D switch prevents VSAFE from updating the checksum files created by MSAV. The /V switch removes VSAFE from memory. And the /? switch displays Help information.

As for any memory resident program, the disadvantage of running VSAFE is that it uses conventional memory. VSAFE can use as much as 44KB of conventional memory. The amount of memory actually used by VSAFE depends on whether expanded (EMS) or extended (XMS) memory is available on your system, as shown in figure 17-13. As you can see, VSAFE uses 44KB of conventional memory if no extended or expanded memory is available. If extended memory is available, VSAFE uses 23KB of conventional memory. And VSAFE uses only 7KB of conventional memory if expanded memory is available. If you want to use VSAFE but aren't sure how to configure your system's memory, refer to chapter 25.

If you use *Windows* and you want to use VSAFE, you should add the following line to your WIN.INI file:

```
load=mwavtsr.exe
```

This loads a program that enables VSAFE to display pop-up messages while *Windows* is running. Once you've added this line to WIN.INI, you'll need to restart *Windows* to make it active.

The format of the VSAFE command

```
VSAFE [switches]
```

Switch meanings

`/1`	Sets the HD-low-level-format option. This option warns of any attempt to low-level format a hard disk. It is on by default.
`/2`	Sets the Resident option. This option warns of any program attempting to become memory resident. It is off by default.
`/3`	Sets the General-write-protect option. This option prevents all disk writes. It is off by default.
`/4`	Sets the Check-executable-files option. This option checks for viruses whenever an executable file is accessed. It is on by default. If this option is off, VSAFE will still scan an executable file whenever it's executed.
`/5`	Sets the Boot-sector-viruses option. This option checks for boot sector viruses. It is on by default.
`/6`	Sets the Protect-HD-boot-sector option. This option warns of any attempt to alter the boot sector on a hard disk. It is on by default.
`/7`	Sets the Protect-FD-boot-sector option. This option warns of any attempt to alter the boot sector of a diskette. It is off by default.
`/8`	Sets the Protect-executable-files option. This option warns of any attempt to modify executable files. It is off by default.

Note: Switches 1 through 8 can be followed by + or - to indicate that the option is being turned on or off; if no + or - sign is used, + is assumed.

`/NE`	Tells VSAFE not to use expanded memory.
`/NX`	Tells VSAFE not to use extended memory.
`/Ax`	Sets the hotkey to Alt+*x*.
`/Cx`	Sets the hotkey to Ctrl+*x*.
`/N`	Allows network drivers to be loaded after VSAFE.
`/D`	Tells VSAFE not to create checksums for new executable files.
`/U`	Removes VSAFE from memory.
`/?`	Displays Help information.

A typical VSAFE command in an AUTOEXEC.BAT file

```
vsafe /4- /cv
```

Figure 17-11 The VSAFE command

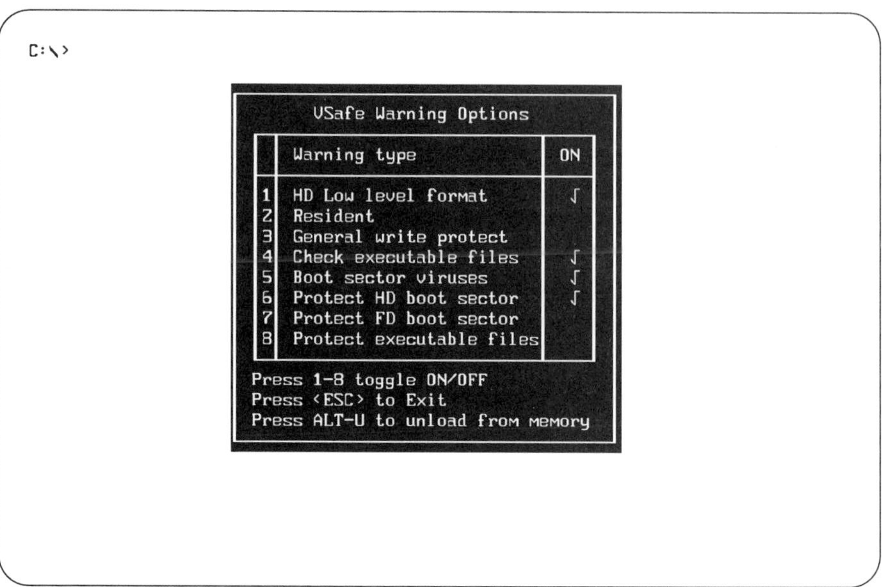

Figure 17-12 The VSAFE pop-up dialog box

How to keep Microsoft Anti-Virus up to date Because new viruses are frequently discovered, Microsoft Anti-Virus is designed so that it can be updated periodically. You can update MSAV by purchasing an update package from Central Point Software or by obtaining the update files from Central Point's bulletin board or Central Point's Compuserve forum. Updates are released four times a year.

Some perspective on Microsoft Anti-Virus

I hope this chapter has raised your awareness of computer viruses without causing you to become paranoid. The fact is that the vast majority of computers today have never been affected by a virus, and the chances are they probably never will. So you don't need to run out right away and buy DOS 6.0 or an anti-virus program.

Nonetheless, if you're already using DOS 6.0, it makes sense to take advantage of its anti-virus capabilities. At the least, I recommend you run MSAV once right away to make sure you don't already have a virus on your system. And consider including the VSAFE command in your AUTOEXEC.BAT file to prevent viruses from entering your system. If you take these precautions, you can be fairly certain that a virus will never infect your system.

	Conventional memory	Extended memory (XMS)	Expanded memory (EMS)
No XMS or EMS available	44KB		
XMS available but no EMS	23KB	23KB	
EMS available	7KB		64KB

Figure 17-13 Memory requirements for the VSAFE command

Terms

computer virus
self-replicate
trojan horse
dropper
boot sector virus
program infector virus
boot sector
loader program
partition table
hotkey

Objectives

1. Describe the two types of computer viruses and how they spread.
2. List the five ways you can protect your PC from becoming infected by a virus.
3. Scan your system for viruses using MSAV.
4. Add a VSAFE command to your AUTOEXEC.BAT file to prevent viruses from entering your system.

Chapter 18

DoubleSpace

DoubleSpace is a feature of DOS 6.0 that significantly increases the capacity of a disk drive by compressing data that's stored on it. Although the degree of compression depends on the contents of your files, DoubleSpace can typically double the capacity of your disk drive. In other words, if you have an 80MB drive, DoubleSpace can usually let you store 160MB of data on it. If you use a large number of files that compress unusually well, the increase in capacity may be even greater.

DoubleSpace compression is entirely transparent to your application programs. When you use DoubleSpace, DOS automatically compresses data as it writes it to the disk and automatically decompresses it as it reads data from the disk. That way, your application programs are unaware that the data is stored on disk in a compressed format.

Contrary to what you might expect, DoubleSpace probably won't slow down your computer, either. Although it does takes a small amount of time to compress and decompress data as it's written to and read from the disk, this overhead is offset by the fact that fewer disk accesses are required. For example, suppose a 20KB word processing document is compressed so that it requires only 10KB of disk storage. When you open this document, DOS must access the disk to read the file. In uncompressed form, DOS would have to read 80 disk sectors. In compressed form, DOS would only have to read 40 disk sectors. In most cases, the amount of time saved by not having to read the additional disk sectors is more than the extra time needed to decompress the data. The net result is that DoubleSpace not only increases your disk capacity, but it often speeds up disk access as well.

In this chapter, you'll learn how to set up and use DoubleSpace on your system. First, I'll explain some basic DoubleSpace concepts and show you how to use DoubleSpace's Express-setup feature to compress your C drive. Then, I'll show you how to use some of DoubleSpace's more advanced features, like creating additional compressed drives, changing the size of compressed drives, and using compressed diskettes.

Text before compression

It was the best of times, it was the worst of times, it was the age of wisdom, it was the age of foolishness, it was the epoch of belief, it was the epoch of incredulity,

Text after compression

It was the best of times, i♦wor♦age♦wisdom♦fool♦hness♦epoch♦belief♦
incredulity,

Compression statistics

Characters before compression:	170
Characters after compression:	79
Compression ratio:	2.2 to 1.0

Figure 18-1 How DoubleSpace compresses text

How DoubleSpace works

DoubleSpace is almost completely transparent. Once you set it up, it does most of its work behind the scenes. So unless you intend to use some of its advanced features, you don't really need to understand the details of how it works. Even so, I think you'll gain the most benefit from DoubleSpace if you have a basic understanding of how it manages to squeeze 160MB of data into an 80MB disk drive.

How DoubleSpace compresses data The basis of DoubleSpace's operation is a disk compression algorithm known as *Lempel-Ziv*, named after the two Israeli computer scientists that developed it. Nearly all disk compression products (such as *Stacker* and *PKZIP*) are based on this algorithm. Simply put, Lempel-Ziv searches data for repeating strings of characters. When found, a repeated string is replaced by a *token* that indicates the length and location of the original string.

To illustrate, figure 18-1 shows how Lempel-Ziv compression might be applied to a small text file. Here, you can see the file in both its uncompressed and compressed forms. In the compressed file, the tokens are represented by small black diamonds. In an actual compressed file, each token contains two encoded numbers: a length and an offset. The length indicates the number of characters that have been replaced by the token, and the offset indicates how many characters to count back to find the repeated text. In figure 18-1, the first token would be <10,26>. So it would be replaced by the 10-character string "t was the " found by counting backwards 26 characters from the token. The next token would be <24,27>, which identifies the 24-character string "st of times, it was the " found 27 characters before the token.

Type of file	Files compressed	Compression ratio
Program	76 .EXE and .COM files totaling 3,106,621 bytes	1.4 to 1.0
Word Processing	71 *WordPerfect* files totaling 511,998 bytes	2.6 to 1.0
Spreadsheet	73 *Lotus 1-2-3* files totaling 953,206 bytes	3.2 to 1.0
Database	10 *Dbase IV* files totaling 12,229,594 bytes	4.7 to 1.0

Figure 18-2 Typical compression results for various types of files

In figure 18-1, the original text required 170 characters. After compression, the text required only 79 characters including the tokens. Thus, the *compression ratio* in this case is 170 to 79, or about 2.2 to 1. This rate of compression is typical for text files. Some files, such as database files and graphics files, compress at much greater rates. Figure 18-2 shows the results of an informal test I did on my own system. As you can see, DoubleSpace was able to compress database files the most and program files the least.

To illustrate the effect of using DoubleSpace on an entire drive, figure 18-3 shows the Chkdsk output from my system before and after I compressed my C drive. In the top part of the figure, you can see that my 80MB disk drive had approximately 8MB of free space before I used DoubleSpace. After DoubleSpace, Chkdsk reports that my C drive is a 144MB drive with about 67MB of free disk space, as you can see in the bottom part of the figure.

The way DoubleSpace reports the size of a compressed drive can be confusing because it uses compression ratios in two ways. First, DoubleSpace calculates the portion of the disk that contains files based on the actual compression ratio achieved for those files. Second, it calculates the amount of free space on the compressed drive using an estimated compression ratio of 2 to 1. The actual amount of free space depends on how much the files you add to the drive can be compressed. For example, if you add database files that compress at 4.5 to 1, you'll actually be able to store more data than is indicated in figure 18-3. On the other hand, if you add program files that compress at 1.4 to 1, you'll be able to store less data. If you wish, you can change the compression ratio DoubleSpace uses to report total disk space and free disk space. You'll learn how to do that later in this chapter.

You might be wondering why the Chkdsk report shows that the space allocated to the files on the drive compressed with DoubleSpace is more than the space

The Check-disk command display for my C drive before compressing it with DoubleSpace

```
C:\>chkdsk

Volume DOS-C       created 12-11-1992 4:05p
Volume Serial Number is 17CD-2D36

  83941376 bytes total disk space
     79872 bytes in 2 hidden files
     98304 bytes in 146 directories
  75024384 bytes in 3188 user files
   8738816 bytes available on disk

      2048 bytes in each allocation unit
     40987 total allocation units on disk
      4267 available allocation units on disk

    655360 total bytes memory
    565680 bytes free

C:\>
```

The Check-disk command display for my C drive after compressing it with DoubleSpace

```
C:\>chkdsk

Volume DOS-C       created 12-11-1992 4:15p
Volume Serial Number is 13F8-4465

 150929408 bytes total disk space
     81920 bytes in 3 hidden files
    303104 bytes in 146 directories
  80707584 bytes in 3188 user files
  69836800 bytes available on disk

      8192 bytes in each allocation unit
     16763 total allocation units on disk
      6864 available allocation units on disk

    655360 total bytes memory
    546640 bytes free
DoubleSpace is checking drive C.

DoubleSpace found no errors on drive C.

C:\>
```

Figure 18-3 How Chkdsk reports the increased capacity for a drive compressed with DoubleSpace

```
C:\DOS\>dir e*.* /c

 Volume in drive C is DOS-C
 Volume Serial Number is 17CD-2D36
 Directory of C:\DOS

EGA      SYS       4885 12-06-92   6:00a    2.0 to 1.0
EGA      CPI      58870 12-06-92   6:00a    2.5 to 1.0
EDIT     COM        413 12-06-92   6:00a   16.0 to 1.0
EXPAND   EXE      16129 12-06-92   6:00a    1.0 to 1.0
EDLIN    EXE      12642 04-09-91   5:00a    1.7 to 1.0
EXE2BIN  EXE       8424 04-09-91   5:00a    2.5 to 1.0
EDIT     HLP      17898 12-06-92   6:00a    1.0 to 1.0
EMM386   EXE     114782 12-06-92   6:00a    2.4 to 1.0
                   2.0 to 1.0 average compression ratio
        8 file(s)      234043 bytes
                     23584768 bytes free

C:\DOS\>
```

Figure 18-4 How to use the Dir command with the /C switch to display the compression ratio for individual files

allocated to the files before the drive was compressed. For example, the space allocated to user files on the uncompressed drive is about 71MB and about 77MB on the compressed drive. To understand this, you have to keep in mind that you don't really have a 144MB drive. But if you did, it would take about 77MB to store the files that take up 71MB on an 80MB drive. That's because on an 80MB drive, disk storage is allocated in 2KB clusters, and on a 144MB drive, it's allocated in 8KB clusters. That means that, in general, more space is wasted on each file. DoubleSpace reclaims this wasted space by allocating disk space using individual sectors (512 bytes) rather than clusters. So in reality, the 144MB DoubleSpace drive wastes less space than the 80MB uncompressed drive. But to maintain compatibility with DOS application programs, DoubleSpace reports that the files are allocated using full 8KB clusters.

This also explains why the compression ratio for individual files may seem unusually high. For example, figure 18-4 shows the compression ratio for all the files in the DOS directory that start with the letter E. To get this information, I entered the Dir command with the /C switch. The right-most column of the display gives the compression ratio for each file. Notice that the compression ratio for EDIT.COM is 16 to 1. Again, that's because it's comparing the space allocated to the file on the 80MB drive, which uses 4KB clusters, to the space allocated to the file on the 144MB drive, which uses 8KB clusters. Because the file is so small, a large amount of space would be wasted if the 144MB drive actually allocated a full 8KB cluster for this file.

But because DoubleSpace allocates space one sector at a time, only one sector (512 bytes) is allocated to this file instead of one cluster (8,192 bytes). So DoubleSpace reports the compression ratio for the file as 16 to 1. Keep in mind that only very small files will report compression ratios that high.

How DoubleSpace implements a compressed drive When you use DoubleSpace to compress a drive, it treats the drive as if it has a higher capacity. You saw that illustrated in the Chkdsk output in figure 18-3. The way DoubleSpace actually implements a compressed drive, however, is quite confusing. But it's essential that you have a basic understanding of how it works.

Figure 18-5 shows a conceptual view of an 80MB drive before and after DoubleSpace is installed. Here, the C drive has 8MB of free space before DoubleSpace compression, with 72MB used by files and directories. After the DoubleSpace compression, the drive contains a 78MB file called the *Compressed Volume File*, or *CVF*, that contains all of the original 72MB of files in compressed form. The remaining 2MB of space is reserved for files that can't be stored in the CVF. I'll tell you more about these files in a minute.

To access the files in the CVF, DoubleSpace treats the CVF as a separate drive. Since the files in the CVF were originally on drive C, DoubleSpace assigns the letter C to the CVF. In figure 18-5, 77MB of drive C is used by files and directories and the remaining 67MB is free space. Because the CVF is now drive C, DoubleSpace has to assign another drive letter to the drive that contains the CVF, called the *host drive*. In figure 8-4, DoubleSpace assigned the drive letter H to the compressed volume. (*H* is easy to remember if you think of it as the *H*ost drive.) So when you access a file on drive C after DoubleSpace compression, DOS actually accesses data stored in the CVF on drive H.

If you display the directory for drive H, as in figure 18-6, it will tell you that drive H is host for drive C. You should also notice the files in this directory listing. The first two, IO.SYS and MSDOS.SYS, are systems files that are needed to boot the system. (These files are also hidden files. That's why I included the /AH switch on the Dir command.) Because your system treats the host drive (drive H in this example) as the boot drive when it begins the boot process, these files must remain in the root directory of the host drive. That's why DoubleSpace reserves space outside of the CVF on the host drive. Early in the boot process, however, the system recognizes that the drive is host to a compressed drive. At that point, the boot continues from the C drive. As a result, your CONFIG.SYS and AUTOEXEC.BAT files belong in the root directory of the C drive, not on the host drive.

The other three files on the host drive, DBLSPACE.BIN, DBLSPACE.INI, and DBLSPACE.000, are placed there by DoubleSpace during its setup process . DBLSPACE.BIN is the portion of DOS that manages DoubleSpace drives. DBLSPACE.INI is a text file that contains settings that tell DBLSPACE.BIN, among other things, what drive letters to use when it activates compressed drives. Both of these files must reside on the host drive in the space reserved outside the CVF. The third file, DBLSPACE.000, is the Compressed Volume File.

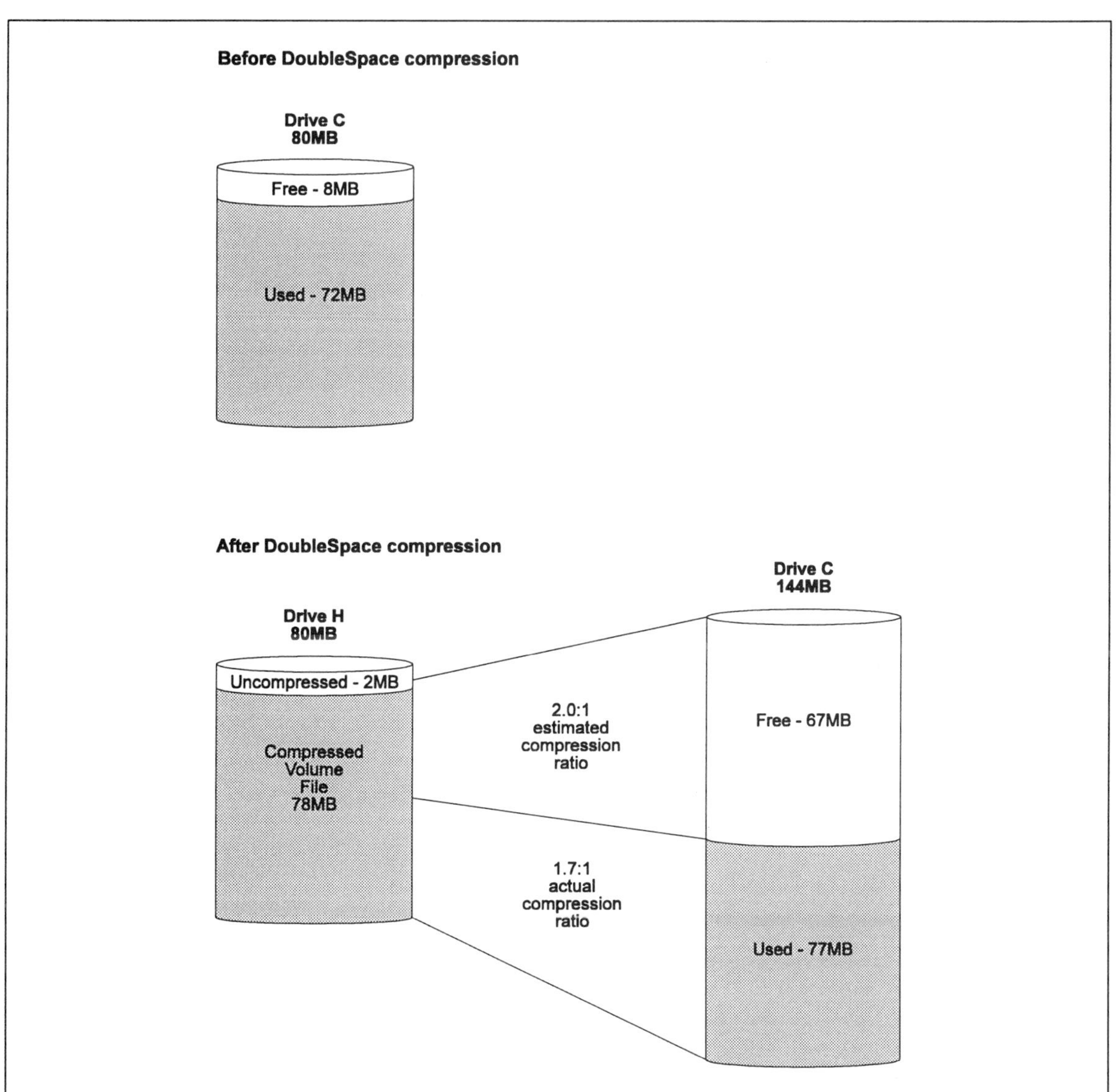

Figure 18-5 How DoubleSpace implements a compressed drive

Incidentally, if you have *Microsoft Windows* installed on your system and you use a permanent swap file, it will also appear in the root directory of the host drive. That's because *Windows'* permanent swap file cannot be compressed.

```
C:\>dir h: /ah

 Volume in drive H is HOST_FOR_C
 Volume Serial Number is 198F-63EE
 Directory of H:\

IO       SYS      40038 12-06-92   6:00a
MSDOS    SYS      37480 12-06-92   6:00a
DBLSPACE BIN      51246 12-06-92   6:00a
DBLSPACE INI         91 12-17-92  11:00a
DBLSPACE 000   81151488 12-17-92  11:15a
        5 file(s)   81131008 bytes
                     2582528 bytes free

C:\>
```

Figure 18-6 The contents of the host drive

How DoubleSpace assigns drive letters In the example in figure 18-5, I illustrated a single host drive with one compressed drive on it. In this common DoubleSpace setup, the drive letters assigned by DoubleSpace are easy enough to deal with: the compressed drive is drive C and the host drive is drive H. However, you can create more than one compressed drive on a single host, and you can have multiple host drives. Then, the way DoubleSpace assigns drive letters is more complicated. Figure 18-7 summarizes the rules DoubleSpace follows when it assigns drive letters.

The first rule in figure 18-7 describes how DoubleSpace assigns host drive letters. When you first run DoubleSpace, it counts the number of hard drives on your system. Then, it sets aside one host drive letter for each drive, starting with H. Contrary to what you might expect, however, it doesn't assign host drive letters by starting with H and working up. Instead, it starts with the highest host drive letter and works down. For example, suppose your PC has three hard drives: C, D, and E. When you run DoubleSpace setup, DoubleSpace sets aside drive letters H, I, and J to use for host drives. Then, when DoubleSpace compresses drive C, it uses drive J for the host drive. (DoubleSpace compresses drive C first by default. You'll see how that works in a minute.)

DoubleSpace assigns the host drive letters for the remaining drives in the order that you compress them. So, if you compress drive D, then compress drive E, the host drive for D will be I and the host drive for E will be H. On the other hand, if you compress drive E, then compress drive D, the host drive for E will be I and the host drive for D will be H. Because of this, I recommend you compress your drives in sequence so that your host drive letters will be assigned in sequence.

1. Host drives are assigned a range of drive letters starting with H. The host drive letters are assigned from highest to lowest, so that if there are three drives to be compressed (C, D, and E), the host for C will be J. Then, the host for the next drive to be compressed (usually D) will be I, and the host for the last drive (usually E) will be H.
2. When you compress an existing drive, DoubleSpace uses the original drive letter for the compressed drive and assigns the host drive letter according to rule 1.
3. When you create an empty compressed drive, it is assigned the highest available drive letter below H. The first empty compressed drive is assigned drive letter G, the next is assigned drive letter F, and so on. If there are no available drive letters below H, the next available drive letter above the drive letters used for the host drives is used.

Figure 18-7 How DoubleSpace assigns drive letters

The second rule in figure 18-7 simply says that when you compress an existing drive, DoubleSpace assigns the new compressed drive the drive letter used by the original, uncompressed drive. That way, you can access the data on the drive by referring to the original drive letter.

The third rule describes how DoubleSpace assigns drive letters when you create an empty compressed drive on a host drive. If possible, DoubleSpace uses the highest unassigned drive letter below H. So the first empty compressed drive you create will be drive G, the next will be drive F, and so on. If there aren't any unassigned drive letters below H, DoubleSpace uses the next available drive letter above the host drive letters. Thus, if the highest assigned host drive letter is K, DoubleSpace will assign drive L to the new compressed drive.

Fortunately, you can display a list of the current drive assignments for your system by entering this DBLSPACE command:

```
C:\>dblspace /list
```

This command creates a list like the one in figure 18-8. Here, you can see that host drive H contains two compressed hard drives, accessed as drives C and G. Drives D, E, and F are available for DoubleSpace to use for additional compressed drives. By the way, the DBLSPACE command has many other switches you can use to perform a variety of functions. I'll present them later in this chapter.

If your PC is connected to a network, you should realize that the output from the DBLSPACE /LIST command doesn't include network drives. So if you're connected to a PC network and the procedure that you use to log in to a network server assigns the drive letters you use to access network drives, you need to be careful that the network drive assignments don't conflict with DoubleSpace's drive assignments. If you think this may be a problem on your system, you should discuss DoubleSpace with your network administrator before installing it.

```
C:\>dblspace /list
Drive  Type                          Total Free  Total Size  CVF Filename
-----  ----------------------------  ----------  ----------  ----------------
  A    Floppy drive                     0.05 MB     1.39 MB
  C    Compressed hard drive           30.98 MB   106.83 MB  H:\DBLSPACE.000
  D    Available for DoubleSpace
  E    Available for DoubleSpace
  F    Available for DoubleSpace
  G    Compressed hard drive           44.49 MB    44.49 MB  H:\DBLSPACE.001
  H    Local hard drive                 2.38 MB    80.05 MB

C:\>
```

Figure 18-8 How to display a list of current drive assignments

How to compress your C drive

Now that you know a little about how DoubleSpace works, you're ready to set it up. DoubleSpace setup takes about a minute for each megabyte of data on your hard disk, so be sure to allow plenty of time. If you have more than 100MB of data on your hard drive, you might want to start DoubleSpace setup before you go home for the night and let it run unattended. In any event, before you start DoubleSpace setup, I recommend you do a complete backup of your hard drive. Although DoubleSpace setup is very reliable, it's always a good idea to do a backup before making major changes to your system. You should also run Chkdsk to make sure there are no allocation errors on your disk. DoubleSpace will run Chkdsk early in the setup process, but you're better off if you run it first and correct any errors it reports.

In addition, you should also use the Mem command to find out if you have enough available memory to use DoubleSpace. DoubleSpace requires about 44KB of internal memory. If you have a 386 or better computer, odds are you have enough free space in the *upper memory area* to accomodate DoubleSpace without reducing the amount of conventional memory available to your application programs. To find out, type MEM at the DOS prompt. The next to last line of the resulting display shows the size of the largest upper memory block, like this:

```
Largest free upper memory block          78K    (80256 bytes)
```

If this block is larger than 44KB, you don't need to worry about DoubleSpace's memory requirements. If it's less than 44KB, you should carefully consider whether or not you can afford to give up conventional memory for DoubleSpace. (If you have a 386 or better computer and the Mem command reports 0KB of upper memory space, your CONFIG.SYS file may not be properly set up to support upper memory. In that case, you should read chapter 25 before you proceed. There, you'll learn how to set up your CONFIG.SYS file to make the best use of all available memory.)

To start DoubleSpace setup, simply type DBLSPACE at the DOS prompt. DoubleSpace responds by displaying the welcome screen shown in part 1 of figure 18-9. After reading this screen, press the Enter key to proceed to the menu shown in part 2 of figure 18-9. This menu lets you pick one of two setup operations: Express-setup and Custom-setup. Express-setup compresses all of the data on your C drive, leaving only a small amount of free space on the host drive. Custom-setup lets you change the drive to compress or the amount of free space to leave on the host drive. In most cases, you should select Express-setup. If you want to change the amount of free space on the host drive or compress another drive, you can do that later.

When you select Express-setup, DoubleSpace displays the confirmation screen shown in part 3 of figure 18-9. This screen provides an estimate of how long the setup will take, and gives you one last chance to exit before proceeding. To proceed, press C. When you do, DoubleSpace runs Chkdsk to make sure your disk has no allocation errors. Next, DoubleSpace alters your CONFIG.SYS and AUTOEXEC.BAT files and reboots your computer. This loads the DBLSPACE.BIN file and restarts DoubleSpace.

After DoubleSpace setup has restarted, it creates the Compressed Volume File and begins compressing your files, moving them one by one into the CVF. Part 4 of figure 18-9 shows the progress screen DoubleSpace displays as it executes. As DoubleSpace compresses your files, it expands the CVF to include the newly freed space. When it's finished, the CVF will fill the drive except for the space it reserves for uncompressed files.

When DoubleSpace is finished compressing your files, it invokes *Microsoft Defrag* to optimize the compressed drive. Part 5 of figure 18-9 shows the progress screen displayed by Defrag as it works. You'll learn about Defrag in chapter 19, so I won't explain this screen in detail here.

Finally, when DoubleSpace setup is complete, it displays the screen shown in part 6 of figure 18-9. Here, you can see the amount of free space available on drive C before compression, the amount of free space available after compression, the overall compression ratio, and the elapsed time. Notice the message, "DoubleSpace has created a new drive H that contains 2.0 MB of uncompressed space." This message is a little misleading. What DoubleSpace actually did was create a new compressed drive, then change the drive letter assignments so that the new drive is accessed as drive C and the original drive is accessed as drive H.

When you press the Enter key, DoubleSpace restores your original CONFIG.SYS and AUTOEXEC.BAT files and restarts your computer. Once your computer has rebooted, you can access the compressed drive C. You'll probably never need to access the host drive, but I recommend you enter the following commands just to see what's on it:

```
C:\>dir h:

C:\>dir h: /ah
```

Part 1:

To compress your C drive, enter DBLSPACE at the DOS prompt. Then, DoubleSpace displays its opening screen. Press the Enter key to continue.

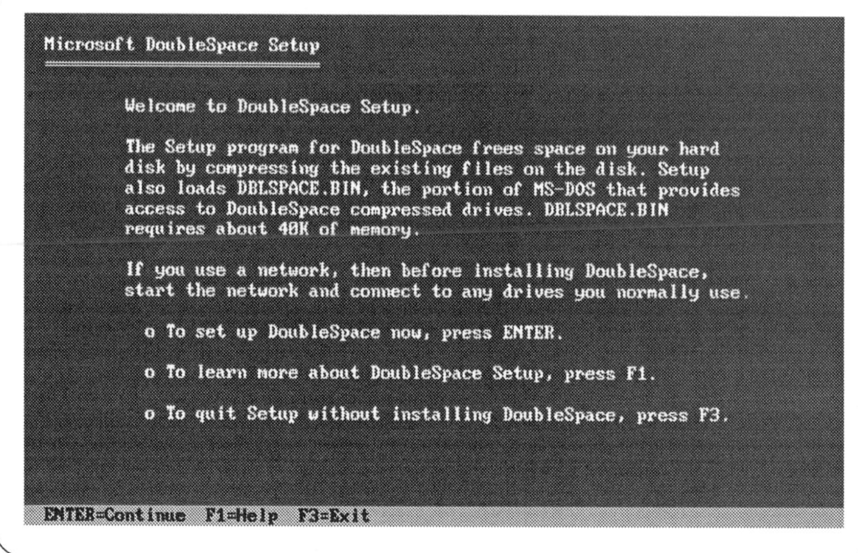

Part 2:

Select Express-setup from the menu and press the Enter key to continue.

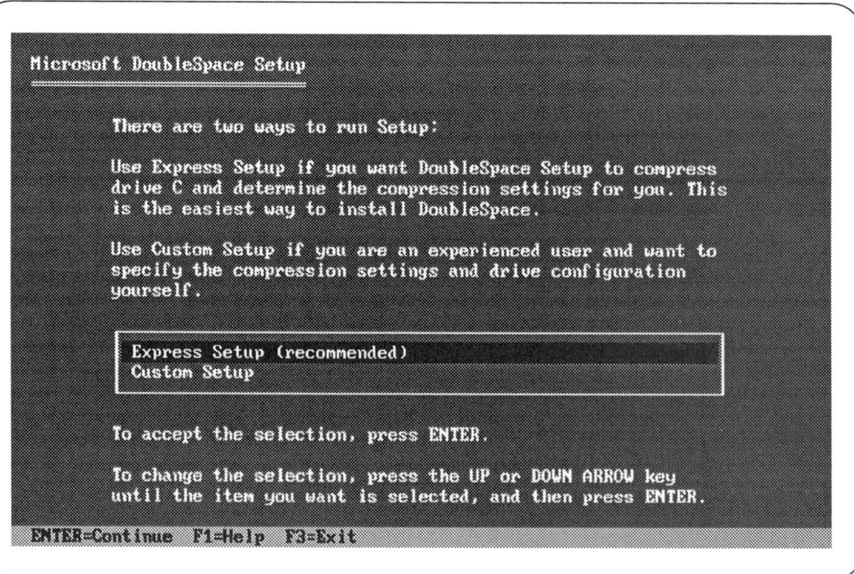

Figure 18-9 How to compress your C drive (parts 1 and 2 of 6)

Part 3:

Before DoubleSpace compresses your C drive, it displays a confirmation screen. Press C to compress your C drive, or press the Escape key to return to the setup menu.

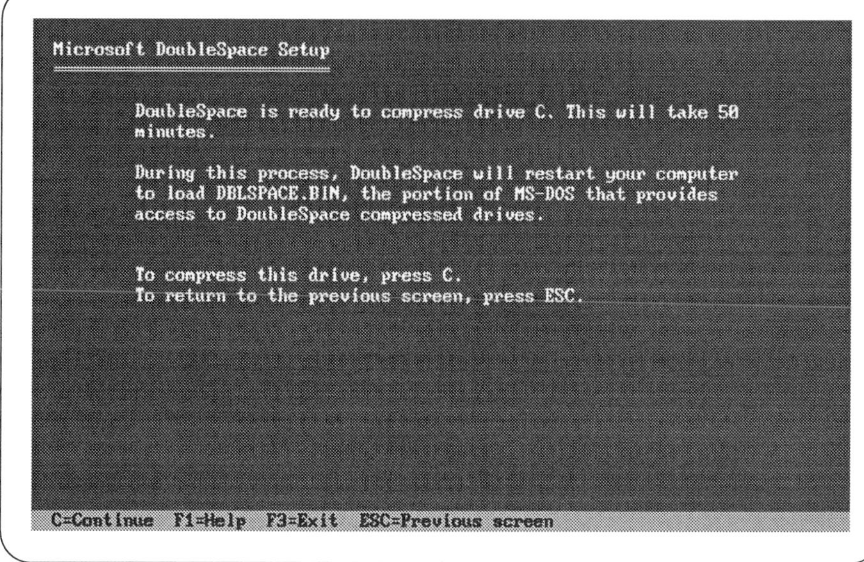

Part 4:

As DoubleSpace compresses files and moves them into the CVF, it displays its progress.

```
Microsoft DoubleSpace Setup

DoubleSpace is now compressing drive C.

Start time:              1:26:12pm
Current time:            1:29:21pm
Estimated finish time:   1:49pm

Time left:               About 20 minutes.

Currently Compressing:   C:\DOS\GRAPHICS.PRO

                         13% complete

Compressing files...
```

Figure 18-9 How to compress your C drive (parts 3 and 4 of 6)

Part 5:

When DoubleSpace finishes compressing your files, it invokes Microsoft Defrag to optimize the compressed drive.

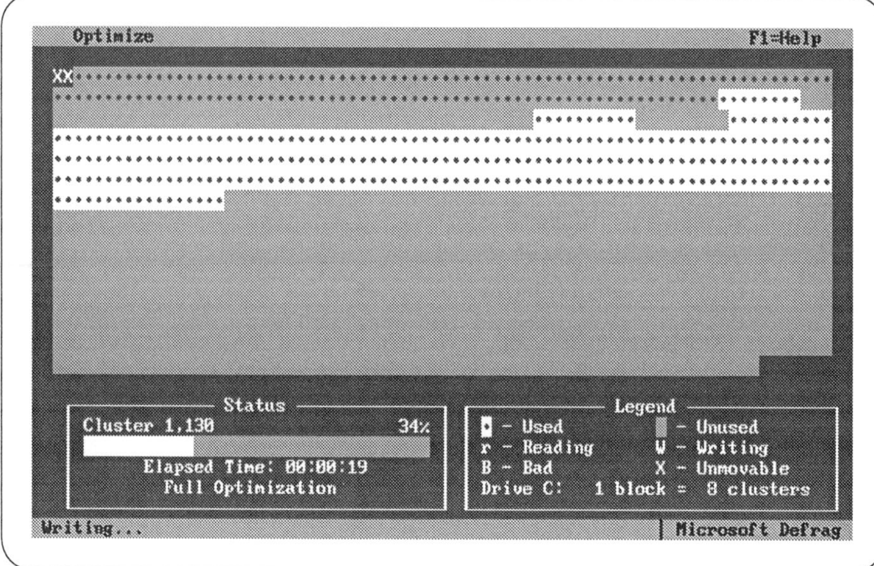

Part 6:

When DoubleSpace setup is finished, it displays information about the compressed drive. Press the Enter key to exit from DoubleSpace and restart your computer so you can access the compressed drive.

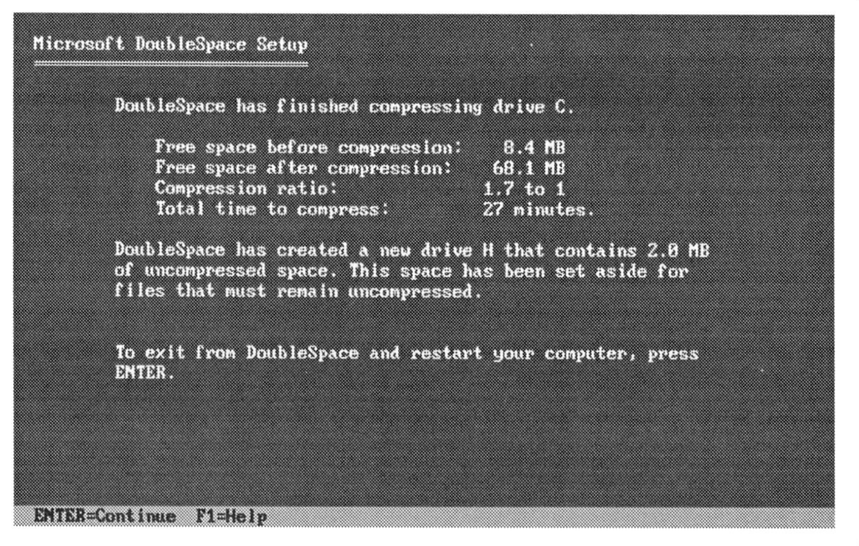

Figure 18-9 How to compress your C drive (parts 5 and 6 of 6)

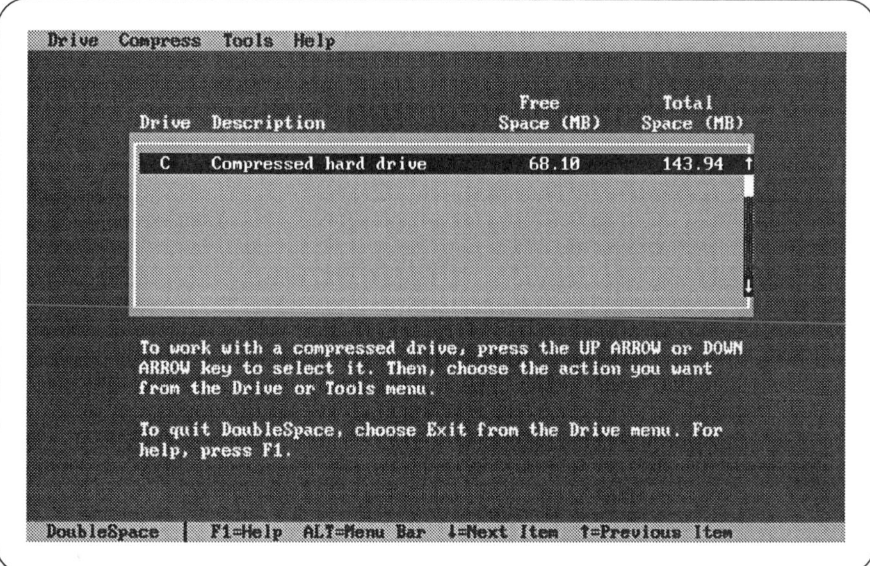

Figure 18-10 The DoubleSpace drive list

You saw the output from this second command in figure 18-6. Then, run a Chkdsk command on drive C to confirm the amount of space available on the compressed drive. The output from this command should look like the output in the bottom part of figure 18-3. If your system is like most, Chkdsk will report that the new C drive has about twice the capacity as your original uncompressed C drive.

How to use the DoubleSpace program

Once you've compressed your C drive, you won't need to use DoubleSpace often. Still, there are some occasions when you'll need to use it. In particular, if you want to create additional compressed drives or change the size of your existing compressed drives, you'll need to use DoubleSpace. If you use compressed diskettes, you'll have to use DoubleSpace to access them. And you may occasionally need to use DoubleSpace for routine maintenance of your compressed drives.

You can execute these and other DoubleSpace functions in two ways. First, you can enter DBLSPACE at the command prompt. Then, you can select the function you want from the menus DoubleSpace provides. Second, you can you can use options on the DBLSPACE command to invoke functions directly from the command line.

How to use the DoubleSpace menus When you enter DBLSPACE without any options, DoubleSpace displays the screen shown in figure 18-10. The center portion of this screen displays a list of the DoubleSpace drives that exist on your system. In this case, there is only one DoubleSpace drive: drive C. If you have other compressed drives, they'll be listed here too. If you have more than one compressed drive, you can use the Arrow keys to select the one you want to work on.

The menu bar on the top line of the DoubleSpace display lists four pull-down menus: Drive, Compress, Tools, and Help. You can access these menus by clicking on them with the mouse. Or you can use an Alt+key combination (Alt+D for Drive, Alt+C for Compress, Alt+T for Tools, and Alt+H for Help). Figures 18-11, 18-12, and 18-13 present the Drive, Compress, and Tools menus and a description of their functions. I'll describe most of these functions later in this chapter. The Help menu lets you access extensive on-line help information for DoubleSpace. Because it's easy to use, I won't describe it here.

DoubleSpace command line options All of the functions that are available from the DoubleSpace menus shown in figures 18-11 through 18-13 can be invoked directly from the command line by using optional switches on the DBLSPACE command. In addition, there's one function that's accessible only from the command line: displaying a list of the current drive assignments. This function is useful when you want to see how DoubleSpace has assigned drive letters to compressed drives and host drives, as I showed you earlier in this chapter.

Figure 18-14 shows the DBLSPACE command format you use for each of these functions. For most of these functions, I recommend you use the DoubleSpace menus rather than the command line options. You're more likely to use the command line options in batch files. For example, you might include the command

```
dblspace /chkdsk c:
```

in your AUTOEXEC.BAT file to check your C drive's internal structure every day when you start your machine. Or, you might create a MOUNT.BAT batch file that contains the command

```
dblspace /mount a:
```

Then, whenever you insert a compressed diskette in drive A, you simply type MOUNT to mount the drive.

Although some of the options in figure 18-14 might not be clear to you now, they will make more sense when you read about the functions they perform. As I describe each these functions, I'll illustrate them primarily with the DoubleSpace menus. But I'll also show you how to invoke each function directly from the command line.

The Drive menu

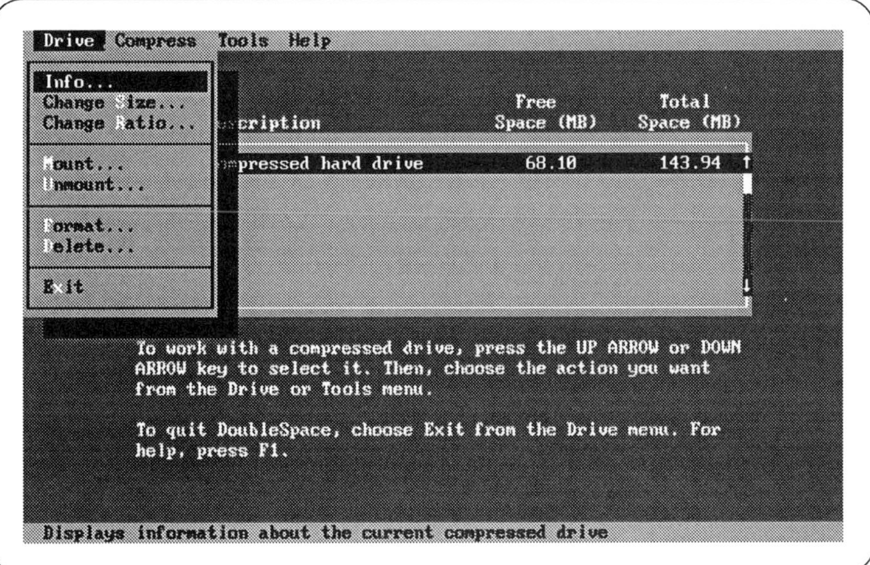

Menu item	**Description**
Info	Displays information about a compressed volume.
Change Size	Changes a compressed volume's size.
Change Ratio	Changes the estimated compression ratio used to calculate free space on the volume.
Mount	Mounts a compressed drive.
Unmount	Unmounts a compressed drive.
Format	Formats a compressed drive, erasing all existing data in the process. DoubleSpace does this automatically when it compresses a drive, so the only reason to format a compressed drive is to erase its contents. DoubleSpace won't let you format your compressed C drive.
Delete	Removes the compressed drive's CVF. This not only erases its contents, but permanently removes the drive as well. As for Format, DoubleSpace won't let you delete your compressed C drive. But you might want to use this function to remove other compressed drives you've created on your hard disk or compressed drives you've created on diskette.
Exit	Exits from the DoubleSpace program.

Figure 18-11 Drive menu functions

The Compress menu

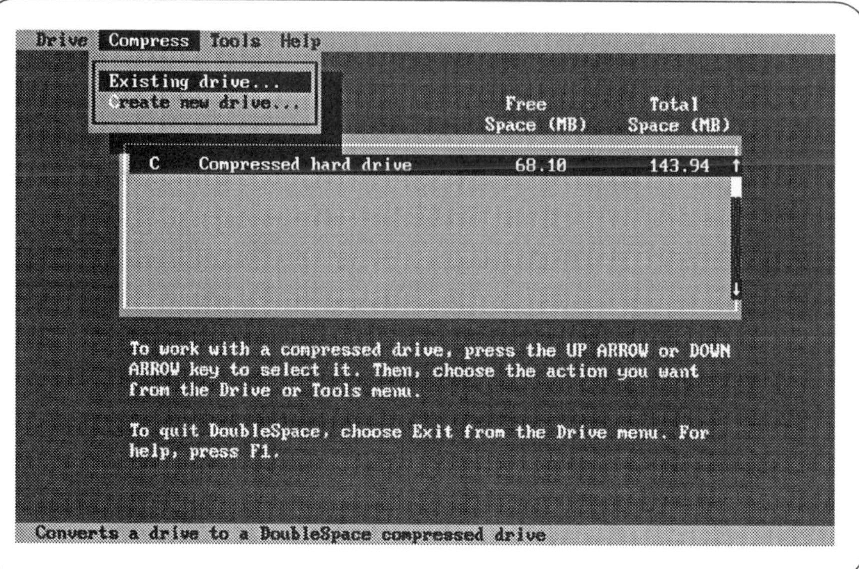

Menu item	Description
Existing drive	Creates a compressed drive using disk space that's already occupied by data. DoubleSpace creates the compressed drive by compressing the existing data and moving it into the compressed drive.
Create new drive	Creates an empty compressed drive using existing free space.

Figure 18-12 Compress menu functions

The Tools menu

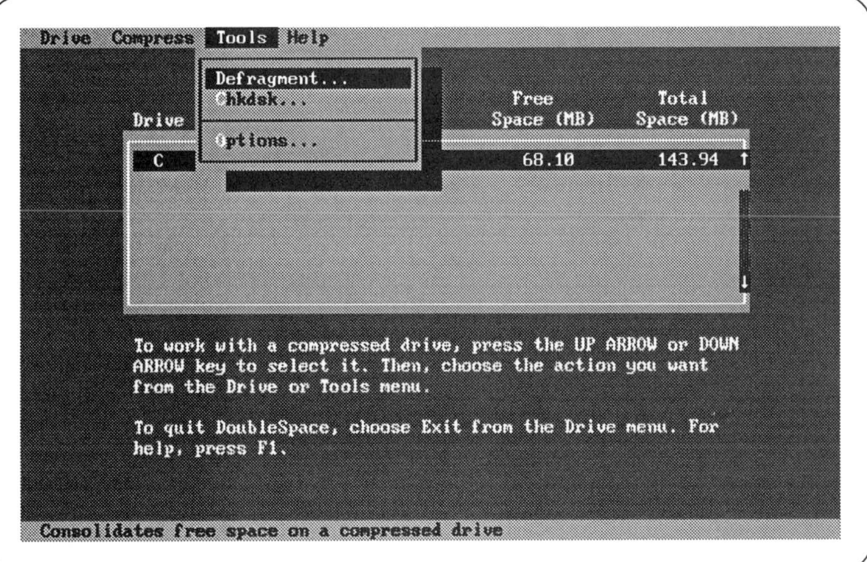

Menu item	Description
Defragment	Reorganizes the contents of a compressed drive so that all of the available free space is grouped together at the end of the volume rather than scattered throughout it.
Chkdsk	Performs the equivalent of a DOS Chkdsk command for a compressed drive.
Options	Lets you change some DoubleSpace options that apply only in unusual situations.

Figure 18-13 Tools menu functions

The DoubleSpace command format	Explanation
`DBLSPACE /INFO drive:`	Displays drive information.
`DBLSPACE /SIZE=size drive:` `DBLSPACE /SIZE /RESERVE=size drive:`	Changes the drive size.
`DBLSPACE /RATIO=ratio drive:`	Changes a drive's compression ratio.
`DBLSPACE /MOUNT=nnn drive: [/NEWDRIVE=drive]`	Mounts a compressed drive.
`DBLSPACE /UNMOUNT drive:`	Unmounts a compressed drive.
`DBLSPACE /FORMAT drive:`	Formats a compressed drive.
`DBLSPACE /DELETE drive:`	Deletes a compressed drive.
`DBLSPACE /COMPRESS drive: [/NEWDRIVE=drive] [/RESERVE=size]`	Compresses an existing drive.
`DBLSPACE /CREATE drive: [/NEWDRIVE=drive] [/SIZE=size]` `DBLSPACE /CREATE drive: [/NEWDRIVE=drive] [/RESERVE=size]`	Creates an empty compressed drive.
`DBLSPACE /DEFRAG drive:`	Defragments a compressed drive.
`DBLSPACE /CHKDSK drive:`	Checks the internal structure of a compressed drive.
`DBLSPACE /LIST`	Displays a drive map.

Figure 18-14 The DoubleSpace command

How to manage a compressed drive

Of the 14 functions available from DoubleSpace's menus, you'll use only six of them on a regular basis to manage your compressed drives. Three of them are on the Drive menu: Info, Change-size, and Change-ratio. The other three are on the Tools menu: Defrag, MaxCompress, and Chkdsk. In addition to these functions, you'll also want to back up a compressed drive regularly. So I'll tell you the best way to do that too.

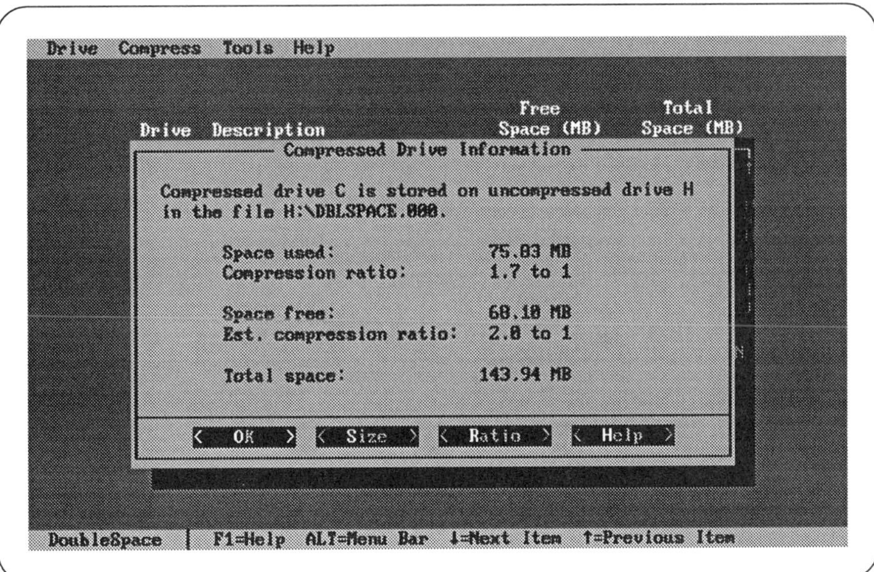

Figure 18-15 Compressed drive information

How to display information about a compressed drive You can display information about a compressed drive by highlighting that drive in the drive list, then selecting the Drive menu's Info function. When you do, DoubleSpace displays the drive information shown in figure 18-15.

The top part of the drive information box tells you the uncompressed host drive (H) where the compressed drive (C) is stored and the name of the Compressed Volume File (DBLSPACE.000). Then, it shows space information for the compressed drive. In this example, the compressed drive has a total capacity of approximately 144MB, with about 75.8MB used and about 68MB of free space.

Notice that the compression ratio for the space used on the drive is 1.7 to 1. However, the amount of free space on the compressed drive is calculated based on an estimated compression ratio of 2.0. This underscores the fact that the amount of free space reported for a compressed drive is only an estimate. The amount of data you can actually store in that free space depends on how much that data can be compressed. Since I've already stored all of my programs on drive C, I expect that most of the additional files I place on drive C will compress 2.0 to 1 or better. So 68MB is a realistic estimate of free space for this drive. As you'll see in a moment, however, you can change the ratio DoubleSpace uses to estimate the remaining free space.

You can obtain the same information from the command line by using this command:

```
C:\>dblspace /info c:
```

When you do, DoubleSpace displays the information for drive C.

How to change the size of a compressed drive You can use the Drive menu's Change-size function to increase or decrease the size of a compressed volume. DoubleSpace does this by changing the amount of disk space on the host drive that's allocated to the Compressed Volume File. By increasing this space, you increase the capacity of the compressed drive. This is called *growing* the drive. Similarly, decreasing the size of the CVF decreases the capacity of the compressed drive. This is called *shrinking* the drive.

You'll probably never use this function if you use only one compressed drive and you don't need to store any files on the uncompressed portion of the host drive. However, if you want to create a second compressed drive on the host drive, you'll first have to shrink the first compressed drive to make room on the host for a second. Or, if for some reason you must store a file on an uncompressed drive, you may need to shrink a compressed drive to increase the free space on the host drive.

There are limits to how much you can grow or shrink a compressed drive. Because the CVF must fit on the host drive, you can grow it only as much as the free space on the host drive will allow. Thus, when the host drive is full, you can't grow the compressed drive any further. And because the CVF must be large enough to accommodate all of the data it contains, you can shrink a compressed drive only until its free space reaches 0.

When you select the Change-size function, DoubleSpace displays the dialog shown in part 1 of figure 18-16. This dialog shows the space usage for both the compressed drive and the host drive. Contrary to what you might expect, you don't change the size of a compressed drive by specifying a new total capacity for it. Instead, you change the size of a compressed drive by changing the amount of free space left on the host drive. That makes sense when you remember that the total capacity and the amount of free space for a compressed drive are just estimates based on the anticipated compression ratio. In contrast, the amount of free space remaining on the host drive is concrete. By changing it, you increase or decrease the actual size of the compressed drive's CVF, and that in turn changes the size of the compressed drive.

In part 1 of figure 18-16, you can see that the Change-size dialog displays the minimum and maximum amount free for the host drive (in this case, 0.54MB and 36.34MB). As you would expect, the free space you specify for the host drive must fall between these two values. When you type a new free space amount for the host

Part 1:

To change the size of a compressed drive, select the Change-size function from the Drive menu. Then, DoubleSpace displays the current space usage for the compressed drive and the host drive.

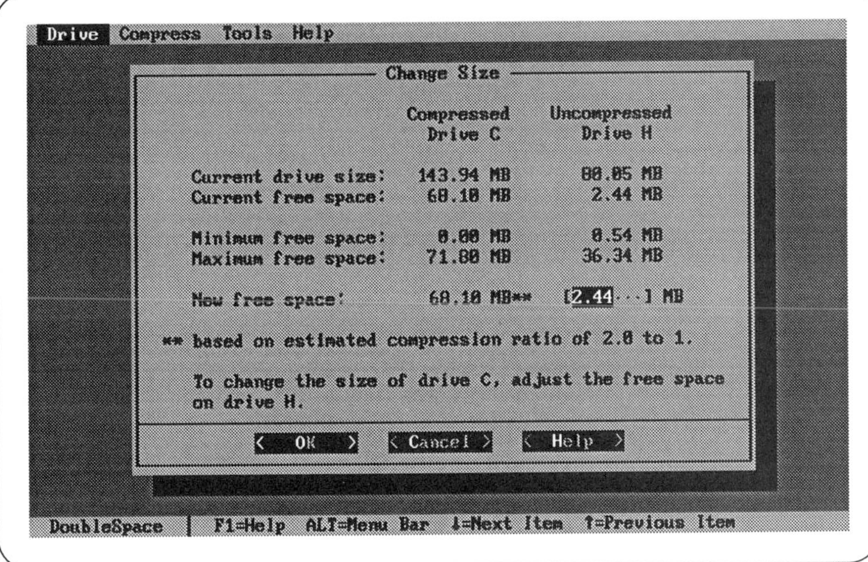

Part 2:

Enter a new value for the free space on the host drive. The value must be between the maximum and minimum free space values in the display. DoubleSpace shows how this will affect the free space on the compressed drive. Press the Enter key to continue.

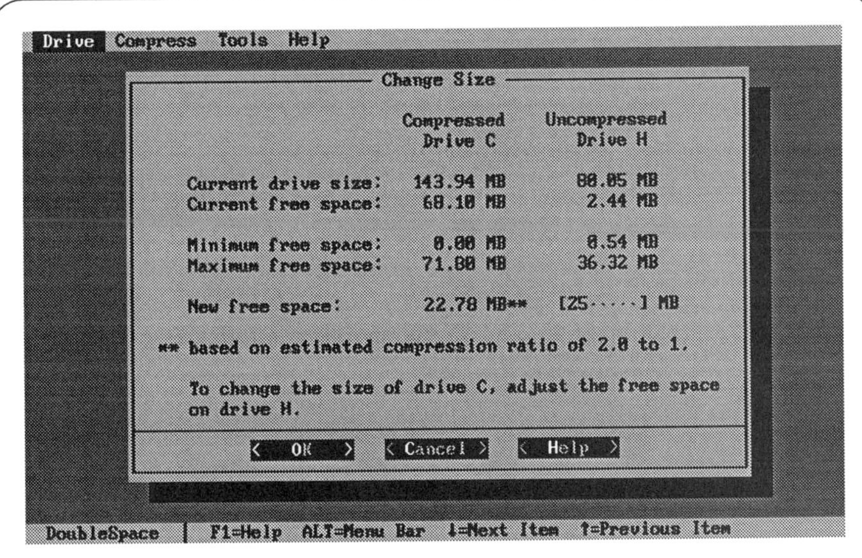

Figure 18-16 How to change the size of a compressed drive (parts 1 and 2 of 3)

Part 3:

After DoubleSpace resizes your disk, it displays the new values for free space and total space on the compressed drive.

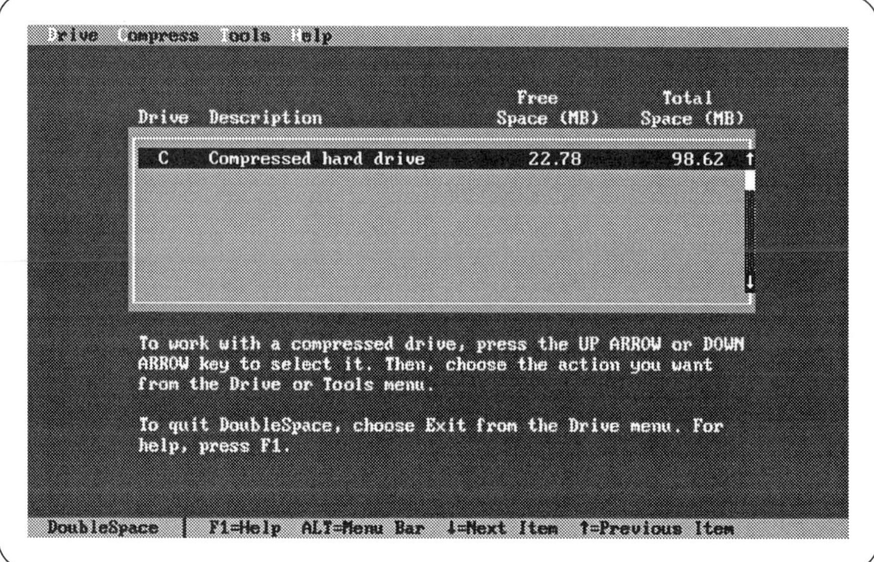

Figure 18-16 How to change the size of a compressed drive (part 3 of 3)

drive, DoubleSpace automatically updates the new free space shown for the compressed drive. For example, in part 2 of figure 18-16, I changed the free space value for the host drive to 25MB. DoubleSpace shows that will reduce the amount of free space on the compressed drive from 68MB to under 23MB, based on an estimated compression ratio of 2.0 to 1.

When you've entered the correct value for the free space to leave on the host, press the Enter key to resize the compressed disk. This operation should take only a few seconds. When DoubleSpace is finished, it redisplays the drive list, as part 3 of figure 18-16 shows. Here, you can see that the total capacity of the C drive is now over 98MB, with under 23MB of free space.

You can use the /SIZE switch on the DBLSPACE command to change the size of a drive directly from the command line. To do that, just specify the new size for the compressed drive's Compressed Volume File on the /SIZE switch, like this:

```
C:\>dblspace /size=50 c:
```

This command changes the size of the C drive's CVF to 50MB. Note that you specify the size of the CVF, not the total capacity of the compressed drive. The resulting capacity for the compressed drive will depend on the estimated compression ratio.

Alternatively, you can use the /RESERVE switch along with the /SIZE switch to resize a compressed drive. Because the /RESERVE switch specifies the amount of free space to leave on the host drive, it works just like the Change-size dialog in figure 18-16. For example, this command,

```
C:\>dblspace /size /reserve=25 c:
```

adjusts the size of the compressed drive so that 25MB of free space is left on the host drive.

How to change a drive's estimated compression ratio You use the Change-ratio function to change the compression ratio that DoubleSpace uses to estimate the amount of free space available on a compressed drive. When you create a compressed drive, DoubleSpace sets the initial value for the compression ratio at 2.0 to 1. If you think that the actual compression ratio for most of your files will be significantly different, you might want to change the compression ratio so that the free space estimate is more realistic.

Part 1 of figure 18-17 shows the dialog DoubleSpace displays when you select the Change-ratio function. As you can see, this dialog displays the current estimated compression ratio and the actual compression ratio for the files already on the drive. Then, it lets you enter a new compression ratio. You can enter any number between 1.0 and 4.1. Here, I changed the ratio from 2.0 to 2.5.

When you change the compression ratio, DoubleSpace updates the drive list, as shown in part 2 of figure 18-17. Here, you can see that DoubleSpace now estimates the amount of free space on drive C as almost 25MB and the total capacity as 100MB.

Notice that both the Change-size function and the Change-ratio function change the amount of free space and the total capacity for a compressed drive. The difference is that the Change-size function actually changes the amount of space available in the compressed drive by increasing or decreasing the size of the CVF. In contrast, the Change-ratio function changes only the estimate of free space and total capacity. If this estimate is inaccurate, you can't depend on the free space and total space values.

You can change the compression ratio from the command line by using the /RATIO switch, like this:

```
C:\>dblspace /ratio=1.7 c:
```

This command changes the estimated compression ratio for the C drive to 1.7 to 1.

How to defragment a compressed drive A *fragmented file* is a file that has clusters in several different areas on a disk. In other words, fragmented files are not stored in adjacent disk clusters. Fragmentation is a common condition under DOS because of the way DOS allocates space to new files. Fragmentation occurs for both compressed and uncompressed drives.

One side effect of fragmentation is that the free space on the disk is scattered across the disk, intermixed with clusters that are occupied by files. On an uncompressed drive, that's not usually a problem because DOS can allocate free

Part 1:

To change the compression ratio, select the Change-ratio function from the Drive menu. Then, enter the new compression ratio.

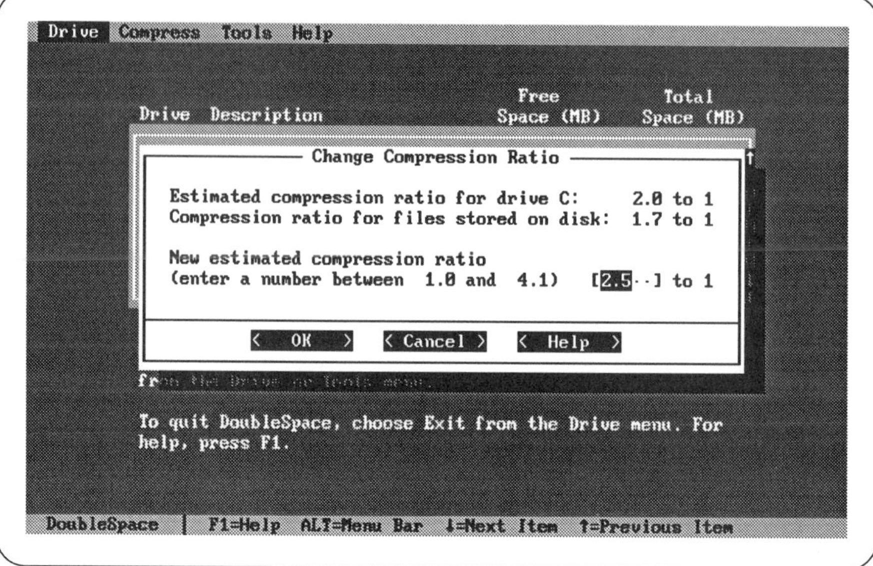

Part 2:

DoubleSpace recalculates the free space and total space values for the compressed drive based on the new compression ratio.

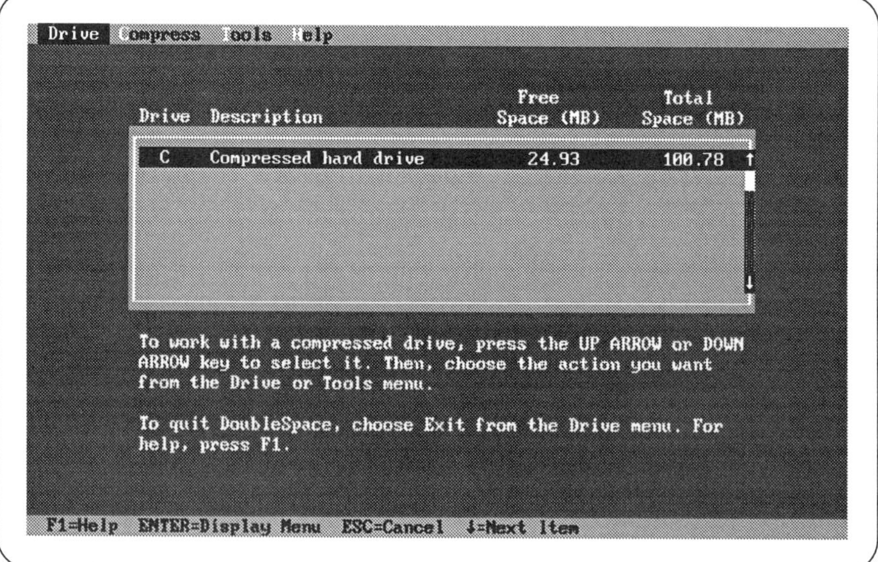

Figure 18-17 How to change the compression ratio for a compressed drive

clusters without regard to fragmentation. However, fragmentation on a compressed drive can be a problem if you're considering shrinking the drive to free up space on the host. That's because DoubleSpace can shrink a compressed drive only if there is enough contiguous free space available at the end of the drive. Free space that's intermixed with file clusters cannot be returned to the host drive when DoubleSpace shrinks the CVF.

As a result, you should always *defragment* a compressed drive before you reduce its size. You can do that with DoubleSpace by selecting the Tools menu's Defrag function or by entering a DBLSPACE command with the /DEFRAGMENT switch at the command prompt. Or, you can defragment the drive using *Microsoft Defrag*, which does a more thorough job. (You'll learn about *Microsoft Defrag* in the next chapter.)

How to check the internal structure of a compressed drive The Chkdsk function available from the DoubleSpace Tools menu is similar to the DOS Chkdsk command. It checks the internal structure of a compressed drive to make sure that there are no inconsistencies. And it can correct any errors it detects.

If you use the Chkdsk command regularly, you won't need to use the DoubleSpace Chkdsk function. That's because Chkdsk performs this function automatically when it detects a compressed drive. If you look back to figure 18-3, you'll see that the last two lines in the Chkdsk display for the compressed drive indicate that the Chkdsk function has been performed.

How to back up a compressed drive Because of the way DoubleSpace assigns drive letters to compressed drives and host drives, you might be confused about how to back up the data on a compressed drive. Should you back up the data from the compressed drive, the host drive, or both? The answer is simple: you should back up the data from the compressed drive. That way, you'll be able to restore individual files from your backups. If you back up the data from the host drive, the entire compressed drive will be contained on the backup media in a single file (the CVF), so you won't be able to do selective restores.

Of course, if you have important uncompressed data on the host drive, you'll want to back it up too. If that's the case, be sure to configure your backup program so it excludes the CVF. The easiest way to do that is to exclude hidden files from the backup. Then, since the CVF is a hidden file, it won't be backed up.

How to use more than one compressed drive

So far, I've assumed that your system has just one compressed drive on it. After you use Express-setup to compress your C drive, that's what you'll have. However, DoubleSpace will let you create additional compressed drives. To do that, you use either the Existing-drive function or the Create-new-drive function from the Compress menu, or you can invoke these functions using command line switches.

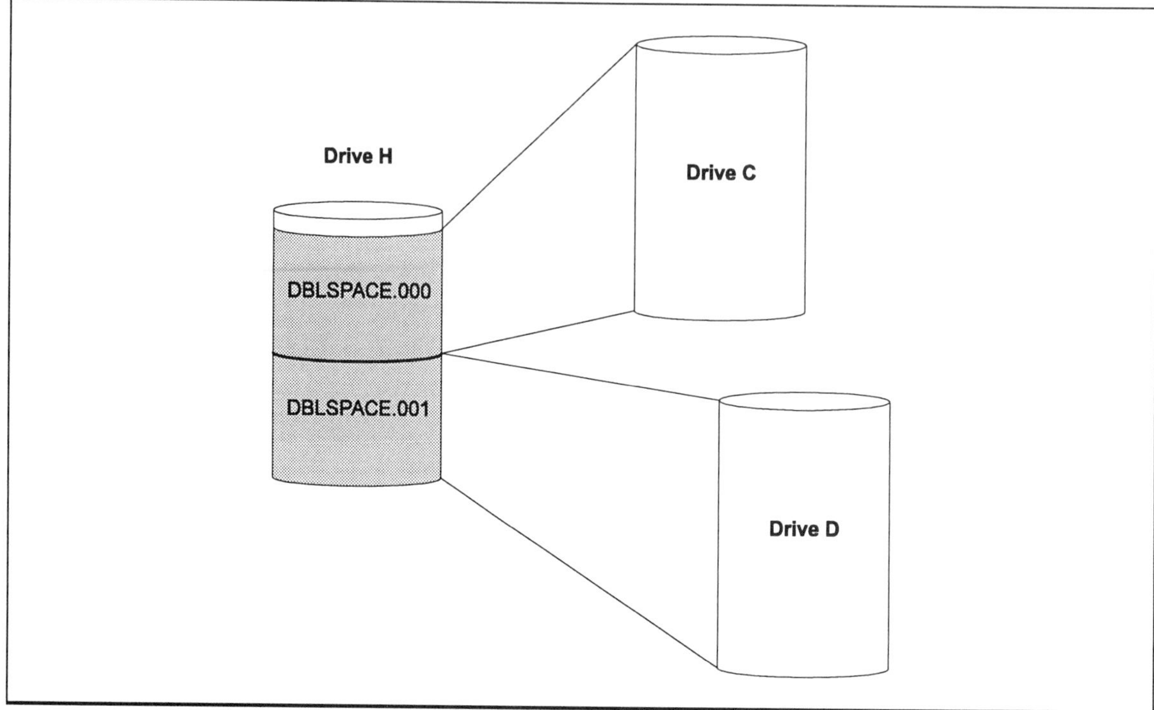

Figure 18-18 How a single drive can host two DoubleSpace drives

The easiest way to set up more than one compressed drive is to create a second compressed drive on the same host drive as your first compressed drive. Figure 18-18 illustrates this arrangement. Here, I've created two compressed drives, C and D, on the host drive, H. Notice that DoubleSpace assigns a different name to the Compressed Volume File for each compressed drive. So DBLSPACE.000 is the CVF for the C drive, and DBLSPACE.001 is the CVF for the D drive.

If your PC has more than one hard drive, each drive can host one or more compressed drives. For example, figure 18-19 shows a system that has two hard drives. (Actually, the system has only one drive, but it's partitioned into two drives.) Here, each drive hosts one compressed drive. So the host for drive C is drive I, and the host for drive D is H. Of course, each host drive could be host to more than one compressed drive. That's an unlikely setup, though.

If you've set up an extended partition and logical drive so that you can store your program files on one drive and your data files on the other, you should consider removing the extended partition and using the arrangement in figure 18-18 rather than keeping the extended partition and using the arrangement in figure 18-19. Placing two compressed drives in a single large partition is more flexible than placing one

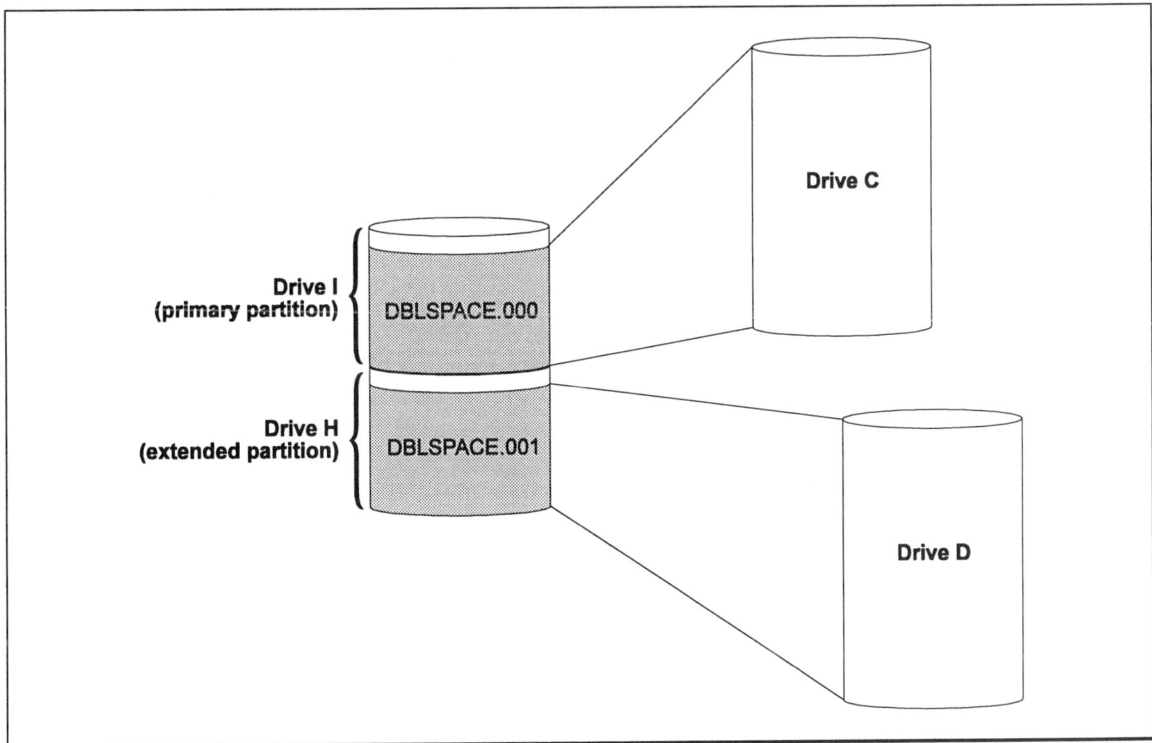

Figure 18-19 How two hard drives can each host a DoubleSpace drive

compressed drive in each of two smaller partitions. That's because DoubleSpace lets you adjust the size of a compressed drive using its Change-size function. In contrast, you have to do a complete backup of both compressed drives, redefine the partition sizes, format the new partitions, recreate the compressed drives, and restore the backup to change the size of a partition.

How to create an empty compressed drive Before you can create a second compressed drive on a host drive, you must shrink the first compressed drive to free up space. To do that, you use the Drive menu's Change-size function as I illustrated in figure 18-16. There, I told DoubleSpace to free up 25MB of space on the host drive (H).

Figure 18-20 shows an example of using DoubleSpace to create an empty compressed drive after space was freed up on the host drive. Part 1 shows the initial DoubleSpace setup with a single compressed C drive. When you start the Create-new-drive function, DoubleSpace displays a list of the available host drives on your system like the one shown in part 2 of figure 18-20. Because this system has only one hard drive, there's only one available drive. It has 25MB of free space, and

Part 1:

To create an empty DoubleSpace drive, select the Create-new-drive function from the Compress menu.

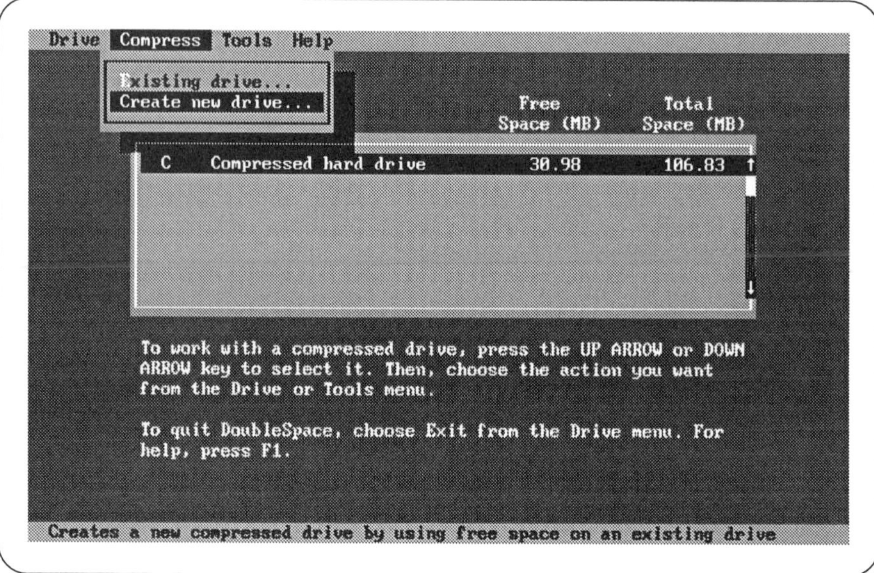

Part 2:

DoubleSpace displays a list of the available host drives on your system. Highlight the drive you want to host the new compressed drive and press the Enter key.

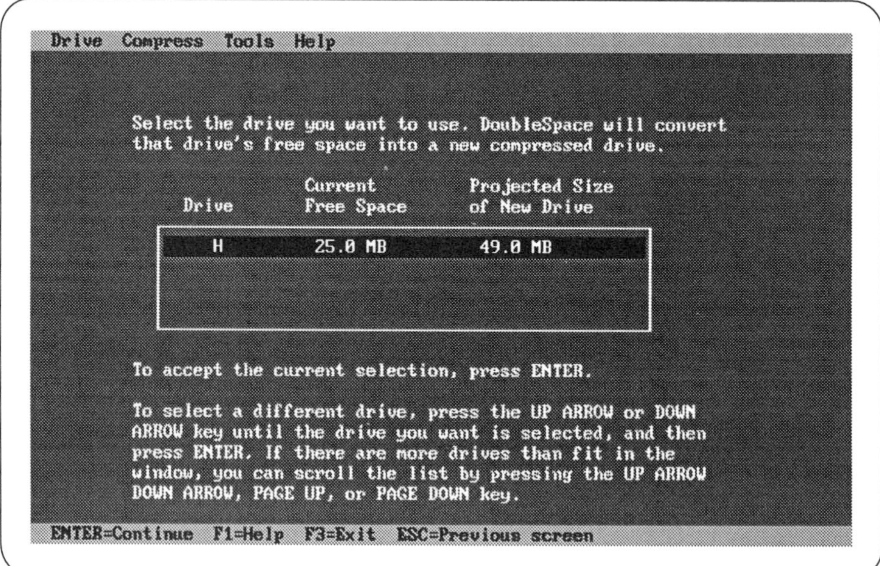

Figure 18-20 How to create an empty DoubleSpace drive (parts 1 and 2 of 5)

Part 3:

DoubleSpace displays its default settings for free space, compression ratio, and drive letter. Change these settings if you want to, then highlight Continue and press the Enter key.

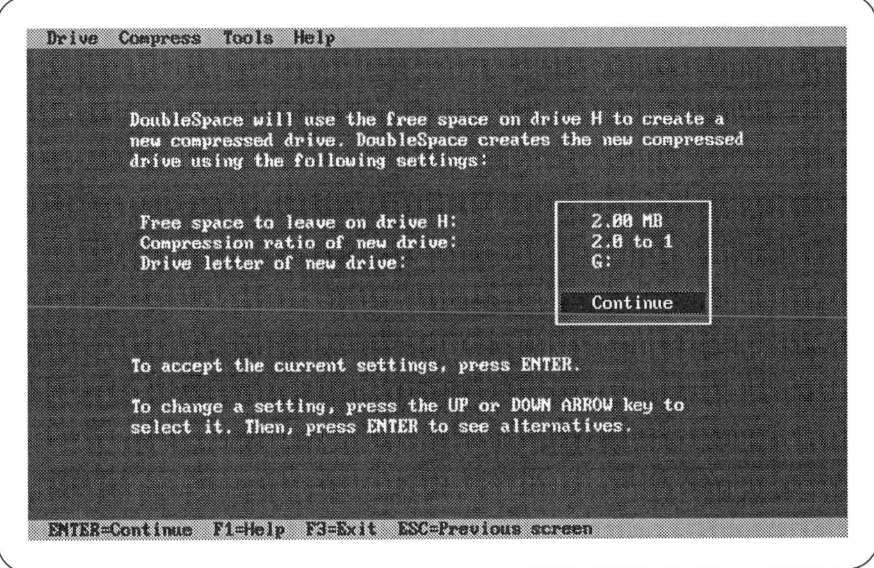

Part 4:

Before creating the new drive, DoubleSpace displays a confirmation screen. Read this screen carefully, then press C to create the new drive, or press the Esc key to change the compression settings.

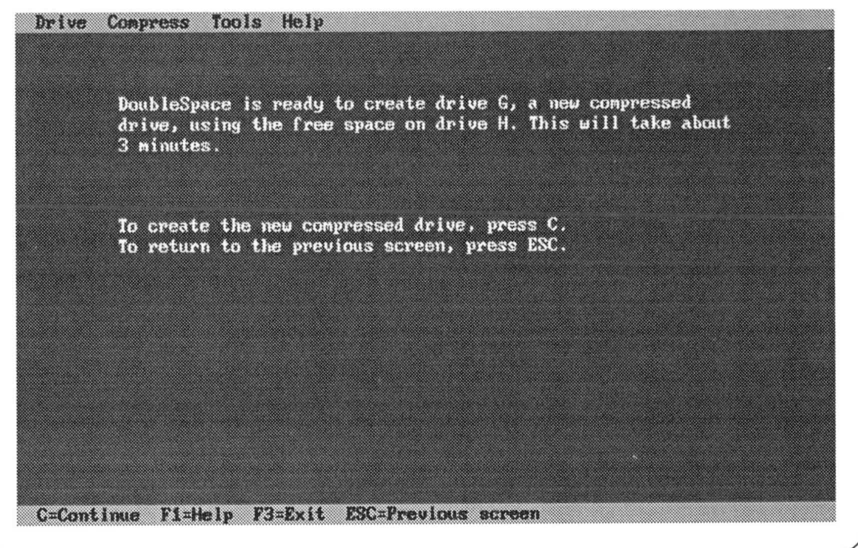

Figure 18-20 How to create an empty DoubleSpace drive (parts 3 and 4 of 5)

Part 5:

DoubleSpace displays a variety of messages as it creates the new drive. When it's done, it displays the free space and total space values for the new drive.

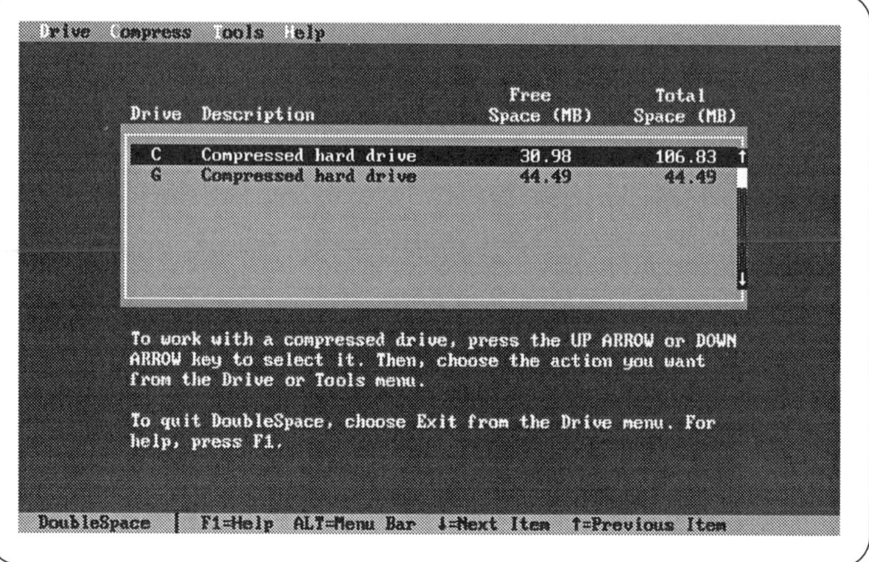

Figure 18-20 How to create an empty DoubleSpace drive (part 5 of 5)

DoubleSpace estimates that you can create a 49MB compressed drive if you use all of it. Since there's only one available host drive, you can continue simply by pressing the Enter key. If DoubleSpace displays more than one available host drive, select it using the Up and Down arrow keys, then press the Enter key.

Next, DoubleSpace displays the compression settings screen shown in part 3 of figure 18-20. The Free-space setting specifies how much free space to leave on the host drive. In most cases, you should accept the setting suggested by DoubleSpace. However, if you know you want to store additional uncompressed files on the host, or if you want to create a third compressed drive on the same host, you can increase this value. The Compression-ratio setting specifies the compression ratio DoubleSpace will use to estimate the capacity and amount of free space for the drive. The default value for this setting, 2.0, is usually adequate.

The drive-letter setting indicates the drive letter you'll use to access data stored on the new compressed drive. Following the rules presented in figure 18-7 for assigning drive letters, DoubleSpace suggests drive letter G. Although you can change this setting if you want to, I'll leave it at G for this example. In a few moments, I'll show you how to change the drive letter for an existing compressed drive.

To change one of these settings, use the Up and Down arrow keys to highlight the setting, then type a new value. To continue, highlight the word "Continue" and press the Enter key. Then, DoubleSpace displays the confirmation screen shown in part 4 of figure 18-20. After you read this screen carefully to make sure DoubleSpace is going to do what you thought it would do, press C to create the new drive. Or, if you want to change the settings, you can press the Esc key to redisplay the settings screen.

Because there's no data to compress, it shouldn't take more than a few minutes to create an empty compressed drive. As DoubleSpace creates the drive, it displays a variety of status messages that inform you of its progress. When it finishes, it redisplays the drive list as shown in part 5 of figure 18-20. Here, you can see that the new drive G has been created with a total capacity of 44.49MB, all of which is free space.

How to compress an existing drive If your PC has more than one hard drive, you can use the Compress menu's Existing-drive function to create a compressed drive on each of your additional hard drives. You can use this function only once on each drive; once you've created a compressed drive, you use the Create-new-drive function to create additional drives on the same host.

Figure 18-21 shows an example of compressing an existing drive. This example was created on a system configured like figure 18-20, with two hard drives. When I installed DoubleSpace, Express-setup compressed all the files on drive C, using drive I as the host. In figure 18-21, I'll compress the files on drive D.

When you select the Existing-drive function from the Compress menu, DoubleSpace displays a list of all the drives that aren't compressed. For this example, only one drive is eligible: drive D. It currently has 41MB of free space, and DoubleSpace estimates that the compressed drive D will have 91MB of free space.

When you press the Enter key to compress an existing drive, DoubleSpace displays the settings screen shown in part 2 of figure 18-21. Here, you can specify the amount of free space to leave on the host drive and the drive letter to use for the host. In most cases, you'll accept DoubleSpace's suggestions for both of these settings. Notice that there's no setting for the compression ratio. If you want to change the compression ratio from the default, you'll have to use the Drive menu's Change-ratio function after you compress the drive.

After you confirm the settings, DoubleSpace displays a confirmation screen like the one shown in part 3 of figure 18-21. Again, you should read this screen carefully to make sure you understand what DoubleSpace is going to do. Then, press C to compress the drive. DoubleSpace then runs Chkdsk, compresses your files, defragments the drive, and resizes the compressed drive. When it's finished, it displays the status screen shown in part 4 of figure 18-21. Then, when you press the Enter key, DoubleSpace reboots your PC so you can access the new compressed drive.

How to change DoubleSpace drive assignments Earlier, I mentioned that you can override DoubleSpace's drive assignment when you create a new empty compressed drive. For example, in part 3 of figure 18-20, DoubleSpace suggested drive G to use for a new compressed drive. If you know you want to use a different

Part 1:

To compress an existing drive, select the Existing-drive function from the Compress menu. Then, DoubleSpace displays the current free space for the drive and the projected free space for the drive after it's compressed. Press the Enter key to compress the drive.

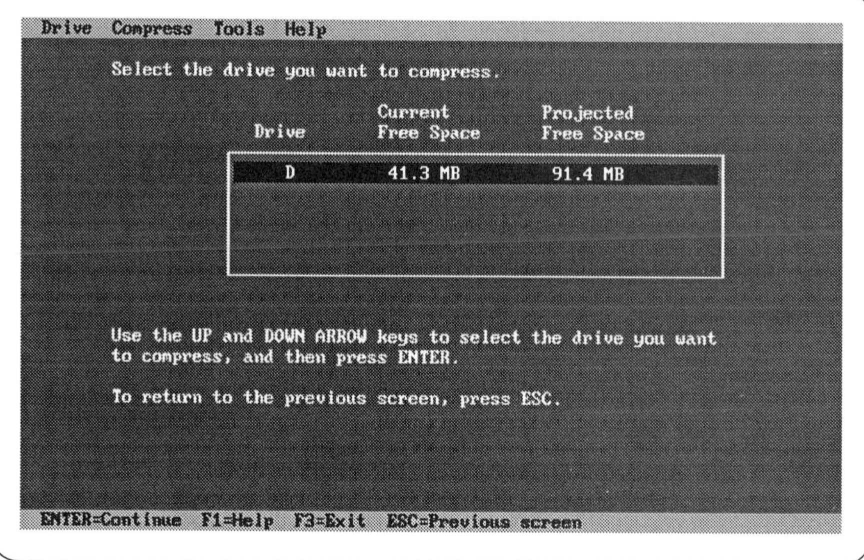

Part 2:

DoubleSpace displays its default settings for free space and drive letter. Change these values if you want to, then highlight Continue and press the Enter key to continue.

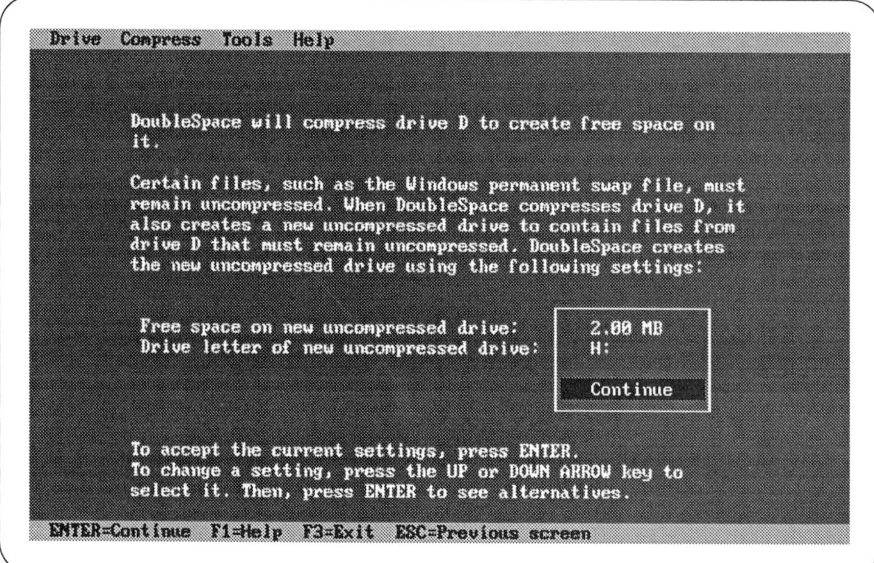

Figure 18-21 How to compress an existing drive (parts 1 and 2 of 4)

Part 3:

Before compressing the drive, DoubleSpace displays a confirmation screen. Read this screen carefully, then press C to compress the drive, or press the Escape key to change the compression settings.

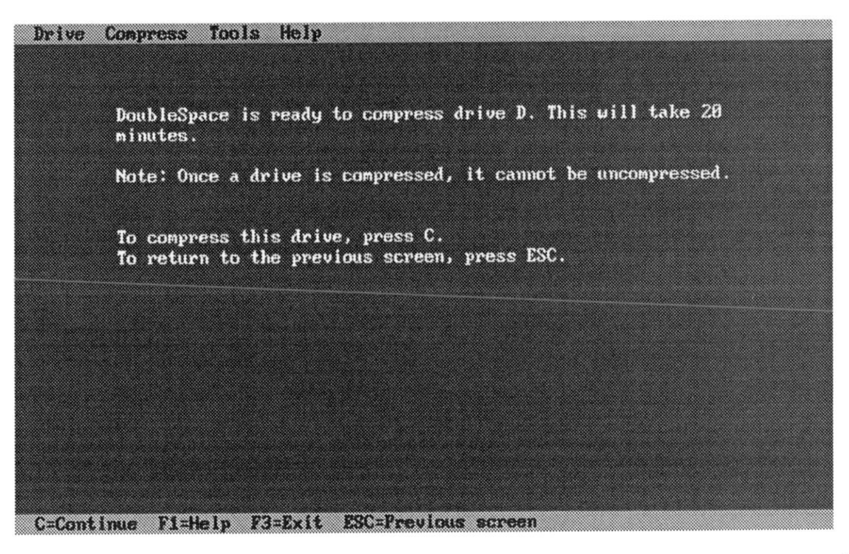
Drive Compress Tools Help
DoubleSpace is ready to compress drive D. This will take 20 minutes.
Note: Once a drive is compressed, it cannot be uncompressed.
To compress this drive, press C.
To return to the previous screen, press ESC.
C=Continue F1=Help F3=Exit ESC=Previous screen

Part 4:

When DoubleSpace finishes compressing the drive, it displays information on the drive. To exit from DoubleSpace and restart you system so you can access the compressed drive, press the Enter key.

```
DoubleSpace has finished compressing drive D.

    Free space before compression:   41.3 MB
    Free space after compression:    82.9 MB
    Compression ratio:              1.7 to 1
    Total time to compress:         14 minutes.

DoubleSpace has created a new drive K that contains 2.0 MB
of uncompressed space. This space has been set aside for
files that must remain uncompressed.

To exit from DoubleSpace and restart your computer, press
ENTER.

ENTER=Continue  F1=Help
```

Figure 18-21 How to compress an existing drive (parts 3 and 4 of 4)

```
C:\>dblspace /unmount g:
DoubleSpace has unmounted drive G.

C:\>dblspace /mount=001 h: /new=d:
DoubleSpace is mounting drive D.
DoubleSpace has mounted drive D.

C:\>dblspace /list
Drive  Type                       Total Free  Total Size  CVF Filename
-----  -------------------------  ----------  ----------- ----------------
  A    Floppy drive                  0.05 MB     1.39 MB
  C    Compressed hard drive        30.98 MB   106.83 MB  H:\DBLSPACE.000
  D    Compressed hard drive        44.49 MB    44.49 MB  H:\DBLSPACE.001
  E    Available for DoubleSpace
  F    Available for DoubleSpace
  G    Available for DoubleSpace
  H    Local hard drive              2.38 MB    80.05 MB

C:\>
```

Figure 18-22 How to change DoubleSpace's drive assignments by unmounting and then remounting a drive

drive letter before you create the drive, you can change it here. If you decide later to change the drive letter, you have to use two DBLSPACE commands in sequence: one with the /UNMOUNT switch, the other with the /MOUNT switch and a new drive letter. (Although the DoubleSpace Drive menu includes unmount and mount functions, they don't let you specify a different drive letter. So to change the drive letter assigned to a compressed volume, you must use the command line switches instead.)

To illustrate, figure 18-22 shows a sequence of DBLSPACE commands that changes the drive letter assigned to a compressed drive from G to D. The first command is this:

```
C:\>dblspace /unmount g:
```

This command tells DoubleSpace to *unmount* drive G, which makes it temporarily inaccessible.

The next command,

```
C:\>dblspace /mount=001 h: /new=d:
```

mounts the compressed drive, this time assigning it drive letter D. Here, the /MOUNT=001 switch specifies which Compressed Volume File to mount. The 001

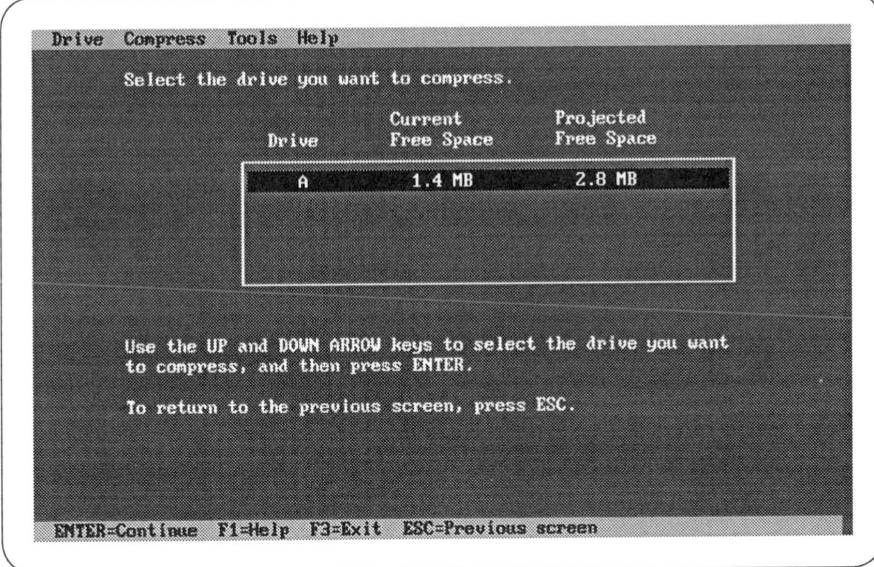

Figure 18-23 How to create a compressed diskette

corresponds to the extension in the CVF file name DBLSPACE.001. Next, the drive letter (H:) tells DoubleSpace which drive contains the CVF to be mounted. Finally, the /NEW=D: switch tells DoubleSpace to assign drive D to the compressed drive being mounted.

I included the third command in figure 18-22 (DBLSPACE /LIST) only so you can verify the effect of the /UNMOUNT and /MOUNT switches. You can see that drive D has been assigned to the second compressed drive hosted on drive H, and drive G is not assigned.

How to use compressed diskettes

DoubleSpace can not only increase the capacity of a hard disk, but it can increase the capacity of diskettes as well. Thus, you can store 2.5MB or more of data on a 1.44MB diskette. Unfortunately, there are some restrictions, as I'll explain in a moment.

To create a compressed diskette, first insert a formatted diskette in the diskette drive. Then, start DoubleSpace and select Existing-drive from the Compress menu. As figure 18-23 shows, DoubleSpace lists the diskette drive as a possible host drive for the compressed drive. Press the Enter key to create the compressed drive. If the diskette is empty, this will only take a moment. If the diskette has data on it, you'll have to wait while DoubleSpace compresses it.

```
C:\>type a:readthis.txt
This disk has been compressed by MS-DOS 6 DoubleSpace.

To make this disk's contents accessible, change to this drive and then type
   DBLSPACE/MOUNT
at the command prompt.

C:\>
```

Figure 18-24 The contents of the READTHIS.TXT file on a compressed diskette

When DoubleSpace compresses a diskette, it adds a file named READTHIS.TXT to the host diskette's root directory. This file contains the message shown in figure 18-24. It's added to the diskette so you can easily tell which diskettes you've compressed.

Notice that the READTHIS.TXT file indicates that you must use a DBLSPACE /MOUNT command to access the compressed data. Just as when you compress data on a hard disk, DoubleSpace automatically mounts a compressed diskette drive when you create it. So if you immediately exit from DoubleSpace, you can access the compressed diskette drive as drive A. However, DoubleSpace doesn't automatically mount compressed diskette drives when you start your PC like it mounts compressed hard drives. But it does keep track of which diskette is in the drive, and automatically unmounts the compressed drive if you remove the diskette or replace it with another diskette. As a result, to access a diskette in drive A you've previously compressed, you must first type this command:

```
C:\>dblspace /mount
```

If the diskette is in the B drive, use the command,

```
C:\>dblspace /mount b:
```

Figure 18-25 shows two batch files you might want to create if you plan on using compressed diskettes regularly. (If you don't understand how these batch files work, don't worry. I'll show you how to use the new commands and techniques they present in chapter 27.) The first, COMPRESS.BAT, compresses a diskette. To use it to compress a diskette in drive A, type

```
C:\>compress
```

To compress a diskette in drive B, type

```
C:\>compress b:
```

The COMPRESS.BAT batch file

```
echo off
if "%1" == "" if exist a:readthis.txt goto error
if not "%1" == "" if exist %1readthis.txt goto error
dblspace /compress %1
goto end
:error
echo The diskette in drive %1 is already compressed!
:end
```

The MOUNT.BAT batch file

```
echo off
if "%1" == "" if exist a:readthis.txt goto mount
if exist %1readthis.txt goto mount
echo The diskette in drive %1 is not compressed!
goto end
:mount
dblspace /mount %1
:end
```

Figure 18-25 Two batch files for working with compressed diskettes

COMPRESS.BAT first checks to make sure the diskette isn't already compressed by looking for the READTHIS.TXT file. Then, it issues a DBLSPACE /COMPRESS command to compress the diskette.

The second batch file in figure 18-25 mounts a compressed diskette. To use this batch file to mount a diskette in drive A, type

```
C:\>mount
```

To mount a diskette in drive B, type

```
C:\>mount b:
```

Like COMPRESS.BAT, MOUNT.BAT first checks to see if the diskette is compressed by looking for the READTHIS.TXT file. Then, it issues a DBLSPACE /MOUNT command to mount the diskette.

I mentioned earlier that there are restrictions on how you can use compressed diskettes. The first one is obvious: any data you store in a compressed diskette can be accessed only by a PC running DOS 6.0. So you can't use a compressed diskette to share data with a PC that's using an earlier DOS version.

The second restriction applies only to *Windows* users. Because you can't run DoubleSpace from within windows, you must mount any compressed diskette you want to access *before* you start *Windows*. So if you're in *Windows* and realize that you

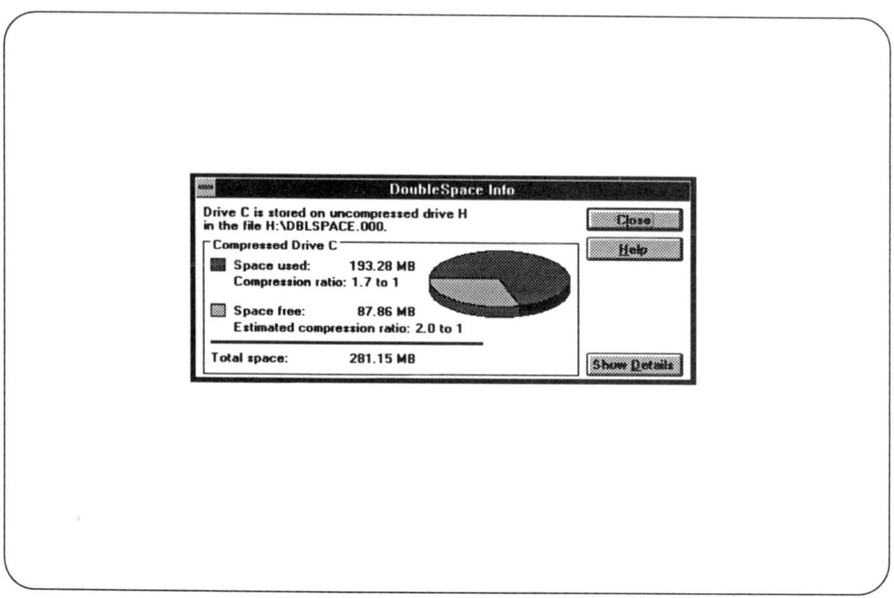

Figure 18-26 The *Windows* DoubleSpace-info dialog box

want to access a compressed diskette that's not mounted, you must end your *Windows* session, mount the diskette, and restart *Windows*. Then, if you want to access a different compressed diskette, you must quit *Windows* again. Unfortunately, this restriction is severe enough that if you're a *Windows* user, you probably won't use compressed diskettes much.

DoubleSpace and *Windows*

Although you can't run the DoubleSpace program from within *Windows,* you can display information about your compressed drives from *Windows*. To do that, you first select the compressed drive you want to display from the File Manager. Then, you select the DoubleSpace-info option from the Tools menu. When you do, *Windows* displays the dialog box shown in figure 18-26. Here, *Windows* displays basic information about the compressed drive: how much space is used, how much space is free, the total size of the compressed volume, the compression ratios for the existing files, and the estimated compression ratio used to calculate the free space. The pie chart lets you quickly see how full the compressed drive is.

If you select one or more files in File Manager before you invoke DoubleSpace-info, you can click the Show-details button to display the actual compression ratio for the selected files. This information is the same as the information displayed by the Dir command's /C switch.

Unfortunately, the DoubleSpace-info dialog is the only *Windows* support provided by DoubleSpace. To perform any other DoubleSpace function, you must first exit from *Windows*.

Some perspective on DoubleSpace

I realize that this chapter has presented a lot of new ideas, and that you may be overwhelmed by the many details involved with setting up and using DoubleSpace. If so, I suggest you start by running DoubleSpace's Express-setup to compress your C drive. Then, use it for awhile without worrying about DoubleSpace's other features. After you've gained some experience and confidence with DoubleSpace, you can learn how to create additional DoubleSpace drives or use compressed diskettes if you want to.

As you may know, several commercial utility programs provide disk compression that's similar to DoubleSpace. The best known of these programs are Stacker by Stac Electronics and *SuperStor* by AddStor, Inc. Would you be better off using one of these programs rather than DoubleSpace? Probably not. These programs may achieve slightly better compression ratios and slightly better performance than DoubleSpace, but because DoubleSpace is an integral part of DOS, it's easier to install and manage than commercial alternatives. So if you're considering purchasing one of these utilities, I suggest you upgrade to DOS 6.0 and use DoubleSpace instead. If you already have one of these utilities and you're upgrading to DOS 6.0 for other reasons, you might consider converting to DoubleSpace.

Terms

Lempel-Ziv algorithm
token
compression ratio
Compressed Volume File
shrinking a drive
fragmented file
defragment
CVF
host drive
upper memory area
growing a drive
unmount
mount

Objectives

1. Explain how DoubleSpace compresses data.
2. Explain how DoubleSpace implements a compressed drive.
3. List the three rules DoubleSpace follows when it assigns drive letters.
4. Use DoubleSpace Express-setup to compress your C drive.

5. Use the DoubleSpace menus or command line options to perform the following tasks:

   a. Display information about a compressed drive
   b. Change the size of a compressed drive
   c. Change a drive's estimated compression ratio
   d. Create an empty compressed drive
   e. Compress an existing drive
   f. Compress a diskette

Chapter 19

Microsoft Defrag

As you use your PC to create and delete files, a condition know as *fragmentation* is likely to occur. Fragmentation occurs when the clusters allocated to a file aren't adjacent to one another. This can happen when you create a new file or when you add records to a file. When you create a file, DOS uses the first available disk space it finds. If this space isn't large enough for the entire file, DOS stores as much of the file as it can in that space, then looks for the next available space. DOS continues in this way until the entire file is stored on disk. When you add records to a file, DOS tries to store the new records in the space that's already allocated to the file. If the records don't fit, DOS looks for the next available disk space.

Fragmentation can slow down the performance of a hard drive. If, for example, a file is divided into three fragments, the read/write heads have to move to three different disk locations to retrieve the file. If the file isn't fragmented, the read/write heads have to move only once. When many of the files on a drive are heavily fragmented, the decrease in speed can be noticeable.

Fragmentation can also contribute to other disk problems. For example, if a drive's File Allocation Table is damaged, resulting in lost clusters or cross-linked files, the problem is more difficult to correct if the drive is heavily fragmented. Fragmentation also reduces the chances of successfully undeleting a file.

Before DOS 6.0, the only way to restore a hard drive to an unfragmented condition was to do a complete backup of your hard drive, reformat the hard drive, then do a complete restore. Alternatively, you could purchase a commercial disk utility such as *PC Tools* by Central Point Software or *The Norton Utilities* by Symantec. Both of these utility packages include programs that can *defragment* a drive in place. Now, you can defragment a drive using *Microsoft Defrag*, a utility program that comes with DOS 6.0. (Microsoft Defrag is actually a subset of the *Speed Disk* program that comes with *The Norton Utilities*.)

What Microsoft Defrag does

Microsoft Defrag (which I'll refer to from now on simply as Defrag) restores your drive to an unfragmented state. It can use one of two *optimization methods* to do this. The first method, called *Full-optimization*, rearranges all the files on your drive so that none of them are fragmented. In addition, it moves all the files to the front of the drive so that all the free space is together at the back of the drive. The second method, called *Unfragment-files-only*, defragments your files but doesn't move them to the front of the drive. As a result, this method leaves free space intermixed with your files. As you might guess, the Unfragment-files-only method is faster then the Full-optimization method.

Defrag also lets you sort your files as it defragments them. Although various sort options are available, you'll probably want to sort them into alphabetical order by file name. Then, when you list them with the Dir command, you can find particular files more easily. Of course when you add files, the new files won't be in the order you specified when you defragmented the drive. For that reason, you may not want to sort your files using Defrag. Instead, you can use the /O switch on the Dir command to display files in the order you want.

How to defragment your files

To defragment your files, run Defrag by entering this command at the DOS prompt (*Windows* must not be currently running):

```
C:\>defrag
```

When you do, Defrag displays the drive selection screen shown in part 1 of figure 19-1. Here, you select the drive you want to defragment.

When you select the drive, Defrag analyzes it to determine the degree of fragmentation, then displays a dialog box like the one in part 2 of figure 19-1. Here, Defrag notes that 99 percent of my C drive is not fragmented, so it recommends the Unfragment-files-only method. If the drive is severely fragmented, Defrag will recommend the Full-optimization method. You have two options at this point: (1) you can select Optimize to defragment the drive using the recommended method, or (2) you can select Configure to activate the Optimize menu. The Optimize menu lets you change the Defrag options, including the optimization method, or exit from the program. I'll show you this menu in a minute. You can also press the Esc key from the dialog box in part 2 of figure 19-1 to activate the Optimize menu.

If you select Optimize, Defrag begins defragmenting the drive. As it executes, it displays a map like the one in part 3 of figure 19-1. This map indicates which portions of the drive are occupied by files and which portions contain free space. (The legend near the bottom right of the screen summarizes the symbols used in this map.) As Defrag works, it updates the map so you can see which portions of the drive are being relocated. In addition, the status bar near the bottom left of the screen indicates Defrag's progress.

Part 1:

When you enter the Defrag command at the DOS prompt, Defrag displays its drive selection screen. To select a drive, highlight it, then press the Enter key.

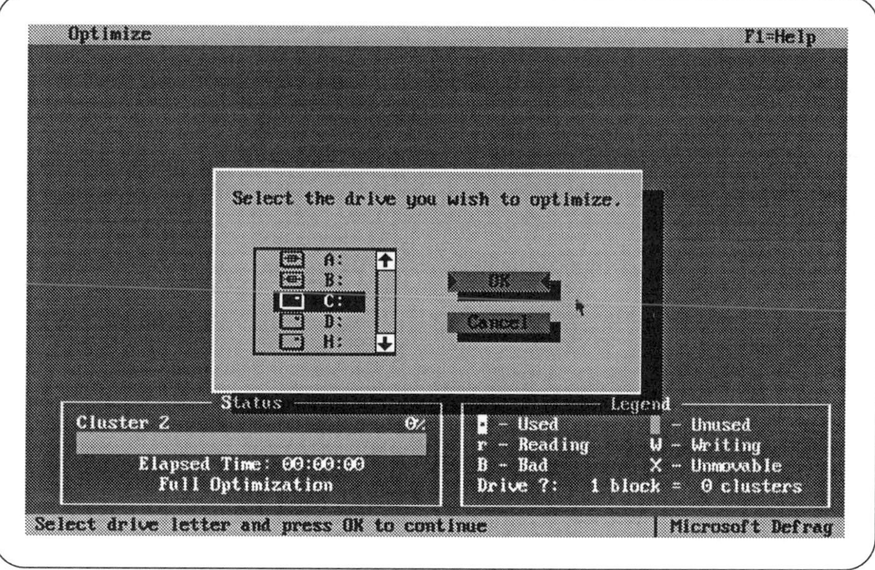

Part 2:

Defrag analyzes the drive you selected, then recommends an optimization method. Select Optimize to accept Defrag's recommendation and defragment the drive, or select Configure to specify Defrag options.

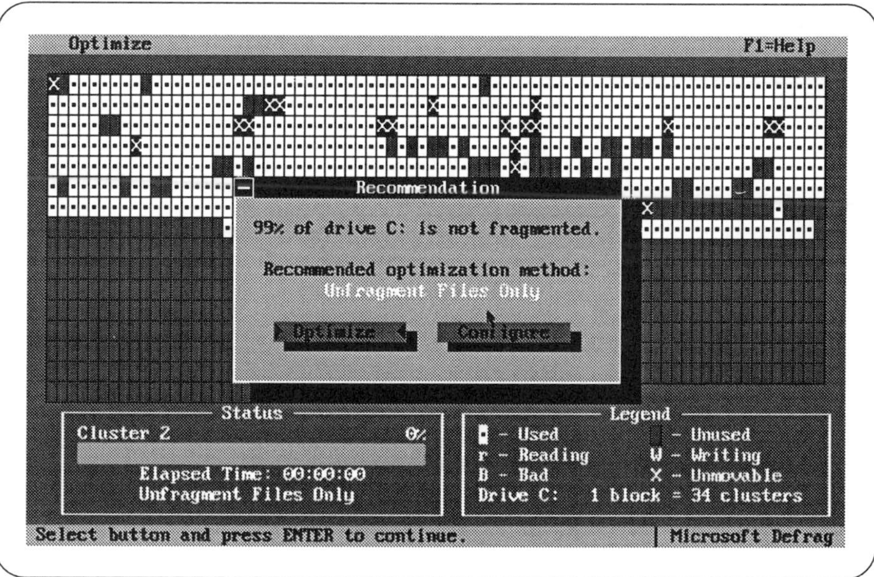

Figure 19-1 How to use Defrag to defragment a drive (parts 1 and 2 of 3)

Part 3:

As Defrag executes, it displays a map that shows the layout of the files on the drive. This map is updated as Defrag relocates the files.

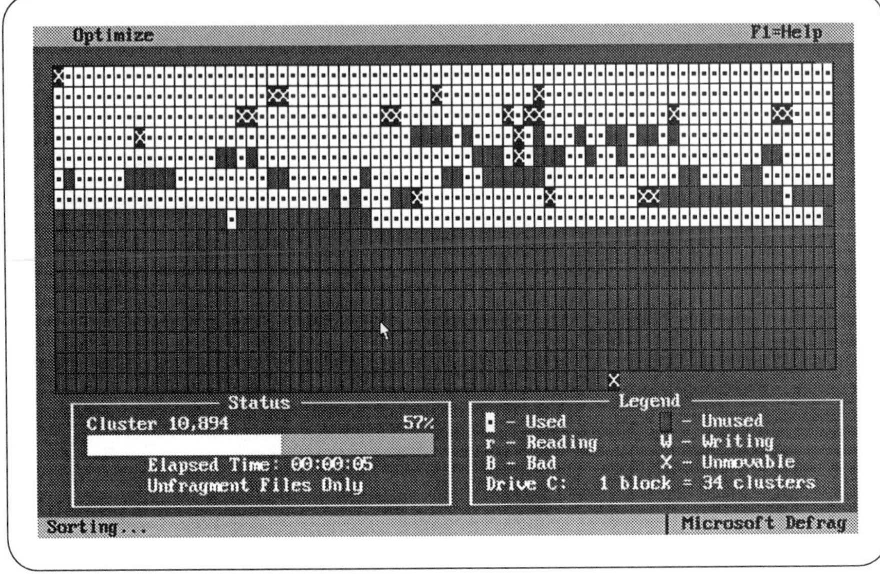

Figure 19-1 How to use Defrag to defragment a drive (part 3 of 3)

How to use Defrag menu options

The only menu that's available from Defrag is the Optimize menu, shown in figure 19-2. Although the Optimize menu option is displayed on all the Defrag screens, you can activate it only by selecting Configure from the recommendation display shown in part 2 of figure 19-1. From this menu, you can begin defragmenting the drive by selecting the Begin-optimization function, or you can change the drive to defragment by selecting the Drive function. You've already seen these functions, so I'll focus on the next three Optimize menu functions.

If you select the Optimization-method function, Defrag displays the screen shown in figure 19-3. Here, you select one of Defrag's optimization methods: Full-optimization or Unfragment-files-only. You use this screen to change the optimization method Defrag recommends after it initially analyzes your drive.

If you select the File-sort function, Defrag displays the screen shown in figure 19-4. Here, you can tell Defrag to sort your files by file name, extension, date and time, or size. In addition, you can specify ascending or descending sort order. So if you want your files sorted alphabetically by name, select Name and Ascending. To sort your files by size so that the largest files appear first, select Size and Descending.

The Optimize menu

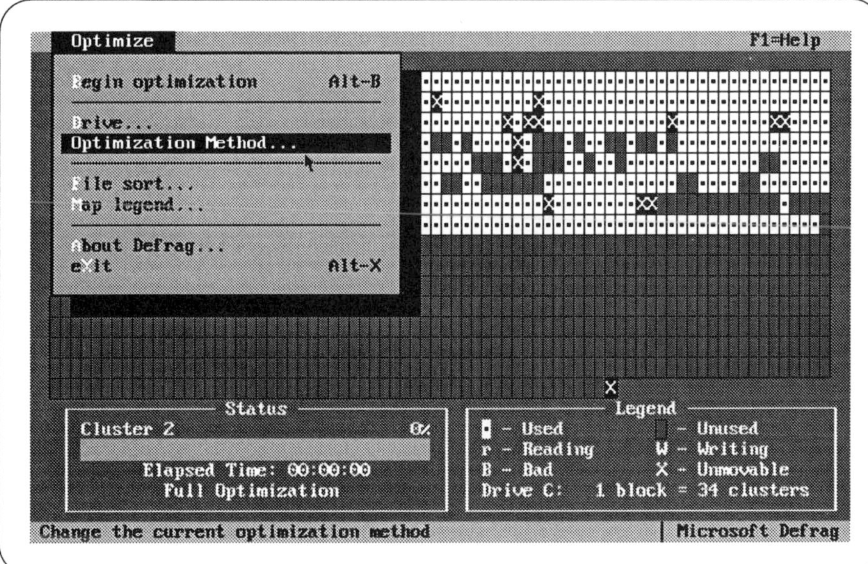

Menu item	**Description**
Begin optimization	Defragments the specified drive.
Drive	Changes the drive to defragment.
Optimization Method	Changes the method Defrag will use to defragment the drive.
File sort	Specifies the order in which Defrag will sort the files on the drive as it defragments them.
Map legend	Displays a description of the symbols Defrag uses in the map it displays as it defragments a drive.
About Defrag	Displays information about Defrag.
Exit	Returns you to the DOS prompt.

Figure 19-2 Optimize menu functions

Figure 19-3 How to select the optimization method

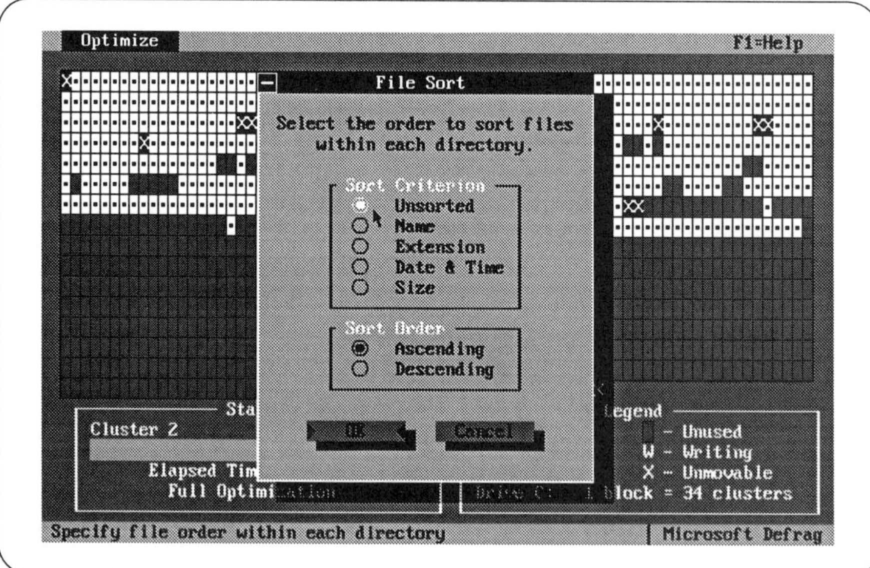

Figure 19-4 How to specify a sort order

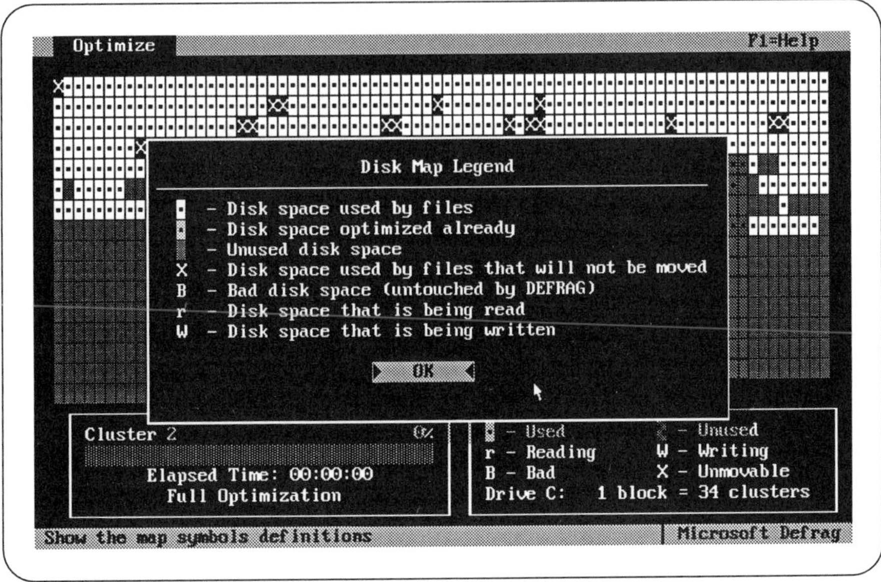

Figure 19-5 The disk map legend

As I mentioned earlier, the legend near the bottom right of the screen summarizes the symbols used in the map Defrag displays as it executes. If you want a more complete description of these symbols, you can select the Map-legend function from the Optimize menu. Then, Defrag displays the legend shown in figure 19-5.

How to use Defrag command line options

Figure 19-6 shows the command line options you can use with the Defrag command. If you specify both a drive and an optimization method on the command line, Defrag will begin defragmenting the drive immediately, bypassing the first two screens shown in figure 19-1. As a result, these switches are most useful if you want to run Defrag from a batch file.

Defrag and *DoubleSpace* drives

If you've used *DoubleSpace* to compress the data on your hard drive, you might be confused about the difference between the Defrag command and the Defrag function provided by DoubleSpace. Although they perform similar functions, there's a critical difference between the two. The DOS Defrag command defragments files by reorganizing the File Allocation Table, which keeps track of how clusters are allocated to files. In contrast, the DoubleSpace Defrag function defragments a

The format of the Defrag command

```
DEFRAG [drive:] [switches]
```

Switch meanings

/F	Defragments the drive using the Full-optimization method.
/U	Defragments the drive using the Unfragment-files-only method.
/S:order	Sorts files using the specified order. For *order* you can specify:

N	Ascending sort order by name
-N	Descending sort order by name
E	Ascending sort order by extension
-E	Descending sort order by extension
D	Ascending sort order by date
-D	Descending sort order by date
S	Ascending sort order by size
-S	Descending sort order by size

The /S switch is valid only if the /U switch is also specified. The colon preceding *order* is optional.

/B	Reboots the computer when the drive is defragmented.
/LCD	Uses an LCD color scheme for portable computers.
/BW	Uses a black and white color scheme for monochrome monitors.
/G0	Does not use graphics characters or a simulated graphics mouse cursor.

Example 1: A Defrag command that defragments the C drive using the Unfragment-files-only method.

```
defrag c: /u
```

Example 2: A Defrag command that defragments the C drive using the Full-optimization method.

```
defrag c: /f
```

Example 3: A Defrag command that defragments the C drive using the Full-optimization method and sorts files into name sequence.

```
defrag c: /f /sn
```

Figure 19-6 The Defrag command

compressed drive by reorganizing the internal structure of the Compressed Volume File. So it doesn't affect the File Allocation Table.

When you use the DOS Defrag command to defragment a compressed drive, Defrag automatically runs the DoubleSpace Defrag function after defragmenting the File Allocation Table. As a result, you'll want to use the DOS Defrag command rather than the DoubleSpace Defrag function to defragment a compressed drive.

Some perspective on Defrag

I mentioned at the start of this chapter that Microsoft Defrag is a scaled-back version of the *Speed Disk* program that comes with *The Norton Utilities*, licensed by Microsoft from Symantec. *Speed Disk* has several features that Defrag doesn't. For example, *Speed Disk* has five optimization methods rather than Defrag's two. In addition to Full-optimization and Unfragment-files-only, *Speed Disk* provides: Full-with-DIR's-first, which does a full optimization and locates all of your directory files at the front of your drive; Full-with-File-reorder, which does a full optimization and groups files that are in the same subdirectory together; and Unfragment-free-space, which doesn't defragment your files, but moves all the free space to the end of the drive. In addition, *Speed Disk* lets you place specific files at the front of the drive. For example, you might place your program files at the front of the drive.

Other commercial utility programs, such as *PC Tools*, come with disk defragmenters that are similar to *Speed Disk*. If you already have one of these utilities, I recommend you continue using it rather than switching to Microsoft Defrag. Just remember that if you're using DoubleSpace to implement compressed drives, you need to use its Defrag function after you've used your utility to defragment the drive.

Terms

fragmentation
defragment
optimization method
Full-optimization method
Unfragment-files-only method

Objectives

1. Describe the two methods for defragmenting a drive provided by Microsoft Defrag.
2. Defragment the hard drives on your system using either of the two methods provided by Microsoft Defrag.

Chapter 20

Interlnk and Power

DOS 6.0 includes two new utility programs that are designed for users of portable computers. The first, called *Interlnk*, lets you connect two computers so you can copy files between them or access one of the computer's printers from the other computer. Interlnk is similar to commercial file transfer utilities such as Traveling Software's *LapLink Pro*. The second program, called *Power*, extends the life of your portable's battery by shutting down certain system functions when the system is idle.

Although the two computers you connect with Interlnk can both be desktop or portable computers, you'll almost certainly use Interlnk to connect a portable computer to a desktop computer. For example, you might take a portable computer with you on a sales trip, using it to record orders, take notes, and track trip expenses. When you return to the office, you can use Interlnk to copy the files from your portable computer to your desktop computer. You can also use Interlnk to copy files from the desktop computer to the portable computer. For example, you might copy a report document from your desktop computer to your portable computer so you can work on it during your trip. Once you invest the time to get Interlnk set up properly, I think you'll find it's easier to share files using Interlnk than it is to copy them from one computer to the other using diskettes.

Although it's possible to use Interlnk to connect two desktop computers, it's unlikely that you'll want to. And Power is of no use for desktop computers. So you'll probably want to read this chapter only if you own a portable computer or are considering purchasing one in the near future.

How to use Interlnk

To use Interlnk properly, you need to understand the configuration shown in figure 20-1. Here, you can see that a cable is used to connect a portable computer to a desktop computer. With Interlnk, one of these computers is called the *client*, and the other is called the *server*. In figure 20-1, you can see that the portable computer is operating as the client and the desktop computer is operating as the server. The client computer is running a program named Interlnk, while the server computer is running a program named Intersvr.

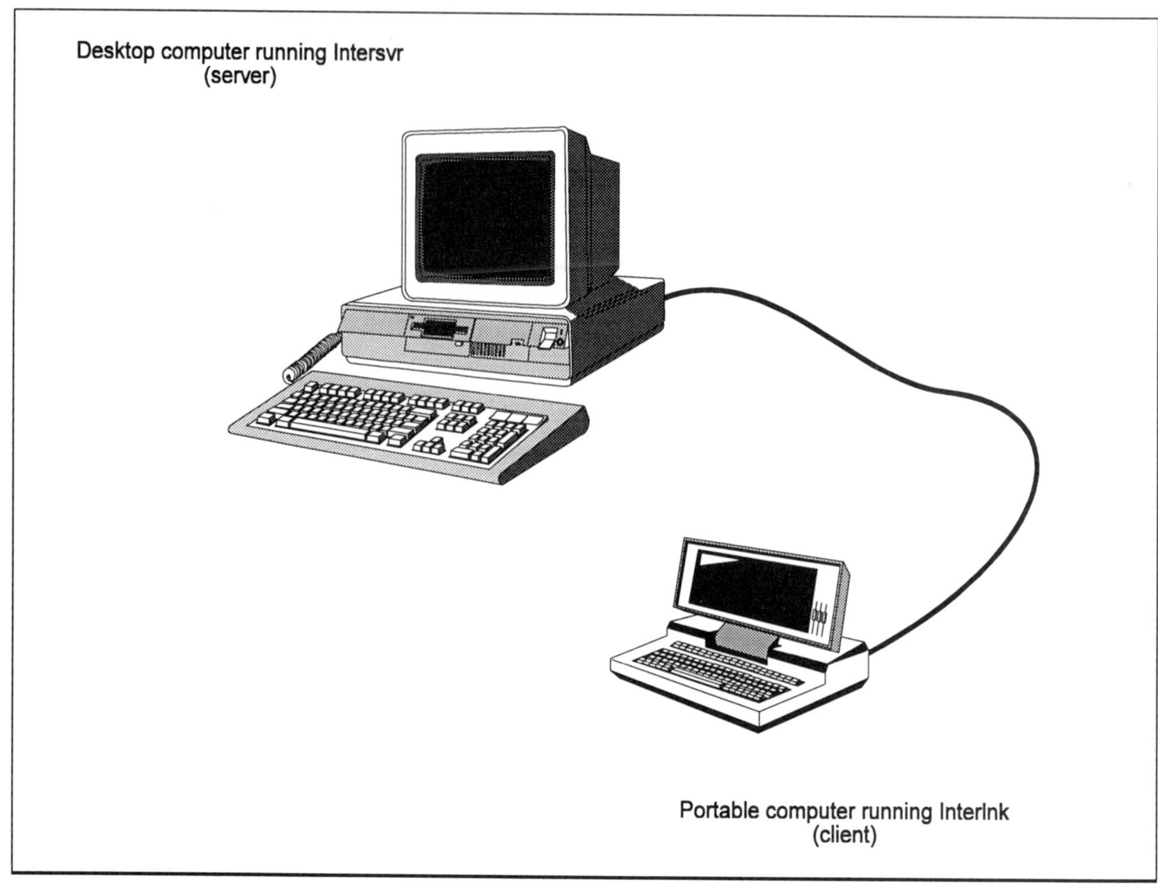

Figure 20-1 How to connect a portable computer to a desktop computer

It's important to realize that while an Interlnk session is active, you cannot use the server computer. Instead, you must work from the client computer to access the server's drives and printers. That's because the server computer is tied up running the Intersvr program. To use the server computer for other work, you must first exit the Intersvr program. That ends the Interlnk session, so the server's drives and printers are no longer available from the client. In contrast, Interlnk runs as a *memory resident program*, so it doesn't tie up the client computer.

Throughout this chapter, I'll refer to the client computer as a portable computer, and the server computer as a desktop computer. I want you to realize that although this is the most common way to use Interlnk, it's not the only way. It's possible to set up Interlnk so that the portable computer is the server and the desktop computer is the client. In that case, you would work from your desktop computer to access files on the portable. And, if you use Interlnk to connect two portable computers or to connect two desktop computers, you must designate one of the computers as the client and the other as the server.

Drives and printers on the desktop server computer	
A:	1.2MB diskette drive
B:	1.44MB diskette drive
C:	85MB hard drive
D:	85MB hard drive
LPT1:	Laser printer

Drives and printers on the portable client computer	
A:	1.44MB diskette drive
C:	80MB hard drive

Drives and printers available from the portable client computer after the Interlnk session is established	
A:	Portable's A drive (1.44MB diskette drive)
C:	Portable's C drive (80MB hard drive)
D:	Desktop's A drive (1.2MB diskette drive)
E:	Desktop's B drive (1.44MB diskette drive)
F:	Desktop's C drive (85MB hard drive)
G:	Desktop's D drive (85MB hard drive)
LPT2:	Desktop's LPT1 printer (laser printer)

Figure 20-2 How Interlnk redirects server drives and printers using available client drive letters and printer ports

As I've mentioned, once Interlnk is set up and running, you work at the portable computer to access the desktop computer's disk drives. Interlnk makes this possible by *redirecting* the desktop computer's disk drives to drive letters that aren't used on the portable computer. Similarly, Interlnk redirects printers on the desktop computer to printer port names (such as LPT1) that aren't used on the portable computer.

To illustrate, figure 20-2 shows the drive and printer ports used by a desktop computer and a portable computer. As you can see, the desktop computer has two diskette drives (A and B), two hard drives (C and D), and a printer (LPT1). The portable computer has just one diskette drive (A) and one hard drive (C). It has no printers.

To access drives on the portable and desktop computer and to access the desktop computer's printer, you use the drive and printer assignments listed in the bottom portion of figure 20-2. As you can see, each drive on the desktop computer is assigned the next available drive letter on the laptop computer. And the printer on the desktop computer is assigned the next available printer port. So, if you enter the command

```
c:\>dir f:
```

on the portable computer, DOS will display a directory listing of the desktop computer's C drive.

Example 1: How to copy all files from the portable computer's DATA directory to the LAPTOP directory on the desktop computer's C drive.

```
copy c:\data\*.* f:\laptop\*.*
```

Example 2: How to copy all *Lotus 1-2-3* files from the 123DATA directory on the desktop computer's C drive to the portable computer's DATA directory.

```
copy f:\123data\*.123 c:\data
```

Example 3: How to print a copy of the portable computer's AUTOEXEC.BAT file on the desktop computer's printer.

```
C:\>print autoexec.bat
Name of output device: LPT2
```

Figure 20-3 How to use DOS commands to access a desktop computer's disk drive and printer from a portable computer

Figure 20-3 shows a variety of commands you might use to access drives and printers on the desktop computer. The first example shows how you can use a Copy command to copy a file from the portable computer's C drive to the desktop computer's C drive. The second example shows a Copy command that does the reverse: it copies a file from the desktop computer's C drive to the portable computer's C drive. And the third example shows how you can print the contents of one of the portable computer's files on the desktop computer's printer.

Figure 20-4 shows the steps you follow to set up and use Interlnk. The hardest part of using Interlnk is figuring out how to connect your portable and desktop computers using the proper cable (step 1), copying the Interlnk files to the portable computer (step 2), and setting up the CONFIG.SYS file on the portable computer so it can load Interlnk (step 3). Fortunately, you only have to do steps 2 and 3 once. And connecting the computers together is easy enough once you've figured out which connectors to use, and you've obtained the correct cable.

How to connect your computers To use Interlnk, you must first connect your desktop and portable computers using a special cable that attaches to the computers' serial or parallel ports. Before you purchase this cable, you need to determine what types of ports are available on each computer. You can usually do that by examining the port connectors on the back of the computer. (For portable computers, the ports may be on the side rather than on the back.)

Figure 20-5 shows the types of connectors most commonly used for each type of port. As you can see, parallel ports usually use a 25-pin female connector, while serial ports use 25-pin or 9-pin male connectors. Most desktop computers have one parallel port that uses a 25-pin female connector and two serial ports: one with a 25-pin male

1. Connect your portable computer to your desktop computer using the correct cable.
2. If necessary, copy the Interlnk files to the portable computer.
3. Add a Device command for the Interlnk device driver to the portable computer's CONFIG.SYS file.
4. Start the Intersvr program on the desktop computer.
5. Reboot the portable computer.
6. Note the drive usage indicated on the portable and desktop computer monitors.

Figure 20-4 Six steps for setting up and using Interlnk

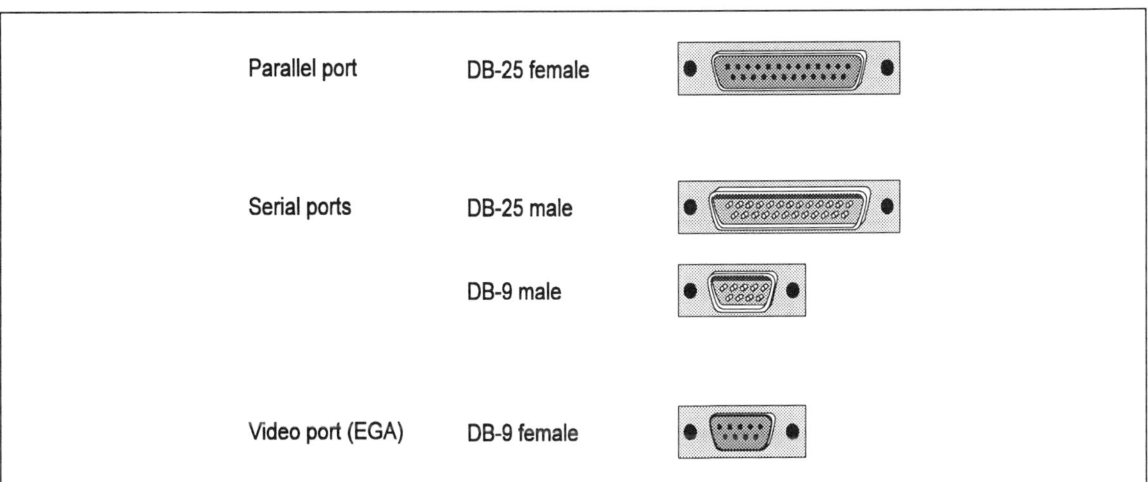

Figure 20-5 How to identify your computer's port connectors

connector, the other with a 9-pin male connector. And most portable computers have one parallel port (25-pin female connector) and one serial port with a 9-pin male connector. I included the 9-pin female connector in figure 20-5 because you need to know that this type of connector is usually used to connect an EGA monitor to its controller card. If you connect this video port to another computer's serial port, you may damage one or both computers.

To connect your computers using the serial ports, you need to purchase a *null-modem cable*. This type of cable should be available from any computer store or office supply store that stocks computer equipment. When you buy it, make sure it has the combination of 25-pin or 9-pin connectors on each end that you need to connect your computers. For example, to connect a 25-pin serial port to a 9-pin serial port, you need a null-modem cable with a 25-pin female connector on one end and a 9-pin female connector on the other. The most flexible type of null-modem cable has both types of connectors on both ends.

To connect your computers using the parallel ports, you need to purchase a *bi-directional parallel cable*. These cables are more difficult to find than null-modem cables, but a knowledgeable computer dealer should be able to get one for you.

The easiest way to connect computers for Interlnk is to use the serial ports. That's not only because a null-modem cable is easier to find than a bi-directional parallel cable, but also because most desktop computers have at least one of their two serial ports free. In contrast, most desktop computers have only one parallel port, and there's usually a printer attached to it. On the other hand, Interlnk works between two and four times faster when you use parallel ports rather than serial ports. So, if you plan on using Interlnk frequently, it may be worth the extra effort to set up Interlnk so it works over parallel ports.

If your desktop computer's parallel port is used by a printer, there are three ways you can use Interlnk with parallel ports. The first way is to simply unplug the printer whenever you need to use Interlnk. This is okay, but you run the risk of damaging the connectors if you do it often.

The second way is to use a switchbox, as shown in figure 20-6. A switchbox lets you switch the desktop computer's parallel port between the printer and the portable computer. Whenever you want to use Interlnk, you simply attach the free end of the bi-directional cable to the portable computer and turn the switch to connect the portable computer to the desktop computer. As you can see in the figure, you need an additional cable to use a switchbox.

The third way to use Interlnk with parallel ports is to purchase and install a second parallel port on the desktop computer. Believe it or not, a second parallel port is usually less expensive than a switchbox. The drawback is that you have to take your computer apart to install the port. If you're not technically inclined, you should have a computer technician install the port for you.

How to copy the Interlnk files to your portable computer Interlnk consists of two files: INTERLNK.EXE and INTERSVR.EXE. To use Interlnk, these files should exist on both the desktop and the portable computer. Both files are included in the DOS directory under DOS 6.0, so this isn't a problem if you've installed DOS 6.0 on both computers. However, if one of the computers uses an earlier version of DOS, you must copy the Interlnk files to it. You can do that by copying the files to a diskette, or you can use Interlnk's *remote installation* feature.

Figure 20-7 summarizes a procedure you can follow to use Interlnk's remote installation feature to copy Interlnk's files to your portable computer. First, you must connect the computers via their serial ports using a null-modem cable. Remote installation won't work using a parallel connection. Once the cable is connected, type this command at the desktop computer:

```
C:\>intersvr /rcopy
```

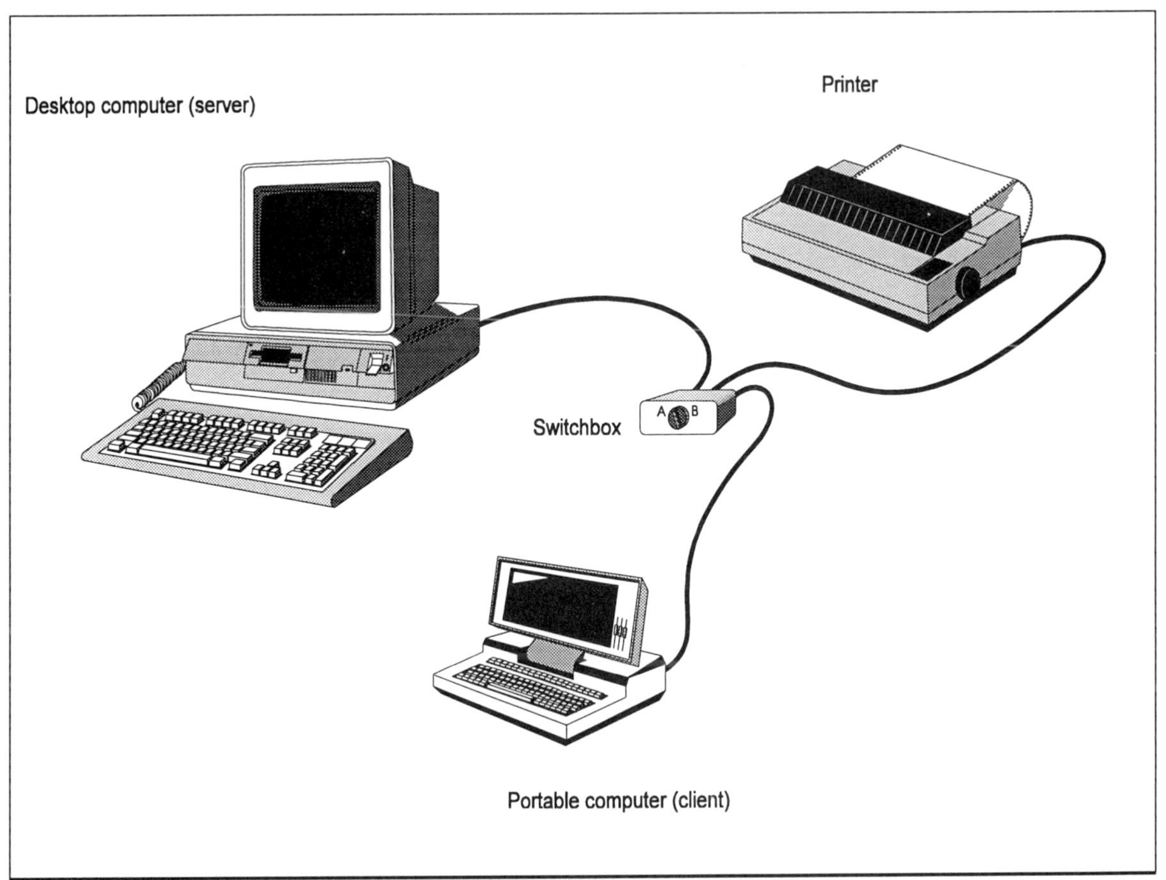

Figure 20-6 How to use a switchbox to connect a printer and a portable computer to a desktop computer's parallel port

When you do, Intersvr displays the screen shown in part 1 of figure 20-8. Here, you select the serial port you've used for the connection, then press the Enter key.

Intersvr then displays the screen shown in part 2 of figure 20-8. This screen tells you to enter two commands on the other computer's keyboard. The first command, Mode, sets up the proper communication parameters for the other computer's serial port. The second command, Ctty, redirects the other computer's command input so that it receives commands from the serial port. Once you've typed these commands, Intersvr begins sending commands to the other computer that cause it to copy the Interlnk files over the serial port. While it works, you'll see the screen shown in part 3 of figure 20-8.

1. Connect the computers via their serial ports using a null-modem cable.
2. At the desktop computer, type the following command:

   ```
   C:\>intersvr /rcopy
   ```

   Follow the instructions on the screen.
3. When the remote installation is complete, verify that the files were copied by typing this command on the portable computer:

   ```
   C:\>dir inter*.*
   ```

   You should see directory entries for two files: INTERLNK.EXE and INTERSVR.EXE.
4. Copy the Interlnk files to your DOS directory using this command at the portable computer:

   ```
   C:\>copy inter*.* \dos
   ```

5. Delete the Interlnk files from your root directory using this command at the portable computer:

   ```
   C:\>del inter*.*
   ```

Figure 20-7 A procedure for using Interlnk's remote installation feature

Figure 20-9 shows what the screen on your portable computer will look like after the remote installation is finished. Here, you can see the Mode and Ctty commands I entered to begin the remote installation. The messages after the Ctty command were displayed by the remote installation procedure as the files were copied.

The remaining steps in figure 20-7 verify that the remote installation was successful and move the files from the root directory to the DOS directory. I recommend you do this simply because it's best to keep as few files as possible in your root directory.

How to set up your portable computer's CONFIG.SYS file To set up your portable computer so that it works as the Interlnk client, you must add a Device command to it's CONFIG.SYS file. This Device command loads the Interlnk *device driver*, INTERLNK.EXE, into memory when you boot your portable computer.

Figure 20-10 shows the format of the Device command for loading Interlnk along with an explanation of the switches you can use with it. And figure 20-11 shows a typical CONFIG.SYS file with a Device command that loads the INTERLNK.EXE device driver. In this example, the only switch I specified for Interlnk is /AUTO. When you use this switch, Interlnk checks to see if a session can be established with the other computer. To establish a session, the cable must be properly connected to both computers, and the Intersvr program must be running on the other computer. (I'll show you how to start the Intersvr program in a moment.) If a session can't be established, Interlnk removes itself from memory.

Part 1:

When you enter INTERSVR /RCOPY, Intersvr displays the opening screen for its remote installation feature. To continue, highlight the correct port and press the Enter key.

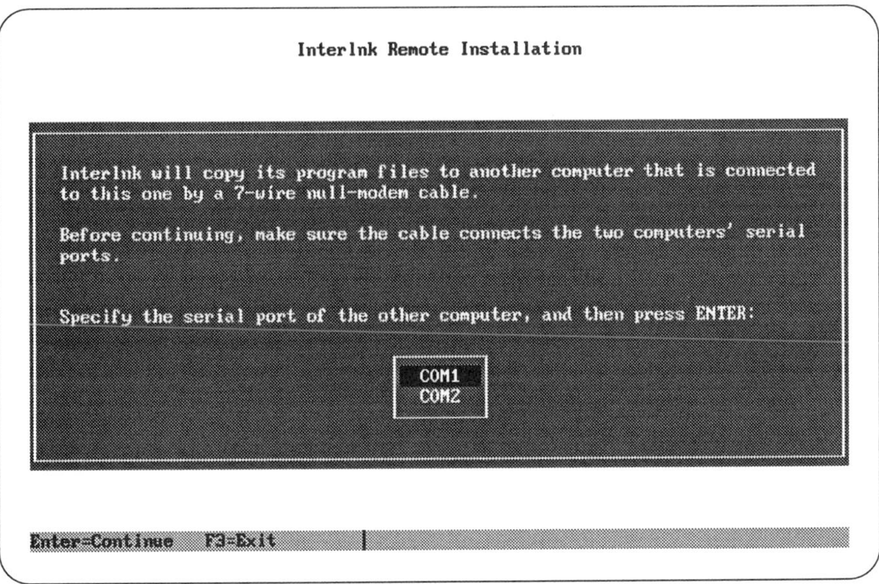

Part 2:

Intersvr instructs you to enter two commands on the other computer: Mode and Ctty.

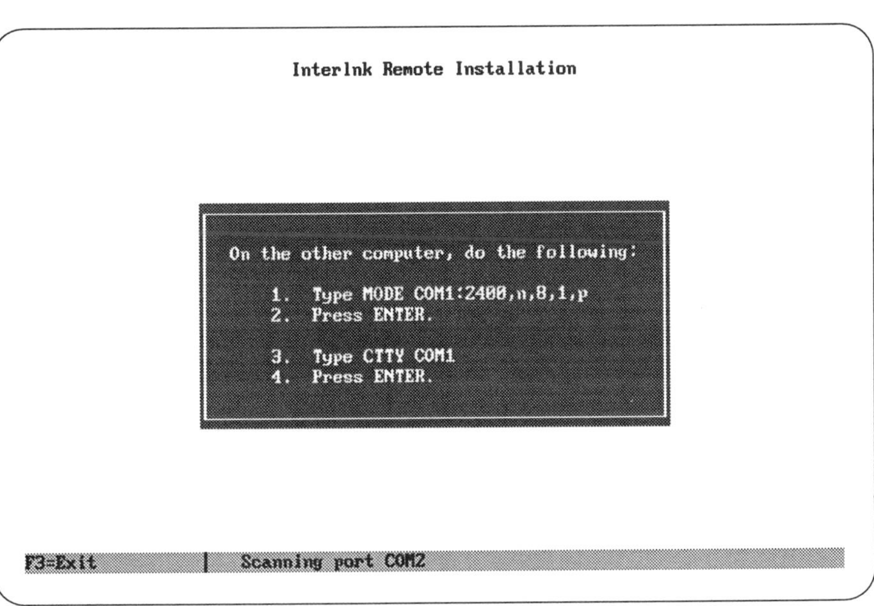

Figure 20-8 How to use Interlnk's remote installation feature (parts 1 and 2 of 3)

Part 3:

After you enter the Mode and Ctty commands, Intersvr copies the Interlnk files to the other computer.

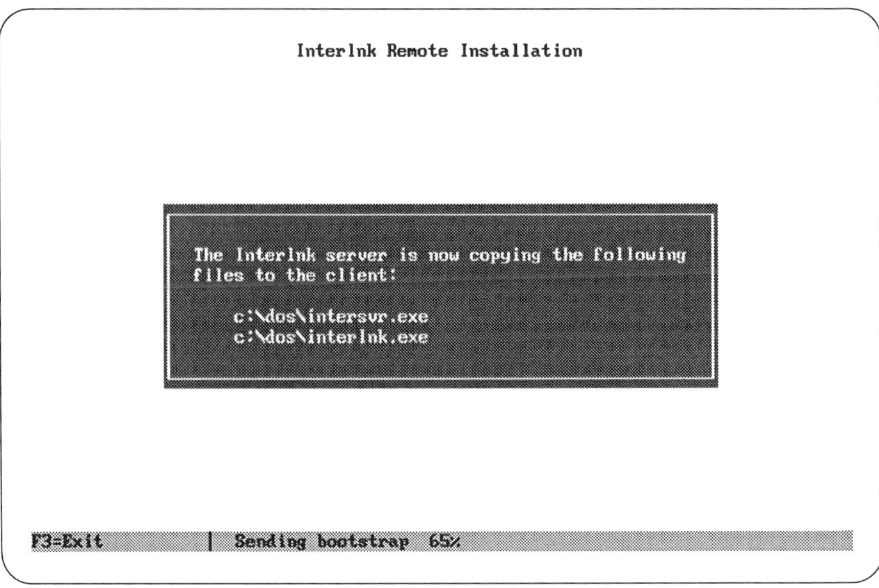
Interlnk Remote Installation
The Interlnk server is now copying the following files to the client:
c:\dos\intersvr.exe
c:\dos\interlnk.exe
F3=Exit
Sending bootstrap 65%

Figure 20-8 How to use Interlnk's remote installation feature (part 3 of 3)

```
C:\>mode com1:2400,n,8,1,p

Resident portion of MODE loaded

COM1: 2400,n,8,1,p

C:\>ctty com1
Loading bootstrap
Receiving INTERSVR.EXE (37266) 100%
Receiving INTERLNK.EXE (17133) 100%

C:\>
```

Figure 20-9 The display on the portable computer when Interlnk has finished the remote installation

The format of the Device command for loading the Interlnk driver

```
DEVICE=C:\DOS\INTERLNK.EXE [switches]
```

Switch meanings

`/AUTO`	Loads Interlnk into memory only if Intersvr is already running on the other computer.
`/NOSCAN`	Loads Interlnk into memory whether or not Intersvr is running on the other computer. If Intersvr isn't running when Interlnk is loaded, you can start a session by running Intersrv on the other computer, then typing INTERLNK at the command prompt.

Note: If you omit both /AUTO and /NOSCAN, Interlnk checks to see if Intersvr is running on the other computer when it's loaded into memory. If it's not, Interlnk remains loaded in memory. To establish a session later, you must run Intersrv on the other computer, then type INTERLNK at the command prompt.

`/LPT[:n]`	Establishes the session using a parallel port. If you specify a port number (such as /LPT:1), Interlnk will use just that port. Otherwise, Interlnk will search all available parallel ports to establish the session. This switch saves about 2KB of memory because Interlnk knows that it doesn't have to load the portion of the program that supports serial ports.
`/COM[:n]`	Establishes the session using a serial port. If you specify a port number (such as /COM:1), Interlnk will use just that port. Otherwise, Interlnk will search all available serial ports to establish the session. This switch saves about 1.5KB of memory because Interlnk knows that it doesn't have to load the portion of the program that supports parallel ports.

*Note: If your computer has a serial mouse, you should specify /LPT or /COM:*n *to avoid conflicts with the mouse.*

`/NOPRINTER`	Disables printer access. This will save about 200 bytes of memory.
`/DRIVES=n`	Specifies the number of server drives you want to access from the client. The default is 3. If your server has more than three drives (including diskette drives), you should specify a larger number.
`/V`	Specifies that a more reliable method should be used for the serial port. Use this switch only if you encounter problems when using a serial port.
`/BAUD:rate`	Specifies a slower transmission speed for a serial connection. Rate can be 9600, 19200, 38400, 57600, or 115200. The default is 115200. Use this switch only if you encounter problems when using a serial port.
`/LOW`	Specifies that Interlnk should not be loaded into upper memory. By default, Interlnk is loaded into upper memory if possible. If you're encountering a problem that you think might be related to upper memory, try using this switch.

Figure 20-10 The Device command for loading Interlnk

```
files=100
device=c:\dos\himem.sys
device=c:\dos\emm386.exe ram
dos=high,umb
devicehigh=c:\mouse\mouse.sys
device=c:\dos\interlnk.exe /auto
```

Figure 20-11 A CONFIG.SYS file that loads the Interlnk device driver

In most cases, you'll use the /AUTO switch on the Device command for loading Interlnk so the driver doesn't occupy any internal memory unless you're using it. But there are two other ways you can establish an Interlnk session. If you include the /NOSCAN switch on the Device command that loads Interlnk, Interlnk doesn't check to see if a session can be established when it's loaded into memory. To establish a session, then, you must enter the Interlnk command at the command prompt on the portable computer. But first, you must make sure the cable is properly connected to both computers, and you must start the Intersvr program on the desktop computer. If you omit both /AUTO and /NOSCAN, Interlnk establishes a session when it's loaded if possible. If it can't establish a session immediately, it remains in memory. Then, when you've connected the computers and started Intersvr on the desktop computer, you can establish a session by entering the Interlnk command on the portable.

The only other switch in figure 20-10 you might need to use is /DRIVES. This switch is often necessary when your desktop computer has two hard drives and you want to access the second drive. By default, Interlnk will access only the first three drives on the desktop computer. If the desktop computer has two diskette drives, that means the portable will be able to access both diskette drives and the first hard disk (drives A, B, and C). To access additional drives, you must use the /DRIVES switch to increase the number of drives you can access. (Alternatively, you can use the drives parameter or the /X switch on the Intersvr command to specify which drives can be accessed from the portable computer, as I'll explain in a moment.)

Most of the other switches in figure 20-10 are useful only in unusual situations. If you're extremely tight on memory, you might be able to free up a few thousand bytes by using the /NOPRINTER and the /COM or /LPT switches. You should also use the /LPT switch or a /COM switch that specifies a serial port if you use a serial mouse. And if you're having trouble establishing a connection over a serial port, the /V or /BAUD switches might help. But in most cases, you won't need to use any of these switches.

How to start the Intersvr program To establish an Interlnk session, you must run the Intersvr program on the desktop computer. If you specify the /AUTO switch on the Device command that loads Interlnk on the portable computer, you

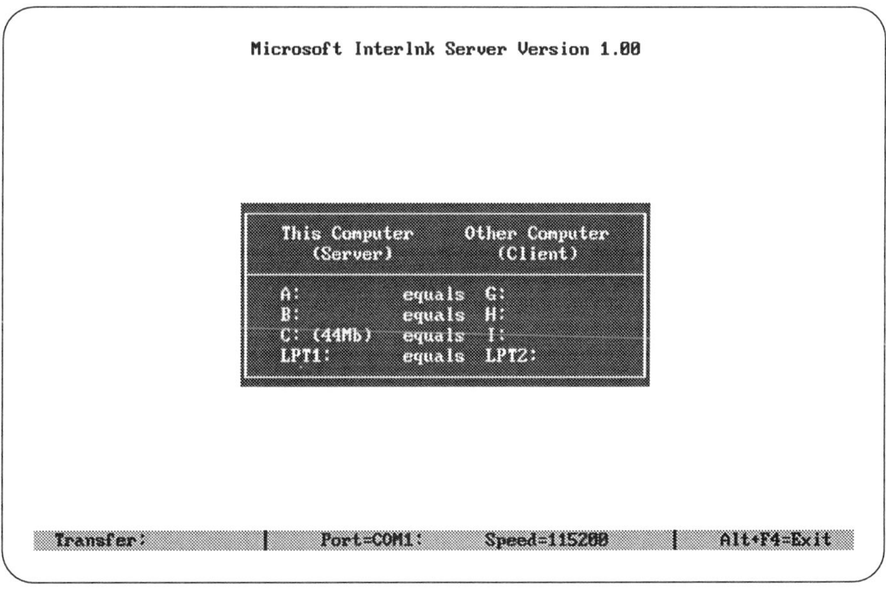

Figure 20-12 The screen that's displayed when you start Intersvr

must run Intersvr on the desktop computer before you boot the portable. Otherwise, you can run Intersvr anytime before or after you start your portable.

To start the Intersvr program, just type INTERSVR at the command prompt. When you do, Intersvr displays a status screen like the one in figure 20-12. As you can see, the server's A, B, and C drives have been redirected to the client's D, E, and F drives, and the printer connected to LPT1 on the server has been redirected to the client's printer port LPT2. Also notice on this screen that you can exit from the Intersvr program by pressing the Alt+F4 key combination.

Figure 20-13 shows the complete format of the Intersvr command, and figure 20-14 shows four examples of how it's used. (I already showed you how to use the /RCOPY switch for remote installation, so I won't mention it here.) Usually, you use the Intersvr command without any parameters, as shown in the first example in figure 20-14. Like Interlnk, some of Intersvr's switches are designed to free up a few thousand bytes of memory (/COM and /LPT), and some are useful when you're having trouble communicating over a serial port (/V and /BAUD). You're not likely to use these switches. However, you may need to use the drives parameter or the /X switch to control which drives are made available to the portable computer.

The drives parameter lets you specify that only specific drives should be made available to the portable computer. For example, suppose your desktop computer has four drives, two diskette drives and two hard drives, and you want to access only the

The format of the Intersvr command

```
INTERSVR [drives] [switches]
```

Explanation

`drives`	Makes only specific drives available to the other computer, in the order listed. If omitted, all drives are made available.
`/X=drive`	Specifies a drive that will not be made available. Use /X only if you do not specify *drives*.
`/LPT[:n]`	Establishes the session using a parallel port. If you specify a port number (such as /LPT:1), Intersvr will use just that port. Otherwise, Intersvr will search all available parallel ports to establish the session. This switch saves memory because Intersvr knows that it doesn't have to load the portion of the program that supports serial ports.
`/COM[:n]`	Establishes the session using a serial port. If you specify a port number (such as /COM:1), Intersvr will use just that port. Otherwise, Intersvr will search all available serial ports to establish the session. This switch saves memory because Intersvr knows that it doesn't have to load the portion of the program that supports parallel ports.
`/V`	Specifies that a more reliable method should be used for the serial port. Use this switch only if you encounter problems when using a serial port.
`/BAUD:rate`	Specifies a slower transmission speed for a serial connection. *Rate* can be 9600, 19200, 38400, 57600, or 115200. The default is 115200. Use this switch only if you encounter problems when using a serial port.
`/B`	Displays Interlnk screens in black and white. Use this switch if you have a monochrome monitor and can't read the Intersvr display.
`/RCOPY`	Copies the Interlnk files to the other computer. This works only with a serial connection using a null modem.

Figure 20-13 The Intersvr command

D drive from the portable computer. The second example shows how you can do this. Here, I specified that only the D drive should be made available. The third example shows that you can specify more than one drive in the drives parameter. Here, I specified that both hard drives (C and D) should be made available.

The /X switch is the opposite of the drives parameter. It specifies that a certain drive should *not* be made available to the portable computer. In the fourth example, I included two /X switches: one excluding drive A, the other excluding drive B. The result of this Intersvr command is the same as the command in the third example: only drives C and D will be available.

Example 1: A basic Intersvr command.

```
C:\>intersvr
```

Example 2: An Intersvr command that makes just drive D available to the other computer.

```
C:\>intersvr d:
```

Example 3: An Intersvr command that makes just drives C and D available to the other computer.

```
C:\>intersvr c: d:
```

Example 4: An Intersvr command that makes all drives other than A and B available to the other computer.

```
C:\>intersvr /x=a /x=b
```

Figure 20-14 How to use the Intersvr command

How to use the Interlnk command You already know that you must include a Device command in the portable computer's CONFIG.SYS file to load the Interlnk device driver. And, if an Interlnk session isn't established when the drive is loaded, you have to enter the Interlnk command to establish the session. You can also use the Interlnk command to display the status of the Interlnk session or to change the drives that are currently accessible. You probably won't do this often, but you may need to once in a while.

Figure 20-15 shows the format of the Interlnk command and three examples of how it's used. If you use it without parameters, as shown in the first example, Interlnk displays the status of the Interlnk session. Figure 20-16 shows an example of this display. You can use it to double-check which drives and printers are currently in use.

The second example shows how to change a drive assignment. Here, I specified that drive D on the portable computer should be used to access drive F on the desktop computer. Any desktop drive that was previously linked to drive D becomes unavailable.

The third example shows how to disconnect a drive. Here, I specified drive D for the portable computer, but I omitted the drive specification for the desktop computer. After issuing this command, drive D will be invalid.

Interlnk restrictions When you use Interlnk, there are several restrictions you should know about. First, you cannot use any of the commands listed in figure 20-17 during an Interlnk session. To use these commands, you first have to terminate the Intersvr program by pressing Alt+F4.

The format of the Interlnk command

```
INTERLNK [client-drive=server-drive]
```

Example 1: An Interlnk command that displays the status of the session.

```
C:\>interlnk
```

Example 2: An Interlnk command that makes server drive F available as drive D.

```
C:\>interlnk d=f
```

Example 3: An Interlnk command that disconnects drive D.

```
C:\>interlnk d=
```

Figure 20-15 How to use the Interlnk command

The second restriction applies when you use Intersvr under *Windows* or with the task swapping feature of the DOS shell. In short, Intersvr temporarily disables multi-tasking and task swapping. So, once you start Intersvr, you won't be able to use these features.

The third restriction applies if you're running a version of DOS before 6.0 on the client computer. In that case, you might not be able to use some of the features that are available with more recent releases of DOS. In particular, if you're using DOS 3.3 or an earlier version of DOS, you can't access partitions larger than 32MB. So if the hard disk on your server is divided into partitions larger than 32MB, you won't be able to access those drives from the client using Interlnk.

The last restriction has to do with the types of drives you can access from your client computer using Interlnk. In general, you can't access any drive that's already redirected. For example, you can't access network drives or CD-ROM drives.

How to use Power

One of the most frustrating aspects of using a portable computer is limited battery life. Most portables can run for only two to four hours without recharging the battery. Just how long your portable computer will run between battery charges depends mostly on the size of the battery and the amount of power required by the computer's components. The larger the battery and the lower the power consumption, the longer the battery life.

Most portable computers have built-in features designed to extend the life of the battery. These power reduction features usually blank the screen and shut down the hard disk after a period of inactivity. Some portables also reduce the speed of the processor and shut down other system components. Until recently, the techniques

```
Microsoft Interlnk version 1.00

Port=LPT1

This Computer    Other Computer
  (Client)          (Server)
-------------    --------------
     D:    equals    A:
     E:    equals    B:
     F:    equals    C: (120MB) MSDOS6
     LPT1: equals    LPT2:
```

Figure 20-16 Interlnk's display indicates the drives and printers that are available

CHKDSK	FORMAT
DEFRAG	MIRROR
DISKCOMP	SYS
DISKCOPY	UNDELETE
FDISK	UNFORMAT

Figure 20-17 DOS commands that don't work during an Interlnk session

used to reduce power consumption varied from one portable computer manufacturer to the next. But in 1992, Intel and Microsoft agreed on a common standard for power reduction, called *Advanced Power Management*, or *APM*. Many newer portable computers are compatible with APM and come with a program called *Power*. The Power program is also available with DOS 6.0.

Although you can use Power with portable computers that aren't compatible with APM, Power is most effective with computers that are compatible with it. Microsoft estimates that Power can extend battery life by 25 percent for computers that are compatible with APM. For computers that aren't compatible with APM, Microsoft estimates about 5 percent power savings.

To use the Power program, you must add a Device command to your CONFIG.SYS file. Figure 20-18 shows the format of the Device command for loading Power, and figure 20-19 shows a typical CONFIG.SYS file that loads Power. In most cases, you don't need to use any of the Power switches. They simply change the level of power conservation provided by Power. For example, the /ADV:MAX switch provides the highest level of power conservation, but might slow down your

The format of the Device command for loading the Power driver

```
DEVICE=C:\DOS\POWER.EXE [switches]
```

Switch meanings

/ADV:MAX	Attempts to maximize power conservation, even if system performance is reduced.
/ADV:REG	Attempts to balance power conservation with system performance. This is the default.
/ADV:MIN	Conserves power only when system performance will not be reduced.
/STD	If your system supports the APM specifications, /STD uses only the power management features provided by the hardware. If not, /STD disables power management.
/OFF	Disables power management.

Figure 20-18 The Device command for loading Power

```
files=100
device=c:\dos\himem.sys
device=c:\dos\emm386.exe ram
dos=high,umb
devicehigh=c:\mouse\mouse.sys
device=c:\dos\interlnk.exe /auto
device=c:\dos\power.exe
```

Figure 20-19 A CONFIG.SYS file that loads Power

computer's operations. The /ADV:MIN switch is the opposite: it provides the least amount of power conservation, but doesn't slow down your system. The default level, /ADV:REG, attempts to provide a balance between system performance and power conservation.

Some perspective on Interlnk and Power

Several commercial utility programs are available that provide file transfer capabilities that are more advanced than Interlnk. For example, *LapLink Pro* by

Traveling Software provides all of the features of Interlnk. In addition, it lets you access network drives from your portable computer, it lets you communicate over a modem, and it uses data compression techniques to increase its transmission speed. In my own informal testing, I've found *LapLink Pro* to be about 15 percent faster than Interlnk. If you frequently exchange data between portable and desktop computers, you should at least consider purchasing a program such as *LapLink Pro*. However, for occasional use, you'll probably find Interlnk more than adequate.

As for Power, its function is often provided by a utility program that's included with your portable. If that's the case, you're probably better off using the utility that came with your portable because it's designed to work with your computer.

Terms

client
server
memory resident program
redirection
null-modem cable
bi-directional parallel cable
remote installation
device driver
Advanced Power Management
APM

Objectives

1. Identify the ports on your desktop and portable computer and determine what type of cable and connectors you need to use Interlnk.
2. If necessary, copy the Interlnk files to your portable computer. If your desktop and portable computers are connected through serial ports, do this using Interlnk's remote installation feature.
3. Set up your portable computer's CONFIG.SYS file so it can load Interlnk.
4. Start an Interlnk session. How you do this will depend on the switches you use on the Interlnk Device command.
5. Given file specifications, copy files from your portable computer to your desktop computer and from your desktop computer to your portable computer, and print files on the printer attached to your desktop computer from your portable computer.
6. Use the Interlnk command to display the status of your Interlnk session, change a drive assignment, or disconnect a drive.
7. Set up your portable computer's CONFIG.SYS file so it loads Power.

Chapter 21

Microsoft Diagnostics

DOS 6.0 includes a utility program called *Microsoft Diagnostics*, or *MSD*, that's designed to collect and display technical information about your PC. For example, MSD can display the type of processor chip your computer uses, the manufacturer of your BIOS, the type of video adapter your computer has, and so on. Microsoft also includes MSD with *Windows* 3.1. So you already have MSD if you have *Windows* 3.1, whether or not you're using DOS 6.0.

Frankly, most of the information displayed by MSD is useful only to computer specialists. In this chapter, I'll show you how to use MSD to display some basic information you might find interesting and occasionally useful. But I won't describe every item of information displayed by MSD because understanding and using that information requires a level of technical background that's beyond the scope of this book.

To start Microsoft Diagnostics, simply enter MSD at the command prompt. If you're running *Windows*, you should exit from it before you start MSD. If you don't, MSD will display a screen telling you that some of the values it displays may not be accurate. So if you want accurate values, be sure to run MSD from outside of *Windows*.

When you enter the MSD command, MSD displays the screen shown in figure 21-1. This screen displays some basic information about your computer system. For example, it indicates that my computer is an American Megatrend 486DX system with 640KB of conventional memory and 3328KB of exptended memory (1932KB is currently available), it has a Tseng VGA card, no network, it's running MS-DOS version 6.0, and it has a Serial Mouse, three disk drives, one parallel port, and two serial ports.

How to display system information

Each of the buttons on the MSD main screen display more detailed information about your system. You can select each button by clicking on it with a mouse or by pressing the highlighted letter. For example, if you click on the Computer button or select it by pressing the letter P, MSD displays the additional computer information shown in

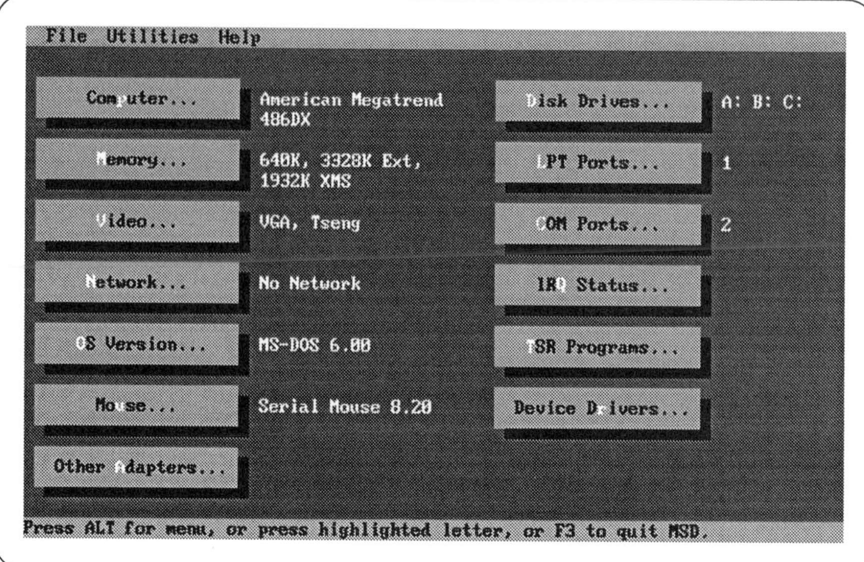

Figure 21-1 MSD's main screen shows basic information about your system

figure 21-2. Here, you can see detailed information about your computer's BIOS, as well as additional information about the processor and other system components.

Figure 21-3 shows the information that's displayed when you click on the Disk button or select it by pressing the letter D. Here, MSD displays basic information about your disk drives, such as the total size and amount of free space. In addition, MSD shows detailed disk drive information, such as the number of cylinders and heads, the number of bytes per sector and the number of sectors per track, and the CMOS disk type.

Each of the other buttons in figure 21-1 displays system information at a similar level of detail. I won't show you samples of these displays, but feel free to explore them on your own.

How to use the File and Utilities menus

The File and Utilities menus provide several additional MSD functions you might use from time to time. To pull down one of these menus, click on it with the mouse or use an Alt+key combination (Alt+F for the File menu, Alt+U for the Utilities menu). Then, to select a function, click on it with the mouse or press the highlighted letter.

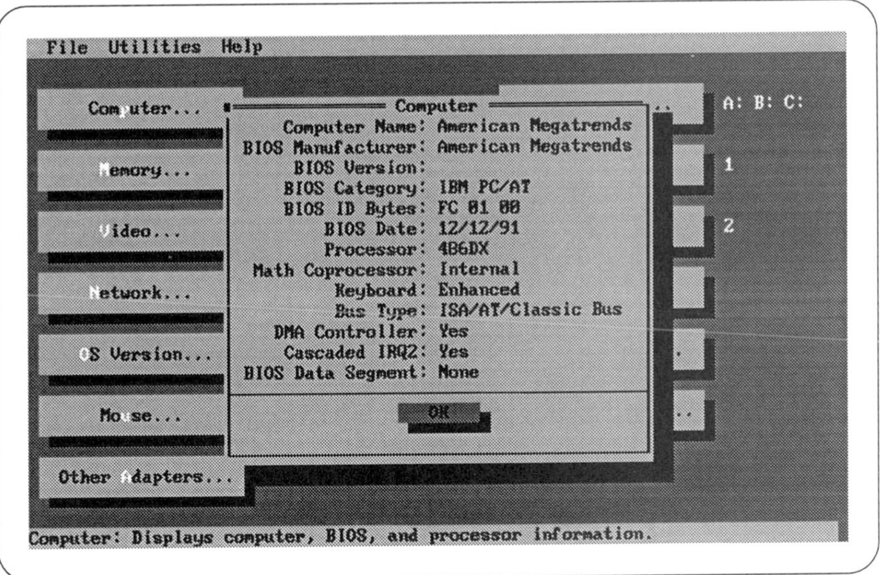

Figure 21-2 The Computer button displays information about the computer, BIOS, and processor

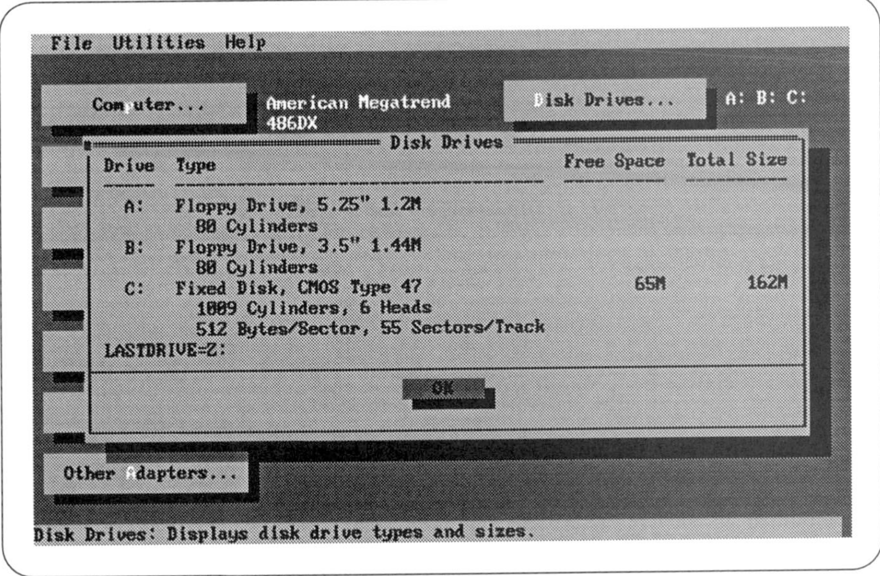

Figure 21-3 The Disk-drives button displays information about the disk drives

The File menu

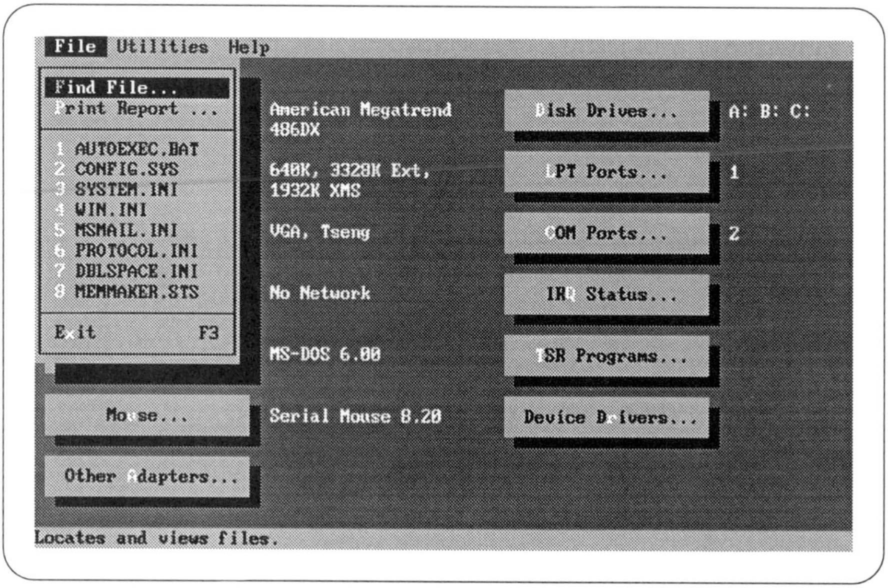

Menu item	Description
Find File	Searches your disk for files that match the file specification you supply.
Print Report	Prints a report that contains selected system information.
1 through 8	Displays the file indicated.
Exit	Exits from MSD.

Figure 21-4 File menu functions

Figure 21-4 shows the File menu. The Find-file function searches your entire disk for particular file names. Because you can perform a similar function using the Dir command with the /S switch, you probably won't use this function often. The numbered file names in the menu display the contents of system files such as AUTOEXEC.BAT and CONFIG.SYS. Because you can't edit these files from MSD, you probably won't use this function often, either.

The File menu function you're most likely to use is Print-report. It creates a report that contains the information displayed by MSD. You can select what information to include, and you can print the report or save it in a file that you can print later.

The Utilities menu

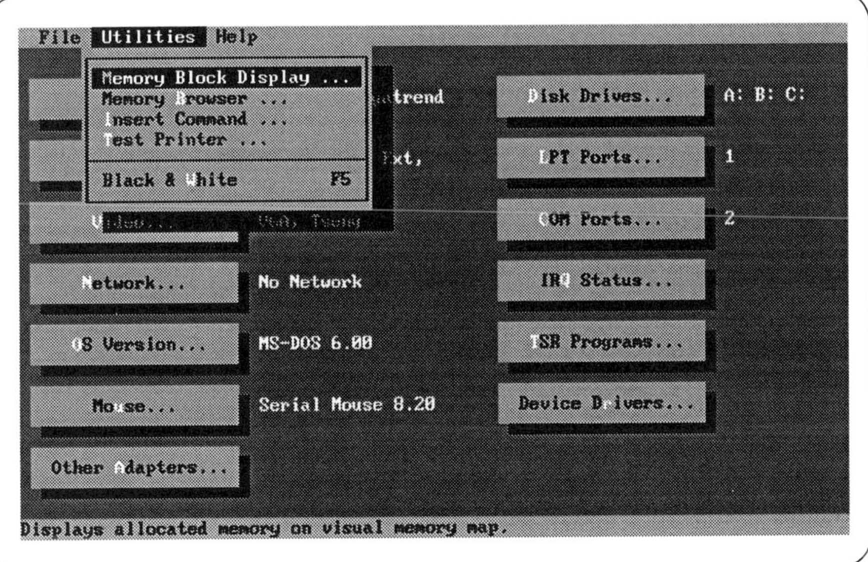

Menu item	Description
Memory Block Display	Displays the locations of areas of allocated memory and a memory map.
Memory Browser	Lets you browse areas of your system's internal memory.
Insert Command	Lets you add a Files, Buffers, or Set command to your AUTOEXEC.BAT file.
Test Printer	Sends a test page to your printer to determine if it's working properly.
Black & White	Changes MSD's displays to black and white.

Figure 21-5 Utilities menu functions

Figure 21-5 shows the Utilities menu. The first two functions, Memory-block-display and Memory-browser, display information about your system's internal memory. The Insert-command function lets you add a Files, Buffers, or Set command to your AUTOEXEC.BAT or CONFIG.SYS file. The Test-printer function sends a test page to your printer so you can determine if it's operating properly. This function is useful because it works for Postscript printers as well as standard dot-matrix or

The format of the MSD command

```
MSD [switches]
```

Switch meanings

`/B`	Runs MSD in black and white mode for monochrome monitors.
`/I`	Bypasses initial hardware detection. This is useful if some incompatible hardware component causes MSD to fail.
`/F file-spec`	Creates a report including name and address information entered by the user.
`/P file-spec`	Creates a report without prompting for user name and address information.
`/S [file-spec]`	Creates a summary report. If *file-spec* is omitted, the report is displayed on the screen.

Figure 21-6 The MSD command

Hewlett-Packard compatible laser printers. And the Black-and-white function changes the display to black and white.

How to use MSD command line switches

Figure 21-6 shows the switches you can use with the MSD command. The first, /B, displays MSD's screens in black and white. It's useful if you have a monochrome monitor. The second, /I, skips MSD's initial hardware detection routines. If your system hangs up when you start MSD, try using this switch. It's possible for some non-standard hardware to cause MSD to fail.

You use MSD's remaining three switches to create various reports. The /S switch creates a summary report like the one shown in figure 21-7. This report is useful to find out basic system information, such as how many disk drives you have, what type of processor you have, or what type of video display you have.

The /F and /P switches create detailed reports. The difference is that /F prompts you to enter name and address information and /P doesn't. Figure 21-8 shows you how to use MSD with the /F switch. Here, you can enter your name, company, address, phone number, and a comment. Then, MSD prepares a report file. This report is 24 pages long on my system, so you probably won't want to print it. But you might want to examine it with the Edit command or save it so you can print it later.

```
C:\>msd /s
      Computer: American Megatrend, 486DX
        Memory: 640K, 3328K Ext, 1932K XMS
         Video: VGA, Tseng
       Network: No Network
    OS Version: MS-DOS 6.00
         Mouse: Serial Mouse 8.20
Other Adapters:
   Disk Drives: A: B: C:
     LPT Ports: 1
     COM Ports: 2

C:\>
```

Figure 21-7 An MSD summary report

```
C:\>msd /f a:doug.msd

MSD Microsoft Diagnostics Version 2.01
Copyright (C) Microsoft Corporation 1990-92

Please enter your Name, Company Name,
Address (two lines), City, State, ZIP code
telephone number, and comment on the lines below:

        Name: Doug Lowe
Company Name: Mike Murach & Associates, Inc.
    Address1:
    Address2:
 City/ST/Zip:
     Country:
       Phone:
    Comments: Doug's PC

Generating Report ...

Page 24

C:\>
```

Figure 21-8 How to use MSD to create a report on diskette

Some perspective on Microsoft Diagnostics

I said at the start of this chapter that most of the information displayed by MSD is useful only to computer specialists. That's because understanding what the information means requires more technical knowledge than most computer users have. Even so, there are occasions when MSD can be useful even for a casual user. For example, suppose you purchase a hardware component such as a CD-ROM drive or a scanner. The installation procedures for such components often require that you determine a free *Interrupt Request Line*, or *IRQ*. You can use MSD's IRQ Status function to find out which IRQ's are available.

Because the information contained in an MSD report can be useful when trying to solve a hardware problem, it's not a bad idea to create an MSD report on diskette *before* a problem develops. Then, should a hardware problem occur, you'll have the MSD report if you need it. For example, if your disk drive fails completely, you can use the MSD report to determine how the drive was configured.

Terms

Interrupt Request Line
IRQ

Objectives

1. Use MSD to display technical information about your PC.
2. Use MSD to create a detailed report on diskette in case your computer develops a hardware problem.

Section 6

Configuring your system

The chapters in this section present a variety of DOS skills that you might need from time to time. Because you probably won't need to use these skills on a daily basis, you don't have to read any of these chapters until the need arises. As a result, you can think of this section as a reference section. If you do need to learn one or more of the skills presented in this section, the chapters are here for you. And you can read them in whatever sequence you prefer.

In chapter 22, you'll learn how to partition and format a hard disk. Most new disk drives are formatted at the factory, so you'll probably need to do these tasks only if you want to change the way your disk is partitioned. In chapter 23, you'll learn how to upgrade to DOS 6.0. In chapter 24, you'll learn how to use the special DOS commands for the CONFIG.SYS and AUTOEXEC.BAT files. And in chapter 25, you'll learn how to make the most efficient use of your computer's memory.

Chapter 22

How to partition and format a hard disk

At one time, it was common for a new PC to come with unpartitioned and unformatted disks. Then, you had to partition and format the disk yourself before you could use the computer. Today, nearly all PCs come with disks that are partitioned and formatted by the manufacturer, with DOS (and probably *Windows*) already installed. Still, you may occasionally need to partition and format a hard disk yourself. For example, you might decide to change the size of existing partitions on your hard disk. To do that, you have to partition and reformat your disk. You might also need to partition and format a disk to recover from a disk error you can't otherwise correct.

In this chapter, you'll learn how to prepare a hard disk for use by partitioning and formatting it. This preparation can require up to three phases: (1) low-level formatting, (2) partitioning, and (3) high-level formatting. As you will see, you can use the DOS Fdisk program for phase 2 and the DOS Format command for phase 3. However, DOS doesn't include software for low-level formatting.

Before I begin, I want to point out that the procedures I'll describe in this chapter will destroy any existing data on your hard disk. If you're partitioning and formatting a brand new hard disk, that's not a problem. But if you're changing the partition structure of an existing hard disk, be sure to do a complete backup before you begin. When you finish, you'll have to restore this backup data to make your PC usable again.

How to do the low-level formatting

Low-level formatting prepares the surface of a hard disk for use. It actually creates the tracks on the hard disk, and it defines the sectors on the disk. It also assigns numbers to the sectors so they can be accessed.

When you buy a PC or a hard disk, the low-level formatting is usually done by the manufacturer, so you can skip this phase of disk preparation. In addition, you should realize that for the most common type of disk drive sold today, IDE drives, low-level formatting can be performed *only* at the factory. So if you have an IDE drive, you can't low-level format it yourself anyway. In all likelihood, the only time you'll need to do a low-level format is when an older, non-IDE disk drive develops errors that persist after you repartition and reformat the drive using the DOS Fdisk and Format commands. In that case, performing a low-level format may correct the problem by redefining the locations of the disk's sectors and tracks.

Assuming you need to do a low-level format, the first step is to remove your computer's case and find the *defect table* printed on the disk drive. This table indicates which areas of the disk were identified as unusable by the factory. Once you've found the defect table, you can run the low-level format program. If you don't want to run your PC with the case open, just write down the values from the defect table before you put the case back on. When you do the low-level format, you'll enter the values from the defect table so those areas won't be used.

The procedure for running the low-level format program varies from one system to the next. If your disk came with a low-level formatting program on diskette, you should use it to do the low-level format. If not, you might be able to use the low-level formatting program included in your computer's BIOS (the built-in program that supports low-level operations for I/O devices). The procedure for starting the BIOS low-level format program depends on the manufacturer and version of the BIOS. For some BIOS chips, you can press the Delete key while your system is booting to access a setup program. Then, you can use the setup program's menus to start the low-level format program. For other BIOS chips, you must boot your PC from a DOS diskette that contains the Debug program. Then, you start the Debug program and enter a G command along with the memory address that indicates the start of the low-level format program. You'll have to consult your computer's operating manual to determine that address.

Once again, I want to stress that you should not attempt to perform a low-level format on an IDE drive. These drives have formatting requirements that are beyond the capabilities of the controllers supplied with the drive. As a result, they must be formatted with special equipment at the factory. (There are a few disk utility packages that can do a low-level format on certain IDE drives. If you think you need to low-level format an IDE drive, contact the manufacturer to find out if such software is available. But don't attempt it if you're not sure.)

DOS partitions

Originally, DOS provided the ability to divide a hard disk into two or more *partitions* so you could have more than one operating system on your hard disk. That way, you could define one partition and put DOS in it. And you could define another partition for another operating system, such as Unix or CP/M. Although some people still use this capability so that they can run DOS and OS/2 together on the same system, you'll probably never use partitions for this purpose.

That doesn't mean you can forget about partitions, though, because you must create at least one partition for DOS before you can use a hard disk. You must create this DOS partition even if it's the only one on the entire disk. And if you want to divide a hard disk into two or more drives, you must create a second partition for the additional drives.

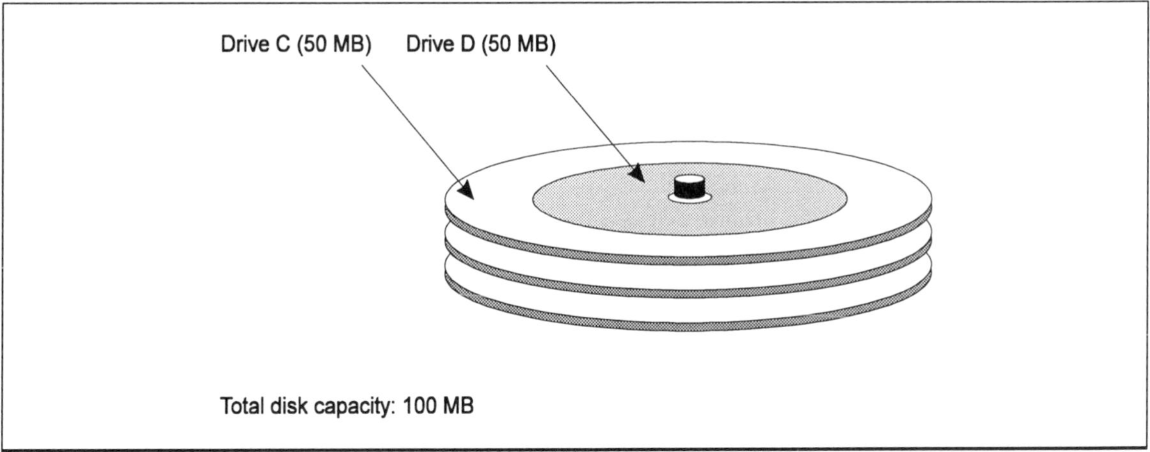

Figure 22-1 Two drives on one hard disk

Figure 22-1 shows an example of how a hard disk can be divided into two drives. Here, a 100MB hard disk is partitioned into two 50MB drives. These drives are referred to as drive C and drive D, and each is in a separate partition.

The primary partition, the extended partition, and logical drives If you want to set up a hard disk as one drive, you create a single partition called the primary partition. This partition will use the entire hard disk. After it has been set up, the primary partition is referred to as drive C.

You might expect that to create additional drives, you simply create an additional partition for each one. But that's not the case. If you want to create two or more drives on a hard disk, you set up two disk partitions: a primary partition and an *extended partition*. Then, you subdivide the extended partition into one or more *logical drives,* as illustrated in figure 22-2. Here, two logical drives are defined in the extended partition: drive D and drive E. If you define only one logical drive in the extended partition, it is referred to as drive D.

The DOS Fdisk program To create a partition on a hard disk, you use a DOS program called Fdisk. It lets you specify the amount of disk space you want to use for the primary and extended partitions. And it lets you define logical drives in the extended partition.

If you have DOS 4.0 or an earlier version, the Fdisk program measures disk capacities in cylinders, not in megabytes. So to determine the number of cylinders you want to use for each partition or logical drive, you must perform a few calculations. If, for example, you have a 40MB disk that has 824 cylinders, you divide 40 into 824 to determine that there are approximately 20.6 cylinders for each megabyte. Then, if you want to create a 30MB C drive and a 10MB D drive, you

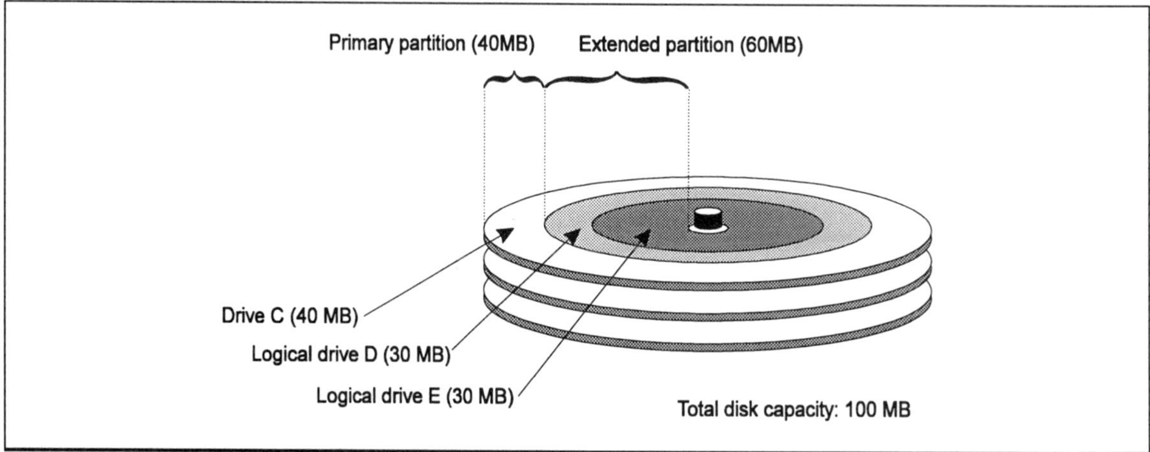

Figure 22-2 Three drives on one hard disk

know that the primary partition must use 618 cylinders and that the extended partition and logical drive D must use 206 cylinders.

If you have DOS 5.0 or a later version, the Fdisk program measures the disk capacity in megabytes and in a percentage of total disk space. As a result, you don't have to calculate the number of cylinders for each partition. You can just enter the number of megabytes or the percentage of total disk space you want to use for each partition and logical drive.

Beginning with DOS 5.0, you can create partitions as large 2GB (2 billion bytes). So you shouldn't have a problem partitioning even the largest disk drive in any way you wish. However, if you're using an earlier version of DOS, you need to be aware of the partition size limits spelled out in figure 22-3. As you can see, DOS versions prior to 3.3 didn't support extended partitions at all, and the primary partition was limited to 32MB. So if you had a disk larger than 32MB, you had to use special software such as *Disk Manager* to access it under DOS. Extended partitions were introduced with DOS 3.3, but each logical drive was limited to 32MB. So, you would have to divide a 90MB drive into three 30MB drives to access it under DOS 3.3. DOS 4.0 increased the 32MB drive size limit to 512MB. So, with DOS 4.0, you could support a 90MB drive in a single partition, but you would still have to partition drives larger than 512MB. Note that with DOS 4.0, the support for partitions larger than 32MB is provided by the Share program. So if you use partitions larger than 32MB, you must include the Share command in your AUTOEXEC.BAT file. With DOS 5.0, the limit was extended to 2GB, and the share program is not required.

DOS version	Partitioning limits
Before 3.3	1. Only one primary partition allowed. No extended partition. 2. Maximum size of primary partition: 32MB. 3. To use drives larger than 32MB, disk partitioning software such as *Disk Manager* is required.
3.3	1. One primary and one extended partition allowed. 2. Maximum size of primary partition and each logical drive within extended partition: 32MB.
4.0	1. One primary and one extended partition allowed. 2. Maximum size of primary partition and each logical drive within extended partition: 512MB. 3. Must include Share program in AUTOEXEC.BAT if primary partition or logical drive exceeds 32MB.
5.0 and later	1. One primary and one extended partition allowed. 2. Maximum size of primary partition and each logical drive within extended partition: 2GB. 3. Share program not required.

Figure 22-3 Partition limits for various DOS versions

How to use the Fdisk program to partition a hard disk when you use DOS 4.0 or later

To set up the partitions and logical drives for a hard disk, you use the DOS Fdisk program. To get this program going, you start your PC using the DOS system diskette in the A drive. Next, you enter FDISK at the command prompt. When the program starts, it displays a menu. Then, if you're going to create two partitions on your hard disk, you do the three steps shown in the procedure in figure 22-4. If you're going to create only a primary partition, you do just step 1.

Figures 22-5 through 22-7 show you how to use the Fdisk program that comes with DOS 6.0 to accomplish the tasks listed in figure 22-4. The Fdisk program for DOS 4.0 and 5.0 is nearly identical to the DOS 6.0 Fdisk program. After I show how you to use the DOS 6.0 Fdisk program, I'll present some of the differences for the DOS 3.3 Fdisk program and earlier versions of Fdisk.

1. Create the primary partition.
2. Create the extended partition and the logical drives.
3. Specify the active partition.

Figure 22-4 The procedure for partitioning a hard disk into two or more drives

How to create the primary partition Figure 22-5 shows how to use the Fdisk program to create the primary partition on a hard disk. Part 1 presents the opening menu Fdisk displays when you first start it. From this menu, you select the Create-DOS-partition option by entering the number 1. Then, Fdisk displays the menu in part 2. From this menu, you select the Create-primary-DOS-partition option by entering the number 1 again.

If there's already a primary partition on the hard disk, Fdisk displays a message. Then, if you want to create a new primary partition to replace the existing one, you must first delete the existing primary partition using the third option on the opening Fdisk menu.

If there isn't already a primary partition on the disk, Fdisk displays the screen shown in part 3 of figure 22-5. Then, if you want to use the maximum size for the partition, you enter the letter Y. In this case, Fdisk creates a primary partition using all the space available on the disk. It also makes this partition the active partition so you don't have to activate it in a separate step.

If you want to create a primary partition that's smaller than the maximum size so you can create an extended partition later, you enter the letter N as shown in part 3 of figure 22-5. Fdisk then displays the screen shown in part 4. This screen shows the total size of the hard disk and the amount of space available for the primary partition. At this screen, you enter the size of the primary partition you want to create. You can specify the size in megabytes by entering a number or as a percentage of the total disk space by entering a number followed by a percent sign. In figure 22-5, I specified that the primary partition should be 50MB, which is half the total available disk space.

Fdisk then displays the screen shown in part 5 to verify that it created the primary partition you specified. When you press the Esc key, Fdisk returns you to the opening Fdisk menu.

Part 1:

To start the Fdisk program, start your PC using the system diskette in drive A. Then, enter FDISK at the command prompt. When it displays its opening menu, select the Create-DOS-partition option by entering the number 1.

```
                    MS-DOS Version 6
                 Fixed Disk Setup Program
          (C)Copyright Microsoft Corp. 1983 - 1993

                      FDISK Options

Current fixed disk drive: 1

Choose one of the following:

1. Create DOS partition or Logical DOS Drive
2. Set active partition
3. Delete partition or Logical DOS Drive
4. Display partition information


Enter choice: [1]




Press Esc to exit FDISK
```

Part 2:

When Fdisk displays its menu for creating a partition or logical drive, select the Create-primary-DOS-partition option by entering the number 1.

```
          Create DOS Partition or Logical DOS Drive

Current fixed disk drive: 1

Choose one of the following:

1. Create Primary DOS Partition
2. Create Extended DOS Partition
3. Create Logical DOS Drive(s) in the Extended DOS Partition


Enter choice: [1]




Press Esc to return to FDISK Options
```

Figure 22-5 How to use Fdisk to create a primary partition (parts 1 and 2 of 5)

Part 3:

Fdisk asks you if you want to use all the available space for the partition. If so, enter Y. If you want to use some of the space for an extended partition, enter N.

```
                    Create Primary DOS Partition

Current fixed disk drive: 1

Do you wish to use the maximum available size for a Primary DOS Partition
and make the partition active (Y/N).....................? [N]







Press Esc to return to FDISK Options
```

Part 4:

If you specified that you want to use only a portion of the available space for the partition, Fdisk prompts you to enter the amount of space to use. Enter the size of the partition in megabytes or in a percentage of total disk space.

```
                    Create Primary DOS Partition

Current fixed disk drive: 1




Total disk space is  100 Mbytes (1 Mbyte = 1048576 bytes)
Maximum space available for partition is  100 Mbytes (100%)


Enter partition size in Mbytes or percent of disk space (%) to
create a Primary DOS Partition..................................: [   50]

No partitions defined


Press Esc to return to FDISK Options
```

Figure 22-5 How to use Fdisk to create a primary partition (parts 3 and 4 of 5)

Part 5:

After Fdisk creates the primary partition, it displays a verification screen. To exit from this screen and return to the Fdisk opening menu, press the Esc key.

```
                    Create Primary DOS Partition

Current fixed disk drive: 1

Partition  Status   Type    Volume Label  Mbytes   System   Usage
 C: 1              PRI DOS                    50   UNKNOWN    50%




Primary DOS Partition created


Press Esc to continue
```

Figure 22-5 How to use Fdisk to create a primary partition (part 5 of 5)

How to create the extended partition and logical drives Figure 22-6 shows you how to create an extended partition and logical drives on a hard disk. First, you select the Create-DOS-partition option from the opening Fdisk menu as illustrated in part 1. Then, you select the Create-extended-DOS-partition option as illustrated in part 2. DOS then displays the screen shown in part 3. This screen gives information about the primary partition, the total size of the hard disk, and the maximum space available for the extended partition. Here, you enter the amount of space you want to use for the partition, again, either in megabytes or as a percentage of total disk space. Because you can create only one extended partition on a disk drive, you'll almost always specify all the remaining disk space here. When Fdisk has created the extended partition, it displays the screen shown in part 4.

When you press the Esc key to exit from the screen shown in part 4, Fdisk displays the screen shown in part 5. This screen indicates that no logical drives have been defined for the extended partition and asks you for the amount of space to use for the first logical drive. It also shows the total size of the extended partition and the amount of space available to create a new logical drive. In this case, I specified that all the available space should be used for the logical drive. That way, the extended partition will contain only one drive. To create more than one logical drive in the extended partition, just specify a logical drive size that's less than the maximum. Then, the remaining space will be available for additional logical drives. After you

Part 1:

From Fdisk's opening menu, select the Create-DOS-partition option by entering the number 1.

```
                    MS-DOS Version 6
                 Fixed Disk Setup Program
          (C)Copyright Microsoft Corp. 1983 - 1993

                      FDISK Options

Current fixed disk drive: 1

Choose one of the following:

1. Create DOS partition or Logical DOS Drive
2. Set active partition
3. Delete partition or Logical DOS Drive
4. Display partition information



Enter choice: [1]






Press Esc to exit FDISK
```

Part 2:

When Fdisk displays its menu for creating a partition or logical drive, select the Create-extended-partition option by entering the number 2.

```
          Create DOS Partition or Logical DOS Drive

Current fixed disk drive: 1

Choose one of the following:

1. Create Primary DOS Partition
2. Create Extended DOS Partition
3. Create Logical DOS Drive(s) in the Extended DOS Partition



Enter choice: [2]






Press Esc to return to FDISK Options
```

Figure 22-6 How to use Fdisk to create an extended partition and logical drive (parts 1 and 2 of 6)

Part 3:

Enter the size of the partition you want to create in megabytes or as a percentage of total disk space.

```
                     Create Extended DOS Partition

Current fixed disk drive: 1

Partition  Status   Type    Volume Label  Mbytes   System   Usage
 C: 1              PRI DOS                   50    UNKNOWN    50%



Total disk space is  100 Mbytes (1 Mbyte = 1048576 bytes)
Maximum space available for partition is   50 Mbytes ( 50%)


Enter partition size in Mbytes or percent of disk space (%) to
create an Extended DOS Partition.............................: [  50]



Press Esc to return to FDISK Options
```

Part 4:

After Fdisk creates the extended partition, it displays a verification screen. To define the logical drives in the partition, press the Esc key.

```
                     Create Extended DOS Partition

Current fixed disk drive: 1

Partition  Status   Type    Volume Label  Mbytes   System   Usage
 C: 1              PRI DOS                   50    UNKNOWN    50%
    2              EXT DOS                   50    UNKNOWN    50%






Extended DOS Partition created


Press Esc to continue
```

Figure 22-6 How to use Fdisk to create an extended partition and logical drive (parts 3 and 4 of 6)

Part 5:

Fdisk prompts you for the size of the first logical drive. Enter the size in megabytes or as a percentage of the total disk space.

```
        Create Logical DOS Drive(s) in the Extended DOS Partition



No logical drives defined



Total Extended DOS Partition size is   50 Mbytes (1 MByte = 1048576 bytes)
Maximum space available for logical drive is   50 Mbytes (100%)

Enter logical drive size in Mbytes or percent of disk space (%)...[  50]


Press Esc to return to FDISK Options
```

Part 6:

After Fdisk creates the logical drive, it displays a verification screen. To return to the Fdisk opening menu or to define another logical drive, press the Esc key.

```
        Create Logical DOS Drive(s) in the Extended DOS Partition

Drv Volume Label  Mbytes  System   Usage
D:                    50  UNKNOWN   100%



    All available space in the Extended DOS Partition
    is assigned to logical drives.
    Press Esc to continue
```

Figure 22-6 How to use Fdisk to create an extended partition and logical drive (parts 5 and 6 of 6)

enter a value, Fdisk displays a screen like the one in part 6 to verify that it created the logical drive you specified. Then, when you press the Esc key, Fdisk returns you to either the opening Fdisk menu or to the screen in part 5 so you can enter the value for the next logical drive.

How to specify an active partition If you didn't use the maximum size for the primary partition when you created it, you must specify an *active partition* before you're finished with the Fdisk program. The active partition is the one that will be used to boot your PC. You should specify your primary partition as your active partition; you can't make the extended partition active.

Figure 22-7 shows how to specify an active partition. First, you select the Set-active-partition option from the opening Fdisk menu as illustrated in part 1. From the screen in part 2, you enter the number 1 to specify the primary partition as the active partition. Fdisk then displays the screen shown in part 3. Here, the letter A in the status column of the screen verifies that the primary partition is the active partition. Then, you press the Esc key twice to exit from the Fdisk program.

How to partition a hard disk when you use earlier versions of DOS

If you understand the procedure for using Fdisk with DOS 4.0 and later, you shouldn't have any trouble partitioning a hard disk when you use an earlier version of DOS. However, there are a few differences you should be aware of when you use an earlier version of DOS.

When you use DOS 3.3 Because DOS 3.3 uses 16-bit numbers to identify sectors on a hard disk, it can't access disk drives that are larger than 32MB. In case you'd like to know why, it's because a 16-bit binary number has a maximum value of 65,536. Since the standard sector size that DOS 3.3 uses for a hard disk is 512 bytes, the total number of sectors (65,536) times the sector size (512 bytes) equals the maximum disk size of 33,554,432 bytes, or 32MB. (DOS 4.0 and later versions overcome this limit by using 32-bit numbers to identify sectors.)

If you have a hard disk with more than 32MB, you must divide it into two partitions: one primary partition for drive C and one extended partition. Then, you must define at least one logical drive in the extended partition. And if the extended partition is more than 32MB, you must further divide it into logical drives D, E, and so on. If, for example, you have an 90MB hard disk, you can divide it into a 30MB primary partition (drive C) and a 60MB extended partition. Then, you can divide the extended partition into two 30MB logical drives (drives D and E) or three 20MB logical drives (drives D, E, and F).

If your hard disk is less than 32MB, you don't have to divide it into two partitions; you only have to define a primary partition. But if you want to divide the hard disk into two partitions so you can have two or more drives, you can do so.

Part 1:

From Fdisk's opening screen, select the Set-active-partition option by entering the number 2.

```
                         MS-DOS Version 6
                     Fixed Disk Setup Program
              (C)Copyright Microsoft Corp. 1983 - 1993

                           FDISK Options

Current fixed disk drive: 1

Choose one of the following:

1. Create DOS partition or Logical DOS Drive
2. Set active partition
3. Delete partition or Logical DOS Drive
4. Display partition information



Enter choice: [2]






Press Esc to exit FDISK
```

Part 2:

Fdisk displays the partitions on the drive. To specify the primary partition as the active partition, enter the number 1.

```
                      Set Active Partition

Current fixed disk drive: 1

Partition  Status   Type    Volume Label  Mbytes   System    Usage
 C: 1              PRI DOS                    50   UNKNOWN     50%
    2              EXT DOS                    50   UNKNOWN     50%


Total disk space is  100 Mbytes (1 Mbyte = 1048576 bytes)

Enter the number of the partition you want to make active..........: [1]




Press Esc to return to FDISK Options
```

Figure 22-7 How to use Fdisk to specify the active partition (parts 1 and 2 of 3)

Part 3:

After Fdisk makes the primary partition active, it displays a verification screen. To return to the Fdisk opening menu and exit from the Fdisk program, press the Esc key twice.

```
                         Set Active Partition

Current fixed disk drive: 1

Partition  Status   Type    Volume Label  Mbytes   System   Usage
 C: 1        A     PRI DOS                   50    UNKNOWN    50%
    2              EXT DOS                   50    UNKNOWN    50%


Total disk space is  100 Mbytes (1 Mbyte = 1048576 bytes)




Partition 1 made active


Press Esc to continue
```

Figure 22-7 How to use Fdisk to specify the active partition (part 3 of 3)

Other than restricting you to 32MB partitions, the DOS 3.3 Fdisk program works much like later versions of Fdisk. The only other significant difference is that DOS 3.3 Fdisk measures disk space in cylinders rather than megabytes or a percentage of total disk space. For example, DOS 3.3 Fdisk might indicate that the total disk space for a 40MB drive is 820 cylinders, and the maximum partition size is 656 cylinders. Unfortunately, you have to calculate the number of cylinders to use if you want to create a partition that's smaller than 32MB.

When you use versions of DOS before 3.3 If you use a version of DOS before DOS 3.3, you can't use the Fdisk program to create an extended partition or logical drives. As a result, these versions of DOS can support only a hard disk with a capacity of up to 32MB. To get around this limitation, you have to use special software that creates non-standard partitions. You also have to set up a special device driver in the CONFIG.SYS file to recognize the non-standard partitioning. The documentation that comes with the disk partitioning software should explain how to do this.

Frankly, if you're using a version of DOS earlier than 3.3 and you have a disk drive larger than 32MB, you should upgrade to DOS 6.0 right away. DOS 6.0's Fdisk program supports the larger disk drive more reliably and more flexibly than non-standard partitioning software.

The Format command for formatting drive C

```
A:\>format c: /s /v
```

The Format command for formatting drive D

```
A:\>format d: /v
```

Figure 22-8 How to use the Format command for the high-level formatting of a hard disk

How to use the Format command to do the high-level formatting

In chapter 8, you learned how to use the DOS Format command for formatting diskettes. When you use this command to format a hard disk, DOS creates the root directory and the *File Allocation Table* (*FAT*) for the hard disk. It also scans the entire disk surface for bad sectors and locks them out in the FAT. This formatting process is called *high-level formatting*.

Figure 22-8 shows the commands you use to format the drives on a hard disk. To format drive C, you start your PC from drive A using the DOS system diskette. Then, you enter the first command. Here, the /S switch causes the command to transfer the system files to the hard disk. The /V switch causes the command to ask for a volume label for the disk after the disk has been formatted. At that time, you should supply a label like DISK-VOL-C.

Once you've formatted drive C, you can restore your backups to the new C drive. Alternatively, you can create a DOS directory, copy all the DOS files to that directory, set up the AUTOEXEC.BAT file with a Path command that includes the DOS directory, and restart the PC from the hard disk. Next, you can format the other logical drives using the second Format command shown in figure 22-8. (To format logical drives other than D, just substitute the correct drive letter.)

Some perspective on partitioning and formatting

You shouldn't have any trouble partitioning and formatting a hard disk if you go about it carefully and methodically. Because you should have to do this job only once or twice in the life of a PC, speed isn't the goal. You just want to get the hard disk set up right.

If you don't like the way the partitions are set up on your PC, you can change them whenever you want to. However, it's a time consuming procedure if your hard disk is already full of programs and data. To repartition your hard disk, start by backing up all the programs and data on the hard disk to diskettes. Next, use the Fdisk program to delete your existing partitions and logical drives and define your new partitions and logical drives. Then, use the Format command to reformat the new drives you defined on the hard disk. Finally, use the Restore function of the backup program to restore the files to the appropriate drives. Because this takes time and care, you should have a good reason for changing the partitions of your hard disk before you undertake this procedure.

One of the best reasons for changing the partitions is to prepare for DoubleSpace. If you've read chapter 18, you know that DoubleSpace lets you create one or more compressed drives on a single drive. Unlike logical drives created by Fdisk, it's easy to change the size of a compressed drive created by DoubleSpace. So if your disk currently has two or more drives, you should consider combining them into one large partition before running DoubleSpace.

Terms

low-level formatting
defect table
partition
primary partition
extended partition
logical drive
active partition
File Allocation Table
FAT
high-level formatting

Objectives

1. Find out if you can do a low-level format on your hard disk and, if so, how to do it.
2. Describe the relationships between a primary partition and a secondary partition, and between and secondary partition and its logical drives.
3. Create a primary partition, extended partition, and one or more logical drives on your hard disk.
4. Perform a high-level format on drive C and on any logical drives.

Chapter 23

How to upgrade to DOS 6.0

In this chapter, you'll learn how to install DOS 6.0 on your computer. When you purchase a new computer, it will most likely have DOS 6.0 already installed on it. So you need to read this chapter only if your computer already has an earlier version of DOS you wish to upgrade.

You can purchase the DOS 6.0 upgrade package from just about any store that stocks computer software, so you shouldn't have any trouble obtaining it. In the upgrade package, you'll find detailed instructions for installing DOS. So in this chapter, I'll give you just an overview of the procedure you follow, plus offer some advice you won't find in the manual.

A procedure for upgrading to DOS 6.0

DOS 6.0 comes with a Setup program that copies the DOS files from the distribution diskettes to your hard disk and sets up your AUTOEXEC.BAT and CONFIG.SYS files automatically. However, there's more to completely installing DOS 6.0 than just running the Setup program. Figure 23-1 lists a complete DOS 6.0 upgrade procedure.

The first step when upgrading to DOS 6.0 is to do a complete backup of your hard disk. Because the DOS 6.0 Setup program is reliable, you probably won't need to resort to using this backup to recover from a problem. Still, experience has taught me to never make major changes to a PC without a backup. And installing a new version of DOS certainly qualifies as a major change.

The second step is to remove any memory resident programs from your AUTOEXEC.BAT file and restart your computer. For example, if your AUTOEXEC.BAT file starts an anti-virus program, a delete tracking program, or any other memory resident software, remove it by deleting the line entirely or by adding the word REM to the beginning of the line. The Setup program, unfortunately, can be adversely affected by these programs. When you've completed the installation, you can edit your AUTOEXEC.BAT file to reactivate these programs.

Next, you should make sure you have two blank diskettes before you proceed. DOS uses these diskettes during installation to store information that can later help you remove DOS 6.0 from your computer if you encounter a problem. This is possible because the DOS 6.0 Setup program doesn't delete your current version of DOS. Instead, it moves the contents of your DOS directory to a directory named OLD_DOS.1. Then, it copies critical information about your system to the uninstall diskettes. If for some reason you need to revert to your old DOS version, you can boot your PC from this diskette and follow the instructions it displays. (Incidentally, the diskettes don't have to be formatted. Setup will format them for you if you insert unformatted diskettes.)

The fourth step in figure 23-1 is to run the Setup program from the installation diskettes. Then, you follow the instructions that Setup displays on the screen. For the most part, this is simply a matter of inserting the correct installation diskette into your diskette drive when prompted by Setup. Setup also asks you to make a few choices, such as whether not to install the DOS or *Windows* versions (or both versions) of Microsoft Backup, Microsoft Anti-Virus, and Undelete.

When Setup finishes, the next step you should take is to create a bootable diskette that you can use to access your system in case something goes wrong with your hard disk. You can let Setup create the diskette for you by invoking it with the /F switch. (You'll learn more about Setup switches and the diskette created by the /F switch later in this chapter.) Or, you can format the diskette using the Format command with the /S switch, then copy the important files to the diskette. Which ever method you use, you should make sure you have access to your backup program from diskette. If there's not enough room for it on the bootable diskette, you'll have to copy it to a separate diskette.

Once you've created the emergency diskette, you should do another complete system backup. This is especially important if you're going to do either of the next two steps because they make major changes to your hard disk. If you skip this second backup and a problem develops, you'll have to restore from your pre-DOS 6.0 backup, then install DOS 6.0 again.

The eighth step is to use DoubleSpace to compress the data on your hard disk. DoubleSpace is described in detail in chapter 18, and you shouldn't proceed with this step until you've read that chapter. The ninth step is to use MemMaker to automatically create memory management commands in your CONFIG.SYS file. MemMaker is described in detail in chapter 25, and once again, you shouldn't proceed until you've read that chapter. Both of these steps are optional. If you don't want or need the disk compression provided by DoubleSpace, you can skip step eight for now. You can always run DoubleSpace later. And if you don't want to use MemMaker's automatic memory configuration, you can skip step nine.

The last step in the installation process is to complete your registration card and mail it in. While you're at it, you should consider sending in the coupon for the DOS 6.0 supplemental diskette. This diskette includes commands that are no longer included with DOS, but are still compatible with DOS 6.0. Figure 23-2 lists these commands. If you used Setup to upgrade from DOS 5.0, you already have all these commands because Setup doesn't remove them from your DOS directory. So there's no need to send in the coupon. But if you upgraded from an earlier version of DOS, you won't have all of them. In particular, you won't have the Mirror command.

1. Do a complete backup of your hard disk.
2. Remove any memory resident programs from your AUTOEXEC.BAT file and restart your computer.
3. Make sure you have two blank diskettes to use as the uninstall diskettes during the next step. They don't have to be formatted.
4. Insert the DOS 6.0 installation diskette labeled "Setup Disk 1" into drive A, and run the Setup program by entering this command:

   ```
   C:\>a:setup
   ```
5. Follow the instructions on the screen. When prompted, insert the blank uninstall diskettes.
6. When Setup is complete, create a bootable DOS 6.0 emergency diskette by typing the command

   ```
   C:\>setup /f
   ```

   and the Setup program will copy a subset of DOS to diskette for you. See figure 23-4 for a list of the files Setup copies.

   Alternatively, you can enter the command

   ```
   C:\>format /s
   ```

   Then, you can copy whatever commands and programs you want to the diskette.

   Note: You may want to tailor the diskette created by SETUP /F so it includes other utilities. For example, you may want to copy the backup program you used in step 1 to the diskette. If your backup program won't fit on the diskette, place it on a separate diskette.
7. Do a complete backup of your system.
8. If you wish, run DoubleSpace to compress your hard disk.
9. If you wish, run MemMaker to optimize your memory configuration.
10. Send in the product registration card and, if you wish, the supplemental diskette coupon.

Figure 23-1 A procedure for upgrading to DOS 6.0

Although most of the features of this command have been added to other commands in DOS 6.0, the feature that provides recovery protection for your hard disk's partition table isn't included anywhere in DOS 6.0.

How to use advanced features of the Setup command

Figure 23-3 shows that the Setup command has a variety of switches. Ordinarily, you don't need to use any of these switches. However, each of them might be handy in certain circumstances. If you have any problems running Setup, check these switches to see if any of them might help.

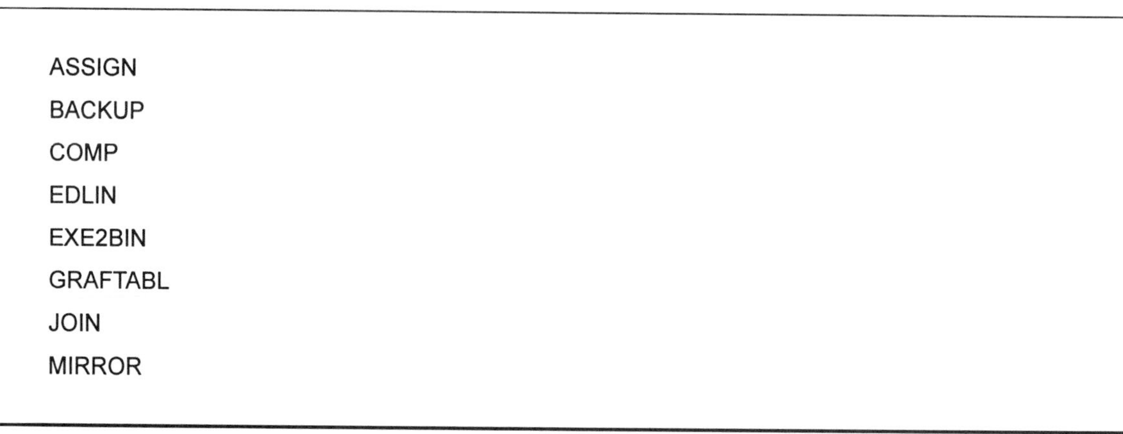

ASSIGN
BACKUP
COMP
EDLIN
EXE2BIN
GRAFTABL
JOIN
MIRROR

Figure 23-2 External DOS commands that are included on the DOS 6.0 supplemental diskette

Although most of the Setup switches shown in figure 23-3 are designed for problem solving, two of them are more generally useful. The /F switch installs a small subset of DOS 6.0 on a diskette. The diskette created by SETUP /F includes the files shown in figure 23-4. If you wish, you can delete some of these files to make room for other programs you'd prefer to have access to in an emergency.

The /E switch is useful if, when you install DOS 6.0, you don't install the optional DOS 6.0 utilities (Microsoft Backup, Microsoft Anti-Virus, and Microsoft Undelete) and you later decide you want them, or if you install DOS 6.0 on a system that doesn't have *Microsoft Windows* and you install *Windows* later. It lets you install either the *Windows* or DOS versions of these programs. (Setup will prompt you for the versions you want to install.) If you install the *Windows* versions, it also adds the Microsoft Tools group to the program manager and updates the File Manager menus so you can access the utilities.

How to retrieve files from the installation disks

Although unlikely, you might need to retrieve a file from one of the installation diskettes. For example, you might accidentally delete a file in your DOS directory. Or, Chkdsk might report that one of your DOS files is damaged, so you have to delete it. When that happens, you can easily retrieve the lost DOS files from the installation disks. To find out which disk contains the file you need, you can insert each of the disks until you find the file. Or, you can check the PACKING.LST file that's stored on Disk 1. It lists the files on each installation disk.

Many of the files on the installation disks are stored in a compressed format, so they must be uncompressed before you can use them. All of these compressed files

The format of the Setup command

```
SETUP [/B] [/E] [/F] [/G] [/H] [/I] [/M] [/Q] [/U]
```

Switch meanings

/B	Displays screens in monochrome.
/E	Installs just the Windows or DOS versions of Microsoft Backup, Microsoft Anti-Virus, and Microsoft Undelete. If necessary, adds the Microsoft Tools group to the *Windows* Program Manager, and creates additional menu items in the *Windows* File Manager.
/F	Installs a minimum subset of DOS onto a diskette.
/G	Does not create an uninstall disk.
/H	Uses default setup options, bypassing user prompts.
/I	Turns off hardware detection. Use this if some unusual hardware device causes Setup to hang up your system.
/M	Installs a minimal DOS system. Use this if you are tight on disk space.
/Q	Copies the DOS 6.0 files to a hard disk, but doesn't copy the hidden files necessary to start DOS (IO.SYS and MSDOS.SYS). To do that, you must use the Sys command. Use this switch if Setup isn't able to install the system files.
/U	Installs DOS even if Setup detects disk partitions that might be incompatible. Use this if your hard disk contains Novell, Unix, or Xenix partitions.

Example 1: A Setup command that creates a bootable diskette.

```
A:\>setup /f
```

Example 2: A Setup command that lets you add the optional DOS 6.0 utilities.

```
A:\>setup /e
```

Figure 23-3 Advanced options for the DOS 6.0 Setup command

have an underscore (_) as the last character of the file's extension. For example, the ANSI.SYS file is stored in compressed form on the installation disks as ANSI.SY_. Similarly, the Move command is stored as MOVE.EX_. To uncompress a compressed file, you use the Expand command shown in figure 23-5.

```
C:\>dir a:

 Volume in drive A is STARTUP
 Volume Serial Number is 1A51-4552
 Directory of A:\

COMMAND  COM     52925 02-12-93   6:00a
ATTRIB   EXE     11165 02-12-93   6:00a
DEBUG    EXE     15715 02-12-93   6:00a
EXPAND   EXE     16129 02-12-93   6:00a
FDISK    EXE     29333 02-12-93   6:00a
FORMAT   COM     22717 02-12-93   6:00a
RESTORE  EXE     38294 02-12-93   6:00a
SYS      COM      9379 02-12-93   6:00a
CHKDSK   EXE     12908 02-12-93   6:00a
EDIT     COM       413 02-12-93   6:00a
QBASIC   EXE    194309 02-12-93   6:00a
MSD      EXE    158470 02-12-93   6:00a
XCOPY    EXE     15820 02-12-93   6:00a
DBLSPACE EXE    273068 02-12-93   6:00a
MSAV     EXE    172198 02-12-93   6:00a
       15 file(s)    1022843 bytes
                      301056 bytes free
```

Figure 23-4 The contents of a diskette created by a Setup command with the /F switch

One file you might want to retrieve from the installation disks right away is EGA.IN_. This file contains the DOS 6.0 version of DOSSHELL.INI, a control file that keeps track of options and menu structures for the DOS shell. The DOS 6.0 version of this file includes a disk utilities menu that lets you access the new DOS 6.0 utilities. If Setup finds an existing DOSSHELL.INI file in your DOS directory, it doesn't copy the DOS 6.0 version. That's because if it did, you'd loose any program items you've added to its menus. If you don't mind losing the changes you've made to the DOS shell and you want the DOS 6.0 version of DOSSHELL.INI, you can use the Expand command shown in figure 23-5 to retrieve it. (EGA.IN_ is located on Disk 2.) Before you do that, though, you'll want to note the program items you've added to the menus.

The format of the Expand command

```
EXPAND compressed-file [compressed-file...] target-spec
```

Explanation

`compressed-file`	The name of a compressed file you want to retrieve from a DOS installation diskette. The last character of the file extension is always an underscore (_).
`target-spec`	The location where DOS is to place the uncompressed file. When you expand a single file, you can change its name by specifying a file name here. When you specify more than one compressed file by using wildcards or multiple file specifications, *target-spec* must not include a file name.

An Expand command that retrieves the file EGA.IN_ from the installation disks and changes its name to DOSSHELL.INI

```
expand a:\ega.in_ dosshell.ini
```

Figure 23-5 How to use the Expand command to retrieve files from the installation disks

Some perspective on upgrading to DOS 6.0

You shouldn't have any trouble upgrading to DOS 6.0 if you go about it carefully and methodically. Microsoft conducted extensive tests of the Setup program on thousands of different PCs, so it's unlikely that you'll encounter any compatibility problems. If you do encounter a problem while running Setup, you can get help by contacting Microsoft using the procedures spelled out in the *User's Guide and Reference,* which comes with DOS 6.0.

Objective

Upgrade your system to DOS 6.0 using the procedure outlined in this chapter.

Chapter 24

Commands for the CONFIG.SYS and AUTOEXEC.BAT files

In chapter 5, you learned that the startup procedure for a PC uses three files that are stored in the root directory of drive C. First, resident DOS is loaded from the COMMAND.COM file. Second, DOS executes the commands in the CONFIG.SYS file. Third, DOS executes the commands in the AUTOEXEC.BAT file.

In chapter 5, you also learned how to set up an AUTOEXEC.BAT file. In chapters 10 and 11, you learned about other commands that you can put in the AUTOEXEC.BAT file. Also in chapter 11, you learned how to use two commands that you can put in the CONFIG.SYS file to improve performance.

In this chapter, you'll learn more about setting up your CONFIG.SYS and AUTOEXEC.BAT files. You'll learn about the various commands that DOS provides for these files and how you can best use them on your system. Because there are so many varieties of computer systems available and people use their computers in a nearly endless variety of ways, it's just not possible to make blanket recommendations for CONFIG.SYS and AUTOEXEC.BAT files that apply to everyone. As a result, you should read through this chapter to see if any of the commands it presents would be useful to you. Before you begin, it might be a good idea to print a copy of your current CONFIG.SYS and AUTOEXEC.BAT files so you can compare them with the examples you'll see here.

This chapter isn't the last one in this book that will cover CONFIG.SYS and AUTOEXEC.BAT features. Many of the CONFIG.SYS commands are related to making the best use of internal memory. Because memory management is itself a complicated subject, I'll discuss it separately in the next chapter. In addition, some of the AUTOEXEC.BAT files you'll see in this chapter use batch file features you haven't learned about yet. If these batch files confuse you, you can skip ahead to chapter 27 to learn how those features work.

Fortunately, once you set up your CONFIG.SYS and AUTOEXEC.BAT files properly, you shouldn't have to change them unless you change some of the hardware components of your PC or you add a program to your system. If, for example, you add a mouse or a CD-ROM drive to your PC, you may have to add one or more commands to your CONFIG.SYS or AUTOEXEC.BAT file. Similarly, if you add a new application program to your system, you may have to add a command to the CONFIG.SYS file that provides for a special requirement of that program.

Today, the installation programs that come with most application programs and utilities automatically modify the CONFIG.SYS and AUTOEXEC.BAT files. When you install new software, it's always a good idea to examine your CONFIG.SYS and AUTOEXEC.BAT files to see what changes the software may have made. In some cases, you may discover that the installation routine has added a command that conflicts with an existing CONFIG.SYS or AUTOEXEC.BAT command.

One final word of warning before I proceed. Always make a backup copy of your CONFIG.SYS and AUTOEXEC.BAT files before you modify them. You may want to revert to your existing CONFIG.SYS or AUTOEXEC.BAT file, and you won't be able to do that if you don't make a backup copy.

DOS 5.0/6.0 commands for the CONFIG.SYS file

If you look through the manual that comes with your version of DOS, you'll find a number of commands that are designed specifically for the CONFIG.SYS file. For instance, figure 24-1 lists the fourteen commands that DOS 5.0 provides for the CONFIG.SYS file. (DOS 6.0 includes all these commands, plus some new ones that I'll cover later in this chapter). Each of these commands is useful in certain situations, but you probably won't need them all. Here, I'll describe just the ones that are the most widely used.

Figure 24-2 presents two CONFIG.SYS files that use some of these commands. The first example is a basic CONFIG.SYS file that can be used with any version of DOS. You're already familiar with the Buffers command, so I'll cover only the Files and Device commands here. The second example includes commands unique to DOS 5.0 and 6.0 for optimizing memory. I'll cover the Lastdrive and Devicehigh commands here. In the next chapter, I'll expand on the Devicehigh command and I'll present the Dos command. In addition to the commands presented in these two examples, I'll also cover the Fcbs, Shell, and Drivparm commands.

The Files command The Files command controls the number of files that DOS will allow to be open at one time. More specifically, the Files command specifies the number of *file handles* that should be created. Although it's an oversimplification, you can think of a file handle as an area of internal memory that DOS uses to keep track of an open file. When a program opens a file, DOS assigns an available file handle to the file. Then, when the program closes the file, DOS frees the file handle so it can be used for another file.

Command format	Function
`BREAK [ON|OFF]`	Enables or disables the Ctrl+C function.
`BUFFERS=buffers[,secondary]`	Sets the number of buffers DOS uses for disk access.
`COUNTRY=parameters`	Specifies the international format DOS uses for time, date, currency, and so on.
`DEVICE=file-spec [parameters]`	Installs a device driver.
`DEVICEHIGH=file-spec [parameters]`	(DOS 5.0 and later) Installs a device driver into upper memory.
`DOS=[HIGH|LOW][,UMB|NOUMB]`	(DOS 5.0 and later) Loads a portion of resident DOS into high memory and/or enables support for upper memory.
`DRIVPARM=/D:number [parameters]`	Specifies parameters for drives.
`FCBS=number`	Specifies the number of File Control Blocks for compatibility with older programs.
`FILES=number`	Specifies the number of files that may be open simultaneously.
`INSTALL=file-spec [parameters]`	(DOS 4.0 and later) Loads certain memory resident programs with less overhead than when started from AUTOEXEC.BAT. With DOS 5.0, it's even more efficient to load memory resident programs using the Loadhigh command as described in chapter 25.
`LASTDRIVE=letter`	Specifies the highest drive letter that can be used by DOS.
`REM remark-text`	Identifies a remark in a CONFIG.SYS file.
`SHELL=file-spec [parameters]`	Specifies the location of the COMMAND.COM file and lets you increase the size of the DOS environment space.
`STACKS=number`	Controls the number of stacks DOS uses for handling special internal operations called *hardware interrupts.*

Figure 24-1 CONFIG.SYS commands

Example 1: A basic CONFIG.SYS file for all DOS versions.

```
files=20
buffers=20
device=c:\dos\ansi.sys
```

Example 2: A CONFIG.SYS file that uses DOS 5.0/6.0 memory management commands and the DOS 5.0 version of Smartdrv.

```
files=20
device=c:\dos\himem.sys
dos=high,umb
devicehigh=c:\dos\ansi.sys
devicehigh=c:\dos\smartdrv.sys 2048 512
devicehigh=c:\dos\setver.exe
install=c:\dos\fastopen.exe c:=50
lastdrive=z
```

Figure 24-2 Two examples of CONFIG.SYS files

The number of files typically open while you're using an application program is more than you might expect. For instance, an application program may open several program files, one or more data files, a backup file for each data file, and several temporary files. If the Files command doesn't provide for all the files that a program tries to open, the program won't work.

If the CONFIG.SYS file doesn't contain a Files command, DOS automatically creates eight file handles. This is inadequate for most modern application programs. If, for example, you try to start *WordPerfect* with only eight file handles, you get an error message that says the system doesn't have enough file handles. To correct the problem, you must change the Files command in the CONFIG.SYS file so it provides for 20 or more open files. Then, to put this change into effect, you have to restart your system.

When you install an application program that requires more than the DOS default of eight file handles, the installation program that comes with the application program is likely to insert an appropriate Files command in your CONFIG.SYS file automatically. As a result, you may never have to add a Files command to your CONFIG.SYS file or modify the old one. Not all programs take care of this for you, though, so you should know how to enter this command when you need it.

The Fcbs command The Fcbs command is required only if you use a very old program. To understand why it's required, you need to realize that when DOS was first introduced, it didn't support subdirectories. (Subdirectories weren't considered necessary because the largest storage device for the original IBM PC was a 360KB diskette drive.) So the *File Control Blocks*, or *FCBs*, it used to keep track of open files didn't provide for directory information.

When IBM introduced DOS 2.0 along with the IBM PC/XT, subdirectories were added to make it easier to manage files on the XT's 10MB hard drive. Because File Control Blocks can't keep track of which directory a file is in, Microsoft used a different method of keeping track of files: file handles. Microsoft immediately began recommending that programmers convert to the file handles method of accessing files rather than the FCB method, so it's unlikely that you have a program that uses FCBs. If you do, however, you may encounter a problem if you use a program that tries to use more FCBs than the DOS default of four. If so, add an Fcbs command to your CONFIG.SYS file to increase the number of File Control Blocks that can be used.

The Device and Devicehigh commands The Device command lets you load special programs called *device drivers*. These device drivers provide support for hardware components like a mouse, a CD-ROM drive, or extended memory. They can also provide support for special hardware and software features like disk caching.

The Devicehigh command is similar to the Device command, but lets you use internal memory more efficiently. You'll learn more about the distinction between Device and Devicehigh in the next chapter. For the purposes of this chapter, you can think of them as interchangeable. (But don't try to use the Devicehigh command until you've read the next chapter.)

Figure 24-3 lists the device drivers that come with DOS 6.0. Of these, the five you're most likely to use are the ANSI.SYS, HIMEM.SYS, EMM386.EXE, SETVER.EXE, and SMARTDRV.SYS drivers. I already covered SMARTDRV.SYS in chapter 11, and I'll cover HIMEM.SYS and EMM386.EXE in chapter 25 and ANSI.SYS in chapter 27. So the only one of these five drives I'll present in this chapter is SETVER.EXE. You'll use the rest of the DOS 6.0 drivers only in unusual situations. I'll show you how to use DRIVER.SYS and RAMDRIVE.SYS later in this chapter.

As you can see in figure 24-1, a Device or Devicehigh command begins with the keyword followed by an equal sign (=). Then, it lists the drive, path, and complete file name of the driver you want to use. After the driver specification, the command can also include parameters and switches that are specific to the device driver.

In the examples in figure 24-2, you can see several examples of Device and Devicehigh commands. In the first example, a Device command loads the ANSI.SYS device driver. And the second example includes several Devicehigh commands to load other drivers.

The Shell command The Shell command, shown in figure 24-4, specifies the location of the DOS command processor, COMMAND.COM. If this file is in your root directory, you don't need a Shell command in your CONFIG.SYS file. If you want to remove COMMAND.COM from your root directory and place it in your DOS directory, you must use a Shell command. The syntax of the Shell command is a little peculiar because it requires you to specify the location of COMMAND.COM twice. First, you must provide a complete file specification for COMMAND.COM,

Device driver	Function
ANSI.SYS	Provides enhanced display capabilities you can access from batch files. Some older programs require ANSI.SYS to be installed. Chapter 27 describes ANSI.SYS in detail.
DBLSPACE.SYS	(DOS 6.0) Moves the DoubleSpace control program into upper memory or to low conventional memory. Described in chapter 25.
DISPLAY.SYS	Provides support for international character sets.
DRIVER.SYS	Lets you support external diskette drives or create logical drive letters that refer to internal diskette drives.
EGA.SYS	(DOS 5.0 and later) Provides support for the DOS shell task swapper when you're using an EGA monitor.
EMM386.EXE	(DOS 5.0 and later) Provides support for expanded memory, upper memory, and Weitek coprocessors. Described in chapter 25.
HIMEM.SYS	(DOS 5.0 and later) Provides support for extended memory. Described in chapter 25.
INTERLNK.EXE	(DOS 6.0) Provides file transfer capabilities. Described in chapter 20.
POWER.EXE	(DOS 6.0) Provides power management support for portable computers. Described in chapter 20.
PRINTER.SYS	Provides printer support for international character sets.
RAMDRIVE.SYS	Simulates a disk drive using internal memory.
SETVER.EXE	Lets older programs that require a specific DOS version operate with a newer version of DOS.
SMARTDRV.SYS	(DOS 4.0 and 5.0 only) Creates a disk cache using extended or expanded memory. Described in chapter 11.

Figure 24-3 The device drivers provided with DOS

including the drive and directory, immediately after the equal sign. Then, you must provide the drive and directory again as the first parameter.

Besides specifying the location of COMMAND.COM, the Shell command has another important function as well. It lets you specify the size of the *environment*. The environment is an area of internal memory that's set aside to hold *environment variables*. Later in this chapter, I'll show you how you can use environment variables in your AUTOEXEC.BAT file to control certain aspects of DOS' operation. And in chapter 27, you'll learn how to use environment variables in other batch files.

The format of the SHELL command

```
SHELL=C:\DOS\COMMAND.COM C:\DOS [/E:number] /P
```

Explanation

`C:\DOS\COMMAND.COM`	The DOS command processor.
`C:\DOS`	The drive and directory location of COMMAND.COM.
`/E:number`	Specifies the number of bytes to reserve for the DOS environment, which DOS uses to store the directory search path and environment variables. Number can be from 160 to 32768. The default is 256.
`/P`	Specifies that this is the primary command processor, so you can't use the Exit command to exit from it. This switch is required.

A Shell command that specifies that COMMAND.COM should create a 512-byte environment

```
shell=c:\dos\command.com /e:512 /p
```

Figure 24-4 The Shell command

By default, DOS reserves only 256 bytes for the environment. In many cases, that's not enough. To understand why, you need to realize that the settings you specify for both the Path and the Prompt commands are stored in the environment along with other environment variables you create. If you specify more than a few directories in your Path command or use a complicated prompt, you'll quickly reduce the amount of space left in the environment to the point where 256 bytes isn't enough to create additional environment variables.

To prevent that from happening, you can use the /E switch on the Shell command. The example in figure 24-4 shows a Shell command that creates a 512-byte environment. Notice that I also specified /P. It's required when you use the Shell command.

The Drivparm command The Drivparm command, shown in figure 24-5, lets you use certain non-standard devices on your PC. Probably the only use you'll have for this command is if you need to install a 3-1/2 inch diskette drive in a PC that was manufactured before 3-1/2 inch drives were available. On these PCs, the BIOS chip, which provides the low-level support needed to use diskette drives, isn't aware of 3-1/2 inch drives. But you can use a 3-1/2 inch drive in one of those older machines if you include a Drivparm command like the one in figure 24-5 in your CONFIG.SYS file.

The Lastdrive command When you start your PC, DOS sets aside about 100 bytes of internal memory to keep track of each disk drive on your system. This includes diskettes, hard disks, logical drives in a hard disk's extended partition, logical drives created by the RAMDRIVE.SYS and DRIVER.SYS device drivers, and compressed drives created with DoubleSpace. DOS assigns a drive letter to each of these drives.

When your PC is connected to a network, you need to reserve additional drive letters that can be assigned to drives that are located on other PCs attached to the network. To do that, you use the Lastdrive command. You can reserve a total of 26 drives by including this command in your CONFIG.SYS file:

```
lastdrive=z
```

Keep in mind that since each drive requires about 100 bytes of internal memory, you shouldn't specify a value that's larger than necessary. For example, if you have three drives on your PC (A through C) and you want to be able to access three network drives (D through F), specify LASTDRIVE=F in your CONFIG.SYS file.

How to use three device drivers provided with DOS

Earlier, I mentioned that three of the device drivers provided with DOS, DRIVER.SYS, RAMDRIVE.SYS, and SETVER.EXE, are useful in certain situations. Now, I'll show you how to use these drivers.

How to use DRIVER.SYS As you already know, you can use the Diskcopy command to copy the entire contents of one diskette to another using a single drive. For example, if you enter the command

```
C:\>diskcopy a: a:
```

Diskcopy will copy the contents of the source diskette to the target diskette, prompting you when necessary to insert each diskette in drive A.

The DRIVER.SYS device driver lets you do similar operations using other DOS commands. It creates an additional drive letter you can use to refer to an existing diskette drive. When you use DRIVER.SYS, DOS treats the diskette drive as if it were two distinct drives, prompting you to swap diskettes in and out of the drive as necessary. For example, suppose you have both a 1.44MB (drive A) and a 1.2MB diskette drive (drive B), and one hard disk (drive C). With DRIVER.SYS, you can create a second drive letter for the 1.44MB drive and a second drive letter for the 1.2MB drive by including the two commands shown in the example in figure 24-6.

When you use DRIVER.SYS, DOS assigns the next available drive letter to use as the second drive letter for the device you specify. Thus, in this example, DOS would assign D as the second drive letter for drive A and E as the second drive letter for drive B. If you watch your screen when you reboot your computer, you can confirm these drive letter assignments by reading the messages displayed by DRIVER.SYS.

The format of the Drivparm command

```
DRIVPARM=/D:drive [/F:factor] [/I] [/C]
```

Switch meanings

`/D:drive`	Specifies the drive number. Drive A is 0, drive B is 1, drive C is 2, and so on.
`/F:factor`	Specifies the type of drive. *Factor* is a number from 0 to 9, as follows:

0	360KB (or smaller) diskette drive (5.25")
1	1.2MB diskette drive (5.25")
2	720KB diskette drive (3.5")
5	Hard disk
6	Tape drive
7	1.44MB diskette drive (3.5")
8	Optical disk
9	2.88MB diskette drive (3.5")

If you omit /F, the default is 2.

`/I`	Enables support for 3.5" diskette drives on PCs that don't have ROM BIOS support for 3.5" drives.
`/C`	Specifies whether or not the drive can detect if the drive door is open or closed. Check the documentation that comes with the disk drive to determine if the drive can do this.

A Drivparm command that provides support for a 3.5" diskette as drive B on a system whose ROM BIOS doesn't support 3.5" diskettes

```
drivparm /d:1 /f:7 /i /c
```

Figure 24-5 The Drivparm command

Once you've set up a second drive letter for a diskette drive, you can use the Xcopy command to copy all the files from one 1.44MB diskette to another like this:

```
C:\>xcopy a:*.* d:*.* /s
```

Here, DOS will read in as many files from the A disk as possible. Then, it will ask you to insert the disk for drive D so it can write the files. DOS will ask you to swap disks as often as necessary to complete the copy operation.

Why would you want to copy diskettes in this way, rather than simply using the Diskcopy command? Because if the diskette has only a small amount of data on it, it's considerably faster to copy it with Xcopy than with Diskcopy. Diskcopy has to copy every sector on the disk, whether or not every sector actually contains data, but Xcopy

The format of the Device command for DRIVER.SYS

```
DEVICE=C:\DOS\DRIVER.SYS /D:drive [/F:factor] [/C]
```

Switch meanings

`/D:drive`	Specifies the drive number. Drive A is 0, drive B is 1, drive C is 2, and so on.
`/F:factor`	Specifies the type of drive. *Factor* is a number from 0 to 9, as follows: 0 360KB (or smaller) diskette drive (5.25") 1 1.2MB diskette drive (5.25") 2 720KB diskette drive (3.5") 7 1.44MB diskette drive (3.5") 9 2.88MB diskette drive (3.5") If you omit /F, the default is 2.
`/C`	Specifies whether or not the drive can detect if the drive door is open or closed. Check the documentation that comes with the disk drive to determine if the drive can do this.

Two Device commands for DRIVER.SYS that create logical drives that can be used to access drives A and B

```
device=c:\dos\driver.sys /d:0
device=c:\dos\driver.sys /d:1
```

Figure 24-6 The Device command for DRIVER.SYS

copies only those sectors that contain data. So if you frequently need to duplicate diskettes that don't have much data on them, you might want to consider using DRIVER.SYS.

By the way, the advantage of using the Xcopy command over the Copy command is significant when you use DRIVER.SYS. Because the Copy command copies files one at a time, you'd have to swap diskettes once for each file you copy. In contrast, Xcopy reads as many files as possible from drive A before asking you to swap diskettes.

Note that DRIVER.SYS is useful only when you have two diskette drives. If you have only one drive, DOS automatically provides this capability for you by assigning both diskette drive letters, A and B, to the diskette drive. DOS prompts you to swap diskettes whenever necessary. If you have only one diskette drive, try entering this command:

```
C:\>dir b:
```

Then, notice how DOS prompts you to insert the diskette for drive B.

How to use RAMDRIVE.SYS The RAMDRIVE.SYS device driver lets you set aside a certain amount of internal memory to use for a *RAM disk.* A RAM disk is a simulated hard disk. Because the data you store on a RAM disk is in internal memory rather than on an actual disk drive, it's lost whenever you power down or reboot your PC. As a result, RAM disks aren't safe for storing data files. Instead, RAM disks are usually used to store program files. Because data in internal memory can be accessed much faster than data on a hard disk, your programs will run much faster if you place their program files on a RAM disk.

Historically, RAM disks were among the first programs that could make use of the extended memory that was available on IBM ATs. As a result, it was common to use a RAM disk because that was the only way to take advantage of extended memory. Although some modern DOS programs (such as *Lotus 1-2-3*) can take advantage of extended memory, most programs still can't. But DOS versions 4.0 and later come with a program that makes even better use of extended memory than RAMDRIVE.SYS: Smartdrive. So if you have extended memory and DOS version 4.0 or later, I recommend you do *not* use a RAM disk. Instead, allocate as much of your extended memory as possible to Smartdrive.

I'll show you how to use RAMDRIVE.SYS here primarily because you may come across an older system that doesn't have a current version of DOS. Or, you might come across a system that does have a current DOS version, but still uses a RAM disk that was set up years ago before Smartdrive was available.

Figure 24-7 shows the Device command you use to set up a RAM disk. As you can see, the RAMDRIVE.SYS driver has three parameters and two switches. The first parameter specifies the size of the drive in KB. Usually, this is the only parameter you'll use. The other two parameters specify the size of each simulated disk sector and the number of root directory entries to allow. As for the switches, /E tells RAMDRIVE.SYS to create the RAM drive using extended memory, while /A specifies expanded memory. If you omit both switches, RAMDRIVE.SYS uses conventional memory.

Once you've added the Device command to CONFIG.SYS, you must restart your computer to create the RAM disk. When it's created, you can access the RAM disk as if it were another hard disk. You can copy files to it, create directories on it, run programs from it, and so on. Unlike a real hard disk, it's not necessary to format a RAM disk.

It's common to include commands in your AUTOEXEC.BAT file to copy files to the RAM disk. For example, if you want to run all of your batch files from the RAM disk, include a command like this in your AUTOEXEC.BAT file:

```
copy c:\util\*.bat d:
```

(This assumes that RAMDRIVE.SYS assigned drive letter D to the RAM drive. You'll have to watch your screen as your computer processes CONFIG.SYS to verify the drive letter RAMDRIVE.SYS uses.)

How to use SETVER.EXE Some application programs require a particular version of DOS because they depend on a DOS feature that was introduced with that version. For example, a program that uses the DOS networking features introduced with version 3.1 can't be run under an earlier version of DOS. Usually, a program like this will test to make sure that the version of DOS running on your machine is 3.1 or later.

Unfortunately, some programs make the mistake of testing for a *specific* version of DOS. For example, a program designed to run only under DOS 5.0 might display a message like this if you try to run it under DOS 6.0:

```
Incorrect DOS version
```

Sometimes, it's appropriate for a program to test for a specific DOS version. But in most cases, it's just a programming error. The programmers who developed the software could just as easily have tested for a specific DOS version or any later version since Microsoft goes to great lengths to insure that each new version of DOS will support programs that ran under previous versions.

With DOS 5.0, Microsoft introduced the SETVER.EXE driver to get around this problem. SETVER.EXE loads a table of program names and DOS version numbers into internal memory. Then, whenever a program asks DOS to report its version number, SETVER scans the version table to see if the program is in the table. If so, SETVER reports the version number from the table rather than the actual DOS version. As a result, the program is fooled into thinking that an earlier version of DOS is being used.

Figure 24-8 shows the Device command you use for the SETVER.EXE driver and the Setver command, which you use to add or delete entries from the Setver table. To use the SETVER.EXE driver, all you do is add the following Device command to your CONFIG.SYS file:

```
device=c:\dos\setver.exe
```

When you first use the SETVER.EXE driver, it loads a default version table that's supplied with DOS. To add programs to this table or to remove programs from the table, you use the Setver command as shown in the two examples in figure 24-8. The version table changes you make using the Setver command won't be effective until you reboot your computer.

If you upgrade to DOS 6.0, you may need to use the SETVER.EXE driver to use the DOS commands that are no longer provided with DOS, such as Edlin and Mirror. When the DOS 6.0 Setup program updates your DOS directory, it leaves the older versions of these programs in your DOS directory and creates entries for them in the version table. That way, you can continue to use them even though they were designed for an earlier DOS version. If you want to continue to use these programs without the SETVER.EXE driver, you can order the supplemental program diskette by using the coupon found at the back of your DOS 6.0 manual. The versions of these programs shipped on the supplemental diskette do not require SETVER.EXE to run under DOS 6.0.

The format of the Device command for RAMDRIVE.SYS

```
DEVICE=C:\DOS\RAMDRIVE.SYS disk-size sector-size num-entries [/E] [/A]
```

Explanation

`disk-size` Specifies the size of the RAM disk to create in KB. *Disk-size* can range from 16 to 4096 (4MB). The default is 64.

`sector-size` Specifies the size of each RAM disk sector in bytes. You can specify 128, 256, or 512. The default is 512. If you specify *sector-size*, you must also specify *disk-size*.

`num-entries` Specifies the number of files and directories to allow in the RAM drive's root directory. *Num-entries* can range from 2 to 1024. The default is 64. If you specify *num-entries*, you must also specify *sector-size* and *disk-size*.

`/E` Creates the RAM disk in extended memory.

`/A` Creates the RAM disk in expanded memory.

Note: You can't specify both /E and /A. If you omit both, the RAM disk is created in conventional memory. Also, the RAMDRIVE.SYS driver is named VDISK.SYS in some versions of DOS. The parameters are the same.

Example 1: A Device command for RAMDRIVE.SYS that creates a 512KB RAM drive using extended memory.

```
device=c:\dos\ramdrive.sys 512 /e
```

Example 2: A Device command for RAMDRIVE.SYS that creates a 4MB RAM drive in extended memory using 512-byte sectors and allows a maximum of 128 root directory entries.

```
device=c:\dos\ramdrive.sys 4096 512 128 /e
```

Figure 24-7 The Device command for RAMDRIVE.SYS

Commands for the AUTOEXEC.BAT file

Based on what you learned in earlier chapters, you should be able to set up simple AUTOEXEC.BAT files like those in figure 24-9. These files include DOS commands, and they include commands that start other batch files and commands that start programs. In the second example in figure 24-9, for example, Dosshell is a command that starts the DOS shell.

The format of the Device command for SETVER.EXE

```
DEVICE=C:\DOS\SETVER.EXE
```

The Setver command to change the version table

```
SETVER [file-name] [version] [/D]
```

Explanation

`file-name`	Specifies the file name for the program you want to add to or delete from the version table. If you omit *file-name*, Setver lists all the programs in the version table.
`version`	Specifies the value that DOS should report when the program asks DOS for the version. Used only when adding a program to the version table.
`/D`	Removes a program from the version table. Not valid when *version* is used.

Note: If you use the Setver command to change the version table, the change won't be in effect until you reboot your computer.

Example 1: A Setver command that adds an entry to the version table for a program named OLDPROG.EXE, which requires DOS version 3.2.

```
C:\>setver oldprog.exe 3.2
```

Example 2: A Setver command that removes the version table entry for OLDPROG.EXE.

```
C:\>setver oldprog.exe /d
```

Figure 24-8 The Device command for SETVER.EXE and the Setver command

Now, I want to show you how to use three commands that come with DOS that are particularly useful in your AUTOEXEC.BAT file. You've already been introduced to the first, Prompt, but you don't know how to use it to create anything other than the basic pg prompt. The other two commands are Set and Mouse.

The Prompt command As you already know, you use the Prompt command to specify the text that DOS displays in the command prompt. The basic prompt I recommended in chapter 5 displays the current drive and path followed by a greater-than sign, like this:

```
C:\DOS>
```

To specify this prompt, you include this command in your AUTOEXEC.BAT file:

```
prompt $p$g
```

An AUTOEXEC.BAT file for DOS 3.3

```
prompt $p$g
path c:\dos;c:\util
c:\dos\fastopen c:=50
```

An AUTOEXEC.BAT file for DOS 5.0 and 6.0

```
prompt $p$g
path c:\dos;c:\util
c:\dos\smartdrv 3084 512
c:\dos\doskey
c:\dos\dosshell
```

Figure 24-9 Basic AUTOEXEC.BAT files for DOS 3.3 and DOS 5.0/6.0

Here, $p is a code that tells DOS to display the current drive and path, and $g is a code that tells DOS to display a greater-than sign. (You have to use $g because if you use a greater-than sign in a DOS command, DOS assumes that you want to redirect the command's output to a device or file. You'll learn about redirection in chapter 26.)

Figure 24-10 shows the Prompt command and all the codes you can use with it. As you can see, Prompt provides codes that let you insert the date and time, the current drive, the current path (which includes the drive), and the DOS version. In addition, it provides codes that let you insert special characters like greater-than and less-than signs, equal signs, vertical bars, and dollar signs. You can also use $_ to create a prompt that displays on more than one line, $h to backspace over information already displayed, and $e to create special codes used by the ANSI.SYS device driver.

Figure 24-10 also includes three sample prompts. The first is the basic pg prompt you're already familiar with. The second displays a two-line prompt that consists of the date and time on one line and the current drive and directory followed by a greater-than sign on the second line. The three $h codes in the prompt erase the hundredths of seconds from the time displayed by $t. When you use this Prompt command, DOS will display a prompt that looks something like this:

```
Sat 01-30-1993 15:53:16
C:\DOS>
```

The third prompt in the figure uses ANSI.SYS commands to display the time and date in white characters on a blue background on the top line of the screen. This prompt will work only if you've installed the ANSI.SYS device driver using a Device command in your CONFIG.SYS file.

The format of the Prompt command

```
PROMPT prompt-text
```

Explanation

`prompt-text` The text you want to appear in the DOS prompt. It may include the following codes:

$B	| (vertical bar)
$Q	= (equal sign)
$G	> (greater-than sign)
$L	< (less-than sign)
$$	$ (dollar sign)
$D	The current date
$T	The current time
$P	The current path
$N	The current drive
$V	The DOS version number
$_	Start a new line
$H	Backspace over previous text
$E	Escape character (for ANSI.SYS)

Example 1: A Prompt command that creates a standard prompt that includes the current path.

```
prompt $p$g
```

Example 2: A Prompt command that creates a two-line prompt that displays the date and time on one line and the current path on the next.

```
prompt $d  $t$h$h$h$_$p$g
```

Example 3: A Prompt command that uses ANSI.SYS commands to create a prompt that displays the time and date against a blue background on the top line of the screen.

```
prompt $e[s$e[H$e[37;44m$e[K$t$h$h$h$e[58C$d$e[37;40m$e[u$p$g
```

Figure 24-10 The PROMPT command

The format of the Set command for AUTOEXEC.BAT

```
SET [variable=[text]]
```

Explanation

`variable`	The name of the environment variable whose value is to be set. If you omit variable, Set displays the current value of all environment variables.
`text`	The text to be associated with the variable. If *text* is omitted, Set deletes the variable.

Example 1: A Set command that sets the TEMP variable, which tells DOS where to create temporary files.

```
set temp=c:\temp
```

Example 2: A Set command that sets the DIRCMD variable, which specifies a default format for the Dir command.

```
set dircmd=/o:n /p
```

Figure 24-11 The Set command for AUTOEXEC.BAT

If you think you might like to create your own customized prompt, you can experiment with the Prompt command directly from the command prompt. Each time you enter a different Prompt command, the DOS prompt immediately changes so you can see the effect of your command. Once you've settled on a prompt you like, you can add the Prompt command to your AUTOEXEC.BAT file.

The Set command The Set command lets you specify a value for an *environment variable*. Environment variables are used in two ways. First, you can use environment variables when you create advanced batch files. You'll learn how to do that in chapter 27. Second, environment variables are used to control the actions of certain programs, including several DOS commands. It is for this second use that you're more likely to add a Set command to your AUTOEXEC.BAT file.

Figure 24-11 shows the Set command. To set the value of an environment variable, you type the name of the variable followed by an equal sign and the text you want assigned to the variable. Be sure not to make the common mistake of typing a space before and after the equal sign. If you do, the space before the equal sign will be considered part of the variable name, and the space following the variable will be considered part of the environment variable's value.

The two examples in figure 24-11 set a value for two environment variables that are used by DOS commands. The first environment variable, TEMP, specifies the location for any temporary files that are created by DOS commands and other programs. (Temporary files are created by DOS commands whenever you use piping, which you'll learn about in chapter 26.) In addition, many application programs use the TEMP variable to specify the location of temporary files as well. In the first example in figure 24-11, I specified C:\TEMP as the location for temporary files. Note that for programs to use the TEMP variable, the directory it specifies must exist.

Example 2 in figure 24-11 sets the DIRCMD variable, which provides default switches for the Dir command. In chapter 7, you learned how you can use switches to control the Dir command's output, to sort the list into name, date, or size sequence, or to limit the listing to files with certain attributes. If you find that you use certain switches just about every time you use the Dir command, you can use the DIRCMD variable to specify them as default switches. In figure 24-11, I specified /O:N and /P as default Dir switches. That way, my directory listings will always list files in alphabetical order, and the directory listing will always pause when the screen is filled.

The Mouse command DOS 6.0 includes the Mouse command, which lets you use a mouse with DOS utilities such as Edit, Microsoft Backup, and Microsoft Defrag. To use it, just add the following line to your AUTOEXEC.BAT file:

```
mouse
```

If your mouse is not Microsoft compatible, you should use the mouse driver that came with it instead of the Mouse command. In addition, if you add the Mouse command to your AUTOEXEC.BAT file, be sure to remove any older mouse drivers from your CONFIG.SYS or AUTOEXEC.BAT files.

New configuration features for DOS 6.0

With DOS 6.0, Microsoft introduced several enhancements that give you more flexibility when you set up your CONFIG.SYS and AUTOEXEC.BAT files. First, DOS 6.0 lets you bypass all or selected lines of your CONFIG.SYS file. Second, you can specify that certain CONFIG.SYS commands are optional so that DOS will ask you each time you start your computer whether or not to process them. Third, DOS 6.0 introduced two new CONFIG.SYS commands you might use from time to time: Set and Switch. And fourth, DOS 6.0 lets you set up *configuration menus* that let you choose one of several alternative configurations when you start your PC. This feature, called *multiple configuration*, adds five additional commands you can use in CONFIG.SYS.

How to bypass CONFIG.SYS and AUTOEXEC.BAT If you encounter a problem with a hardware device, an application program, or some aspect of DOS, it's often useful to do a *clean boot*; that is, to start your system without a CONFIG.SYS or AUTOEXEC.BAT file. That way, you can isolate the exact cause of the problem without being concerned about the effects of device drivers that might be resident in memory. With versions of DOS before 6.0, the only way to do a clean boot is to

How to bypass CONFIG.SYS and AUTOEXEC.BAT altogether

When DOS displays the message

```
Starting MS-DOS...
```

press and release the F5 key, or press and hold the Shift key.

How to selectively bypass CONFIG.SYS commands

When DOS displays the message

```
Starting MS-DOS...
```

press and release the F8 key.

Figure 24-12 How to bypass configuration settings under DOS 6.0

temporarily rename your CONFIG.SYS and AUTOEXEC.BAT files so DOS won't recognize them at startup. For example, you could enter the two commands

```
C:\>rename config.sys *.sav
C:\>rename autoexec.bat *.sav
```

and reboot your system. Then, DOS will boot clean, without processing CONFIG.SYS or AUTOEXEC.BAT. (If an error in your CONFIG.SYS file prevents DOS from starting, you may have to boot from a system diskette. Then you can rename the CONFIG.SYS and AUTOEXEC.BAT files on your C drive and reboot.)

With DOS 6.0, it's much easier to do a clean boot. Figure 24-12 lists the configuration bypass options DOS 6.0 provides. As you can see, you can cause DOS to completely ignore your CONFIG.SYS and AUTOEXEC.BAT files simply by pressing and releasing the F5 key when DOS displays its startup message:

```
Starting MS-DOS...
```

Alternatively, you can press and hold the Shift key. Either way, the effect is the same.

Of course, there are potential problems that can arise when you use your system after a clean boot. For example, because the Path command in AUTOEXEC.BAT isn't processed, the default path (C:\DOS) will be used. Similarly, the default prompt (C>) will be used. Any environment variables you created with Set commands in your AUTOEXEC.BAT file won't be available. And any device drivers you load with Device or Devicehigh commands in your CONFIG.SYS file won't be available. But at least you'll be able to access your system so you can correct whatever problem has come up.

If you suspect that the problem might be in a particular line in your CONFIG.SYS file, you can have DOS process the commands in your CONFIG.SYS

```
shell=c:\dos\command.com c:\dos\ /e:512 /p
files=100
lastdrive=z
device=c:\dos\himem.sys
device=c:\dos\emm386.exe ram
dos=high,umb
device?=c:\dos\ramdrive.sys 1024 /e
device?=c:\dos\driver.sys /d:0
device?=c:\dos\driver.sys /d:1
```

Figure 24-13 How to use optional commands in a DOS 6.0 CONFIG.SYS file

file one at a time. To do that, just press the F8 key when DOS displays the "Starting MS-DOS..." message. DOS displays each line in your CONFIG.SYS file, like this:

```
DEVICE=C:\DOS\RAMDRIVE.SYS [Y,N]?
```

Then, you can press Y to tell DOS to process the command, or you can press N to tell DOS to skip the command. With this feature, you can eliminate CONFIG.SYS commands one at a time until you've found the source of the problem.

After DOS has processed the entire CONFIG.SYS file in this way, it will ask if you want to execute your AUTOEXEC.BAT file:

```
Process AUTOEXEC.BAT [Y,N]?
```

Unfortunately, DOS 6.0 doesn't provide line-by-line prompting for the commands in AUTOEXEC.BAT. But if you suspect a problem in your AUTOEXEC.BAT file, you can always answer N here, then manually enter the commands in your AUTOEXEC.BAT file one at a time to isolate the problem.

How to create optional CONFIG.SYS commands If you have one or two CONFIG.SYS commands that you need only occasionally, you can make them optional by following the command's keyword with a question mark, just before the equals sign. For example, figure 24-13 shows a CONFIG.SYS file with three optional commands:

```
device?=c:\dos\ramdrive.sys 1024 /e
device?=c:\dos\driver.sys /d:0
device?=c:\dos\driver.sys /d:1
```

When DOS encounters a CONFIG.SYS command with a question mark, it asks the user whether or not to process it, like this:

```
DEVICE=C:\DOS\DRIVER.SYS /D:0 [Y,N]?
```

If you press Y, DOS processes the command. If you press N, DOS skips the command.

The format of the Set command for CONFIG.SYS (DOS 6.0)

```
SET variable=text
```

Explanation

`variable`	The name of the environment variable whose value is to be set.
`text`	The text to be associated with the variable.

Example 1: A Set command that establishes the DOS search path.

```
set path=c:\dos;c:\util
```

Example 2: A Set command that sets the DOS prompt.

```
set prompt=$p$g
```

Figure 24-14 The Set command for CONFIG.SYS (DOS 6.0)

If you have a genuine need for optional CONFIG.SYS commands, you should consider creating a configuration menu instead. I'll show you how to do that in few moments. But first, I want to show you two new CONFIG.SYS commands provided by DOS 6.0

Two new DOS 6.0 CONFIG.SYS commands With DOS 6.0, there are two new commands you can use in your CONFIG.SYS file. The first, Set, has the same function as the Set command you normally use in your AUTOEXEC.BAT file. It creates environment variables and assigns values to them. Figure 24-14 shows the CONFIG.SYS Set command. The only difference between this command and the DOS Set command shown in figure 24-11 is that the variable name and the text value are required when you use Set in a CONFIG.SYS file.

The Set command examples in figure 24-14 show two uses for environment variables that you might not expect. The first sets the Path variable, which sets up the DOS search path in the same way you would set it up using the Path command in your AUTOEXEC.BAT file. The second sets the PROMPT variable, serving the same function as the DOS Prompt command. Whether you set the path and prompt in CONFIG.SYS or in AUTOEXEC.BAT is a matter of preference. Neither method has a compelling advantage over the other.

The format of the Switches command (DOS 6.0)

```
SWITCHES=[/N] [/F] [/W] [/K]
```

Switch meanings

/N	Prevents the user from bypassing CONFIG.SYS commands by pressing F5, F8, or the Shift key when the "Starting MS-DOS..." message is displayed.
/F	Disables the two-second delay normally taken when the "Starting MS-DOS..." message is displayed.
/W	Indicates that the WINA20.386 file is not in the root directory. Use only with *Windows* 3.0 when you've moved the WINA20.386 file out of the root directory.
/K	Tells DOS to cause an AT-style enhanced keyboard to behave as if it were an older PC-style keyboard. Use only when you have a program that doesn't work with your keyboard.

Figure 24-15 The Switches command (DOS 6.0 only)

Figure 24-15 shows the other new CONFIG.SYS command, Switches. This command lets you set four switches that control the operation of DOS. The first two are related to the configuration bypassing features that were presented in figure 24-12. If you don't want to allow the user to bypass CONFIG.SYS and AUTOEXEC.BAT, include SWITCHES=/N in your CONFIG.SYS file. Then, pressing the F5, F8, or Shift key when DOS displays its "Starting MS-DOS..." message will have no effect. If you include SWITCHES=/F, DOS will skip its usual two-second delay following the "Starting MS-DOS..." message. This makes DOS boot faster, but makes it more difficult to interrupt by pressing the F5, F8, or Shift key. The other options for the Switches command are for unusual situations you're unlikely to encounter.

How to create configuration menus If you find yourself frequently changing your CONFIG.SYS file, or if you routinely alternate between several CONFIG.SYS files, you should consider using the DOS 6.0 multiple configuration feature to create a configuration menu. The idea behind a configuration menu is simple. First, you add commands to your CONFIG.SYS file to create a menu of configuration choices. Next, you associate a set of CONFIG.SYS commands with each choice. Then, when you boot your PC, DOS displays the configuration menu and lets you pick one of the menu choices. DOS then processes the CONFIG.SYS commands you associated with the selection you chose.

```
[menu]
menuitem=plain-DOS,Plain DOS
menuitem=RAM-drive,DOS with RAM Drive
menudefault=plain-DOS,10
menucolor=15,1
numlock=on

[plain-DOS]
device=c:\dos\himem.sys
device=c:\dos\emm386.exe ram
dos=high,umb
shell=c:\dos\command.com c:\dos\ /e:512 /p
files=100
lastdrive=z

[RAM-drive]
device=c:\dos\himem.sys
device=c:\dos\emm386.exe ram
dos=high,umb
shell=c:\dos\command.com c:\dos\ /e:512 /p
files=100
lastdrive=z
device=c:\dos\ramdrive.sys 1024 /e
```

Figure 24-16 A CONFIG.SYS file that uses the DOS 6.0 multiple configuration feature to create a simple configuration menu

For example, figure 24-16 shows a simple CONFIG.SYS file that creates a configuration menu with two choices: one starts the PC without a RAM drive, the other starts the PC with a RAM drive. As you can see, the CONFIG.SYS file is divided into three blocks of commands labeled [menu], [plain-DOS], and [RAM-drive]. The Menu block contains one Menuitem command for each of the menu choices. Notice that the Plain-DOS and RAM-drive block names appear in the Menuitem commands. The Plain-DOS block contains the CONFIG.SYS commands that are processed if the user picks the first menu item, and the RAM-drive block contains the commands processed if the user picks the second menu item. As you can see, the only difference between these blocks is the Device command that loads the RAMDRIVE.SYS device driver.

Figure 24-17 shows the menu displayed when your start your PC with this CONFIG.SYS file. Here, you can pick one of the menu choices by typing 1 or 2. Or, you can use the F5 key to bypass the CONFIG.SYS and AUTOEXEC.BAT files altogether or the F8 key to confirm each CONFIG.SYS command.

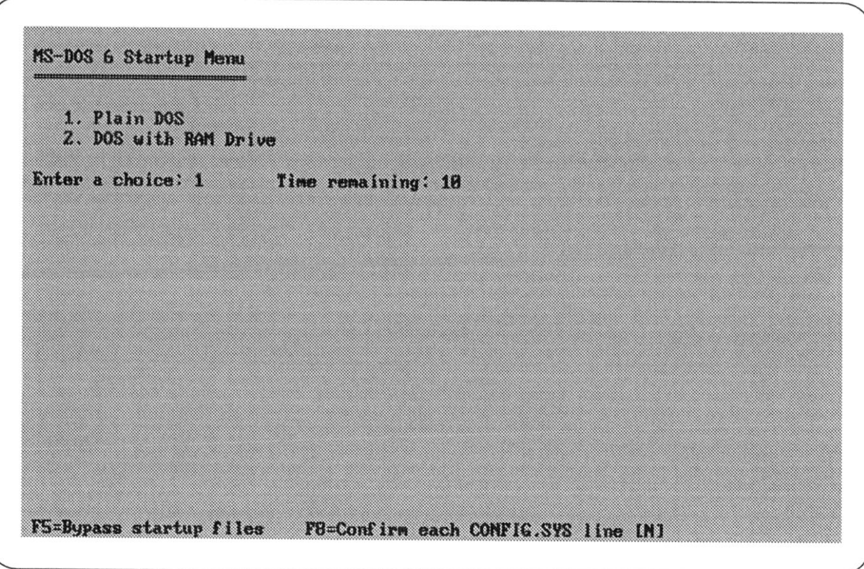

Figure 24-17 The configuration menu displayed by the CONFIG.SYS file shown in figure 24-16

The two parts of figure 24-18 list all the commands you can use to set up configuration menus. You use the commands in part 1 to identify the blocks that can appear in a CONFIG.SYS file. Notice that two block names have special meaning. The Menu block contains the commands that define the main configuration menu. (I'll show you how to create second-level configuration menus, called *submenus*, in a moment.) And the Common block contains commands that are processed no matter which menu selection the user picks. All other blocks have names you create.

The commands in part 2 of figure 24-18 let you create more complicated configuration menus. Rather than explain each of these commands individually, I'll show you how to use them in the examples in figures 24-19 through 24-23. For example, the CONFIG.SYS file in figure 24-19 uses the Menudefault command to specify a default menu item that's automatically chosen if the user doesn't do anything within 10 seconds. It uses a Menucolor command to cause the menu to display with white characters on a blue background. And it uses the Numlock command to automatically set Numlock mode. That makes it easier to select a menu item using the numeric keypad.

You may have noticed in figure 24-16 that most of the commands in the Plain-DOS and RAM-drive blocks are identical. In figure 24-19, I placed all the CONFIG.SYS commands that are related to memory management in a block named

Command	Function
`[MENU]`	Marks the beginning of the Menu block, which contains the CONFIG.SYS commands that define the menu.
`[COMMON]`	Marks the beginning of the Common block, which contains CONFIG.SYS commands that are processed no matter which menu option the user selects.
`[block]`	Marks the beginning of a configuration block that contains either the CONFIG.SYS commands for one of the blocks specified in the Menu block, or the menu definition commands for a submenu specified in the Menu block. The name you create can be up to 70 characters long and can include any characters other than the following: `(space) \ / , ; = [ ]`

Figure 24-18 CONFIG.SYS commands for the DOS 6.0 multiple configuration feature (part 1 of 2)

Memory and I placed the other common commands in the block named Common. Then, the first command in both the Plain-DOS and RAM-drive blocks is this:

```
include memory
```

This causes DOS to copy the commands from the Memory block as if they were coded at the same location as the Include command. The commands in the Common block are processed *after* the commands in the Plain-DOS or RAM-drive blocks are processed.

You might be wondering why I didn't just place the memory management commands in the Common block rather than create a separate Memory block for them. The answer has to do with the memory management features you'll learn about in the next chapter. Simply put, the Device command for the RAMDRIVE.SYS driver specifies the /E switch, which tells RAMDRIVE.SYS to create the RAM drive using extended memory. Before this command will work, you must first activate extended memory by loading the HIMEM.SYS device driver. So, the Device command for HIMEM.SYS must come before the Device command for RAMDRIVE.SYS. I made sure of that by placing the HIMEM.SYS Device command and the other memory management commands in the Memory block. Then, the Include command places these commands *before* the Device command for RAMDRIVE.SYS. If I had placed the Device command for HIMEM.SYS in the Common block, it would have been processed *after* the Device command for RAMDRIVE.SYS, and the /E switch would have been invalid.

Note: The following configuration commands can be used only in the Menu block or a block identified by a Submenu command as a submenu.

Command	Function
`MENUITEM=block-name[,menu-text]`	Creates a menu item identified on the screen by menu-text. If the user selects this menu item, the block specified by *block-name* is processed.
`SUBMENU=block-name[,menu-text]`	Creates a menu item identified on the screen by *menu-text*. If the user selects this menu item, the submenu defined in *block-name* is displayed.
`MENUCOLOR=text[,background]`	Specifies the colors for the menu display. *Text* and *background* are both numbers from 0 to 15, as follows: 0 Black; 1 Blue; 2 Green; 3 Cyan; 4 Red; 5 Magenta; 6 Brown; 7 White; 8 Gray; 9 Bright blue; 10 Bright green; 11 Bright cyan; 12 Bright red; 13 Bright magenta; 14 Yellow; 15 Bright white Colors 8 through 15 blink on some displays.
`MENUDEFAULT=block-name[,time]`	Specifies the default menu selection. *Time* specifies a time-out value after which the default is automatically processed.
`NUMLOCK=ON`	Specifies that the keyboard is to be forced into Numlock mode so that numbers can be typed more easily.
`INCLUDE=block-name`	Copies the commands from *block-name* into the current block.

Color table for MENUCOLOR:

0	Black	8	Gray
1	Blue	9	Bright blue
2	Green	10	Bright green
3	Cyan	11	Bright cyan
4	Red	12	Bright red
5	Magenta	13	Bright magenta
6	Brown	14	Yellow
7	White	15	Bright white

Figure 24-18 CONFIG.SYS commands for the DOS 6.0 multiple configuration feature (part 2 of 2)

```
[menu]
menuitem=plain-DOS,Plain DOS
menuitem=RAM-drive,DOS with RAM Drive
menudefault=plain-DOS,10
menucolor=15,1
numlock=on

[plain-DOS]
include memory

[RAM-drive]
include memory
device=c:\dos\ramdrive.sys 1024 /e

[memory]
device=c:\dos\himem.sys
device=c:\dos\emm386.exe ram
dos=high,umb

[common]
shell=c:\dos\command.com c:\dos\ /e:512 /p
files=100
lastdrive=z
```

Figure 24-19 A CONFIG.SYS file that uses the DOS 6.0 multiple configuration feature to create a more sophisticated configuration menu

How to test for the current configuration from AUTOEXEC.BAT

When the user picks a configuration menu selection, DOS sets an environment variable named CONFIG to the name of the block associated with the menu item. As a result, you can test this variable in your AUTOEXEC.BAT file to process different batch file commands depending on the configuration selected by the user.

You'll learn how to test environment variables in a batch file in chapter 27. For now, I want to show you a simple example that uses a configuration menu that lets the user pick one of several application programs to be started initially. Figure 24-20 shows a CONFIG.SYS file that displays this configuration menu:

```
1. Lotus 123
2. WordPerfect
```

In the CONFIG.SYS file, the configuration blocks corresponding to these menu items are empty. As a result, the same CONFIG.SYS commands are processed no matter what menu item the user picks. But in the AUTOEXEC.BAT file, the If commands are used to test the value of the CONFIG environment variable. Then, *Lotus 1-2-3* or *WordPerfect* is started according to the user's choice. (Don't worry if you don't understand all the commands in the AUTOEXEC.BAT file in this example. They'll be explained in detail in chapter 27.)

The CONFIG.SYS file

```
[menu]
menuitem=123,Lotus 123
menuitem=WP,WordPerfect
menucolor=15,1

[123]
[WP]

[common]
device=c:\dos\himem.sys
device=c:\dos\emm386.exe ram
dos=high,umb
shell=c:\dos\command.com c:\dos\ /e:512 /p
files=100
```

The AUTOEXEC.BAT file

```
@echo off
path c:\dos;c:\util
if "%config%"=="123" goto 123
if "%config%"=="WP" goto WP
dosshell
goto EXIT
:123
cd \123
123
goto EXIT
:WP
cd \wp51
wp
:EXIT
```

Figure 24-20 How to use the DOS 6.0 multiple configuration feature to select an application program

How to create submenus If you really want to build flexibility into your CONFIG.SYS file, you can create a series of *submenus* that are displayed in response to main menu selections. For example, suppose in addition to selecting whether or not to use a RAM Drive, you want to select whether or not to use DRIVER.SYS to create logical drives to access your A and B diskette drives. You could create a configuration menu with four choices, like this:

```
1. Plain DOS
2. Plain DOS with logical diskette drives
3. DOS with RAM drive
4. DOS with RAM drive and logical diskette drives
```

Although this menu would probably be manageable, what if you had a third selection, such as whether or not to access a network? Or what if one of the selections had more than two choices? Submenus can make configuration choices like these easier for the user to deal with. And, since you can't create more than ten menu items in one menu, submenus are a must if you have more than ten possible configurations.

Figure 24-21 shows a CONFIG.SYS file that uses a main configuration menu and two submenus. Figure 24-22 shows the menus displayed by this file. To create a menu item that leads to a submenu rather than to a block of CONFIG.SYS commands, you use a Submenu command rather than a Menuitem command. Other than typing Submenu rather than Menuitem, the command is the same: it specifies a block name and the text that's displayed on the menu. However, the block it names doesn't contain CONFIG.SYS commands. Instead, it contains another set of menu commands that create the submenu.

The structure of the CONFIG.SYS file in figure 24-21 is straightforward. The first three blocks, Menu, Plain-DOS, and RAM-drive, define the main configuration menu and the two submenus. Then, the next four blocks define each of the four possible configurations: Plain-DOS-with-driver, Plain-DOS-without-driver, RAM-drive-with-driver, and RAM-drive-without-driver. Finally, the last two blocks contain the commands for memory management and the other CONFIG.SYS commands common to all configurations.

Some perspective on the CONFIG.SYS and AUTOEXEC.BAT files

Once you get your CONFIG.SYS and AUTOEXEC.BAT files set up right, you shouldn't have to change them unless you make changes to your system's hardware or software. Fortunately, most hardware components and software packages that require specific commands in CONFIG.SYS or AUTOEXEC.BAT come with complete instructions for installation. Some software packages even include installation programs that make the required changes to the CONFIG.SYS and AUTOEXEC.BAT files for you. You should always check the results of these installation programs, however, to make sure they don't introduce conflicts into your CONFIG.SYS or AUTOEXEC.BAT file.

If you've just switched to DOS 6.0, you might be tempted to jump right into creating a complicated CONFIG.SYS file with several levels of submenus. I recommend you don't do that unless you really have complicated configuration needs. For most users, configuration menus aren't necessary. And for those users who do need configuration menus, most won't need submenus.

```
[menu]
submenu=plain-DOS,Plain DOS
submenu=RAM-drive,DOS with RAM Drive
menudefault=plain-DOS,10
menucolor=15,1
numlock=on

[plain-DOS]
menuitem=plain-DOS-with-driver,Create logical diskette drives D and E
menuitem=plain-DOS-without-driver,Do not create logical diskette drives
menudefault=plain-DOS-with-driver,10

[RAM-drive]
menuitem=RAM-drive-with-driver,Create logical diskette drives E and F
menuitem=RAM-drive-without-driver,Do not create logical diskette drives
menudefault=RAM-drive-with-driver,10

[plain-DOS-with-driver]
include memory
device=c:\dos\driver.sys /d:0
device=c:\dos\driver.sys /d:1

[plain-DOS-without-driver]
include memory

[RAM-drive-with-driver]
include memory
device=c:\dos\ramdrive.sys 1024 /e
device=c:\dos\driver.sys /d:0
device=c:\dos\driver.sys /d:1

[RAM-drive-without-driver]
include memory
device=c:\dos\ramdrive.sys 1024 /e

[memory]
device=c:\dos\himem.sys
device=c:\dos\emm386.exe ram
dos=high,umb

[common]
shell=c:\dos\command.com c:\dos\ /e:512 /p
country=001,437,c:\dos\country.sys
stacks=9,256
files=100
lastdrive=Z
```

Figure 24-21 How to use submenus in a DOS 6.0 CONFIG.SYS file

Part 1:

When you start your system using the CONFIG.SYS file in figure 24-21, the main configuration menu is displayed.

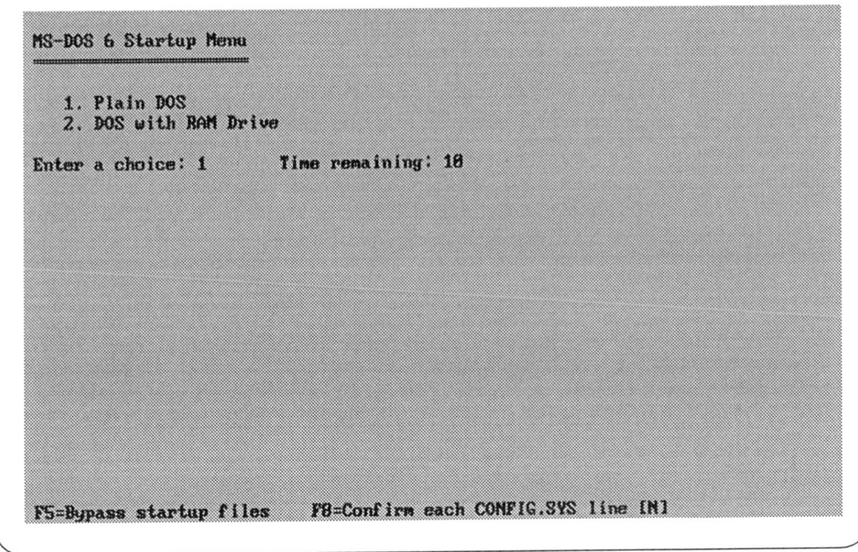

Part 2:

If you select option 1 from the main configuration menu, the Plain-DOS submenu is displayed.

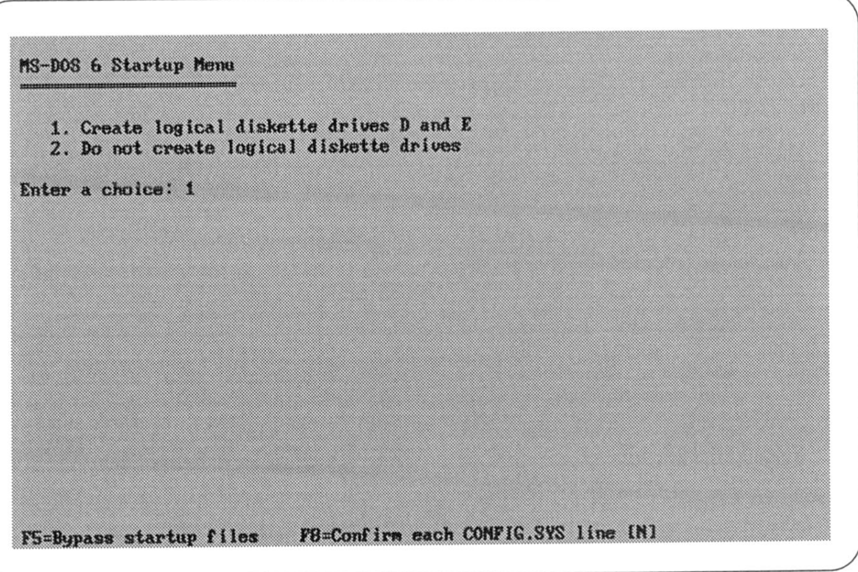

Figure 24-22 The menus displayed by the CONFIG.SYS file shown in figure 24-21

Although this chapter is large, it isn't by any means the final word on system configuration. For example, I've only hinted at the complications involved in setting up your CONFIG.SYS and AUTOEXEC.BAT files to make the most efficient use of internal memory. You'll learn more about that subject in the next chapter. And you'll learn how to use advanced batch file commands in chapter 27.

Terms

file handle
File Control Block
FCB
device driver
environment
environment variable
RAM disk
configuration menu
multiple configuration feature
clean boot
submenu

Objectives

1. If you're using DOS 5.0 or 6.0, add the DOS 5.0/6.0 commands presented in this chapter to your CONFIG.SYS file as necessary.
2. When necessary, add the appropriate Device command for loading any of the three device drivers presented in this chapter to your CONFIG.SYS file.
3. Include the appropriate commands in your AUTOEXEC.BAT file to set the command prompt, set environment variables, and use a mouse with the DOS utilities.
4. If you're using DOS 6.0, use its new configuration features to do the following:
    a. Start your system without using the CONFIG.SYS and AUTOEXEC.BAT files.
    b. Create optional commands in your CONFIG.SYS file.
    c. Use the Set command to set environment variables.
5. If you're using DOS 6.0 and you use two or more system configurations regularly, create configuration menus using the DOS 6.0 multiple configuration feature.

Chapter 25

How to make the most efficient use of your PC's memory

In chapter 24, you learned how to control your computer's configuration by using commands in the CONFIG.SYS and AUTOEXEC.BAT files. In this chapter, you'll learn more about one of the most important application of those commands: optimizing your memory. Here, you'll learn about the various types of memory that are available on your PC. Then, you'll learn how to use the CONFIG.SYS and AUTOEXEC.BAT commands supplied with DOS 5.0 and 6.0 that let you use your memory as efficiently as possible. Finally, you'll learn about a new feature of DOS 6.0 called *MemMaker*, which automatically sets up your CONFIG.SYS and AUTOEXEC.BAT files to use memory efficiently.

Although it's possible to optimize your memory use if you're using a version of DOS earlier than 5.0, you have to use a third-party memory manager such as Quarterdeck's *QEMM-386*. In this chapter, I'll focus on the standard memory optimization features provided with DOS 5.0 and 6.0.

When you install DOS 5.0 or 6.0, the Setup program may insert some of the commands you'll learn about in this chapter into your CONFIG.SYS and AUTOEXEC.BAT files automatically. Still, to set your computer up so it uses memory as efficiently as possible, you need to understand each of these commands so you can decide which ones are appropriate for your situation.

Understanding internal memory

When IBM introduced the original PC in 1981, it could support a maximum of 1MB of internal memory. Of that 1MB, 384KB was reserved for use by the system, leaving only 640KB of internal memory available to application programs. Still, in those days, most people thought that 640KB was more than any program would ever require. At the time, that was probably a reasonable opinion. After all, the PC's 640KB limit was ten times the limit of most popular computers at the time.

It didn't take long, however, for software to grow until it filled the 640KB. From then on, the 640KB limit became one of the most frustrating limitations of DOS. Although Intel's processor chips can support additional memory, DOS still enforces the 640KB limit to remain compatible with programs written for earlier versions. (The 286 processor could support up to 16MB of internal memory, and the 386 and 486 chips can support up to 4GB, or four billion, bytes of internal memory.) Memory beyond 640KB can be accessed, but special techniques such as the ones you'll learn in this chapter are required.

Before you can learn how to use memory optimization techniques, you need to understand the various types of memory you can have on a PC. Figure 25-1 shows the types of memory present in a typical PC with 4MB of total memory. As you can see, the 4MB of memory consists of three distinct types of memory: conventional memory, upper memory and adapter RAM/ROM, and extended memory. In addition, you can see that the first 64KB portion of extended memory is called the High Memory Area, or HMA.

To find out how much memory of each type you have on your system, you can use the Mem command as shown in figure 25-2. Here, you can see that this computer has 640KB of conventional memory, 155KB of upper memory and 229KB of adapter RAM/ROM (which together total 384KB), and 3,072KB (3MB) of extended memory. These memory totals add up to a total of 4,096KB (4MB). You can also see that DOS is resident in the high memory area. (This output is from DOS 6.0. Earlier versions of Mem show less information.) Now, I'll describe the differences between these various types of PC memory and explain how DOS uses each.

Conventional memory Simply put, *conventional memory* is the first 640KB of internal memory on your PC. This memory is sometimes called *base memory*. Application programs can access conventional memory without using any special techniques. For example, when you run *Lotus 1-2-3*, its program code is loaded into conventional memory so your PC can execute it. Then, when you instruct *123* to retrieve a worksheet file, it copies the contents of the worksheet file from disk into conventional memory. When you close the worksheet file, the conventional memory it used is released so that it can be used to retrieve another file. And when you quit *123*, the conventional memory occupied by its program code is released so you can run another program.

Unfortunately, not all 640KB of conventional memory is available for your application programs. That's because DOS uses some of this memory for itself. In addition, any device drivers you load with Device commands in your CONFIG.SYS file and memory resident programs you start in your AUTOEXEC.BAT file are loaded into conventional memory. This reduces the amount of conventional memory available for your programs. For example, the Mem output in figure 25-2 shows that only 613KB of the 640KB of conventional memory is available for programs. The other 27KB is used by DOS.

The main goal of optimizing your memory is to increase the amount of conventional memory available to your application programs. To do this, you move

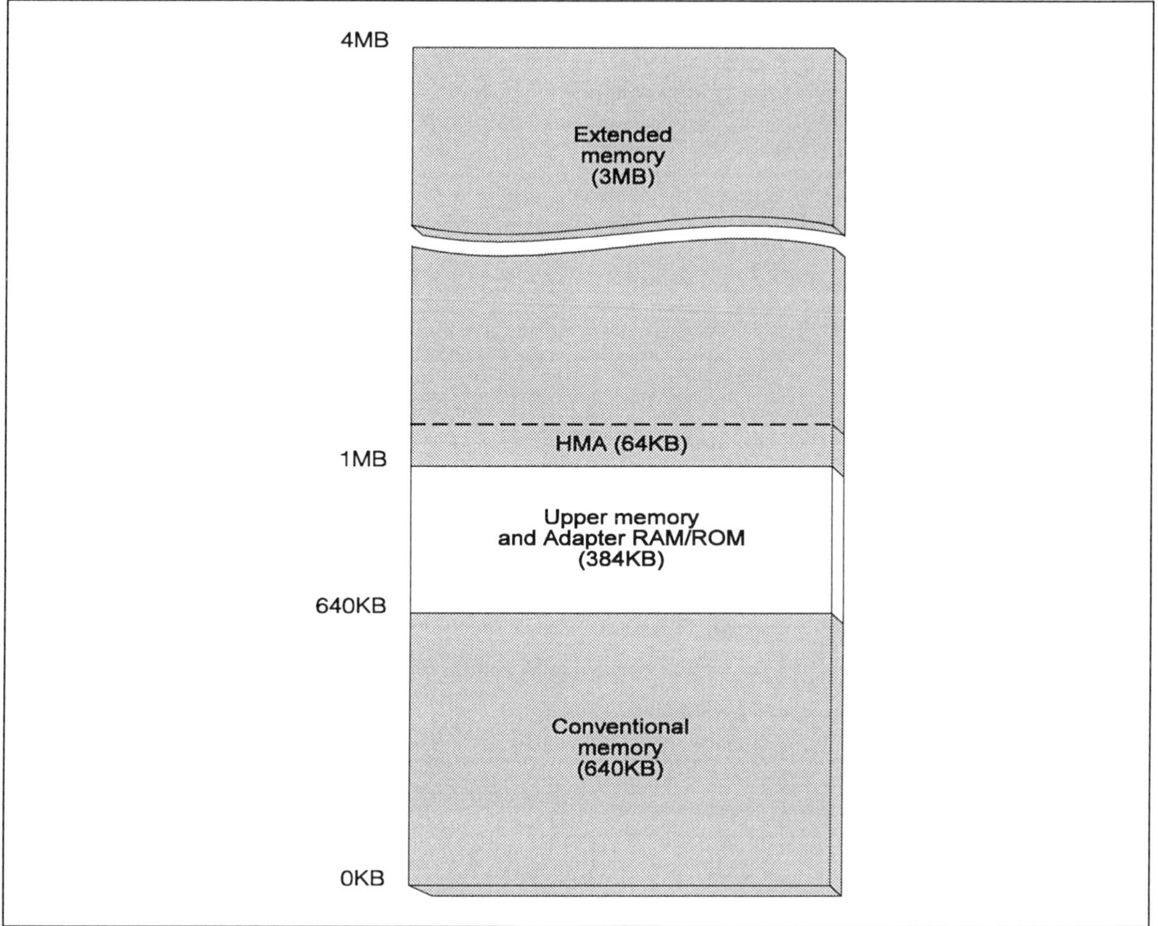

Figure 25-1 How PC memory is organized

portions of DOS, the device drivers, and memory resident programs out of conventional memory and into one of the other areas of memory shown in figure 25-1. The result is increased conventional memory for your application programs. By using the memory optimization techniques available with DOS 5.0 and 6.0, you can often increase the amount of available conventional memory by as much as 100KB. (The Mem output in figure 25-2 is for a computer whose memory configuration has already been optimized using the techniques you'll learn in this chapter. Without this optimization, the amount of conventional memory available to programs would be more like 550KB.)

```
C:\>mem

Memory Type          Total =  Used  +  Free
----------------   ------   ------   ------
Conventional         640K     27K     613K
Upper                155K     91K      64K
Adapter RAM/ROM      229K    229K       0K
Extended (XMS)      3072K   1140K    1930K
----------------   ------   ------   ------
Total memory        4096K   1472K    2624K

Total under 1 MB     795K    103K     692K

Largest executable program size       613K  (627808 bytes)
Largest free upper memory block        78K   (80256 bytes)
MS-DOS is resident in the high memory area.
```

Figure 25-2 Output from the DOS 6.0 Mem command

Upper memory and adapter RAM/ROM To many PC users, the 384KB *upper memory area* is a mystery. The designers of the PC set aside this 384KB for use by the system hardware. At the time, they didn't need that much memory for hardware support. The original IBM PC used the top 64KB of the upper memory area for the ROM BIOS (the program that provides low-level support for I/O devices, stored in read-only memory) and the bottom 128KB to support monochrome and CGA graphics adapters. That left 192KB of the upper memory area unused. Unfortunately, the unused portion of the upper memory area was just wasted space.

As new hardware was introduced, new portions of the upper memory area were dedicated to their use. For example, a small portion of the upper memory area was used to support the hard disk when the PC/XT was introduced. When the AT was introduced, additional portions of the upper memory area were used to support its EGA graphics adapter. And when the VGA graphics adapter was introduced with the IBM PS/2, still more of the upper memory area was appropriated.

Figure 25-3 shows the portions of the upper memory area used by various video adapters and other hardware devices. You don't need to worry about the details of which upper memory areas are used by which adapters. For now, I just want you to see that the amount of unused memory in the upper memory area depends on the type of hardware your computer uses. And, I want you to notice that even today, large portions of the upper memory area are still unused.

In most computers, these unused portions of the upper memory area don't physically exist. In other words, there are no memory chips that correspond to these areas. However, an advanced feature of the 386 and 486 processor chips make it possible to substitute extended memory for the unused portions of the upper memory area. Then, when a program uses a memory address that's in a portion of the upper

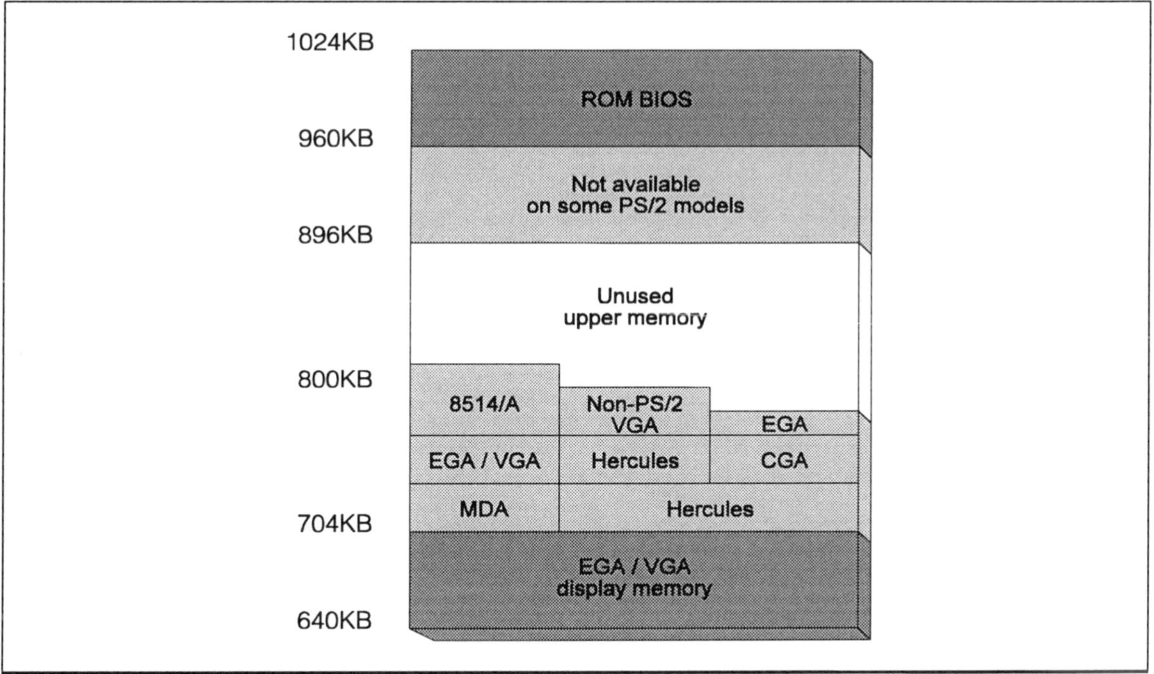

Figure 25-3 The upper memory area

memory area that has been *mapped* to extended memory, the processor translates the address into a valid extended memory address and accesses extended memory instead.

As you can see in figure 25-2, the DOS 6.0 Mem command divides the upper memory area into two parts: *upper memory* and *adapter RAM/ROM*. This distinction reflects the portion of the upper memory area that is actually used by video adapters, the system BIOS, and other hardware devices (adapter RAM/ROM), and the portion that's available for use by a 386 or 486 processor (upper memory). In this example, 320KB of the upper memory area is used and 64KB is available. The amounts listed for adapter RAM/ROM and upper memory always add up to 384KB, the total size of the upper memory area.

Each contiguous portion of the upper memory area that can be mapped safely to extended memory is called an *Upper Memory Block*, or *UMB*. Both DOS 5.0 and 6.0 can use these Upper Memory Blocks to load device drivers and memory resident programs. Because there's no absolute way to determine which portions of the upper memory area are used and which are free, both DOS 5.0 and 6.0 must scan it to locate UMBs. On a typical system, DOS 5.0 is able to recover about 90KB of the upper memory area. Because DOS 6.0 does a more thorough scan of upper memory, it can typically recover about 155KB.

Extended memory In a PC, any memory above the 1MB line is *extended memory*. Because the 8088 processor can support a maximum of 1MB of memory, you can't have extended memory on a PC based on that processor (that is, an IBM PC or XT). Extended memory is possible only on computers that have a 286 or better processor.

As you already know, extended memory can be used only by those programs that are specifically designed to support it. DOS can support extended memory in four ways. First, DOS can use extended memory to create a disk cache using Smartdrive or a RAM disk using RAMDRIVE.SYS. Second, DOS can use extended memory to recover unused portions of the upper memory area. Third, DOS can load itself into the first 64KB of extended memory, the HMA. And fourth, DOS can use extended memory to simulate an older type of memory called *expanded memory*. You learned about Smartdrive in chapter 11 and you learned about RAMDRIVE.SYS in the last chapter, so I won't describe them here. You'll learn about the last two uses for extended memory in a few moments. Naturally, all of these uses reduce the amount of extended memory available to other programs that might be able to use it, such as current versions of *Lotus 1-2-3* or *Microsoft Windows*. But the benefit of freeing up conventional memory is usually worth the cost of a small amount of extended memory.

By the way, most programs that access extended memory do so using a standard protocol called the *eXtended Memory Specification*, or *XMS*. That's why the Mem output in figure 25-2 lists the extended memory as XMS memory.

The High Memory Area (HMA) The first 64KB of extended memory is called the *High Memory Area*, or *HMA*. Because of a quirk in the way 286 and higher processors address memory, it's possible to access this memory from DOS with some slick programming. DOS 5.0 and 6.0 can take advantage of this quirk by loading themselves into the HMA. This frees up about 55KB of conventional memory. I'll show you how to do that later in this chapter.

Expanded memory Even before the introduction of the AT with its extended memory capabilities, many spreadsheet users were running out of conventional memory. As a result, three companies, Lotus, Intel, and Microsoft, developed the *LIM Expanded Memory Specification* (*EMS*), a technique for accessing additional memory called *expanded memory*. Because extended memory is both faster and more flexible than expanded memory, expanded memory isn't used much anymore. But if you have an older PC that has an expanded memory card, you may have to configure your PC to use expanded memory. And if you have an old program that supports expanded memory but not extended memory, you may have to configure your extended memory so that it simulates expanded memory.

Figure 25-4 shows how expanded memory works. Expanded memory is not directly accessible by the processor. Instead, it's contained on an expansion card that's installed on the computer's I/O bus. Strictly speaking, expanded memory is more like an I/O device than internal memory. To access expanded memory, its

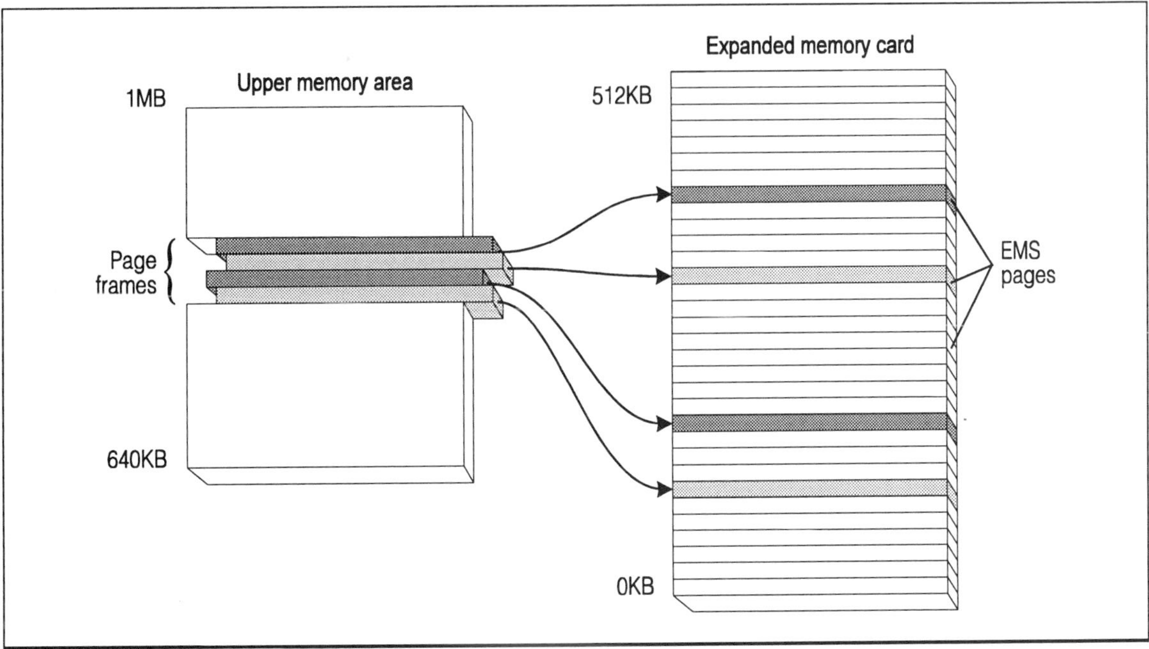

Figure 25-4 How expanded memory works

contents are read from the expanded memory card into an area of internal memory called a *page frame* in much the same way that data is read from a disk into an internal memory buffer. Then, the processor can access the data in the page frame. This is one of the reasons that expanded memory is slower than extended memory. To access data in expanded memory, it has to be copied from the EMS card into the page frame.

The memory on an EMS card is divided into 16KB *pages.* An application program can access data in EMS memory four pages, or 64KB, at a time. The page frames in internal memory are also 16KB. As you can see in figure 25-4, EMS uses 64KB of upper memory to create four page frames.

Although it's not illustrated in figure 25-4, the EMS card is accessed via the PC's I/O bus, which slows the operation dramatically. That's because the standard PC I/O bus operates at a relatively slow speed of 8Mhz regardless of the clock speed of the processor. In contrast, extended memory (and conventional memory) is accessed at the processor's clock speed. So if you have a 33Mhz processor, your PC can access extended memory more than four times as fast as it can access expanded memory. The speed penalty for simulating expanded memory with extended memory is not as dramatic. Still, because of the extra overhead involved with setting up a page frame and moving data to and from it, it's better to use extended memory rather than expanded memory with programs that can use either.

DOS 5.0 commands for optimizing memory use

Now that you understand the various types of memory your PC can access, you're ready to learn how to configure DOS so it makes the best use of the memory you have. DOS 5.0 introduced several device drivers and commands that you can use to optimize memory use. In this section, I'll present the techniques you use to move DOS into the High Memory Area and to load device drivers and memory resident programs into upper memory.

Figure 25-5 shows two CONFIG.SYS files that use the DOS 5.0 memory management commands. The first is for a 286-based computer with at least 384KB of extended memory. It includes the commands necessary to activate extended memory and the High Memory Area and move as much of DOS as possible into it. The second is for a 386 or 486 computer. It not only moves DOS into the HMA, but activates the Upper Memory Blocks and loads the ANSI.SYS and SETVER.EXE drivers into upper memory, thus freeing up even more conventional memory.

You can use the commands you'll learn here with DOS 6.0 as well as DOS 5.0. Keep in mind, however, that DOS 6.0 comes with a sophisticated memory configuration program called *MemMaker* that carefully examines your system memory and the programs you use and sets up your CONFIG.SYS and AUTOEXEC.BAT files for you. In most cases, the simple techniques you'll learn here can optimize your memory as well as MemMaker can. However, in more complex situations, MemMaker can almost always free up more conventional memory than you could on your own. (By the way, the formats of the the Devicehigh and Loadhigh commands have been changed under DOS 6.0 so MemMaker can make more efficient use of upper memory. However, DOS 6.0 still supports the DOS 5.0 syntax for these commands.)

Before I continue, I want to stress the importance of creating a clean boot diskette before you make changes to your AUTOEXEC.BAT or CONFIG.SYS files. You probably won't encounter any problems when you optimize your memory, but if you do, you'll need a clean boot diskette to fix the problem. To make a clean boot diskette, format a diskette using this command:

```
C:\>format a: /s
```

Then, copy your current CONFIG.SYS and AUTOEXEC.BAT files to the diskette. To make sure it works, test the boot diskette by leaving it in your A drive and restarting your computer.

The HIMEM.SYS device driver The first command in both of the CONFIG.SYS files in figure 25-5 is a Device command that loads a device driver named HIMEM.SYS. This driver provides support for extended memory so it can be used more reliably by application programs and DOS. This driver also lets DOS access the High Memory Area. If you have a PC that has a 286, 386, or 486 processor, you should have this command in your CONFIG.SYS file. When you install DOS 5.0 or 6.0, the Setup program automatically adds a Device command for HIMEM.SYS for you. So you probably won't have to add it yourself.

A DOS 5.0/6.0 CONFIG.SYS file for a 286 computer

```
device=c:\dos\himem.sys
dos=high
device=c:\dos\ansi.sys
device=c:\dos\setver.exe
files=20
buffers=20
lastdrive=z
```

A DOS 5.0/6.0 CONFIG.SYS file for a 386 or 486 computer

```
device=c:\dos\himem.sys
device=c:\dos\emm386.exe /noems
dos=high,umb
devicehigh=c:\dos\ansi.sys
devicehigh=c:\dos\setver.exe
files=20
buffers=20
lastdrive=z
```

Figure 25-5 Two CONFIG.SYS files to optimize memory under DOS 5.0 or 6.0

Figure 25-6 shows the format of the Device command for HIMEM.SYS. Although the HIMEM.SYS driver has several switches, you probably won't ever need them. That's because the driver works on most PCs without using a switch. If HIMEM.SYS requires a switch for your PC, the DOS 5.0 and 6.0 Setup programs should be able to add it for you. For example, if you have an IBM PS/2 computer, the Setup program adds this switch: /MACHINE:PS2.

The EMM386.EXE device driver The second command in the CONFIG.SYS file for 386 and 486 systems in figure 25-5 is the Device command you use to install the EMM386.EXE device driver. Figure 25-7 shows the format of the Device command to load EMM386.EXE. If your computer uses a 386 or 486 processor, you should include this command in your CONFIG.SYS file. As its name suggests, however, it requires a 386 or better computer. So you shouldn't include it if your computer uses a 286 processor. The DOS 5.0 and 6.0 Setup programs do not add this command to CONFIG.SYS, so you need to add it yourself.

EMM386.EXE provides two basic functions. First, it searches the upper memory area to locate unused portions from which it can create Upper Memory Blocks. These blocks can be used later to load device drivers and memory resident programs. This feature is enabled when you specify the /NOEMS switch or the /RAM switch. If you

The format of the Device command for HIMEM.SYS

```
DEVICE=C:\DOS\HIMEM.SYS [switches]
```

Note: Although HIMEM.SYS has several switches, the DOS Setup program should add them automatically if your computer needs them.

Figure 25-6 The Device command for HIMEM.SYS

want EMM386.EXE to provide UMB support only, use the /NOEMS switch as shown in the first example in figure 25-7. If you want EMM386 to provide UMB support and to simulate expanded memory as I'll explain next, use the /RAM switch.

Second, EMM386.EXE lets you convert extended memory into expanded memory (EMS). That way, programs that can use EMS can take advantage of the extended memory that's already installed in a PC. If you use EMM386.EXE for this purpose, EMM386 will set aside a 64KB block of upper memory to use for the page frame. Because this memory could be better used to load device drivers and memory resident programs, you should use EMM386 to simulate expanded memory only if you use a program that can't use extended memory directly. The second example in figure 25-7 shows a Device command that sets up EMM386.EXE to support UMBs and to simulate 512KB of expanded memory.

Note that if you omit both /RAM and /NOEMS, EMM386.EXE simulates expanded memory but does not provide support for UMBs. Because UMBs can usually free up additional conventional memory, you should almost always use either the /RAM or /NOEMS switch.

The Dos command Both CONFIG.SYS files in figure 25-5 include the Dos command. Figure 25-8 shows the format of this command. How you use it depends on whether your PC uses a 286 processor or a 386 or newer processor. If you have a 286 processor, you should specify DOS=HIGH as in the first example. That causes much of the resident portion of DOS to be loaded into the High Memory Area (the first 64KB of extended memory). As a result, DOS uses less conventional memory so more memory is available for other programs. If you specify DOS=HIGH, you must also include a Device command to load HIMEM.SYS.

If your computer uses a 386 or 486 processor, you should specify DOS=HIGH,UMB, as the second example in figure 25-8 shows. This tells DOS to load itself into the HMA and to activate support for Upper Memory Blocks. Then, you can later use Devicehigh commands to use the UMBs. To use this form of the Dos command, you must include Device commands for both HIMEM.SYS and EMM386.EXE. The DOS 5.0 and 6.0 Setup programs add a DOS=HIGH command to your CONFIG.SYS file, but you'll have to add UMB yourself.

The format of the Device command for EMM386.EXE (386 and 486 computers only)

```
DEVICE=C:\DOS\EMM386.EXE [EMS-memory] [/RAM] [/NOEMS]
```

Explanation

`EMS-memory`	Specifies the amount of expanded memory you want EMM386 to simulate. Omit EMS-memory if you don't want expanded memory.
`/RAM`	Tells EMM386 to create simulated expanded memory and to activate support for Upper Memory Blocks.
`/NOEMS`	Tells EMM386 to activate support for Upper Memory Blocks, but not to create simulated expanded memory.

Notes

1. A Device command to load HIMEM.SYS must precede this command.
2. You cannot specify both /RAM and /NOEMS. If you omit both, EMM386 creates simulated expanded memory but does not activate support for Upper Memory Blocks.
3. EMM386.EXE has other switches that give you precise control over its operation, but you're unlikely to need them. For more information, consult the DOS 5.0 manual or DOS 6.0 on-line Help.

Example 1: A Device command that loads the EMM386.EXE driver to activate upper memory but not to provide expanded memory.

```
device=c:\dos\emm386.exe /noems
```

Example 2: A Device command that loads the EMM386.EXE driver to activate upper memory and to provide 512KB of expanded memory.

```
device=c:\dos\emm386.exe 512 /ram
```

Figure 25-7 The Device command for EMM386.EXE

The Devicehigh command Figure 25-9 shows the Devicehigh command. Like the Device command, the Devicehigh command loads device drivers. But instead of loading them into conventional memory, the Devicehigh command loads them into Upper Memory Blocks, provided there's a UMB large enough to hold the device driver. In the second CONFIG.SYS file in figure 25-5, I used Devicehigh commands to load the ANSI.SYS and SETVER.EXE device drivers into upper memory. This frees up about 5KB of conventional memory. If you use larger device drivers, Devicehigh can save more memory.

The format of the Dos command

```
DOS={HIGH|LOW} [,{UMB|NOUMB}]
```

Explanation

HIGH	Tells DOS to load itself into the High Memory Area. You must also include a Device command for HIMEM.SYS.
LOW	Tells DOS to not use the High Memory Area. This is the default.
UMB	Tells DOS to allow device drivers and memory resident programs to be loaded into Upper Memory Blocks. You must also include a Device command for EMM386.EXE.
NOUMB	Tells DOS to not allow device drivers and memory resident programs to be loaded into Upper Memory Blocks. This is the default.

Example 1: A Dos command that loads DOS into the HMA.

```
dos=high
```

Example 2: A Dos command that loads DOS into the HMA and enables UMBs.

```
dos=high,umb
```

Figure 25-8 The Dos command

When you use the Devicehigh command, you don't have to worry about whether or not you have enough upper memory to hold the device drivers you want to use. That's because if the Devicehigh command sees that there's not enough upper memory to load a driver, it loads it into conventional memory instead. As a result, I suggest you change all the Device commands (except the commands that load HIMEM.SYS and EMM386.EXE) to Devicehigh commands. In rare cases, you may encounter an upper memory conflict that causes problems. I'll show you how to resolve such problems in a moment.

Any Devicehigh commands in your CONFIG.SYS file must come after the Device commands for HIMEM.SYS and EMM386.EXE. Because the DOS 6.0 Setup program adds a Device command for SETVER.EXE to the beginning of your CONFIG.SYS file, you should move this command so that it follows the Device commands for HIMEM.SYS and EMM386.EXE before you change it to a Devicehigh command.

The format of the Devicehigh command

```
DEVICEHIGH=file-spec [parameters]
```
or
```
DEVICEHIGH SIZE=size file-spec [parameters]
```

Explanation

`file-spec`	The complete file specification for the device driver.
`parameters`	Any parameters or switches required by the device driver.
`SIZE=size`	Specifies the minimum amount of memory that must be available before DOS will attempt to load the driver into upper memory. Required only for drivers that allocate additional memory after loading.

Notes

1. You must include Device commands for HIMEM.SYS and EMM386.EXE before you use a Devicehigh command.
2. You cannot load the HIMEM.SYS and EMM386.EXE drivers using Devicehigh commands. You can use Devicehigh for any other driver supplied with DOS.

Two Devicehigh commands that load the ANSI.SYS and SETVER.EXE drivers into upper memory

```
devicehigh=c:\dos\ansi.sys
devicehigh=c:\dos\setver.exe
```

Figure 25-9 The Devicehigh command

If you use DOS 6.0 and have installed DoubleSpace, you may have noticed that DoubleSpace added the following Devicehigh command for DBLSPACE.SYS to your CONFIG.SYS file:

```
DEVICEHIGH=C:\DOS\DBLSPACE.SYS /MOVE
```

This command relocates the DoubleSpace program, contained in the file DBLSPACE.BIN, into upper memory if possible. It's necessary because DoubleSpace loads itself into conventional memory when your computer boots. DoubleSpace can't load itself into upper memory because support for upper memory isn't activated until the HIMEM.SYS and EMM386.EXE drivers are loaded. Incidentally, this Devicehigh command is required even if upper memory is not available on your computer. So don't remove it.

The format of the Loadhigh command

```
LOADHIGH program [parameters]
```
or
```
LH program [parameters]
```

Explanation

`program`	The name of the memory resident program to be loaded into upper memory.
`parameters`	Any parameters or switches required by the program.

Two Loadhigh commands that run the Doskey and Fastopen commands in upper memory

```
lh doskey
lh fastopen c:=50
```

Figure 25-10 The Loadhigh command

The Loadhigh command Figure 25-10 shows the Loadhigh (LH) command. This command provides the same type of function as the Devicehigh command. But you put it in the AUTOEXEC.BAT file instead of the CONFIG.SYS file, and you use it to load programs instead of device drivers into Upper Memory Blocks. You can, for example, use Loadhigh to load DOS utilities, like Fastopen and Doskey. Like the Devicehigh command, the Loadhigh command loads the program into conventional memory if not enough upper memory is available. So I suggest you add LH to the beginning of every command in your AUTOEXEC.BAT file that loads a memory resident program. Figure 25-11 shows a typical AUTOEXEC.BAT file that uses the Loadhigh command.

How to resolve upper memory conflicts

If you have a 386 or 486 computer and you use only the device drivers and memory resident programs that come with DOS, you should be able to load all of them into upper memory without encountering any problems. However, if you use device drivers or memory resident programs that come with some hardware device or an application program, you may encounter problems when you try to load them into upper memory. If you encounter a problem like this under DOS 6.0, you can use MemMaker to resolve the problem. With DOS 5.0, though, you'll have to resolve the problem yourself.

The most common type of upper memory conflict is caused by device drivers or programs that acquire additional memory after they've been loaded. For example,

```
prompt $p$g
path c:\dos;c:\util
lh c:\fastopen c:=50
lh c:\dos\smartdrv 2048 512
lh c:\dos\doskey
lh c:\dos\dosshell
```

Figure 25-11 An AUTOEXEC.BAT file that loads programs into upper memory

suppose a mouse device driver named MOUSE.SYS acquires additional memory after it's loaded. DOS might try to load the program into an Upper Memory Block that's large enough to hold the driver in its initial size. But when the driver tries to acquire additional memory, it will fail if there's not enough extra memory available in the UMB. Another type of problem occurs when a program simply won't work when it's loaded into upper memory.

For both types of problems, the symptom you'll most likely notice is that your system will lock up. That's why it's so important that you make sure you have a bootable system diskette available before you modify your CONFIG.SYS and AUTOEXEC.BAT files. If your system locks up because of an upper memory conflict and you don't have a clean boot disk, you won't be able to access your computer at all.

Figure 25-12 shows a five-step procedure you can follow to resolve upper memory conflicts. The first step is to remove all programs from upper memory by editing your CONFIG.SYS and AUTOEXEC files. In CONFIG.SYS, change all Devicehigh commands to Device commands. In AUTOEXEC.BAT, remove the Loadhigh command wherever it occurs. Then, reboot your computer. This should load all the same device drivers and memory resident programs, but they'll all be loaded into conventional memory rather than upper memory. So there shouldn't be any conflicts.

Next, use the Mem command with the /C switch to list the details of each loaded program's memory usage. Because the output of the Mem command is lengthy, I added >PRN to the command so the command's output would be redirected to the printer. You'll learn more about redirecting DOS command output in the next chapter.

Figure 25-13 shows the DOS 5.0 MEM /C command's output. (The DOS 6.0 MEM /C command uses a different display format.) As you can see, the output is in two parts. The first shows how DOS is using conventional memory, and the second shows how DOS is using upper memory. For both parts, the first column of output lists the name of each program that's using a block of memory. Then, the second column gives the size of the block. For example, you can see that ANSI.SYS is using a block of conventional memory that is 4,192 blocks long. You can also see that three blocks of conventional memory totaling 604,640 bytes are free and two blocks of upper memory totaling 67,840 bytes are free.

1. Remove all programs from upper memory by editing CONFIG.SYS and replacing all Devicehigh commands with Device commands, and by editing AUTOEXEC.BAT and removing the Loadhigh or LH keyword from all commands. Reboot your computer.
2. Enter this command:

   ```
   C:\>mem /c >prn
   ```

   Save the printout for use in later steps.
3. Identify which device driver or memory resident program is causing the problem by reintroducing resident programs into upper memory one at a time until the system fails again. To reintroduce a program into upper memory, change it's CONFIG.SYS Device command to a Devicehigh command or add LH to the beginning of its AUTOEXEC.BAT startup command and reboot your computer.
4. If the problem is caused by a device driver, find the size of the driver in the Mem output you created in step 1 and add it to the Devicehigh command using a size parameter, as follows:

   ```
   devicehigh size=3bb0 c:\dos\mouse.sys
   ```

   Then, reboot your computer. If the size parameter doesn't solve the problem, replace the Devicehigh command with a Device command.

   If the problem is caused by a memory resident program loaded from AUTOEXEC.BAT, you can't load it into upper memory.
5. Repeat steps 3 through 4 until all device and memory resident programs have been tested.

Figure 25-12 The procedure for finding and correcting problems caused by upper memory conflicts

The third column of the Mem output gives the size of each memory block in *hexadecimal notation*, or *hex*. Hex represents the base-sixteen numbering system that is often used by programmers and other computer specialists when they work with computer memory. As you'll soon see, you may have to use these hex values to resolve upper memory conflicts.

Once you've printed the Mem command's output, you reintroduce your programs into upper memory one at a time, rebooting your computer each time you add a Devicehigh or Loadhigh command. When your computer locks up, you've found the program that's caused the problem.

If the problem was caused by a Devicehigh command, add a Size parameter to make sure DOS doesn't try to load the driver if there isn't enough upper memory for it. To find out the value to specify in the Size parameter, find the driver in the MEM /C output. The Size value you use is the hex size specified for that driver. For example, in figure 25-13, you can see that the hex size for the MOUSE.SYS driver is 3BB0. So, you would write the Devicehigh command for the driver like this:

```
Devicehigh size=3bb0 c:\dos\mouse.sys
```

After you've added this line to your CONFIG.SYS file, reboot your system again.

The Mem command for listing the memory used by loaded programs

```
C:\>mem /c >prn
```

The output from the Mem command

```
Conventional Memory :
  Name                 Size in Decimal       Size in Hex
-------------       ---------------------   -------------
  MSDOS               17440       ( 17.0K)       4420
  HIMEM                1072       (  1.0K)        430
  EMM386               3232       (  3.2K)        CA0
  SETVER                400       (  0.4K)        190
  ANSI                 4192       (  4.1K)       1060
  MOUSE               15280       ( 14.9K)       3BB0
  COMMAND              2624       (  2.6K)        A40
  SHARE                6192       (  6.0K)       1830
  FREE                   64       (  0.1K)         40
  FREE                  160       (  0.2K)         A0
  FREE               604416       (590.3K)      93900

Total  FREE :        604640       (590.5K)

Upper Memory :

  Name                 Size in Decimal       Size in Hex
-------------       ---------------------   -------------
  SYSTEM             167472       (163.5K)      28E30
  SMARTDRV            26768       ( 26.1K)       6890
  FREE                   32       (  0.0K)         20
  FREE                67808       ( 66.2K)      108E0

Total  FREE :         67840       ( 66.3K)

Total bytes available to programs (Conventional+Upper) :     672480   (656.7K)
Largest executable program size :                            604416   (590.3K)
Largest available upper memory block :                        67808   ( 66.2K)

   3407872 bytes total contiguous extended memory
         0 bytes available contiguous extended memory
   2088960 bytes available XMS memory
           MS-DOS resident in High Memory Area
```

Figure 25-13 Output from the MEM /C command

If adding the Size parameter doesn't correct the problem, you'll have to change the Devicehigh command for the problem driver back to a Device command. In other words, you won't be able to load that driver into upper memory. You'll have to leave it in conventional memory. Finally, repeat the previous steps for any remaining programs that you want to install into upper memory.

There's yet another type of upper memory conflict that can occur, which the procedure in figure 25-12 doesn't address. This problem happens when you have enough total upper memory to load all your programs, but not all of them are loaded into upper memory. Often, this happens because of the order in which you load the programs. For example, if you load several small device drivers before a big one, there might not be enough contiguous upper memory left to load the big driver. You can often solve this problem simply by rearranging the Devicehigh commands in your CONFIG.SYS file so that the largest device drivers are loaded first. This is the type of upper memory problem that DOS 6.0's MemMaker is designed to handle best.

MemMaker

I've already mentioned several times in this chapter that DOS 6.0 comes with a program called *MemMaker* that automates the task of optimizing your memory configuration. MemMaker works by first restarting your computer so it can monitor each of the device drivers and memory resident programs loaded by your CONFIG.SYS and AUTOEXEC.BAT files, collecting statistics about the amount of memory each uses. Then, MemMaker considers hundreds, sometimes even thousands, of possible combinations of where in memory to load each device driver and program. From these combinations, MemMaker picks the one that leaves you with the most conventional memory available for application programs. Then, it alters your CONFIG.SYS and AUTOEXEC.BAT files, restarts your computer again, and tests its configuration to make sure it works properly.

If the output from the MEM /C command lists any programs using conventional memory other than MSDOS, COMMAND, HIMEM, or EMM386, you should run MemMaker to see if it can improve your memory configuration. In simple situations where you use only the device drivers and memory resident programs provided with DOS, you can often achieve results as good as MemMaker's simply by loading HIMEM.SYS and EMM386.EXE, specifying DOS=HIGH,UMB, and loading all your drivers and memory resident programs into upper memory by changing all your Device commands to Devicehigh commands and using Loadhigh commands in your AUTOEXEC.BAT file. Even so, it won't hurt to run MemMaker just to see if it improves your configuration. If it doesn't, you can always revert to your current CONFIG.SYS and AUTOEXEC.BAT files.

Because MemMaker works by controlling the exact placement of programs in the upper memory area, you can use it only on 386 and 486 systems that have extended memory. So if you have an older 286 or 8088 system or if your computer doesn't have extended memory, you can't use MemMaker.

The CONFIG.SYS file

```
device=c:\DOS\himem.sys
device=c:\dos\emm386.exe noems
dos=high,umb
device=c:\dos\setver.exe
device=c:\dos\ansi.sys
device=c:\dos\ramdrive.sys 512 /e
device=C:\dos\dblspace.sys /move
shell=c:\dos\command.com c:\dos /e:512 /p
buffers=17,0
files=100
stacks=9,256
lastdrive=z
fcbs=16,8
```

The AUTOEXEC.BAT file

```
@echo off
cls
prompt $p$g
path c:\dos;c:\util;c:\pctools;c:\lantasti
set pctools=c:\pctools\data
vsafe
smartdrv.exe 2048
share
mouse
doskey
print /d:prn
undelete /sc /sd
cpsched
desktop /r
aex irq=15 iobase=300 verbose
ailanbio
redir %netid% logins=3
```

Figure 25-14 An unoptimized system configuration (part 1 of 2)

How to optimize your memory with MemMaker Figure 25-14 shows the CONFIG.SYS and AUTOEXEC.BAT files for a system on which I will run MemMaker to optimize memory, along with the output produced by the Mem command for this configuration. These configuration files are more complicated than the ones I've shown previously. In particular, the AUTOEXEC.BAT file in this

Output from the Mem command

```
Memory Type        Total =  Used  +  Free
----------------  ------  ------  ------
Conventional        640K    211K    429K
Upper               155K     36K    120K
Adapter RAM/ROM     229K    229K      0K
Extended (XMS)    15360K   2971K  12389K
----------------  ------  ------  ------
Total memory      16384K   3446K  12938K

Total under 1 MB    795K    247K    549K

Largest executable program size      429K  (439072 bytes)
Largest free upper memory block      119K  (122320 bytes)
MS-DOS is resident in the high memory area.
```

Figure 25-14 An unoptimized system configuration (part 2 of 2)

example loads a number of memory resident programs that aren't included with DOS. It loads several memory resident programs that come with the popular utility software, *PC Tools* (CPSCHED and DESKTOP). And it includes the commands necessary to connect the PC to a Lantastic local area network (AEX, AILANBIO, and REDIR).

I made the configuration files in figure 25-14 unusually complex to demonstrate the benefit of MemMaker in complex configurations. You can see from the Mem command output in part 2 of figure 25-14 that this configuration leaves only 429KB of free conventional memory. Because there are so many memory resident programs loaded by this AUTOEXEC.BAT file, there's no way to get this figure back up to 600KB or more. But you can free up about 100KB of conventional memory if you move the right device drivers and memory resident programs into upper memory. Just using Devicehigh and Loadhigh commands won't result in the most efficient configuration, but MemMaker can consider thousands of possible memory configurations using these configuration files and pick the best one.

Before you run MemMaker, it pays to take a look at your CONFIG.SYS and AUTOEXEC.BAT files to see if they load any unnecessary device drivers or memory resident programs. If so, remove them before you start MemMaker. In addition, if your AUTOEXEC.BAT file ends with a command that starts an application program or a shell (like Dosshell), temporarily disable it by typing REM at the beginning of the line. (Be sure to leave a space between the word REM and the first letter of the command.) When MemMaker is finished, you can edit the new AUTOEXEC.BAT file to reinstate the command.

The seven parts of figure 25-15 show various screens displayed by MemMaker as it optimizes your memory configuration. To start MemMaker, you simply enter this command:

```
C:\>memmaker
```

Then, MemMaker displays the welcome screen shown in part 1 of figure 25-15. This screen explains what MemMaker is and gives you a chance to exit the program if you don't want to proceed.

When you press the Enter key to proceed, MemMaker displays the screen shown in part 2. Here, you can choose one of MemMaker's two modes of operation: Express-setup or Custom-setup. Usually, you'll run MemMaker in Express-setup mode so it uses its default option settings. I'll show you the advanced option settings you can control through Custom-setup mode in a few moments.

The next screen displayed by MemMaker, shown in part 3 of figure 25-15, asks whether or not you have any programs that need access to expanded memory. The answer you provide determines how MemMaker configures the EMM386.EXE device driver.

Next, MemMaker displays the screen shown in part 4 of figure 25-15. Here, MemMaker is about to restart your computer so it can monitor your device drivers and memory resident programs as they're loaded. When you press the Enter key, your computer will go through its normal startup process, and you'll see the status messages normally displayed by your device drivers and memory resident programs. Then, the MemMaker program will automatically be restarted, and you'll see the screen shown in part 5 of figure 25-15. Here, MemMaker is using the information it gathered when your computer restarted to determine the optimum memory configuration for your system.

As you can see, MemMaker considered 22,823 possible configurations before deciding on the optimum one. In simple configurations, MemMaker may have to consider only a few alternative configurations. But in more complex situations, MemMaker may consider even more. For example, if I had answered "Yes" to the expanded memory option in part 3 of figure 25-15, MemMaker would have considered more than 32,000 combinations.

When MemMaker has determined the best configuration, it modifies your CONFIG.SYS and AUTOEXEC.BAT files and restarts your computer again. As it does, you should again watch the status messages displayed by your device drivers and memory resident programs. Watch especially for any error message. When the MemMaker program automatically restarts after rebooting your computer, it displays the screen in part 6 of figure 25-15. Here, MemMaker asks if your system started properly. If you noticed any unusual messages when your system started, answer "No" to this question and follow the instructions MemMaker provides.

Assuming your system started properly, MemMaker then displays the summary table shown in part 7 of figure 25-15. Here, you can see a comparison of memory usage before and after MemMaker was run. As you can see, MemMaker was able to recover 103,334 bytes of conventional memory (that's just over 100KB) by moving

Part 1:

When you start MemMaker, it displays its welcome screen.

```
Microsoft MemMaker

Welcome to MemMaker.

MemMaker optimizes your system's memory by moving memory-resident
programs and device drivers into the upper memory area. This
frees conventional memory for use by applications.

After you run MemMaker, your computer's memory will remain
optimized until you add or remove memory-resident programs or
device drivers. For an optimum memory configuration, run MemMaker
again after making any such changes.

MemMaker displays options as highlighted text. (For example, you
can change the "Continue" option below.) To cycle through the
available options, press SPACEBAR. When MemMaker displays the
option you want, press ENTER.

For help while you are running MemMaker, press F1.

          Continue or Exit? Continue

ENTER=Accept Selection  SPACEBAR=Change Selection  F1=Help  F3=Exit
```

Part 2:

When you press the Enter key, MemMaker asks you to choose whether you want it to run Express-setup or Custom-setup mode. Unless you want to change MemMaker's defaults, choose Express-setup.

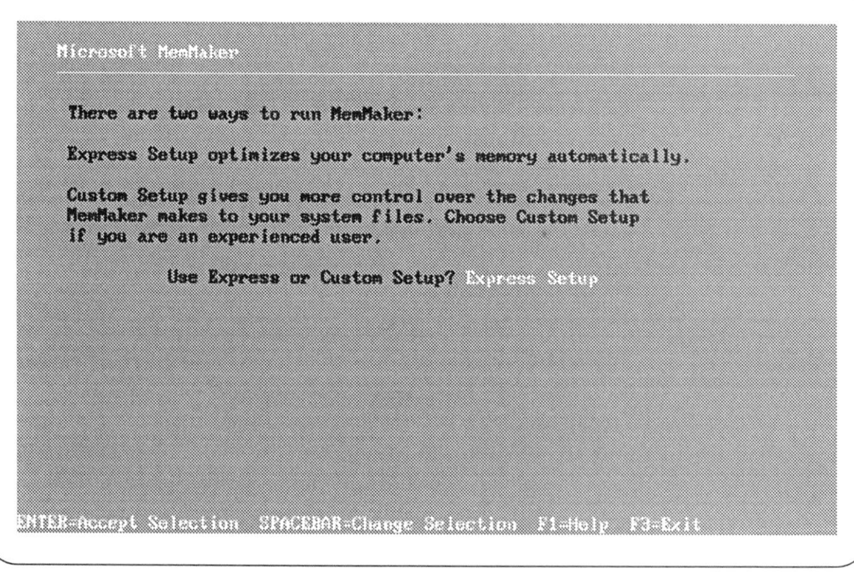

Figure 25-15 How to use MemMaker to optimize your memory configuration (parts 1and 2 of 7)

Part 3:

Next, MemMaker asks you if you use any programs that need expanded memory. If not, press the Enter key. Otherwise, enter Yes.

```
Microsoft MemMaker

If you use any programs that require expanded memory (EMS), answer
Yes to the following question. Answering Yes makes expanded memory
available, but might not free as much conventional memory.

If none of your programs need expanded memory, answer No to the
following question. Answering No makes expanded memory unavailable,
but can free more conventional memory.

If you are not sure whether your programs require expanded memory,
answer No. If you later discover that a program needs expanded
memory, run MemMaker again and answer Yes to this question.

Do you use any programs that need expanded memory (EMS)? No

ENTER=Accept Selection  SPACEBAR=Change Selection  F1=Help  F3=Exit
```

Part 4:

Before MemMaker restarts your computer to monitor the memory resident programs that are installed by your CONFIG.SYS and AUTOEXEC.BAT files, it displays an information screen. Press the Enter key when you're ready to restart your computer.

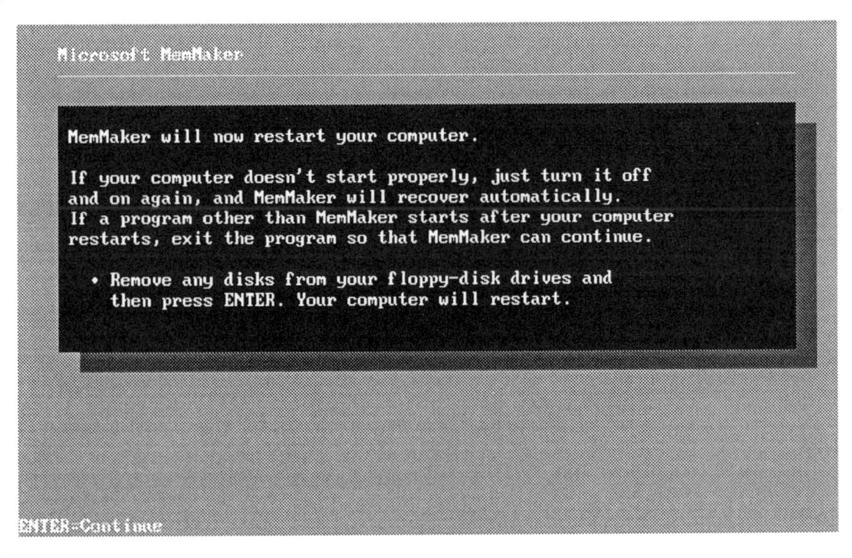

Microsoft MemMaker
MemMaker will now restart your computer.
If your computer doesn't start properly, just turn it off
and on again, and MemMaker will recover automatically.
If a program other than MemMaker starts after your computer
restarts, exit the program so that MemMaker can continue.
• Remove any disks from your floppy-disk drives and
then press ENTER. Your computer will restart.
ENTER=Continue

Figure 25-15 How to use MemMaker to optimize your memory configuration (parts 3 and 4 of 7)

Part 5:

After MemMaker restarts your computer, it checks various configuration combinations to determine which one is optimum. Then, it restarts your computer again.

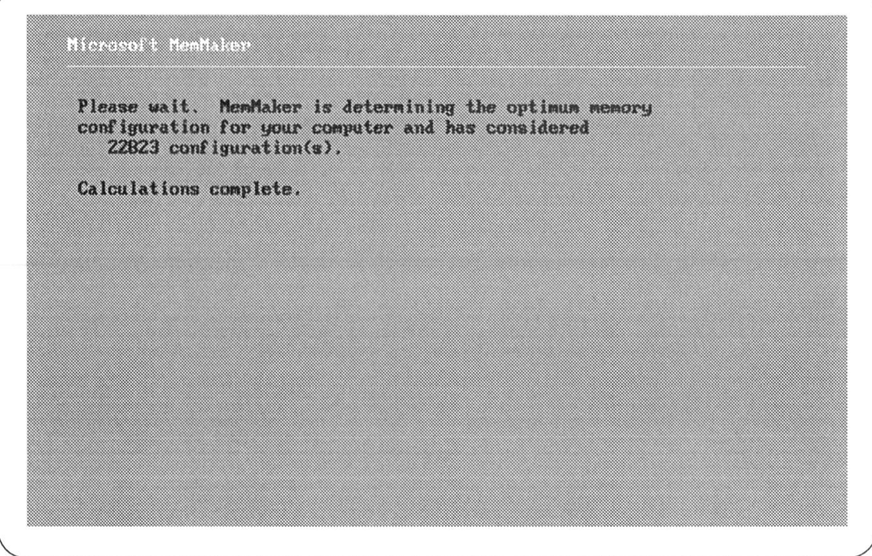

Part 6:

After your computer has restarted the second time, MemMaker asks you if it appears to be operating correctly. If you noticed any unusual error messages during startup, enter No.

```
Microsoft MemMaker

Your computer has just restarted with its new memory configuration.
Some or all of your device drivers and memory-resident programs
are now running in upper memory.

If your system appears to be working properly, choose "Yes."
If you noticed any unusual messages when your computer started,
or if your system is not working properly, choose "No."

Does your system appear to be working properly? Yes

ENTER=Accept Selection  SPACEBAR=Change Selection  F1=Help  F3=Exit
```

Figure 25-15 How to use MemMaker to optimize your memory configuration (parts 5 and 6 of 7)

Part 7:

When it's finished, MemMaker displays a table showing your computer's memory usage before and after running MemMaker.

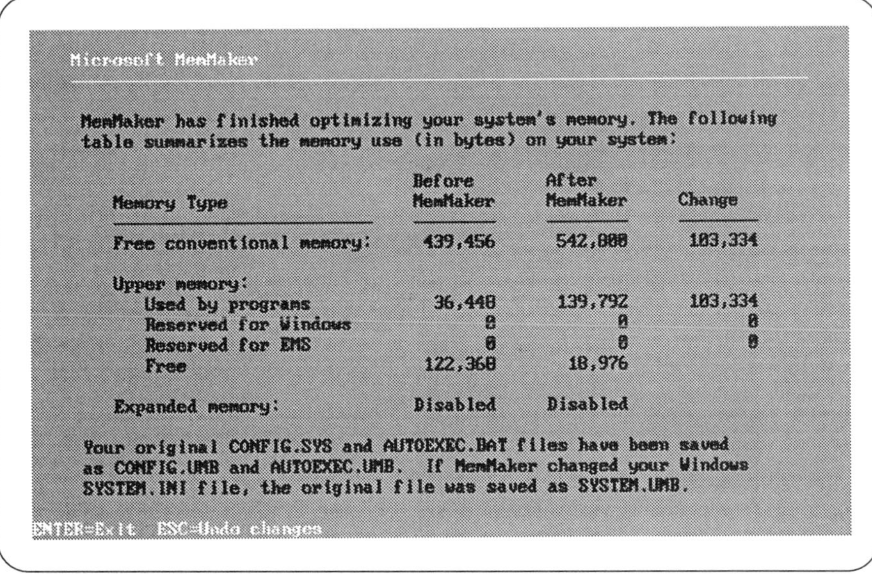

Figure 25-15 How to use MemMaker to optimize your memory configuration (part 7 of 7)

certain device drivers and memory resident programs into upper memory. The amount of conventional memory available for application programs has increased from 439,456 bytes (429KB) to 542,800 bytes (530KB).

Figure 25-16 shows the CONFIG.SYS and AUTOEXEC.BAT files and the Mem command output after MemMaker has been run. Here, the changes MemMaker made to CONFIG.SYS and AUTOEXEC.BAT are all in uppercase letters. As you can see, MemMaker rearranged the CONFIG.SYS commands, changed some of the Device commands in CONFIG.SYS to Devicehigh commands, and added LH to some of the AUTOEXEC.BAT commands that load memory resident programs. (If you're wondering why MemMaker loads only some of the device drivers and memory resident programs into upper memory, it's because not all of them fit there.) Notice also that MemMaker used the /L switch to specify the location in upper memory where each device driver or memory resident program is to be loaded. This switch, along with several other new switches, was added to the Devicehigh and Loadhigh commands with DOS 6.0 so that MemMaker can control the placement of upper memory programs. Although you could manually add these switches to Devicehigh and Loadhigh commands, there's little reason to do so since MemMaker does it automatically.

How to use MemMaker's custom setup options If you select Custom-setup rather than Express-setup when you start MemMaker, MemMaker

The CONFIG.SYS file

```
DEVICE=C:\DOS\himem.sys
DEVICE=C:\DOS\EMM386.EXE NOEMS
buffers=17,0
files=100
dos=UMB
lastdrive=z
fcbs=16,0
dos=HIGH
DEVICE=C:\DOS\SETVER.EXE
DEVICEHIGH /L:1,9072 =C:\DOS\ANSI.SYS
DEVICEHIGH /L:1,5888 =C:\DOS\RAMDRIVE.SYS 512 /E
DEVICEHIGH /L:1,44528 =C:\DOS\DBLSPACE.SYS /MOVE
shell=c:\dos\command.com c:\dos /e:512 /p
stacks=9,256
```

The AUTOEXEC.BAT file

```
@echo off
cls
prompt $p$g
path c:\dos;c:\util;c:\pctools;c:\lantasti
set pctools=c:\pctools\data
LH /L:1,63088 vsafe
LH /L:0;1,42400 /S smartdrv.exe 2048
share
LH /L:1,56928 mouse
LH /L:1,6400 doskey
LH /L:1,16192 print /d:prn
undelete /sc /sd
LH /L:0;1,7648 /S cpsched
desktop /r
LH /L:1,13728 aex irq=15 iobase=300 verbose
LH /L:1,18848 ailanbio
redir  logins=3
```

Figure 25-16 The sample configuration after it has been optimized by MemMaker (part 1 of 2)

displays the options screen shown in the top part of figure 25-17. Here, you can specify several advanced options that affect how MemMaker optimizes your memory. Figure 25-17 also describes what each of these options does and when it's appropriate to change the default. If any of these options apply to you, you can change them from this screen.

Output from the Mem command

```
Memory Type        Total =  Used   +  Free
----------------  ------   ------   ------
Conventional        640K     110K     530K
Upper               155K     137K      19K
Adapter RAM/ROM     229K     229K       0K
Extended (XMS)    15360K    2971K   12389K
----------------  ------   ------   ------
Total memory      16384K    3447K   12937K

Total under 1 MB    795K     247K     548K

Largest executable program size       530K  (542416 bytes)
Largest free upper memory block        18K   (18624 bytes)
MS-DOS is resident in the high memory area.
```

Figure 25-16 The sample configuration after it has been optimized by MemMaker (part 2 of 2)

How to use MemMaker with multiple configurations MemMaker is one of two significant new configuration features introduced with DOS 6.0. The other is support for multiple configurations through the use of configuration menus, which you learned about in the last chapter. Unfortunately, these two new configuration features don't work well together. In other words, MemMaker doesn't know how to deal with CONFIG.SYS files that contain multiple configurations.

Figure 25-18 shows a procedure you can follow to use MemMaker when you have multiple configurations. In short, this procedure requires that you run MemMaker against each configuration separately. To do that, you make separate CONFIG.SYS and AUTOEXEC.BAT files for each configuration and edit the files to remove the configuration menu commands and any other commands that don't apply to that configuration. Then, you run MemMaker using each set of CONFIG.SYS and AUTOEXEC.BAT files. Finally, you combine the CONFIG.SYS and AUTOEXEC.BAT files modified by MemMaker, adding back in the commands that define your configuration menu. The exact details for how you do this depend on how you set up your CONFIG.SYS file. But it will be easier if you avoid Include commands and the Common block, so that each configuration block is completely self-contained.

The Advanced-options screen

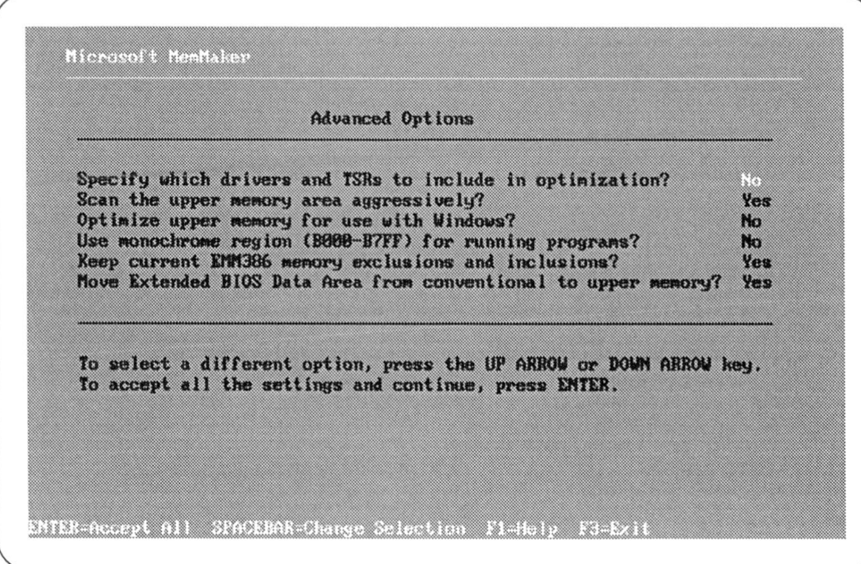

Custom-setup option	Description
Specify which drivers and TSRs to include in optimization?	If you're having trouble with a particular driver or memory resident program, specify Yes for this option. Then, when MemMaker prompts you for each driver or program, tell it to exclude the one you're having problems with.
Scan the upper memory area aggressively?	If your system locks up when you restart it, specify No for this option. This tells MemMaker to avoid using the portions of upper memory that most often cause conflicts.
Optimize upper memory for use with Windows?	If you run DOS applications from within *Windows*, specify Yes for this option. This will make more conventional memory available for DOS applications run from within *Windows*, but may result in less conventional memory for applications run outside of *Windows*.
Use monochrome region (B000-B7FF) for running programs?	If you use an EGA or a true VGA monitor (not super VGA), specify Yes for this option to free up additional upper memory.

Figure 25-17 How to set advanced options for MemMaker (part 1 of 2)

Custom-setup option	Description
Keep current EMM386 memory exclusions and inclusions?	If you specified options for EMM386.EXE to exclude or include certain portions of memory, specify Yes for this option if you want MemMaker to retain those exclusions.
Move Extended BIOS Data Area from conventional to upper memory?	This option frees up 1KB of conventional memory by moving the Extended BIOS Data Area to upper memory. Specify No for this option if this causes your system to fail.

Figure 25-17 How to set advanced options for MemMaker (part 2 of 2)

Some perspective on the CONFIG.SYS and AUTOEXEC.BAT files

Once you get your CONFIG.SYS and AUTOEXEC.BAT files set up so they use memory efficiently, you shouldn't have to change them unless you make changes to the hardware or software of your system. For example, if you add a hardware component that requires a device driver, you should load it with a Devicehigh command, then restart your computer to see if everything still works. If you used MemMaker to optimize your memory, you can run it again with the new device driver so it can determine a new optimum configuration.

Terms

conventional memory
base memory
upper memory area
upper memory
adapter RAM/ROM
Upper Memory Block
UMB
extended memory
eXtended Memory Specification
XMS
High Memory Area
HMA
LIM Expanded Memory Specification
EMS
expanded memory
page frame
page
hexadecimal notation
hex

Objectives

1. In general terms, explain how each of these types of memory can be used on your PC:

   conventional memory
   upper memory
   adapter RAM/ROM
   the High Memory Area
   extended memory
   expanded memory

1. Create a copy of CONFIG.SYS and AUTOEXEC.BAT for each configuration you have, using commands such as these:

```
copy config.sys config1.sys
copy config.sys config2.sys
copy config.sys config3.sys
copy autoexec.bat auto1.bat
copy autoexec.bat auto2.bat
copy autoexec.bat auto3.bat
```

   Also, create a backup copy of the CONFIG.SYS and AUTOEXEC.BAT using extensions other than BAK or UMB:

```
copy config.sys config.sav
copy autoexec.bat autoexec.sav
```

2. Edit each copy of CONFIG.SYS and AUTOEXEC.BAT, removing all lines that don't apply to the configuration. For CONFIG.SYS, be sure to account for commands in the Common block and any blocks specified in Include commands.

3 Run MemMaker for each configuration by renaming the files, with commands such as these:

```
copy config1.sys config.sys
copy auto1.bat autoexec.bat
```

   Reboot to make sure the configuration files are correct, then run MemMaker. When it's done, rename the configuration files back to their original file names:

```
copy config.sys config1.sys
copy autoexec.bat auto1.bat
```

4. Combine the optimized configuration files to recreate your multiple configuration.

Figure 25-18 A procedure for using MemMaker with multiple configurations

2. If you're using DOS 5.0, use the following commands in your CONFIG.SYS and AUTOEXEC.BAT files where appropriate:

   device=c:\dos\himem.sys
   device=c:\dos\emm386.exe
   dos=high,umb
   devicehigh
   lh

3. If you're using DOS 6.0, use MemMaker to optimize your memory configuration.

Section 7

Advanced DOS skills

The two chapters in this section show you how to use advanced features of DOS. Chapter 26 shows you how to use advanced DOS commands and command techniques. Then, chapter 27 shows you how to create advanced batch files, including batch files that use ANSI.SYS to create professional-looking screens. Chapter 27 also shows you how to create and use DOSKEY macros, which are similar to batch files.

Most users will never need to use any of the features presented in this section. However, I recommend you at least skim through these chapters so you'll have a general idea of what these DOS features do. Then, if you do encounter a need for one of them, you can read the appropriate chapter in greater detail.

Chapter 26

Advanced DOS commands and techniques

In this chapter, you'll learn about some of the DOS commands and techniques that haven't been presented in earlier chapters. First, you'll learn how to use several DOS commands that are occasionally useful. Then, you'll learn how to use a set of related DOS command techniques that can be surprisingly useful in certain circumstances: redirection, filters, and piping.

Advanced DOS commands

DOS provides several commands that are useful in special situations. The Attrib command lets you change a file's attributes. The Replace command selectively copies files from a source directory based on whether corresponding files exist in the target directory. The FC command lets you compare files to see if they are identical. The Subst command lets you use a single drive letter as shorthand for an entire subdirectory path. And the Append command extends the power of the Path command to data files and program overlays.

The Attrib command In chapter 9, you learned that DOS maintains an *archive bit* for each file on your system. The archive bit indicates whether or not a file has changed since the last backup. This file characteristic is called its *archive attribute.* Backup utilities use the archive attribute to perform incremental backups.

Actually, the archive attribute is one of four *file attributes* maintained by DOS for each file on your PC. The other three attributes are *read-only*, *hidden*, and *system.* The Attrib command, shown in figure 26-1, lets you set or clear these attributes for one or more files. With DOS 5.0 and 6.0, you can set or clear any of the file attributes, and you can use the /S switch to change the attributes of files not just in the specified directory, but in subdirectories as well. With earlier versions of DOS, the Attrib command lets you change only the read-only and the archive attribute, and it doesn't provide the /S switch.

A file that has the read-only attribute can't be deleted, modified, replaced, or renamed. You might want to set this attribute for a file like a master document or spreadsheet so it can't be changed or deleted accidentally. Then, you can use an application program to read the file into internal memory, but you can't replace the file on disk. If you try to, DOS issues an error message. To write the file, you must either use a new file name or turn off the read-only attribute for the existing file.

The hidden attribute causes a file to be left out of most DOS file operations. Thus, the file doesn't appear in directory listings, and the file can't be deleted, copied, or renamed. Since you usually want files to appear in directory listings, you probably won't want to use this attribute. You shouldn't use the system file attribute for your own files, either. It's reserved for DOS system files.

Incidentally, the four file attributes can't be changed completely independently of one another. In particular, you can't change the read-only or archive attribute of a hidden or system file. So you must remove the hidden or system attribute to change the read-only or archive attribute.

The Replace command The Replace command, shown in figure 26-2, is similar to the Copy and Xcopy commands. Its purpose is to let you update the files in a directory by replacing existing files or adding new files. Like Xcopy, it was introduced with version 3.2 of DOS. You're most likely to need the Replace command if you're involved in maintaining software on several computers. In that case, the Replace command is sometimes the most efficient method for distributing software updates.

The first example in figure 26-2 shows how you can use the Replace command to replace existing files. Here, all the files on the C drive are replaced with files from the diskette in drive A. This Replace command copies a file from the source specification only if a file with the same name exists in the target specification. Because this command can't change the names of the files it copies, you can't type a file name in the target specification. If you want the Replace command to prompt you before replacing each file, you can add the /P switch.

The /S switch in this example works differently from what you might expect. Instead of applying to the source directory, as it does with Xcopy, the /S switch applies to the target. In other words, Replace looks in the target directory and all subdirectories subordinate to it for file names that match files in the source directory. As a result, all the files you want to update with Replace should be in a single source directory.

The second example in figure 26-2 shows how you can use the Replace command with the /U switch to replace files with more recent versions of themselves. Here, files on the C drive are replaced with more current versions from the diskette in drive A. The /U switch tells the Replace command to copy a file from the source directory only if a file with the same name exists in the target directory and if the source file has a more recent date and time than the corresponding target file.

The third example in figure 26-2 shows how you can use the Replace command with the /A switch to add files to a directory. Here, any files on the source diskette in

The format of the Attrib command

```
ATTRIB [±R] [+±A] [±S] [±H] file-spec [/S]
```

Explanation

`+R` `-R`	Sets (+R) or clears (-R) the read-only attribute. When the read-only attribute is set, the file can be read but not changed, deleted, or renamed.
`+A` `-A`	Sets (+A) or clears (-A) the archive attribute. The archive attribute is set whenever the file is modified in any way. It is used primarily by backup programs to control incremental backups.
`+S` `-S`	(DOS 5.0 and 6.0 only) Sets (+S) or clears (-S) the system attribute, which marks the file as a system file.
`+H` `-H`	(DOS 5.0 and 6.0 only) Sets (+H) or clears (-H) the hidden attribute. When the hidden attribute is set, the file will not be displayed by the Dir command and cannot be deleted, copied, or renamed.
`file-spec`	Identifies the file or files whose attributes are to be changed.
`/S`	(DOS 5.0 and 6.0 only) Changes the attributes of files in the specified directory and in any subdirectories subordinate to the specified directory.

Example 1: An Attrib command that turns on the read-only attribute of a file named TEMPLATE.WK1.

```
C:\WK1>attr +r template.wk1
```

Example 2: An Attrib command that turns off the read-only attribute of all files in the current directory.

```
C:\DOC>attr -r *.*
```

Example 3: An Attrib command that turns off the archive attribute of all *.BAK files on the current drive.

```
C:\>attr -a *.BAK /s
```

Figure 26-1 The Attrib command

drive A that don't exist on the C drive are added. Note that you can't use the /S switch with the /A switch. So the replace command will add a file to the target directory even if a file with the same name already exists in a subdirectory of the target directory.

Note that although you can't use the /U and /A switches together, you might sometimes want to use two Replace commands in sequence, one with the /U switch,

The format of the Replace command

```
REPLACE source-spec target-spec [/U] [/A] [/P] [/S]
```

Explanation

`source-spec`	Identifies the files to be copied.
`target-spec`	Identifies the location where the files are to be copied.
`/U`	Updates files only if the file in *source-spec* has a more recent time and date than the corresponding file in *target-spec*.
`/A`	Copies only those files that exist in *source-spec* but not in *target-spec*. Can't be used with /U or /S.
`/P`	Prompts the user before replacing each file.
`/S`	Replaces not only files from the directory specified in *target-spec*, but also any files in subdirectories subordinate to the target directory.

Example 1: A Replace command that updates all files in the MMA directory with corresponding files from drive A.

```
C:\>replace a:*.* c:\mma /s
```

Example 2: A Replace command that replaces files in the MMA directory with more current files from drive A.

```
C:\>replace a:*.* c:\mma /u /s
```

Example 3: A Replace command that adds any files from drive A that don't already exist in the MMA directory.

```
C:\>replace a:*.* c:\mma /a /s
```

Figure 26-2 The Replace command

the other with the /A switch. This sequence of commands would ensure that the target contains a complete set of current files from the source directory. First, any files for which there are newer versions in the source directory are copied to the target directory. Then, any new files in the source directory are copied to the target directory. The only files that would not be copied by one or the other of these two commands are files for which a more current version already existed in the target directory.

The FC command Figure 26-3 shows the FC command, which lets you compare one or more files to find out if they are identical. Although FC has a variety of switches that can be useful in some situations, you'll usually use it without any

The format of the FC command

```
FC file-spec-1 file-spec-2 [/A] [/B] [/C] [/L] [/LBn]
                           [/N] [/T] [/W] [/nnn]
```

Explanation

file-spec-1	Identifies one or more files to be compared with *file-spec-2*.
file-spec-2	Identifies the file to be compared with each file specified in *file-spec-1*.
/A	Displays abbreviated output.
/B	Performs a binary comparison, the default for program files.
/C	Ignores case.
/L	Compares files line by line, resynchronizing lines after a mismatch is detected. This is the default for non-program files.
/LBn	Like /L, but sets the internal line buffer to hold *n* lines. The default is 100. The comparison is canceled if the number of consecutive lines that are different exceeds this number.
/N	Displays line numbers.
/T	Does not convert tabs to spaces. If you omit this switch, FC converts tabs to spaces, with tab stops every eight characters.
/W	Ignores extraneous white space (tabs and spaces).
/nnn	Specifies how many consecutive lines must match before FC considers the comparison resynchronized. The default is 2.

Example 1: An FC command that compares the file CONFIG.SYS with the file CONFIG.OLD.

```
C:\>fc config.sys config.old
```

Example 2: An FC command that compares all the files named CONFIG with CONFIG.SYS, disregarding extraneous white space.

```
C:\>fc config.* config.sys /w
```

Figure 26-3 The FC command

switches as in the first example. Here, the file CONFIG.SYS is compared with the file CONFIG.OLD. If the files are identical, the FC command will tell you. Otherwise, it will display the differences. Usually, you're not interested in what the differences are, just whether or not the files are identical. Unfortunately, though, there's no way to suppress the detailed display of file differences.

The second example in figure 26-3 shows how you can use wildcards in the first file specification. When you do, all the files that match the wildcard specification are compared with the single file you specify in the second file specification. In this case, files named CONFIG with any extension are compared with the CONFIG.SYS file. Because the file CONFIG.SYS matches the CONFIG.* file specification, the files compared against CONFIG.SYS will include the CONFIG.SYS file itself. This does not cause an error.

The Subst command The Subst command, shown in figure 26-4, lets you use a single drive letter to refer to a complete directory path. For example, the first example in figure 26-4 lets you access the files in C:\DATA as if they were on a separate drive B. The main reason to use the Subst command is if you need to access a file in a directory on a hard drive from a program that doesn't recognize DOS directories. For example, if you use an old program that recognizes only the diskette drives A and B, you can use a Subst command like the one in the first example to enable that program to access data in a hard disk directory. Note that the drive letter you assign can be a drive that exists on your system. However, if you specify an existing drive in the Subst command, you can no longer access the data on that drive. To cancel a substitution, enter the Subst command with the /D switch, as in the second example in figure 26-4.

Another situation where you might want to use the Subst command is when you want to install a program that requires you to install it from drive A, but your A drive is the wrong format. For example, suppose you need to install a program from 5-1/4 inch diskettes on a system with a 3-1/2 inch A drive and a 5-1/4 inch B drive. If the installation program requires that you install the program from drive A, you can issue a Subst command like the one in the third example in figure 26-4 to access the 5-1/4 inch drive as drive A. Notice that since a directory path is required for this command, you have to use a backslash to indicate that the substitution applies to the B drive's root directory.

Some people use Subst simply because it's more convenient to type a single drive letter rather than a full directory path. As a general rule, I don't think that's a good idea because of the confusion it can cause. For example, suppose you use a Subst command so you can access your C:\DATA directory as drive D. Months later you might forget that drive D is not a separate drive, but rather a directory on the C drive. Then, you might make the mistake of deleting the files in the C:\DATA directory, thinking they are unnecessary duplicates of the files that appear in the root directory of your D drive.

The Join command The Join command, shown in figure 26-5, is the opposite of the Subst command. Instead of letting you use a single drive letter to refer to a directory path, the Join command lets you use a directory path to refer to a drive letter. Thus, when you execute the Join command shown in the first example in figure 26-5, it will appear as if the D drive is actually a subdirectory named \DRIVE-D on the C drive. To cancel the join, use a Join command with the /D switch like the one in the second example.

The format of the Subst command

```
SUBST drive: path
```
or
```
SUBST drive: /D
```
or
```
SUBST
```

Explanation

`drive`	Specifies the drive letter that will be used to refer to the specified path.
`path`	Specifies a directory that will be referred to as *drive*.
`/D`	Specifies that the drive substitution is to be canceled.

Notes

1. If you omit all parameters, Subst displays the current substitutions.
2. The following commands should not be used on drives created by the Subst command:

ASSIGN	DISKCOPY	RESTORE
BACKUP	FDISK	RECOVER
CHKDSK	FORMAT	SYS
DEFRAG	LABEL	UNDELETE /S
DISKCOMP	MIRROR	

3. You can't issue a Subst command while *Windows* is running.

Example 1: A Subst command that specifies that the directory C:\DATA can be referred to as drive B.

```
C:\>subst b: c:\data
```

Example 2: A Subst command that cancels the substitution in example 1.

```
C:\>subst b: /d
```

Example 3: A Subst command that accesses drive B using drive letter A.

```
C:\>subst a: b:\
```

Figure 26-4 The Subst command

The format of the Join command

```
JOIN drive: path
```
or
```
JOIN drive: /D
```
or
```
JOIN
```

Explanation

`drive`	Specifies the drive letter that will be accessed via the specified path.
`path`	Specifies a directory path that will be used to access *drive*.
`/D`	Specifies that the join is to be canceled.

Notes

1. If you omit all parameters, Join displays the current joins.
2. Join has the same command restrictions as the Subst command listed in figure 26-4.
3. You can't issue a Join command while *Windows* is running.
4. Under DOS 6.0, the Join command is available only on the supplemental program diskette.

Example 1: A Join command that specifies that the drive D should be accessed as the DRIVE-D directory on the C drive.

```
C:\>join d: c:\drive-d
```

Example 2: A Join command that cancels the substitution in example 1.

```
C:\>join d: /d
```

Figure 26-5 The Join command

Like Subst, Join is most useful for older programs that have limitations on retrieving files. For example, the program I used to capture many of the screen images for this book can retrieve files only from the current drive. It lets you access any directory on the drive, but it won't let you access a different drive. By using a Join command, I can access files from other drives as if they were in a subdirectory on the current drive.

The Append command The Append command, shown in figure 26-6, can be used to set up a path that DOS uses when it's looking for data files. Then, if DOS

The format of the Append command

```
APPEND path [;path...] [/X | /X:ON | /X:OFF]
               [/PATH:ON | /PATH:OFF] [/E]
```

Explanation

`path`	Specifies one or more directories that DOS is to search for data files and program overlays.
`/X or /X:ON`	Searches for program files using the Append path. The Append directories are searched *before* the directories specified on the Path command. To use this feature, you must use /X:ON in the first Append command you issue after starting your computer.
`/X:OFF`	Searches the Append path only when opening data files or program overlays. This is the default.
`/PATH:ON`	Searches the Append path even if a complete path is specified for the file.
`/PATH:OFF`	Doesn't search the Append path.
`/E`	Places the Append directories in an environment variable named APPEND. To use this feature, you must first use /E on an Append command with no other parameters. Then, issue another Append command to specify the Append directories.

An Append command that sets up an Append path that includes three data directories

```
C:\>append d:\wk1;d:\doc;d:\q&a
```

Figure 26-6 The Append command

can't find a file in the current directory, it looks through the directories specified in the Append command. This is comparable to what DOS does when it looks through the directories given in the Path command for a program or command file. The example in figure 26-6 shows how to set up an Append path that includes three data directories.

The Append command is sometimes useful with programs that require you to change to the program's directory before running the program. These programs often load overlay files that must be in the current directory. With the Append command, DOS can find these overlay files even if they're not in the current directory by searching the Append path. Most newer programs avoid this requirement, so you probably won't need to use Append for this reason.

In general, you shouldn't use the Append command because it introduces confusion that may lead to operational errors. For example, suppose you have a file name that exists in two or more directories in the Append path. When you open this file from an application program, you won't know for certain which version of the file you've accessed unless you know the order of the directories in the Append path. Your application program will give no indication of which directory it retrieved the file from. And if you use your application's Save-as function to save the file under a new name, the new file will probably be saved in the current directory rather than in the directory that it retrieved the original file from.

If you do use the Append command, you need to realize that if you use the /X:ON switch, the DOS search sequence for program files is changed. When you use APPEND /X:ON, DOS searches for program files first in the current directory, then in the directories listed in the Append command, and finally in the directories listed in the Path command.

The Mode command In chapter 11, you learned how to use the Mode command to increase the speed of your keyboard's repeat rate (called the *typamatic rate*). Figure 26-7 shows that the Mode command has many additional options that let you control various aspects of your computer's I/O devices. In particular, you can use the Mode command to display the status of devices, to change the lines per inch or characters per line settings for an IBM or Epson-compatible dot matrix printer, to set up communication parameters for a serial port, to redirect printer output to a serial port, and to set the number of lines on the screen for an EGA or VGA monitor. If you need to use one of these commands on a regular basis, you should include it in your AUTOEXEC.BAT file.

Commands you'll rarely use In addition to the commands you've learned so far, DOS provides several other commands that you'll rarely, if ever, need to use. These commands either perform such unusual functions that it's unlikely you'd need to use them, or they've been replaced by more sophisticated commands that perform similar functions. Figure 26-8 summarizes these commands.

Redirection, filters, and piping

Experienced DOS users often use two techniques known as redirection and piping along with special DOS programs called filters to perform specific functions. Although these techniques might at first appear baffling, I think that once you understand how they work, you'll agree that they can be occasionally useful.

How to redirect a command's input and output *Redirection* is a technique that lets you send command output to some device other than the monitor. The device can be another physical device, such as a printer or a communications port, or it can be a file. For example, you can redirect the Type command's output so that instead of displaying a file's contents on the monitor, the output is printed. Or,

The Mode command to display the status of devices

```
MODE /STATUS
```

The Mode command to configure a printer

```
MODE LPTn[:] [COLS=n] [LINES=n]
```

Configures the IBM- or Epson-compatible printer specified by LPT*n* (LPT1, LPT2, or LPT3). The COLS value is the number of columns per line (80 or 132), and the LINES value is the number of lines per inch (6 or 8).

Example: `C:\>mode lpt1 cols=132`

The Mode command to configure a serial port

```
MODE COMn[:] [BAUD=b] [PARITY=p] [DATA=d] [STOP=s]
```

or

```
MODE COMn[:] b,p,d,s
```

Configures the communication parameters for a serial port. *B* sets the baud rate and is usually specified as 12 (1200 baud), 24 (2400 baud), 48 (4800 baud), 96 (9600 baud), or 19 (19,200 baud). *P* sets the parity and can be N for no parity, E for even parity, or O for odd parity. *D* sets the number of data bits, usually 7 or 8. *S* sets the number of stop bits, usually 1 or 2.

Example: `mode com1: 24,n,8,1`

The Mode command to redirect printer output to a serial port

```
MODE LPTn[:]=COMn[:]
```

Redirects output intended for LPT*n* to the specified serial port. You should first configure the serial port's communication settings.

Example: `mode lpt1:=com2:`

Figure 26-7 The Mode command (part 1 of 2)

you can use redirection to save the output from the Dir command in a file. Redirection also lets you receive command input from some device other than the keyboard or from a file.

To understand redirection, you need to know about the DOS concepts of *standard output* and *standard input*. Whenever a command writes information to standard output, DOS copies the information to the current standard output device. Usually, that's your monitor. However, DOS lets you substitute some other device, or even a file, for standard output. Then, the command's standard output will be sent to

The Mode command to set the number of lines for an EGA or VGA display

```
MODE CON[:] LINES=n
```

Sets the number of lines to display on the screen. For EGA, *n* can be 25 or 43. For VGA, *n* can be 25, 43, or 50. ANSI.SYS must be installed for this to work.

Example: `mode con: lines=43`

The Mode command to set the keyboard typamatic rate

```
MODE CON[:] RATE=n DELAY=n
```

Controls how many times a key is repeated in a second (RATE) and the delay before a keystroke is repeated when a key is held down (DELAY). The RATE value can be from 1 to 32. The DELAY value can be from 1 to 8 for DOS 4.0 and from 1 to 4 for DOS 5.0 and 6.0.

Example: `mode con: rate=32 delay=2`

Figure 26-7 The Mode command (part 2 of 2)

the redirected device or file rather than to the monitor. Similarly, whenever a command requests information from standard input, DOS reads the information from the current standard input device. Usually, this is the keyboard. But again, DOS lets you substitute some other device or a file for standard input. Then, the command obtains its input from the redirected source.

The standard output and input facility is available to any DOS program, not just the commands that come with DOS. Most application programs bypass standard output and input so that they can make more efficient use of the monitor and keyboard. However, many simple utility programs use standard output and input. If they do, you can use redirection with them as well as with DOS commands.

To use redirection, you type *redirection symbols* following the command whose input or output you want to redirect. You use the greater-than symbol (>) to redirect a command's standard output, and the less-than symbol (<) to redirect a command's standard input. After the redirection symbol, you type the name of the device or file you want the input or output redirected to.

When you use redirection, you must often use *device names* too. For example, PRN is the device name for the printer. If you have two printers, you can identify them as LPT1 and LPT2. The device name CON refers to the keyboard for input and the monitor for output. One other device name you might occasionally use for output is NUL, which represents a null device. Any output you redirect to NUL is simply discarded. (Redirecting output to NUL is sometimes useful in a batch file to avoid cluttering the screen with unnecessary messages.)

Command format	Function
`ASSIGN drive-1=drive-2`	Substitutes the second drive letter for the first drive letter. If you issue the command with no parameters, all drive assignments are canceled. This command has been replaced with the Subst command.
`COMP file-1 file-2`	Compares two files. This command has been replaced with the FC command, which provides more control over the type of comparison to be done.
`CTTY device`	Redirects the DOS console functions to the specified device. *Device* can be NUL, PRN, LPT1, LPT2, LPT3, CON, AUX, COM1, COM2, COM3, or COM4. CTTY NUL is sometimes used in batch files to suppress command output. CTTY NUL must be followed by CTTY CON to restore the DOS console.
`DISKCOMP drive-1 drive-2`	Compares the contents of one diskette with the contents of another one on a sector by sector basis. If the diskettes aren't identical, this command displays the side and track number of any sectors that differ.
`VERIFY [ON|OFF]`	Turns the DOS verify feature on or off. This feature verifies that data has been successfully written to disk after a write operation. If you don't specify a parameter, DOS tells you whether this feature is on or off. This feature actually provides inadequate protection against I/O errors, yet significantly reduces disk performance. As a result, you should not use it.

Figure 26-8 DOS commands you'll rarely use

To illustrate how redirection works, figure 26-9 shows four examples of redirection. The first example redirects the standard output of a Tree command to the printer (PRN). Thus, the tree listing is printed rather than displayed on the monitor. The second example uses the Type command to send the contents of a file named README.TXT to the printer.

The third example uses redirection to delete all the files in the TEMP directory without requiring the user to confirm the deletion. Here, the contents of the file

Example 1: A Tree command whose output is redirected to the printer.

```
C:\>tree >prn
```

Example 2: A Type command that prints the contents of the README.TXT file on the printer.

```
C:\>type readme.txt >prn
```

Example 3: A Del command that deletes all the files in the \TEMP directory without user intervention.

```
C:\>del \temp\*.* <c:\utility\y.txt
```

Example 4: A Time command whose output is appended to a file named TIMER.TXT and whose input is redirected to a file named ENTER.TXT.

```
C:\>time <c:\util\enter.txt >>timer.txt
```

Figure 26-9 How to use redirection

Y.TXT in the UTILITY directory are used for the standard input source for the Del command. For this command to work properly, you must first create a Y.TXT file that contains a single line with the letter Y. (In a few moments, I'll show you a more advanced technique that doesn't require the Y.TXT file.)

The fourth example shows how you can use two greater-than signs to append redirected output to an existing file. Here, the standard output from the Time command is added to the end of the TIMER.TXT file. If TIMER.TXT doesn't already exist, it will be created. In addition, the Time command's standard input is redirected to the ENTER.TXT file. Before you use this command, you must first create the ENTER.TXT file. It should contain nothing except a single empty line.

How to use filters A *filter* is a program that reads data from standard input, modifies it in some way, and writes it back to standard output. DOS provides three filters: More, Sort, and Find. The More filter reads data from standard input, then writes it unchanged to standard output, stopping whenever the screen is full. You can then press any key to display the next screen of data. The Sort filter reads data from standard input, sorts it, then writes it back to standard output. And the Find filter reads data from standard input and writes only those lines that match a given character string to standard output.

All three of these filters are designed to operate on text files, not word processing, spreadsheet, or database files. To present input data to a filter, you have to use redirection (or an advanced form of redirection called piping, which I'll explain in a moment).

Filter	Function
`MORE`	Displays one screen of output at a time.
`SORT [/R] [/+n]`	Sorts lines from the input source before writing it to the output source. If you specify /R, the input is sorted into reverse order. If you specify /+*n*, input is sorted on the character in column *n.* If you omit /+*n*, the input is sorted on the character in column 1.
`FIND [/N] [/I] "string" [file-spec...]`	Displays all lines from the input source that contain the specified string. If you specify /N, Find displays line numbers. If you specify /I, Find ignores case. (Unlike other filters, Find has an optional *file-spec* parameter that follows *"string"*, so you can specify an input file without using the redirection symbol.)

Example 1: A More filter that displays the README.TXT file one screen at a time.

```
C:\>more <readme.txt
```

Example 2: A Sort filter that sorts the file VENDORS.TXT, placing the sorted data in SORTVEND.TXT.

```
C:\>sort <vendors.txt >sortvend.txt
```

Example 3: A Find filter that searches the file VENDORS.TXT for the string "MMA" and displays the line numbers along with the lines that contain the string.

```
C:\>find /n "MMA" <vendors.txt
```

Example 4: A Find filter that searches the files VENDORS1.TXT and VENDORS2.TXT for the string "MMA," using the *file-spec* parameter rather than input redirection.

```
C:\>find "MMA" vendors1.txt vendors2.txt
```

Figure 26-10 How to use DOS filters

Figure 26-10 shows the three DOS filters along with four examples of how they're used. The first example uses the More filter to display a file named README.TXT. If you occasionally use the Type command to display text files and are annoyed by data scrolling off the screen before you've had a chance to read it, this use of the More filter should prove helpful.

The second example in figure 26-10 shows how to sort a file using the Sort filter. Here, input redirection is used to specify VENDORS.TXT as the input file, and output redirection is used to specify SORTVEND.TXT as the output file. Because I didn't include the /R or /+*n* switch on the filter, the records are sorted in ascending order based on the character in column 1 of each record.

The third example shows how to use the Find filter to display lines that contain a particular character string, in this case "MMA." The /N switch is specified so the line numbers will be displayed along with the lines containing the string. The fourth example shows a peculiarity of the Find filter that lets it read input from one or more files specified as parameters, rather than from redirected standard input. Here, both files VENDORS1.TXT and VENDORS2.TXT are searched for occurrences of "MMA." Strictly speaking, Find is acting as a command rather than as a Filter in example 4 since no input redirection is used.

How to use piping *Piping* is a technique where the standard output from one command is used as the standard input to another command. For example, suppose you pipe the output of a Dir command into the Sort filter. The result is a sorted display of the files in a directory.

To pipe the output from one command to another, you type both commands on the same command line and separate them with the *pipe symbol* (|). When DOS executes the first command, it redirects its output to a temporary file on disk. Then, DOS executes the second command, redirecting its input to the temporary file that was created by the first command. When the second command finishes, DOS deletes the temporary file.

Figure 26-11 shows six examples of pipes. In the first example, the output of a Type command is piped to the More filter. As a result, the file is displayed one screen at a time. This has the same effect as example 1 in figure 26-10, but it's actually less efficient because it first copies the entire README.TXT file to a temporary file before displaying it. Still, it demonstrates the basic operation of piping.

The second example in figure 26-11 shows how you can pipe the output of an Echo command into a Del command to delete all the files in a directory without having to create a Y.TXT file.

In the third and fourth examples in figure 26-11, the output of a Dir command is piped to the Sort filter. As a result, the directory is sorted before it is displayed or printed. In the fifth example, the sorted directory output is piped to the More filter so it's displayed one screen at a time. Note that these particular uses of piping are more suitable for older versions of DOS that don't support the Dir command's /O or /P switches.

In the last example in figure 26-11, you can see how to use piping and the Find filter to do something with the Chkdsk command that it was never intended to do. When you use the /V switch with Chkdsk, it displays a list of all the files in all the directories on the disk. In this example, piping is used so the output of the Chkdsk command goes through the Find filter. Then, Find removes all files except those named BUDGET93.WK1. Because the Chkdsk command displays the path along with the file name, this use of piping can help you find all files with a specific name.

Example 1: A pipe that's used to display a text file one screen at a time.

```
C:\>type readme.txt | more
```

Example 2: A pipe that's used to force the output of an Echo command into a Del command.

```
C:\>echo Y | del \temp\*.*
```

Example 3: A pipe that's used to sort the output from a Dir command.

```
C:\>dir | sort
```

Example 4: A pipe that's used to sort the output from a Dir command, redirecting the output to a printer.

```
C:\>dir | sort >prn
```

Example 5: A pipe that's used to sort the output from a Dir command and display the results one screen at a time via another pipe and the More filter.

```
C:\>dir | sort | more
```

Example 6: A pipe that's used with a Find filter to find all occurrences of a file named BUDGET93.WK1, no matter what directory it's in.

```
C:\>chkdsk /v | find "BUDGET93.WK1"
```

Note: If you have DOS 5.0 or later, you can perform the functions illustrated by examples 3 through 6 using the /O, /P, and /S switches of the Dir command.

Figure 26-11 How to use pipes

However, you must use uppercase letters in the character string within the Find command because the file names in directories are stored in uppercase letters. Also, because you can't use wildcards with this command, it's only useful when you can remember the exact spelling of a file name. (If you have DOS 5.0 or 6.0, this type of file search is better done with the /S switch of the Dir command.)

Some perspective on advanced DOS commands and techniques

As you read this chapter, you may have come to the conclusion that you'll never use any of the commands or techniques presented here. That's certainly possible since none of these commands are essential to the day-to-day activities of most PC users. On the other hand, you may have discovered a command or technique here that's exactly what you need to accomplish some important task. In any event, the value of some of these commands and techniques may become more apparent when you read the next chapter where you'll learn how to create sophisticated batch files.

Terms

archive bit
archive attribute
file attribute
read-only attribute
hidden attribute
system attribute
typamatic rate
redirection
standard output
standard input
redirection symbol
device name
filter
piping
pipe symbol

Objectives

1. Use the Attrib, FC, Replace, Subst, Join, Append, and Mode commands to solve specific problems or accomplish specific tasks as the need arises.
2. Use redirection to print the results of any DOS command or to save the results of any DOS command in a file.
3. Use the More, Sort, and Find filters and the piping techniques presented in this chapter as the need arises.

Chapter 27

Advanced batch file techniques

In chapter 6, you learned how to create simple batch files to start your application programs. And elsewhere in this book, you've learned how to set up the AUTOEXEC.BAT file. So far, though, you haven't learned how to use any of the special DOS commands and techniques that are designed specifically to be used with batch files. In this chapter, you will. You'll learn how to write batch files that can use parameters entered on the command line, test command line parameters to make sure they're valid, prompt the user for input, and more.

You'll also learn how to use the special commands for the ANSI.SYS device driver that can give your batch files a more professional appearance. Although, strictly speaking, ANSI.SYS isn't a batch file facility, you can use it with the Echo command to create more attractive displays. Finally, you'll learn how to use the Doskey macro facility, which lets you create short batch files that are always available in memory.

If you have a background in programming, you'll probably be frustrated by the many limitations you'll face as you develop batch files. Although you can use simple condition tests, Goto commands, and For loops, the DOS batch file facility lacks such basic programming concepts as expressions and arithmetic operators. Simple tasks, such as running a particular program every Friday, are possible only with a lot of effort. In many cases, you may be able to find an inexpensive utility program that can solve a batch file problem in a more straightforward manner. Or, you might be better off using a real programming language such as QBasic, which comes with DOS.

Batch file commands

Figure 27-1 lists the DOS commands that are designed to be used with batch files. You're already familiar with two uses for the Echo command. You use it to tell DOS whether the commands in a batch file should be displayed as they're executed and to display a message on the screen. But you may not be familiar with the third form of the Echo command shown in figure 27-1, which simply displays a blank line on the screen. Notice that a period must immediately follow the keyword Echo. If you type a space before the period, Echo will display a period on the screen.

You may also not be aware that although the ECHO OFF command suppresses command echoing for all commands, you can suppress the echo of a specific command by typing an at sign (@) immediately before the keyword. This technique is often used with the Echo command itself, like this:

```
@echo off
```

That way, the ECHO OFF command won't be displayed when you run the batch file.

The next command, Rem, is provided so you can add remarks to your batch files. Usually, this isn't necessary. But because the batch file techniques you'll learn in this chapter can be cryptic, you may want to consider using an occasional Rem command to explain what's going on. All the batch file examples you'll see in this chapter include a Rem command immediately after the @ECHO OFF command to give a brief description of the batch file and any parameters it requires.

You use the Pause command to stop the execution of a batch file. When the Pause command is executed, it displays the message "Press any key to continue..." Usually, you'll precede the Pause command with an Echo command that displays other instructions for the user. Then, when the user presses any key, the batch file continues. For example, if your batch file writes data to a diskette, you might want to include a sequence of commands similar to this:

```
echo Insert the sample diskette.
pause
copy c:\sample\*.* a:
```

Then, the user will be given a chance to change diskettes before the batch file copies files to it.

I'll explain each of the remaining commands in figure 27-1 as I present specific batch programming techniques.

How to use replaceable parameters As you already know, you can use replaceable parameters in a batch file to access parameters typed on the command line when the batch file is invoked. To use a replaceable parameter, you type a percent sign (%) followed by the sequence number of the parameter you want to use. For example, to access the first parameter on the command line you type %1, to access the second parameter you type %2, and so on. You can access up to nine parameters in this way.

The Shift command lets you shift the parameter values one position to the left. So, the parameter that was %2 becomes %1, the parameter that was %3 becomes %2, and so on. The value for the original first parameter (%1) is discarded. The SHOWALL.BAT file shown in figure 27-2 should help you understand how the Shift command works. This batch file displays the value of the %1 parameter using an Echo command. Then, it issues a Shift command and, if the new %1 parameter is not empty, branches to the :LOOP label to repeat the process. If you compare the

Command format	Function
`ECHO [ON|OFF]`	Turns the command-echoing feature on or off. (You can suppress the display of any specific command by adding the @ symbol to the beginning of the command.)
`ECHO [message]`	Displays *message* on the screen even when Echo is off.
`ECHO.`	Displays a blank line.
`REM [remark-text]`	Includes a remark in a batch file to help document the batch file's function.
`PAUSE`	Stops the execution of the batch file and displays the message, "Press any key to continue . . ."
`SHIFT`	Moves the parameters given in the command line that starts the batch file one position to the left. For example, %2 becomes %1, %3 becomes %2, and so on. The previous %1 parameter is lost.
`IF [NOT] condition command`	Executes *command* only if *condition* is true. If NOT is specified, executes *command* only if *condition* is not true. See figure 27-4 for details.
`GOTO label`	Skips from this command to the specified label.
`:label`	Sets up a label that can be used in a Goto command.
`FOR %%v IN (set) DO command`	Executes *command* once for each member of *set*. The variable specified as %%*v* is set to the value of each member of the set before *command* is executed. See figure 27-6 for details.
`CALL file-spec [parameters]`	Executes the commands in the batch file specified by *file-spec*, then returns to the batch file that issued the Call command.
`CHOICE [/C:keys] [/S] [/N]` `[/T:c,nn] text`	Displays the specified text, then waits for the user to press one of the keys listed in the /C switch. When the Choice command completes, the errorlevel code will be set to indicate the user's choice. See figure 27-9 for details.

Figure 27-1 Commands for advanced batch files

The SHOWALL.BAT file

```
@echo off
rem SHOWALL.BAT — Echoes each parameter typed on the command line
:loop
echo %1
shift
if not "%1"=="" goto loop
```

How the batch file works

```
C:\UTIL>showall It was the best of times
It
was
the
best
of
times
C:\UTIL>
```

Figure 27-2 A batch file that illustrates how the Shift command works

parameters I specified on the Showall command to invoke this batch file with the output displayed by the Echo commands, I don't think you'll have any trouble understanding what the Shift command does. (If you don't understand the :LOOP label, the If command, or the Goto command in this batch file, don't worry. You'll see how these commands work soon enough.)

Although you can access only nine parameters at a time, you can include more than nine parameters on the command line. If you do, the only way to access the parameters after the ninth one is by using the Shift command. Batch files that use ten or more parameters are uncommon, though.

You're more likely to use the Shift command to make it easier to deal with a variable number of parameters. For example, the COPYA.BAT file shown in figure 27-3 copies one or more files to the diskette in drive A. This batch file will work with any number of command line parameters.

Notice in this batch file that in addition to starting with an @ECHO OFF command, I silenced the output from the Copy command by redirecting its output to NUL. This is commonly done in batch files so you can supply your own, more meaningful output. In this case, I suppressed the output from the Copy command because it isn't very informative. It displays a message indicating how many files were copied, but not the name of the file or where it was copied. Instead, I displayed this information myself using an Echo command just before the Copy command. If

The COPYA.BAT file

```
@echo off
rem COPYA.BAT – Copies all specified files to drive A
:loop
echo copying %1 to a:
copy %1 a: >nul
shift
if not "%1"=="" goto loop
```

How the batch file works

```
C:\UTIL>copya oct93.wk3 nov93.wk3 dec93.wk3
copying oct93.wk3 to a:
copying nov93.wk3 to a:
copying dec93.wk3 to a:
```

Figure 27-3 A batch file that uses the Shift command to deal with a variable number of parameters

the Copy command encounters an error, the error message it displays will still be visible. Because error messages are not displayed using standard output, they're not redirected.

There's one other replaceable parameter you should know about: %0. This parameter is always set to the name of the batch file that's running. This might be useful if you want to display the name of the batch file in its output. You can also use the %0 parameter to cause a batch program to run itself.

How to use labels and the Goto command The batch files in figures 27-2 and 27-3 both use a Goto command to implement a basic looping structure. In both cases, the Goto command is embedded in an If command so it's executed only if the condition in the If command is true. And in both cases, the Goto command transfers control of the batch file to the *label* named LOOP, which appears before the Goto command in the batch file. The label doesn't have to come before the Goto command, however. Later in this chapter, you'll see examples of batch files that use the Goto command to branch forward, bypassing commands that should be executed only under certain conditions.

To create a batch file label, type a colon followed by the name of the label. Although you can type a label as long as you want, only the first eight characters are significant. So the two labels :BATCH-LABEL-1 and :BATCH-LABEL-2 are considered to be the same. Notice that when you refer to a label in a Goto command, you omit the colon.

How to use the If command The If command is a standard command in most programming languages. When the condition in the If command is true, the specified command is executed. Usually, you'll use a Goto command within an If command to control looping. That's how the batch files in figures 27-2 and 27-3 work.

Unfortunately, the conditions you can express in an If command are not as flexible as the conditions you can express in most programming languages. Figure 27-4 summarizes the three types of conditions you can use in an If command. As you can see, a condition can test the setting of the *errorlevel code* for a previous command, it can test the existence of a particular file, or it can test whether two character strings are equal.

The errorlevel code is a value maintained by DOS that indicates the completion status of the last command executed. Whenever a DOS command ends, it sets the errorlevel code to a numeric value ranging from 0 to 255. Although most commands always set the errorlevel code to 0, some set it to different values to indicate the success or failure of the command. And some communicate specific information via the errorlevel code, such as an action taken by the operator. You can test the value of the errorlevel code with an If command like the one in the first example in figure 27-4. Here, the batch file will branch to the label ERROR if the errorlevel code is 1 or more.

You have to be careful when you want to test for several possible errorlevel values because the IF ERRORLEVEL condition is true not just if the errorlevel code is equal to the value you specify, but also if it's greater than the value you specify. For example, suppose you use a program that can return three possible errorlevel codes, 1, 2, and 3, and you want to branch to three labels, ERROR1, ERROR2, or ERROR3, depending on the errorlevel code returned by the program. If you used the If command

```
if errorlevel 1 goto error1
```

the batch file would branch to ERROR1 for all three errorlevel values because 2 and 3 are greater than one.

The second example in figure 27-4 shows how you can easily test for multiple errorlevel values by testing the values in reverse order from highest to lowest. Here, the batch file branches to the label ERROR1 if the value of errorlevel is 1, ERROR2 if the value of errorlevel is 2, and ERROR3 if the value of errorlevel is 3 or more.

The third example shows how you can test for the existence of a file. Here, I used a replaceable parameter to supply the file name. And I used the keyword NOT to negate the entire condition. As a result, this condition is true if the specified file does *not* exist.

The fourth and fifth examples show how you can test the value of one string to see if it's equal to another. Notice that you must specify two consecutive equals signs for this test. (If you have any experience using the C programming language, this syntax should be familiar.) Although it's not always a requirement, it's a good practice to enclose both strings in quotation marks. That way, you don't have to worry about whether or not either string contains special characters that make

Condition format	Explanation
`ERRORLEVEL n`	This condition is true if the errorlevel code returned by the previous command is greater than or equal to *n*.
`EXIST file-spec`	This condition is true if the specified file exists.
`"string-1"=="string-2"`	This condition is true if the two strings are identical. The quotes are not always required, but they usually improve the reliability of the condition test.

Example 1: An If command that branches to the label ERROR if the previous command's errorlevel code is 1 or more.

```
if errorlevel 1 goto error
```

Example 2: If commands that branch to the labels ERROR1, ERROR2, or ERROR3 if the errorlevel code is 1, 2, or 3.

```
if errorlevel 3 goto error3
if errorlevel 2 goto error2
if errorlevel 1 goto error1
```

Example 3: An If command that branches to the label NOFILE if the file identified by the first command line parameter does not exist.

```
if not exist %1 goto nofile
```

Example 4: An If command that branches to the label DRIVEA if the first parameter is the letter A.

```
if "%1"=="A" goto drivea
```

Example 5: An If command that branches to the label NOPARM if the first parameter is not supplied.

```
if "%1"=="" goto noparm
```

Figure 27-4 Condition tests you can perform with the If command

quotation marks mandatory. The fourth example tests the value of a replaceable parameter to see if it's equal to the string "A". Even within the quotation marks, DOS recognizes that the percent sign marks a replaceable parameter and substitutes the parameter's value.

The fifth example shows how you can test a string for a null value by coding two adjacent quotation marks. If the user doesn't supply a value for the first parameter,

DOS will replace %1 with an empty string. Then, the If command effectively becomes this:

```
if "" == "" goto noparm
```

Because the two strings are both empty, the condition is true and the batch file branches to the label NOPARM.

How to use environment variables In chapter 24, you learned how to use the Set command to set a value for an environment variable. Two environment variables, DIRCMD and TEMP, are used by DOS to control certain aspects of its operation. Other environment variables are used by certain application or utility programs to control their operations. But you can also create your own environment variables in your batch files to control their operations.

When you create your own environment variables, you can use any name you wish for the variable name. For example, all of the following Set commands are valid:

```
set root=c:\
set target-dir=d:\test
set md$=44
```

To see a list of all the currently defined environment variables, use the Set command without any parameters. And to delete an environment variable, type the variable name on the Set command followed by an equal sign, but no value like this:

```
set root=
```

In this example, the ROOT variable is deleted.

Figure 27-5 shows a batch file that copies several files to the destination specified in the first parameter. This batch file is similar to the COPYA.BAT file I presented in figure 27-3. But instead of including the destination in the batch file, the COPYLIST.BAT file uses the first parameter as the destination. Because this parameter is lost the first time the Shift command is executed, the file uses an environment variable to keep track of the destination specified in the first parameter. Notice that to use the value of an environment variable, you must type a percent sign before and after the variable name.

You may recall from chapter 24 that DOS sets aside a relatively small amount of memory, called the *environment*, for environment variables. If you make extensive use of environment variables in your batch files, you may need to increase the size of the environment. To do that, you need to include a Shell command in your CONFIG.SYS file.

How to use the For command Figure 27-6 presents the format of the For command. To understand how it works, you first need to understand its parameters. The first parameter, %%*v*, is a variable. Although you can use any name you wish for the For variable, it's common to use %%V. Note that when you use For in a batch file, you must precede the variable name with two percent signs. The second

The COPYLIST.BAT file

```
@echo off
rem COPYLIST.BAT – Copies specified files to the specified directory
set dest=%1
shift
:loop
echo copying %1 to %dest%
copy %1 %dest% >nul
shift
if not "%1"=="" goto loop
```

How the batch file works

```
C:\UTIL>copylist c:\4q93 oct93.wk3 nov93.wk3 dec93.wk3
copying oct93.wk3 to c:\4q93
copying nov93.wk3 to c:\4q93
copying dec93.wk3 to c:\4q93
```

Figure 27-5 A batch file that uses an environment variable to store a parameter value

parameter, *set*, is simply one or more file names or text strings separated by spaces, comas, or semicolons. And the third parameter, *command*, can be any command along with that command's parameters, other than another For command. The keywords IN and DO that separate the parameters are required and help describe what the For command does.

When you issue the For command, it executes the command that follows the DO keyword once for each member of the set you specify. Each time the DO command is executed, the For command assigns the value of the next member of the set to the *%%v* variable. So, if you include the *%%v* variable as a parameter on the DO command, the command operates with a different parameter each time it's executed. For example, the first example in figure 27-6 prints the contents of the AUTOEXEC.BAT and CONFIG.SYS files.

Of course, if you use the For command in a batch file, you're likely to use a replaceable parameter for the set on which the command will operate. So, if you entered the two file names as parameters, you could print the two files using the command in the second example in figure 27-6. Note that, in this example, the DO command will execute exactly two times: once for each file name entered on the command line. If you want to execute the command for a variable number of files, you can use wildcards.

The format of the For command

```
FOR %%v IN (set) DO command
```

Explanation

`%%v`	A variable that's set to the value of the next member of *set* before *command* is executed.
`set`	One or more file names or strings separated by spaces, commas, or semicolons.
`command`	Any DOS command along with its parameters, except another For command.

Example 1: A For command that prints the AUTOEXEC.BAT and CONFIG.SYS files.

```
for %%v in (autoexec.bat config.sys) do print %%v
```

Example 2: A For command that prints the two files specified as parameters.

```
for %%v in (%1 %2) do print %%v
```

Example 3: A For command that copies each file that matches the file specification in %1 to drive A if the file doesn't already exist.

```
for %%v in (%1) do if not exist a:%%v copy %%v a:
```

Figure 27-6 The For command

If you use a wildcard in a member of the set, DOS repeats the DO command for every file that matches the specification. For example, suppose you want to copy a group of files to diskette. To do that, you could use the For command in the third example in figure 27-6. Notice that I specified %1 for the set in this command. So, if I entered a file specification with a wildcard as the first parameter, this command would copy each file that matches the specification to diskette. Actually, this commands copies a file only if it doesn't already exist on the diskette. That's because I used an If command within the DO command to test for the existence of each file.

Figure 27-7 shows an example of a batch file that uses a For command. This batch files lists all the directories in the DOS path one line at a time. Here, I specified the value of the PATH environment variable as the set. Because this variable contains the name of each directory in the path separated by semicolons, the For command considers each directory to be a separate value for the set. As a result, the Echo command lists each path directory on a separate line.

Figure 27-8 shows how you can use the For command to do simple parameter checking. In this case, I want to make sure the user specifies a valid diskette drive

The SHOWPATH.BAT file

```
@echo off
rem SHOWPATH.BAT – Shows path directories on separate lines
echo.
echo DOS will search for programs in the following directories:
echo.
for %%v in (%path%) do echo    %%v
echo.
```

How the batch file works

```
C:\>showpath

DOS will search for programs in the following directories:

    C:\DOS
    C:\UTIL
    C:\PCTOOLS
```

Figure 27-7 A batch file that uses the For command to display all the directories in the DOS path

letter as the batch file's first parameter. At first, this might seem like a simple task because the drive letter can be A or B. But the user may use uppercase or lowercase letters and may or may not follow the drive letter with a colon. As a result, there are eight correct ways to enter this parameter: A, a, A:, a:, B, b, B:, or b:. The first batch file in figure 27-8 shows how tedious it is to test for all eight of these values using If commands. The second batch file shows how you can test for all eight values using a single For command.

How to use the Call command The Call command lets you execute a batch file from a batch file. Then, when the second batch file has been executed, DOS returns to the next command in the first batch file. When you execute a batch file from a batch file without using the Call command, DOS executes the second batch file, but never returns to finish executing the first one. If that isn't what you want, you must use the Call command.

How to use the Choice command DOS 6.0 introduced a new batch file command, Choice, that lets you control your batch file's processing based on the user's input. The Choice command, presented in figure 27-9, displays the text you specify, then waits for the user to press one of the keys you specify. You specify the list of valid keys using the /C switch. If you omit /C, the defaults are Y and N.

The PARMIF.BAT file

```
@echo off
rem PARMIF.BAT — Checks %1 for valid diskette drive spec using If commands
if "%1"=="A"  set dest=%1
if "%1"=="A:" set dest=%1
if "%1"=="a"  set dest=%1
if "%1"=="a:" set dest=%1
if "%1"=="B"  set dest=%1
if "%1"=="B:" set dest=%1
if "%1"=="b"  set dest=%1
if "%1"=="b:" set dest=%1
if "%dest%"=="" goto nodest
echo You specified drive %dest%.
goto exit
:nodest
echo You did not specify a valid diskette drive.
:exit
set dest=
```

The PARMFOR.BAT file

```
@echo off
rem PARMFOR.BAT — Checks %1 for valid diskette drive spec using a For command
for %%v in (A A: a a: B B: b b:) do if "%1"=="%%v" set dest=%1
if "%dest%"=="" goto nodest
echo You specified drive %dest%.
goto exit
:nodest
echo You did not specify a valid diskette drive.
:exit
set dest=
```

Figure 27-8 The For command can make it easier to validate batch file parameters

After the user presses a valid key, the Choice command sets the value of the errorlevel code to a number that corresponds to the order of the keys in the Choice command. For example, if the valid choices are Y and N, the errorlevel code is set to 1 if the user types Y and 2 if the user types N. (Normally, the Choice command doesn't care whether the user types uppercase or lowercase letters, but you can make Choice case sensitive by using the /S switch.)

Figure 27-10 shows an AUTOEXEC.BAT file that uses the Choice command to ask whether the user wants to start the DOS shell. If so, the batch file issues the Dosshell command. Otherwise, the batch file branches around this command to the EXIT label. The Choice command in this batch file is this:

```
choice /t:y,10 Start the DOS shell?
```

The format of the Choice command

```
CHOICE [/C:keys] [/S] [/N] [/T:c,nn] text
```

Explanation

`/C:keys`	Specifies a list of valid keys. If /C is omitted, the only valid keys are Y and N.
`/S`	Specifies that a key must be entered in the case indicated in the /C switch.
`/N`	Doesn't display a list of the valid keys.
`/T:c,nn`	Provides a default choice, *c*, if the user doesn't enter a valid key before *nn* seconds have elapsed.
`text`	The text you want to display on the screen.

Figure 27-9 The Choice command

The AUTOEXEC.BAT file

```
@echo off
path c:\dos;c:\util
prompt $p$g
smartdrv 2048
echo.
choice /t:y,10 Start the DOS shell?
if errorlevel 2 goto exit
dosshell
:exit
```

What the user sees

```
Start the DOS shell? [Y,N]
```

Figure 27-10 An AUTOEXEC.BAT file that uses the Choice command

Here, I didn't specify the /C switch, so the default keys are Y and N. I did, however, specify the /T switch to provide a time-out default value. In this case, if the user doesn't press any key in 10 seconds, Y is assumed.

Figure 27-11 shows how you can use the Choice command to create a simple menu. Here, the MENU1.BAT file displays a list of menu selections. Then, a Choice command prompts the user for input. In this case, I didn't specify a time-out. However, I did use the /N switch so that the Choice command doesn't display the list

The MENU1.BAT file

```
@echo off
cls
echo 1.  Lotus 123
echo 2.  WordPerfect
echo 3.  DOS shell
echo.
choice /c:123 /n Enter your choice:
if errorlevel 3 goto shell
if errorlevel 2 goto wp
123
goto exit
:wp
wp
goto exit
:shell
dosshell
:exit
```

What the user sees

```
1.  Lotus 123
2.  WordPerfect
3.  DOS shell

Enter your choice:
```

Figure 27-11 A batch file that displays a menu of application programs

of valid keys. (They're displayed by the Echo commands, so there's no need to display them again.) Following the Choice command, If commands test the errorlevel code to determine what action to take. Notice that I tested the errorlevel values in reverse order: first 3, then 2. I didn't bother to test for 1 because if the errorlevel value isn't greater than 2, it's 1.

If you're using a DOS version prior to 6.0, the Choice command isn't available. However, you can create a similar command I'll call Getyn. To create the Getyn command, you must first use a word processor or text editor to create the file shown in the top part of figure 27-12. Then, you use the Debug command as shown to create the GETYN.COM program file. Since you must enter the GETYN.SCR file *exactly* as shown, be sure to proof your file against figure 27-12 before you use it with the Debug command. The bottom portion of figure 27-12 shows how you can use the Getyn command in a batch file. (In case you're interested, Debug is a DOS command that's often used by programmers to create simple program files like this one. And the

The GETYN.SCR file

```
e 100 b4 08 cd 21 88 c2 3c 59
e 108 74 10 3c 79 74 0c 3c 4e
e 110 74 04 3c 6e 75 ea b3 00
e 118 eb 02 b3 01 b4 02 cd 21
e 120 b2 0d cd 21 b2 0a cd 21
e 128 88 d8 b4 4c cd 21
r cx
2e
n getyn.com
w
q
```

A Debug command to create GETYN.COM

```
C:\UTIL>debug <getyn.scr
```

How to use GETYN in a batch file

```
echo Start the DOS shell?
getyn
if not errorlevel 1 goto exit
dosshell
:exit
```

Figure 27-12 How to create and use GETYN.COM

GETYN.SCR file contains the machine instructions used by the GETYN command as well as commands that direct the Debug program to copy these instructions.)

How to use ANSI.SYS

In chapter 24, you learned how to load the ANSI.SYS device driver using a Device command in your CONFIG.SYS file. If you load this driver, you can use special codes in your batch files to improve the appearance of your batch file's output. These codes are often called *escape sequences* because they all begin with a special character called the *escape character*. (Actually, they all begin with an escape character followed by a left bracket.) As a general rule, you should avoid using ANSI.SYS escape sequences because they make your batch files more complicated and they require that you load the ANSI.SYS driver, which occupies about 4KB of memory. If you run a batch file that includes ANSI.SYS escape sequences while ANSI.SYS isn't loaded, your screen will be cluttered up with the non-functioning

Escape sequence	Example	Function
`Esc[row;colH`	`Esc[5,20H`	Moves the cursor to the specified line and column position. The top line is line 0, and the left-most column is column 0. The example moves the cursor to column 20 of line 5.
`Esc[nA`	`Esc[1A`	Moves the cursor up the specified number of lines. The example moves the cursor up one line. If the cursor is already at the top of the screen, this sequence is ignored.
`Esc[nB`	`Esc[1B`	Moves the cursor down the specified number of lines. The example moves the cursor down one line. If the cursor is already at the bottom of the screen, this sequence is ignored.
`Esc[nC`	`Esc[10C`	Moves the cursor right the specified number of columns. The example moves the cursor right 10 columns. If the cursor is already at the right edge of the screen, this sequence is ignored.
`Esc[nD`	`Esc[10D`	Moves the cursor left the specified number of columns. The example moves the cursor left 10 columns. If the cursor is already at the left edge of the screen, this sequence is ignored.
`Esc[s`	`Esc[s`	Saves the current cursor position.
`Esc[u`	`Esc[u`	Restores a previously saved cursor position.
`Esc[2J`	`Esc[2J`	Clears the displays. The cursor is moved to the home position (line 0, column 0).
`Esc[K`	`Esc[K`	Erases the current line from the current cursor position to the end of the line.

Figure 27-13 ANSI.SYS escape sequences (part 1 of 2)

escape sequences. Nevertheless, if you want to create batch files with a professional appearance, ANSI.SYS can help you do it.

Figure 27-13 lists the ANSI.SYS escape sequences you're most likely to use in your batch files. As you can see, these escape sequences let you move the cursor, save and restore the cursor position, clear the entire screen or just one line, change the text attributes of the characters displayed on your screen, and change the foreground and background colors of the display. In this figure, the word Esc stands for the escape character. In other words, the escape sequence to erase the current line consists of three characters: an escape character, a left bracket, and an uppercase K. This escape

Escape sequence	Example	Function
`Esc[a;...;am`	`Esc[34;46m`	Sets one or more display attributes. *A* can be any number from the following list:

Text attributes

0	Normal
1	Bold
4	Underscore (monochrome only)
5	Blink
7	Reverse video
8	No display

Foreground	Background	Color
30	40	Black
31	41	Red
32	42	Green
33	43	Yellow
34	44	Blue
35	45	Magenta
36	46	Cyan
37	47	White

The example sets the display to blue characters on a cyan background.

Figure 27-13 ANSI.SYS escape sequences (part 2 of 2)

sequence is shown in figure 27-13 as Esc[K. By the way, the required letters in the escape sequences must be entered in the case indicated in figure 27-13. So Esc[k isn't a valid escape sequence.

One of the difficulties in using ANSI.SYS escape sequences is adding escape characters to your file. That's because when you press the Esc key on your keyboard, most text editors interpret it as an editing command. As a result, you must follow special procedures to add escape characters to a batch file. Figure 27-14 shows the procedures you follow when you use the DOS 5.0/6.0 Edit command or Edlin. It also suggests a procedure you can try when using other text editors. Note that how the escape character actually appears on your screen depends on the text editor you're using. For example, if you use the Edit command, the escape character will display as a left arrow (←).

EDIT	Press the Ctrl and P keys together, then release them and press the Esc key. The escape character will display as a left arrow (←).
EDLIN	Press the Ctrl and V keys together, then release them and type the [character. The escape character will display as ^V[when you enter it. If you redisplay the line, it's displayed as ^[.
Other programs	Try holding down the Alt key and typing 27 on the numeric keypad.
For the Prompt command	Just type $e. Prompt translates this code into an escape character for you.

Figure 27-14 How to enter an escape character into a text file

Figure 27-14 also shows that if you use ANSI.SYS escape sequences in a Prompt command, you don't have to worry about these special procedures. That's because the Prompt command interprets the code $e as an escape character. So, to use the escape sequence that clears the current line in a Prompt command, you would type $e[K.

Figure 27-15 shows the Prompt command I introduced in chapter 24 and explains what each ANSI.SYS escape sequence and prompt code does. The prompt that results from this command displays the current time and date on the top line of the display in white characters on a blue background. Then, it displays the usual pg prompt information on the current line.

Figures 27-16 and 27-17 show a more ambitious use of ANSI.SYS to create an elaborate menu system. Figure 27-16 shows the batch file that displays the two menus in figure 27-17. When the batch file is first run, the menu in part 1 is displayed, offering the user three choices: *WordPerfect*, *Lotus 1-2-3*, or DOS Utilities. If the user picks DOS Utilities, a second menu pops up over the first to display a menu of DOS utilities as in the second part of figure 27-17. The user can return to the first menu by pressing the Esc key. From the main menu, the user can press the Esc key to exit to DOS.

Besides the use of ANSI.SYS escape sequences, there are two things I want you to notice about the batch file in figure 27-16. First, I used special characters to create the borders around the menus. Figure 27-18 lists the special characters you can use to create borders like these. As you can see, these characters include portions of boxes made from single lines, double lines, or a combination of single and double lines. To enter one of these characters, hold down the Alt key and type the three-digit code for the character using the numeric keypad. For example, to enter the single-line top-left-corner character, hold down the Alt key and type 218 on the numeric keypad. Then, when you release the Alt key, the special character will appear.

The Prompt command

```
prompt $e[s$e[H$e[37;44m$e[K$t$h$h$h$e[58C$d$e[37;40m$e[u$p$g
```

What each ANSI.SYS escape sequence and Prompt code does

`$e[s`	Saves the cursor position.
`$e[H`	Moves the cursor to the home position.
`$e[37;44m`	Sets the screen colors to white on blue.
`$e[K`	Erases the line, changing the entire line to white on blue.
`$t`	Displays the time.
`$h$h$h`	Backspaces over the hundredths of seconds.
`$e[58C`	Moves the cursor 58 columns to the right.
`$d`	Displays the date.
`$e[37;40m`	Sets the screen colors to white on black.
`$e[u`	Restores the original cursor position.
`$p$g`	Displays the path and a greater-than sign.

Figure 27-15 A Prompt command that uses ANSI.SYS codes

Second, notice how I used escape characters in the Choice command not only to include an ANSI.SYS escape sequence, but also to specify that the Esc key is a valid response for the Choice command. The first Choice command in figure 27-16 is this:

```
choice /c123← /n ←[21;20fEnter your choice:
```

Here, the escape character in the /C switch specifies that the valid user responses are 1, 2, 3, or the Esc key. The second Choice command in figure 27-16 is similar.

How to create and use macros

As you already know, the Doskey command that comes with DOS 5.0 and 6.0 makes it easier to enter commands at the DOS prompt by allowing you to use editing keys and letting you recall previous commands. In addition, Doskey lets you create *macros,* which are similar to batch files but are stored in internal memory rather than as separate files. The advantage of macros over batch files is that they execute faster because they're stored in internal memory. In addition, if you create a macro with the same name as an internal command, DOS will execute your macro rather than the

```
@echo off
:start
rem set up screen colors
echo ←[34;46m
cls
echo ←[37;44m
echo ←[5;20f┌─────────────────────────────────────┐
echo ←[6;20f│            MAIN MENU                │←[40m ←[44m
echo ←[7;20f├─────────────────────────────────────┤←[40m ←[44m
echo ←[8;20f│                                     │←[40m ← [44m
echo ←[9;20f│       1. Word Perfect 5.1           │←[40m ←[44m
echo ←[10;20f│       2. Lotus 1-2-3 3.4            │←[40m ←[44m
echo ←[11;20f│       3. DOS Utilities              │←[40m ←[44m
echo ←[12;20f│                                     │←[40m ←[44m
echo ←[13;20f│                                     │←[40m ←[44m
echo ←[14;20f└─────────────────────────────────────┘←[40m
echo ←[15;22f                                        ←[34;46m
echo ←[22;20fPress ESC to Exit
choice /c123← /n ←[21;20fEnter your choice:
if errorlevel 4 goto exit
if errorlevel 3 goto menu3
if errorlevel 2 goto menu2
if errorlevel 1 goto menu1
:menu1
cls
call c:\util\wp.bat
goto start
:menu2
cls
call c:\util\123.bat
goto start
```

Figure 27-16 A batch file that uses ANSI.SYS to create a menu system (part 1 of 2)

```
:menu3
rem set up screen colors
echo ←[34;46m
echo ←[37;44m
echo ←[8;25f┌──────────────────────────────────────┐
echo ←[9;25f│           DOS Utilities              │←[40m ←[44m
echo ←[10;25f├──────────────────────────────────────┤←[40m ←[44m
echo ←[11;25f│                                      │←[40m ←[44m
echo ←[12;25f│       1. Check hard disk             │←[40m ←[44m
echo ←[13;25f│       2. Format a diskette           │←[40m ←[44m
echo ←[14;25f│       3. Microsoft Backup            │←[40m ←[44m
echo ←[15;25f│                                      │←[40m ←[44m
echo ←[16;25f│                                      │←[40m ←[44m
echo ←[17;25f└──────────────────────────────────────┘←[40m
echo ←[18;27f                                        ←[34;46m
echo ←[22;20fPress ESC to return to main menu
choice /c123← /n ←[21;20fEnter your choice: ←[D
if errorlevel 4 goto start
if errorlevel 3 goto dos3
if errorlevel 2 goto dos2
if errorlevel 1 goto dos1

:dos1
rem Check hard disk
echo ←[37;40m
cls
chkdsk c:
pause
goto start

:dos2
rem Format diskette
echo ←[37;40m
cls
format a:
goto start

:dos3
rem Microsoft Backup
msbackup
goto start

:exit
echo ←[37;40m
cls
```

Figure 27-16 A batch file that uses ANSI.SYS to create a menu system (part 2 of 2)

Part 1:

When you run the batch file in figure 27-16, it displays a main menu with three options.

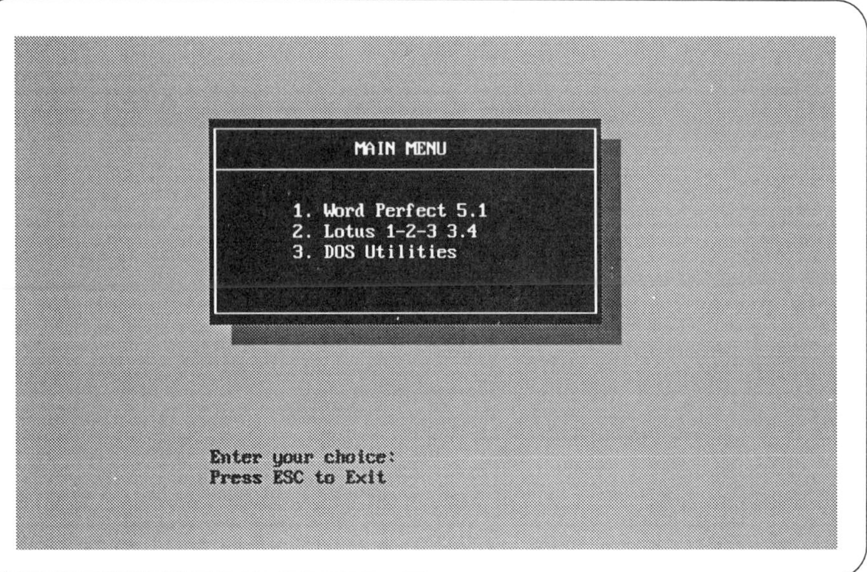

Part 2:

If you select option 3 from the main menu, the batch file displays another menu of DOS utilities.

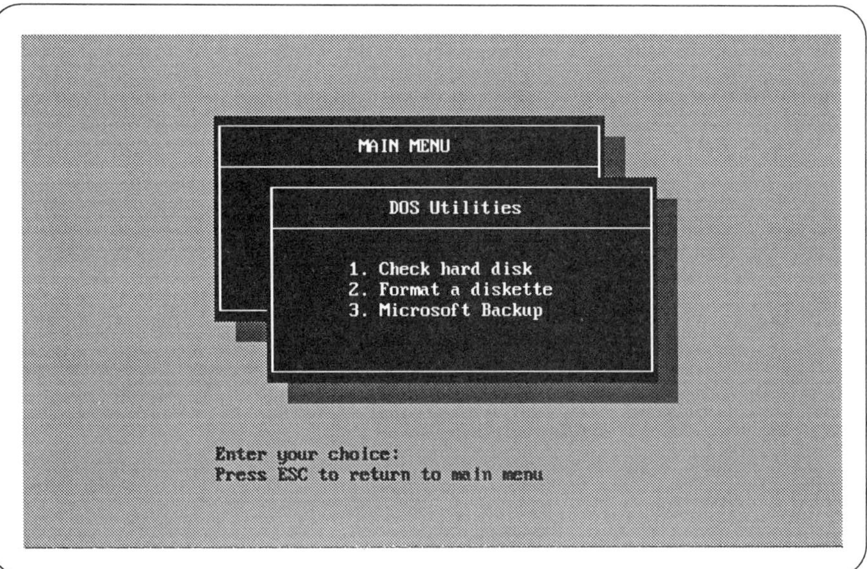

Figure 27-17 The menus displayed by the batch file in figure 27-16

Box segment	Single		Double		Mixed			
Horizontal	196	─	205	═				
Vertical	179	│	186	║				
Top left	218	┌	201	╔	214	╓	213	╒
Top right	191	┐	187	╗	183	╖	184	╕
Bottom left	192	└	200	╚	211	╙	212	╘
Bottom right	217	┘	188	╝	189	╜	190	╛
Middle left	195	├	204	╠	199	╟	198	╞
Middle right	180	┤	185	╣	182	╢	181	╡
Top middle	194	┬	203	╦	210	╥	209	╤
Bottom middle	193	┴	202	╩	208	╨	207	╧
Center cross	197	┼	206	╬	215	╫	216	╪

Other useful extended ASCII characters

176	░	220	▄
177	▒	221	▌
178	▓	222	▐
219	█	223	▀

Figure 27-18 Extended ASCII characters used to draw boxes and other shapes

command. The disadvantage of macros is that they must be relatively short and they can't include labels or Goto commands.

Figure 27-19 shows the various forms of the Doskey command you use to work with macros. The first format is the one you use to define a macro. Figure 27-20 shows the special symbols you can use when you define a Doskey macro, along with some examples. (You can enter the letters in these symbols in uppercase or lowercase. I used uppercase here so you can distinguish the letter L from the number 1.) Doskey uses these symbols rather than the ones you already know about so you can include Doskey commands that define macros in a batch file. If Doskey used the same symbols you use for batch files, DOS wouldn't know if the symbols were part of the batch file or part of the macro definition.

Doskey command format	Explanation
`DOSKEY macro-name=[text]`	Defines a macro.
`DOSKEY macro-name=`	Deletes a macro definition.
`DOSKEY /REINSTALL`	Deletes all macro definitions.
`DOSKEY /BUFSIZE=size`	Specifies the size of the macro buffer. The default is 512 bytes.
`DOSKEY /MACROS`	Lists the current macros.

Figure 27-19 The Doskey command

The first example in figure 27-20 shows you how to create a macro named +R that sets the read-only attribute for a file. To invoke this macro, you would use it as if it were a command, like this:

```
C:\DATA>+r 92final.wk3
```

Here, the macro sets the read-only attribute for the file 92FINAL.WK3. This macro uses the symbols $1 and $2 to stand for replaceable parameters in the same way you use %1 and %2 in a batch file. (I included the $2 parameter in this macro so you can use the Attrib command's /S switch when you use the +R macro.)

The macro in the second example uses $1 and $2 to provide for two replaceable parameters. In addition, it uses $T to separate the two commands used in the macro. And the macro in the third example uses $L to redirect the output of a command through the More filter.

The Doskey switches shown in figure 27-19 are useful when you work with macros. To erase all your macros, you use the /REINSTALL switch. If you need to increase the size of the buffer Doskey uses to store macros, use the /BUFSIZE switch. And to display the current macros, you use the /MACROS switch.

Figure 27-21 shows how you can save the current macros in a batch file. First, you enter the Doskey command using the /MACROS switch, and you redirect the command output to a file. The second portion of the figure shows the contents of the file that's created by the command. If you save this file as a batch file, you can then execute it to load the macro definitions. But first, you must modify the file and add the appropriate Doskey commands as shown in the third portion of figure 27-21. Here, the first Doskey command without any parameters loads the DOSKEY program, and each line that follows defines a macro. If you call this batch file from your AUTOEXEC.BAT file, the DOSKEY program and the macro definitions will be loaded automatically when you start your PC.

Character	Function
`$G`	Redirects output; equivalent to the (>) redirection symbol.
`$L`	Redirects input; equivalent to the (<) redirection symbol.
`$B`	Pipes output to the next command; equivalent to the (|) pipe symbol.
`$T`	Separates commands in a macro definition.
`$1 - $9`	Replaceable parameters that are equivalent to the (%) replaceable parameters you use in batch files.
`$*`	Represents everything typed on the command line following the command macro name.

Example 1: A Doskey command that creates a macro named +R that sets the read-only attribute for the specified file.

```
doskey +r=attrib +r $1 $2
```

Example 2: A Doskey command that copies the user-specified files to the specified target, then deletes the original files.

```
doskey move=copy $1 $2 $T del $1
```

Example 3: A Doskey command that displays text files one screen at a time by redirecting the file into the More filter.

```
doskey view=more $L$1
```

Figure 27-20 Special characters you can use in macros

Some perspective on advanced batch files

Although you can create sophisticated batch files using the facilities DOS provides, I think you'll agree that the most useful batch files are often the simplest. For example, you can create simple batch files that solve the basic problem of starting an application program from any directory without using any of the commands or techniques you've learned about in this chapter. And you can often create batch files that automate routine tasks like backing up your critical files to a network drive using only a few of the commands and techniques you've learned here.

Still, there are occasions when it pays to spend the time necessary to develop a sophisticated batch file. This is especially true if you're creating a batch file to automate a process that's vital to your business. Then, it pays to think through all the unexpected conditions that might cause an unsophisticated batch file to fail. For example, what if a key file doesn't exist? Or what if a file you're copying already exists in the target directory? Or what if a user types an invalid file name as a parameter?

The Doskey command to save the current macros in a batch file

```
C:\UTIL>doskey /macros >mac.bat
```

The resulting batch file

```
+R=attrib +r $1 $2
-R=attrib -r $1 $2
+H=attrib +h $1 $2
-H=attrib -h $1 $2
+A=attrib +a $1 $2
-A=attrib -a $1 $2
+ALL=attrib +r +h +s +a $1 $2
-ALL=attrib -r -h -s -a $1 $2
```

The batch file after it has been modified to load the macros

```
doskey
doskey +R=attrib +r $1 $2
doskey -R=attrib -r $1 $2
doskey +H=attrib +h $1 $2
doskey -H=attrib -h $1 $2
doskey +A=attrib +a $1 $2
doskey -A=attrib -a $1 $2
doskey +ALL=attrib +r +h +s +a $1 $2
doskey -ALL=attrib -r -h -s -a $1 $2
```

Figure 27-21 How to save the current macros in a file

Also keep in mind that advanced batch files often make it possible to transfer your knowledge of DOS to a less knowledgeable user. For example, if you are responsible for supporting unsophisticated users who use their PCs to access files on a network, you can set up a series of batch files to let them log on and off the network, access certain directories and printers, and start network application programs. These batch files let the unsophisticated user access advanced features of DOS without knowing anything other than the name of the batch files.

Terms

label
errorlevel code
environment
escape sequence
escape character
macro

Objectives

1. Given some task that must be automated, create an appropriate batch file using any of the advanced commands and techniques presented in this chapter.
2. Create a batch file that includes ANSI.SYS escape sequences to produce professional-looking output.
3. Create Doskey macros to simplify your most frequently used commands.

Appendix A

Command reference

This appendix summarizes the formats and functions of every command available under DOS. For each command, this appendix gives the MS-DOS version when the command first became available. If you're using some other manufacturer's version of DOS, you may have to check your DOS manual to see whether a command or option is available to you.

This appendix is divided into two sections. The first section presents all the commands that are available from the DOS prompt or in batch files. The second section presents all the commands that you can use in your CONFIG.SYS file, including the commands that load the device drivers that come with DOS.

DOS commands

The APPEND command

Function: Sets up a search path for data files.

DOS version: 3.2

Format:

```
APPEND path[;path...] [/X|/X:ON|/X:OFF]
        [/PATH:ON|/PATH:OFF] [/E]
```

Explanation:

path[;path...]	One or more directory paths to search for data files.
/X:ON	Searches specified directories for programs as well as data files.
/X:OFF	Does not search specified directories for programs.
/PATH:ON	Searches even if explicit path is specified for file.
/PATH:OFF	Does not search if explicit path is specified for file.
/E	Stores the path in an environment variable named APPEND.

The ASSIGN command

Function: Substitutes one drive letter for another. SUBST is preferred for this function.

DOS version: 3.0

Format:

```
APPEND drive-1=drive-2
```

Explanation:

drive-1	The drive you wish to access using a substituted drive letter.
drive-2	The substitute drive letter you wish to use to access *drive-1*.

The ATTRIB command

Function: Sets file attributes.

DOS version: 3.3.

Format:

```
ATTRIB [+R|-R] [+A|-A] [+S|-S] [+H|-H] file-spec [/S]
```

Explanation:

+R -R	Sets or resets the read-only attribute.
+A -A	Sets or resets the archive attribute.
+S -S	Sets or resets the system attribute (5.0 and later).
+H -H	Sets or resets the hidden attribute (5.0 and later).
file-spec	The files whose attributes are to be set.
/S	Set file attributes in subdirectories (5.0 and later).

The BACKUP command

Function: Backs up files.

DOS version: 2.0.

Format:
```
BACKUP source-spec target-spec [/A] [/D:date] [/F[:size]]
       [/L[:file-spec]] [/M] [/S] [/T:time]
```

Explanation:

source-spec	The files to back up.
target-spec	The drive to back up to.
/A	Appended backup (3.3 and later).
/D:date	Backs up files modified since the specified date.
/F[:size]	Formats if necessary; see FORMAT for size values (3.3 and later).
/L[:file-spec]	Creates a log file; default is BACKUP.LOG in root directory.
/M	Backs up modified files.
/S	Backs up subdirectories.
/T:time	Backs up files modified since the specified time; use with /D.

The BREAK command

Function: Activates or deactivates Ctrl+C checking.

DOS version: 1.0

Format:
```
BREAK [ON|OFF]
```

The CALL command

Function: Used in batch files to invoke another batch file.

DOS version: 3.3

Format:
```
CALL batch-file [parameters...]
```

Explanation:

batch-file	The name of the batch file to invoke.
parameters	Parameters passed to the batch file.

The CD (CHDIR) command

Function: Changes the current directory.

DOS version: 2.0.

Format:
```
CD [drive:][path]
```
or
```
CHDIR [drive:][path]
```

Explanation:

drive:	The drive on which you want to change the current directory.
path	The directory you want to make current.

The CHCP command

Function: Changes the active code page. To use this command, you must include a DEVICE command to load DISPLAY.SYS in your CONFIG.SYS file, and you must include an NLSFUNC and MODE CON CP PREP command in your AUTOEXEC.BAT file.

DOS version: 3.3

Format: `CHCP nnn`

Explanation:

nnn	The three-digit code page. The default is 437 (U.S. English).

The CHKDSK command

Function: Check the disk for errors in the FAT or directory structure.

DOS version: 1.0

Format: `CHKDSK [drive:] [/F] [/V]`

Explanation:

drive:	The drive to check.
/F	Corrects errors.
/V	Lists all files on *drive.*

The CHOICE command

Function: Prompts the user to make a selection, then sets the errorlevel code to indicate the user's choice. (This command is used in batch files.)

DOS version: 6.0

Format: `CHOICE [/C:keys] [/N] [/S] [/T:c,nn] [text]`

Explanation:

/C:keys	A list of keys the user can press.
/N	Does not display the prompt of valid keys.
/S	Case sensitive.
/T:c,nn	Defaults to choice *c* after *nn* seconds.
text	The text to be displayed.

The CLS command

Function: Clear the screen.

DOS version: 2.0

Format: `CLS`

The COMMAND command

Function: Invokes a second copy of COMMAND.COM.

DOS version: 1.0

Format:
```
COMMAND [path] [device] [/E:nnnnn] [/C command]
        [/K file-name] [/MSG] [/P]
```

Explanation:

path	The directory that contains COMMAND.COM.
device	A device to use for console I/O. CON is the default.
/E:nnnnn	Reserves *nnnnn* bytes for the environment. The default is 256.
/C command	Executes the specified command.
/K file-name	Runs the specified batch file instead of AUTOEXEC.BAT.
/MSG	Avoids diskette swapping by storing all error messages in internal memory. Used only when running DOS from diskette.
/P	Makes the command processor permanent. Use only in a SHELL command in the CONFIG.SYS file.

The COMP command

Function: Compares two files.

DOS version: 3.3

Format:
```
COMP file-spec-1 file-spec-2 [/A] [/C] [/D] [/L] [/N=n]
```

Explanation:

file-spec-1	The first file or set of files to be compared.
file-spec-2	The second file or set of files to be compared.
/A	Displays differences using ASCII characters.
/C	Ignores case.
/D	Displays differences using decimal codes (default is hexadecimal).
/L	Displays line numbers for differences (default is byte offset).
/N=n	Compares first *n* lines.

The COPY command

Function: Copies one or more files.

DOS version: 1.0

Format: `COPY source-spec [+source-spec...] [target-spec] [/A|/B] [/V]`

Explanation:

source-spec	One or more files to copy.
+source-spec	Combines several files into one file.
target-spec	The location where the files are to be copied.
/A	Treat each file as an ASCII file when combining files.
/B	Treat each file as a binary file when combining files.
/V	Verify writes (not recommended).

The CTTY command

Function: Sets up an alternate console device for your system.

DOS version: 2.0

Format: `CTTY device`

Explanation:

device	The device to use for the console (AUX, COM1, COM2, COM3, COM4, CON, LPT1, LPT2, LPT3, PRN). The default is CON.

The DATE command

Function: Sets the system date.

DOS version: 1.0

Format: `DATE [mm-dd-yy]`

Explanation:

mm-dd-yy	The date. If omitted, DATE prompts you to enter the date.

The DBLSPACE /CHKDSK command

Function: Checks the internal structure of a compressed drive.

DOS version: 6.0

Format: `DBLSPACE /CHKDSK [/F] [drive:]`

Explanation:

/F	Corrects errors.
drive:	The drive to be checked.

The DBLSPACE /COMPRESS command

Function: Compresses the specified drive.

DOS version: 6.0

Format:
```
DBLSPACE /COMPRESS drive1: [/NEWDRIVE=drive2:]
          [/RESERVE=size]
```

Explanation:

drive1:	The drive to compress.
/NEWDRIVE=drive2:	The drive letter to assign to the new compressed drive.
/RESERVE=size	Space to leave free on the host drive.

The DBLSPACE /CREATE command

Function: Creates an empty compressed drive.

DOS version: 6.0

Format:
```
DBLSPACE /CREATE drive1: [/NEWDRIVE=drive2:]
          [/SIZE=size|/RESERVE=size]
```

Explanation:

drive1:	The uncompressed drive that will host the compressed drive.
/NEWDRIVE=drive2:	The drive letter to assign to the new compressed drive.
/SIZE=size	Amount of host drive space to use for compressed drive.
/RESERVE=size	Space to leave free on the host drive.

The DBLSPACE /DEFRAGMENT command

Function: Defragments a compressed drive.

DOS version: 6.0

Function:
```
DBLSPACE /DEFRAGMENT [drive:]
```

Explanation

drive:	The drive to defragment.

The DBLSPACE /DELETE command

Function: Deletes a compressed drive.

DOS version: 6.0

Format:
```
DBLSPACE /DELETE drive:
```

Explanation:

drive:	The drive to delete.

The DBLSPACE /FORMAT command

Function: Formats a compressed drive. This is not required when creating a compressed drive, but can be used later to erase all of the files on the drive.

DOS version: 6.0

Format: `DBLSPACE /FORMAT drive:`

Explanation:

drive:	The drive to format.

The DBLSPACE /INFO command

Function: Displays information about the specified drive.

DOS version: 6.0

Format: `DBLSPACE [/INFO] drive:`

Explanation:

drive:	The drive whose information is to be displayed.

The DBLSPACE /LIST command

Function: Lists information about disk drives.

DOS version: 6.0

Format: `DBLSPACE /LIST`

The DBLSPACE /MOUNT command

Function: Mounts a compressed drive.

DOS version: 6.0

Format: `DBLSPACE /MOUNT[=nnn] [drive:] [/NEWDRIVE=drive:]`

Explanation:

/MOUNT[=nnn]	The DBLSPACE.*nnn* file to be mounted. The default is DBLSPACE.000.
drive:	The drive where the DBLSPACE.nnn file resides.
/NEWDRIVE=drive:	The drive letter assigned to the compressed drive.

The DBLSPACE /RATIO command

Function: Changes the estimated compression ratio for a compressed drive.

DOS version: 6.0

Format: `DBLSPACE /RATIO[=r.r] [drive:|/ALL]`

Explanation:

/RATIO[=r.r]	The new compression ratio.
drive:	The drive whose compression ratio is to be changed.
/ALL	Changes the compression ratio of all compressed drives.

The DBLSPACE /SIZE command

Function: Changes the size of a compressed drive.

DOS version: 6.0

Format: `DBLSPACE /SIZE[=size|/RESERVE=size] [drive:]`

Explanation:

/SIZE[=size]	Amount of host space to use for the compressed drive.
/RESERVE=size	The amount of free space to leave on the host.
drive:	The drive whose size is to be changed.

The DBLSPACE /UNMOUNT command

Function: Unmounts the specified drive.

DOS version: 6.0

Format: `DBLSPACE /UNMOUNT [drive:]`

Explanation:

drive:	The drive to unmount.

The DEBUG command

Function: Creates and tests executable files.

DOS version: 2.0

Format: `DEBUG [file-name [parameters]]`

Explanation:

file-name	The program file to debug.
parameters	Passes parameters to *file-name*.

Subcommands:

?	Displays list of commands.
A [addr]	Prompts for assembler commands to be loaded at specified address.
E addr [list]	Enters one or more bytes of hex data at the specified address.
N file-spec	Specifies a file name for a W command.
Q	Quits DEBUG.
R register	Displays the specified register value and prompts you for a new value.
W address	Writes data at the specified address to file named in N command. The length must be loaded into the CS register with an R command.

The DEFRAG command

Function: Defragments a drive.

DOS version: 6.0

Format: `DEFRAG [drive:] [/F|/U] [/S:order] [/B] [/H] [/SKIPHIGH] [/LCD|/BW|/G0]`

Explanation:

drive:	The drive to defragment.
/F	Defragments files and eliminates embedded free space.
/U	Defragments files but doesn't eliminate embedded free space.
/S:order	Sorts the files into the specified order:

N	Name	N-	Reverse name
E	Extension	E-	Reverse extension
D	Date	D-	Reverse date
S	Size	S-	Reverse size

/B	Reboots when finished.
/H	Moves hidden files.
/SKIPHIGH	Does not use upper memory, even if available.
/LCD	Uses LCD color scheme.
/BW	Uses black and white color scheme.
/G0	Does not use graphics characters.

The DEL (ERASE) command

Function: Deletes a file.

DOS version: 1.0

Format: `DEL [file-spec] [/P]`
or `ERASE [file-spec] [/P]`

Explanation:

file-spec	One or more files to delete.
/P	Confirms each file before it's deleted. (4.0 and later).

The DELTREE command

Function: Deletes a directory tree.

DOS version: 6.0

Format: `DELTREE path [path...] [/Y]`

Explanation:

path	One or more directories to be deleted.
/Y	Does not prompt before deleting subdirectory.

The DIR command

Function: Displays a listing of the files in a directory.

DOS version: 1.0

Format:
```
DIR [file-spec] [/A[:attrib...]] [/B] [/C] [/CH] [/L]
    [/O[:order...] [/P] [/S] [/W]
```

Explanation:

file-spec — The directory or files to list.

/A[:attrib...] — Lists files whose attributes match the attributes you specify (5.0 and later). *Attrib* can be:

+R	-R	Lists files with or without the read-only attribute.
+A	-A	Lists files with or without the archive attribute.
+S	-S	Lists files with or without the system attribute.
+H	-H	Lists files with or without the hidden attribute.

/B	Lists in brief format with file names only.
/C	Displays the compression ratio if the file is on a compressed drive.
/CH	Displays the compression ratio using the host drive's cluster size.
/L	Uses lowercase letters.

The DIR command (continued)

/O[:order...]	Lists files in the specified order (5.0 and later). *Order* can be:
	N -N Name order, alphabetical or reverse.
	E -E Extension order, alphabetical or reverse.
	D -D Date order, oldest first or last.
	S -S Size order, smallest first or last.
	G -G Directories first or last.
/P	Pauses when the screen is full.
/S	Display subdirectories (5.0 and later).
/W	Displays listing in wide format.

The DISKCOMP command

Function: Compares two diskettes.

DOS version: 3.2

Format: `DISKCOMP drive-1: drive-2: [/1] [/8]`

Explanation:

drive-1:	The first drive to be compared.
drive-2:	The second drive to be compared.
/1	Single-sided diskette (DOS 1.0 compatibility).
/8	Eight-sector diskette (DOS 1.0 compatibility).

The DISKCOPY command

Function: Copies a diskette.

DOS version: 2.0

Format: `DISKCOPY drive-1: drive-2: [/1] [/V]`

Explanation:

drive-1:	The disk to be copied.
drive-2:	The disk to be created.
/1	Single-sided diskette (DOS 1.0 compatibility).
/V	Verify writes (not recommended).

The DOSKEY command

Function: Provides command editing and macros.

DOS version: 5.0

Format:

```
DOSKEY [/REINSTALL] [/BUFSIZE=size] [/MACROS] [/HISTORY]
       [/INSERT|/OVERSTRIKE] [macro-name=text]
```

Explanation:

/REINSTALL	Loads a new copy of DOSKEY, clearing the buffer and erasing macros.
/BUFSIZE=size	Sets the size of the buffer. The default is 512.
/MACROS	Lists all current macros.
/HISTORY	Lists all commands stored in the buffer.
/INSERT	Places the keyboard in insert mode.
/OVERSTRIKE	Places the keyboard in typeover mode.
macro-name=text	Creates a DOSKEY macro.

Macro symbols:

$G	Redirects output (equivalent to >).
GG	Redirects and appends output (equivalent to >>).
$L	Redirects input (equivalent to <).
$B	Pipes output to next command (equivalent to |).
$T	Separates commands.
$$	Specifies the dollar sign character.
$1 - $9	Command line parameters like %1-%9 in batch files.
$*	Represents all command line parameters.

The DOSSHELL command

Function: Invokes the DOS shell.

DOS version: 4.0

Format:

```
DOSSHELL [/T|/G] [/B]
```

Explanation:

/T	Starts DOS shell in text mode.
/G	Starts DOS shell in graphics mode.
/B	Displays in black and white.

The ECHO command

Function: Activates or deactivates command echoing, or displays a message.

DOS version: 2.0

Format: `ECHO [ON|OFF|message]`

Explanation:

ON	Activates command echoing.
OFF	Deactivates command echoing.
message	Displays the message.

Note: Preceding a command with the @ symbol suppresses echoing for that command. Batch files usually begin with an @ECHO OFF command.

The EDIT command

Function: Edits a text file.

DOS version: 5.0

Format: `EDIT file-spec [/B] [/G] [/H] [/NOHI]`

Explanation:

file-spec	The file to be edited.
/B	Displays in black and white.
/G	Uses fast screen display for CGA monitors.
/H	Uses maximum screen resolution.
/NOHI	Supports older eight-color monitors.

The EDLIN command

Function: Edits a file.

DOS version: 1.0

Format: `EDLIN file-spec`

Explanation:

file-spec	The file to be edited.

Subcommands:

?	Displays a list of commands.
line	Changes a specific line.
D	Deletes the current line.
*line*D	Deletes the specified line.
line-1,*line-2*D	Deletes a range of lines.
E	Saves changes and ends.
I	Inserts lines before the current line.
*line*I	Inserts lines before the specified line.

The EDLIN command (continued)

L	Lists the file.
*line-1,line-2*L	Lists a range of lines.
Q	Quits without saving changes.

The EMM386 command

Function: When entered as a command, activates or deactivates EMS or Weitek support.

DOS version: 5.0

Format: `EMM386 [ON|OFF|AUTO] [W=ON|W=OFF]`

Explanation:

ON	Activates EMS support.
OFF	Deactivates EMS support.
AUTO	Activates EMS support when a program requests it.
W=ON	Activates Weitek processor support.
W=OFF	Deactivates Weitek processor support.

The EXIT command

Function: Exits a secondary command processor.

DOS version: 2.0

Format: `EXIT`

The EXPAND command

Function: Expands program files from the distribution diskettes.

DOS version: 5.0

Format: `EXPAND file-spec [file-spec...] target-spec`

Explanation:

file-spec	One or more files to be expanded. Wildcards not allowed.
target-spec	The directory where uncompressed files are to be written.

The FASTHELP command

Function: Provides brief help information.

DOS version: 6.0

Format: `FASTHELP [command]`
or `command /?`

Explanation:

command	The command for which you want to display brief help information.

The FASTOPEN command

Function: Sets up internal cache for directory entries.

DOS version: 3.3

Format:
```
FASTOPEN drive:=entries... [/X]
```
or
```
FASTOPEN drive:=(entries,buffers)... [/X]
```

Explanation:

drive:	One or more drives for which directory entries are to be cached.
entries	The number of directory entries to cache.
buffers	The number of continuous space buffers to provide (4.0 only).
/X	Uses expanded memory (4.0 and later).

The FC command

Function: Compares two files.

DOS version: 2.0

Format:
```
FC file-spec-1 file-spec-2 [/A] [/C] [/L] [/LBn] [/N]
   [/T] [/W] [/nnn]
```
or
```
FC file-spec-1 file-spec-2 [/B]
```

Explanation:

file-spec-1	The first file to be compared.
file-spec-2	The second file to be compared.
/A	Abbreviated output.
/B	Binary comparison.
/C	Ignores case.
/L	Line-by-line comparison.
/LBn	Sets size of buffer used to resynchronize files. The default is 100.
/N	Displays line numbers.
/T	Does not expand tabs to spaces.
/W	Ignores white space.
/nnn	Number of lines that must match to resynchronize files. The default is 2.

The FDISK command

Function: Configures hard disk partitions and logical drives.

DOS version: 2.0

Format:
```
FDISK [/STATUS]
```

Explanation:

/STATUS	Displays the current partition table.

The FIND command

Function: Searches files for a specified text string.

DOS version: 2.0

Format: `FIND [/C] [/I] [/N] [/V] "string" file-spec`

Explanation:

file-spec	One or more files to be searched. If omitted, FIND works as a filter.
"string"	The characters to be located.
/C	Displays count only.
/I	Ignores case.
/N	Displays line numbers.
/V	Displays lines that do *not* contain the specified string.

The FOR command

Function: Executes a DOS command once for each member of a set. (This command is used in batch files.)

DOS version: 2.0

Format: `FOR %%v IN (set) DO command [parameters]`

Explanation:

%%v	A variable whose value is set to each member of *set*.
set	A set of values separated by spaces or semicolons. May include file specifications with wildcards.
command	A command that's executed once for each member of *set*.
parameters	Parameters passed to *command*. Usually includes %%v.

The FORMAT command

Function: Formats a disk.

DOS version: 1.0

Format:

```
FORMAT drive: [/1] [/4] [/8] [/N:sectors] [/T:tracks]
       [/F:{360|1200|1.2|720|1440|1.44|2880|2.88}]
       [/S] [/B] [/Q] [/U] [/V:label]
```

Explanation:

drive:	The drive to be formatted.
/1	Formats a single-sided disk.
/4	Format 360KB in 1.2MB drive.
/8	Formats an eight-sector disk.
/N:sectors	Number of sectors.
/T:tracks	Number of tracks.

The FORMAT command (continued)

/F:360	Formats 360KB diskette (4.0 and later).
/F:1200 or /F:1.2	Formats 1.2MB diskette (4.0 and later).
/F:720	Formats 720KB diskette (4.0 and later).
/F:1440 or /F:1.44	Formats 1.44MB diskette (4.0 and later.).
/F:2880 or /F:2.88	Formats 2.88MB diskette (4.0 and later).
/S	Transfers system files.
/B	Reserves room for system files transferred later with SYS.
/Q	Quick format (5.0 and later).
/U	Unconditional format (can't be unformatted) (5.0 and later).
/V:label	The volume label.

The GOTO command

Function: Transfers control to a batch file label. (This command is used in batch files.)

DOS version: 2.0

Format: `GOTO label`

Explanation:

label	A label that appears elsewhere in the batch file.

The GRAPHICS command

Function: Enables the Print-screen key to print graphics screens.

DOS version: 2.0

Format: `GRAPHICS [type] [file-spec] [/B] [/LCD] [/PB:STD|/PB:LCD] [/R]`

Explanation:

type	The printer type. Consult manual for values.
file-spec	The graphics profile file. Default is GRAPHICS.PRO.
/B	Prints background color.
/LCD	Uses LCD display aspect ratio.
/PB:STD	Uses standard print box size.
/PB:LCD	Uses LCD print box size.
/R	Prints characters white on black rather than black on white.

The GRAFTABL command

Function: Enables extended characters when code pages are used with CGA monitors.

DOS version: 3.0

Format: `GRAFTABL nnn`

Explanation:

nnn	The code page. The default is 437 (U.S. English).

The HELP command

Function: Displays help information.

DOS version: 5.0

Format: `HELP [command-name] [/B] [/G] [/H] [/NOHI]`

Explanation:

command-name	The command for which help is to be displayed.
/B	Displays in black and white.
/G	Uses fast screen display for CGA monitors.
/H	Uses maximum screen resolution.
/NOHI	Supports older eight-color monitors.

The INTERLNK command

Function: Redirects a drive on a client computer to a server drive.

DOS version: 6.0

Format: `INTERLNK [client-drive:=[server-drive:]]`

Explanation:

client-drive:	The client drive to be reassigned.
server-drive:	The server drive.

The INTERSVR command

Function: Starts an Interlnk server.

DOS version: 6.0

Format:

```
INTERSVR [drive:...] [/X=drive:...] [/LPT[:n] [/COM[:n]
         [/BAUD:rate] [/B] [/V]
```

or `INTERSVR /RCOPY`

Explanation:

drive:	One or more drives to be made available to the client.
/X=drive:	Excludes the specified drive or drives.
/LPT[:n]	Uses a parallel port to establish the connection.
/COM[:n]	Uses a serial port to establish the connection.

The INTERSVR command (continued)

/BAUD:rate	Specifies the baud rate for a serial connection. Rate can be 9600, 19200, 38400, 57600, or 115200.
/B	Displays in black and white.
/V	Uses a more reliable method for serial communications.
/RCOPY	Installs the Interlnk files to the client.

The IF command

Function: Executes a command if a condition is true. (This command is used in batch files.)

DOS version: 2.0

Format: **`IF [NOT] ERRORLEVEL nnn command`**
or **`IF [NOT] string-1==string-2 command`**
or **`IF [NOT] EXIST file-spec command`**

Explanation:

ERRORLEVEL nnn	Executes *command* if errorlevel code is greater than or equal to *nnn*.
string-1==string-2	Executes *command* if *string-1* is equal to *string-2*.
EXIST file-spec	Executes *command* if the specified file exists.
NOT	Executes *command* if the specified condition is *not* true.
command	The DOS command to be executed conditionally.

The JOIN command

Function: Substitutes a path specification for a drive.

DOS version: 3.1

Format: **`JOIN drive: [path|/D]`**

Explanation:

drive:	The drive to be accessed via a path specification.
path	The path that will be used to access the drive.
/D	Cancels a previous JOIN command for the specified drive.

The KEYB command

Function:	Configures a keyboard for a specific language.	
DOS version:	3.3	
Format:	`KEYB keyboard-code [,codepage] [,file-spec] [/E] [/ID:nnn]`	
Explanation:	keyboard-code	The keyboard code. Consult manual for values.
	codepage	The code page. Consult manual for values.
	file-spec	The keyboard definition file. The default is KEYBOARD.SYS.
	/E	Supports enhanced keyboards on PC and XT-class computers.
	/ID:nnn	The layout for countries that support two layouts.

The LABEL command

Function:	Creates a volume label for a disk drive.	
DOS version:	3.0	
Format:	`LABEL [drive:] [label]`	
Explanation:	drive:	The drive you want to label. The default is the current drive.
	label	The label you want to use for the drive.

The LOADHI command

Function:	Loads a program in upper memory.	
DOS version:	5.0	
Format:	`LOADHI command`	
or	`LH command`	
Explanation:	command	Any external DOS command.

The MD (MKDIR) command

Function:	Creates a directory.	
DOS version:	2.0	
Format:	`MD path`	
or	`MKDIR path`	
Explanation:	path	The directory to be created.

The MEM command

Function: Displays memory information.

DOS version: 4.0

Format: `MEM [/C] [/D] [/F] [/M module] [/P]`

Explanation:

/C	Shows memory use by class (low, upper, extended) (5.0 and later).
/D	Shows memory used by programs and drivers (5.0 and later).
/F	Shows information about free memory (6.0).
/M module	Shows information about a particular module (6.0).
/P	Under DOS 5.0, shows memory used by programs. Under DOS 6.0, pauses the display when the screen is full.

The MEMMAKER command

Function: Determines the optimum memory configuration.

DOS version: 6.0

Format: `MEMMAKER [/B] [/BATCH] [/SWAP:drive] [/T] [/UNDO] [/W:n,m]`

Explanation:

/B	Displays in black and white.
/BATCH	Unattended mode.
/SWAP:drive	Specifies the boot drive if swapped by a compression program. Not required for *DoubleSpace*, *SuperStor*, or *Stacker 2.0*.
/T	Disables detection of IBM Token Ring networks.
/UNDO	Tells MemMaker to undo its most recent changes.
/W:n,m	Reserves two areas of upper memory for *Windows* translation buffers.

The MIRROR command

Function: Protects against certain types of errors.

DOS version: 5.0 only

Format: `MIRROR drive:  [/Tdrive] [/U] [/1] [/PARTN]`

Explanation:

drive:	The disk to be protected.
/Tdrive	Enables delete tracking.
/U	Unloads delete tracking.
/1	Keeps only one generation of Mirror data.
/PARTN	Backs up the disk's partition table to a diskette.

The MODE command (configure printer)

Function: Configures a printer.

DOS version: 3.2

Format: `MODE LPTn: c,l,r`
or `MODE LPTn: [COLS=c] [LINES=l] [RETRY=r]`

Explanation:

LPTn:	The printer port to configure.
c	Columns per line (80 or 132).
l	Lines per inch (6 or 8).
r	Retry action: E to return error, B to return busy, P to retry, R to return ready, or N to take no action.

The MODE command (configure serial port)

Function: Configures a serial port.

DOS version: 3.2

Format: `MODE COMn: b,p,d,s,r`
or `MODE COMn: [BAUD=b] [PARITY=p] [DATA=d] [STOP=s] [RETRY=r]`

Explanation:

COMn:	The serial port to configure.
b	The baud rate: 12 (1200), 24 (2400), 48 (4800), 96 (9600), or 19 (19,200).
p	Parity: N (none), E (even), or O (odd).
d	Data bits: 5, 6, 7, or 8.
s	Stop bits: 1, 1.5, or 2.
r	Retry action: E to return error, B to return busy, P to retry, R to return ready, or N to take no action.

The MODE command (display device status)

Function: Displays the status of a device.

DOS version: 3.2

Format: `MODE [device] [/STATUS]`

Explanation:

device	The device whose status you wish to display.
/STATUS	Displays status of redirected printers.

The MODE command (redirect printer)

Function: Redirects printer output to a serial port.

DOS version: 3.2

Format: `MODE LPTn:=COMn:`

Explanation:

LPTn:	The printer you want to redirect.
COMn:	The serial port to send printer output to.

The MODE command (set device code pages)

Function: Sets up device code pages.

DOS version: 3.2

Format: `MODE device CODEPAGE PREPARE=((codepage...) file-spec)`
or `MODE device CODEPAGE SELECT=codepage`
or `MODE device CODEPAGE REFRESH`
or `MODE device CODEPAGE [/STATUS]`

Explanation:

device	The device: CON, LPT1, LPT2, or LPT3.
PREPARE	Prepares the listed code pages.
codepage	The code page. See manual for valid code pages.
file-spec	The .CPI file that contains the code pages.
SELECT=codepage	Selects a code page to use for the device.
REFRESH	Refreshes the code pages.
/STATUS	Lists the code pages currently prepared for the device.

The MODE command (set display mode)

Function: Configures the display adapter.

DOS version: 3.2

Format: `MODE [display-type] [,shift] [,T]`
or `MODE CON [COLS=c] [LINES=c]`

Explanation:

display-type	Display type: 40, 80, BW40, BW80, CO40, CO80, or MONO.
shift	Shifts a CGA display left (L) or right (R).
T	Displays a test pattern to align display.
COLS=c	Columns per line: 40 or 80.
LINES=c	Lines per screen: 25, 43, or 50.

The MODE command (set typamatic rate)

Function: Sets the keyboard repeat rate.

DOS version: 4.0

Format: `MODE CON: RATE=r DELAY=d`

Explanation:

RATE=r	The rate at which characters repeat (1 to 32).
DELAY=d	The delay before repeating a keystroke (1 to 4).

The MORE command

Function: Displays output one screen at a time.

DOS version: 2.0

Format: `MORE`

Note: More is a filter, so it must be used with a pipe or input redirection.

The MOVE command

Function: Moves files from one location to another.

DOS version: 6.0

Format: `MOVE source-spec [source-spec...] target-spec [/Y]`

Explanation:

source-spec	One or more files to move.
target-spec	The directory where the files are to be moved. If only one file is moved, *target-spec* may specify a new file name.
/Y	Does not prompt to create a directory.

The MSAV command

Function: Scans your system for computer viruses.

DOS version: 6.0

Format:

```
MSAV [drive...] [/S|/C] [/R] [/A|/L] [/N] [/P] [/F]
     [/lines] [/color] [/FF] [/BF] [/NF] [/BT] [/VIDEO]
```

Explanation:

drive	One ore more drives to scan.
/S	Scans the specified drives (this is the default).
/C	Scans and cleans the specified drives.
/R	Creates a report.
/A	Scans all drives except A and B.
/L	Scans all local drives except A and B.

The MSAV command(continued)

/N	Uses command-line interface and suppresses informational messages.
/P	Uses command-line interface.
/F	Suppresses file name display (used with /N or /P).
/lines	Number of lines on screen: 25, 28, 43, 50, or 60.
/color	Color scheme: BW, MONO, LCD, or IN (always run in color).
/FF	Uses fast display for CGA monitors.
/BF	Uses BIOS font to avoid graphics problems.
/NF	Does not use graphics characters.
/BT	Allows graphics mouse under Windows.
/VIDEO	Displays help information for video and mouse options.

The MSBACKUP command

Function: Backs up and restores data on a hard disk. Replaces the BACKUP and RESTORE commands.

DOS version: 6.0

Format: `MSBACKUP [setup-file] [/BW|/LCD|/MDA]`

Explanation:

setup-file	Specifies the setup file to use for the backup.
/BW	Displays in black and white.
/LCD	Uses an LCD color scheme.
/MDA	Monochrome display.

The MSCDEX command

Function: Provides support for CD-ROM drives.

DOS version: 6.0

Format: `MSCDEX /D:sig... [/E] [/K] [/S] [/V] [/L:drive] [/M:number]`

Explanation:

/D:sig	The signature of the CD-ROM driver (must match the signature specified on the /D switch for the CONFIG.SYS Device command that loads the driver).
/E	Uses expanded memory for sector buffers.
/K	Recognizes Kanjii-encoded CD-ROM volumes.
/S	Shares CD-ROM drives on network servers.
/V	Displays memory statistics.
/L:drive	The drive letter assigned to the CD-ROM drive.
/M:number	The number of sector buffers.

The MSD command

Function: Displays system information.

DOS version: 6.0 (also included with *Windows* 3.1)

Format: `MSD [/B] [/I] [/F file-spec] [/P file-spec] [/S [file-spec]]`

Explanation:

/B	Displays in black and white.
/I	Bypasses initial hardware detection.
/F file-spec	Creates a report using name and address information entered by the user.
/P file-spec	Creates a report without name and address information.
/S [file-spec]	Creates a summary report on the screen or in the specified file.

The NLSFUNC command

Function: Enables national language support.

DOS version: 3.3

Format: `NLSFUNC [file-spec]`

Explanation:

file-spec	The file that contains country information. The default is COUNTRY.SYS.

The PATH command

Function: Sets up a directory search sequence for commands or programs.

DOS version: 2.0

Format: `PATH [path [;path...]]`

Explanation:

path	One or more directories to include in the search path.

The PAUSE command

Function: Pauses execution of a batch file until the user presses a key.

DOS version: 2.0

Format: `PAUSE`

The POWER command

Function: Conserves power on portable computers. POWER.EXE must first be loaded in CONFIG.SYS.

DOS version: 6.0

Format: `POWER [/ADV:MAX|/ADV:REG|/ADV:MIN|/STD|/OFF]`

Explanation:

/ADV:MAX	Maximizes power conservation even if performance is reduced.
/ADV:REG	Balances power conservation with performance.
/ADV:MIN	Conserves power only when performance is not reduced.
/STD	Uses APM standards only.
/OFF	Disables power management.

The PRINT command

Function: Prints a text file.

DOS version: 2.0

Format:

```
PRINT file-spec... [/D:device] [/C] [/P] [/T]
      [/B:size] [/U:ticks] [/M:ticks] [/S:ticks] [/Q:size]
```

Explanation:

file-spec	One or more files to print.
/D:device	The printer device.
/C	Removes files from print queue.
/P	Adds files to print queue.
/T	Cancels the printing of all files.
/B:size	The size of the buffer. The default is 512 bytes. Maximum is 16384.
/U:ticks	Clock ticks to wait for printer to be available (1-255).
/M:ticks	Clock ticks allowed to print one character (1-255).
/S:ticks	Clock ticks allocated for background printing (1-255).
/Q:size	Maximum number of files in print queue.

The PROMPT command

Function: Configures the DOS prompt.

DOS version: 2.0

Format: `PROMPT text`

Explanation:

text — The prompt text. May include the following special characters:

$Q	= (equal sign)	$G	> (greater-than)
$$	$ (dollar sign)	$L	< (less-than)
$T	Current time	$B	| (pipe)
$D	Current date	$_	Return
$P	Current drive and path	$E	Escape (ANSI)
$V	DOS version	$H	Backspace
$N	Current drive		

The QBASIC command

Function: Invokes the Quick Basic interpreter.

DOS version: 5.0

Format:

```
QBASIC file-spec [/B] [/G] [/H] [/NOHI] [/EDITOR]
       [/MBF] [/RUN]
```

Explanation:

file-spec	The file to be loaded.
/B	Displays in black and white.
/G	Uses fast screen display for CGA monitors.
/H	Uses maximum screen resolution.
/NOHI	Supports older eight-color monitors.
/EDITOR	Invokes the MS-DOS editor.
/MBF	Converts CVD, CVS, MKD$, and MKS$ functions to CVD functions.
/RUN	Runs the program.

The RD (RMDIR) command

Function: Deletes a directory.

DOS version: 2.0

Format: `RD directory-spec`
or `RMDIR directory-spec`

Explanation: directory-spec — The directory to be removed. It must be empty.

The RECOVER command

Function: Recovers unreadable files. This command can often do more harm than good, so it should be avoided.

DOS version: 2.0

Format: `RECOVER [drive:|file-spec]`

Explanation:

drive:	The drive to recover.
file-spec	The file to recover.

The REM command

Function: Includes a remark in a batch file.

DOS version: 2.0

Format: `REM remark`

Explanation:

remark	Any remark text you wish. Do not include redirection symbols (>, <, or |).

The REN (RENAME) command

Function: Renames a file.

DOS version: 1.0

Format: `REN source-spec target-spec`
or `RENAME source-spec target-spec`

Explanation:

source-spec	One or more files to be renamed.
target-spec	The new name for the file or files.

The REPLACE command

Function: Copies files selectively.

DOS version: 3.2

Format: `REPLACE source-spec target-spec [/A] [/P] [/R] [/S] [/U] [/W]`

Explanation:

source-spec	The files to be copied.
target-spec	The location of existing files.
/A	Adds new files only.
/P	Prompts before replacing existing files.
/R	Replaces read-only files.
/S	Searches target subdirectories.
/U	Updates older files only.
/W	Pauses before beginning.

The RESTORE command

Function: Restores files copied by the BACKUP command.

DOS version: 2.0

Format:

```
RESTORE source-spec target-spec [/A:date] [/B:date] [/D]
        [/E:time]  [L:time] [/M] [/N] [/P] [/S]
```

Explanation:

source-spec	The drive that contains the backup diskettes.
target-spec	One or more files to be restored.
/A:date	Restores only files modified on or after *date*.
/B:date	Restores only files modified on or before *date*.
/D	Displays a list of files on the backup diskette without restoring.
/E:time	Restores only files modified at or before *time*. Use with /B.
/L:time	Restores only files modified at or after *time*. Use with /A.
/M	Restores only files modified since last backup.
/N	Restores only files that do not exist on the target drive.
/P	Prompts before overwriting files that have been modified since the last backup.
/S	Restores subdirectories.

The SET command

Function: Sets the value of an environment variable.

DOS version: 2.0

Format:

```
SET [variable[=string]]
```

Explanation:

variable	The environment variable to be set. If omitted, all variables are listed.
string	The new value for the variable. If omitted, the variable is deleted.

The SETVER command

Function: Sets the DOS version reported for specific programs.

DOS version: 5.0

Format:

```
   SETVER [directory-path] [file-name n.nn]
or SETVER [directory-path] [file-name [/DELETE [/QUIET]]]
```

Explanation:

directory-path	The path that contains SETVER.EXE.
file-name	The program to which DOS should report a different version number.
n.nn	The version to report for the specified program.
/DELETE	Remove a SETVER table entry. May be abbreviated /D.
/QUIET	Do not display SETVER messages when removing an entry.

The SHARE command

Function: Provides shared access to files and support for large partitions under DOS 4.0.

DOS version: 3.0

Format: `SHARE [/F:space] [/L:locks]`

Explanation:

/F:space	Size of the area used to store file sharing information. The default is 2048.
/L:locks	The number of files that can be locked at one time. The default is 20.

The SHIFT command

Function: Shifts batch file parameters left one position.

DOS version: 2.0

Format: `SHIFT`

The SMARTDRV command

Function: Caches disk I/O for improved performance.

DOS version: 6.0 (DOS 5.0 used the SMARTDRV.SYS device driver; *Windows* 3.1 uses an earlier version of the Smartdrv command.)

Format:

```
SMARTDRV [[drive[+|-]]...] [/E:size] [initial-size]
         [minimum-size]] [/B:buffer]
         [/C] [/R] [/L] [/Q] [/V] [/S]
```

Explanation:

drive[+|-]	Activates or deactivates caching for the specified drive. *Drive* by itself activates read caching; *drive+* activates read and write caching; *drive-* deactivates caching.
/E:size	Specifies the cache element size: 1024, 2048, 4096, or 8192. The default is 8192.
initial-size	The amount of memory initially allocated to the cache.
minimum-size	The minimum size of the cache when *Windows* is running.
/B:buffer	The size of the read-ahead buffer. Can be any multiple of *size*. The default is 16KB.
/C	Writes cached data to disk.
/R	Resets the cache.
/L	Does not use upper memory.
/Q	Does not display startup messages.
/V	Displays verbose startup messages.
/S	Displays status information.

The SORT command

Function: Sorts the lines in a text file.

DOS version: 2.0

Format: `SORT [/R] [/+column]`

Explanation:

/R	Sorts in reverse order.
/+column	Sorts on a specific column.

Note: Sort is a filter, so it must be used with redirection or piping.

The SUBST command

Function: Substitutes a drive letter for a directory.

DOS version: 3.1

Format: `SUBST [drive: [path|/D]`

Explanation:

drive:	The drive letter used to refer to the path.
path	The path to be accessed via the drive letter.
/D	Deletes the substitution.

The SYS command

Function: Transfers the operating system files to a formatted diskette.

DOS version: 1.0

Format: `SYS [source-spec] drive:`

Explanation:

source-spec	The drive and directory that contains the system files (4.0 and later).
drive:	The drive where the system files are to be copied.

The TIME command

Function: Sets the system time.

DOS version: 1.0

Format: `TIME hh:mm:ss[.hh] [A|P]`

Explanation:

hh:mm:ss[.hh]	The time (hours, minutes, seconds, hundredths of seconds).
A or P	AM or PM (4.0 and later).

The TREE command

Function: Displays the directory structure.

DOS version: 2.0

Format: `TREE [drive:] [/A] [/F]`

Explanation:

drive:	The drive whose directory structure is to be listed.
/A	Does not use line drawing characters.
/F	Lists file names (3.2 and later).

The TRUENAME command

Function: Displays the complete name of a path, ignoring SUBST, ASSIGN, or JOIN commands or network reassignments. (This command is undocumented.)

DOS version: 4.0

Format: `TRUENAME [file-spec]`

Explanation:

file-spec	The drive, directory, or file whose true name you want to display.

The TYPE command

Function: Displays a text file.

DOS version: 1.0

Format: `TYPE file-name`

Explanation:

file-name	The file to be displayed.

The UNDELETE command

Function: Undeletes a file and enables delete tracking and delete sentry under DOS 6.0.

DOS version: 5.0

Format:

```
UNDELETE [file-spec] [/DOS|/DT|/DS] [/LIST|/ALL|/LOAD|
         /UNLOAD|/PURGE[drive]|/STATUS|/S[drive]|
         /Tdrive[-entries]]
```

Explanation:

file-spec	The file or files to undelete.
/LIST	Lists the files that can be undeleted.
/ALL	Undeletes all files.
/DOS	Ignores delete tracking and delete sentry.
/DT	Undeletes only files deleted while delete tracking was active.
/DS	Undeletes only files deleted while delete sentry was active (6.0).

The UNDELETE command (continued)

/LOAD	Loads UNDELETE into memory (6.0).
/UNLOAD	Removes UNDELETE from memory (6.0).
/PURGE[drive]	Deletes files in the specified drive's sentry directory (6.0).
/STATUS	Displays the delete protection currently in effect (6.0).
/S[drive]	Enables delete sentry for the specified drive (6.0).
/Tdrive	Enables delete tracking for the specified drive (6.0).
-entries	The number of files to track with delete tracking (6.0).

The UNFORMAT command

Function: Recovers data from an accidentally formatted disk.

DOS version: 5.0

Format: `UNFORMAT drive: [/J]`
or `UNFORMAT drive: [/U] [/TEST] [/L] [/P]`
or `UNFORMAT /PARTN [/L]`

Explanation:

drive:	The drive to be unformatted.
/J	Verifies the accuracy of the Mirror file without unformatting.
/U	Unformats the disk without the Mirror file.
/TEST	Determines if the disk can be unformatted with a Mirror file.
/L	Without /PARTN, lists files and directories on disk. With /PARTN, lists the partition table.
/P	Prints output messages on LPT1.
/PARTN	Recreates the partition table using the MIRROR /PARTN diskette.

The VER command

Function: Displays the DOS version.

DOS version: 2.0

Format: `VER`

The VERIFY command

Function: Activates or deactivates write verification.

DOS version: 2.0

Format: `VERIFY [ON|OFF]`

The VOL command

Function: Displays a disk's volume label and serial number.

DOS version: 2.0

Format: `VOL [drive:]`

Explanation:

drive:	The drive whose volume information is to be displayed.

The VSAFE command

Function: Provides memory resident virus detection.

DOS version: 6.0

Format: `VSAFE [/option[+|-]... [/NE] [/NX] [/AX] [/CX] [/N] [/D] [/U]`

Explanation:

/option [+|-] Enables or disables the specified option, as follows:

1	Detects low-level format of hard disk.
2	Detects program attempting to become resident.
3	Write protects hard disk.
4	Scans program files when executed.
5	Checks for boot sector viruses.
6	Protects hard disk boot sector.
7	Protects floppy disk boot sector.
8	Protects executable files.

/NE	Does not use expanded memory.
/NX	Does not use extended memory.
/Ax	Sets hotkey to Alt+*x*.
/Cx	Sets hotkey to Ctrl+*x*.
/N	Allows network drivers to be loaded after VSAFE.
/D	Tells VSAFE not to create checksums for new executable files.
/U	Removes VSAFE from memory.

The XCOPY command

Function: Copies one or more files.

DOS version: 3.2

Format:

```
XCOPY source-spec target-spec [/A|/M] [/D:date]
      [/P] [/S[/E]] [/V] [/W]
```

Explanation:

source-spec	One or more files to copy.
target-spec	The location where the files are to be copied.
/A	Copies only if Archive; leaves Archive bit set.
/M	Copies only if Archive; resets Archive bit.
/D:date	Copies files modified after the specified date.
/P	Prompts to confirm each file.
/S	Copies subdirectories.
/E	Creates subdirectories even when empty.
/V	Verifies writes (not recommended).
/W	Pauses before beginning.

CONFIG.SYS commands

The ANSI.SYS device driver

Function: Provides extended display support.

DOS version: 2.0

Format: `DEVICE[HIGH]=C:\DOS\ANSI.SYS [/X] [/K]`

Explanation:

/X	For extended keyboards, allows duplicated keys to be remapped separately.
/K	Ignores extended keys.

ESC sequences:

ESC[*l*,*c*H	Moves cursor to line *l* and column *c*.
ESC[*l*,*c*f	Moves cursor to line *l* and column *c* (same as above).
ESC[*n*A	Moves cursor up *n* lines.
ESC[*n*B	Moves cursor down *n* lines.
ESC[*n*C	Moves cursor forward *n* columns.
ESC[*n*D	Moves cursor backwards *n* columns.
ESC[s	Saves cursor position.
ESC[r	Restores cursor position.
ESC[2J	Clears the screen.
ESC[K	Erases to the end of the line.
ESC[*n;n*...m	Sets text attributes. *N* can be:

0	Plain	30	Black text	40	Black background
1	Bold	31	Red text	41	Red background
4	Underscore	32	Green text	42	Green background
5	Blink	33	Yellow text	43	Yellow background
7	Reverse	34	Blue text	44	Blue background
8	Hidden	35	Magenta text	45	Magenta background
		36	Cyan text	46	Cyan background
		37	White text	47	White background

ESC[*n*h — Sets display mode. *N* can be:

0	40×25 mono text	13	320×200 color graphics
1	40×25 color text	14	640×200 16-color graphics
2	80×25 mono text	15	640×350 mono graphics
3	80×25 color text	16	640×350 16-color graphics
4	320×200 4-color graphics	17	640×480 mono graphics
5	320×200 mono graphics	18	640×480 16-color graphics
6	640×200 mono graphics	19	640×480 256-color graphics
7	Enables line wrapping		

ESC[=*n*l	Rests mode. *N* can be any of the above.
ESC[*c*;*string*;...p	Remaps the key specified by *c* to *string*. Consult your manual for the proper code for each key on your keyboard.

The BREAK command

Function: Activates or deactivates Ctrl+C checking.

DOS version: 1.0

Format: `BREAK [ON|OFF]`

The BUFFERS command

Function: Sets aside internal memory to use as disk buffers.

DOS version: 2.0

Format: `BUFFERS=n[,m]`

Explanation:

n	The number of buffers to set up (1 to 99). Each buffer is 512 bytes.
m	For DOS 4.0, the number of read-ahead buffers. For DOS 5.0 and later, the number of secondary buffers.

The COUNTRY command

Function: Establishes international conventions for dates, times, etc.

DOS version: 2.1

Format: `COUNTRY=country[,[codepage][,[file-spec]]]`

Explanation:

country	The country code. See manual for valid country codes.
codepage	The code page. See manual for valid code pages.
file-spec	The country file. The default is COUNTRY.SYS in the root directory.

The DEVICE command

Function: Loads a device driver into conventional memory.

DOS version: 2.0

Format: `DEVICE=file-spec [parameters]`

Explanation:

file-spec	The device driver file.
parameters	Parameters used by the device driver.

The DEVICEHIGH command

Function: Loads a device driver, using upper memory if possible.

DOS version: 5.0

Format:
```
DEVICEHIGH=file-spec [parameters]
```
or
```
DEVICEHIGH SIZE=hexsize file-spec [parameters]
```

Explanation:

file-spec	The device driver file.
parameters	Parameters used by the device driver.
SIZE=hexsize	The minimum size of an upper memory block that can be used to load the driver.

Note: DOS 6.0 supports additional switches for the DEVICEHIGH command that are intended for use by MemMaker.

The DISPLAY.SYS device driver

Function: Enables code-page switching.

DOS version: 3.3

Format:
```
DEVICE[HIGH]=C:\DOS\DISPLAY.SYS
                CON:=(type,codepage, {count|(count,subfonts)} )
```

Explanation:

type	Display type: EGA or LCD. EGA supports EGA and VGA displays.
codepage	The code page. See the manual for values.
count	The number of additional code pages supported by the display.
subfonts	The number of subfonts supported by the display.

The DOS command

Function: Specifies that DOS should use the high memory area and/or enables access to upper memory.

DOS version: 5.0

Format:
```
DOS=[HIGH|LOW],[UMB|NOUMB]
```

Explanation:

HIGH	Loads DOS into the high memory area.
LOW	Does not load DOS into the high memory area. This is the default.
UMB	Enables upper memory support.
NOUMB	Does not enable upper memory support. This is the default.

The DBLSPACE.SYS device driver

Function: Relocates the DoubleSpace program.

DOS version: 6.0

Format:

```
DEVICE[HIGH]=C:\DOS\DBLSPACE.SYS /MOVE
```

Explanation:

/MOVE	Relocates the DBLSPACE.BIN program. If you use a DEVICEHIGH command, relocates DBLSPACE.BIN to upper memory.

The DRIVER.SYS device driver

Function: Creates a logical drive that can be used to access a diskette drive.

DOS version: 3.2

Format:

```
DEVICE=C:\DOS\DRIVER.SYS /D:drive [/C] [/F:factor]
        [/H:heads] [/S:sectors] [/T:tracks]
```

Explanation:

/D:drive	The drive number (0 is A, 1 is B, etc.).
/C	The drive is able to detect if the drive door is open or closed.
/F:factor	The type of drive:

0	360KB
1	1.2MB
2	720KB
7	1.44MB
9	2.88MB

/H:heads	The number of heads in the drive.
/S:sectors	The number of sectors per track.
/T:tracks	The number of tracks per side.

The DRIVPARM command

Function: Configures block devices.

DOS version: 5.0

Format:

```
DRIVPARM=/D:drive [/C] [/F:factor] [/I] [/N]
          [/H:heads] [/S:sectors] [/T:tracks]
```

Explanation:

/D:drive	The drive number (0 is A, 1 is B, etc.).
/C	The drive is able to detect if the drive door is open or closed.
/F:factor	The type of drive:

0	360KB	6	Tape drive
1	1.2MB	7	1.44MB
2	720KB	8	Optical disk
5	Hard disk	9	2.88MB

The DRIVPARM command (continued)

/I	Supports 3.5" drives on systems with older BIOS chips.
/N	Non-removable device.
/H:heads	The number of heads in the drive.
/S:sectors	The number of sectors per track.
/T:tracks	The number of tracks per side.

The EGA.SYS device driver

Function: Allows the DOSSHELL Task Swapper to work with EGA displays.

DOS version: 5.0

Format: `DEVICE=C:\DOS\EGA.SYS`

The EMM386.EXE device driver

Function: Provides simulated expanded memory and support for upper memory.

DOS version: 5.0

Format:

```
DEVICE=C:\DOS\EMM386.EXE [ON|OFF|AUTO] [memory] [RAM|NOEMS]
        [W=ON|W=OFF] [Mx|FRAME=addr|Paddr] [Pn=addr]
        [X=mmmm-nnnn] [I=mmmm-nnnn]
        [B=addr] [L=nnn] [A=nnn] [H=nnn] [D=nnn]
```

Explanation:

ON	Activates EMS support.
OFF	Deactivates EMS support.
AUTO	Activates EMS support when a program requests it.
memory	The amount of EMS memory to allocate.
RAM	Provides both EMS and upper memory support.
NOEMS	Provides upper memory but not EMS support. The default is to provide EMS but not upper memory support.
W=ON	Activates Weitek processor support.
W=OFF	Deactivates Weitek processor support.
Mx	The address of the page frame. *X* can be 1-14, as follows:

1	C000h	6	D400h	11	8400h
2	C400h	7	D800h	12	8800h
3	C800h	8	DC00h	13	8C00h
4	CC00h	9	E000h	14	9000h
5	D000h				

FRAME=addr	The address of the page frame.

The EMM386.EXE device driver (continued)

/Paddr	The address of the page frame.
/Pn=addr	The address of the specified page.
/X=mmmm-nnnn	Excludes the specified address range from the EMS page frame.
/I=mmmm-nnnn	Includes the specified address range in the EMS page or upper memory.
/B=addr	The lowest available address to use for EMS banking (1000h-4000h).
/L=nnn	Guarantees that *nnn*KB of XMS memory will be available.
/A=nnn	Specifies the number of alternate registers sets for multi-tasking. The default is 7.
/H=nnn	Specifies the number of handles EMS386.EXE can use. The default is 64.
/D=nnn	Reserves *nnn*KB of memory for DMA buffering.

The FCBS command

Function: Specifies the number of FCB structures to support.

DOS version: 3.0

Format: `FCBS=x`

Explanation: x — The number of FCB structures to support (1-255). The default is 4.

The FILES command

Function: Specifies the number of files that can be open simultaneously.

DOS version: 2.0

Format: `FILES=x`

Explanation: x — The number of files that can be open simultaneously (8-255). The default is 4.

The HIMEM.SYS device driver

Function: Manages extended memory.

DOS version: 5.0

Format:

```
DEVICE=C:\DOS\HIMEM.SYS [/HMAMIN=m] [/NUMHANDLES=n]
        [INT15=xxxx] [/MACHINE:code] [/A20CONTROL:ON|OFF]
        [/SHADOWRAM:ON|OFF] [CPUCLOCK:ON|OFF]
```

Explanation: /HMAMIN=n — The amount of memory a program must request to access the HMA.

The HIMEM.SYS device driver (continued)

/NUMHANDLES=n	The number of EMS handles that can be used simultaneously.
/INT15=xxxx	The amount of memory to allocate to the INT15 interface.
/MACHINE:code	Specifies that an A20 handler for a specific machine should be used. Consult the manual for more information.
/A20CONTROL:[ON|OFF]	ON activates the A20 handler even if A20 is in use. The default is OFF.
/SHADOWRAM:[ON|OFF]	OFF disables shadow RAM for use by HIMEM.SYS. The default is ON.
/CPUCLOCK:[ON|OFF]	ON corrects a clock speed problem that occurs on some systems. The default is OFF.

The INCLUDE command

Function: Copies configuration commands from another block.

DOS version: 6.0

Format: `INCLUDE block-name`

Explanation:

block-name	The name of the block to be copied.

The INSTALL command

Function: Loads a memory resident program from CONFIG.SYS rather than AUTOEXEC.BAT.

DOS version: 4.0

Format: `INSTALL file-spec [parameters]`

Explanation:

file-spec	The program file.
parameters	Parameters for the program.

The INTERLNK.EXE device driver

Function: Loads Interlnk so your computer can function as an Interlnk client.

DOS version: 6.0

Format:

```
DEVICE[HIGH]=C:\DOS\INTERLNK.EXE [/AUTO|/NOSCAN]
                [/NOPRINTER] [/LPT[:n]] [/COM[:n]] [/BAUD:rate]
                [/V] [/LOW]
```

Explanation:

/AUTO	Loads only if Intersvr is detected on the server computer.
/NOSCAN	Loads without scanning for Intersvr on the server computer.
/NOPRINTER	Does not redirect printers.
/LPT[:n]	Uses a parallel port to establish the connection.
/COM[:n]	Uses a serial port to establish the connection.
/BAUD:rate	Specifies the baud rate for a serial connection. *Rate* can be 9600, 19200, 38400, 57600, or 115200.
/V	Uses a more reliable method for serial communications.
/LOW	Loads into conventional memory even if upper memory is available.

The LASTDRIVE command

Function: Specifies the highest drive letter allowed.

DOS version: 3.0

Format:

```
LASTDRIVE=drive
```

Explanation:

drive	The highest drive letter allowed. The default is one greater than the last drive actually installed on the system.

The MENUCOLOR command

Function: Specifies the foreground and background colors for configuration menus.

DOS version: 6.0

Format: `MENUCOLOR=foreground[,background]`

Explanation:

foreground — The foreground color.

background — The background color.

Foreground or *background* can be any of the following:

0	Black	8	Gray
1	Blue	9	Bright blue
2	Green	10	Bright green
3	Cyan	11	Bright cyan
4	Red	12	Bright red
5	Magenta	13	Bright magenta
6	Brown	14	Yellow
7	White	15	Bright white

The MENUDEFAULT command

Function: Specifies a default choice and a time-out value for a configuration menu.

DOS version: 6.0

Format: `MENUDEFAULT=block-name[,time]`

Explanation:

block-name — The name of the default configuration block.

time — The number of seconds to wait before using the default block.

The MENUITEM command

Function: Defines an item on a configuration menu.

DOS version: 6.0

Format: `MENUITEM=block-name[,menu-text]`

Explanation:

block-name — The name of the configuration block used if the users selects this menu item.

menu-text — The text displayed for the menu item. If omitted, *block-name* is displayed.

The SUBMENU command

Function: Defines a submenu.

DOS version: 6.0

Format:
```
SUBMENU=block-name[,menu-text]
```

Explanation:

block-name	The name of the configuration block that contains the submenu displayed if the users selects this menu item.
menu-text	The text displayed for the menu item. If omitted, *block-name* is displayed.

The POWER.EXE device driver

Function: Conserves power on portable computers.

DOS version: 6.0

Format:
```
DEVICE[HIGH]=C:\DOS\POWER.EXE
              [/ADV:MAX|/ADV:REG|/ADV:MIN|/STD|/OFF] [/LOW]
```

Explanation:

/ADV:MAX	Maximizes power conservation even if performance is reduced.
/ADV:REG	Balances power conservation with performance.
/ADV:MIN	Conserves power only when performance is not reduced.
/STD	Uses APM standards only.
/OFF	Disables power management.
/LOW	Loads into conventional memory even if upper memory is available.

The PRINTER.SYS device driver

Function: Supports code-page switching for printers.

DOS version: 3.2

Format:
```
DEVICE[HIGH]=C:\DOS\PRINTER.SYS LPTx:=(type,codepage,count)
```

Explanation:

LPTx	The printer port.
type	Display type: EGA or LCD. EGA supports EGA and VGA displays.
codepage	The code page. See manual for values.
count	The number of additional code pages supported by the printer.

The RAMDRIVE device driver

Function: Creates a RAM disk.

DOS version: 5.0

Format: `DEVICE[HIGH]=C:\DOS\RAMDRIVE.SYS size sector entries [/E|/A]`

Explanation:

size	The size in KB of the RAM drive (16 to 4096). The default is 64.
sector	The sector size (128, 256, or 512). The default is 512.
entries	The size of the root directory (2 to 1024). The default is 64.
/E	Uses extended memory.
/A	Uses expanded memory.

The SETVER.EXE device driver

Function: Loads the version table. Use the SETVER command to maintain the version table.

DOS version: 5.0

Format: `DEVICE[HIGH]=C:\DOS\SETVER.EXE`

The SHELL command

Function: Specifies the location of the DOS command processor.

DOS version: 2.0

Format: `SHELL=file-name [parameters]`

Explanation:

file-name	The program file for the command processor, usually COMMAND.COM.
parameters	Parameters for the command processor. For COMMAND.COM's parameters, see the COMMAND entry in the DOS commands section of this appendix.

The SMARTDRV.EXE device driver

Function: Performs double-buffering.

DOS version: 6.0

Format: `DEVICE[HIGH]=C:\DOS\SMARTDRV.EXE /DOUBLE_BUFFER`

Explanation:

/DOUBLE_BUFFER	Double-buffers disk I/O. Required only for certain drive types.

The SMARTDRV.SYS device driver

Function: Caches disk I/O for improved performance.

DOS version: DOS 5.0 only (DOS 6.0 uses the SMARTDRV command instead)

Format: `DEVICE[HIGH]=SMARTDRV [initial-size [minimum-size]] [/A]`

Explanation:

initial-size	The size of the cache in KB. The default is 256.
minimum-size	The minimum size of the cache when *Windows* is running.
/A	Uses expanded memory rather than extended memory.

The STACKS command

Function: Specifies the number of stacks to provide.

DOS version: 3.2

Format: `STACKS=number,size`

Explanation:

number	The number of stacks to provide (8 to 64).
size	The size of each stack (0 or 32 to 512).

The SWITCHES command

Function: Sets certain configuration options.

DOS version: 5.0

Format: `SWITCHES=[/K] [/N] [/F] [/W]`

Explanation:

/K	Causes enhanced keyboard to emulate a conventional keyboard.
/N	Suppresses F5 and F8 keys at startup (6.0).
/F	Suppresses two-second delay at startup (6.0).
/W	Indicates that WINA20.386 is not in the root directory (*Windows* 3.0 only).

Appendix B

A checklist for periodic maintenance of your PC

Throughout this book, I've presented a variety of DOS functions that should be performed periodically to keep your PC in efficient operating condition. In this appendix, I've gathered those tasks together in the form of a checklist you can follow when you perform this periodic maintenance. Just how often "periodically" is depends on how extensively you use your PC. For most users, it's appropriate to work through this checklist every three to six months. Other users might need to do it more often.

Partition and directory maintenance

- ___ Evaluate your partition structure and reorganize it if a change is warranted.
- ___ Evaluate your directory structure. Remove unnecessary directories. Consolidate directories where appropriate.
- ___ Delete unnecessary temporary and backup files (*.TMP, *.BAK, etc.). Use the Dir command with the /S switch to locate them.
- ___ Delete unnecessary files or archive them to tape or diskette.
- ___ Use the Dir command to display the contents of your C drive's root directory and remove any unnecessary files.

Backup and recovery

- ___ Run Chkdsk against all drives and correct any errors that are detected. Also, note the amount of free space on each drive. If it's low, delete additional files or consider compressing the drive with DoubleSpace if you haven't already done so.
- ___ If you're using DOS 6.0, run DEFRAG against all drives to defragment them.
- ___ If you are using DOS 6.0, run MSAV against all drives to detect and remove any virus infections.
- ___ Review your backup procedures to make sure they are still adequate.
- ___ Perform a complete backup of all drives.
- ___ If you have a bootable system diskette, boot your PC from it to make sure it's working properly. If not, create a new bootable system diskette.
- ___ Use the MIRROR /PARTN command to write a copy of your current partition structure to diskette. (If you have already done this, do it again to make sure the diskette is current.)

Memory configuration

- ___ If you have a 386 or better PC, review CONFIG.SYS to make sure it includes the commands necessary to load DOS into the high memory area and activate upper memory.
- ___ Evaluate each device driver and memory resident program loaded by CONFIG.SYS and AUTOEXEC.BAT. Remove any that are unnecessary and reboot your PC. (Be sure to make a backup copy of these files before editing them.)
- ___ Review the size of the cache set up by Smartdrive and adjust it as necessary.
- ___ Run the Mem command to determine how much conventional memory is available to application programs.
- ___ If you're using DOS 6.0, run MemMaker to see if it can free additional conventional memory.
- ___ If you're not using DOS 6.0, or if you chose not to run MemMaker, convert all your Device commands to Devicehigh commands except the ones for EMM386.EXE and HIMEM.SYS.

Index

C

D

E

M

T

Order/Comment Form

Your opinions count

If you have any comments, criticisms, or suggestions for us, I'm eager to get them. And if you find any errors in this book, typographical or otherwise, please point them out so we can correct them in the next printing. Thanks for your help.

Book title: *The Only DOS Book You'll Ever Need (Second Edition)*

Dear Mike: ______________________________________

____

____

____

____

____

____

____

Our Ironclad Guarantee

To our customers who order directly from us: You must be satisfied. Our books must work for you, or you can send them back for a full refund...no questions asked.

Name (& Title, if any) ______________________

Company (if company address) ______________________

Street address ______________________

City, State, Zip ______________________

Phone number (including area code) ______________________

Fax number (if you fax your order to us) ______________________

Qty	Product code and title		*Price
____	DOSR	**The Only DOS Book You'll Ever Need**	$27.50
____	LDSR	**The Least You Need to Know about DOS**	20.00
____	LWIN	**The Least You Need to Know about Windows 3.1**	20.00
____	C95N	**Crash Course: Windows 95 & NT 4.0**	10.00
____	CCW8	**Crash Course: Word 97**	15.00
____	CCX8	**Crash Course: Excel 97**	15.00
____	CCW7	**Crash Course: Word 95**	15.00
____	CCX7	**Crash Course: Excel 95**	15.00
____	PRW7	**Work like a PRO with Word for Windows 95**	25.00
____	PRX7	**Work like a PRO with Excel for Windows 95**	25.00

☐ Bill my company for the books plus UPS shipping and handling (and sales tax within CA). P.O.# ______________________

☐ I want to **SAVE 10%** by paying in advance.
Charge to my ____Visa ____MasterCard ____American Express:

Card number ______________________

Valid thru (mo/yr) ______________________

Cardowner's signature ______________________

☐ I want to **SAVE 10% plus shipping and handling**. Here's my check for the books minus 10% ($____________). California residents, please add sales tax to your total. (Offer valid in U.S.)

*Prices are subject to change. Please call for current prices.

To order more quickly,

Call toll-free
1-800-221-5528
(Weekdays, 8 to 5 Pac. Time)

Fax: 1-209-440-0963

Mike Murach & Associates, Inc.
2560 West Shaw Lane, Suite 101
Fresno, California 93711-2765
(209) 440-9071

NO POSTAGE
NECESSARY
IF MAILED
IN THE
UNITED STATES

BUSINESS REPLY MAIL

FIRST-CLASS MAIL PERMIT NO. 3063 FRESNO, CA

POSTAGE WILL BE PAID BY ADDRESSEE

Mike Murach & Associates, Inc.
2560 W SHAW LN STE 101
FRESNO CA 93711-9866